COLONIAL FAMILIES OF MARYLAND II

They Came, They Flourished, and Some Moved On

COLONIAL FAMILIES OF MARYLAND II

They Came, They Flourished, and Some Moved On

Robert W. Barnes

CLEARFIELD

Copyright © 2014
Robert W. Barnes
All Rights Reserved.

Published for Clearfield Company by
Genealogical Publishing Company
Baltimore, Maryland
2014

ISBN 978-0-8063-5705-8

To Vern Skinner, Jr.

Colonial Families of Maryland II

Contents

Introduction..ix

Acknowledgements..x

Families Included x

Bibliography...xiv

Colonial Families of Maryland II..1

Index..239

Colonial Families of Maryland II

Introduction

This book is dedicated to Vern Skinner, whose careful, scholarly research has made thousands of records accessible to researchers across the world, especially those who are unable to visit the repositories where the original records are held.

The families in this volume were found in many counties, but primarily Baltimore and Anne Arundel Counties. Others have researched families in Western and Southern Maryland, and on the Eastern Shore. Some families have been followed beyond the Revolutionary War period, and some have appeared for one or two generations and then moved on. It has not always been possible to trace their destination, but they are presented here in the hope that they may help researchers elsewhere find the missing generations in their ancestry.

Sometimes when the male line of a family has died out, I have attempted to trace one or two generations of the descendants of the daughters.

Some colonial women were married two, three, or more times, and I have designated these ladies as Matriarchs, and traced the descendants of all their marriages.

I have used church, land, court and probate records as well as newspapers in an attempt to present as full a picture of the lives and times of those included in this book. No author likes to think he could possibly have made a mistake—but, in spite of careful checking, if I have made an error, I would like to know. I will acknowledge the researcher's comments, and errors will be corrected in print, probably in the Maryland Genealogical Society's *Journal*.

It has been said that finding the answer to one genealogical question raises at least one more question. One recurring problem when dealing with early families is the variations in spelling—not only of family names but of first names as well. 'Sam'l' is easily interpreted as 'Samuel,' but does 'Edw.' mean 'Edward' or 'Edwin?' Some families have a number of isolated family members that cannot be connected. The Daughaday family is a case in point. The family has several ties to the Taylor family, but I have not been able to do more than present several clusters of relationships. There is a theory that Matriarch Ann [-?-] Vickory Plowman was descended from the Stevenson, Haile and King families, I have not found solid documentary evidence to support the theory. The essential tenets of the theory are presented here. Finally there is the possibility that Edward Stevenson's wife Mary was a relative of a Richard King because Edward and Mary named one of their sons Richard King Stevenson. I researched three Richard Kings, all of whom had some connection to Maryland, but to date no connection to Edward and Mary Stevenson has been found. All of these theories are presented in the hope that future research may reveal the proofs.

An interesting parallel pattern of fathers naming sons arose when I found that Nicholas Leake of Baltimore County had a son named Gilbert Francis Yaxley Leake, and that an earlier Nicholas Leake of Yaxley Hall, England, named his illegitimate son Gilbert Francis Yaxley Leake also.

I would point out that in the case of Peden's *St. John's and St. George's Parish Register*, I have used his page numbers and not the page numbers that appeared in Lucy H. Harrison earlier transcription of the parish register at the Maryland Historical Society.

Acknowledgements

As the bibliography will show I am indebted to the work of many authors, notably Vern Skinner and Henry C. Peden, Jr. I am also grateful for the patience shown by my friends and family, especially my wife, Catherine, and my friends Allender Sybert, Robert K. Headley, and Isaac Becker-Howell, who have listened patiently—oh, so patiently—while I talked about my work, offering advice when it was asked for, and sometimes just listening to my interminable 'progress reports.'

I am indebted to Michael McCormick and the staff of the Reference and Research Department at the Maryland State Archives, and to Dr. Patricia D. Anderson, Francis O'Neill, and the library staff at the Maryland Historical Society, all of whom have provided excellent places to work.

As always, I am grateful for the staff at the Genealogical Publishing Company, for publishing my work and for helping me to make sure it is the best possible book. Thank you, Michael Tepper, Joe Garonzik, and Eileen Perkins.

Finally I want to thank all of those researchers whose material has contributed to this work. James Cheyne's web site on the Cheyne family has been very helpful. David Watkins provided a wealth of information on the English ancestry of Francis Watkins. All of those whose work I have found helpful are mentioned in the text.

Families Included

Airey of Talbot County.
Andrews of Kent County.
Ashley of Kent County.
Assa Notes. See Matriarch Dinah [-?-] Nuthead Devoran Oley Assa.
Atkinson of Baltimore County.
Auld Notes. See Piper Family of Anne Arundel Co.
Bagford of Baltimore County.
Barton Family of Baltimore County.
Benger Notes. See Matriarch Deborah of Baltimore County.
Berry Notes. See Goddard Family.
Barnet Bond of Baltimore County.
Charles Bond of Baltimore County.

Colonial Families of Maryland II

Bradford of Baltimore County.
Brogden Notes. See Mahan of Baltimore County.
Bull of Baltimore County.
Burke of Baltimore County.
Busk of Baltimore County.
Cannon of Baltimore County.
Cantwell of Baltimore County.
Carback of Baltimore County.
Carrington of Baltimore County.
Chadwell of Baltimore County.
Cheyne of Baltimore County.
Cobb Family of Baltimore County.
Cockayne of Talbot County.
Cogell Notes. See Matriarch Elizabeth [-?-] Cogell Dorman Swimdell.
Cole Notes. See Litton.
Connor Notes. See Carrington of Baltimore County.
Corbin of Baltimore County.
Coulter of Cecil and Baltimore Counties.
Cowan of Baltimore County.
Jacob Cox of Baltimore County.
William Cox of Baltimore County.
Dare of Calvert and Anne Arundel Counties.
Daughaday of Baltimore County.
Daugherty of Baltimore County
Debruler of Kent and Baltimore Counties.
Devoran Notes. See Matriarch Dinah [-?-] Nuthead Devoran Oley Assa.
Dixon Notes. See Matriarch Jane [-?-] Waites Dixon Long
Dorman Notes. See Matriarch Elizabeth [-?-] Cogell Dorman Swindell
Duhadaway of Anne Arundel County.
Duskin of Baltimore County.
Eastwood of Baltimore County.
Edwards of Anne Arundel County.
Emson Notes. See Matriarch Rebecca [-?-] Daniell Emson Cobb Hawkins
Farmer Notes. See Emson of Baltimore County
Ferguson of Montgomey County.
Field of Baltimore County.
Ford Notes. See Grant of Baltimore County.
Fitsimmons of Baltimore County.
Fugate of Baltimore County.
Garland of Baltimore County.
Giles of Anne Arundel and Baltimore Counties.
Goddard of Dorchester County.
Golding of Baltimore County.
Goldsborough Notes. See Piper of Anne Arundel County.
Grangett Notes. See Lavely of Baltimore County.
Grant of Baltimore County.
Gray Notes. See Mahan of Baltimore County.
Haddin of Anne Arundel County.
Haile Notes. See Grant of Baltimore County; also Matriarch Ann [-?-] Vickory Plowman..

Hall Notes. See Andrews of Kent County.
Hambleton Family of Baltimore County.
Hamill of Charles County.
Harrington Notes. See Piper of Anne Arundel County.
Harryman of Baltimore County
Hatherly of Anne Arundel County.
Hawkins Notes. See Matriarch Rebecca [-?-] Daniell Emson Cobb Hawkins
Hayes Notes. See Matriarch Jane [-?-] Waites Dixon Long.
Hayes Notes. See Norrington of Baltimore County.
Hearn of Anne Arundel County.
Heighe of Calvert County.
Hennis of Baltimore County.
Hickson of Baltimore County.
Hinton Notes. See Matriarch Elizabeth [-?-] Sampson Bagford Hinton Stone
Hitchcock of Baltimore County.
Hook, Joseph, of Baltimore County.
Hook, Rudolph, of Baltimore County.
Hughes of Baltimore County.
Johnson Notes. See Matriarch Deborah of Baltimore County.
Morgan Jones of Anne Arundel County.
Thomas Jones of Baltimore County,
Jones Notes. See Chadwell of Baltimore County.
Kenley of Baltimore and Harford County.
Henry King of Baltimore County.
Richard King Families of Maryland.
Knight of Baltimore County.
Knowlman of Kent County.
Lee Notes. See Hickson of Baltimore Count.
Leeke of Anne Arundel and Baltimore Counties
Leroy Notes. See Atkinson Familyof Baltimore.
Levely of Baltimore County.
Litton of Baltimore County.
Lomax of Baltimore County.
Long Notes. See Matriarch Jane [-?-] Waites Dixon Long.
Mahane of Baltimore County.
Mallonnee of Baltimore County.
Marchant Notes. See Sweeting of Baltimore County.
Matriarch Ann [-?-] Vickory Plowman of Baltimore County,
Matriarch Deborah [-?-] Johnson Benger of Baltimore County
Matriarch Dinah [-?-] Nuthead Devoran Oley Assa.
Matriarch Elizabeth [-?-] Cogell Dorman Swindell.
Matriarch Elizabeth [-?-] Sampson Bagford Hinton Stone of Baltimore County.
Matriarch Jane [-?-] Waites Dixon Long of Baltimore County.
Matriarch Rebecca [-?-] Daniell Emson Cobb Hawkins of Baltimore County.
Matthews Notes. See Hughes of Baltimore County.
Maxwell of Baltimore County.
McClain of Baltimore County.
McQueen of Baltimore County.
Merryman of Baltimore Co.
Merryman Notes. See Matriarch Ann [-?-] Vickory Plowman.

Mohler of Baltimore County.
Moran of Charles and St. Mary's Counties.
Morris of Baltimore County.
Morton Notes. See Lavely of Baltimore County.
Munday Notes. See Temple of Baltimore County.
Nichols of Cecil County.
Norrington of Baltimore County.
Norris Notes. See Norrington of Baltimore County.
Nuthead Notes. See Matriarch Dinah [-?-] Nuthead Devoran Oley Assa.
Oakley of Baltimore County.
Ogg of Baltimore County.
Oley Notes. See Matriarch Dinah [-?-] Nuthead Devoran Oley Assa.
Paulson Notes. See Matriarch Rebecca [-?-] Daniell Emson Cobb Hawkins
Peacock Notes. See Sickelmore of Baltimore County.
Peake Notes. See Matriarch Jane [-?-] Waites Dixon Long of Baltimore County.
Peale of Maryland.
Pickering of Anne Arundel County.
Piper of Anne Arundel County.
Plowman Notes. See Matriarch Anne [-?-] Vickory Plowman.
Polk Notes. See Peale of Maryland.
Popejoy of Baltimore County.
Porter Notes. See Carrington of Baltimore County.
Powell Notes. See Temple of Baltimore County.
Prebble of Baltimore County.
Purnall Notes. See Pickering of Anne Aundel County.
Rankin Notes. See Bull Family of Baltimore County.
Rathell of Talbot County.
Raven Notes. See Ward of Baltimore County.
Rhodes Notes. See Hughes of Baltimore County.
Robinson Notes. See Peale of Maryland.
Rogers of New England and Anne Arundel County.
Rowles of Anne Arundel, Baltimore, and Queen Anne's Counties
Scott Notes. See Matriarch Deborah of Baltimore County.
Scrivener Notes. See Pickering of Anne Arundel County.
Scudamore Notes. See Matriarch Jane [-?-] Waites Dixon Long.
Shaw Notes. See Matriarch Deborah of Baltimore County.
Sickelmore Family of Baltimore County.
Simes Notes. See Peale of Maryland.
Simmons Family of Anne Arundel County.
Simpson of Baltimore County.
Sing Notes: See Richard Taylor of Baltimore County
Sligh of Baltimore and Anne Arundel Counties.
Anthony Smith of Anne Arundel County.
James Smith of Anne Arundel County.
Stevenson Notes. See Matriarch Ann [-?-] Vickory Plowman
Sweeting of Baltimore County.
Sweeting Notes: see Lavely of Baltimore County.
Swindell Notes. See Matriarch Elizabeth [-?-] Cogell Dorman Swindell.
Tanzey of Anne Arundel and Baltimore Counties and North Carolina.
Taylor Notes. See Emson.

Colonial Families of Maryland II

Richard Taylor of Baltimore County.
Tebedo of Anne Arundel County.
Temple of Baltimore County.
Tolley of Baltimore County.
Tongue of Anne Arundel County.
Towson Notes. See Mahan of Baltimore County.
Tucker of Baltimore County.
Turner of Cecil and Baltimore Counties.
Tye Notes. See Hitchcock of Baltimore County.
Vickory Notes. See Matriarch Anne [-?-] Vickory Plowman.
Vine Notes. See Litton of Baltimore County.
Ward of Anne Arundel County.
Ward of Baltimore County.
Ward Notes. See Sicklemore of Baltimore County.
Watkins of Baltimore County.
West of Anne Arundel County.
Whayland Family of Baltimore County
Whipps of Calvert and Anne Arundel Counties.
Whitaker Notes. See Matriarch Rebecca [-?-] Daniell Emson Cobb Hawkins.
White Notes. See Cobb of Baltimore County.
Wiley Notes: See Richard Taylor of Baltimore County.
Wilkinson of Baltimore County.
Wineman Notes. See Lavely of Baltimore County.

Bibliography

AACR: F. Edward Wright, *Anne Arundel County Church Records of the 17th and 18th Centuries,* Lewes [Del.]: Colonial Roots, 2004.
AAJU: Anne Arundel County Court (Judgments Records), 1703-1844. MSA C 91.
AALC: Anne Arundel County Court (Land Commissions), 1716-1829. MSA C94
AALR: Anne Arundel County Court (Land Records), 1662-1851. MSA C97. See also *Abstracts of Anne Arundel County Land Records,* Pub by the Anne Arundel County Genealogical Society.
AAML: Anne Arundel County Court (Marriage Licenses), 1777-1851, MSA C 113.
AAMR: Henry C. Peden and Veronica Clarke Peden, *Anne Arundel County Marriage References, 1658-1800,* Lewes [Del.]: Colonial Roots, 2009.
AAWB: Anne Arundel County Register Of Wills (Wills) 1777-1980. MSA CM 122.
Adomanis: James Admonais, *Annarundell County Free School, 1723-1912,* Arnold,[Md.]:The Maryland Center for the Study of History, © 2000 by James Adomanis.
Alumni Cantabrigensis. Comp. by Joseph A. Venn. Cambridge University Press, 1927
Anne Arundel County Court (Coroner's Inquests, 1787-1790), MSA C 58.
Archer Notes: Archer, G. W., "Early Land Grants, Surveys, and Deeds – 1648-1730: Extracts from Maryland Rent Rolls and Land Records Comiled by Louis Dow Scisco," typescript in the possession of the author.
ARMD:Archives of Maryland. Vol. 1-, Baltimore: The Maryland Historical Society, 1893-
Arps, Walter E., Jr., *Heirs and Orphans: Anne Arundel Co., Maryland Distributions, 1788-1838.* Silver Spring: Westminster: Family Line Publications, © 1985.
AWAP: Peter Wilson Coldham. *American Wills and Administrations Proved in London,*

1611-1857. Baltimore: Genealogical Publishing Co., 2007.
BAAB: Baltimore County Register of Wills (Administration Bonds), 1667-1851, MSA C264.
BAAD: Baltimore County Register of Wills (Administration Accounts), 1674-1851, MSA C258.
BACP: Baltimore County Court (Proceedings), 1682-1756, MSA C 400.
BACT: Baltimore County Court (Chattel Records), 1750-1814. MSA C298; 1770-1773, MSA CM 133.
BADB: Baltimore Co. Debt Books: See Land Office (Debt Books), 1733-1775, MSA S 12; 1753-1774, MSA SM 124. N.B.: a Debt Book for 1750 is in the Calvert Papers at the MdHS.
BAEJ; Baltimore County Ejectment Papers: See Provincial Court (Ejectment Papers), MSA S 549. (OS: Oversize).
BAGA: Baltimore County Register of Wills (Guardian Accounts), 1786-1851, MSA C 333..
BALC: Baltimore County Court (Land Commissions) 1727-1831, MSA C 350.
BALR: Baltimore County Court (Land Records), 1661-1851, MSA C352.
Baltz, Shirley V., *The Quays of the City: An Account of the Bustling 18th Century Port of Annapolis.* Annapolis: The Liberty Tree, Ltd. 1975.
BAMI: Baltimore County Court (Minutes), 1755-1851, MSA C376
BAML: Baltimore County Court (Marriage Licenses), 1777-1751, MSA C376.
BAOC: Baltimore Co. Register of Wills (Orphans Court Proceedings) 1777-1851, MSA C 396
BAPE: Baltimore County Register of Wills (Petitions) 1780-1789, MSA C399
Barnes, Robert, *Colonial Families of Anne Arundel County,* Westminster: Family Line Publications, accessed on CD-ROM FTM CD#184.
BARP: Peden, Henry C., Jr. *Revolutionary Patriots of Baltimore Town and Baltimore County 1775-1783.* Westminster: Family Line Publications, accessed on CD-ROM FTM CD#133.
BAWB: Baltimore County Register of Wills (Wills) 1666-1851, MSA C 435, Libers 4 -20 abst. by Annie Walker Burns.
BCD: Baltimore City Directories, various years.
BCF: Robert W. Barnes, *Baltimore County Families, 1659-1759,* Baltimore: Genealogical Publishing Co., 1989.
BDML: Edward C. Papenfuse, et al. *A Biographical Dictionary of the Maryland Legislature, 1635-1789.* 2 vols. Baltimore: The Johns Hopkins University Press, 1979, 1985.
Berry, Ellen T., and David A. Berry, *Early Ohio Settlers, Purchasers of Land in Southwestern Ohio, 1800-1840.* Baltimore: Genealogical Publishing Co., 1986
BFD: Balances of Final Distributions (Balance Books), 7 vols. MSA
BIND: Baltimore Co. Register of Wills (Indentures) 1794-1913, MSA C 337
BINV: Baltimore Co. Register of Wills (Inventories) 1661-1851, MSA C 340.
BRCO: Peter Wilson Coldham, *The Bristol Registers of Servants Sent to Foreign Plantations, 1654-1686.* Baltimore: Genealogical Publishing Co., 1988.
Calendar of Maryland State Papers. Annapolis: The Maryland Hall of Records Commission, 1943-1958.
.... *No. 1: The Black Books,* Repr. Baltimore: Genealogical Publishing Co., 1967.
.... *No. 2: The Brown Books.*
.... *No. 3: The Red Books.*
........*No. 5: Executive Miscellanea*

Carothers, Bettie Stirling, *1776 Census of Maryland,* Lutherville [MD]: The Author, n.d.
Carothers, Bettie Stirling, and Robert W. Barnes.,*1783 Tax List of Baltimore County, Maryland. 1783 Tax List of Baltimore Co., Maryland,* Lutherville, Bettie Stirling Carothers, 1978.
Carothers, Bettie Stirling, *1783 Tax List of Maryland: Part 1: Cecil, Talbot, Harford and Calvert Counties,* Lutherville [Md.]: Carothers, 1977
CBEB: Peter Wilson Coldham, *British Emigrants in Bondage,* Baltimore: Genealogical Publishing Co., © 2005, available on CD-ROM.
CD-ROM DCD#103: *Maryland Militia in the War of 1812.* 8 vols., available from Lewes {Del.] Colonial Roots.
CECH: Henry C. Peden, Jr. *Early Anglican Church Records of Cecil County.* Westminster: Family Line Publications, 1990.
CELR: Cecil County. Court (Land Records) 1674-1792, MSA C626 See also June D. Brown, *Cecil County, Maryland Land Records, 1673-1751,* Westminster: Family Line Publications, 1998.
CHLR: Charles County Court (Land Records) 1658-1844, MSA C70.
CHWB: Charles County Register of Wills (Wills) 1665-1825, MSA C 6812.
Clark, Raymond B., Jr. *Baltimore Co. Tax Lists, 1699-1706,*
CMSP: See *Calendar of Maryland State Papers.*
Colonial Abstracts of Lancaster County, Virginia: See: Beverly Fleet, *Virginia Colonial Abstracts; Three Volumes Published in Four* (1937-1949) Repr.: Baltimore: Genealogical Publishing Co., 2010.
Commission Book No. 1: Governor and Council (Commission Record), 1726-1786, MSA 1080
Commission Book 2: Governor and Council (Commission Record), 1733-1773, (also called Liber 82 J.R) MSA 1080; indexed in *MdHM* 26:138ff.
Cummins, Virginia Raymond, *Hamilton County, Ohio Court And Other Records Volumes 1 & 2),* General Printing Co., 1967
DOLR: Dorchester County Court (Land Records) 1669-1851, MSA C 710.
EAQG: *Encyclopedia of American Quaker Genealogy;* accessed on CD-ROM GPC CD#192: Encyclopedia of Quaker Genealogy
"Emigrants from America to Liverpool," *New England Historic and Genealogical Register:* 1911
ESVR: F. Edward Wright, *Maryland Eastern Shore Vital Records,* 5 vols., 1648-1825, accessed on CD-ROM FTM CD#178.
Final Distribution Books: See BFD.
FTM CD#19: *Egle's Notes and Queries: Historical, Biographical, and Genealogical Relating Chiefly to Central Pennsylvania,* accessed on CD-ROM FTM CD#19.
FTM CD#133: Maryland and Delaware Revolutionary Patriots. Westminster: Family Line Publications.
FTM CD#166: *Church Records: Selected Areas of Pennsylvania,* Westminster: Family Line Publications.
FTM CD#178: *Maryland and Delaware Church Records.* Westminster: Family Line Publications.
FTM CD#184: Colonial Families of Maryland, Westminster: Family Line Publications.
FTM CD#206: Maryland Probate Records,
FTM CD#209: Pennsylvania Wills, Westminster: Family Line Publications.
FTM CD#512: *Pennsylvania Colonial Records, 1600s-1800s.* Baltimore: Genealogical Publishing Co..
FRLR: Frederick County Court (Land Records) 1748-1847, MSA C 814.

Colonial Families of Maryland II

Ghirelli, Michael, *List of Emigrants to America, 1682-1692*. (1986) Repr.: Baltimore: Genealogical Publishing Co. 1989.

GSV: Dawn Thomas and Robert W. Barnes. *The Green Spring Valley: Its History and Heritage*, 2 vols.. Baltimore: Maryland Historical Society, 1975

HAML: John Harlan Livezey and Helene Maynard Davis, *Harford Co. Marriage Licenses, 1777-1865*, Westminster: Family Line Publications, 1993.

HAMR: Henry C. Peden, Jr., and Veronica Clarke Peden, *Harford County Marriage References and Family Relationships, 1774-1824*. Lewes: Colonial Roots, 2011.

HAOC: Henry C. Peden, Jr. *Abstracts of Orphans Court Proceedings, 1778-1800, Harford County, Maryland*. Westminster: Family Line Publications, 1990.

Harrison, Lucy H. "St. John's and St. George's Parish Register." MS. at MdHS. See *SJSG*.

Harrison, Lucy H., "St. John's and St. George's Parish Vestry Proceedings: MS at MdHS.

Harrison, "St. John's Parish, Prince George's Co., Register: See *PGKG*.

HAWB: Harford County Register of Wills (Wills) 1774-1976, MdSCA CM 599, See Ralph H. Morgan, *Harford County Wills, 1774-1880, Harford County Maryland*, Westminster: Family Line Publications, 1990.

Hayward, Mary Ellen, and R. Kent Lancaster. *A Guide to the Markers and Burials, 1775-1943* [of Baltimore's Westminster Cemetery Westminster Presbyterian Church]. Baltimore: Westminster Preservation Trust, 1984.

Heads of Families at the First Census of the United States Taken in the Year 1790: Maryland, United States Bureau of the Census (1907) Repr.: Baltimore: Genealogical Publishing Co., 2004

Historic Graves, Private Burial Grounds, and Cemeteries of Kent County, Maryland. Silver Spring: Family Line Publications, n.d.

Horvath, George J., Jr. *The Particular Assessment Lists for Baltimore and Carroll Counties, 1798.* Silver Spring: Family Line Publications, 1986.

IBCP: Henry C. Peden, Jr. *Inhabitants of Baltimore Co., 1763-1773*. Westminster: Family Line Publications, 1989.

IBCW: F. Edward Wright. *Inhabitants of Baltimore Co., 1692-1763.* Silver Spring: Family Line Publications, 1987.

INAC: Prerogative Court (Inventories and Accounts) 1674-1718, MSA S 536. Accessed at V. L. Skinner, Jr......

INCE: Henry C. Peden, Jr., *Inhabitants of Cecil County, 1649-1774*. Westminster: Family Line Publications, 1993.

INKE: Henry C. Peden, Jr. *Inhabitants of Kent County, Maryland, 1637-1787.* Westminster: Family Line Publications, 1994.

Jourdan, *Early Family. of Southern Maryland*. 10 vols., Lewes, Colonial Roots. Volumes 1-6 available in CD-ROM FTM CD#184.

Kaminkow, Marion J. *Original lists of Emigrants in Bondage from London to the American Colonies, 1719-1744,* edited with introduction by Marion and Jack Kaminkow (1967) Repr. By Baltimore: Genealogical Publishing Co.

Kaminkow, Jack, and Marion Kaminow. *List of Emigrants to America, 1718-1759.* Repr. Baltimore: Genealogical Publishing Co., 1989.

KEBI: Kent County Court (Bonds and Indentures) 1694=1782. MSA C 1928.

KELR; Kent County Court (Land Records) 1648-1790. MSA C 1068.

KESP: St. Paul's Parish, Kent Co.: see *F. Edward Wright. Maryland Eastern Shore Vital Records,* , 5 vols..

KPMV: Peter Wilson Coldham. *The King's Passengers to Maryland and Virginia.* Westminster: Family Line Publications, © 1997 by Peter Wilson Coldham.

Letzer and Russo: *The Diary of William Faris; The Daily Life of an Annapolis Silversmith* Edited by Mark B. Letzer and Jean B. Russo. Baltimore: The Oress at the Maryland Historical Society, 2003.

Mallick, *Sketches:* Sallie A. Mallick *Sketches of Citizens from Baltimore City and Baltimore County.* Westminster: Family Line Publications, 1989.

Marine, William, *The British Invasion of Maryland.* Repr.: Baltimore: Genealogical Publishing Co.,, available on CD-ROM FTM CD#521: Maryland Settlers and Soldiers.

Maryland Genealogies. 2 vols. Baltimore: Genealogical Publishing Co., available on CD-Rom FTM CD#195: *Maryland Genealogies and Marriages.*

MBR: *Maryland Bible Records.* Henry C. Peden, Jr. 7 vols. Westminster: Family Line Publications.

MCHP: Chancery Court (Chancery Papers), var. d., MSA S 512.

MCHR: Chancery Court (Chancery Record), 1668-1852, MSA S 517; See also Debbie Hooper. *Abstracts of Chancery Court Records of Maryland 1669-1782,* Westminster: Family Line Publications, 1996).

MCW: Maryland Calendar of Wills, Vols. 1-8 comp. by Jane Baldwin Cotton. Baltimore: Kohn and Pollock, 1904. Vols 9-16 comp. and pub. Westminster: Family Line Publications

MDAD: Prerogative Court (Accounts) 1718-1777, MSA S 531; abst. by V. L. Skinner, Jr., accessed at CD-ROM FTM CD#206.

MDTP: Prerogative Court (Testamentary Proceedings) 1657-1777, MSA S 529; abstracted by V. L. Skinner, Jr., in *Abstracts of the Testamentary Proceedings of the Prerogative Court of Maryand.* 42 vols. Baltimore: Clearfield Co., 2004-2012.

Memoirs of the Dead and the Tomb's Remembrancer (1806) Repr.: Westminster: Family Line Publications, 1989.

MGSB: Maryland Genealogical Society Bulletin. periodical

MINV: Prerogative Court (Inventories) 1718-1777, MSA S 534; abst. by V. L. Skinner, Jr., accessed at CD-ROM FTM CD#206

Moller; Shirley Middleton Moller, *Prince George's County, Maryland, Marriage Refercnces and Family Reationships.* Lewes [Del.]. Colonial Roots, © 2009.

MPL: Land Office (Patent Record) 1637-1979, MSA S 11.

MRR: Maryland Rent Roll: Baltimore and Anne Arundel Counties. Baltimore: Genealogical Publishing Co. 1976.

MWB: Prerogative Court (Wills) 1635-1777, MSA S 538, accessed at CD-ROM FTM CD#206, including those abstracted in the *Maryland Calendar of Wills.* Libers 23-31 have also been abstracted by Carson Abst. by Gibb) and are accessible at Maryland State Archives/Reference and Research/Probate Records.

NGSQ: National Genealogical Society Quarterly .periodical

The Notebook: publication of the Baltimore County Genealogical Society.

PASC: David Faris. *Plantagenet Ancestos of 17th Century Colonists.* Baltimore: Genealogical Publishing Co., 1996.

PCLR: Provincial Court (Land Records), 1658-1777, MSA S 552.

Peden, Henry C., Jr. *Baltimore City Deaths and Burials, 1834-1840.* Westminster: Family Line Publications, 1998.

Peden, Henry C., Jr. *A Collection of Maryland Church Records.* Westminster: Family Line Publications, ©1997, accessed on CD-ROM FTM CD#178.

Peden, Henry C., Jr., *Heirs and Legatees of Harford County, Maryland, 1802-1846.* (1988) Repr.: Westminster: Family Line Publications, 2000.

Peden, Henry C., Jr. *Marylanders to Carolina*. Westminster: Family Line Publications, 1994.
Peden, Henry C., Jr. *Marylanders to Kentucky, 1775-1825*. Westminster: Family Line Publications, 1991.
Peden, Henry C., Jr. *More Marylanders to Carolna*. Westminster: Family Line Publications Westminster: Family Line Publications, 1999
Peden, Henry C., Jr. *More Marylanders to Kentucky, 1178-1828*. Westminster: Family Line Publications, 1997
Peden, Henry C., Jr. *Presbyterian Records of Baltimore,* Westminster: Family Line Publications, © 1995, accessed on CD-ROM FTM CD#178.
Reamy, Bill, and Martha Reamy. *St. George's Parish Register 1689-1793*. Silver Spring: Family Line Publications, 1988, accessed on CD-ROM FTM CD#178
Reamy, Bill, and Martha Reamy *St. Paul's Parish Register*. Westminster: Family Line Publications, accessed on CD-ROM FTM CD#178
PGKG: Helen W. Brown, *Index to King George Parish, Prince George's County,* Westminster: Family Line Publications, n.d.
PGQA: Helen W. Brown, *Index to St. Barnabas Church, Queen Anne Parish, Prince George's Co.*, Westminster: Family Line Publications, n.d.
QRNM: Henry C. Peden, Jr., *Quaker Records of Northern Maryland,* Westminster: Family Line Publications, 1993,accessed on CD-ROM FTM CD#178
QRSM: Henry C. Peden, Jr., *Quaker Records of Southern Maryland,* Westminster: Family Line Publications, 1992, accessed on CD-ROM FTM CD#178
Rent Roll: Land Office (Rent Rolls) 1639-1776, MSA S 18.
RPAA: Henry C. Peden, Jr. *Revolutionary Patriots of Anne Arundel County, 1775-1783.* Westminster: Family Line Publications, accessed on CD-ROM FTM CD#133.
RPCH; Henry C. Peden, Jr., *Revolutionary Patriots of Charles County,* accessed on CD-ROM FTM CD#133.
RPCV: Henry C. Peden, Jr., *Revolutionary Patriots of Calvert County,* accessed on CD-ROM FTM CD#133.
RPHA: Henry C. Peden, Jr. *Revolutionary Patriots of Harford County.* accessed on CD-ROM FTM CD#133.
RPKE: Henry C. Peden, Jr., *Revolutionary Patriots of Kent County.* accessed on CD-ROM FTM CD#133.
RPPG: Henry C. Peden, Jr., *Revolutionary Patriots of Prince George's Count.* accessed on CD-ROM FTM CD#133.*y*
Saint Barnabas Church, Queen Anne Parish, Prince George's Co. See PGKG.
Scharf, John Thomas. *History of Baltimore City and County*. (1881). Repr. in two vols.: Baltimore: Clearfield Co., 1997.
Scisco: Louis Dow Scisco, *Baltimore County Land Records, 1665-1687*. Baltimore: Clearfield Co. 1992
SJSG: Henry C. Peden, Jr., *St. John's and St. George's Parish Register, 1696-1851.* Westminster: Family Line Publications, 1987.
Skinner, Vern L., Jr.: his abstracts of Inventories and Accounts, Maryland Inventories, and Maryland Accounts, are accessible on CD-ROM FTM CD#206.
Skinner, Vern L., Jr.: Abstracts of the Prerogative Court of Maryland, Libers 37-74, 5 vols., Westminster: Family Line Publications, and Westminster: Willow Bend Books.
Skordas: Gust Skordas, *Early Settlers of Maryland, 1633-1680,* Baltimore: Genealogical Publishing Co., 1979
SOCD: David Dobson, *Scots on the Chesapeake*. Baltimore: Genealogical Publishing Co.

SPKE: St. Paul's Parish Register, accessed on CD-ROM, FTM CD#178.
Stein, Charles Frances, *History of Calvert County Maryland,* 3rd ed., The Author, Baltimore, MD, 1976.
TALC: Talbot County Court (Land Commissions), 1702-1793, MSA C1878
TALR: Talbot County Court (Land Records), 1662-1851, MSA C 1880.
Third Haven Meeting, Society of Friends. See *ESVR.*
Votes and Proceedings of sessions of the Lower House and House of Delegates, including notes, minutes, roll calls, and bills and amendments discussed. Arranged chronologically. The Journal series is a printed edition of Proceedings, 1777-1841 MSA S975.
Warfield, *Founders:* John D. Warfield. *Founders of Anne Arundel and Howard Counties* (1905). Repr. Baltimore: Regional Publishing Co., 1967.
WCES: F. Edward Wright. *Citizens of the Eastern Shore of Maryland, 1659-1750.* Silver Spring: Family Line Publications, 1986.
Wright, *Inhabitants of Baltimore Co.*
Wright, F. Edward, *Maryland Militia in the War of 1812: Anne Arundel Co.,* accessed on CD-ROM DCD#103
Wright, F. Edward, *Maryland Militia in the War of 1812. Vol. 3, Harford and Cecil Counties,* accessed on CD-ROM DCD#103
Wright, F. Edward, *Judgment Records of Dorchester, Queen Anne's, and Talbot Counties,* Lewes: Colonial Roots, 2001.
Wright. F. Edward, *Quaker Minutes of the Eastern Shore, 1676-1779,* Lewes [Del/]: Colonial Roots, 2003.
Wyand, Jeffrey A., and Florence L. Wyand, *Colonial Maryland Naturalizations,* Baltimore: Genealogical Publishing Co., 1975
YASP: Publications of the Yorkshire Archaeological Society.

The Airey Family of Talbot County

1. Jonathan Airey died by 1704 when David Airey, administrator, was summoned to render accounts (MDTP 20:67).

Jonathan Arey was in Talbot Co. by 21 August 1688 when he witnessed two deeds (TALR 5:180, 183). On 1 January 1688 Richard Dudley and wife Eleanor conveyed 100 a. *Dudley' Choice* to Jonathan and David Arey (TALR 5:212).

Jonathan was probably the father of: **2. David**; and **3. Joseph**.

2. David Airey or Arey, probably son of Jonathan (1), died about 1714. David Arey married, 1st, Hannah Jadwyn, Jr., on 11 January 1795 at Third Haven Meeting (Wright, *Quaker Minutes of the Eastern Shore:* 16). He married, 2nd, Elizabeth Cook on 9 d. 12 m. 1707 at Tuckahoe Meeting House ("Third Haven Meeting" on *ESVR* 1:54).

Sarah Kindred, aged 53 of Talbot Co. deposed on 18 August 1747 that she had married her first husband Philip Morgan no more than 40 years earlier and that David Arey had married Elizabeth Cook some time in the 'foure part' of the same winter and that their daughter Esther was not born until a considerable time after they were married (TALR 17:117).

At the June 1698 Talbot Co. Court, Thomas Wallis, an orphan boy bound to David Arey was judged to be ten years old and was to earn the trade of a cordwainer. At the March 1705 Talbot County Court, John Barnes, who had married the widow of William Viney, petitioned the court that David Arey retained Godfrey Viney, son of William, in his service and refused to deliver him to the petitioner and his mother. The boy was ordered discharged (Wright, *Judgment Records of... Talbot Co.:* 137, 145).

David Arey witnessed a deed on 13 February 1699 (TALR 8:19). David Arey and Emanuel Jackson were appointed trustees of the will of John Jadwin, proved 24 April 1707 (MDTP 19C:212). On 20 d. 6 m. 1705 John Jadwin, Edward Clark and Benjamin Parrott conveyed to George Bowes, David Arey and Abraham Morgan, trustees, three acres of land on which the meeting house and graveyard of the people called Quakers stood (TALR 9:340).

On 24 March 1704/5 David Arey paid £0.7.6 for the alienation of 118 a., part of *Roeclift*, which Jonathan Airey had purchased from William Hemsley (TALR 9:288). David and Elizabeth Arey, on 3 March 1708 conv. 100 a., the northern part of *Dudley's Choice*, to John Harrington, planter (TALR 11:72).

David Arey of Talbot Co., in his will made 19 January 1714, left his plantation *Sinefield*, to his brother Joseph where he and his wife were living. Joseph and his wife to have the care of his daughters Esther and Deborah, and he mentioned the Quaker Quarterly Meeting (MWB 14:68, abst. in *Md. Cal. of Wills* 4:34). Deborah Arey married Benjamin Parratt on 27 d. 7 m. 1728 at Tuckahoe Meeting (Third Haven Meeting," *ESVR* 1:94).

On 5 October 1716 Joseph Arey, executor, filed an account of the estate of David Arey of Talbot Co. (INAC 37C:154).

David and Elizabeth were the parents of: **4. Easter,** b. about 1708; **5. Deborah,** b. about 1709/10. David Harrington of Queen Anne's Co., planter, aged 47, deposed on 18 Aug 1747 that some 37 years earlier he had gone to live with David Arey of Talbot Co., and that time Deborah Arey, daughter of Elizabeth was not more that 5 or 6 months of age (TALR 17:117). Deborah Arey and Benjamin Parratt were m. on 27 d. 7 m. 1728 at Tuckahoe Meeting House ("Third Haven Meeting" on *ESVR* 1:94).

3. Joseph Airey, orphan boy, probably son of Jonathan (1), was listed as a servant in the May 1696 inventory of William Finney of Talbot Co. (INAC 13B:152). Joseph Arey of Talbot Co., planter, m. Mary Baynard on 10 d. 9 m. 1708 at Tuckahoe Creek Meeting ("Third Haven Meeting" on *ESVR* 1:55). Joseph 'Arey.' Quaker, married, 2nd, by 10 August 1725, Jane, Quaker, widow and executrix, of Benjamin Parrott of Talbot Co. (MDAD 7:44, 525). Joseph Arey and Jane Parratt declared their intention to marry on 27 d. 3 m. 1725 and again on 30 d. 4 m. 1725, and they were given liberty to marry (Wright. *Quaker Minutes of the Eastern Shore:* 39).

Jane Airey, of Talbot Co., wife of Joseph, affirmed between 14 June and 17 July 1729 when she witnessed a deed (DOLR 8 Old: 432). William Scott, Quaker, and 'Jean' Arey declared their intention to marry on 31 d. 10 m. 1729, and on 25 d. 12 m. 1729 it was reported that the marriage had been decently accomplished (Wright. *Quaker Minutes of the Eastern Shore:* 41).

On 24 March 1725 Airey was a creditor listed in the account of Col. Robert Grundy of Talbot Co. On 12 February 1727 Airey was one of the appraisers of John Hankin (MINV 13:20).

Joseph Arey died leaving a will dated 6 November 1728 and proved 18 December 1728. His sons-in-law Eliazer and William Parratt were to have *Sullop* after the death of his wife Jane. His son Jonathan was to have personalty (MWB 19:574, abst. in *Md. Cal. of Wills* 6:91).

Joseph Arey died by 7 March 1728/9 when John Loveday and Edward Nedels appraised his personal estate at £107.5.4. Jonathan Arey and Joshua Clarke signed as next of kin. Jane Arey, the administratrix, filed the inventory on 19 March 1728 (MINV 13:460). An additional inventory totaling £31.4.2 was compiled by Nedles and Loveday on 22 August 1729. Jane Scott filed the inventory on 8 Sep 1730 (MDAD 7:260).

On 8 September 1730 Jane Scott, Quaker, wife of William Scott, filed an account of the estate of Joseph Arey. She cited an inventory of £107.5.4, and listed payments of £48.2.7. The deceased was cited as executor of Esther Arey, and payments were made to James Powell who married Hannah Parrott, daughter of Benjamin Parrott. The deceased had two children who were dead (MDAD 10:425). On 1 June 1731 Jane Scott, Quaker, filed another account, listing payments of £13.1.3. His son Jonathan Airey was listed as a legatee (MDAD 11:163).

Joseph and Jane were the parents of: **6. Jonathan; 7.** probably **David**, living 3 November 1728; **8.** probably **Mary**, living 3 November 1728; **9.** |-?-|, deceased; and **10.** |-?-|, deceased.

4. Easter Arey, daughter of David (2) and Elizabeth, was born about 1708. William Tharp of Talbot Co., aged 65, deposed on 18 August 1747 that Esther, daughter of David and Elizabeth, was born about 12 months after David and Elizabeth had been married (TALR 17:117).

Esther Arey of Talbot Co. died leaving a will dated 3 November 1728 and proved 18 December 1728. Her brother-in-law Benjamin Parratt and his heirs were to have 500 a. *Parker's Park.* She left her cousin Jonathan Arey and his heirs 300 a. *Morgan's Reserve.* She left her cousin David 125 a. *David's Ridge,* and if he died without issue, to her cousin Mary Arey. Her Uncle Joseph Arey and brother-in-law Benjamin Parratt were named executors. Edward Nedles, George Golt, and Procello Bradbury witnessed the will (MWB 19:600 abst. in *Md. Cal. of Wills* 6:96).

On 14 May 1748 Anthony Roe who had married Jane, sister of Benjamin Parrott, and Hannah Dobson, widow, another sister of Benjamin Parrott, stated that Esther Airey's will was invalid because she had been a minor under 21 (TALR 17:117).

6. Jonathan Airey, son of Joseph (3) and Jane, was left 300 a. *Morgan's* Reserve by his cousin Easter Arey. On 15 April 1761 John Tillotson of Queen Anne's Co. made his will appointing his wife Sarah and cousin Jonathan Airey as guardians of his children (MWB 38:620 abst. in *Md. Cal. of Wills* 14:215-316).

Jonathan Arey of Queen Anne's Co. died leaving a will dated 8 December 1767 and proved 28 December 1767. He named his cousins Sarah, William, and John Tillotson, and his friend Edward Chetham. He disposed of *Roclift and David's Ridge* on Tuckahoe Creek on Choptank River, Talbot Co. John Tillotson was named as executor. John Coursey, Michael Green, Philip Saintee, and Abraham Delahunt witnessed the will (MWB 36:247, abst. in *Md. Cal. of Wills* 14:24).

Unplaced:
Mary Airey and John Covington were married on 13 July 1731 in St. Luke's Parish, Queen Anne's Co. (*ESVR* 2:48).

= = 0 = =

The Andrews Family
With Notes on the Hall Family

1. Samuel Andrews, of Kent Co., school master, on 9 April 1725 purchased land from Thomas Tyer of Kent Co., and his wife Johanna (KELR JS#W:472-452) Andrews and his wife Mary, on 18 August 1727 conveyed to William Thomas, 100 acres of the northern part of a tract called *Hillingsworth* (KELR JS#X:104).

On 8 September 1723 Andrews was listed as a creditor of the estate of James Ringgold of Kent Co. (MDAD 5:240). In 1725 Andrews registered a cattle mark (*WCES:* 33). On 21 March 1725 Andrews testified in court about the behavior of Dominick Kenslaugh, laborer ("Criminal Records of Kent County," *MGSB* 36:405).

On 13 March 1749 Edward Hall of Kent Co., planter, and his wife Mary, Michael Hall of the same county, planter, and his wife Martha, conveyed land to Joseph Nicholson of the same county, Gent., stating that whereas Samuel Andrews, late of Kent Co., deceased, had died seized and possessed of 100 acres being the uppermost moiety of 200 acres heretofore the estate of John Hudson late of the same county, deceased, which after the death of said Samuel Andrews descended to his daughters Mary and Martha who married Edward Hall and Michael Hall (KELR JS#26:284).

Samuel and Mary Andrews had two daughters, born in St. Paul's Parish, Kent Co. (*ESVR* 1:13): **2. Martha**, married Michael Hall; **3. Mary Ann**, b. 28 February 1726, married Edward Hall.

2. Martha Andrews, daughter of Samuel (1) and Mary, married Michael Hall.

Michael Hall is shown in the Kent Co. Debt Book of 1747 as owning *Pentridge* (*INKE,* 54).

Michael and Martha were the parents of two children, born in St. Paul's Parish, Kent Co. (*ESVR* 2: 24): **4. Sarah**, b. 23 January 1748; and **5. James**, b. 3 February 1750.

3. Mary Ann Andrews, son of Samuel (1) and Mary, married Edward Hall.

On 13 March 1749 Edward Hall of Kent Co., planter, and his wife Mary, and Michael Hall of the same county, planter, and his wife Martha, conveyed to Joseph Nicholson of the same county, Gent.: Whereas Samuel Andrews, late of Kent Co., deceased, died, seized and possessed of 100 acres being the uppermost moiety of 200 acres heretofore the estate of John Hudson late of the same county deceased, which after the death of said Samuel Andrews descended to his daus. Mary and Martha who married Edward Hall and Michael Hall (KELR JS#26:284).

In the 1783 Assessment List of Kent Co. an Edward Hall owned part of *Doe Neck*, in the 3rd District (*INKE*, 76).

Edward and Mary Hall were the parents of two children, whose births were recorded in St. Paul's Parish (*ESVR* 2: 24, 3:14): **6. Mary**, b. 27 November 1739; and **7. Samuel**, b. 14 December 1752.

== 0 ==

The Ashley Family[1]

A. William Ashley was the father of:
1. John Ashley.

1. John Ashley, son of William (A), was born about 1618 in Lancaster, Gloucestershire, England, and died about 1671 in Rappahannock County, Va. About 1645 he married Jane Cooper, daughter of Sir John of Rockbourne Cooper, son of Sir John Cooper, Esq., son of Richard Cooper, son of Sir John Cooper.

John and Jane were the parents of: **2. Thomas A.**, Sr., b. about 1660 in Lancaster Co., Va., and d. after 1747 in Chowan, Bertie County, N. C.; **3. Charles**, b. about 1669; and **4. Isaac**, Sr., b. about 1667.

4. Isaac Ashley, Sr., son of John (1) and Jane, was born about 1667 in Lancaster Co., Virginia, and died by 29 March 1708/09 in Kent Co., Md. He married Elizabeth [-?-], about 1689. She died after 30 May 1709.

Ashley died leaving a will dated 24 January 1708/9 and proved 29 March 1709. His son John and heirs were to have either his dwelling plantation was that seated by William Hubert. His son Isaac was to have the one that John refused. His sons Thomas and William and youngest son Abraham and their heirs were each to have 100 a. If any of his sons were to die, his portion was to pass to his daughter [unnamed]. His wife Elizabeth was named executrix and was to have personalty for life. William Hopkins, John Beck, Jr., Mary Beck, Sr., and Mary Beck Jr. witnessed the will (MWB 12, part 2: 9, abst. in *Md. Cal. of Wills* 3:125).

Elizabeth Ashley of Kent Co., widow and relict of Isaac Ashley, deceased, conveyed to her children, John Ashley, Isaac Ashley, Mary Ashley, Thomas Ashley,

---

[1] Unless otherwise noted the basic outline of this family was created by Chris Hinckley in "All in the Family Tree," accessed on Ancestry. (hinx88@centurylink.net).

Elizabeth Ashley, William Ashley, Ann Ashley and Abraham Ashley of the county afsd., cattle [listed] when they become the age of 21, deed dated 30th of 5th month (July) 1709. KELR JSN:152).

Isaac and Elizabeth were the parents of the following children, all born in St. Paul's Parish (*ESVR* 1:13): **5. William,** b. 27 July 1699; **6. John,** b. 21 September 1689; **7. Isaac,** b 24 August 1691; **8. Mary,** b. 12 August 1693; **9. Thomas,** b. 18 April 1695; **10. Elizabeth,** b. 26 May 1697; **11. Ann,** b. 2 January 1700/1; and **12 Abraham,** b. 26 March 1704.

5. William Ashley, son of Isaac (4), was born 27 July 1699 in St. Paul's Parish, Kent Co., and died there by January 1753.

William Ashley died leaving a will dated 20 August 1752 and proved 23 January 1753. His eldest son William was to have land, provided he paid the testator's two youngest sons Joshua and John Jons Ashley each £20 at age 21. All his single children were to share equally. His wife Mary was to have £12 to bring up the two small children. His wife and son William were named executors. Thomas Catline, John Jones, and Thomas Jones witnessed the will (MWB 28:457, abst. in *Md. Cal. of Wills* 10:253).

In 1753 his estate was appraised by John Reed, Sr. and N. Ricketts, and valued at £104.8.8. Adam Gray and Matthew Zuille signed as creditors. Isaac Ashley and Thomas Ashley signed as next of kin. Mary Ashley and William Ashley, executors, filed the inventory on 11 Aug 1753 (MINV 55:75). On 8 April 1754, distribution of his estate was made by Mary Ashley and William Ashley, executors (BFD 1:118).

William and Mary were the parents of (*ESVR* 1:17): **13. Jane,** b. 13 July 1729; **14: William,** b. 10 February 1731; **15. Mary,** b. 15 August 1734; **16. Joshua;** and **17. John Jones.**

6. John Ashley, Sr., son of Isaac (4) and Elizabeth, was born 21 September 1689 in St. Paul's Parish, Kent Co. and died there in 1740. On 14 August 1714 in St. Paul's Parish, Kent Co. he married Martha Wroth (*ESVR* 1:13). She was a daughter of James and Mary ([-?-]) Wroth, and was born in 1695.

John Ashley died leaving a will dated 10 December 1739 and proved 13 April 1740. His sons Isaac and John were to have the dwelling plantation *Ashley Loot,* but his wife was to have a life interest in the tract. If his sons were to die without issue, the tract was to pass to his daughters Mary Dollerhead and Hannah. Daughters Mary Dollerhead and Martha Body were each to have one shilling. His granddaughter Martha Body was to have personalty at age 16. His wife and son Isaac were named executors. Thomas Cathling, William Bagshaw, and William Ashley witnessed the will (MWB 22:204, abst. in *Md. Cal. of Wills* 8:90).

John and Martha were the parents of (*ESVR* 1:14): **18. [-?-],** b. 3 August 1717 in St. Paul's Parish; **19. [-?-],** b. 26 February 1719/20 in St. Paul's Parish; **20. Isaac; 21. John., Jr.,** b. 26 February 1719/20; **22. Mary,** m. [-?-] Dolllerhed; **23. Hannah;** and **24. Martha,** m. [-?-] Body.

7. Isaac Ashley, son of Isaac (4), was born 24 August 1691 in St. Paul's Parish and died there in 1749. He married Mary Wroth in St. Paul's Parish on 9 July 1714 (*ESVR* 1:13).

Isaac Ashley of Kent Co., died by 25 July 1749, when his estate was appraised by Samuel Groome and Richard Kinnard, and valued at £19.15.5. No creditors listed. John

Ashley and Mary [Mutsey?] signed as next of kin. Mary Ashley, administratrix, filed the inventory on 27 September 1749 (MINV 43:403).
Isaac and Mary were the parents of (*ESVR* 1:14, 17, 18): **25. Sarah**, b. 6 August 1717; **26. James**, b. 7 March 1726; **27. Ann**, b. 15 February 1727; **28. Isaac**, b. 6 May 1731; **29. Jacob**, b. 5 October 1733; and **30.** [-?-], daughter, b. 1 January 1735).

9. Thomas Ashley, son of Isaac (4) and Elizabeth, was born 18 April 1695; He married Elizabeth [-?-].
Thomas and Elizabeth were the parents of (*ESVR* 1:13, 16): **31. Thomas**, b. 5 November 1725; **32. Elizabeth**, b. 2 May 1728; **33. Abraham**, b. 10 March 1730; **34. Mary**, b. 13 August 1733; and **35. Sarah**, b. 8 December 1735.

20. Isaac Ashley, son of John (6), was born in St. Paul's Parish, and died by 5 April 1755, when his estate was appraised by Richard Kinword and William Browning, and valued at £81.14.6. John Ashley and Matthew Zuille signed as creditors. Thomas Ashley

and Elisabeth Norten signed as next of kin. Margaret Ashley, executrix, filed the inventory on 24 May 1755 (MINV 60:308).
Isaac Ashley died leaving a will dated 7 March 1755 and proved 12 February 1755/6. His sons Benjamin and Isaac were to have the 100 a. on which the testator lived, being part of *Ashley Lot*. His two sons and two daughters, Phebe and Mary were to have his estate divided among them; they were to stay on the plantation with their mother-in-law until they were able to shift for themselves. Rachel Ashley *alias* Rachel Canaday was to have furniture. Daughters Elizabeth Bowyer, Sarah Godding were to have stock; daughter Ann Money was to have cattle and his wife Margaret was to have stock and as named executrix. Thomas Catlin, William Ashley and Sophia Ashley witnessed the will which was proven in the presence of Benjamin Ashley, the heir at law (MWB 29:531, abst. in *Md. Cal. of Wills* 11:107).
Margaret Ashley filed an account of Isaac's estate on 4 February 1756. She cited the inventory as given above and listed payments of £30.4.4 (MDAD 39:105). On 1 August 1758 Margaret distributed his estate (BFD 2:86).
Isaac was the father of: **36. Benjamin; 37. Isaac; 38. Phebe; 39. Mary; 40. Rachel**, m. [-?-] Canaday; **41. Elizabeth**, m. [-?-] Bowyer; **42. Sarah**, m. [-?-] Godding; and **43. Ann**, m. [-?-] Money.

21. John Ashley, Jr., son of John (6) and Martha, was born 26 February 1719/20 in St. Paul's Parish, and died there in June 1767. He married Mary [-?-] by 1766. She married 2nd, Robert Roberts.
Ashley died leaving a will dated 1 June 1767 and proved 16 July 1767. He named his wife Mary and children John, Daniel, Nancy, and Milcah. He mentioned Col. Edward Lloyd and Richard Frisby, and he mentioned *Ashley's Lot,* bought from John Browning. His wife Mary was named executrix. John Green, Richard Frisby, and Kinvin Wroth witnessed the will (MWB 36:48, abst. in *Md. Cal. of Wills* 14:6).
On 5 November 1767 his estate was appraised by John Wickes and Jean Yeates, and valued at £272.11.1.William Slubey, Jr. and Thomas Ringgold & Co. signed as creditors. William Ashley signed as next of kin. Mary Ashley, executrix, filed the undated inventory (MINV 94:322). On 30 April 1768 his estate was appraised again by John Wickes and Marmaduke Tilden, and valued at £65.2.0.Thomas Ringgold & Co. and

Morgan & Slubey, Jr. signed as creditors. William Ashley and John Jones Ashley signed as next of kin. Mary Roberts, wife of Robert Roberts, Executrix, filed the undated inventory (MINV 98:161).

Mary Roberts filed an account of John Ashley's estate on 28 February 1769. She cited the two inventories as given and listed payments of £24.4.7 (MDAD 61:45).

John and Mary were the parents of: **44. John;** **45. Daniel,** b. about 1755; **46. Nancy;** and **47. Milcah,** (who may be the Milcah Ashley who was m. "Tues. eve. last by Rev. Woolley," to Richard W. Pipen (Chestertown *Telegraphe* 10 February 1826).

45. Daniel Ashley (Not David as originally believed), son of John (21) and Mary, was born about 1755, and died 1810 in Kent Co. He married Ann Emerich on 8 November 1781 in Kent Co.

On 23 August 1781 Daniel Ashley was listed as a New Recruit in the Continental Army (*RPKE*:5).

Daniel and Ann were the parents of: **48. Isaiah,** b. about 1782 in Kent Co.

48. Isaiah Ashley, son of Daniel (45) and Ann, was born about 1782 in Kent Co., and died there in 1866. He married Mary Dudley on 5 November 1804 in Kent Co. She was born about 1790 in Maryland.

Isaiah and Mary were the parents of: **49. Lemuel Washington,** b. about 1820; **50. John Dudley,** b. about 1814 in Md.; m. Levina Ann Adkinson on 22 October 1839 in Kent Co.; **51. Thomas Wroth,** b. October 1823 in Kent Co.; **52. Eliza Ann,** b. 1805 in Kent Co.; **53. James David,** b. 1810 in Kent Co.; **54. Joseph,** b. about 1812; **55. Benjamin,** b. about 1821; and **56. David C.,** b. 21 March 1819, d. 7 December 1911; m. Mary Ann [-?-], b. 18 October 1823, d. 9 January 1907. Both are buried in the Ashley Cemetery in Piney Neck, near Rock Hall (*Historic Graves, Private Burial Grounds and Cemeteries of Kent County, Maryland*. Silver Spring: Family Line Publications, n.d.: 18).

Unplaced:
William Ashley of Kent Co. died by 19 October 1774 when Sophia Ashley, the administratrix, filed an account of his estate citing an inventory of £64.8.5, and listing payments of £72.8.11. (MDAD 71:332).

== 0 ==

The Atkinson Family

1. Stephen Atkinson married Ann Wilton. He had a fulling mill on Conestoga Creek from 1720 to 1730. He died leaving a will dated 14 September 1739 and proved in Lancaster Co., Pa. ("Atkinson Family Data," *Egle's Notes and Queries Annual Volume*, 1899: 54, accessed on FTM CD#19: *Egle's Notes and Queries*).

On 2 d. 2 m. 1723 Atkinson requested a grant of a parcel of land lying in the Barrens beyond his plantation where it would be convenient to erect a fulling mill. Secretary Logan wrote to Isaac Taylor about it. The grant was confirmed on 15 f/ 4 m. 2727 (Minute Book I, in "Early Pennsylvania Land Records," pp. 721, 749, accessed in FTM CD#512: *Pennsylvania Colonial Records*).

Colonial Families of Maryland II

Stephen Atkinson of Lancaster Twp. died leaving a will dated 14 September 1739 and proved 31 July 1742. He named his wife. Anne Atkinson, and children: Mathew, Thomas, Joshua and Samuel. Anne Atkinson was the executrix (Lancaster County Will Book 1732-1785. accessed on FTM CD#209: Pennsylvania Wills).

Stephen and Ann were the parents of: **2. Matthew; 3. Elizabeth,** m. Thomas Doyle; **4. Jane,** m. Joshua Minshall; and **5. |-?-|,** daughter, m. Samuel Reed.

2. Matthew Atkinson, son of Stephen and Ann, died testate in 1756 in Lancaster Co. He married 1st, [-?-] [-?-], and 2nd, Margaret, daughter of Thomas Thornborough of Lancaster Co., who died testate in Lancaster co. on 20 July 1758. Margaret Atkinson died in 1798 leaving a will dated 7 September 1798 ("Atkinson Family Data").

Mathew Atkinson of Lampeter Twp. died leaving a will dated 7 April 1756 and proved 7 December 1756. He named his wife Margaret Atkinson and his children: Stephen and Wilton. He mentioned but did not name his daughters. Stephen and Wilton Atkinson were named executors (Lancaster County Will Book 1732-1785. accessed on FTM CD#209: Pennsylvania Wills).

Matthew Atkinson was the father of: **6. Stephen; 7. Wilton; 8. Ann.** m. [-?-] Davis; **9. Margaret; 10. Matthew;** and **11. Hannah,** m. James Brown

7. Wilton Atkinson, son of Matthew (2) (probably by his first wife), married Ann Maria Leroy at St. James Episcopal Church, Lancaster, on 14 April 1762 (Register of St. James Episcopal Church, accessed on FTM CD#166: *Church Records: Selected Areas of Pennsylvania*).

Anna Maria Leroy, daughter of Abraham, married 'William' Atkinson of Baltimore Co., and from 1796 to 1819 was found in Baltimore. Mary Atkinson in 1796 was listed as a watchmaker on the south Side of Second St. In 1807 A. Atkinson was a clock and watch maker at 33 Market Space (Baltimore City Directories 1796, 1809).

Anne Maria Atkinson died leaving a will dated 8 January 1822 and proved 5 May 1823. She named her grandsons Leroy Atkinson and Thomas Conway and a granddaughter Amelia Conway. Her son-in-law and grandson Thomas Conway were executors. James Camp, James Halett and G. W. [Miller?] witnessed the will (BAWB 11:573, abst. by Burns).

'William' (or Wilton) and Ann Maria were the parents of three sons and two daughters [They also had a grandson Leroy Atkinson] ("Atkinson Family Data"): **12. Thomas Wilton,** b. 8 June 1766, bapt. 5 Oct 1766; sponsor Elizabeth Hendle (First Reformed Congregation of Lancaster Co., Pa., accessed on FTM CD#166: *Church Records: Selected Areas of Pennsylvania*); **13. Matthew Abraham; 14. William Benjamin,** b. 8 June 1766, bapt. 5 October 1766 at the Reformed Church, Lancaster; **15. Sarah,** m. William Conway on 25 Aug 1792 (Reamy and Reamy, *St. Paul's Parish Register:* 65). They were the parents of (Reamy and Reamy, *St. Paul's Parish Register:* 83, 116, 127): Maria Cecilia, b. 9 Sep 1793, bur. 1 March 1798; Charles William Augustus, b.8 Dec 1798; they also had a son Thomas Conway and a daughter Amelia Conway, both b. by 1822.

(Notes on the Leroy Family)

Abraham Leroy, a Swiss clock maker, lived in Lancaster Co., Pa., between 1757 and 1765. Abraham Le Roy of Lancaster Borough died leaving a will dated 9 February 1765

and proved 25 February 1765. He named his mother: Anna Maria LeRoy, and his sisters: Salome and Elizabeth LeRoy, and Anna, wife of William Atkinson. Paul Weitzel and Salome LeRoy were named executors (Lancaster Co., Pa. Wills 1732-1785, accessed on FTM CD#209: Pennsylvania Wills).

He was the father of: **Anna Maria**; **Salome**; and **Elizabeth**.

== 0 ==

The Bagford Family of Baltimore County

1. James Bagford died by 1720. He married Elizabeth [-?-], widow of Richard Sampson. Elizabeth married 3rd, Samuel Hinton, and 4th, Thomas Stone.

James Bagford first appeared in Baltimore Co. when he and John Downes were sureties for Elizabeth Sampson's administration bond (MDTP 22:475). On 26 May 1735 Sarah James, aged about 64 years, deposed that 18 or 19 years earlier Bagford had married Elizabeth (now the widow of Thomas Stone, deceased), and that she (Sarah James) had been sent for as a midwife to Elizabeth Bagford, and had delivered her of a son James Bagford, now living with his mother, and that James Bagford, Sr., was present at the birth (BALR HWS#M: 237).

In August 1718 James Bagford and wife Elizabeth were named guardians of Henry Yanston, son of Lawrence (BACP IS#C: 4).

Bagford died by 1720 when wife Elizabeth had married 3rd, Samuel Hinton whose will of 4 April 1720 named son-in-law James Bagford.

James and Elizabeth were the parents of: **2. James**.

2. James Bagford, son of James and Elizabeth (1), was born about 1716. He married Comfort [-?-].

By his mother's will, James Bagford had inherited one-half of *Bachelor's Delight*. On 10 September 1741 James Bagford and his wife Comfort conveyed 133 a. *Bachelor's Delight* to Patrick Lynch (BALR TB#A: 38). Bagford conveyed 100 a. of *Bachelor's Delight* to Robuck Lynch on 8 July 1744 (BALR TB#C: 642).

In 1737 James Bagford was in the household of John Sampson in Patapsco Lower Hundred (*IBCW*: 24).

Unplaced:

Miss Backford, one of the twin daughters of Mr. and Mrs. Backford of Garrison Forest, died early Tuesday morning. She had been bitten by a stray dog, and died of hydrophobia (*Maryland Journal and Baltimore Advertiser* 12 June 1789).

William Bagford signed the petition for the removal of the county seat from Joppa to Baltimore Town. In 1773 he was head of a household in Back River upper Hundred. Richard Hiser and two Negroes, Harry and Hannah, were listed with him. (*IBCP*: 30, 50). In 1778 he was a Non-Juror to the Oath of Allegiance (*BARP*: 10). In 1783 he was listed with seven white inhabitants in Middle River Upper and Back River Upper Hundred (Carothers, *1783 Tax List of Baltimore County, Maryland*: 49).

== 0 ==

Colonial Families of Maryland II

The Barton Family of Baltimore County

1. Lewis Barton was transported to Maryland as a servant by 1674 He died by 4 March 1692/3. He married Joan (or Judith) [-?-], who married 2nd, William Farfarr (MDTP 16:13).

Barton was in Baltimore County by 17 March 1681/2 when he witnessed the will of William Hill (MWB 4:73).

On 11 May 1688 Thomas James of Baltimore Co., planter, conv. 136 a. *James Pasture* to Lewis Barton. Sarah James consented (BALR RM#HS: 498). The tract was later held by William Farfarr for Barton's orphans.

William and Joan Farfarr posted an administration bond on Barton's estate on 4 March 1692/3, with Francis Watkins, John Hayes, Michael Gormacon, and Robert Gardner.

Lewis and Joan were the parents of: **2. Lewis**, d. by November 1716.

2. Lewis Barton, son of Lewis (1) and Joan, died by November 1716. He married Sarah Dorman, daughter of Selah Dorman, and granddaughter of Daniel and Elizabeth Swindell. In August 1692 her grandmother Elizabeth Swindell conveyed one-half of her estate to Sarah Barton.

In 1700 Barton was a taxable in North Side of Patapsco Hundred (Clark1:11).

On 29 November 1709 Lewis Barton conveyed the whole 136 a. of *James Pasture* to Andrew Anderson (BALR TR#A: 35).

Thomas Cannon and John Filredman [Fitzredmond?] appraised the personal estate of Lewis Barton on 9 November 1716, and said the goods and chattels were worth £19.11.3. John and Elizabeth Ensor approved the will, and Selah Dorman was mentioned (INAC 38B:158).

On 20 July 1780 Thomas Gibbons, age 93, deposed that a daughter of Selah Dorman and his wife (a daughter of Daniel and Elizabeth Swindell), had married a certain Lewis Barton. Gibbons added that he had been well acquainted with Selah Dorman Barton and he always understood that he was son of Lewis Barton and his wife, and that Lewis and his wife were the parents of Selah Dorman Barton, who in turn m. Comfort, and was the father of Greenbury Barton (BACT 1773-1784:399).

Lewis Barton and his wife were the parents of: **3. Selah Dorman.**

3. Selah Dorman Barton, son of Lewis (2) and Sarah, died by 1757. He married, 1st, on 27 December 1730, Rebecca Biddison, and 2nd, on 24 January 1733, Comfort Roberts. She married, 2nd, James Lynch on 18 November 1762 (Reamy and Reamy, *St. Paul's Parish Register:* 1:30, 31; *SJSG:* 109).

On 18 August 1736 Selah Barton conveyed 100 a. *Inloes* and 120 a. *Selah's Point* to Thomas Stansbury. Barton's wife Comfort consented (BALR IS#IK: 273).

On 28 May 1738 Selah Barton received a payment out of the estate of Robert Gardiner of Baltimore Co., and in 10 November 1738 he was paid from the estate of Cornelius Angling of BA Co. (MDAD 16:61, 353).

Selah Barton patented 45 a. *Barton's Mount* on 30 January 1745 (MPL PT#2:157). On 19 September 1750 Selah Barton conveyed 15½ a. of this tract to James Brown. His wife Comfort consented (BALR TR#D: 22).

Comfort Lynch, relict of Selah Dorman Barton, and aged 64, deposed on 20 July 1780, stating that she had been married to Selah Dorman Barton by Rev. William Hooper. She always understood that her husband was the son of Lewis Barton and his wife Sarah, who was a daughter of Selah Dorman. The said Selah Dorman had another daughter who m. Michael Gorman but there were no descendants of that marriage. The deponent stated that her husband (Selah Dorman Barton) held lands which formerly belonged to Selah Dorman, and her husband was the only child of his father, and the only descendants of Selah Dorman are the deponent's children. She stated that her husband claimed that Tobias Stansbury had caused him to get in liquor at Edward Day's, and Stansbury got him to write a deed for the said land, but when her husband got sober, he would not convey the land. Greenbury Barton was her son by Selah Dorman Barton (BACT 1773-1784:400).

Benjamin Roberts, age 50, deposed on 13 January 1784 that he heard his father John Roberts or Camel (who was over 90 when he died), say that one of Daniel Swindell's daughters had married Michael Gorman, and that Selah Dorman had married the other daughter. The deponent's father stated that Selah Dorman's daughter had married Lewis Barton, and their son Selah Dorman Barton had married Comfort Roberts, sister of the deponent. Daniel Swindell's land was called *Daniel's Plains* (BACT 1773-1784:401).

The personal estate of Selah Barton was appraised at £91.3.0 by Abraham Andrew and George Simmons. Lewis and Greenbury Barton signed as next of kin, and Comfort Barton, the administratrix, filed the inventory on 25 July 1757 (MINV 63;417).

On 27 September 1762 Barton's estate was administered by Comfort Barton; the deceased left nine children (BAAD 6:128). The sureties were John Roberts and Mark Guishard. An inventory of £91.3.0 was cited and payments came to £55.6.3. Nine children were mentioned, but none were named (MDAD 48:267). In March 1763 William Andrew was approved as security for the balance of his estate (BACP 1763).

According to the deposition of Thomas Gibbons and others, Selah and Comfort were the parents of (Reamy and Reamy, *St. Paul's Parish Register:* 1:16): **4. Lewis**, b. 24 February 1737; **5. Greenbury**, b. 6 November 1739; **6. Asael**, b. 14 April 1741; **7. Selah**, b. 10 February 1743; **8. Joshua**, b. 22 November 1745; and **9-12. Four others** (These could have been daughters).

4. Lewis Barton, son of Selah (3) and Comfort, was born on 24 February 1737. He married Johanna Simmons on 30 June 1757 (*SJSG:* 101). She was a daughter of George 'Simmonds' (BAAD 6:188; MDAD 64:81).

Lewis Barton witnessed the will of Thomas Miles of Orange Co., N. C., when it was made 14 March 1766 (MWB 36:43).

On 9 December 1780 Lewis Barton, who had taken the Oath of Fidelity, formally quit possession of *Daniel's Plains*, which Greenbury Barton had formerly paid for. Possession was symbolized by delivery of twig and turf (BALR WG#F: 83). (N.B.: He is not listed in Peden's *BARP*).

Lewis and Johanna were the parents of (Reamy and Reamy, *St. George's Parish Register:* 80): **13. James**, b. 19 February 1758.

5. Greenbury Barton, son of Selah Dorman (3) and Comfort, was born 6 November 1739, and was living in 1780. He married Ann [-?-], possibly a granddaughter of Phillip Pettibone of Anne Arundel Co., whose administration account of 18 May 1775 mentioned an unnamed granddaughter, wife of Greenbury Barton (MDAD 72:108).

Greenbury Barton, aged 40, deposed on 13 September 1773, about the beginning tree of *Gassaway's Ridge*, and stated he had been an overseer to Rev. Hugh Dean (BALR WG#A:268). He petitioned the court for a land commission to determine the boundaries of *Daniel's Plains* on 14 March 1780 (BALR WG#V: 601-604).

In 1778 he was a Non-Juror to the Oath of Fidelity (*BARP:* 16).

In 1783 Greenbury Barton was listed in Back River Lower Hundred, Baltimore Co., as owning 100 a. *Daniel's Plains*. His household consisted of four free males and six white inhabitants (Carothers, *1783 Tax List of Baltimore County:* 1).

Greenbury Barton died by 15 April 1812 when his estate was administered by Ann Barton; she retained $931.51 as her thirds, and paid $310.50 to each of the children named below (BAAD 19:28).

Ann Barton, widow of Greenbury, died leaving a will dated 16 July 1808 and proved 25 June 1816, leaving her entire estate to her son Thomas, who was named executor. Robert Stewart, J. M. Dorsey, and Robert S. T. Stewart witnessed the will (BAWB 10:186, abst. by Burns). On 9 August 1816 her estate was administered by the executor Thomas Barton; no heirs were named (BAAD 20:461).

Greenbury and Ann were the parents of (*SJSG:* 75, 76): **14. Cathender**, b. 4 April 1768; **15. Thomas**, b. 4 June 1769; **16. Celia**, b. 27 November 1771; **17. Priscilla**, the wife of James Galloway; **18. Nicholas; 19. Aquila; 20. Elizabeth**, wife of Samuel Losey; and **21. Mary**, wife of James Brady.

6. Asael Barton, son of Selah (3) and Comfort, was born 14 April 1741. He married Ann Holt on 29 August 1769 (*SJSG:* 259).

In 1778 he was a Non-Juror to the Oath of Fidelity (*BARP:* 16).

In 1783 Asael Barton, with no land and two white males and seven white inhabitants was listed in the Baltimore Co. Assessment List for Gunpowder Upper Hundred (Carothers, *1783 Tax List of Baltimore County:* 27).

On 26 January 1787 Clare Young and Rebecca Young leased 52 ¾ a. *Nanjemoy* to Asael Barton, carpenter, for 21 years, provided that he plant an apple orchard of 100 trees and clear and put into meadow as much land as possible (BALR WG#BB:18).

7. Selah Barton, son of Selah (3) and Comfort, was born 10 February 1743. He married, 1st, Ann [-?-] by January 1772. He may have married, 2nd, Susanna [-?-].

In 1778 he was a Non-Juror to the Oath of Fidelity (*BARP:* 16).

Selah Dorman was named as one of the heirs of John Sudden on 14 September 1782 (BAAD 8:95). He may be the 'Sillis' Barton, who in 1783 was listed in Middle River Lower Hundred with no land, but three free white males and 10 white inhabitants in his household (Carothers, *1783 Tax List of Baltimore County:* 37).

Selah died by 6 April 1816 when his estate was administered by Susannah Barton; no heirs were named (BAAD 20:313).

Selah [Cealidge] and Ann were the parents of (Reamy and Reamy, *St. Paul's Parish Register:* 25): **22. Rachel**, b. 8 January 1772.

8. Joshua Barton, son of Selah (3) and Comfort, was born 22 November 1745 and died by 6 March 1779 when an administration bond was posted by his administratrix, Sarah Barton, with Wm. Pilott and Greenbury Barton (BAAD 5:2).

The widow and administratrix, Sarah, now wife of John Roberts, administered the estate on 25 April 1789; she retained £34.12.10 for her thirds, and paid £16.18.7 each to daughters of the deceased, Sarah and Mary, wife of Thomas Jarman (BAAD 9:326).

Joshua (and Sarah) were the parents of: **23. Joshua** (not yet 14 on 17 February 1788 when he was made a ward of John Roberts); **24. Rachel** (not yet 14 on 17 February 1788 was also made a ward of John Roberts BOCP 2:55); **25. Sarah** (was unmarried in 1789; she may have been the Sarah who m. Josias Pitts); and **26. Mary**, m. Thomas Jarman.

17. Nicholas Barton, son of Greenbury (5), on 7 August 1794 was bound to Jonathan Harrison, carpenter and joiner (BIND 1:53).

Unplaced:

Elizabeth Barton married. 1st, William Wright on 7 May 1727, 2nd, on 28 May1741 James Greer, and 3rd, on 26 January 1742, Heathcote Pickett (*SJSG:* 12, 28, 49).

James Barton and Temperance Rollo were married on 8 October 1730 (*SJSG:* 68). On 20 October 1734 Temperance was named as a daughter of Archibald Rollo (MWB 21:319 abst. in *Md. Cal. of Wills* 7:126).

James Barton and Sarah Everett were married on 19 December 1756 (*SJSG:* 101).

John Barton, m. on 23 May 1738, Ann Hitchcock (*SJSG:* 104). She was a daughter of William Hitchcock (BALR TB#C: 664).

John Barton and Dorothy Nice were married by license dated 31 May 1783 (BAML). This was evidently a second marriage. Dorothy m. 2nd, Philip Fews or Foos. John Barton died leaving a will dated 8 February 1784 and proved 13 March 1784. He named his wife Dorothy and mentioned three sons (but not by name). He mentioned a tract of land in Harford Co., being part of *Barton's Lot.* His wife Dorothy was to be executrix. George Dandell (Bandell?), Thomas Brown, and John Bortels (Bartels?) witnessed the will (BAWB 4:19, abst. by Burns). On 9 February 1785 Dorothy Barton administered his estate (BAAD 8:178). Dorothy and Philip Foos were married by license dated 5 November 1785 (BAML). On 18 June 1791 Dorothy 'Fews,' formerly Barton, administered the estate (BAAD 10:400).

Barton, John, m. by 26 October 1798 Ann, daughter of Jesse Biddle (BALR WG#58:247).

Seth Barton, merchant, and Sally Maxwell were m. last Thurs. eve. (*Maryland Journal and Baltimore Advertiser* 21 December 1790; *Maryland Gazette or Baltimore General Advertiser* 21 December 1790).

Susanna Barton (formerly Sharp), on 28 d. 3 m. 1789 was charged with marrying outside the society ("Minutes of Gunpowder Meeting," *QRNM:*86). [No other marriage reference found].

== = 0 = =

The Barnett Bond Family of Baltimore County

1. **Barnet Bond** (#20 in *BCF*), died by April 1749. He married Alice [-?-], who married, 2nd, William Grimes, who died by April 1771.

In 1744 Barnett Bond surveyed 694a, *Bond's Care,* which was later patented by his son Thomas on 5 October 1772 (MPL BC#42:441; BC#45: 183).

For some years Barnet Bond was the master of a ship carrying transported felons to America, and in 1743 he was arraigned on a charge of murder on the high seas. After a lengthy trial he was acquitted (*AWAP:* 188).

Barnet Bond, formerly of Md., but now of Limehouse, Middlesex, mariner, died leaving a will dated 25 January 1742, and proved 20 April 1749. He left his freehold estates in Md. including one near Gunpowder River, one near the head of Bush River, and one in Nodd Forest called *The Land of Nod,* to be divided: one-third to his wife Alice, and two-thirds to his daughter Mary and such other child as his wife may now be pregnant with. His wife was to be executrix and trustee, but if she remarried, his cousin William Bond was to be trustee. The will was witnessed by Charles Barnard, John Lugg and Thomas Coulthred. The will was proved on 20 April 1749 by the relict, now wife of William Grimes, who made an affidavit that the testator had only one daughter, Mary, now living (AWAP: 187-188).

Alice Grimes, widow, age 55, late of London, now of Baltimore County, deposed on 4 April 1771 that in 1736 she was married by a Rev. Foster to Barnett Bond then residing in London. By Barnet Bond she had issue: William, Barnet, Mary, and Thomas

Colonial Families of Maryland II

Bond. Her sons William and Barnett died in their infancy before 1743, and as of 1 Jan 1765 Thomas Bond is her only son living. Her husband Barnet Bond was a mariner and master of a vessel, *Coomes* that he sailed from London to Md. After the death of his father, William Bond, which happened about 3 years after her [the deponent's] marriage Barnet continued to sail from London to this province until the year 1745, when he died in VA. After Barnet's death the deponent married William Grimes who is also dead (BAEJ: "Thomas Bond: *Harritt's Fancy, Laurence, Buck Range,* and *Addition*").

Thomas and Alice were the parents of: **2. William**, d. by 1743; **3. Barnett**, d. by 1743; **4. Mary**, living in 1749; and **5. Thomas**, d. by September 1797.

5. Thomas Bond, son of Barnet (1) and Alice, as "Thomas Bond of Middle River Neck, age 56 years, was buried. 30 May 1794 (*SJSG*:116). He married, 1st, in February 1768 Sarah Bond (*SJSG*:231). He married 2nd, on 24 July 1783 Sarah Jordan (Marr. Returns of Rev. William West, Scharf Papers, MS.1999 at MdHS) She married 2nd, James Gregory on 7 May 1796 (Marriage Register of Rev. Lewis Richards, MS.690 at MdHS).

Thomas Bond of Barnett was listed in the 1783 Assessment List for Middle River Lower Hundred as owning 500 a. *Bond's Care*. His household consisted of six free white males and nine white inhabitants (Carothers, *1783 Tax List of Baltimore County*:37).

On 9 September 1797 Bond's estate was administered by Sarah Bond, the wife of James Gregory (BAAD 12:307). Sarah Gregory administered his estate again on 31 January 1798. William Bond was one of the minor children (BAAD 12:364).

Bond's estate was administered again on 14 August 1800 by James Gregory. The widow received her thirds of 78.7.9 current money; Elizabeth Bond who m. Daniel Reese was paid in full: 20.6.3; Barnet Bond, Thomas Bond, Hugh Hughes who m. Ann Bond and James Bond, each received 14.17.5 current money. The accountant was guardian of Tobias, Ali, Joshua, and Mary Bond, and on their behalf retained 69.12.8 (BAAD 13:316).

On 7 June 1818 Aaron Helmkin and wife Elizabeth said that they and the defendants hereinafter named were tenants in common of certain lands: *Bond's Care, Buck's Range,* and *Windley's Rest* (Baltimore Co. Chancery Paper # 68). One-seventh of the land belonged to the orator; one-seventh of the land belonged to them in right of the oratrix; one-seventh of the land belonged to James and Alice Thomas in right of the said Alice; one -seventh of the land belonged to Thomas Bond; another seventh of the land belonged to John Hughes. One-ninth belonged to Joseph Griffin; one-ninth to Elizabeth Christopher. Two-sixty-thirds parts belonged to Daniel Reese and wife Elizabeth Reese; and two-sixty-thirds parts to Bernard or Barnet Bond (Baltimore Co. Chancery Paper # 68).

On 24 July 1818 Aaron Helmkin filed a petition; mentioned that Daniel Reese and wife Elizabeth were non-residents of the state; now they have discovered that John Hughes is another non-resident of the state (Baltimore Co. Chancery Paper # 68).

On 5 February 1819 Aaron Helmkin and wife Mary petitioned the court against James Thomas and wife Alice, Thomas Bond, John Hughes, Elizabeth Christopher, Joseph Griffin, Bernard Bond, and Daniel Reese and wife Elizabeth, praying for a partition of certain lands. Since the filing of the original petition, Thomas Bond, Elizabeth Christopher and Joseph Griffin had continued to cut or threatened to cut timber on the land (Baltimore Co. Chancery Paper # 68).

On 12 April 1819 Elizabeth Christopher replied that she owned part of *Bonds Care* and *Bucks Range*; and that about 25 years ago Thomas Bond, who owned the land died, leaving as children, his heirs at law: Barnet; Thomas; Betty/Elizabeth, married before the death of Thomas Bond, one Daniel Reese; in 1801 they assigned their land to Solomon Disney. Their share was transferred by several conveyances to James Christopher, late husband of the deponent, and to Aaron Helmking; James; Nancy; Alice, m. James

Thomas (Their response was filed on 18 July 1820); Tobias, d. without issue; Mary, m. Aaron Helmking, one of the complainants; and Joshua, d. without issue (Baltimore Co. Chancery Paper # 68).

Sarah Gregory died by 8 September 1830 when Barnet Bond and Thomas Bond, her heirs and legal representatives, renounced the right to administer and asked that letters be granted to Joshua Bond. Edward F. Carter witnessed for Barnet Bond and Wm. W. Carter witnessed for Thomas Bond (Baltimore City Renunciations).

Thomas and his first wife, Sarah (Bond) were the parents of (Bond Notes in the Francis S. Hayward Genealogical Collection, MdHS Genealogical Collection G-5024): **6. Barnet,** b. 1769, m. Ruth Hughes by license dated 12 Jan 1790; **7. Thomas,** said to have m. Maria [-?-]; **8. James,** merchant of Baltimore, m. by license 11 July 1799, Julia McCord; **9. Elizabeth,** m. Daniel Reese by license dated 21 July 1790 (In 1801 they assigned their land to Solomon Disney. Their share was transferred by several conveyances to James Christopher, late husband of Elizabeth Christopher, the deponent, and to Aaron Helmking); **10. Ann,** m. Hugh Hughes by 18 August 1800 (She left one heir: John Hughes, who deeded his interest in 1100 a. to Barnet Bond in 1820).

Thomas Bond and his second wife, Sarah (Jordan), were the parents of: **11. Tobias,** b. 1785, m. but d. s.p. by 1819; **12. Ali[ce],** b. 1787, m. by license 3 Jan 1805, James Thomas; **13. Joshua,** b. 1789, m. but d. s.p. by 1819 (He got a share of *Bucks Range* and other land as heir of his deceased brothers Tobias and James. He deed this land to Aaron Helmkin in 1818); **14. William,** b. 1791, d. about 1798; and **15. Mary,** b. 1793.

==0==

The Charles Bond Family of Baltimore County

1. Charles Bond (not placed in *BCF* died by 1766. He married Elinor [-?-].

On 13 September 1762 Charles Bond assigned 113 a. *Teague's Revenge* to Joseph Sutton (BALR B#K: 464).

On 16 [month not given] 1766 Elinor Bond, administratrix, with will attached, posted an administration bond for £500. Chas. Bond and Edw. Bond were sureties (BAAB 1:190). On 16 March 1767 John Hughes and Joseph Sutton appraised Bond's estate at £347.4.2. John Allbny [*sic*] and John Hughs signed as the greatest creditors, and Charles and Edward Bond signed as next of kin. Elenor Bond filed the inventory on 7 April 1767 MINV 91:253).

'Ellonor' Bond administered the estate on 10 May 1770. The heirs were son Charles, son Abraham; the deceased left seven children in all (BAAD 6:230). The same day the estate of £347.4.2, was distributed by Mrs. Eleanor Bond, with Edward Bond and Charles Bond as sureties (BFD 5:370).

Elinor Bond recorded receipts from her children, for their share of the estate of their father, Charles Bond: on 2 April 1770 Susanna Bond received £23.13.10. On 28 August 1772 William Thompson received £6.4.4. On 31 October 1774 George Bond rec'd £29.4.4. On 1 November 1774 John Bond received £29.4.4, Abraham Bond received £1.9.8 and £24.19.0, Barzilla Bond received £29.2.8, Edward Bond received £1.9.8 and £27.13.0, and Charles Bond received £1.9.8 (having earlier received £27.19.0 on 23 June 1770. All receipts were recorded on 6 December 1774 (BACT 4:135 ff.)

Charles and Elinor were the parents of (Reamy and Reamy, *St. George's Parish Register:* 61): **2. Susanna,** b. 1 September 1737; **3. Charles,** b. 21 November 1739; **4. George; 5. John; 6. Abraham; 7. Barzilla;** and **8. Edward.**

3. Charles Bond, probably the son of Charles (1) and Elinor, was born on 21 November 1739 (Reamy and Reamy, *St. George's Parish Register:* 61). He married Sarah [-?-].

He died leaving a will dated 25 October 1784 and proved 6 October 1784 [*sic*]. Wife Sarah was to have one-third of the estate; the remainder to his children: eldest daughter Eliz., eldest son Edward, and youngest son Barzilla. Wife Sarah, Edward Bond and Joshua Grover to be executors. Benj. Grover, Wm. Hendrix and Eliza Hendrix witnessed the will (BAWB 3:556).

On 6 October 1784 Sarah Bond and Jos. Grover posted a bond for £1,000. Edw. Bond and Thos. Rutledge were sureties (BAAB 5:15).

In 1785 Josiah Grover and Sarah Bond were executors. Sarah Bond had married Nicholas Miller, who lived in Pennsylvania. Edward Bond, surety for the executors, asked the court to grant him counter security (Bond, Charles, 1785, BPET Box 1, Folder 17).

Joseph Grover administered the estate on 13 October 1785 (BAAD 8:189). He administered the estate on 19 April 1788, and paid one-third of the balance, and retained the other two-thirds as guardian of the children (BAAD 9:197).

Charles Bond was the father of: **9. Elizabeth; 10. Edward;** and **11. Barzilla [Bazil].**

8. Edward Bond, son of Charles (1) and Elinor, died by March 1797. He married Ruth Sampson on 23 March 1769 (*SJSG:* 135).

Edward Bond died leaving a will dated 14 January 1797 and proved 22 March 1797. He mentioned but did not name his wife. He named his sons Charles, George, and Edward, a daughter Eleanor, and three children by his daughter Mary. He mentioned other children but not by name. He mentioned a tract named *Cabin Field.* Abraham Sampson, Thomas Marshal, and Elijah Thompson witnessed the will (BAWB 5:497, abst. by Burns).

On 28 March 1798 Charles Bond administered the estate (BAAD 12:398). An account filed 24 November 1798 mentioned a legacy of £10.0.0 to Mary Freeland (BAAD 12:517).

Edward and Ruth were the parents of: **12. Charles; 13. George; 14. Edward; 15. Eleanor; 16. Mary,** and perhaps others.

9. Elizabeth Bond, daughter of Charles (3) Bond, deceased, had been a ward of James Campbell, who resigned and on 22 February 1787 Josias Grover was appointed guardian. Edward Bond and Thomas Rutledge were sureties (BAOC 2:15).

10. Edward Bond, son of Charles (3) Bond, deceased, had been a ward of James Campbell, who, on 22 February 1787 resigned, Josias Grover was appointed guardian. Edward Bond and Thomas Rutledge were sureties (BAOC 2:15) In April 1793, Edward Bond, orphan of Charles, chose Thomas Ayres as his guardian BAOC 3:39).

11. Bazil Bond, son of Charles (3) Bond, deceased, had been a ward to James Campbell, who resigned and on 22 February 1787 Josias Grover was appointed guardian. Edward Bond and Thomas Rutledge were sureties (BAOC 2:15). In April 1793, Bazil Bond, orphan of Charles, chose Thomas Ayres as his guardian BAOC 3:39).

==0==

The Bradford Family of Baltimore County

B. William Bradford, Parish Officer of St. Ann's Church, London, had at least three children (Walter Preston. *History of Harford County.* Baltimore, 1901): **A. John;**

Colonial Families of Maryland II

Hannah, m. Joseph Presbury and had James Presbury who came to Md.; and **Samuel**, Dean of Westminster and Bishop of Rochester.

A. John Bradford, son of William (B): was a merchant of London. He married Mary, daughter of Matthew Skinner of London. They were the parents of (Preston. *Harford Co.*): **1. William.**

1. William Bradford, son of John (A) and Mary, schoolmaster, was in Baltimore Co. by 2 June 1724 when he purchased 323 a., being one-half of *Enlargement,* from Abraham Whiteacre (BALR IS#G: 329). He died by 21 March 1757. He married 1ˢᵗ Elizabeth Lightbody. William Bradford and his second wife, Catherine Osborne, made a prenuptial agreement on 4 May 1751 (BACT TR#E: 37). She was a daughter of Henry Rhodes, and when Bradford died by 2 May 1761, she was noted as being the mother of Benjamin Osborne (BALR B#1: 107).

He may be the same William Bradford who in 1721 at the time of his levy, petitioned the court that he was a servant whose time expired on 16 September 1721, but William the progenitor was known to have been a married man with a son in 1718 (BACP IS#TW#3:16).

He was on the Grand Jury in 1737 and also on the petit jury (*IBCW:* 27, 28).On 20 April 1739 he was styled "Gentleman" in the will of Benjamin Jones of St. John's Parish (MCW 8:36). In 1750 as Capt. William Bradford he was nominated by the Vestrymen and Churchwardens of St. John's Parish to serve as Inspector of Tobacco for the Otterpoint Warehouse on Bush River (*CMSP Black Books,* item 678).

On 6 March 1722 Peter Whitacre and his wife Frances conveyed 64½ a. of *The Enlargement* to William Bradford (BALR IS#G: 120). On 2 June 1724 Abraham Whiteacre of Baltimore Co., planter, conveyed 32 a. being one-half of *Enlargement* to William Bradford, schoolmaster (BALR IS#G: 329). On 9 June 1726 John McComas and wife Anne conveyed 20 a. part *Come By Chance* to William Bradford, in exchange for 20 a. part *Enlargement* (BALR IS#H:239, 244). On 7 November 1739 Ann McComas, widow, conveyed 1 a. part *Come By Chance* to William Bradford (BALR HWS#1-A: 305). On 27 November 1740 Diana Jones of Baltimore Co., widow of Benjamin Jones, conveyed 81 a. and 50 a. of *Division, part of Turkey Hills and Strawberry Hills* to William Bradford, who had originally bought the lands from Benjamin Jones on 1 November 1738; by his last will and testament Jones had directed his wife to conveyed the land to William Bradford (BALR HWS#1-A: 481).

On 21 October 1749 Bradford conveyed to his son John George Bradford part of two tracts: *Strawberry Hills* and *Turkey Hills,* which had been conveyed to Bradford by the executors of Benjamin Jones (BALR TR#C: 315).

In 1750 he owned 76 a. *Enlargement,* 200 a. *Bradford's Barrens,* 20 a. of *Come By Chance,* and 6 a. of *Turkey Hills and Strawberry Hills* (Baltimore Co. Debt Book for 1750).

In 1754 he was listed as Capt. William Bradford in the Debt Book, and as the owner of part *Enlargement, Bradford Barrens,* part *Come By Chance,* and part of *Osburn Addition (IBCW:* 61).

He died by 21 March 1757 when an administration bond was posted by George Bradford, with Alexander and Aaron McComas (MDTP 36:376).When he died his estate was inventoried at £71.12.4 (MINV 65:37). George Bradford administered William's estate on 3 March 1760. He cited an inventory of £71.12.4, and listed payments of £76.3.2 (MDAD 44:228).

Catherine Bradford died by 20 September 1776 when her estate was administered by Amos Hollis who cited an inventory of £42.3.9, and listed payments of £7.0.0 (MDAD 72:349).

William and Elizabeth were the parents of (*SJSG:* 8, 10, 25, 26, 27, 28, 92); **2. Joseph,** b. 15 January 1718, d. 28 February 1718; **3. John George,** later called George, b. 3 September 1720 or 1721; **4. Susanna,** b. 7 June 1724, m. John Norris on 3 April 1744; **5. Mary,** b. 18 September 1727; **6. Martha,** b. 13 April 1731, m. James Amos on 20 November 1750; and **7. William,** b. 1739, d. 12 February 1794, aged 55, m. 16 February 1764, Sarah McComas.

3. John George (later called George) Bradford, son of William (1) and Elizabeth, was born 3 September 1720 or 1721.He married Margaret Bonfield on 3 December 1746 (*SJSG:* 67).

He had been indicted for bastardy on 3 December 1746 (BACP TB&TR#1:230). In 1750 he owned 135 a. *Turkey Hills and Strawberry Hills* (Baltimore Co. Debt Book for 1750).

John George and Margaret were the parents of (*SJSG:* 67): **8. William,** b. 20 May 1748.

7. William Bradford, son of William (1) and Elizabeth, was born 1739 and died 12 February 1794, aged 55. He married Sarah McComas on 16 February 1764 (*SJSG;* 226).

When Daniel McComas' estate was administered on 31 October 1766 one of the heirs was a daughter who had married William Bradford (BAAD 7:192).

In 1776 Capt. William Bradford, aged 40 was living in Bush River Lower Hundred, Harford Co. With him were his wife Sarah, aged 30, John Johnson, a servant, aged 20, William Williamson, aged 14, and the children listed below (Carothers, *1776 Census of Md:* 133).

In 1783 William Bradford, assessor, was listed in Bush River Lower Hundred, Harford Co., owning 371 a., part *Littleton,* and with 11 whites in his household (Carothers, *1783 Tax List of Maryland:*95).

William and Sarah were the parents of: **9. Martha,** aged 12 in 1776, m. Godfrey Waters on 13 November 1787 (*SJSG:* 148); **10. Elizabeth,** aged 10 in 1776; **11. Mary,** aged 8 in 1776, m. Henry Watters by license dated 31 December 1800 (*HAMR:*221); **12. Sarah, Jr.,** aged 6 in 1776, m. James Fullerton on 143 January 1791 (*HAMR:*76); **13. George,** aged 4 in 1776; and **14. Samuel,** aged 2 in 1776.

13. George Bradford, son of William (7) and Sarah, was born about 1772 and died in 1854. He and Susanna McComas, daughter of James and Elizabeth (Hillen) McComas, were married by license dated 26 May 1801 (*HAMR:*27; *SJSG:* 147, 155).

14. Samuel Bradford, son of William (7) and Sarah, was born in 1774 and died in 1849. He and Jane Bond were married by license dated 21 July 1803 (*HAMR:*27).

Unplaced:
Bradford, George, and Margaret Talbot were m. by lic. dated 20 April 1785 (HAML). Margaret Bradford (formerly Talbot), on 5 d. 11 m. 1789 produced a paper condemning her outgoing in marriage ("Minutes of Deer Creek Meeting," *QRNM:*147).

==0==

The Bull Family of Baltimore County
With Notes on the Rankin Family

Colonial Families of Maryland II

References: A: The First Parish Register of St. George's Tombland, Norwich. By George Branwhite Jay. Norwich: A. H. Goose, 1891. Pp. 152, 153, 172. **B:** Bull entries in IGI, 1988 ed. **C:** CMSP: The Black Books. **D:** The Register of the Freemen of Norwich, 1548-1713. By Percy Millican. Norwich: Jarrold and Sons, Ltd., 1934. **E:** The Freemen of Norwich, 1714-1752. By Percy Millican. The Norfolk Record Society, 1952.

A. Edward Bull of St. George's Tombland, Norwich, Norfolk, m. Mary [-?-].
Edward Bull was apprenticed to Willo. Weston, Sherman[?], on 25 February 1703 (D:120).
Edward and Mary were the parents of (A; B): **[-?-], daughter**, bur. 11 May 1704; **Deborah**, bapt. 18 May 1704; **Peter**, bapt. 6 September 1705; was a barber as of 21 August 1728: E:6); **Stephen**, bapt. 13 July 1707; **John**, bapt. 26 June 1709; **Mgt [Margaret?]**, bapt. 5 February 1712; **Edward**, bapt. 23 September 1716; and **1. Constantine**, bapt. 24 May 1719.

1. Constantine Bull, son of Edward (A) and Mary, was bapt. 24 May 1719 at St. George's Tombland, Norwich (A). He was buried 5 December 1792 in his 78th year (Letzer and Russo, *Diary of William Faris:* 137). He married by 20 May 1764 Catherine Walker of Rothrop Hall, Dalton, York, when their son William Horatio was born (Reamy and Reamy, *St. Paul's Parish Register:* 1:22)
Constantine Bull, son of Edward Bull, shearman, was a Grocer of Norwich on 9 May 1741 (E:36). He was in Maryland by 29 May 1749 when his name appears on a list of bills of exchange (*CMSP: The Black Books:* item 566). Constantine Bull advertised he had goods for sale next door to William Roberts' store (Annapolis *Maryland Gazette* 13 July 1748). In 1760 Bull was identified as a school teacher when he appeared in a court action (Letzer and Russo: 137). On 21 April 1761 he was listed as an inhabitant of Chestertown who signed a petition for a free market (*CMSP: The Black Books:* item 1124). In October 1765 he advertised he had been in Cecil County jail for debt, and would apply to the next Assembly for relief (Annapolis *Maryland Gazette* 23 October 1755). He was released by the last Session (Annapolis *Maryland Gazette* 3 June 1756). In November 1758 he was living in Chestertown when he advertised he would sell a servant woman's time (Annapolis *Maryland Gazette* 30 November 1758). On 21 April 1761 he and other inhabitants of Chestertown petitioned for permission to hold a market there on Wednesdays and Saturdays (*CMSP: The Black Books:* item 1124).
From 1766 to 1768 he was Registrar of St. Paul's Parish. In 1768 he signed the petition in favor of removing the county seat of Baltimore Co. from Joppa to Baltimore Town (*ARMD* 61:559). In 1767 he signed a petition on behalf of some German inhabitants who had been unfairly treated by some of the Magistrates owing to the Germans' inability to speak English. The petition specifically exonerated William Aisquith (*IBCP:* 26). On 3 February 1767 he and Catherine Bull witnessed the will of Deborah Smith, wife of Joseph Smith f Baltimore Co. (MWB 36:169, abst. in *Md. Cal. of Wills* 14:17).
William and Catherine (Walker) Bull were the parents of: **2. Mary**, m. 1st, on 25 February 1771 George Rankin, b. in that part of Great Britain called England (Reamy and Reamy, *St. Paul's Parish Register:* 1:37), and 2nd, Charles Wallace; **3. Catherine**, b. 18 November 1752 at St. Mary Anne's Parish, Cecil Co. (*CECH:* 64); **4. Constantine Cooke**, b. 22 September 1761 in St. Anne's Parish, Anne Arundel County (*AACR:* 104); and **5. William Horatio**, b. 20 May 1764, bapt. 1 July 1764.

2. Mary Bull, daughter of Constantine (1) and Catherine (Walker) Bull, married George Rankin, native of England, on 25 February 1771 in St. Paul's Parish, Baltimore Co. (Reamy and Reamy, *St. Paul's Parish Register:* 1:37). Rankin, former Clerk of the

Corporation and the General Court, died in 1788 with no property. She married 2nd, by license dated 26 April 1798 Charles Wallace, b. 1727, d. 1812, a member of the State Legislature (*BDML* 2:854-856: AAML). In his Diary, William Faris noted that Wallis was 71 and Mrs. Mary Rankin was 40 or 45 years of age (Letzer and Russo: 287).

In June 1784 she informed the public that she intended to open a school on Monday, the seventh day of June instant, agreeably to her former advertisement, and being advised that a well regulated boarding school is very desirable, she likewise offered to keep a boarding school in this city where the greatest attention and care will be given to the morals as well as education of all young ladies entrusted to [her] management (Annapolis *Maryland Gazette* 1 June 1784). Later she placed this notice: 'that being unable to discharge her debts, she gives this public notice to all her creditors that she intended to apply to Anne Arundel County Court ...for the benefit of the act for the relief of insolvent debtors (Annapolis *Maryland Gazette* 10 Jan 1788).

Mary Rankin of Annapolis on 14 March 1788 petitioned the Justices of the Anne Arundel County Court that she was very much indebted, so she was applying to 'Your Worships' for the benefits of an Act respecting insolvent debtors. She had placed an advertisement in the Maryland Journal and Baltimore Advertiser, and she now submits a list of her property and debts, including Thomas Wall for his daughter's boarding; 20 volumes of bound books, a picture of her daughter Dolly. On 19 March 1788 Mary Rankin took an oath that she would deliver all her property to her creditors. Burton Whetcroft and William Whetcroft posted bond that Burton Whetcroft would carry out his duties as trustee. On 20 March 1788 Burton Whetcroft swore he would carry out the duties of trustee. On 30 March 1788 Whetcroft testified that he had received all of Mary Rankin's property (Insolvent Debtors, Anne Arundel Co., 1788 to 1804).

By George Rankin, Mary was the mother of (AACR:104): **6. Catherine Walker**, b. 29 September 1773, d. 8 Sep 1774 in St. Anne's Parish, Anne Arundel Co.; **7. Mary Walker**, b. 1775, died by 1813, m. Leonard Sellman by license dated 23 June 1804 (AAML)..

== 0 ==

The Burke Family of Baltimore County

See also: Robert Barnes. *Baltimore County Families, 1659-1759.* Baltimore: Genealogical Publishing Co.,1989. See also Robert Barnes, "The Burke Family," *The Notebook* 5 (2) (June 1989) 102.

1. Ulick Burke was born about 1690 in Ireland, and died 20 April 1762 in Md. He married, 1st, about 1711 Elizabeth [-?-]. She was born about 1692. As Ulick Buck he married, 2nd, Mary Leekings on 14 May 1732 (*SJSG:* 41). He married 3rd, by 5 May 1761 Elizabeth [-?-].

Mary Leekings was the mother of Elizabeth Leekings, born 14 May 1732 (*SJSG:* 17).

In November 1724 Edward and Jane Cox conveyed 100 a. *Cox's Forest* to Ulick Burke (BALR IS#G: 298). Burke's will, dated 5 May 1761, left this same land to his wife Elizabeth; his daughter Mary Ryland; and his grandchildren Ulick and Thomas Burke.

In June 1731 Burke was indicted for 'unlawful cohabitation' with Mary Leekings (BACP HWS#7:156). In 1737 he was head of a household, with two slaves, in the Upper Hundred, North of Gunpowder (*IBCW:* 18).

In a legal dispute over the testimony of one William Johnson, John Cretin and Darby Tool and others deposed on 29 and 30 November 1756 before the Governor and Council that they never heard any one say that Ulick Burk or any other Burk would do all that lay in his power towards furnishing any persons with arms and ammunition to assist the French (*ARMD* 31: 170, 171).

Ulick Burke was probably the 'Muck' Burk who signed the petition for the removal of the county seat to Baltimore Town in 1760 (*IBCP:* 30).

Ulick Burke died leaving a will dated 5 May 1761 and proved 22 April 1761. His wife Elizabeth was to have 100 a. of his dwelling plantation for life and at her death it was to pass to his grandson Ulick Burk; if the grandson should die without issue, then to his brother Thomas Burk. His wife was to have one-third of his personal estate and a Negro fellow George. his granddaughter Elizabeth Taylor was to have a bed and a dividend of his Catholic books, 100 a. *Coxes Forrest* adjacent the 100 a. willed to his grandson Ulick Burk, and if she d. s. p., then to her mother, Margaret Miles. His daughter Mary Ryland was to have 100 a. leased to him by Esquire Tasker adjacent the plantation he lived on and a dividend of his Catholic books. The rest of his books were to be divided between Thomas Miles and Nicholas Ryland. His grandchildren Thomas, Richard, Elizabeth, and Sarah Burk, were to have 20 sh. equally divided. Margaret Miles was to have the residue of his personal estate. Son-in-law Thomas Miles, was to be exec. William Parish, Jr., Jacob Johnson, Thomas Franklin witnessed the will (BAWB 2:117).

Thomas Miles, Jr., posted an administration bond for £1000.0.0 on 30 March 1762 with Peter Miles and William Parish as securities (BAAB 1:87). Some time before 28 March 1763 John Talbott and William Bosley appraised 'Ellick' Burk's personal estate at £162.3.6. Mary Ryland and Ulick Burk signed as next of kin. Thomas Miles, Jr., filed the inventory on 28 March 1763 (MINV 80:63). Miles filed an account of the estate on 30 January 1764. The widow was to have her thirds, and the accountant as to keep the balance (BAAD 6:81).

Ulick and Elizabeth were the parents of (*PGQA*): **2. Thomas,** b. 4 November 1712; **3. Richard,** b. about 1714; **4. Mary,** b. 1717, m. Nicholas Ryland; **5. Margaret,** b. 10 November 1720 in Prince George Co., Md., d. 14 December 1796 in Harford Co., Md.; she m. 1st, John Taylor, who d. by 18 May 1741, and by whom she had a daughter Elizabeth, and 2nd, on 11 October 1744 Thomas Miles (*SJSG:* 191).

Ulick and Mary (Leekings) were the parents of: **6. Richard,** b. 1740 in Baltimore Co., Md.

2. Thomas Burke, son of Ulick (1) and Elizabeth, was born 4 November 1712 in Saint Barnabas Church, Queen Anne Parish, Prince George's Co., Md., and died by 21 December 1771 in Baltimore Co., MD. He married Sarah Sicklemore on 14 April 1737 (*SJSG:* 35). She was a daughter of Sutton and Constant (Love) Sicklemore, and was born 21 March 1714 in Baltimore Co., Md.

Thomas Burke was charged with bastardy at the June 1733 Court, for begetting a child on the body of Sarah Owings (BACP (BACP HWS#9:136).

On 24 July 1739 Thomas Bladen granted Thomas Burke a lease on part of *Blathnia Cambria* for the lifetimes of Thomas Burke, his wife Sarah, and Richard Burke, son of Ulick Burke who was father of said Thomas (BALR HWS#1-A:327).

On 21 December 1771 Sarah Burke, administratrix of Thomas Burke, posted bond to administer his estate. Ulick Burke and Thomas Burke were sureties (BAAB 1:154). His estate was appraised by Jacob Johnson and Thomas Franklin on 5 June 1772 and the inventory was filed on 19 June of that year. It mentioned the widow who was 55, and also mentioned 100 a. *Blathnia Cambria* (MINV 109:174).

Thomas and Sarah were the parents of (*SJSG:* 70: **7. Ulick** ["W." in the Parish Register], b. 30 January 1740, d. 1784 in Baltimore Co.; **8. Elizabeth,** b. 5 May 1745; she may be the Elizabeth Burke who m. Jos. Legatt on 6 May 1766 (*SJSG:* 114); **9. Thomas,** b. 17 November 1747; **10. Sarah,** b. about 1749; and **11. Richard,** b. about 1751.

7. Ulick Burke, son of Thomas (2) and Sarah, was born 30 January 1740, and died 1784 in Baltimore Co., Md. On 8 November 1764, as "W." Burke he married Mary Lemmon, daughter of Alexis Lemmon (*SJSG:*112; BAWB 4:151, abst. by Burns).

Ulick Burke took the Oath of Allegiance before the Hon. Robert Simmons in 1778. He could not write so he made his mark (*BARP:* 36).

In 1783 Ulick Burke was listed in Mine Run Hundred, with seven white males and nine white inhabitants as owning 230 acres, part *Bladen's Manor* and *Cox's Forest* (Carothers; *1783 Tax List of Baltimore County:* 65).

Mary Burke, and Moses Lemmon, on 12 August 1784 posted bond for £500.0.0 to administer the estate of Ulick Burke, with Elexus Lemmon and John Lemmon as sureties (BAAB 5:10). Mary Burke and Moses Lemmon filed accounts of Burke's estate on 15 November 1785 and 21 August 1790 (BAAD 8:183, 10:193).

In Dec 1785 Mary Burke, relict of Ulick Burke, and Moses Lemmon petitioned the Lower House of the Assembly praying an Act would be passed allowing them to dispose of part of the real estate of the said Burk in order to pay his debts (Votes and Proceedings, Nov 1785, p. 58).

Ulick and Mary were the parents of: **12. Thomas,** b. 3 May 1773, d. 27 April 1858; m. Elizabeth [-?-].

9. Thomas Burke, son of Thomas (2) and Sarah (Sicklemore) Burke, was born 17 November 1747. He married Delilah Peacock on 21 June 1772 (*SJSG:* 70, 141). Thomas and Sarah may have been the parents of: **13. John.**

12. Thomas Burke, "eldest son and heir at law" of Ulick (7) Burke, was born 3 May 1773 and died 27 April 1858. He married Elizabeth [-?-].

On 13 October 1798 he conveyed to Mary Burke part of *Blathnia Cambria,* which was conveyed to Ulick Burke [Thomas Burke's grandfather] by Daniel Dulany. Thomas' wife Elizabeth consented (BALR WG#71:280).

Thomas Burke may have moved to Frederick Co. by 13 August 1804 when he purchased part of *Cromwell and Murray's Hope* from Joshua Chilcoat and wife Sarah of Union Twp., Huntingdon County (BALR WG#83:88).

13. John Burke, probably son of Thomas (9) and Delilah (Peacock), and Susanna Templeton were married by license dated 28 Dec 1796 (HAML). The marriage as performed on 25 May 1797 by Rev. John Allen (Marr. Returns of Rev. John Allen, MS. at MdSA).

John and Susanna were the parents of (*SJSG:* 189, 197, 198): **14. William Goldsmith,** b. 19 May 1798; **15. John James,** b. 10 March 1803; **16. Elisia Elizabeth,** twin, b. 25 Augu1805; **17. Edward,** twin, b. 25 Aug 1805; and **18. Thomas,** b. 1 April 1808[?].

Unplaced:
Burke, Barbara, and John Bourne were married on 11 October 1744 (*SJSG:* 86).
Burke, John, died by 9 January 1779 when Robert Conway, administrator, posted a bond for £1000.0.0, with Martin Bulger and Wm. Smith as sureties (BAAB 5:1),
Burke, Margaret, died 13 October 1759 (*SJSG:* 78).
Burke, Margaret, petitioned the Orphan's Court, that a number of "children of us being in great distress," an unworthy woman pretended compassion, and on this pretense the petitioner gave up her sister Cealia to her in August Orphans Court. "But how deplorable it must be to see my sister brought up by a Miss Hendricks. Let my sister be discharged from her and be bound to some decent person." NOTE: A Mrs. Grundervil [?] on Fells Point will take her. (Burke, Margaret, Pet BA, n.d.)

Colonial Families of Maryland II

Burk (Burke), Richard, married Ann Ryland on 16 December 1776 ("Richard Burke Bible Record," *MBR* 2:11).

Burk, Sarah, and Thomas Miller were married on 24 July 1748 (*SJSG:* 89). Sarah Burke and "Theophilus Miller" were married on 7 July 1748 (*SJSG:* 125).

Burk, Sarah, and James Hall were married on 17 May 1772 (*SJSG:* 140).

Burke, Thomas, died by 2 March 1787 when Margaret Burke, administratrix, posted an account (BAAD 9:21).

Burk, William, aged 9 next 28 September, on 10 May 1789 was bound to John Peter (BIND 2:19).

Ryland, Nicholas, enlisted in General Pulaski's Legion on 8 May 1778 (*ARMD* 18:593);

== 0 ==

The First John Busk Family of Baltimore County

N.B.: The name is sometimes written as Buck, Burke, or Bush, .

1. John Busk, from Middlesex, was transported to Maryland on the *Patapsco Merchant* in May 1736 (*KPMV:* 69). On 25 February 1736 he had been indicted for breaking into the house of Elizabeth Wingfield and stealing 13 linen handkerchiefs, worth 10 s., six copper-colored ditto, worth 8 s., four yards of printed linen, worth 7 s., and twelve blue and white linen handkerchiefs, worth 8 s. Eleanor Wilford had also been indicted for receiving those stolen goods (Online Proceedings of the Old Bailey, the Central Criminal Court of London, at www.oldbaileytoline.org). He married Ruth [-?-].

On 3 November 1753 he was listed as a creditor of the estate of John Serjeant of Baltimore Co. (MDAD 35:268). On 1 November 1774 Ruth Busk received a payment from the estate of John Cooper (MDAD 71:245).

John Busk was a Non-juror to the Oath of Allegiance in 1778 (*BARP*).

In 1798 Ruth 'Bush' was listed as a pauper in Back River Lower Hundred, with one free male and four white inhabitants in her household (Carothers,*1783 Tax List of Baltimore Co.:* 8).

John Busk and his wife Ruth were the parents of (Reamy and Reamy, *St. Paul's Parish Register:* 18): **2. William,** b. 17 December 1743; **3. James,** b. 10 April 1746; and **4. Elizabeth,** b. 2 May 1750.

3. James Busk, son of John (1) and Ruth, was born 10 April 1746 and died by June 1819.

In 1768 he signed the petition in 1768 favoring the removal of the county seat to Baltimore Town (*ARMD* 61:547). Like his father, James Busk was a Non-juror to the Oath of Allegiance in 1778 (*BARP*).

In 1798 James Busk was listed in the Particular Assessment List of Back River Lower Hundred as occupying 718 a. owned by Tobias Stansbury (Horvath:78). In 1804 he was listed in Back River Lower Hundred as assessed at 125.10.0 (Ports, "The 1804 Assessment List for Back River Lower Hundred," *MGSB* 44 (1) (Winter 2003) 3).

James Busk died leaving a will dated 2 May 1819 and proved 12 June 1819. He left his estate to Nicholas Leeke in trust for his daughter-in-law Rhoda, formerly Rhoda Davis, and her children. Nicholas Leeke was also named executor. John Bush (Busk?) and Hester Bush (Busk?) witnessed the will (BAWB 10:613, abst, by Burns).

James Busk was the father of: **5. Greenbury.**

5. Greenbury Busk (Bush), son of James (3), probably died between 1802 and 1819. He married Rhoda Davis on 17 Aug 1796 (Reamy and Reamy, *St. Paul's Parish Register:*

Colonial Families of Maryland II

327; BAML; the *Maryland Journal and Baltimore Advertiser* of 18 Aug 1796 reported his name as Burke).

Anna Davis died leaving a will dated 9 September 1802 and proved 6 April 1803. She named her granddaughter Anna Busk and her daughter Rhoda Busk. James Busk was named executor. Nicholas Leeke, Ann Ellis, and Hannah Busk witnessed the will (BAWB 7:167, abst. by Burns).

In December 1812 Greenbury 'Burk,' a seaman on the privateer *High Flyer* was wounded in action (Marine, *The British Invasion of Maryland:* 234).

Greenbury and Rhoda were the parents of (Reamy, *St. Paul's Parish Register:* 117): **6. William,** b. 1 February 1798, bapt. 16 April 1798, bur. 18 April 1798; **7. James,** bur. 19 April 1798; and perhaps others.

The Second John Busk Family of Baltimore County

1. John Busk (Burk) John Busk and Eleanor (Helen) Ridden Gash were married on 10 November 1785 (Marr. Returns of Rev. Joseph J. B. Bend, Scharf Papers, MS.1999 at MdHS). Eleanor Busk was living as late as 19 May 1799.

In April 1796 Basil Gash, and Rachel Gash, orphans, age not given, chose John Busk as their guardian (BAOC 3:187).

John Busk died by 19 May 1798 when Eleanor Busk administered his estate and mad a payment to Rachel Gash, ward of John Busk (BAAD 12: 432). She filed a final account on 19 May 1799 and listed a payment made to Basil Gash, orphan of Daniel Gash, another ward of John Busk (BAAD 13:80).

On 11 June 1799 Hannah and John Busk came into court and the court appointed Eleanor Busk as their guardian, who accepted and offered Nicholas Leeke and Basil Gash as her securities (BOCP 4:55). On 11 March 1801 Nicholas Leeke was appointed guardian to Hannah Busk, who accepted. He offered Isaac Atkinson and John Boyer as his securities (BOCP 4:153).

John and Eleanor were the parents of (Reamy ands Reamy, *St. Paul's Parish Register:* 101, 109): **2. Thomas,** b. 20 January and bapt. 20 July 1794; **3. Elenor,** b. 9 June, and bapt. 9 October 1796, and bur. 5 July 1797 (*Memoirs:* 172).

Unplaced:
Mrs. Barbara Busk died last Wed. evening; her funeral was from the house of Nicholas Leake, Ann St., Fell's Point (*Baltimore American* 28 July 1813).
Darby Busk received a payment from the estate of William Harvey on 4 January 1775 (MDAD 71:438).
David Busk on 15 December 1792 had Samuel Solomon, orphan, who would be age 18 on 24 May 1793 bound to him to learn the trade of a boat builder, Samuel, aged 11 [*sic*] on 24 May 1796, formerly bound to David Busk, in Aug 1795 was bound to Jacob Grafflin to learn the trade of sailmaker (BAOC 3:20, 162).
James Busk, orphan, 14 years old on January 6 next, was bound with consent of his mother (unnamed) on 7 August 1805 to Benjamin Buck to learn sailmaking. (BIND 5:358)
John Busk of Baltimore Co. bound himself to William Hamilton on 19 July 1799 until 17 July 1804, when he would be 21 years old, to learn the trade of pilot (BIND 2:85).
John Busk, 14 years old on 10 September 1805, was bound by Justices of the Peace on 2 November 1805 to Thomas Murphy of Baltimore City, of the firm of George Dobbin and Murphy, printers and stationers, until 21 years old to learn the trade of printer (BIND 6:111)

Colonial Families of Maryland II

John Busk and Mrs. Hester Dobbin, all of Baltimore, were married last Thurs.eve. by the Rev. Mr. Dobbin (*Baltimore American* 25 December 1818, *Baltimore Patriot* 26 December 1818). Hester Busk, aged 48 years, died 25 July 1832 (*Baltimore American* 2 Aug 1832).

William Busk, orphan, 10 years old on March 1 last, was bound with consent of his mother (unnamed) on 2 April 1805 to John Welch of Baltimore City until 21 years old to learn the trade of ladies' shoe maker (BIND 5:271)

==0==

The Cannon Family of Baltimore County

1. Thomas Cannon was transported about 1663 (MPL 6:166). He was in Baltimore Co. by 1680 when he claimed land for service (MPL WC#2:391-392). He died by 15 March 1681/2, when Henrietta Cannon posted an administration bond with Peter Ellis and Edward Reeves.

He married Henrietta [-?-], who had previously been married William Robinson and Edward Swanson. She married 4$^{th.}$ by 18 July 1682, Edward Reeves (INAC 1:472, 7C:183, 8:275; BALR RM#HS: 58).

In an undated court minute, Christopher Tapley petitioned that Thomas Cannon be ordered to deliver to Tapley a certain patent that was taken up jointly by Tapley and Levy Wharfe (BALR IS#IK:67). In 1680 Cannon was a surety for George Gunnell, the administrator of Edward Gunnell (MDTP 12A:155). On 25 May 1680 William Vaughan, Robert Elliot, John Hunking, and Jane [?] Jouse, merchants of New England, petitioned that Edward Gunnell had been indebted to the petitioners and George Gunnell, the administrator, had absconded. It was ruled that the bond of James Philips and Thomas Cannon be assigned to the petitioners (MDTP 12:183-4).

On 22 June 1681 Michael Judd, carpenter, and wife Jane conveyed 150 a. of a 300 a. tract called *Collet's Neglect* to Thomas Cannon, planter (BALR IR#AM: 122).

On 12 June 1682 William Osborne exhibited that Thomas Cannon, deceased, had committed an 'unworthy action' against Col. Johnson of Va. Said Osborne was security for said Cannon. Henrietta Canon was granted administration on estate of said Cannon (MDTP 12B:100).

Thomas and Henrietta were the parents of: **2. Thomas,** b. prob. before 1682

2. Thomas Cannon, son of Thomas (1) and Henrietta, was probably born before 1682, although he gave his age as 34 in 1718. In November 1694 he was living with William Ebden in the North Side of Gunpowder Hundred. In 1695 he was listed with Michael Judd in the same Hundred (*IBCW:* 5, 8).

2. Thomas Cannon, son of Thomas (1) and Henrietta, was probably born before 1682, although he gave his age as 34 in 1718. In November 1694 he was living with William Ebden in the North Side of Gunpowder Hundred. In 1695 he was listed with Michael Judd in the same Hundred (*IBCW:* 5, 8).

On 2 August 1698 Thomas Cannon, son of Thomas Cannon, late of Baltimore Co., conveyed 150 a. of *Collett's Neglect* to William Ebden (BALR TR#RA:282).

In 1702 Thomas Cannon, administrator of John Lawrence of Calvert Co., filed an account of the estate (MDTP 19A:177). Cannon, aged c34, deposed on 20 November 1718 concerning the bounds of *Dickson's Neck* (MCHR CL: 464). In January 1714/5 Thomas Cannon was a surety for Thomas Knighton, administrator of Samuel Taylor (MDTP 22:47). In September 1716 he was paid from the estate of Taylor (INAC

37C:111). On 9 November 1716 he was one of the appraisers of the estate of Lewis Barton ((INAC 38B:158).
An inventory for Thomas Cannon was filed in 1720 (MDTP 24:306).Thomas Biddison and John Hillen appraised his personal property at £75.11.10 (MINV 4:310).
He may be the same Thomas Cannon whose inventory was filed in 1727.

==0==

The Cantwell Family of Baltimore County

1. Edward Cantwell may have been the son of Edmund [See below] and Mary. With nine mos. to serve, on 2 May 1696 was listed as a servant in the inventory of Francis Watkins (INAC 14:25-26). He died on 31 March 1721. On 5 December 1699 he married Joan ([-?-]) Chattam, widow of Francis Chattum. Joan married 3rd, on 4 August 1721 Thomas Burchfield (Reamy and Reamy, *St. George's Parish Register:* 5, 21, 22).
Cantwell witnessed the will of Francis Watkins (MWB 7:197). In 1682 he was a taxable in the household of Francis Watkins on the North side of Patapsco Hundred. On 6 May 1701 he received a payment from the estate of Edward Boothby. On 1 July 1704 he was listed as a debtor of Blanch Wells. On 6 March 1705 he was a debtor to the estate of Henry Jackson (INAC 25:177). Later he was paid from the estate of Henry Jackson (INAC 21:113, 25:177, 28:143; MWB 3:604).
Cantwell patented 200 a. *Taylor's Hall* on 2 October 1698, and again in 1703 (MPL 35:360, DD#5:118).
Cantwell died leaving a will dated 29 March 1721 and proved 2 May 1721. His son Edward and his heirs were to have 100 a. *Taylor's Hall*. His wife Johanna was named executrix, and was to have the residue of his estate during her lifetime. John Willson, Eliza Ryley and Lucy Ann Bayly (or Baily) witnessed the will (MWB 16:475 abst. in *Md. Cal. of Wills* 5:60).
Edward and Joan (Johanna) were the parents of (Reamy and Reamy, *St. George's Parish Register:* 7, 8, 9): **2. Lucy (Lucian),** b. 17 January 1700, bapt. 31 May 1702; **3. Edward,** b. 11 January 1702/3; **4. Sarah;** and **5. John.**

3. Edward Cantwell, son of Edward (1) and Joan, was born on 11 January 1702/3 and died by June 1749. He married 1st, Sarah [-?-], and 2nd, on 5 January 1744 Blanch Jackson (Reamy and Reamy, *St. George's Parish Register:* 71). After Edward's death, Blanch married 2nd, on 30 September 1750 John Gray (*SJSG:* 92).
Edward Cantwell of St. Georges Parish, Baltimore Co., died leaving a will dated 30 March 1749 and proved 17 June 1749. His sons John and Edward were to have *Taylors Hall*. 200 a, equally divided; the parcel containing his home to son Edward, his younger son. His personal estate was left to his children, Mary, Sarah, Hannah, Joannah, and Ruth and his sons Edward & John after they come of age. His wife and executrix [not named], was to have one-third of his estate. Luke Griffith, William Cook, and John Sullivan witnessed the will (MWB 26:118, abst. by Gibb).
An administration bond was posted by the executrix, with Guy Little and Jacob Combest (BAAB 1:363). His estate was administered on 2 April and 29 September 1750 (BAAD 5:151, 156).
Edward and Sarah were the parents of (Reamy and Reamy, *St. George's Parish Register:* 28, 29, 34, 38, 48, 49, 55, 61, 79, 83, 106, 108): **6. Mary,** b. 18 February 1725/6; may have married John Handland on 2 July 1749 (*SJSG:* 126); she was probably the Mary Cantwell who was fined 30 shillings for bastardy on 3 March 1746/7 (BACP TB&TR#1:402-403); **7. Sarah,** b. 15 or 16 March 1728; she was charged with bastardy,

confessed and was fined on 4 November 1746 (BACP TB&TR#1:247); on 6 July 1748 the Vestry of St. George's Parish issued a summons to Sarah Cantwell and William Norvil; **8. Hannah**, b. 28 February 1729; **9. Lucy**, b. 21 March 1731, d. 27 January 1739; **10. Johanna**, b. 22 December 1733, prob. d. young; **11. John**, b. 27 April 1734; **12. Johannah**, b. 22 December 1735; married William Collins on 7 November 1751; **13. Ruth**, b. 10 December 1737; married Samuel Sutton on 25 August 1757; they had been charged with unlawful cohabitation on 18 July 1757; and **14. Edward**, b. 28 February 1739; married Mary Vincent on 11 June 1761 (*SJSG:* 107).

5. John Cantwell, son of Edward (1) and Joan, was born by 1721 and was alive as late as 1740. He married Mary Burchfield on 4 February 1732 (Reamy and Reamy, *St. George's Parish Register:* 38. 56).

John and Mary were the parents of (Reamy and Reamy, *St. George's Parish Register:* 44, 49, 56, 63): **15. Johanna**, b. 6 November 1733; **16. John**, b. 27 April 1734 [prob. 1734/5]; **17. Francis**, d. 6 March 1735; **18. Edward**, b. 2 September 1737; and **19. Adam**, b. 6 January 1740.

18. Adam Cantwell, son of John (5) and Mary, was born 6 January 1740. He is said to married Sallie Woody [?], and they are said to have been the parents of: **20. William; 21. Thomas; 22. John; 23. Peter; 24. Malley**, b. about 1765; **25. Hugh**, b. about 1783; and **26. Adam**, b. 14 November 1786 in North Carolina, and d. 21 September 1850.

Unplaced:

Edmund Cantwell is said to have been born about 1626 in Berkshire, England, and to have died 17 January 1685 in New Castle County, Delaware, where he married Mary Dehaes about 1650. She was a daughter of Roelff and Gurtrurie (Jacobsen) Dehaes and was born about 1630. He is referred to as Capt. Cantwell and as having had a command in a 1679 letter written by the Dutch magistrates in New Castle (Peter Stebbins Craig, *The 1693 Census of Swedes on the Delaware*, SAG Publications, 1993: 113). On 25 July 1666 he was left personalty in the will of Francis Wright of Baltimore Co. (MWB 1:298, abst. in *Md. Cal. of Wills* 1:41).

On 12 March 1677, Edmund Cantwell filed an account of the estate of Daniel Mackery of Cecil Co. On 29 March 1679 he was listed in the inventory of John Inglish of Cecil Co. as Capt. Edmond Cantwell, who was to have the land patented with William Price (INAC 5:48, 6:125). In his will, made 8 January 16878 Inglish had named Cantwell as his executor and sole legatee (MWB 2:105, abst. in *Md. Cal. of Wills* 1:92).

Edmund and Mary were the parents of: **Edward**, b. about 1650; **Mary Ann**, b. about 1654; **Jane**, b. about 1656; **William**, b. about 1658; **Nathaniel**, b. about 1662; **Johanna**, b. about 1664; **Elizabeth**, b. about 1667; and **Richard**, b. about 1670 (**N.B.:** Unless otherwise documented, this material is from undocumented material on the internet).

Matthew Cantwell of Baltimore Co. died by 27 February 1762 when Greenbury Dorsey and James Garrettson appraised his personal estate at £41.12.0. Aquila Hall and Robert Adder signed as greatest creditors, and Pattison Cantwell and Mary Davis signed as next of kin. Nicholas Cantwell, administrator, filed the inventory on 10 January 1763 (MINV 80:432).

Nicholas Cantwell and Elizabeth M'Kim were married 23 May [1761?] (Reamy and Reamy, *St. George's Parish Register:* 85).

Colonial Families of Maryland II

Sarah Cantwell, servant of Benjamin Norris, in August 1734 had her petition for freedom dues granted (BACP HWS#9:306). In November 1746 she confessed to bastardy (BACP TB&TR#1:247).

Thomas Cantwell and Sally Smith were married by license dated 27 August 1795 (BAML). James Smith, in his will made 13 December 1800 named his daughter Sarah Cantwell, and her children Catherine Goff Cantwell and James Smith Cantwell (BAWB 6:339, abst. by Burns).

William Cantwell and Mary Baxton [sic] were married on 23 May 1768 (*SJSG:* 116).

==0==

The Carback Family of Baltimore Co.

1. **John Valentine Carback** died by May 1778. He married Mary Harryman on 19 December 1736 (Reamy and Reamy, *St. Paul's Parish Register:* 33), She was a daughter of John Harryman of Baltimore Co. (MDAD 28:53, 30:78, 79).

On 18 February 1741 Thomas Dexter and wife Mary Ann of New Castle Co., Pa., [now Del.] conveyed 50 a. *Molly' Garden* to Valentine Carback (BALR TB#A: 118).

On 8 May 1744 he was listed as a debtor to Luke Stansbury (MDAD 20:156). On 13 July 1751 he was a debtor of Robert North's (MDAD 30:141).

John Carback filed administration accounts of Valentine Carback's estate on 11 May 1778 and 11 February 1792 (BAAD, 8:28, 10:528). In the latter account equal shares of £15.2.1 each were paid to: the accountant (John), Mary, Thomas, Valentine, and Anne Carback now wife of William Rusk.

Mary Carback and John Griffin were married on 27 March 1792 (Marr. Register of Rev. Lewis Richards, MS.690 at MdHS). On 11 September 1793 Margaret [sic] was named as the mother of Henry Carback (BACT 1791-1794, MS 2865/1 at MdHS: 248).

Valentine and Mary were the parents of (Reamy and Reamy, *St. Paul's Parish Register:* 12): **2. Henry,** b. 28 April 1737; **3. Thomas; 4. Valentine,** b. about 1751; **5. John,** b. about 1755; **6. Mary;** and **7. Ann** married William Rusk.

2. **Henry Carback,** son of John Valentine (1), and Mary, was born 28 April 1737. He married Mary [-?-].

In 1776 Henry Carback was a Non-Juror to the Oath of Allegiance (*BARP:* 40). In 1783 Mary Carback was listed in Middle River Lower Hundred with no land, and three free males and seven white inhabitants (Carothers, *Baltimore Co. Tax List 1783:* 38).

Henry Carback died by 1 November 1788 when his estate was administered by Mary Carback who spent money on the three children of the deceased (BAAD 9:248).

Henry and Mary were the parents of: **7. William,** b. 17 August 1763; and **8.** and **9.** whose names are unknown.

3. **Thomas Carback,** son of John Valentine (1) and Mary, was a Non-Juror to the Oath of Allegiance (*BARP:* 40). In 1783 he was listed in Back River Lower Hundred with three free males and six white inhabitants (Carothers, *Baltimore Co. Tax List 1783:* 1).

4. **Valentine Carback,** son of John Valentine (1) and Mary, was born about 1755. Aged c32, he deposed on 2 Dec 1783 that seven or eight years earlier his father Valentine Carback had been living (BALR WG#T: 655).

He was a Non-Juror to the Oath of Allegiance in 1776 (*BARP:* 40). In 1783 he was listed in Back River Lower Hundred, with no land, but four free males and seven white inhabitants (Carothers, *Baltimore Co. Tax List 1783:* 1). In 1798 he was listed in back

River Lower Hundred as occupying 422 a. owned by Ann Stinchcomb (Horvath, *1798 Particular Assessment List:* 78).

5. John Carback, son of John Valentine (1), was born about 1755. Aged c28, he deposed on 2 December 1783 that seven or eight years earlier his father Valentine Carback had been living (BALR WG#T: 655).

On 9 Dec 1777 Archibald Davis, aged 12, was bound to John Carback to get an education and to serve until he was of full age (BAOC 1:5).

In 1783 John Carback owned 50 a. *Molly's Garden* in Back River Lower Hundred. There were three free males and five white inhabitants in his household (Carothers, Baltimore Co. 1783 Tax List). In 1798 he was listed as still owning 50 a. in Back River Lower Hundred (Horvath, *1798 Particular Assessment List,* p.76).

7. William Carback, son of Henry (2) and Mary, was born 17 August 1763, and married Jane Wright, b. 12 April 1770, by license dated 15 November 1785 (BAML). In 1785, Jane Wright (now Jane Carback), was identified as an orphan girl aged 15, who chose William Carback as her guardian (BAOC 1:235; BAGA 1:2; Carback Bible in MGRC 1:16)

Unplaced:
[-?-] Carback married by 19 August 1769 Ruth, daughter of Richard Jones (BAWB 3:161). On 25 June 1770 she had married 2nd, Abraham Green (*SJSG:* 137). As Ruth Carback, now the wife of Abraham Green she was paid a legacy from the estate of Richard Jones on 12 April 1773 (MDAD 69:194).

Ann Carbeck was paid from the estate of Thomas Dulany on 4 December 1741 (MDAD 18:437). Ann Carback and Joseph Wells were married on 30 January 1748 (*SJSG:* 90).

Avarilla Carback was charged with bastardy at the August 1765 Court; Thomas Egleston or Eagleston was summoned to appear (BAMI 1765:18).

Elizabeth Carback and John Parker were married on 3 January 1757 (*SJSG:* 101).

Elizabeth Carback and Thomas Davis were married on 31 January 1758 (*SJSG:* 102).

Mrs. Isabella Carback and Dr. P. Janney, all of Baltimore, were married Thursday, 10th inst. by Rev. Healey (*Federal Gazette and Baltimore Daily Advertiser* 12 November 1814).

Rev. John Carback of the Methodist Episcopal Church was the father of the children listed below. (There may well have been other children). He may be the John Carback who married Jane Rawlings by BAML dated 25 August 1797. He was the father of: Temperance, married by 1829 William Wilkinson; Elizabeth, married by 1836, Henry Hughes; and [E?], married by 1843 Cassie Wilkinson.

John Martin Carback and Frances Mahorne were married on 14 July 1734 (Reamy and Reamy, *St. Paul's Parish Register:* 31). On 5 March 1741 Frances was named as a daughter of John Mahone, and with Watkins James signed John Mahone's inventory as next of kin MWB 22:533 abst. in *Md. Cal. of Wills* 8:193; MDAD 22:207; MINV 32:281). Frances Carback and James Bonaday in May 1758 were reported by Thos. Merrideth as living together in a scandalous manner; they were cited to appear before the next vestry (Harrison, "St. John's and St. George's Parish Vestry Proceedings:" 139). She or another Frances Carback married Francis Wilkins on 18 February 1762 (*SJSG:* 108).

Philip Carback died by 14 July 1748 when Thomas Sligh posted an administration bond. Isaac Risteau and Nathan Nicholson were the sureties (MDTP 32:181).

Colonial Families of Maryland II

Thomas Carback married Anne [-?-]. In 1798 a Thomas Carback was listed in Back River Lower Hundred as occupying 91 a. owned by Thomas Henderson (Horvath, *1798 Particular Assessment List:* 77). Thomas and Anne were the parents of (Reamy and Reamy, *St. Paul's Parish Register:* 74, 107): **William**, b. 15 October, bapt. 20 December 1793 [probably d. young]; and **William**, b. 13 March, bapt. 16 May 1797.

William Carback was named as son of William Ingle, who on 13 October 1746 conveyed him 32½ a. *Small Valley* and all his personal estate after the death of Ingle and his wife Catherine (BALR TB#D:221).

William Carback was listed in Middle River Lower Hundred as occupying 288 a. owned by James Crook (Horvath, *1798 Particular Assessment List:* 42).

== 0 ==

The Carey Family of Baltimore County

1. John Carey was in Baltimore Co. died by June 1764. He married 1st, Abarilla [-?-], and 2nd, Dorothy [-?-].

He was in Baltimore Co. by 13 December 1756 when he purchased 50 acres of *Castle Moore* from Benjamin and Elizabeth Knight (BALR BB#I: 624). On 7 June 1759 John Welch conveyed 60½ a. of *Little Munster* to Carey (BALR (BACT B#G: 476).

John Cary died by 21 May 1764 when Dorothy Cary, administratrix, posted a bond worth £500, with John Stinchcombe and Elijah Owings as sureties (BAAB 1:431).

On 4 June 1764 his estate was inventoried by Joshua Owings and Robert Gilchrest and valued at £182.14.6. J. Ridgely and R. Croxall signed as creditors and Margaret Cary and Is. Carey signed as relatives. Dorothy Carey filed the inventory on 27 August 1764 (MINV 84:209).

Dorothy administered his estate on 2 September 1766 (BAAD 7:202). She also administered his estate on 7 March 1770, stating that the deceased left four children (BAAD 6:224).

On 14 March 1770 Dorothy filed a report of the final distribution of John Carey's estate, with John Stinchcomb and Elijah Owings as her sureties. There was a balance of £93.16.9 to be distributed. The names of the heirs were not given (Final Distribution Books, 5:374).

Dorothy Carey was still living in 1770 when the Baltimore County Debt Book for that year showed she owned *Little Munster* and *Castle Moore* in Baltimore Co.

John Carey was the father of (Reamy and Reamy, *St. Paul's Parish Register:* 19): **2. John**, twin, bapt. 22 December 1751 in St. Paul's Parish; **3. James**, twin, bapt. 22 December 1751; **4.** (poss.) **Eleanor**, married 6 May 1773 Christopher Randall. Their great-grandson was James Ryder Randall, author of "Maryland, My Maryland." (*GSV* 2:84); and **5. [-?-]**, unnamed child.

2. John Carey, son of John and Abarilla, was bapt. 22 December 1751 in St. Paul's Parish. He is probably the oldest son because he was in Cecil County on 24 May 1773, when as son and heir of John Carey of Baltimore County, deceased, he conveyed to Bale and Margaret Randall 50 a. of *Castle Moore* and 61½ a. *Little Munster* (BALR AL#H: 52).

Unplaced

Andrew Carey died by 21 September 1786 when an administration bond on his estate was posted by Samuel Hill, executor, with William Richardson and Jacob Laurence as sureties (BAAB 6:374).

James Carey administered the estates of Abraham Towson and Benj. Iamp, both on 18 September 1754 (BAAD 4:224, 243). He administered Abraham Towson's estate again on 21 November 1754 (BAAB 4:240).

James Carey was in Baltimore County by 1759 when he acquired part of *Cole's Harbour and Todd's Range* from Thomas Sligh and Lot # 5 (or 15) from Edward Fell (BALR B#G:: 461, 464). On 4 March 1760 he conveyed 51 a. *Stone Hill* to George Cole. James' wife Anne gave her consent (BALR (BALR B#H: 111). In 1761 James Carey sold 246 a. of *Sheredine's Search* to Charles Ridgely (BALR B#H, 536). In 1762 Carey conveyed part of *Coles Harbor and Todd's Range* to Hughes and Baxter (BALR (BALR B#H: 536). In 1764 he sold 150 a. *Sheredine's Bottom* to Robert Long (BALR B#N: 291, B#G, 265).

Joshua Carey died by 15 October 1789, when Hugh Finley administered the estate; he administered the estate again on 12 April 1791 (BAAD 10:656, 328).

==0==

The Carrington Family of Baltimore County
With Notes on the Connor and Porter Families

1. **John Carrington** immigrated to Md. some time before 1665 (MPL 9:50). He was definitely here on 10 November 1665 when he witnessed the will of James Strowd (MDTP 12:9). He married by 2 March 1695 Catherine [-?-], who later married John Scutt and by 1705 Matthew Organ.

Carrington did not appear to patent any land after 1679 (Coldham. *Settlers of Maryland, 1679-1783*). On 2 March 1695 John Carrington of Baltimore Co., and wife Katherine, conveyed 100 a. *Monmouth Green* to David Mackelfresh of Anne Arundel Co., mariner (BALR RM#HS: 521). David Mackelfish [sic] of Anne Arundel Co. had patented this land on 10 October 1707 (MPL PL#2:331).

John Carrington of Baltimore Co. died leaving a will dated 22 March 1695 and proved 9 April 1696. His sons John and George and daughter Mary and their heirs were to have 213 a. *Carrington's Increase*, equally. Sons Daniel and Henry and unborn child, and their heirs were to have 200 a. *Carrington's Venture*. Daughter Margaret and her heirs were to have 70 a. *Pleasant Valley*. If she died without heirs, the land was to pass to son Henry. Daughter Ann was left personalty. His wife Catherine was named executrix, and was to have one-third of the personalty. The residue of estate was to be divided among his children equally, daughter Ann excepted. The sons were to be of age at 21 and the daughters at age 16. If the first three children should die without issue, the three last mentioned were to inherit the deceased's portion. Geo. Ashman, Hector Macklane, Joshua Howard and Michael Summer witnessed the will (MWB 7:168).

Catherine Carrington, widow of John Carrington of Baltimore Co., exhibited his will on 21 April 1696 and was granted administration (MDTP 16:145; INAC 14:142). In 1697, as executrix of John Carrington, she exhibited accounts, which mentioned eight children, and also the inventory by appraisers John Gaither & Amos Peirpoint (MDTP 16:235). Her children, Henry, Margaret, and Catherine, were named in the May 1703 will of a later husband, John Scutt.

On 27 April 1705, the Catherine, now wife of Matthew Organ, filed an administration account of Carrington's estate, citing an inventory of £17.14.0, and listing payments of £2.16.6 (INAC 25:48).

John and Catherine were the parents of: **2. John**, b. by 1683 as he was aged 16 or more in 1699; **3. George**, b. by 1687 as he was aged 16 in 1703; **4. Mary; 5. Daniel; 6. Henry**, living 4 May 1703; **7. Margaret**, living on 4 May 1703; may have married 1st Philip Connor, and 2nd David Hagan; **8. Ann**, deposed in January 1693/4 that Robert Parker gotten her with child; and **9. Catherine**, prob. the unborn child mentioned in her father's will; living in 1703.

2. John Carrington, son of John (1) and Catherine, was born by 1683 as he was aged 16 or more in 1699. He was living as late as November 1710.

In 1699, 1702 and 1703 John Carrington was listed in the household of Turla Michael Howen in N. S. Patapsco Hundred (William N. Wilkins, "Baltimore Co. Tax Lists," MS. at MdHS: 7, 21, 46). In 1703 he and George Carrington were at 'the widow Howens' in North Side Patapsco Hundred, along with Timothy White and Timothy Gayne (Wilkins: 63). In 1704 John Carington was in the Household of Isaac Jackson with Edward Teal, N.S. Patapsco (Wilkins: 82). In 1705 he was in the household of Philip Conner, Upper Part of Patapsco (Wilkins: 99). In 1706 he was in the household of Henry Knowles, Upper Part of Patapsco (Wilkins: 115).

On November 1710, he was charged with begetting a bastard on the body of Ann Mackarny (BACP IS#B:187).

3. George Carrington, son of John (1) and Catherine, was born by 1687 as he was aged 16 in 1703, when he was listed with his brother John, at the "Widow Howens'" (She was actually the mother of the two).

6. Henry Carrington, son of John (1) and Catherine, was living 4 May 1703 when he was named in the will of his stepfather, John Scutt. Shortly after August 1719 he took his niece Eleanor Connor, daughter of his sister Margaret and her husband, Philip Connor, to raise *(BCF:*129). On 30 January 1721 he and Thomas Taylor were sureties for Lloyd Harris (BAAB 1:292). On 31 July 1721 he was listed as a debtor to the estate of Alexander Frazer of Baltimore Co. (MDAD 3:434). In June 1726 he was mentioned in the account of Thomas Randall's estate as being involved in being involved in a legal dispute with Thomas Stackmous (MDAD 7:459).

7. Margaret Carrington, daughter of John (1) and Catherine, was living on 4 May 1703; may have married 1st Philip Connor, and 2nd David Hagan.

On 18 Oct 1705 Daniel and Dennis Crowley of Baltimore Co., planters, conveyed 100 a. *Crowley's First Venture* to Philip Connor (BALR RM#GS:578).

Philip Connor, as Philip 'Conway,' died leaving a will dated 6 May 1710 and proved 15 July 1710. He left personal estate to Eliza Burk and James Macklove [*i.e.,* prob. James McClone]. His unnamed wife was named executrix and residuary legatee. William Webster, Matthew Organ, and William Hambleton witnessed the will (MWB 13:141, abst. in *Md. Cal. of Wills* 3:182).

Philip Connor, as Philip 'Conway,' died leaving a will dated 6 May 1710 and proved 15 July 1710. He left personal estate to Eliza Burk and James Macklove [*i.e.,* prob. James McClone]. His unnamed wife was named executrix and residuary legatee. William Webster, Matthew Organ, and William Hambleton witnessed the will (MWB 13:141, abst. in *Md. Cal. of Wills* 3:182).

Margaret Conner, executrix, posted an administration bond on 15 July 1710, with Patrick Murphy and Richard King as sureties (BAAD 1:302).

David Hagan was in Baltimore Co. by June 1719. He married Margaret, widow of Philip Connor, and died by 5 September 1724 when an administration bond was posted by Richard Gist with John Giles and Richard Owings. Richard Gist administered Hagan's estate on 26 August 1725.

Philip and Margaret were the parents of: **10. Eleanor.**

10. Eleanor Connor, daughter of Philip and Margaret (7), was born about 1709 and married Thomas Porter by 13 July 1734. Porter died by about 1779.

Thomas Porter was listed as an indentured servant in the 1725 inventory of John Israel (BINV 5:184).

In August 1719 Thomas Taylor petitioned the court that 3½ years earlier, David Hagan, father-in-law to said Eleanor, then 7 years old, orphan of Philip and Margaret Connor, and god daughter of Thomas Taylor's wife, requested Taylor to raise the child. However Eleanor's uncle, Henry Carrington, took the child, and Taylor's petition to have the child restored to him was rejected (BACP IS#C:215).

On 13 July 1734 Thomas Porter and wife Eleanor conveyed 100 a. *Crowley's First Venture* (which Eleanor's father had bought from the Daniel and Dennis Crowley) to William Rogers (BALR HWS#M:107).

Porter patented the following tracts in Soldier's Delight Hundred: 50 a. *Porter's Hall* in 1732; 19 a. *Porter's Desire* in 1757; and 164 a. *Resurvey on Porter's Desire* in 1762. Porter conv. 80 ¾ a. *Porter's Desire* on 1 March 1768 (BALR B#Q:358).

Thomas and Eleanor were the parents of: **11. Thomas,** b. 2 April 1736 (Reamy and Reamy, *St. Paul's Parish Register,* 1:12); **12. Richard,** d. by June 1789; **13. Elizabeth,** b. 14 June 1747 (Reamy and Reamy, *St. Thomas Parish Register:* 6); and **14. Philip.**

11. Thomas Porter, son of Thomas and Eleanor (10), was born 2 April 1736 in St. Paul's Parish (Reamy and Reamy, *St. Paul's Parish Register,* 1:12). In 1763 as Thomas Porter he was listed in the tax list of St. Thomas' Parish (Reamy and Reamy, *St. Thomas' Parish Register:* 62).

In 1798 Thomas Porter occupied or owned, with George Grundy, 119 a. *part McClains Hills* in Soldier's Delight Hundred. The property contained a one story round log dwelling house, 30 x 14, an old log barn, fit for fuel, 40 x 18, and an old log stable, fit for fuel, 16 x 12 (Horvath, *Particular Assessment Lists:* 49).

12. Richard Porter, son of Thomas and Eleanor (10), died by 13 June 1789. He married Mary [-?-] who survived him. Mary may have been a daughter of John Parrish, whose administration account filed 6 September 1786 named a daughter "wife of Richard Porter" (BAAD 8:307).

In 1763 he was listed as a taxable in St. Thomas' Parish (Reamy and Reamy, *St. Thomas' Parish Register:* 62). In 1778 he was a Non-Juror to the Oath of Allegiance (*BARP:* 214).

Richard Porter died leaving a will dated 29 May 1789 and proved 13 June 1789. He named a son Shadrach and his wife Mary. She was to have his estate real and personal for her life and widowhood. He mentioned "all my sons" and "all my daughters." Francis Lockard, Jean Lockard and Thomas Job witnessed the will (BAWB 4:363, abst. by Richard Miller). Mary and Greenbury Porter filed accounts of the estate of Richard Porter on 20 November 1790 and again on 2 April 1796. Mary retained her legacy (BAAD 10:226, 317).

Mary Porter may be the 'Mury' Porter who was listed in 1798 as living in Soldier's Delight Hundred, on 100 a., part of *McClain's Hills*, with a one story round log dwelling house, 26 x 14, a round log barn 26 x 16, and a round log stable, 16 x 12 (Horvath: 54).

14. Philip Porter, son of Thomas and Eleanor (10) was living as late as 1798.

In 1778 he was a Non-Juror to the Oath of Allegiance (*BARP:* 214). In 1798 he was living in Soldier's Delight Hundred. He owned 50 a. *Porter's Hall*, which contained a one story hewed log house, 16 x 16 (Horvath: 54).

== 0 ==

The Chadwell Family

1. John Chadwell was born by 1645 in England, and died by 1 December 1676 in Baltimore Co., Md. He married by 1670 Katherine [-?-], who married 2nd, Robert Benjer.

John and Michael Shadwell were transported by 1665 by John Dixon, and John Chadwell was in Baltimore Co. by 1670 when he claimed land for service (MPL 8:129, 15:169-179, 16:60, 19:500).

On 1 August 1670 Godfrey Harmer, merchant, and wife Mary, conveyed 100 a. *Harmer's Hope*, on the south side of Salt Peter Creek in Gunpowder R., to John 'Shadwell' (BALR IR#PP:84). In 1673 Chadwell patented 100 a. *Chestnut Neck* in Baltimore Co. In 1674 he patented 36 a. *Bettie's Delight*. In 1675 he patented 80 a. *Chadwell's Range* (MPL 15:79, 18:208, 366).

On 23 March 1675 Chadwell and James Cogell were to appraise the estate of Samuel Tracey (MDTP 7:360). On 8 Oct 1675 he was listed as a debtor to the estate of Thomas Salmon. On 16 Dec 1678 he was listed as a debtor to the estate of Capt. Thomas Todd (INAC 2:160, 7A:279).

Hugh Broadwater, in a nuncupative will filed 4 January 1670 left his entire estate to John and Michael Shadwell equally (MWB 1:420, abst. in *Md. Cal. of Wills* 1:58). On 4 January 1670 Richard Windley of Baltimore Co., aged 24, deposed before John Collier that three years ago the deponent had been with Hugh Broadwater at the house of John Dixon, who bequeathed to Michaell Shadwell brother to John Shadwell. Michael Shadwell has drowned. On the same day Henry Inloes aged 38, deposed that he had been at the house of Mr. John Dixon on Back River, where [-?-] Broadwater was ill and he bequeathed to John Dixon [sic], Michaell Shadwell (since dec'd), and his brother John Shadwell (MDTP 5:29).

The inventory of John Chadwell's goods, chattels and debts was taken 14 December 1676 by taken by James Collyer and Thomas Jones. It showed that he owned two old razors, a fishing line; three old hoes, a parcel of nails, old axes, a parcel of tools, a saddle and bridle, a box of iron, a mill, lbs feathers, a hone; two broken chests, two iron pots; his crop; five cows, four heifers, one year-old bull, two steers, two calves, two mares, a parcel of hogs; a parcel of lumber; he was both debtor and a creditor: bills of Capt. Boston, and Hazlewood, William Caine, Laurence Poole, Christopher Shaw, William Ebden, Robert Gardner, Robert Conner, James Armstrong, James Brockshaw, and desparate debts, in all about 5005 lbs. tob., one trunk, one box, two glass bottles, a parcel of money worth 580 lbs. tob. The value of his estate in tobacco was 24,735 lbs. (INAC 4:23-24).

Katherine Shadwell, the relict, now Katherine Benjer, administered the estate on 9 February 1677. She cited an inventory of 14737 lbs. tob. and listed payments coming to the same amount. She filed an additional account on 8 September 1678, listing additional payments of 3494 lbs. tobacco (INAC 4:632, 10:167).

On 9 October 1677 Robert Benjar, who married Katharine relict and administratrix of John Shadwell, petitioned for John Waterton, Gent., to take the oath of said Katharine as she could not travel to the Office, because of great sickness (MDTP 9A:335).
On 22 May 1688 Simon Jackson of Baltimore Co., who married Elisabeth, the eldest daughter of John Chadwill. was granted administration on his estate, in right of the orphans. Appraisers: Thomas James, John Birens. Francis Watkins, Gent., was to administer oath (MDTP14:72).
On 4 October 1688 Robert Benjar and wife, administratrix of John Chadwell, exhibited additional accounts, proved before Francis Watkins, Gent. (MDTP14:101).
John and Katherine were the parents of: **2. Elisabeth,** married 1st, by 22 May 1688 Simon Jackson, and, 2nd, Thomas Morris (See The Morris Family, elsewhere in this work); and **3. John,** b. by 1670.

3. John Chadwell, son of John (1) and Katherine, was born by 1670 in Baltimore Co., and died there by 21 July 1724 in Baltimore County, Maryland. He married Mary [-?-] some time before September 1701 in Baltimore Co., Md.
In 1677 he took up 45 a. *Chadwell's Outlet* (MPL 20:67). The same year he patented 190 a. *Stanharket* (MPL 20:77). On 1 November 1698 John Chadwell of Baltimore Co., planter, son and heir of John Chadwell, deceased, conveyed 80 a. *Chadwell's Range* to Robert Benger, cordwainer (BALR TR#RA:300). On 10 November 1702 John Chadwell conveyed 100 a. *Pearman's (or Shearman's) Hope* to Daniel Scott (BALR HW#2:213). On 17 September 1701 John Chadwell and his wife Mary conveyed. to Daniel Scott 100 a. *Chestnut Neck* and 190 a. *Stanharket* (BALR HW#2:95).
On 31 December 1700 Chadwell was listed as a debtor to the estate of Joseph Peak of Baltimore Co. (INAC 20:145). On 21 April 1701 John Chadwell made an affidavit That Daniel Scott has put up a locust post in place of a bounded tree of *Swallow's Bill* as the tree had fallen down (BALR HW#2:65).
John and Mary were the parents of: **4. Margaret,** b. by 1700, married John Jones by 21 July 1724; and (poss.) **5. John,** b. 1700.

4. Margaret Chadwell, daughter of John (2) and Mary, was born by 1700, and married John Jones by 21 July 1724. John Jones was born about 1697 and was living on 1 April 1752.
On 21 July 1724 John Jones of Baltimore Co., and wife Margaret, daughter and sole heir of a certain John Chadwell the Younger conveyed *Chestnut Neck* and *Stanharket* (originally surveyed for John Chadwell, Sr.), *Harmer's Hope* and *Hunting Creek* (surveyed for Godfrey Harmer and Oliver Spry and sold to John Chadwell, Sr., grandfather of Margaret Jones) to Daniel Scott the Younger (BALR IS#G:352). In November 1729 John Jones and wife Margaret, conveyed 45 a. *Chadwell's Outlet* to Bloyce Wright. 1729: John Jones and wife conv. *Chadwell's Range* and *Betty's Delight* to Bloyce Wright (BALR IS#K:128, 157).
On 1 April 1752 John Jones, Sr., of Middle River Neck, aged about 55, deposed that about 28 years earlier Bloyce Wright had told him the boundary of *Chadwell's Range* (BALC HWS&BB#4, no. 127).

== 0 ==

The Cheyne Family of Baltimore County

N.B.: The following account of Roderick Cheyne of Echt, Scotland, was taken from the following sources: (i.e. Materials obtained from the Cheyne WebSite, maintained by

James W. Cheyne www.rootsweb.ancestry.com/~cheyne/) (1) Peter John Anderson, M. A. LL.B. *Officers and Graduates of University and King's College, Aberdeen, 1495-1860*, New Spalding Club, Aberdeen, (1893) Masters of Arts, Page 222; (2) Old Parish Register (OPR), Register of Baptisms, Saint Nicholas Parish, Aberdeen, Volume 7, 1704-1734, Church of Scotland, LDS Family History Library, Salt Lake City, Utah, USA, LDS Film 0991136, transcribed by the James W. Cheyne, unless otherwise noted Frame 186; and (3) International Genealogy Index, Aberdeenshire, dated May 1988, LDS Family History Library, Salt Lake City, Utah, USA, Saint Nicholas Parish, Batch ABOUT 111686, Serial 3111.

Roderick Cheyne, Schoolmaster in Echt, Scotland, was born about 1695. He received a Masters of Arts degree from King's College, 1715. The entry in *Officers and Graduates of University & King's College* reads: "Mr. Rodericus Cheyn."

Roderick Cheyne married Jean Walker. On the baptismal entry for his daughter Christian, Jean Walker was referred to as his spouse.

The entry in the Saint Nicholas, Register of Baptisms, Volume 7, 1704-1734, frame 186, reads: "Oct'r 15 (1721) Mr. Roderek Cheyne, School Master at Echt and Jean Walker, his Spouse had a daughter called Christan baptized by Mr. Osborn, witnesses Mr. Arthur Forbes Smith and William Forbes, late Ballie in Aberdeen."

Roderick Cheyne Schoolmaster in Echt and Jean Walker were the parents of: **Christian**, b. 15 October 1721; and **Elizabeth**, b. 26 July 1723.

There is a strong possibility that Roderick Cheyne the schoolmaster of Echt, came to Maryland, and taught school in Baltimore County. Definite proof has yet to be found.

1. Roderick Cheyne, Principal of the Baltimore County Free School evidently did not own any land. He probably lived on the Free School Land, located in the vicinity of Knight's Corner, where the present Philadelphia Road diverges from the Old Philadelphia Road (William B. Marye, "The Old Indian Road," *MdHM* 15:220n).

On 16 October 1744 Cheyne witnessed the will of James Tolley, Baltimore Co. (MWB 23:654). On 8 January 1746 he witnessed the will of Edward Day of Baltimore Co. (MWB 25:4). In 1749 he seems to have been a vestryman of St. John's Parish, and is mentioned again in April 1754 (*SJSG:* 117, 118).

The Annapolis *Maryland Gazette* of 6 January 1757 contained a notice that he was living at the Sign of the White Horse in Baltimore County and had moved from his old house to a new stone house just north of the Nottingham Iron Works, called Mr. Lawson's Works, on the Post road from Philadelphia to Annapolis, where he would continue to keep a tavern. His establishment was half-way between the Sign of the Black Horse at the Head of Bush river, and Baltimore Town. Marye states that this is probably the Red Lion Inn (Marye, *MdHM* 15:221n).

On 19 July 1757 he was listed as a creditor in the estate of Mr. Stephen Onion of Baltimore Co. On 15 April 1759 he was listed as a creditor in the estate of John Casdrop (MDAD 41:110, 43:134; see also MDAD 43:328). On 21 July 1762 he and John Buck appraised the estate of John Wiltshire of Baltimore Co. (MINV 79:96)

In 1773 he was listed as a taxable in Middle River Lower Hundred (*IBCP:* 65)

He may have died by 1783 as the tax list for Middle river Lower Hundred show Elizabeth and Mary 'Chine' (Carothers, *1783 Tax List of Balto. Co.*)

He married Elizabeth [-?-] and was the father of the following children (He was evidently of sufficient social status for the parish registrar to list the godparents of his children, something that was not done for the births of everyone's children) (*SJSG:* 48, 52, 107): **2. Frederick**, b. 7 December 1741; at his baptism, Messrs. William Young and

Colonial Families of Maryland II

Thomas Gassaway were Godfathers and Mrs. Sarah Gassaway was Godmother, d. January 1742; **3. Pamela**, b. 6 February 1743; and **4. Chloe**, b. 24 November 1745 at the Baltimore County Free School.

3. Pamela Cheyne, daughter of Roderick (1) and Elizabeth, was born 6 February 1743, and bapt, at St Johns Church in Trinity Sunday on 20 May 1744; her godparents were Mr. N. Ruxton Gay, Mrs. Christian Deans, and Mrs. Christian Caswell; she married, 1st, John Owen on 12 November 1761; John Owings [sic] died by 2 May 1781 when Pamelia Owings, administratrix, posted a bond worth £10,200, with John Skinner and Moses Galloway as sureties (BINV 1:122). As 'Pamelia' Owings, she and Moses Galloway were m. by lic. dated 6 March 1782 (BAML).

Moses Galloway died leaving a will dated 30 April 1798 and proved 25 July 1798. He named his grandson Moses Galloway, son of his deceased son John; his son William and William's son Robert Christie Galloway; his granddaughter Pamela Cheyne Galloway, daughter of his deceased son James. He mentioned the children of his sons John and James. His wife Pamela and son William were named executors. He named a tract called *Andrew's Care*. George Gouldsmith Presbury, James Marywell, and Robert Hutton (or Button) witnessed the will (BAWB 6:122, abst. by Burns).

Unplaced:
Sarah Cheyne or Chainy married James Murphy on 15 December 1746. A date of 9 Nov 1746 may refer to the date they filed their intention to marry or the date they posted the banns (Peden, *A Closer Look*, 17).

==O==

The Cobb Family of Baltimore County
With Notes on the White Family

1. James Cobb was born about 1651, a servant, was transported to Md. by 1668 (MPL 21:271). He moved to Baltimore Co. by November 1721 when at age 70 he had petitioned the court to be levy free (BAAB 3:625).

He was probably the father of: **2. James**, d. 12 March 1718.

2. James Cobb, probably son of John (1), died 12 March 1718. He married Rebecca [-?-] Ernston [sic] (Emson) on 30 October 1709 (Reamy and Reamy, *St. George's Parish Register:* 14). Rebecca [-?-] had married 1st, John Daniell, who died in Calvert Co. about 1685, and 2nd, by 9 July 1686 James Em(p)son (INAC 9:27). She married 4th, John Hawkins, and 5th, Gregory Farmer.

James Cobb died 12 March 1718 (Reamy and Reamy, *St. George's Parish Register:* 19). His 'executrix' [but he seems to have died intestate] and relict Rebecca, widow of John Hawkins filed an account of his estate on 1 October 1734. She cited an inventory of £121.6.6, and a second inventory of £22.18.4. The estate was distributed with one-third going to the widow, and the balance in equal shares to the children, all of whom were of age: daughter Priscilla Cobb, daughter Frances, wife of Charles Jones, daughter Charity, wife of Zachariah Spencer, daughter Margaret, wife of Seaborn Tucker, and son James Cobb (MDAD 12:476). Another account was filed on 22 July 1737; an inventory of £13.8.0 was cited and daughter Priscilla was now the wife of John White (MDAD 15:354).

James and Rebecca Cobb were the parents of (Reamy and Reamy, *St. George's Parish Register:* 18, 19, 33, 34): **3. Rebecca**, b. 26 March 1710 married John Hawkins,

Colonial Families of Maryland II

Jr.; **4. Priscilla,** married John White; **5. Frances,** married Charles Jones on 26 December 1727 (See The Thomas Jones family elsewhere in this work); **6. Charity** (or **Christiana**), b. 15 April 1712, married Zachariah Spencer on 2 February 1728 (See The Spencer Family elsewhere in this work); **7. Margaret,** b. 15 May 1714, married Seaborn Tucker on 2 April 1730 (See The Tucker Family elsewhere in this work); and **8. James,** b. 16 September 1716.

4. Priscilla Cobb, daughter of James and Rebecca (2), married John White on 18 May 1726. John and Priscilla were the parents of (Reamy and Reamy, *St. George's Parish Register:* 34): **9.John,** b. 2 September 1728; and **10. James,** b. 7 December 1730.

8. James Cobb, son of James (2) and Rebecca, was born 16 September 1716 (Reamy and Reamy, *St. George's Parish Register:* 19, 67). He married, 1st, on 21 January 1734, Ruth Elledge (Reamy and Reamy, *St. Paul's Parish Register:* 31). He married, 2nd, Mary Poge on 18 March 1741.

On 7 June 1738 Cobb conveyed 100 a. *Cobb's Delight* to Samuel Wallis. Cobb's wife Ruth consented (BALR HWS#1-A: 85). On 13 April 1741 James Cobb conveyed 150 a. *Cobb's Chance (*or *Choice)* (a certificate of survey had been dated 1 September 1734) to George Buchanan (BALR HWS#1-A: 476).

James and Ruth were the parents of (Reamy and Reamy, *St. George's Parish Register:* 67): **11. James,** b. 27 November 1735; **12. Joseph,** b. 4 February 1737.

James and Mary were the parents of (Reamy and Reamy, *St. George's Parish Register:* 67): **13. Margaret,** b. 25 December 1742.

== 0 ==

The Cockayne Family of Talbot County

1. Samuel Cockayne of Gilling, Yorkshire, was born about 1662, giving his age as 46 on 3 February 1708; he died in Talbot Co., Md., by June 1717. He married Anne, also aged 46 in February 1708 daughter of William Carter (a brother of Thomas and Richard Carter).

On 3 February 1708 Samuel Cockayne was appointed attorney by other Carter descendants to settle the estate of Richard Carter (PCLR PL#3:135). Samuel and his family were in Talbot Co. by 15 March 1714 when he witnessed a deed (TALR 12:199).

On 5 November 1715 he and his wife Anne sold to Richard Ratcliffe 170 a. part of *Jacob and John's Pasture,* which Richard Carter, deceased, had purchased from John Newnam and his wife Joane (TALR 12:220).

Samuel Cockayne was dead by 8 June 1717 when his widow Ann conveyed part of the inheritance of Richard Carter, deceased, to William, son of said Samuel and Ann (TALR 12:292). In a deed made 29 May 1717, Ann Cockayne stated she was a sister of Mary wife of Christopher Teasdale, and of [-?-], wife of Nathaniel Hargrave, and that Ann, Mary, and [-?-] were daughters of the elder brother of Richard Carter of Talbot Co. deceased (TALR 12:294).

On 1 October 1717 Mr. William Clayton and Mr. Thomas Beswick appraised the personal estate of Samuel Cockayne at £283.1.1. Thomas Cockayne and William Cockayne signed as next of kin (INAC 39A:11). Ann Cockayne, the administratrix, filed an account on 1 November 1720, citing the inventory as above, and listing payments totaling £163.2.11 (MDAD 3:351).

On 24 November 1718 Anne Cockayne, for love, conveyed to her son William 100 a., part of *Poplar Ridge* or in *Finney's Hermitage,* both on Brewer's Branch at the Head of Wye River (TALR 12:345). In November 1721 Ann conveyed property to her son Samuel Cockayne of Talbot Co. Gent., to her daughter Sarah Cockayne, spinster, and to her son Thomas (TALR 13:16, 18, 22, 23, 68).

Samuel and Ann (Carter) Cokayne were the parents of: **2. William; 3. Samuel; 4. Sarah;** and **5. Thomas.**

2. William Cockayne, son of Samuel (1) and Anne, signed the inventory of his father in 1721. He is placed as the oldest son because he was the first child to be conveyed property by his mother.

He died by 3 February 1722 when his estate was appraised by William Cole and Robert (Richard?) Noble at £140.1.4. Thomas Cockayne and Samuel Cockayne signed as next of kin (MINV 8:31). On 30 September 1723 his executrix [*sic:* William seems to have died intestate], Mrs. Susanna Edmondson, wife of Mr. William Edmondson prepared an account of his estate, listing payments of £20.15.6. She filed the account on 21 January 1723/4 (MDAD 9:266).

William may have been the father of: **6. Catherine,** a minor in August 1730 when her guardian, William Edmondson petitioned for the establishment of the land entitled to her (TALC PF#B:143); **7. Christopher**

3. Samuel Cockayne, son of Samuel (1) and Ann, and Sarah Scales were married on 6 June 1738 at St. Peter's Parish, Talbot Co. (*ESVR* 2:76).

Thomas and Sarah were the parents of ("Third Haven Meeting," *ESVR* 2:79): **8. Sarah,** b. 8 November 1738.

5. Thomas Cockayne, son of Samuel (1) and Ann, died testate by 8 April 1741. He married Sarah Harwood.

He was named in a 1721 deed from his mother. On 9 November 1725 Thomas Cockayne, schoolmaster, was mentioned in a petition of Elizabeth Grey, administratrix of Joseph Grey (MDTP 27:228). On 14 September 1735 he was a surety for Grace Harwood, administratrix of Peter Harwood, Jr. (MDTP 30:127). In August 1735 he was one of the Lord Proprietary's justices of the peace (TALR 14:104).

Thomas Cockayne died leaving an undated will proved 27 March 1741. He left one-third of his estate to his wife Sarah. The residue of his estate he left to his children Thomas, Sarah, and Mary. Samuel Cockayne, Thomas Perkins, and Edward Days witnessed the will. The widow made her election to abide by the will (MWB 22:310, abst. in Md. *Cal. of Wills* 8:120).

On 8 April 1741 the will of Thomas Cockayne with the widow's election was filed in the Prerogative Court (MDTP 31:163). Samuel Bond posted bond to administer the estate on 10 July 1741 (MDTP 31:197). His inventory was filed in October 1741 (MDTP 31:224).

Sarah, widow of Thomas Cockayne, died 15 d. 10; married 1755 ("Third Haven Meeting," *ESVR* 3: 61). She left a will dated 4 October and proved 25 November 1755. To son Thos. Cockayne, she left a Negro woman Esther and her three children: Peter, Phill, & Jenny. To son-in-law Joseph Berry she left a Negro boy Abraham in his possession; to son-in-law Peter Harwood, a Negro man Tim in his possession; to son-in-law William Hopkins, Negro girl Ruth. Sons-in-law Joseph Berry and Peter Harwood were named execs. On 25 November 1755, Robert Harwood (Quaker) affirmed that the above is what the said Sarah asked him to write the day before she d.& that she would have executed it but was rendered incapable by the near approach of death (MWB 30:16, abst. by Gibb). .

Colonial Families of Maryland II

Thomas and Sarah [-?-] were the parents of the following, whose births are recorded at Third Haven Meeting (*ESVR* 1:57): **9. Sarah,** b. 2 d. 3 m. 1733; as Sarah Cockayne "the younger," she and Joseph Berry were married on 27 January 1752 ""Third Haven Meeting;" Wright, *Quaker Minutes of the Eastern Shore:* 54); **10. Mary,** b. 16 d., 6 m. 1735, married by 10 m. 1755 Peter Harwood; **11. Thomas,** b. 24 d. 6 m. 1738; and **12. Rebecca,** married William Hopkins.

7. Christopher Cockayne of Talbot Co. may have been a son of William Cockayne (2) and Sarah.

On 13 May 1736 he was conveyed a Negro boy named Bows, and five head of cattle and seven head of sheep by Ann Cockayne, widow, effective on the day of her decease (TALR 14:161). On 29 April 1740 Thomas Perkins of Talbot Co., and his wife Sarah, for love and affection conveyed 100 a., part of *Carter's Farm* to Christopher Cockayne (TALR 14:337).

Christopher Cockayne died leaving a will dated 19 February 1740 and proved 27 March 1741. To his mother Sarah Perkins, his father-in-law Thomas Perkins, and his brothers William, Samuel, and Thomas Perkins he left personalty in the hands of his uncles Thomas and Samuel, John Summerson, William Hagg, John Woodward, Robert Noble, James Doan, and James Clayland. His left his entire real estate to his sister Mary Perkins. John Mail, William Hopkins, and Rebecca Hopkins witnessed the will (MWB 22:309, abst. in *Md. Cal. of Wills* 8:120).

11. Thomas Cockayne, son of Thomas (5) and Sarah, was born 24 d. 6 m. 1738. Thomas Cockayne and Sarah Kemp "the elder," both of Talbot Co., were married on 7 d. 5 m. 1764 at the house of John Kemp in Talbot Co. ("Third Haven Meeting," *ESVR* 3:63).

On 6 January 1756 Peter Harwood, for love and affection, conveyed three Negroes to his grandson Thomas Cockayne (TALR 18:314). On 8 November 1762 Thomas Cockayne, son and heir at law of Thomas Cockayne, late of Talbot Co., deceased, and grandson and heir at law of Anne Cockayne, late of Talbot Co., deceased, and Joseph Berry and his wife Sarah, and Peter Harwood and wife Mary (which Sarah and Mary are the daughters of Thomas Cockayne, deceased), conveyed [various tracts] to James Tilghman (TALR 19:186).

On 30 d. 4 m. 1761 Thomas requested a certificate to the monthly meeting at Duck Creek at Kent Co. on the Delaware. On 26 d. 8 m. 1762 he produced a certificate from Duck Creek signifying his clearness on marriage (Wright, *Quaker Minutes of the Eastern Shore:* 61, 63). On 28 d. 9 m. 1769 Cockayne produced an account of one pair of saddlebags confiscated for priests' demands. On 26 d. 8 m. 1771 Cockayne requested leave to take measures the law directs to recover some debts due him against a person not of 'our society' (Wright, *Quaker Minutes of the Eastern Shore:* 70, 72).

Thomas and Sarah were the parents of ("Third Haven Meeting, *ESVR* 3:62): **12. James,** b. 23 d. 8 m. 1771, "withdrew from the Society;" and **13. Sarah,** b. 28 d. 11 m. 1773,

Unplaced:
Carter Cockayne, with three white inhabitants, was listed in Bay and Mill Hundreds of Talbot Co. as not owning any land (Carothers, *183 Tax List of Maryland:* 45).
Timothy Cockayne died by 1 June 1749 in Queen Anne's Co., when John Fairbank, administrator, posted bond (MDTP 32:267).

==0==

Colonial Families of Maryland II

The Corbin Family of Baltimore County

1. Nicholas Corbin immigrated to Maryland by November 1671 with his wife Elizabeth and daughters Elizabeth and Mary (MPL 16:533). He was buried on 31 December 1696. He married 1st, Elizabeth [-?-], and 2nd, by 30 March 1695 Alice [-?-], who married as her 2nd husband John Barrett.

Lewis Bryan, in his will made 31 January 1676 left personalty to Nicholas Corbin (MWB 5:226 abst. in *Md. Cal. of Wills* 1:190).

On 26 July 1680 Nicholas Corbin patented 200 a. *Corbin's Rest* (MPL 28:24; BALR HWS#M: 13). On 6 March 1688 he patented 100 a. *Corcell Hill* (MPL 25:349, 33:735).

Nicholas Corbin, Sr., of Bear Creek, in 1692 was an original vestryman of St. Paul's Parish, and was buried 31 December 1796 (Reamy and Reamy, *St. Paul's Parish Register:* 152, 161). On 3 September 1693 he was one of the appraisers of Joseph Heathcott's estate (INAC 10:301).

Corbin died leaving a will dated 30 March 1695 and proved 11 May 1697. He left personalty to his daughters Eliza. Roberts and Mary Gostwick. Son Edward was to have 100 a. *Corbin's Mills*. His wife Alice was named executrix, and residuary legatee. Amos Evans, Mary Marton, and Alice Edwards witnessed the will (MWB 7:797 abst. in *Md. Cal. of Wills* 2:126).

Alice Barrett, wife of John Barrett, filed an account of Corbin's estate showing an inventory of £35.5.6, and listing payments of 9408 lbs. tobacco (INAC 20:47).

Nicholas was the father of: **2. Eliza,** came to Md. about 1671, married Thomas Roberts; **3. Mary,** came to Md. by 1671, married Joseph Gostwick; **4. Nicholas, Jr.;** and **5. Edward.**

4. Nicholas Corbin, son of Nicholas (1) and Elizabeth, first appeared in Baltimore Co. Tax Lists in 1684, proving he was born in about 1676/8.

5. Edward Corbin, son of Nicholas (1) was probably born about 1685 as he first appears in the Baltimore Co. Tax List in 1701. He married by 19 September 1716 Jane Wilkinson, daughter of William and Tamar (MWB 14:503 abst. in *Md. Cal. of Wills* 4:162; BALR AL#A:356)..

On 19 September 1716 Edward and Jane conveyed part *Corcell Hill* to John Bowen (BALR TR#A: 431). On 27 March 1722 Edward Corbin and wife Jane of Baltimore Co. conveyed 425 a. *Landisell* and 50 a. *Wilkinson's Spring* to Tamar Wilkinson (BALR IS#G:6). On 10 September 1737 Edward and Jane conveyed 150 a., part *Corbin's Rest*, bequeathed to said Edward in will of Nicholas Corbin, and 50 a. part *Jonas' Range*, to Thomas Sligh (BALR HWS#1-A:13). On 10 Sep 1737 Thomas Sligh and wife Sophia conveyed 100 a. *Cumberland* to Edward Corbin (BALR HWS#M:16).

On 10 April 1747 Edward and Jane conveyed 58 a. *Cumberland* to their son William Wilkinson Corbin (BALR TB#E: 547). On 4 Jan 1749/50 Edward and Jane conveyed 100 a. part of *Cumberland* to Thomas Sligh (BALR TR#C: 363). On 4 Jan 1749/50 Edward and Jane conv. 50 a. *Cumberland* to Edward Corbin, Jr. (BALR TR#C: 365). On 22 May 1758 Edward and Jane, in case of any question, conveyed to Robert Wilkinson *Landisell* which they had already conveyed to his mother, Tamar Wilkinson (BALR B#G:157).

Edward Corbin, Sr., was living in 1769 when he signed the petition to remove the county seat from Joppa to Baltimore Town (Peden, *Inhabitants of Baltimore Co.*, p. 30).

Edward and Jane were the parents of (Reamy and Reamy, *St. Paul's Parish Register:* 2, 3, 4): **6. Nicholas,** b. by 21 June 1717; **7. Edward; 8. William Wilkinson;**

9. Abraham, b. 7 September 1722; **10. Phylisanna,** b. 12 May 1725; **11. Providence,** b. 26 June 1727, married Henry Peregoy on 14 January 1745, and **12. Unity,** b. 2 March 1730, married Robert Green on 21 September 1745.

6. Nicholas Corbin, eldest son of Edward (5) and Jane, Corbin, on 21 June 1717 was named as grandson in the will of John Barrett of Baltimore Co. (MWB 14:544 abst. in *Md. Cal. of Wills* 4:246). He married Eleanor [-?-].

On 3 September 1733 Nicholas Corbin and wife Eleanor conveyed 125 a. *Barrett's Rest,* (which John Barrett had devised by his will of 21 June 1717 to said Corbin), to Philip Sindall (BALR IS#L:421). On 29 March 1755 Nicholas Corbin conveyed his claim to *Dear Bit* and *Barrett's Rest* to John Ensor, Jr. (BALR BB#I: 373).

On 28 Feb 1761 Nicholas Corbin of Frederick Co. patented 18 a. *Corbin's Forest* (MP Certificate#19:580, Certificate#21:621).

In 1766 Nicholas Corbin conveyed. 18 a. part of *Corbin's Forest* to William Winchester (BALR B#P: 253).

7. Edward Corbin, son of Edward (5) and Jane, may be the Edward who died leaving a will dated 14 July 1770 and proved 30 November 1770. He married Mary [-?-].

In 1769 Edward Corbin signed the petition to remove the county seat from Joppa to Baltimore Town (*IBCP:* 32).

Edward Corbin died leaving a will dated 14 July 1770 and proved 30 November 1770. His wife Mary was named executrix and was to have all household furniture and his dwelling plantation for life or her widowhood. After the decease of his wife, his children Eliakim and Mary were to have ten pounds Maryland money, and sons John and Edward were to have five pounds of Maryland money. The residue of his estate was to go to his youngest son Eliakim and his daughters Rachel, Leah, and Mary. Son Edward was to have the dwelling plantation, one-half of one quarter of *Cumberland,* after the decease of his wife. Son John was to have 50 a. *Rochester* on Turkey Branch. Thomas Hale, George Harryman, Jr., and Joseph Syons witnessed the will (BAWB 3:144).

Edward and Mary were the parents of: **13. Edward,** b. 11 April 1746 (*SJSG:* 62); **14. John; 15. Eliakim; 16. Rachel; 17. Leah,** and **18. Mary.**

9. Abraham Corbin, son of Edward (5) and Jane, was born 7 September 1722 in St. Paul's Parish, and died about 1786. He is probably the Abraham who married Rachel Marshall on 4 December 1768.

On 26 September 1798 Rachel Marshall, widow of Abraham Corbin deeded to Joshua Marsh [part of *the Valley of Jehosophat*] (BALR WG#56:152).

Abraham was the father of: **19. Abraham;** on 26 September 1798 Abraham Corbin, one of the heirs of Abraham Corbin, deceased, deeded to Joshua Marsh Lot #10, and part of Lot # 11 in *The Valley of Jehosophat* (BALR WG#56:150); **20. Thomas; 21. Nicholas;** by June 1805 he was in Bourbon Co., Ky., when as one of the heirs of Abraham Corbin, deceased, he sold part of *the Valley of Jehosophat* to Joshua Marsh (BALR WG#66:252); **22. Nathan; 23. Sarah,** married Thomas Marsh, Jr., and **24. Eleanor,** married Beale Marsh.

13. Edward Corbin, son of Edward (7) and Mary, was to have his father's dwelling plantation, one-half of one quarter of *Cumberland,* after the decease of his wife. In 1783 Edward was listed in Middle River and Back River Upper Hundreds as owning 50 a. part of *Cumberland,* and 19 a. part of *Blathany Cambry.* His household consisted of five white inhabitants (Carothers, *1783 Tax List of Baltimore Co.:* 51).

Colonial Families of Maryland II

19. Abraham Corbin, son of Abraham (9), in 1783 was listed in Gunpowder Upper Hundred as owning 200 a. part of *Dulaneys;* his household consisted on four white males and seven white inhabitants (Carothers, *1783 Tax List of Baltimore Co.:*28); on 26 September 1798 as one of the heirs of Abraham Corbin, deceased, he deeded to Joshua Marsh Lot #10, and part of Lot # 11 in *The Valley of Jehosophat* (BALR WG#56:150);.

Unplaced:
Edward Corbin in 1783 was listed as a pauper with two white males and three white females in Baltimore East Hundred (Carothers, *1783 Tax List of Baltimore Co.:*8).
Edward Corbin of Baltimore Co., on 1 August 1795 placed his son Edward, aged 13 years, 6 mos., with Nicholas Lemmon of Westminster, hat maker, for seven years; on 2 June 1795 he placed his son John, aged 12 years, 11 mos., also with Nicholas Lemmon (Frederick Co. Indentures GM&RB#2:33, 48).
John Corbin on 30 August 1722 Archibald Edmondson and wife Jane of Prince George's Co., conveyed 100 a. *Beal's Camp* to John Corbin (BALR IS#G: 188).
John Corbin married by 29 November 1794, Rachel, daughter of George Harrryman (BAWB 5:236; BAOC Petition of George Harryman, 1799).
Vincent Corbin in 1783 was listed in Middle River Upper and Back River Upper Hundreds as owning 62½ a. *Cumberland.* His household consisted of nine white inhabitants (Carothers, *1783 Tax List of Baltimore Co.:*51). He married Mary [-?-]. They were the parents of: Zany, b. January 1778 or 1779, bapt. 8 February 1795 (Reamy and Reamy, *St. Paul's Parish Register:* 85).
William Corbin and Catherine Leary were married by license 14 July 1792 at St. Peter's Catholic Church, Baltimore (*Piet:*130). BAML gives the bride's name as Catharine Maryann Leary.

$==0==$

The Coulter Family of Cecil and Baltimore Counties

Note: There was an early Coulter family in Kent County, but research to date has not been able to establish a relationship.

1. Andrew Coulter died in Cecil Co. prior to 29 April 1776. He married 1st, Hannah Kilpatrick on 28 February1750 in St. Mary Ann's Parish, married 2nd. on 18 November 1767 Sarah Hall at Lewes and Coolspring Presbyterian Church, Lewes, Delaware (Harrison, "St. Mary Ann's Parish Register:" 299; MS at MdHS). *Vital Records of Kent and Sussex Counties, Delaware.* Westminster: Family Line Publications: 124). Sarah may be the Sarah Coulter who was married to Samuel Campbell by license dated 9 November 1786 (CEML).

On 26 July 1763 Andrew Coulter witnessed the will of Thomas Elliot of Charlestown, Cecil Co. (MWB 31:986, abst. in *Md. Cal. of Wills* 12:203). In 1767 he as a surety for Thomas Palmer, executor of Thomas Elliott, in the distribution of the latter's estate (BFD 5:59). On 21 February 1765 he was one of the appraisers of the estate of Elizabeth Mitchell (MINV 88:300). He appraised the estate of James Quail on 10 April 1771 (MINV 109:337).

Andrew Coulter died leaving a will dated 19 April 1776 and proved 29 April 1776. His son Alexander was to have clothing, boarding, schooling, and to be taught a trade, or if he went into business he was to have enough money to start a business out of real and personal estate. Son Andrew was to have boarding for one year and £55. Daughter Elizabeth was to have £50 if she married with her brothers' approval and she was to be maintained and kept until she was 25 years of age if single. Son John was to have £10. Wife Sarah was to have one-third part of the movable estate and the privilege of living in the dwelling house with his daughter Elizabeth during here life; if she remarried she was to have the share the law directed. Thomas Palmer, Samuel Kilpatrick and James Campbell witnessed the will. (MWB 40:670, abst. in *Md. Cal. of Wills* 16:123). [RWB Note: Alexander does not seem to mention any of his children by his second marriage].

On 7 May 1776 Thomas Hughs and James Orrice appraised Coulter's personal estate at £178.16.3. Andrew Coulter and Sarah Coulter signed as next of kin. Samuel Coulter, executor, filed the inventory on 20 July 1776 (MINV 124:275). On 22 August 1776 Samuel Coulter filed a list of debts owing to Andrew Coullter's estate that came to £1132.18.9 (MINV 124:15:88). No final account was found in either the Prerogative Court Accounts or in the Cecil County Administration Accounts.

Alexander and Hannah were the parents of the following children, born in St. Mary Ann's Parish, Cecil Co. (Henry C. Peden, Jr. *Early Anglican Church Records of Cecil County,* Westminster: Family Line Publications, 1990: 67): **2. John**, b. 30 November 1751; **3. Samuel**, b. 6 February 1754; **4. Andrew**, b. 9 April 1756; **5. Alexander**, b. 16 April 1760; **6. Elizabeth**, b. 15 November 1762; she may be the Elizabeth Coulter who married James Tate on 29 January 1782 (Peden, *Presbyterian Records of Baltimore:* 82).

Alexander and Sarah were the parents of (*Vital Records of Kent and Sussex Counties, Delaware.* Westminster: Family Line Publications: 138, 140, 143, 145): **7. James,** bapt. 11 June 1769; **8. Elizabeth**, bapt. 12 November 1771; **9. Andrew**, bapt. 23 June 1774; **10. Andrew**, twin, bapt. 4 August 1776; and **11. Joseph**, twin, bapt. 4 August 1776.

2. John Coulter, son of Alexander (1) and Hannah, was born 30 November 1751. He married Mary McCaskey on 3 February 1788 (Peden, *Presbyterian Records of Baltimore:* 73).

During the Revolutionary War he was a doctor in the Naval Service (*DAR Patriot Index* 157). He was a member of the Maryland Legislature and served on the Baltimore City Council. He was buried in Lot # 5 at the Westminster Presbyterian Graveyard, Baltimore (Hayward and Lancaster: 16).

Dr. John and Mary (McCaskey) Coulter were the parents of (Peden. *Presbyterian Records of Baltimore:* 12, 13, 14, 102): **12. Hannah**, b. 23 October 1788, bapt. 11 January 1789; she may be the 'Ann Coulter,' daughter of the late Dr. John Coulter,' who married Eli Hewitt of Anne Arundel Co. on 25 October 1831 (*Baltimore American* 26 October 1831); **13. John Alexander**, born 3 January 1792, bapt. 13 May 1792; **14. Elizabeth**, twin, b. 17 April 1794, bapt. 9 May 1793; married Capt. Alfred Grayson of the U. S. Marine Corps last evening by Rev. Glendy (*Federal Gazette and Baltimore Daily Advertiser* 13 May 1816). Eliza was a great beauty, who sat for the painter Jarvis, for his "Lady of the Lake;" **15. Mary**, twin, b. 17 April 1794, bapt. 9 May 1793; married Dr. James Page of Baltimore last evening by Rev. Glendy (*Federal Gazette and Baltimore Daily Advertiser* 9 June 1809); **16. Esther**, twin, b. 11 July 17 96, bapt. 16 December 1796; **17. Louisa**, twin, b. 11 July 17896, bapt. 16 December 1796; **18. Susan**, b. 12 March 1798, bapt. 7 December 1798; she may be the Susanna Coulter who married George Fogleman on 9 June 1835 (*Baltimore American* 15 June 1835); **19. John**, b. 9 November180, bapt. 19 March 1801; **20. Henry Stevenson**, b. 24 September 1803, bapt. 26 January 1804; he was in the U. S. Navy when he married Esther, daughter of the late Alexander Coulter, on 1 November 1832 (*Baltimore American* 3 November 1832).

3. Samuel Coulter, son of Andrew (1) and Hannah, was born 6 February 1754. He and Sarah Foster were married by license dated 18 November 1778.

5. Alexander Coulter, son of Andrew (1) and Hannah, was born 16 April 1760 in Cecil Co. and died 3 October 1828 in Baltimore. He married on 29 March 1792 Hetty McCaskey, daughter of Mr. Alexander McCaskey, at Fell's Point (*Maryland Journal and Baltimore Advertiser* 30 March 1792; Register of First Presbyterian Church, Baltimore, MS. at MdHS:4). Hetty, or Esther, McCaskey, was bapt. 27 April 1803, "at age 31 and upwards."

Alexander Coulter was a private in Capt. Sterrett's Independent Merchants Company, Maryland Militia, in 1777 (*BARP*).

On 20 March 1794 John Orrick bound his son Nicholas to Alexander Orrick to learn the trade of a saddler (BIND 1:15.). Other children who were bound to Alexander Coulter to learn the trade of saddler were: John Thompson in 1806, Lewis Littig in 1807, Rufus Griffin in 1812, Jeremiah Spencer in 1815 (BIND 5:549, 6:385, 8:505, 9:432).

Alexander and Esther were the parents of (Peden. *Presbyterian Records of Baltimore:* 13, 14, 100, 103, 108, 113, 119): **21. John Thomas,** b. 5 May 1793, married Deborah Symngton, daughter of James Symington, on 25 January 1820 (*Baltimore American* 27 January 1820); **22. Alexander,** b. 27 January 1795, d. 10 July 1795, aged 4 [*sic*] mos. and 4 days, buried under Westminster Presbyterian Church (Hayward and Lancaster: 16); **23. Andrew,** b. 7 July 1796, bapt. 4 September 1796; **24. Mifflin,** b. 27 November 1798, bapt. 12 April 1799, at age 15 years on November 27 last, was bound by his father Alexander Coulter on 12 Oct 1814 to William Gwynn, of Baltimore City, until 21 years old, to learn the trade of printer (BIND 9:363). He was evidently a Doctor in the U. S. Navy when his infant son Mifflin died at Sykesville, Anne Arundel Co., on 22 July 1834 (*Baltimore American* 26 July 1834); **25. Alexander,** b. 12 July 1802, bapt. 27 April 1803, d 1866, having married Eliza McCalmont Barklie; **26. Delia,** b. 26 September 1804, bapt. 10 March 1805; **27. Mary,** b. 30 August 1807, bapt. 12 November 1807, d. 4 February 1817, aged 9 years, 5 mos., and 5 days, and was buried under Westminster Presbyterian Church (Hayward and Lancaster: 16); **28. Elizabeth,** b. 18 February 1810, bapt. 23 August 1810, d. 14 January 1817, and was buried under Westminster Presbyterian Church (Hayward and Lancaster: 16.), and **29. Esther,** b. 31 December 1812, bapt. 13 July 1814, married Dr. Henry S. Coulter, son of the late Dr. John Coulter (See above), on 1 November 1832. Esther died 7 May 1862 in her 60th year (Hayward and Lancaster: 16; Baltimore *American* 3 November 1832 and 12 May 1862).

Unplaced:
Alexander and Jane Coulter were the parents of (Reamy and Reamy, *St. Paul's Parish Register:* 1:115): Jane, b. 29 January and bapt. 20 February 1798).
Mrs. Elizabeth Coulter of Baltimore died last Tuesday in the 21st year (*Baltimore American* 2 August 1805).
Henry Coulter, and Miss Ann Clarke, both of Annapolis, were married Thurs., 23rd inst. in that City (*Baltimore Telegraphe* 27 September 1802).
John Coulter and Margaret McElroy were married on 3 November 1796, and were the parents of (Peden, *Presbyterian Records of Baltimore:* 14, 73): Mary, b. 14 January 1798, bapt. 15 January 1798).
Mrs. Margaret Coulter of Baltimore died yesterday (*Federal Gazette and Baltimore Daily Advertiser* 24 January 1798).

==0==

Colonial Families of Maryland II

The Cowan Family of Baltimore County

N.B.: The name is sometimes spelled Coin, Cowen, Cowin, or Cowing,

1. **John Cowen** died by 31 October 1749 in Baltimore Co., Md. He married on 25 September 1712 Susanna Teague who died there on 3 April 1741 (Reamy and Reamy, *St. George's Parish Register*: 17, 63).

On 15 April 1743 John Cowen, Sr., conveyed 100 a. *Cowan's Addition* to his son Thomas Cowen (BALR TB#C: 216). On the same day he conveyed 76 a., part of *Cowen's Settlement* to his son, John Cowen, Jr. (BALR TB#C: 216, TB#C:215). In 1750 the heirs of John Cowen owned 100 a., part *Cowin's Settlement* (Baltimore County Debt Book: 8, MS. at MdHS).

John Coin (Cowin) died by 20 January 1748 when Michael Gilbert and Gregory Farmer appraised his personal estate at £103.16.7. John Cowen and Thomas Cowen signed as next of kin. Edward Cowin, the administrator, filed the inventory on 14 October 1749 (MINV 41:97). An administration account was filed by Edward 'Cawin' on 30 October 1749. He cited payments of £18.1.6. The deceased left three children, unnamed (MDAD 27:190).

John and Susanna were the parents of (Reamy and Reamy, *St. George's Parish Register:* 17, 20, 23, 25, 27, 54, 55, 61 64): **2. Sarah,** b. 18 July 1713, d. 27 April 1739; she may have had a daughter Mary b. 20 March 1738; **3. John,** b. 21 May 1715; **4. Elizabeth,** b. 2 February 1715/6, married 22 December 1737 John Denson; **5. Martha,** b. 2 January 1718/9,married Daniel Murdagh on 23 October 1740; **6. Thomas,** b. 26 May 1721; **7. William,** b. 14 April 1723; **9. Edward,** b. 5 June 1725; **9. Elias,** b. 14 February 1726/7; and **10. Susanna,** b. 27 March 1735.

3. **John Cowen,** son of John (1) and Susanna, was born 21 May 1715. He married, 1st, Elizabeth Bond on 22 April 1743. He married 2nd, on 9 March 1745 Elizabeth Wood (Reamy and Reamy, *St. George's Parish Register:* 68, 74).

On 14 March 1767 John 'Coen,' Sr., with the consent of his wife Elizabeth, conveyed 76 a., part of *Coen's Settlement* to William Mitchell (BALR B#P: 497).

His undated will was proved 14 August 1783: in it he named his wife Elizabeth Cowen (nee Wood), eldest son William, and children Benjamin (to have 50 a. *Woods Close*) and Hannah wife of James Seal. He named his mother-in-law Elizabeth Wood. His wife Elizabeth and son Benjamin were named executors. Kent Mitchell, Daniel Anderson, James Mitchell, and Enoch west witnessed the will (HAWB AJ#2:90).

John Cowan had a daughter Sarah who died 27 April 1739 (Reamy, *St. George's Parish Register:* 61).

John and Elizabeth (Wood) Cowen were the parents of (Reamy and Reamy, *St. George's Parish Register:* 74): **11. Hannah,** b. 10 January 1746, married James Seal; **12. William,** b. 19 February 1747; and **13. Benjamin,** who inherited 50 a. *Woods' Close*.

6. **Thomas Cowen,** son of John (1) and Susanna, was born 26 May 1721. On 15 April 1743 John Cowen, Sr., conveyed 100 a. *Cowan's Addition* to his son Thomas Cowen (BALR TB#C: 216). On 14 April 1750: Thomas Cowan of Baltimore Co. conveyed 100 a. *Cowan's Addition* to Edward Mitchell (BALR TR#C: 422).

7. **William Cowen,** son of John (1) and Susanna, was born 14 April 1723. He married about 1746 Judy [-?-], who may have been born about 1724. He may be the William Cowan who married by 3 March 1775 Juliana de Courcy (MCHP # 1375).

Colonial Families of Maryland II

In an attempt to identify Judith, wife of William Cowen, who was age 52 in 1776, research in St. George's Parish registers for all women named Judith born between 1720 and 1730, revealed only (a) Judith Bucknal of Francis and Blanch (Brown), b. 11 April 1730 (p. 35); (b) a John Crow was married to a Judith c.1732, but she is probably too old to have married William, but John d. by 1745 (See *BCF*: Could his widow have married William); and (c) a Charles Williams married a Judith Jones in 1739. There is nothing to show which, if any of these Judiths married William,

No direct proof has been found that the William described below is the son of John, but the evidence found to date has not revealed any other William. The William, age 52, listed in the 1776 Census of Susquehanna Hundred, Harford Co., with Judy, 52, and the children named at the end of this sketch, is almost certainly the William b. 1723, son of John (Carothers, *1776 Census of Maryland;* 116).

Although a study of Baltimore County Land Records failed to show that William Cowan bought any land, but he is listed in Baltimore County Debt Books between 1754 and 1769 as owning 50 a. of *Triple Union* (Card Index to Baltimore County Debt Books, MdSA). A study of deeds showing ownership of *Triple Union* between 1732 and 1748 has failed to reveal anyone owning the tract who had a daughter Judith, yet Cowan could not be found buying the tract, so he may well have inherited it (Card file on Baltimore County tracts in possession of the author).

A Baltimore County Rent Roll for 1733-1774 (MdHR 17,627), compiled Michaelmas, 1753, and carried beyond showed that *Triple Union* was a 350 acre tract surveyed for Thomas White on 5 March 1729, and by 1753 it was held as follows: 100 a. held by Dr. Josias Middlemore, 100 a. held by William Hughes. 75 a. held by William Durbin and 50 a. held by William Cowen. On the opposite page from this entry was an abbreviated chain of title showing how the land had been sold since 1753. No mention was made of William Cowan.

"Rent Roll, #2 for Baltimore and Anne Arundel County," (MdHR 17,611) contained an entry for the same *Triple Union,* with a chain of title from 1730 down to 1750. Of all the persons listed who bought and sold parcels of the tract the only ones who might have earlier owned William Cowan's 50 acres were Abigail Copley who sold 50 a. to William Waller in 1748. She was the widow of Thomas Copley who died 1748 (BALR TR#C:80).

William Waller died leaving a will dated 17 January 1748 and proved 18 April 1749, leaving all of his estate to his wife Elizabeth for her life, and then to his son John. It is possible that the widow Elizabeth married William Cowan, and he held the property as her husband for her lifetime. She could have died about1769 when his name disappears from the Debt Books, and the property might have reverted to John Waller. There is no proof that he had a wife Elizabeth but in the absence of any deeds it would appear that the only way William Cowan could have gained possession of the tract was by inheritance-either in his own right, or that of his wife.

In 1768 William Cowen signed a petition favoring the removal of the county seat from Joppa to Baltimore Town (*Thomas:* 41). As William Cowen or Cowan, he was a Signer of the Association of Freemen in Deer Creek Upper Hundred (*RPHA: 52,* citing Ella Rowe and Joseph Carroll Hopkins, "Men of '76," *Thomas* 25 (3) 323).

William Cowen, aged 52, Judith, aged 52, and Mary, aged 28, Thomas, aged 21, Susannah, aged 18, Edward, aged 18, Stephen, aged 11, and Rachel, aged 11, were listed in Susquehanna Hundred (Carothers, *1776 Census of Maryland:* 116).

In 1783 William Cowan was listed in the assessment list of Susquehanna Hundred with five taxables, but he was not shown as owning any land (Carothers, *1783 Tax List of Maryland:*138). Another[?] William Cowing was listed in the 1783 Tax List of

Gunpowder Upper Hundred with two white males and five taxables, but no land (Carothers; *1783 Tax List of Maryland:* 28).

William and Judith ([-?-]) were the parents of: **14. Mary**, b. about 1748; **15. Thomas**, b. about 1755; **16. Susanna**, b. about 1756; **17. Edward**, b. about 1761; **18. Stephen**, b. about 1765, and **19. Rachel**, b. about 1767

15. Thomas 'Coen,' probably son of William (7) and Judith, was born about 1755, perhaps in Baltimore Co., and died 29 June 1814 in Hamilton Co., Ohio. He married 19 February 1785 (HAML) in Harford Co., Md., to Mary Richardson, born 25 January 1764, did 25 October 1844.

Thomas Cowan was in Harford County in February 1796 when James Cowan, aged 14 on 1 August 1796, was bound to Thomas Cowan until he reached the age of 21, to learn the carpenter's trade, and to read, write and cipher to the age of 3 (Peden, *Abstracts of Orphans Court Proceedings, 1778-1800, Harford County, Maryland:* 57).

Thomas and Mary were the parents of: **10. Josiah**, b. 7 February 1792.

20. Josiah 'Coen,' son of Thomas (15) and Mary (Richardson), was born 7 February 1792 in Harford Co., Md., and died 19 November 1867 in Oak Forest Fran[klin Co., Ind.?]. He married on 7 July 1809 in Hamilton Co., Ohio.

On 17 September 1835 Josiah Coen of Franklin Co., Indiana, purchased land in Ohio, Range 13, Township 11, section 20. He seems to have bought land in the same Range, Township and Section on 14 September 1836. It should be noted that Thomas Coen also of Franklin Co., Indiana, had purchased land in the same section on 29 May 1832. A note after the names of purchasers indicates that the land purchased was east and North of the Second Principal Meridian, Ranges 11-15, Townships 10-23, were lands lying entirely in the present state of Indiana, including Franklin Co., Indiana (Ellen T. Berry and David A. Berry, *Early Ohio Settlers, Purchasers of Land in Southwestern Ohio, 1800-1840,* Baltimore: Genealogical Publishing Co., 1986: 61).

Unplaced Cowens;
Elizabeth Cowan, aged 16, and Ann Cowan, aged 8, were listed in Susquehanna Hundred, living with Elizabeth Brown, aged 46, and Mary Brannon, aged 4 (Carothers, *1776 Census of Maryland:* 110).
George Cowen on 6 June 1764 leased from Joshua Bond 100 a. of *Groom's Chance,* except for the portions already leased to Samuel Talby and William Huggins (BALR B#N:327).
Isabella Cowin, aged 15, was listed in 1776 in Susquehanna Hundred living with Thomas Boyls, aged 40, and Mary Boyls, aged 34 (Carothers, *1776 Census of Maryland:* 109). She and John Carroll were married by license dated 16 Jan 1779 (HAML).
John Cowan, aged 24, Sarah Cowen, aged 24, Mary Cowen, aged 4, John Cowen, Jr., aged 1, and Mark Cowen, aged 1 mo., were listed in Spesutia Lower Hundred (Carothers, *1776 Census of Maryland:* 106).
Mark Cowin, died by 24 November 1770 when John Cowin, administrator, posted a bond worth £200, with Wm. Cox and Amos Garrett as sureties (Garrett did not sign) (BAAB 1:472). On 19 December 1770 Philip Gover and Arthur Ingram appraised his personal estate at £32.4.9. Margaret Allen and Elizabeth Cowin signed as next of kin. John Cowin, administrator, filed the inventory on 2 February 1771 (MINV 105:200).

Colonial Families of Maryland II

William Cowan on 10 September 1803 was deeded 100 a. on the Little Miami River by Hans Lackie (Cummins, *Hamilton Co., Ohio, Court and Other Records* 3: 96).

== 0 ==

The Jacob Cox Family of Baltimore County

1. Jacob Cox was in Baltimore Co. by 25 September 1722 when he married Elizabeth Merryman, daughter of Charles Merryman. He died 1 November 1724 (Reamy and Reamy, *St. Paul's Parish Register:*29, 41). Elizabeth married 2nd, Samuel Smith.

Elizabeth Cox posted and administration bond on 3 May 1725 with Jonas Robinson and John Hayes as sureties. Philip Jones, Jr., and John Eaglestone appraised Jacob Cox's estate on 26 May 1725, and valued his goods at £110.10.11. Charles Merryman and Mary Merryman signed as next of kin (MINV 11:94). Elizabeth Cox filed an account of his estate on 8 November 1726, showing an inventory of £110.11.1, and listing payments of £7.1.11 (MDAD 8:103).

Elizabeth Smith died leaving a will dated 22 June 1770 and proved 7 December 1770. She named her children Merryman Cox, Rachel, Elizabeth (mother of Mary Fowler Smith), John, Charles, Sophia Greenfield, and grandchild, the heir of her son of Jacob Cox, and grandson Thomas Smith. Edmund Talbot, George Stansbury, and Nicholas Nicholas Norwood witnessed the will (MWB 38:111, abst. in *Md. Cal. of Wills* 14:150).

Jacob and Elizabeth were the parents of: **2. Merryman**, b. 22 January 1723/4; and **3. Jacob**, b. 7 July 1725.

2. Merryman Cox, son of Jacob (1) and Elizabeth, was born 22 January 1723/4. On 26 December 1745 he married Honour Hall (Reamy and Reamy, *St. Paul's Parish Register:* 1, 34).

On 30 October 1745 Merryman Cox of Baltimore Co. and his wife Honour, deeded 40 a. *East Humphreys* to Tobias Stansbury (BALR TB#E: 229). On 21 September 1748 Samuel Smith and wife Elizabeth Merryman, Merryman Cox and Jacob Cox sold 40 a. *East Humphreys* to Tobias Stansbury (BALR TR#C: 92). On 15 October 1748 Samuel Smith and wife Elizabeth, Merryman Cox, and Jacob Cox, conveyed 40 a. part *East Humphreys* to Tobias Stansbury (BALR TR#C: 93).

Merryman Cox took the oath of Allegiance in 1778 (*BARP:* 60).

Merriman Cox stated he would not pay the debts of his wife Eleanor (*Maryland Journal and Baltimore Advertiser* 34 April 1780).

3. Jacob Cox, son of Jacob (1) and Elizabeth, was born 7 July 1725 (Reamy and Reamy, *St. Paul's Parish Register:* 3).

On 21 September 1748 Samuel Smith and his wife Elizabeth Merryman, Merryman Cox and Jacob Cox sold 40 a. East Humphreys to Tobias Stansbury (BALR TR#C: 92). Jacob Cox was not married at this time, but Jacob Cox of William was married.

== 0 ==

The William Cox Family of Baltimore County

1. William Cox died in Baltimore Co. by July 1737. He married 1st, by March 1721, Elizabeth [-?-], and 2nd, by March 1727, Mary [-?-], who survived him.

On 4 September 1730 William Rogers and wife Sarah of Baltimore Co. conveyed 50 a. (*Bachelor's Range* to William Cox (BALR IS#L: 184). On 3 August 1736 William

Cox, for love he bore his daughter Elizabeth, wife of Charles Bosley, conveyed her 50 a. *Bachelor's Range* (BALR HWS#M: 418).

William Cox's estate was appraised by Edward Stevenson and Nicholas Haile at £124.2.6. Joseph and Richard Cox signed as next of kin. Thomas Taylor, administrator, filed the inventory on 23 July 1737 (MINV 22:327). William [*sic*] Taylor filed an account of the estate on 12 May 174-. After citing the inventory he listed payments of £129.19/2 (MDAD 20:208).

Mary Cox, possibly the widow of William, who in 1737 had a child who was being nursed [cared for] for six weeks by James Boreing (Baltimore Co. Levy List for 1737). In November 1737 Cox's widow Mary was assigned to Edward Cox for care

William and Elizabeth were the parents of (Reamy and Reamy, *St. Paul's Parish Register:* 9; BACP HWS#1-A:131-132; BACP TB#D:61): **2. Elizabeth**, b. 15 March 1721, married Charles Bosley; on 10 July 1758 Charles Bosley made a will naming his wife Elizabeth and her brother Jacob Cox as executors (MWB 31:750 abst. in *Md. Cal. of Wills* 12:152); **3. Jacob**, b. 11 February 1723; **4. Susannah**, b. 17 July 1726, in November 1737 was bound to Edward Cox; **5. Sarah**, b. 17 November 1728; **6. William**, b. 14 May 1730, in November 1737 was bound to Joseph Cox; and **7. Mary**, b. 31 March 1734; in November 1737 was bound to Edward and Jane Cox and in November 1742 was bound to Charles Bosley.

William and Mary were the parents of: **8. Providence**, b about March 1737; she may be the Providence Cox, who in 1762 was fined for begetting a bastard (BAMI 1775-1763),

3. Jacob Cox, son of William (1) and Elizabeth, was born 11 February 1723. He died in 1798. He married 1st, on 13 December 1744 Elizabeth Gain (*SJSG:* 122). He married, 2nd, Keziah Peregoy. Jacob Cox, aged about 41, deposed on 7 May 1764 (BALR B#N:141). Henry Peregoy, in his will dated 15 February 1802 named his daughter Keziah Cox (BAWB 7:5, abst. by Burns).

In July 1759 he was named as a brother of Charles Bosley's wife Elizabeth (BAWB 2:131).

On 5 March 1745 Jacob Cox of Baltimore Co. conveyed 47 a. *Jacob's Struggle* to Charles Bosley. Jacob's wife Elizabeth consented (BALR TB#E: 12). On 6 March 1749 Jacob Cox and Elizabeth conveyed 50 a. *Bachelor's Choice* to Charles Bosley (BALR TR#C: 391). 2 April 1750 Matthew Hail assigns his lease of *Hail's Park,* part of His Lordship's Reserve Lands, to Jacob Cox (BALR TR#C: 399). Later [date not given] Jacob Cox assigned the lease to James Bosley (BALR AL#1: 52), On 2 April 1757 Jacob Cox and wife Elizabeth conveyed 50 a. *Cox's Range* to Charles Bosley (BALR BB#1: 655).On 27 June 1761 Benjamin Barney of Baltimore Co. with wife Delilah's consent, conveyed 200 a. *Barney's Timber Ridge* to Jacob Cox (BALR B#I: 359). On 1 September 1768 Jacob Cox conveyed 50 a. *Elijah's Lot* to Benjamin Wheeler. His wife Elizabeth consented (BALR B#Q: 601).

In 1778 Jacob Cox was a Non-Juror to the Oath of Fidelity (*BARP:* 59).

Jacob Cox died leaving a will dated 24 June 1798 and proved 31 July 1798. He named his wife Casiah, and children Zebediah,. Dinah Murry, Rachel Marshall, Elizabeth Davis, Jacob, Rebecca Boring, Elijah, Elisha, William, John, and an unborn child. Joshua Tracey and John Perago (Peregoy) were executors. Richard Laughan, Peter Frank, and Samuel Tipton witnessed the will (BAWB 6:121, abst. by Burns).

Jacob Cox was the father of (listed in the order they were mentioned in his will): **9. Zebediah;** married by 4 June 1770, [-?-], daughter of Abraham Vaughn (BAAD 6:217); **10. Dinah**, b. 15 July 1751, married Capt. John Murray; **11. Rachel**, married [-?-]

Marshall; **11. Elizabeth,** married [-?-] Davis; **13. Jacob; 14. Elijah; 15. Elisha,** married Arabella Wheeler; **16. William; 17. John;** and **18.** [-?-], unborn child.

6. William Cox, son of William (1) and Elizabeth, was born 14 May 1730. William Cox, brother of Jacob, gave his age as age 31, when he deposed on 31 May 1764 (BALR B#N: 140). He may have married Ruth, daughter of Joseph Bosley.

William Cox died by 27 January 1767 when John Talbot and Jacob Johnson appraised his personal property at £176.6.0. Jacob Cox and Elizabeth Bosley signed as next of kin. Ruth Cox was the administratrix (MINV 91:262).

Ruth Cox filed an account of Cox's estate on 19 May 1767. She cited the inventory as given and listed payments of £54.7.9. The account mentioned eight children, all minors (MDAD 56:199).

On 19 May 1767 Ruth Cox distributed his estate coming to £176.6.0. Nathan Johnson and Jacob Cox were sureties. The widow received her thirds and the balance went to eight children (unnamed), all minors (BAAD 7:283; BFD 5:19).

15. Elisha Cox, son of Jacob (3), married Arabella Wheeler

David Gist of Clark Co., Ky., sold Elisha Cox of Baltimore Co. 49½ a. of *Gist's Prospect* on 23 June 1798 (BALR WG#55:356).

Unplaced:
William Cox, orphan, petitioned the court that in February 1788 he had been bound to
  James Clark, merchant, to learn the art of a merchant. Cox complained of his
  treatment (BOCP Petition of William Cox, 1791).

==0==

The Dare Family of Calvert County

Sources Checked:
A: Christopher Johnston. Chart of the Dare Family. Johnston Collection, MHS.

1. James Dare was transported to Md. by 1662 (MPL 5:307). He acquired much land. He is stated to have been the father of (*BDML* 1:249, but no documentary proof of his existence has been found): **2. Nathaniel.**

2. Nathaniel Dare, possibly son of James (1), died in 1699. He married by 31 August 1685 Elizabeth [-?-], widow and executrix of Thomas Banks of Calvert Co. (PCJU DS#A: 477; INAC 13B:1; MDTP 13:262). She was a daughter of Thomas Cleverly (*BDML* 1:249).

On 21 February 1685 Nathaniel Dare appraised the estate of James Bowle of Cecil Co. William Dare was to administer the oath to the appraisers (MDTP 13:207). About 1686 he was one of the appraisers of William Gamball of Calvert Co. (MDTP 13:343). He administered the estate of Thomas and Ann Cleverly on 21 May 1687 (MDTP 13:488; INAC 9:280, 382).

On 1 May 1688 Nathaniel Dare witnessed the will of Robert Dixon of "The Clifts," Calvert Co. (MWB 7:51).

Nathaniel and Elizabeth were the parents of (*BDML* 1:249): **3. Nathaniel;** and **4. Amy,** m. [-?-] Battson.

3. Nathaniel Dare, son of Nathaniel (2), was born about 1660. In 1720 he made a deposition, giving his age as about 60 (MCHR CL: 521). He died in Calvert Co. by July 1742. He married Mary [-?-] who died in 1748 (*BDML* 1:249).

On 9 April 1711 Amy Battson, widow of Calvert Co. made a will, and named several children. She left her daughter Amy to the care of her brother and sister Nathaniel and Mary Dare (MWB 16:195).

Nathaniel Dare was a member of the Lower House of the Assembly in 1708, 1711, and 1716 to 1718 (*BDML* 1:250).

He patented 375 a. *Dare's Addition* on 20 May 1735 (MPL PL#6:8, IL#A: 505). He also patented 2, 294 a. *Gideon and Cleverly's Delight* on 17 May 1737 (MPL EI#2:438, EI#5:277).

Nathaniel Dare, Gent., of Calvert Co. died leaving a will dated 9 February 1732 and proved 14 July 1742. He left land to his sons Gideon and Cleverly and named his wife Mary as executrix. She was to have tracts *Hooper's Clift* and *Red Clift*. Amory Babson, Samuel Leson, and John Mackall witnessed the will (MWB 22:499, abst. in *Md. Cal. of Wills* 8:181).

The personal estate of Nathaniel Dare was appraised at £1938.4.5 on 27 January 1742 by James Somervell and John Clare. Gideon and Cleverly Dare signed as next of kin. Mrs. Mary Dare, executrix, filed the inventory on 3 February 1742 (MINV 27:253).

Mary Dare died leaving a will dated 7 June 1748 and proved 17 December 1748. She named her children Gideon and Cleverly Dare, Althea Smith, Kezia Broome, and Charles Clagett's children, born of her daughter Diannah. Son Cleverly was named executor. Isaac Rawlings, John Rigby, and Ellis Dixon witnessed the will (MWB 25:494).

Nathaniel and Mary were the parents of (*BDML* 1:249-250): **5. Gideon,** d. 1757; **6. Cleverly,** was living in 1756 when he witnessed his brother Gideon's will; **7. Alethia,** m., 1st, Walter Smith, and, 2nd, Rev. George Cooke; **8. Keziah,** m. [-?-] Browne; and **9. Diana,** m. Charles Clagett.

5. Gideon Dare, of Calvert Co., son of Nathaniel (3) and Mary, died by July 1757. He married Susanna Parker, daughter of George and Susanna Parker of Calvert Co. Susanna was born 18 Jan 1701 and died in 1774 (A).

Gideon was a Justice of Calvert Co. from 1727 to 1751. He patented 112 a. *Bite the Biter* on 4 May 1740 (MPL LG#B:118). He also patented 112 a. *Ball* on 24 May 1749 (MPL EI#5:721).

Dare left a will dated 15 December 1756 and proved 13 July 1757. He left sterling money to each of his children, Nathaniel, Samuel, Sarah, Gideon, Thomas Cleverly, Alethea, William, Mary Ireland, Susanna Somervell, Parrott, and Diana Dare. He named his grandchildren Susanna Johnson and John Somervile. He named his father Nathaniel Dare. Friends John Gray of the Clifts and John Somervile were to see to a fair division of the estate. Susanna Dare was named executrix. John Gray Clifts, Cleverly Dare, Ella Dixon and Nathaniel Clagett witnessed the will (MWB 30:322).

On 27 November 1757 Samuel Parran and John Somervell appraised Gideon Dare's estate at £893.2.4. Samuel and Gideon Dare signed as next of kin, and Susanna Dare, executrix, filed the inventory of 16 August 1758 (MINV 64:411).

Susanna Dare, executrix, filed an account of the estate on 16 August 1758. She cited the inventory as given and listed payments of £183.4.11 (MDAD 42:74).

Susanna Dare died leaving a will dated May 1765 and proved 6 December 1774. Her son Gideon was to have a Negro girl named Peg, and her son John was to have a Negro girl named Nan. John Somervell, son of James Somervell was left a Negro boy names Jacob The rest of her estate was left to her sons Gideon and John equally. Ellis Dixon, John Cotton, and Graves, Jr. witnessed the will (MWB 40:77, abst. in *Md. Cal. of Wills* 16:17).

Gideon and Susanna were the parents of: **10. Nathaniel**, d. 1764; **11. Samuel**, probably the Samuel who m. Sarah, executrix of Everard Taylor of Calvert Co. by 16 October 1753 (MDAD 35:223); **12. William; 13. Thomas Cleverly; 14. Mary**, m. [-?-] Ireland; **15. Susanna**, m. James Somervell; **16. Gideon; 17. John; 18. Alethea, 19. Elizabeth Parrott; 20. Sarah; 21. Diana;** and **22. Regia**, m. [-?-] Broome.

10. Nathaniel Dare, of Calvert Co., son of Gideon (5) and Susanna, died in Anne Arundel Co. by January 1764. On 29 August 1748 he married Anne [-?-], widow of James Tongue (A).

Nathaniel Dare of Anne Arundel Co. died leaving a will dated 13 November 1763 and proved 17 January 1764. He left one-third of his estate to his wife Ann Dare. He named his son-in-law Thomas [Tongue], sons Nathaniel, Gideon and Richard, and daughter Ann. Wife Anne was named executrix. Jacob Franklin, Quaker, Thomas Grover, and William Kune witnessed the will (MWB 31:1054).

Ann Dare, executrix of Nathaniel Dare of Anne Arundel Co. advertised she would settle his estate (Annapolis *Maryland Gazette* 8 March 1764).

On 29 October 1765, Mrs. Ann Dare, administratrix, late Mrs. Ann Tongue, filed the inventory of James Tongue of Anne Arundel Co. The inventory had been taken on 3 June 1747 (MINV 88:268B).

Benjamin Harrison and John Weems appraised the personal estate of Nathaniel Dare on 31 August 1766 and set a price of £1089.3.8 on his goods and chattels. Samuel Chew and P. Chew signed as next of kin. Ann Dare, executrix, filed the inventory on 17 November 1766 (MINV 89:209).

Mrs. Ann Dare filed an account of Nathaniel Dare's estate on 4 March 1767. She cited an inventory of £1089.3.8, and listed payments coming to £303.5.2. The representatives were Gideon, Ann, and Nathaniel Dare (MDAD 55:344).

Nathaniel and Ann were the parents of (A): **23. Nathaniel**, b. 4 August 1748; **24. Gideon; 25. Richard;** and **26. Ann,** almost certainly the Ann, daughter of Nathaniel Dare who m. James Sollers.

11. Samuel Dare, son of Gideon (5) and Susanna, was probably the Samuel who m. Sarah, executrix of Everard Taylor of Calvert Co. by 16 October 1753 (MDAD 35:223).

Samuel Dare was a private in Capt. John Mackall's Company, 15th Battalion of Calvert Co. Militia, on 12 June 1778, and was also a Private in Capt. Frederick Skinner's Company of Calvert Co. Militia; he took the Oath of Allegiance in 1778 (*RPCV:* 70).

12. William Dare, son of Gideon (5) and Susanna, took the Oath of Allegiance in Calvert Co. in 1778 (*RPCA:* 70). He was probably married and the father of: **24. William, Jr.**

13. Thomas Cleverly Dare, son of Gideon (5) and Susanna, took the Oath of Allegiance in Calvert Co. in 1778 (*RPCV:*70).

16. Gideon Dare, Jr., son of Gideon (5) and Susanna, took the Oath of Allegiance in Calvert Co. in 1778 (*RPCV:*69).

23. Nathaniel Dare, son of Gideon (10) and Ann, was born 4 August 1748. He and Jean Gray were married on 22 January 1778 (Marr. Returns of Rev. Francis Lauder, Scharf Papers, MS.1999 at MdHS).

In 1778 Nathaniel Dare was a private in Capt. Walter Smith's Company of Calvert Co. Militia, and he took the Oath of Allegiance in 1778 (*RPCV:*70).

24. William Dare, Jr., son of William (12) was a First Lieutenant in Capt. Frederick Skinner's Company of Calvert Co. Militia on 16 June 1778. On 12 June 1778 a petition was sent to the House of Delegates to appoint him a captain (*RPCV:* 70).

Unplaced:
Gideon Dare married Elizabeth [-?-]. They were the parents of the following ("West River MM," *AACR:* 190): **Sarah,** b. 9 d. 2 m. 1776; **Priscilla,** b. 17 d. 9 m. 1777; **Thomas Cleaverly,** b. 28 d, 10 m. 1779; **Henry,** b. 18 d. 10 m. 1781; **Elizabeth,** b. 6 d. 9 m. 1783; **Gideon,** b. 8 d. 3 m. 1786; and **William,** b. 18 d. 12 m. 1787.
Gideon Dare m. by 9 May 1798 Elizabeth, daughter of Henry Wilson, whose will of that date named their children Sarah, Rachel, and Elizabeth (BAWB 6:234, abst. by Burns).

== 0 ==

The Daughaday Family of Baltimore County

N.B.: These miscellaneous notes are presented even though the author has not been able to consolidate the account of the family.

A Quaker Daughaday Family

1. [-?-] Daughaday, married [-?-]. They were the parents of the following children, who were accepted into membership in Gunpowder Meeting in 1754, along with their cousins Joseph Taylor, and his cousin Richard Taylor, b. 16 d. 12 m. 1738 ("Minutes of Gunpowder Meeting," *QRNM:*33): 2. **Richard,** b. 28 d. 9 m. 1736; 3. **Joseph,** b. 26 d. 12 m. 1738; and 4. **Rachel,** b. 26 d. 10 m. 1740.

2. Richard Daughaday, born 28 d. 9 m. 1746, was charged with going out in marriage on 6 d. 3 m. 1760 ("Minutes of Gunpowder Meeting," *QRNM:*40). In 1783 he was listed in Middle River and Back River Upper Hundreds as owning 245 a. part of *Taylor's Discovery,* with nine white inhabitants in his household (Carothers, *1783 Tax List of Baltimore Co.:* 52). in 1798 he was listed as owning 145 a. *Taylor's Discovery* with four old houses Horvath, *Particular Assessment Lists:* 34).

3. Joseph Daughaday was b. 26 d. 12 m. 1738. In 1783 as Joseph Daugherday he was listed in Back River Lower Hundred, with one white male and six white inhabitants (Carothers, *1783 Tax List of Baltimore Co.:* 2). Joseph Taylor, owning 888 a. *Continuance,* 718 a. *Taylor's Addition,* and one a. of *Darley Hall* was also listed in Back River Lower Hundred (Carothers, *1783 Tax List of Baltimore Co.:7).*

4. Rachel Daughaday was born 26 d. 10 m. 1740. She married Thomas Floyd on 23 d. 4 m. 1755. John, Richard, and Joseph Daughaday, and Richard and Joseph Taylor were among the witnesses ("Records of Gunpowder Meeting," *QRNM:*36-37). On 29

September 1788 Joseph Taylor, 'for love and good will,' conveyed part *Taylor's Addition* to Richard Floyd (BALR WG#CC:301). On 13 April 1789 Richard Floyd conveyed 51 a. *Taylor's Addition* to Joseph Floyd (BALR WG#DD:240). On 18 July 189 Joseph Floyd and wife Anne conveyed 7¼ a. of the tract to Solomon Hillen (BALR WG#DD:241).

Katherine Daughaday, probably a member of this family, on 19 April 1788 was named as the mother of Joseph, Abraham, Thomas, John, and Richard Daughaday, in the will of Joseph Taylor, who named her sons as cousins (nephews?) (BAWB 4:346).

Thomas Daughaday and John Daughaday were legatees of Joseph Taylor, and in February 1794 chose Richard Taylor as their guardian (BAOC 3:88).
On 7 July 1802 an indenture stated that Joseph Taylor of Baltimore Co. left 200 a. *Taylor's Addition* to Thomas, John, Abraham and Joseph Daughaday (BALR WG#73:435).

The John Daughaday Family

1. John Daughaday married by 10 July 1770 Rachel, widow of George Sater, and daughter of William and Sarah Hamilton (BAAD 6:219, 7:139, 350; 10:414, 514; BAWB 4:304).
On 25 November 1779 John Daughaday, with the consent of his wife Rachel, leased 30 a. *Tully's Adventure* to Edward Tully (BALR WG#E:88). On 27 December 1788 Daughaday and his wife Rachel, formerly the wife of George Sater, deeded to Charles Carroll of Carrollton and John Cockey, the tract *Sater's Addition* (BALR WG#CC:351). In 1785 John Tully Young conveyed 30 a. *Tully's Adventure* and 36½ a. *James Forest* to John Daughaday (BALR WG#DD:520).
On 1 May 1802 John Daughaday and his wife Rachel deeded to Peter Parks part of *Bachelor's Habitation*, part of *Taylor's Direction*, and part of *Knight's Addition* (BALR WG#71:496).
John Daughaday died leaving a will dated 6 November 1803 and proved 19 November 1803. He named his wife Rachel and daughter Helen (Hollin) Daughaday, his son William Hamilton Daughaday and grandchildren Caleb Owings Daughaday and Helen Maria Daughaday. His wife Rachel and daughter Helen were named executors. Gerard Tipton, John T. Holland and Luke Ensor witnessed the will (BAWB 7:256, abst by Burns).
On 25 June 1803 Caleb, Johnza, and Helen Maria Daughaday, orphans of Johnza, came into court and the court appointed Caleb Owing as their guardian, who accepted and offers Samuel Norwood and John Daugharday [sic] as his securities. (BAOC 5:7)
John and Rachel were the parents of: **2. Helen; and 3. William Hamilton.**

== 0 ==

The Margaret (Sing) Daughaday Wiley Family

1. Margaret Sing in 1726 had been named as a granddaughter in the will of Richard Taylor (MWB 19:781 abst. in *Md. Cal. of Wills* 6:131). She had married William Wiley on 23 December 1734 (Reamy and Reamy, *St. Paul's Parish Register:* 31).
She is presumed to have been the mother of a son **2. John Daughaday.**

Colonial Families of Maryland II

2. John Daughaday (Daugherty), is presumed to have been the son of Margaret (1), who had him bound to Samuel Collier in October 1745 to learn the trade of blacksmith (BALR TB#D:331).

Daughaday bought 50 a. *Panther's Ridge* from Benjamin and Elizabeth Knight on 25 February 1754 (BALR B#l:175). On 2 October 1761 Benjamin Long conveyed 50 a. *Knight's Addition* to John Daughaday, blacksmith (BALR B#l: 340). On 8 October 1761 Richard Chenoweth of Baltimore Co. conv. to John Daughaday, blacksmith, 201 a. *Chenoweth's Adventure* also known as *Daughaday's Purchase.* His wife Keziah consented (BALR B#l: 337).

John Daughaday, blacksmith, and Sarah Taylor, were convicted of bastardy in November 1757 (BACP Rough Minutes 1755-1763).

John Daughaday agreed on 10 August 1765 to make bolts and keys where wanted for the window shutters of the church and vestry house (Reamy and Reamy, *St. Thomas Parish Register:* 57, 58). In 1767 John 'Daugherterey' and Richard 'Daugherterey' were listed as taxables in Back River Upper Hundred (Reamy and Reamy. *St. Thomas Parish Register;* 66).

John Daughaday (Dawhody) was listed in Middle River and Back River Upper Hundreds as owning 50 a. *Night's* Addition and 195 a. *Taylor's Direction,* with six white inhabitants in his household (Carothers, *1783 Tax List of Baltimore Co.:* 52). In 7898 John was listed in Back River Upper Hundred as owning 195 a. *Bachelor's Habitation,* 96 a. *Taylor's Direction,* and 50 a. *Knight's Addition,* and 14 slaves. His property was improved by a one story old frame dwelling house, 17 x 40, an old kitchen, 18 x 25, a log meat house, 12x16, and two old barns, fit for fuel (Horvath, *Particular Assessment Lists:* 34).

== 0 ==

The William Daughaday Family

1. William Daugherty m. Mary [-?-].

On 7 November 1745 Amos Garrett, son and heir of Bennett Garrett, deceased, conveyed 268 a. *Thomas and Mary's Repose* and *Roberts Choice,* which Bennett Garrett bought from Thomas Burchfield, to William Daugherty (BALR TB#D: 396).

About 1770 William and several members of the Kimble family held Pew # 13 in St. George's Parish (Reamy and Reamy, *St. George's Parish Register:* 114).

William Daugherty, Sr., died leaving a will dated 19 August 1767 and proved 3 May 1768. His son William was named executor, and was to have all his land and persona estate, except for certain bequests. Daughter Usen was to have £10 Penna. money and personalty at age 16 or marriage. Son George and daughters Margaret and Eleanor were each to have one shilling. John Clark, Nath'l Smith, Samuel Macarty, and James Henderson witnessed the will (BAWB 3:85).

On 3 May 1768 when William Daugherty, administrator with will attached, posted a bond worth £1000, with George Daugherty, Stephen Kimble as sureties (BAAB 1:553).

William and Mary were the Parents of (Reamy and Reamy, *St. George's Parish Register:* 68, 73, 84): 2. **Eleanor,** b. 30 December 1742; m. John Reddell on 23 April 1760; **3. William,** b. 22 April 1745; and 4. **Ufan,** b. 25 January 1753; **5. George;** and **6. Margaret.**

Colonial Families of Maryland II

Unplaced:
Constantine Daughaday: On 17 November 1762 Joseph Henley conveyed 36 a. part *Maiden's Bower* to Constantine Daughaday of Hunterdon Co., N. J. (BALR B#K: 438).
George Daughaday, aged 48, Margaret, aged 30, Samuel, 17, Mary Ann, 3, and Joh, 3 mos., in 1776 were listed in Spesutia Hundred, Harford Co. With them were Martha Brown, aged 3, and one Negro (Carothers, *1776 Census of Md.:* 206). In 1783 George Daugherty, with three whites, was listed in as owning 69 a. *Roberts' Choice,* and 19 a. *Daugherty's Angles* (Carothers, *1783 Tax List of Maryland:* 130).
John Daughaday was listed in 1737 as head of a household in Back River Upper Hundred (Wright, *Inhabitants of Baltimore Co.:* 21). In 1762 and 1763 a John Daughaday was taxed as a bachelor in St. Thomas Parish (Wright, *Inhabitants of Baltimore Co.:* 79, 80).
Margaret Daughtery *alias* Barkey and Stephen Kimble were m. on 22 March 1758 (Reamy and Reamy, *St. George's Parish Register:* 82).
Samuel Daugherty, with two whites, in 1783 was listed as a pauper in Spesutia Lower Hundred (Carothers, *1783 Tax List of Maryland:* 136). He or another Samuel Daugherty, with two whites, was listed in Spesutia upper Hundred as owning 100 a. part *Jericho* (Carothers, *1783 Tax List of Maryland:* 156).

== = 0 = =

The Debruler Family of Baltimore and Kent Counties

1. John Debruler, listed as John 'Debrewlah,' was in Baltimore Co., by 1692 as a taxable in the North Side of Gunpowder Hundred (*IBCW:*2). He, his sons John and William, "and other sons and daughters born in this province, were naturalized on 17 May 1701 (*ARMD* 24:404).

John Debruler (Debrular, Debruly), died leaving a will dated 23 July 1707 and proved 24 April 1710. He named his son George, his daughter Eliza Hopkins, son John, daughter Mary, sons Peter and William at 21 yrs., daughter Rosamond, son Anthony at

21 yrs. and daughter Jane. He left personalty to the boy George Davis. His wife Eliza, executrix, was to have the residue of his estate (MWB 13:840).

John Debruler's estate was administered on 5 May 1711 and 5 June 1711 by Elisabeth Debrular (INAC 32B:167, 32C:55).

John Debruler was the father of (order of birth uncertain): **2. John; 3. William,** not yet 21; **4. George; 5. Eliza,** m. [-?-] Hopkins; **6. Mary; 7. Peter,** not yet 21; **8. Rosamond; 9. Anthony;** and **10. Jane.**

2. John Debrular, son of John (1) and Eliza, married Mary Drunkord, on 12 April 1704 (Reamy and Reamy, *St. George's Parish Register:* 10). He administered the estate of James Drunkord on 3 March 1708 (BAAD 2:167). James Drunckord and Mary Greenfield had been married on 22 December 1700 James died 1 February and was buried 5 February 1704/5 (Reamy and Reamy, St. George's Parish Register: 6, 12).

Debruler was conveyed 116 a. *Little Britain* on 23 May 1728 by John Tilyard (acc. to a later deed in TB#E: 322, he was a grandson of said Green) Tilyard's wife, unnamed, consented (BALR IS#I: 106). John Debruler of St. John's Parish, and his wife Mary, daughter and devisee of Thomas Greenfield, late of St George's Parish, deceased, on 5 March 1728 conveyed 50 a. part *Hazard,* 200 a. granted to Thomas Greenfield on 10 December 1695) to Patrick Ruark, laborer (BALR IS#I: 266). John Debruler made a will on 1 February 1728/9, leaving to wife Mary *Little Britain*, which he had recently bought from John Tilyard (BALR IS#I: 316).

Mary Greenfield Drunckord Debruler died leaving a will dated 4 December 1751 and proved 18 December 1751. She left the land on Little Brittain where she lived to William Dawtridge, and stock to William York. John York, Edward York and James Meade of Edward witnessed the will (MWB 28:237).

3. William Debruler, son of John (1) and Eliza, was naturalized in 1701, but was not 21 when his father made his will.

On 7 May 1722 William Debruler of Kent Co., planter, and his wife Anne, conveyed to Francis Barney of the same county, carpenter, 100 acres, being part of a tract called *Essex*[?] near the head of Church Creek (KELR JS#W:228).

William 'Debrulo' died leaving a will dated 19 May 1721 proved 21 Aug 1722. To his daughter Ann, he left personalty, and one-half of *Essex*. If his daughter died, one-half of Essex to wife Ann, and the other half to his brother Peter. His wife Ann was named executrix and was to have personal estate (MWB 17:186).

William and Anne were the parents of: **11.Ann,** b. 3 July 1719, recorded in Shrewsbury Parish, Kent Co. (*ESVR* 1:43).

4. George Debrular, son of John (1) and Eliza, and Esther Lewis were married 20 October 1713 in St. Paul's Parish, Kent Co. (*ESVR* 1:19). Hester died 23 December 1742 in Baltimore Co.

On 13 October 1725 John Tilyard of Kent Co., carpenter, conv. 80 a. *Sally's Delight* to George Debruler; the tract had formerly been laid out for John Tilyard, grandfather of deceased, and bequeathed to Richard Tilyard, now also deceased father of the afsd John Tilyard (BALR IS#H: 192). On 23 May 1728 Tilliard conveyed part of *God's Providence* to George Debruler; Tilliard's wife Mary consented (BALR IS#I: 172, 175)

Debruler died leaving a will dated 13 January 1734 and proved 23 February 1734. His wife Hester was named executrix and was to have his entire estate for her lifetime. His daughter Elizabeth, wife of William York was left personalty His six sons, William, George, James, John, Benjamin, and Francis, and daughter Elizabeth were to have the remainder of his estate divided equally. Gilbert Crockett, George York. Jr. (Quakers), and Edgar Tipper witnessed the will (MWB 21:397, abst. in *Md. Cal. of Wills* 7:142).

George Debruler was the father of (St. Paul's Parish, Kent Co. (*ESVR* 1:18, 20; *SJSG:*13): **12. Elizabeth,** b. 19 July 1714, m. William York; **13. William,** b. 22 June 1720; **14. George,** b. 22 August 1721; **15. James,** b. 22 February 1723; **16. John; 17. Benjamin, 18. Martha,** b. 6 March 1727/8, d. 16 March 1728; and **19. Francis**, b. 20 September 1729.

7. Peter Debruler, son of John (1) and Eliza, and Margrett Skidmore were married on 22 December 1712 in St. Paul's Parish, Kent Co. (*ESVR* 1:19).

Peter died by May 1749, leaving a son and two daughters: **20. William; 21. Margaret;** and **22. Hannah.**

9. Anthony Debruler, son of John (1) and Eliza, married Elizabeth [-?-]. Could she be the Elizabeth Debruler who married Thomas Jackson in September 1724 (Reamy and

Reamy, St. George's Parish Register: 30)?
Anthony and Elizabeth were the parents of (Reamy and Reamy, *St. George's Parish Register:* 30): **23. Mary**, b. 28 January 1720, and **24. John**, b. 25 January 1724

13. William Debruler, son of George (4) and Esther, was born 22 June 1720, and died by 10 March 1772 in Baltimore Co. He married 1st, Diana, daughter of William Greenfield, on 23 March 1743; he married 2nd, on 7 February 1764 Sarah Watters (*SJSG*:46, 111).

In 1750 he owned *Sally's Delight* and *God's Providence* (BACO Debt Book for 1750).

Debrular died leaving a will dated 16 February 1772 and proved 10 March 1772. He named his wife and son William as executors,. Son George was to have £8.0.0. Sons James and Micajah were to have personalty. Daughters Cordelia Presbury Euohan Debruler were to have personalty, and son William was to have the dwelling Plantation and all other lands. The rest of his personal estate was to pass to his five children: William, James, Micajah, Cordelia and Euphan. John Day of Edward, Wm. Robinson Presbury, and George York of William witnessed the will. (BAWB 3:324).

On 10 March 1772 William Debruler, executor, posted a bond worth £500, with William Presbury, William Robinson Presbury, and John Day of Edward as sureties (BAAB 3:8).

On 1 June 1773 when William Debruler, acting executor, filed an account of his estate citing two inventories of £373.6.6 and £51.5.3, and listing payments of £98.19.1 He named Micajah, James and Ufan Debruler, who received their portions of the estate of their grandfather William Greenfield, and he mentioned Micajah Greenfield, executor of William Debruler (MDAD 68:85).

William and Diana were the parents of (*SJSG:*19. 20, 57): **25. Cordelia/Deliha**, b. 29 March 1744, d. 7 November 1744; **26. Cordelia**, b. 20 November 1748, m. [-?-] Presbury; **27. William**, b. 14 February 1750; **28. Ufaan**, b. 28 August 1752, d. 6

February 1756; **29. James**, twin, b. 30 December 1755; **30. Micajah**, twin, b. 30 December 1755; and **31. Ufaan**, b. 27 April 1759.

16. John Debruler, son of George (4) and Esther, died in Baltimore Co., on 15 April 1729 (*SJSG*:66). On 1 July 1749 Robert Adair posted an administration bond, with W. Dallam and Talbott Risteau as sureties (BAAB 5:381). He married Frances Buredy or Burridge on 18 May 1744 (*SJSG*: 85; Reamy and Reamy, *St. George's Parish Register:* 71 gives the date as 14 May 1744).

John Debruler was made levy free in November 1746 (BACP TB&TR#1:228, 229).

John was the father of (Reamy and Reamy, *St. George's Parish Register:* 74): **32. Sarah**, b. 1 November 1746.

17. Benjamin Debruler, son of George (4) and Esther, married Semelia Jackson.

They were the parents of: **33. Elizabeth**, b. 14 December 1756; and **34. Francis**, b. 6 October 1759.

20. William Debruler, son of Peter (7) and Margaret, inherited a 120 a. tract called *Duns Folley*.

On 16 June 1736 William Debrulear, son of Peter Debrulear, planter, deceased, an orphan, was bound as an apprentice to Thomas Rouse, plasterer, until age 21, he being 12 years old on 16 June (KEBI JS#18:44).

On 15 July 1736 Peter's master Thomas Rouse was allowed to clear 2 a. of *Dun's Folley*. The property had a dwelling house of loggs, 25 feet long and 20 feet wide, old and a log tobacco house rotten and old orchard 40 apple trees and some peach trees and cherry trees and a 12 foot house 'ruff work,' 961 pannels of indifferent good pannells, the year rent at 300 lbs. of tobacco. Wm. Hynson, Benj. Wicks (KEBl JS#18:65)

On 17 June 1740 William Debrular, son of Peter Debrular of Kent Co., deceased, an orphan, was bound to Thomas Salway, ship carpenter, until age 21, as an apprentice to the trade of ship carpenter, he being 16 years old on the above date (KEBI JS#18:255.

21. Margaret Debruler, daughter of Peter (7) and Margaret, on 20 June 1736 was bound as an apprentice to Samuell Thomas, planter, until age 16 or day of marriage, she being 8 years old last April (KEBI JS#18:49).

On 6 May 1749 she conv. 12½a. to Thomas Bowers of said county, one moiety of a tract called *Essex* and devised by William Debruler late of said county to his brother Peter Debruler, father of said Margret as by his last will, 100 sold out of it to Francis Barney. The other moiety was sold to Thomas Bowers by John Arnold and his wife Hannah (KELR JS#26:212).

At March Court 1746 it was presented that Margaret Debrular, spinster, and William Street, planter, on 1 March 1745, and at divers times as well before as since, committed fornication and begot a bastard child. They were each fined 30 shillings (KECR JS#24:361, 362).

Margaret Debruler and William Street were the parents of: Hannah, b. 21 December 1746 (St. Paul's Parish, Kent Co.)

22. Hannah Debruler, daughter of Peter and Margaret, m. John Arnold.

On 17 November 1747 John Arnold of Kent Co., planter, and his wife Hannah, conveyed to Thomas Bowers of said county, planter, one moiety of a part of a tract called *Essex* and devised by William Debruler late of said county to his brother Peter Debruler, father of the said Hannah Arnold by his last will, 12½ a. (KELR JS#26:78).

Unplaced

Elizabeth Debruler and Thomas Jackson were marred in September 1724 (Reamy and Reamy, St. George's Parish Register: 30).

John Debruler on 5 March 1746 conveyed 116 a. part *Little Britain* to Stephen Onion. Deed traces descent of property from Green to Tilyard to Debruler. The conveyance was made on the condition that Debruler and "his now wife" might occupy the property for life (TB#E: 322).

John Debruler was given an allowance in 1772 for supporting Francis and Anthony Debruler, his sons (Baltimore Co. Levy List, 1772).

== 0 ==

The Duhadaway Family of Anne Arundel County

Variations in spelling: Duehataway, Duhataway, Duhadway, and Duhattoway.

1. Jacob Duhadaway married Margaret [-?-]. In 1674 Jacob Duhattoway deposed that he had been born at Dort in Holland under the Dominion of the States General of the united Provinces (*ARMD* 2:460-462).

Jacob 'Dewhattway,' husband of Alice, was transported between 1649 and 1652, and completed his service by 1659 (MPL 4:58-59, 7:182-3).

Jacob was in Anne Arundel Co. by 10 February 1661 when he assigned a parcel of about 50 a. called *Dort* to Richard Galloway (AALR WH#4:17). On 2 April 1663 as Jacob Duhattes he witnessed the will of Richard Talbot (MWB 1:180 abst. in *Md. Cal. of Wills* 1:25).

Jacob and Margaret were the parents of: **2. Jacob,** his birth was registered in the county court; he was bapt. 2 February 1698/9 in St. James' Parish (*AACR:* 150).

2. Jacob Duhadaway, son of Jacob (1) and Margaret, was bapt. 2 February 1698/9 at St. James' Parish (*AACR:*150). He died by February 1726. He married on 16 d., 9m., 1712, Elizabeth, daughter of Edward and Mary Parish, at West River/Cliffs Meeting (*AACR:*192)..

In his will made April 1722 Edward Parish of Anne Arundel Co. left personalty to Jacob Duhadaway provided he would allow certainly legacies to his children (*viz.* grandchildren) Edward, Jacob (at age 21), Margaret, and Mary, at the decease of their mother (MWB 18:158 abst. in *Md. Cal. of Wills* 5:145).

Jacob Duhadaway died leaving a will dated 20 February 1723/4 and proved 14 February 1726. His sons Jacob and Edward and their heirs were to have his entire estate, real and personal. His children were to have certain personalty as expressed in the will of Duhadaway's father-in-law Edward Parrish. His wife Elizabeth was to have one-third of his personal estate, and was named executrix. The other two-thirds of his estate was to go to all his children including the inborn child. Joseph Galloway was named overseer. John Galloway, John Steward, Joseph Galloway, and Deborah Edwards witnessed the will. (MWB 19:269 abst. in *Md. Cal. of Wills* 6:42).

Elizabeth Duhadaway, widow, died leaving a will dated 25 d., 1 m., 1726/7 and proved 17 April 1727. She left her entire estate to her youngest son Thomas, except certain legacies to daus. Mary and Margaret; her son Thomas and daughter Margaret were left to the care of her mother Mary Parrish; daughter Mary to the care of Joseph Richardson, and sons Jacob and Edward to the care of Joseph Galloway, the executor Joseph Rabbling, Mary Maccubbin, and Frances Sands witnessed the will (MWB 19:273 abst. in *Md. Cal. of Wills* 6:43).

Jacob and Elizabeth were the parents of: **3. Jacob; 4. Edward; 5. Margaret; 6. Mary;** and **7. Thomas,** b. after 20 Feb 1723/4 and before 25 d., 1 m., 1726/7.

2. Jacob Duhadaway, son of Jacob (1) and Elizabeth, and Sarah Harris declared their intention to marry on 24 d., 6 m., 1741 (*AAMR:*71). The records of Duck Creek Meeting, Delaware, show a report of an orderly marriage on 31 d. 6 m. 1743 between Jacob Duhadaway and Rachel Corbitt, daughter of Daniel Corbitt on 26 d. 7 m. 1743 having the consent of their parents and relations ("Extracts from Duck Creek Monthly Meeting, 1705-1800," in *Vital Records of Kent and Sussex Counties* in Westminster: Family Line Publications: 10, 72).

On 21 January 1737 Jacob Duhadaway, planter, for £180 sterling conveyed to Joseph Galloway all that tract called *Dort* except for 64 acres earlier sold to Richard Galloway (AALR RD#3:25).

Jacob Duhadaway was granted a certificate of transfer from Cliffs Meeting to Kent on Delaware on 2 d. 3 m. 1740 (*QRSM:*40). On 26 d. 11 m. 1763 a complaint was made that Jacob Duhadaway had drunk strong liquor to excess and had absented himself from the religious meetings ("Extracts from Duck Creek Monthly Meeting, 1705-1800," in *Vital Records of Kent and Sussex Counties:* 21).

Unplaced:
Daniel Duhaddaway on 6 d. 23 m. 1764 had a complaint brought against him from Murtherkill Preparative Meeting that he had married contrary to the rules of the Society ("Extracts from Duck Creek Monthly Meeting, 1705-1800," in *Vital Records of Kent and Sussex Counties:* 21).

==0==

The Duskin Family

1. Dennis Duskin married Mary [-?-] who married 2nd, John Fraser. Fraser died by January 1717.

Dennis and Mary were the parents of (BALR TR#RA:523): **2. Michael**, b. about 1708, was aged 8 on 24 October 1716; and **3. Daniel**, b. about 1711, was aged 8 on 7 April 1717.

2. Michael Duskin, son of Dennis (1) and Mary, was born about 1708 and was aged 8 on 24 October 1716; in January 1717 he was bound by his mother to serve John and Alice Barrett to age 21 (BALR TR#RA:523). He died by September 1768. He married Sarah Johnson on 6 June 1751 (*SJSG:* 93).

On 29 September 1751 he and Abraham Ditto were sureties for Esther Standiford when she posted an administration bond on Skelton Standiford's estate (BAAB 3:453).

Michael Duskin died by 17 August 1767 when Sarah Duskin, administratrix, posted a bond worth £500, with Luke Johnson and Geo. Prickett as sureties (BAAB 1:557).

John Talbott and John Slade appraised Duskin's estate on 14 November 1767, at a value of £153.18.6. Nicholas Hutchins and Richard Frasher signed as next of kin. Sarah Duskin filed the inventory on 11 April 1768 (MINV 97:176).

On 15 April 1768 the Deputy Commissary was ordered to examine the accounts of Sarah 'Duskins,' administratrix of Michael 'Duskins' (MDTP 42:363).

Sarah Duskin filed an account of Michael Duskin's estate on 4 September 1768, citing an inventory of £153.8.6, and listing payments of £34.1.11. Sarah Johnson was listed as a legatee, and the deceased left six children, all minors (MDAD 60:176).

Sarah was living as late as 25 June 1770 when she received a payment from the estate of Thomas Miles the Younger (MDAD 64:75).

Michael and Sarah were the parents of: **4. Michael**, b. 27 October 1752 (*SJSG:*72); and 5-10, five other minor children

3. Daniel Duskin, son of Dennis (1) and Mary, was born about 1711, was aged 8 on 7 April 1717, when he was bound by his mother to serve John and Alice Barrett to age 21 (BALR TR#RA:523).

In 1769 Daniel Duskin signed the petition opposing the removal of the county seat from Joppa to Baltimore Town (*IBCP:* 42, 45).

N.B.: No Duskins were listed in the 1790 Census of Maryland.

==0==

Colonial Families of Maryland II

The Eastwood Family of Baltimore County

N.B.: The name is sometimes written as Yestwood.

1. Michael Eastwood (Yestwood), died 26 May 1739. He married Elizabeth [-?-] on 30 June 1729 (Reamy and Reamy, *St. George's Parish Register:* 44, 57). Elizabeth married 2nd, James Butcher on 15 May 1740 or 1741 (Reamy and Reamy, *St. George's Parish Register:* 63). James and Elizabeth had a daughter Mary, b. 10 November 1741.

In 1737 Michael Eastwood was head of a household in Spesutia Upper Hundred (*IBCW:* 12).

On 25 --- 1738 James Prichard and wife Elizabeth conveyed 25 a. *Margaret's Purchase* to Michael Eastwood which Eastwood left to his heirs (BALR HWS#1-A: 83). Elizabeth Eastwood witnessed the will of Margaret Prichard, widow, on 26 March 1739 (MWB 22:75, abst. in *Md. Cal. of Wills* 8:36).

Michael and Elizabeth were the parents of (Reamy and Reamy, *St. George's Parish Register:* 45, 52, 57, 62): **2. James,** b. 7 June 1730; **3. Hannah,** b. 3 February 1732; **4. Mary,** b. 12 June 1734, d. 1 October 1738; **5. Elizabeth,** b. 2 December 1736, d. 12 September 1738; and **6. Michael,** b. 18 January 1738, d. 18 September 1738.

2. James Eastwood, son of Michael (1) and Elizabeth, was born 7 June 1730, and was bound to John Grafton to age 21 (BACP 1743-1745).

James Eastwood appears in Sheriff Aquila Hall's Assessment Ledger, dated about 1762-1765 (*IBCP:* 18).

3. Hannah Eastwood, daughter of Michael (1) and Elizabeth, was born 3 February 1732, and was bound to Antil and Sarah Deaver (BACP 1743-1745). Hannah may have married Thomas Wilkinson, for on 13 June 1759 Thomas Wilkinson and wife Hannah conveyed to Benjamin Culver, 25 a. *Margaret's Purchase,,* originally laid out in 1724 for Obadiah Pritchett (BALR B#G: 468).

Unplaced:
John Eastwood of Anne Arundel Co. died by February 1721. Elisabeth Eastwood, his administratrix, posted bond on 14 February 1721 with sureties were Thomas Wells, Robert Henderson (MDTP 26:21). She married 2nd, by 1725 Charles Busey when she filed an account of John Eastwood's estate on 10 April 1725. citing an inventory of £32.5.5, and listing payments of £21.8.10 (MDAD 6:323).

==0==

The Edwards Family of Anne Arundel County.

1. Cadwallader Edwards was born about 1685, and died in 1744. He married on 12 April 1710, Catherine [-?-], widow of Henry Bourne, in All Hallow's Parish (*AACR:*68). He married as his second wife Anne ([-?-], who survived him.

In 1705 he constructed the altar and font for St. Anne's Church, Annapolis. Newman added that in 1710 an Act of the Maryland Assembly authorized him to be paid for work done on the State House after it had been destroyed by fire, and in 1711 he was commissioned to make window shutters for the same building. In 1713 he did some work for St. Anne's Church (Harry Wright Newman. *Anne Arundel Gentry, Revised and Augmented,* 2:220).

Edwards and Thomas Jones appraised the estate of Susannah Beard on 20 March 1710 (INAC 32B:50).

On 2 June 1713 Cadwallader Edwards of Annapolis, joiner, mortgaged his dwelling house with its lot, standing in Annapolis, near the Gate House, next to the houses of John Slaughter and Thomas Docwra, to Charles Carroll of Annapolis (AALR IB#2:44).

Ann Edwards, administratrix, filed an inventory of his estate on 22 January 1724. Simon Duff and Samuel Soumain had appraised the estate at £52.15.6 in January 1724. Edward Edwards signed as next of kin (MINV 30:232). Ann, now the wife of Thomas Howard, filed an account of Edwards' estate on 28 April 1748, citing the inventory as given, and listing payments of £20.17.0. (MDAD 22:160).

Cadwallader and Catherine were the parents of (*AACR:* 29, 70): **2. Edward**, b. 7 June 1711 and bapt. 8 July 1711; and **3. Cadwallader**, b. 14 August 1713 and bapt. 16 August 1713 in All Hallow's Parish.

2. Edward Edwards, son of Cadwallader (1) and Catherine, was born 7 June 1711 and bapt. 8 July 1711 in All Hallows Parish. He married 1st, in January 1734 in All Hallows Parish, Jemima Welsh (*AACR:*29, 48, 69). Jemima was bapt. 19 April 1717 in All Hallows Parish, daughter of Robert and Catherine (Lewis) Welsh. Jemima Welsh Edwards died in 1741 (Newman: 221).

When Robert Welsh made his will in 1756 he mentioned the heirs of his daughter Jemima Edwards (Newman: 221).

Edwards married 2nd, Elizabeth (or Elinor) Chilton (or Clinton) on 18 November 1742, at St. Anne's Parish (*AACR:*99). By this marriage he acquired the tract *Bold Venture* which he sold to Richard Barnes on 8 May 1744, with wife Elinor waiving her right of dower (AALR RB#1:383).

Edward Edwards evidently died intestate and there was no formal administration of his estate by his son and heir.

Edward and Eleanor Edwards were mentioned in a deposition of Adderton Skinner (Annapolis *Maryland Gazette* 5 May 1747).

Edward and Jemima (Welsh) Edwards were the parents of (Newman: 222): **4. Edward, Jr.**

4. Edward Edwards, Jr., son of Edward and Jemima, died in 1786, having married Anne ([-?-], born about 1738 in St. Anne's Parish; she may have been a relative of the Linthicum family (Matilda P. Badger, *Genealogy of the Linthicum and Allied Families*).

In 1752 Edward Edwards purchased the mortgage of *Linthicum Walk*, which Thomas Linthicum had mortgaged to Philip Hammond (Newman: 223).

In 1778 Edward Edwards and his son Aquila took the Oath of Allegiance to the State of Maryland (*RPAA:* 59).

Edwards wrote his will on 17 April 1786, and it was filed on 18 May following (AAWB TG#1 (34): 336). Letters of administration on the estate were granted on 19 June 1786 (Newman: 223).

Anne Edwards, Aquila Edwards, William Edwards, Cadwallader Edwards and Jonathan Edwards, executors, advertised they would settle his estate (Annapolis *Maryland Gazette* 6 July 1786).

On 23 September 1793 his estate, with a balance of £1475.14.8, was distributed by his administrator William Edwards. Sureties were Thomas Bicknell and Jonathan Edwards. The balance of the estate was divided into tenths, and distributed to (AADI JG#1:45): children of Jemima Evans; children of Catherine Lusby; William Anderson, husband of Elizabeth Edwards; Sarah Edwards; Cephas Waters, husband of Mary

Edwards; John Linthicum, husband of Mary Edwards [sic]; John Fonerden, husband of Margaret Edwards; William Edwards; Cadwallader Edwards; and Jonathan Edwards.
Edward and Anne ([-?-]) Edwards were the parents of: **5. Catherine**, m. [Edward] Lusby; **6. Elizabeth**, m. William, son of William and Susannah (Meek) Anderson; **7. Jemima**, m. [-?-] Evans; **8. Mary**, m. Cephas Waters, son of John and Mary (Ijams) Waters; **9. Sarah**, m. as his second wife William Anderson who had married her sister Elizabeth; **10. Anne**, m. John Linthicum; **11. Margaret**, m. John Fonerden; **12. Aquila**, d. s.p. William Edwards was the administrator, and advertised he would settle the estate of Aquila Edwards(Annapolis *Maryland Gazette* 25 March 1790).; **13. William**, m. by license dated 20 July 1789 Ann Chalmers (AAML); **14. Cadwallader**, m. in 1786 Sarah Chalmers (AAML); **15. Jonathan**; **16. Edward**, d. s.p (Newman says it was his estate that was distributed on 23 September 1793).

==0==

The Ferguson Family of Montgomery County

1. Duncan Ferguson, a Jacobite, was transported on 28 July 1716 on the *Godspeed*, and arrived in Md. in October 1716 (*SOCD:* 47). He died by 1751, having married Catherine [-?-], who died by 30 August 1779 in Frederick County.

"Donkin" Ferguson purchased 128 a. of *Hamilton's Addition* from Andrew Tanihill on 2 June 1731 (PGLR Q:278).

On 17 January 1745 George Woodhead of Prince George's County named Duncan Ferguson his executor, and sole legatee of all property he might have in the Province or in Great Britain, except tobacco due from Benjamin Harris (MWB 24:327). On 8 March 1747 Duncan Ferguson was one of the freeholders of Prince George's County who sent a petition to Gov. Ogle concerning the needed repairs to the court house at Upper Marlborough (*CMSP: Black Books,* document 531).

Catherine 'Ferguson' filed an administration account of Duncan Ferguson's estate. She cited an inventory of £281.7.9, and listed payments of £70.9.11. The unnamed heirs were all of age (MDAD 34:249).

Catherine Ferguson died in Montgomery Co. leaving a will dated 16 March 1779 and proved 30 Aug 1779. She named her granddaughters Katherine Lovelace, Catherine Lanham, and Ann Skinner Ferguson, and her son John. John Lacklen, Elias Harding and John Wilcoxen (MSA: Montgomery Co. Wills Original, Box A, folder 197).

Duncan and Catherine 'Fargison' were the parents of (PGKG: 258; *Moller:* 181): **2. John**, b. 1725; **3. Mary**, b. 25 August 1732; **4. Catherine**, b. 1734, m. on 28 November 1751 Isaac Walker, b. 1721, d. 1807; **5. Thomas**, b. 16 June 1735; and **6. Elizabeth**, b. 3 May 173-.

2. John Ferguson, son of Duncan (1) and Catherine, was born 1725 and died 1793 in Monongalia Co., Va. He married by 1755 Bersheba or Bathsheba Griffith, born 1839. She was a daughter of Samuel Griffith, Jr., who died 1741 in Calvert Co., and his wife Anne Skinner (*Moller:* 65).

On 24 Oct 1765 John Ferguson patented 280 a. in Prince George's Co. called *Ferguson's Gain* (MPL BC#26:182, BC#30:8).

John, aged 51, and Bathsheba, aged 37, were listed in the 1776 census of St. John's and Prince George's Parishes, with daughters aged 20, 16 14, and 1, and an 8 year old son (Carothers, *1776 Census of Maryland:* 133).

John Ferguson took the Oath of Fidelity before the Hon. William Berry in 1778 (*RPPG:* 112).

Colonial Families of Maryland II

John and Bathsheba 'Faurgeson' were the parents of (PGKG: 330; Moller: 13, 104, 196): **7. Catherine,** b. 1755, m. William Lanham, b. 1750; **8. Ann Skinner,** m. Joseph Wilson; **9. Susannah,** bapt. 19 December 1762; **10. Vialindo [Verlinda?],** bapt. 10 August 1766, m. Zephaniah Beall (Moller, p. 13); and **11. Rebecca,** m. Wiliam Wilson by PGML dated 1 October 1777 (Moller: 196-7).

== 0 ==

The Field Family of Baltimore County

1. John Field, aged 24, of Northampton, husbandman, on 14 January 1722 signed his name when he bound himself to serve Christopher Veale, of Shoreditch, Middlesex, for four years in Maryland (Kaminkow, *List of Emigrants,* p. 78).

He married Catherine Hogg on 23 December 1729 in St. George's Parish, Baltimore, now Harford, Co. (Reamy and Reamy. *St. George's Parish Register:* 32).

John and Catherine were the parents of (Reamy and Reamy, *St. George's Parish Register:* 37, 65): **2. Jo.,** born 28 January 1732; **3. Ann,** b. 12 April 1734.

Unplaced:
Elizabeth Fields died 28 October 1727 (Reamy and Reamy. *St. George's Parish Register:*28.

== 0 ==

The Fitzsimmons Family of Baltimore County

1. Nicholas Fitzsimmons was in Baltimore Co., by 1694, and d. by January 1743/4. He married by 9 June 1697 Martha, widow of Joseph Heathcote and daughter of Capt. Thomas Morgan (MWB 7:392, abst. in *Md. Cal. of Wills* 2:140).

Nicholas Fitzsimmons patented 300 a. *Cordwainer's Hall* on 10 May 1696 (MPL 37:412). On 10 March 1701 Fitzsimmons, a cordwainer, conveyed the land to Richard Cromwell (BALR 11W#2: 157).

On 13 May 1699 William Herbert and his wife conveyed *Ball's Addition* and *Bennett's Range,* formerly taken up by John Bennett, and *Thomas Range,* formerly taken up by John Thomas, to Nicholas Fitzsimmons (BALR HW#2: 21). On 5 March 1705 William Farfarr and wife Johanna conveyed 219 a., part of *Dear Bit,* to Nicholas Fitzsimmons (BALR IR#AM: 37). 6 March 1705/6: Richard Lennox and his wife Mary conv. 200 a. *Lennox' Adventure,* and 218 a. *Maiden's Choice,* (orig. granted to Mary Richardson, now Mary Lennox), to Nicholas Fitzsimmons (BALR IR#AM: 40). On 9 March 1709 Thomas Knighton and wife Dorothy conveyed 100 a. *Knighton's Fancy* to Fitzsimmons (BALR TR#A: 46). In August 1707 Thomas Hooker, with consent of wife Sarah, conveyed 230 a. *Maiden's Choice* to Nicholas Fitzsimmons, cordwainer (BALR RM#HS: 58). On 1 April 1725 Nicholas Fitzsimmons conveyed 200 a. *Lennox' Adventure* and 215 a. *Maiden's Choice* to Richard Lenox, who had earlier conveyed the tract to Fitzsimmons (BALR IS#H: 73).

He was one of the appraisers of the estate of Francis Watkins on 12 May 1696 (INAC 14:25). On 30 May 1698 Nicholas Fitzsimmons witnessed the will of Richard Thompson (MWB 6:140, abst. in *Md. Cal. of Wills* 2:153). He received a payment from the estate of John Greeniffe on 11 July 1710 (INAC 31:271).

In November 1716 Samuel Smallwood petitioned the court that the two children he had entrusted to Nicholas Fitzsimmons be taken away as Fitzsimmons he alleged that

Fitzsimmons had been mistreating them. The petition was rejected, but in August 1718 his sons were taken away. (BACP IS#B:192, 57, IS#1A: 64; IS#C: 2, 5).

Nicholas Fitzsimmons died leaving a will dated 11 October 1743 and proved 2 January 1743/4. He left *Knighton's Fancy* and *Mascall's Rest* to the male heirs of his daughter Flora, wife of Joshua Dorsey. If Flora should die without male heirs, the property was to go to the poor of Anne Arundel Co., who were members of the Church of England or who were Quakers. *Thomas' Range, Bennett's Range*, and *Ball's Addition* were to go to the male heirs of his daughter Mary. Other tracts were to go to the daughters of his daughters. Daughter Mary was to be executrix. John Orrick, Jr., Alex. Cromwell, and Sarah Cromwell witnessed the will (MWB 23:501, abst. in *Md. Cal. of Wills* 8:267).

Nicholas and Martha were the parents of: **2. Flora**, m. Joshua Dorsey on 3 November 1734 (Reamy and Reamy, *St. Paul's Parish Register:* 1:31); and **3. Mary**, m. 9 November 1746 Edward Norwood (Reamy and Reamy, *St. Paul's Parish Register:* 34).

== O ==

The Fugate Family of Baltimore County

N.B.: The name has also been spelled as Fewgate, Fookit, Fowcate, Fucat, and Fuckett

1. Peter Fugate was transported in 1662 (MPL 5:238). On 22 Nove1665 he was listed as a servant in the inventory of Capt. George Gouldsmith (MDTP 2:79-80). He married by 6 January 1690 Frances, daughter of John Mould (BALR RM#HS:329).

'Peter Fowcate' was naturalized on 17 September 1681 (*ARMD* 7:216). In 1673 100 acres *French Plantation* were surveyed for him in Baltimore Co. The tract was later held by Thomas Cord (MPL 15:208; 19:7; *MRR:*10). On 29 December 1685 100 a. *Peter's Addition* was patented to Peter Fucatt (MPL 25:244, 30:306). On 16 October 1686 Peter Fucatt, planter, mortgaged to John Walston, carpenter, for 6 years, the 100 a. *Peter's Addition* lately occupied by Fucatt and the 100 a. adjacent (BALR RM#HS: 208). On 6 January 1690 Peter Fuckett and wife Frances of Baltimore Co. conveyed 100 a. *Peter's Addition* and 100 a. *French Plantation* to Thomas Cord (BALR RM#HS: 329). On 4 July 1694 Peter Fucatt and wife Frances (one of the daughters of John Mould) made their marks when they conveyed 133⅓ a. of *Mould's Success,* the lowermost third of the land to Edward Boothby. The land had come to Frances by descent from her father John (BALR RM#HS: 419).

On 6 May 1681 he received a payment from the estate of Samuel Boston (INACs 7B:59). In 1686 he was a security for George Wells, administrator of Simon Dockins (MDTP 13: 416). Fugate was head of a household in Spesutia Hundred in 1692. John Combest and Jeremiah Smith were with him. In 1694 he was in the household of Edward Boothby. In 1695 he was in the household of Solomon Rice (*IBCW:* 3, 4, 7).

He was mentioned as being dead in the 1701 inventory of Thomas Smith (INAC 28:150).

Peter and Frances were the parents of: **2. (poss.) Easter**, whose banns of marriage to John Davis were pub. 14 October and 12 November 1702 (Reamy and Reamy, *St. George's Parish Register:* 12); **3. Peter**, was on the tax lists for 1694 and 1695, but not thereafter; **4. James; 5. John**, son of Peter, b. 27 Feb 1689 at the head of Musketa Creek (Reamy and Reamy, *St. George's Parish Register:* 1, which gives the name as 'Furat'); and **6. Ann**, daughter of Peter, b. 14 March 1692 at Spesutia Creek (Reamy and Reamy, *St. George's Parish Register:*1, which gave the name as 'Furat').

Colonial Families of Maryland II

4. James Fugate (Fewgate), son of Peter (1) and Frances, was of age in September 1683. He was married by May 1686 to Dorothy [-?-].
In September 1683 James surveyed 200 a. *North Yarmouth* (*MRR:*9). He patented two tracts of land on 14 September 1683: 300 a. *Fugat's Fork* (MPL 25:37), and 200 a. *North Yarmouth* (MPL 25:37, MPL 30:127). In May 1686 he and Dorothy mortgaged *North Yarmouth* to Miles Gibson.
In January 1681 James was named as residuary legatee and executor of Anthony Watson (MWB 4:76, abst. in *Md. Cal. of Wills* 1:139). In 1699 he was a taxable in Spesutia Hundred. In November 1737 he was made exempt from the levy (BACP (BACP HWS#1A: 134). James Fugatt registered a cattle mark on 9 June 1724 (BALR IS#G:303). In 1737 he was at Upper Hundred of North Gunpowder, and the levy list for 1737 showed that he was paid a bounty for squirrels' heads for that year (*IBCW:* 16, 28).
James was prob. the father of: **7. James.**

7. James Fugate, probably son of James (2) and Dorothy, was living as late as 1744. He married Ann [-?-]. Jams Fugate was made exempt from the levy in November 1737 (BACP HWS#1-A: 134).
On 25 November 1742 he leased 108 a. of *My Lady's Manor* from Thomas Brerewood; the lease was to run for the lifetimes of the said James, aged c66, his sons James *alias Peter,* aged 15, and son James, aged 13 (BALR TB#C:108).
On 15 December 1743 John Hooper, aged c44 leased part of *My Lady's Manor,* for his lifetime and that of Mary Fugate now Knowles, aged c20, and Ann Fugate, daughter of James, age c7 (BALR TB#C:440). Hooper, aged c45, leased another portion of *My Lady's Manor* on 30 January 1744, the lease to run for his own lifetime, and those of Mary Fugate, now Knowles, ages 21, and Ann Fugate, daughter of James, aged c8 (BALR TB#D:225).
James and Ann were the parents of (*SJSG:* 10, 36, 46, 91): **8. Sarah,** b. 11 November 172-; **9. Mary,** b. c1722, m. Peter Knowles by 25 Nove1742, when Peter Knowles, aged 26, leased 61½ a. of *My Lady's Manor,* the lease to run for the lifetimes of himself, his wife Mary, aged c19, and their son Peter, aged c1 (BALR TB#C:130); **10. Peter,** b. 1 May 1726; **11. Edward,** b. 14 September 1731, prob. d. young; **12. John,** twin, b. 15 March 1732; **13. Easter,** twin, b. 15 March 1732 (or 1736), m. Dennis Dulany on 23 January 1749; **14. Edward,** b. 10 August 1734; **15. Anne,** b. 23 April 1735, prob. d. young; and **16. Ann,** b. February 1738.

10. Peter Fugate, son of James (7) and Ann, was born 1 May 1726. He was in Frederick Co. by28 February 1756 when he registered a stray horse (FRLR E:1002).
He was named as having married Mary, daughter of David Watson in the latter's will, dated 1 January 1769 (MWB 37:293, abst. in *Md. Cal. of Wills* 14:96). Peter and Mary Fugate signed the inventory of David Watson of Frederick Co. on 21 August 1769 as next of kin (MINV 102:275).
A Peter 'Fuget' was listed in Washington Co., Md., in the 1790 Census, with a household consisting one white male over 16, two white males under 16, two white females, and one slave. Nearby was a John 'Fuget' whose household consisted of one white male over 16, five white males under 16, and one white female (*Heads of Families...1790...Maryland:* 120).

14. Edward Fugate (Fewgate), son of James (7) and Ann, was born 10 August 1734, and died by March 1787. He married Elizabeth Bacon on 12 January 1758. She was born on 23 November 1741, the daughter of Martin and Mary Bacon (*SJSG:* 46, 102).

In 1773 Edward Fugate was listed as a taxable in Mine Run Hundred. He had a servant named Tom (*IBCP:* 72). In 1778 Edward Fugate was a non-juror to the Oath of Allegiance (*BARP:* 94).

Eliz. Fugate posted an administration bond on Edward Fugate's estate on 9 August 1785. Rich. Rode and Edw. Bosman were sureties (BAAB 6:251). On 14 March 1787 Elizabeth Fewgate [*sic*] administered his estate (BAAD 9:25).

Elizabeth Fugate was listed as a head of family in Mine Run Hundred in the 1790 Census of Maryland, Her household consisted of one white male under 16, and four white females (*Heads of Families, 1790, Maryland:* 24).

In 1798 Elizabeth Fugate was living in Mine Run Hundred on 98 a. of *My Lady's Manor*, in a one-story stone dwelling house, 24 x 18, 'out of repair;' a 20 x 65 log kitchen in 'tolerable repair' (Horvath, *Particular Assessment Lists:* 5).

Edward and Elizabeth may have been the parents of: **17. (poss.) Martin**; **18. [-?-]**, a son, b. after 1774; and **19-21.** three daughters.

17. Martin Fugate, tentatively placed as a son of Edward (14) and Elizabeth, was living as late as 1798.

In 1778 Martin Fugate was a non-juror to the Oath of Allegiance (*BARP:*94).

He may be the Martin Fugate listed in Mine Run Hundred in 1783 as owning 168 a. *Perdue's Lot*, with one white male and one white inhabitant (Carothers, *1783 Tax List:* 65).

In 1790 he was listed in Mine Run Hundred, Baltimore Co., with a household consisting of two white males over 16, one white male under 16, and two white females (*Heads of Families...1790...Maryland:* 24). In 1798 Martin Fugate was living in Mine Run Hundred on lots 84, 97, and 51 of *My Lady's Manor*. His property contained a one-story log dwelling house, 16 x 20; an unfinished log barn, 49 x 20, and an old log smith's shop, 22 x 16 (Horvath, *Particular Assessment List:* 5).

Unplaced:

Edward Fugate, suggested by Peden to be the son of Edward (14) and Elizabeth (Bacon) Fugate died in Mason Co., Ky., by 1805. He married Cassandra [-?-], who married 2nd, John Laws in Bourbon Co., Ky., in 1807. Edward and Cassandra were the parents of three daughters, each of whom married men named McKenney, and migrated to Butler Co., Ky. *Kentucky Ancestor* 16 (1): 48, in Peden, *Marylanders to Kentucky:* 53).

== 0 ==

The Garland Family of Baltimore County

1. Henry Garland, married Lydia [-?-].

On 23 December 1708 he witnessed the will of Henry Borck (MWB 12:302, abst. in *Md. Cal. of Wills* 3:114).

Henry and Lydia were the parents of (Reamy and Reamy, *St. George's Parish Register:* 15, 17): **2. Sarah,** b. 2 August 1710, d. August 1714; **3. Elizabeth,** b. 19 January 1710 [1710/11]. d. August 1714; **4. William,** b. 26 January 1712; and **5. (prob.) Henry,** b. c1718.

4. William Garland, son of Henry (1) and Lydia, was born 26 January 1712. He is probably the William Garland who married Bethia Ogg on 10 June 1728 (Reamy and Reamy, *St. George's Parish Register:* 28).

In 1737 William Garland and Henry Garland were in the same household in Spesutia Lower Hundred. In 1739 William Garland was on the Levy List (*IBCW:* 14, 32). In 1741 he was a surety for William Hollis, executor of William Snelson (BAAB 3:459).

Garland died by 31 July 1749 when John Matthews and Daniel Ruff appraised William Garland's personal estate at £207.14.3. William Hollis and George Chancey signed as next of kin. Henry Garland filed the inventory on 3 Aug 1749 (MINV 40:82).

On 1 August 1750 Henry Garland filed an account of his estate citing an inventory of £207.14.3, and listing payments of £16.18.4. The heirs were James, aged 18, Susanna, aged 12, Francis, aged 9, and Catherine, aged 2 (MDAD 28:250). On 12 August 1751 his estate was administered again by Henry Garland; he left four children: James, aged 20; Susannah, 13; Francis, 10; and Catherine 2½ (BAAD 4:276).

William and Bethia were the parents of (Reamy and Reamy, *St. George's Parish Register:* 34. 44, 61): **6. James**, b. 6 November 1730; **7. William**, b. 5 September 1734; **8. Susanna**, b. 29 November 1737, m. Josiah Hitchcock on 20 July 1755 (*SJSG:* 47); they had a daughter Nancy "Ann" Hitchcock who married Rev. John Whitaker and was named as niece in the will of Francis Garland (HAMR; see also below); and **10. Francis** (son), b. 1 January 1741.

5. Henry Garland probably son of Henry (1) and Lydia, is so placed because in 1737 he and William Garland in the same household, and because he administered Henry's estate in 1751. He as born c1718, and married Sarah Herrington on 27 January 1743 (Reamy and Reamy, *St. George's Parish Register:* 69).

On 3 July 1738 he was a debtor to the estate of George Drew (MDAD 16:326). He witnessed the will of William Hollis on 28 December 1753(MWB 31:895, abst. in *Md. Cal. of Wills* 12:182).

Henry Garland, aged about 50, deposed on 4 January 1768, mentioning Thomas Burchfield (BALR B#L:499). In 1768 he signed a petition against the removal of the county seat from Joppa to Baltimore (*IBCP:*41).

Henry Garland died leaving a will dated 21 November 1774 and proved 26 September 1777. He named his cousins Ann and Randal, children of Josias Hitchcock. He named Henry Hitchcock, his nephew Francis Garland, and Thomas Fisher, and all his cousins except William Cole. Josias Hitchcock was named as executor. John Cotter, John Whitacre, and Mary Johnson witnessed the will (HAWB AJ#2:222, abst. by Morgan).

6. James Garland, son of William (4) and Bethia, was born on 6 November 1730. He married Jane Gaddis on 3 February 1761 (Reamy and Reamy, *St. George's Parish Register:* 85).

Jane Garland, administratrix, posted an administration bond for £200.0.0 on James Garland's estate on 3 June 1765, with Henry Garland as surety (BAAB 3:171). On 15 June 1766 William Osborn and Samuel Griffith appraised his personal estate at £83.10.4. Henry Garland and Francis Garland signed as next of kin. 'James' [prob. Jane] Garland, admin., filed the inventory on 20 June 1766 (MINV 90:128).

James and Jane were the parents of (Reamy and Reamy, *St. George's Parish Register:* 85): **11. Catherine**, b. 13 April 1762; she may be the Catherine Garland who married by license dated 8 Oct 1784 to William Fowler (HAML).

10. Francis Garland, son of William (1) and Lydia, as born 1 January 1741.
In 1768 he signed a petition against the removal of the county seat from Joppa to Baltimore (*IBCP:* 41). Henry Garland, in his will made 21 November 1774 named Francis Garland as his nephew (HAWB AJ#222, abst. by Morgan). In 1776 Francis Garland, aged 33, was listed as a taxable in Spesutia Lower Hundred, Harford Co. (Carothers, *1776 Census of Maryland:* 106).
Francis (Frances) Garland died leaving a will dated 26 March 1781 and proved 31 August 1781. He named his niece Ann Whitaker, daughter of his sister Susannah, and his niece Catherine Garland, daughter of his bro. James. Jacob Forwood was named as executor and as trustee for his sister Catherine Garland. John Cosley and John Condrin witnessed the will (HAWB AJ#2:232, abst. by Morgan).

11. Catherine Garland, daughter of James (6) and Jane, was born 13 April 1762. In 1776 at aged 14 she was in the household of James Oliver, aged 60, and his wife Catherine in Harford Lower Hundred, Harford Co. (Carothers, *1776 Census of Maryland:* 100), She may be the Catherine Garland who were married by license dated 8 October 1784 to William Fowler (HAML).

Unplaced:
Jane Garland was named as a servant in the inventory of Col. Nathaniel Uty on 25 February 1675 (INAC 1:580).
Nicholas Garland married Sarah [-?-]. They were the parents of (*SJSG:* 5): Elizabeth, b. 12 September 1717.

== 0 ==

The Giles Family of Anne Arundel and Baltimore Counties.

See also: Louis F. Giles, "The Giles Family of Harford County," *MGSB* 35 (1) (Winter 1994) 3-21.
1. John Giles, progenitor, was in Anne Arundel Co., Md., with his wife Mary in 1687. He died by July 1688.
Skordas lists a John Giles who immigrated prior to 1666 (MPL 9:477), and a John Giles who was transported about 1673 (MPL 17:424).
On 7 July 1688 Mary, widow of John Giles of Anne Arundel Co., was granted administration on his estate. The appraisers were to be Robert Lockwood, John Waters. Col. Thomas Taillor was to administer the oath (MDTP 14:80). On 28 November 1688 Col. Thomas Taillor exhibited oath of Mary Giles administratrix of John Giles. Security: John Waters; he also exhibited the inventory, by the appraisers Robert Lockwood and John Waters (MDTP 14:121).
On 4 August 1697 when Abel Brown deeded part of *Cumberston* to John Giles [the son], the deed mentioned land of the Widow Giles (AALR WH#4:211).
On 18 August 1691 Henry Bonner exhibited [reported] that the widow Giles, administratrix, of John Giles, was very aged and incapable of rendering accounts, and a continuance was granted (MDTP 15A:72).
Mary Giles filed an account of the estate of John Giles on 14 May 1694. She cited an inventory of £74.0.0, and listed payments of 12855 lbs. of tob.(INAC 12:131).
John and Mary were the parents of five children, whose births were recorded at West River Meeting in Anne Arundel Co., Md. (*AACR*:205): **2. Elizabeth,** b. 7 d., 2 m., 1668, by 1684, as his 2nd wife, John Waters (Wattors) (*AAMR;*247); **3. Nathaniel,** b. 10 d., 1

1 mo., 1667; **4. John**, b. 7 d., 11 mo., 1670; **5. Jacob**, b. 11 d., 4 mo., 1673; and **6. Artridge**, b. 4 d., 6 mo., 16(?) at West River Meeting, Anne Arundel Co.; she m. Robert Franklin on 19 d., 8 mo., 1697 (*AACR:*184).

3. Nathaniel Giles, son of John (1) and Mary, was bon 10 d. 1 m. 1687, and died in Baltimore Co. by October 1730. Nathaniel Giles and Elizabeth Harris declared their intention to marry on 3 d. 10 m. 1703, and a second time on 31 s. 10 m. 1703 (*AAMR* cites *QRSM*).

On 25 July 1719 James Mauldin of Calvert Co., Gent., conveyed 500 a. *Friend's Discovery* to Nathaniel Giles (BALR TR#DS: 79). In December 1722 Nathan(iel) Giles conveyed 200 a., *Friend's Discovery*, being "half" of the portion he bought from James Mauldin, to Gerard Hopkins (BALR IS#G: 64).

Nathaniel Giles died leaving a will dated 12 August 1730 and proved 17 October 1730, naming his children, Nathaniel, John, Mary, and Elizabeth, wife of Michael Webster, who was named as a son-in-law by Giles (MWB 20:105).

Michael Webster posted an administration bond on 24 October 1730 with Jacob Giles and Richard Russ (BAAB 3:734).

Nathaniel Giles and Elizabeth were the parents of: **7. Nathaniel; 8. John; 9 Mary,** and **10. Elizabeth,** m. Michael Webster.

4. John Giles, son of John (1) and Mary, was born 7 d. 11 mo. 1670, and died in Baltimore County by 27 November 1725 when an administration bond on his estate was posted by the executors Sarah, John, Nathaniel, and Jacob Giles, with Nathaniel Giles and Melchizedek Murray as sureties (BAAB 3:130).

John Giles married Sarah, daughter of John Welsh on 1 October 1695 in St. James Parish, Anne Arundel Co. (*AACR:*146).

On 27 November 1703 John Wattors of Anne Arundel Co. made his will. He named his brother-in-law John Giles as overseer. Giles was also one of the witnesses (MWB 3:246, abst. in *Md. Cal. of Wills* 3:39).

On 23 March 1704, the Sheriff of Anne Arundel Co. was directed to summon John Giles to affirm that he had none of the effects of Samuel Harwood, deceased, save those items already delivered to Richard Harwood administrator (MDTP 20:33).

On 13 May 1707 Thomas Hawkins and his wife Elisabeth of Baltimore Co., administratrix, of Jacob Giles, exhibited [reported] that said Elisabeth had assigned administration of the said estate to John Giles of Anne Arundel Co., brother of the deceased, and that said John has lately gone to England (MDTP 19C:186).

Some time before 1707 John Giles came to possess 200 a. in Anne Arundel Co., called *Cumber(s)ton*, surveyed in 1676 for John Cumber. He also came to possess 250 a. *Three Sisters*, which had been surveyed for his father-in-law (*MRR:* 35, 252). On 4 August 1697 Abel Brown deeded part of *Cumberston* to John Giles (AALR WH#4:211).

On 17 March 1708 John Giles and his wife Sarah, and Daniel Richardson and wife Elizabeth conveyed to James Heath their interest in 1000 a. *Three Sisters*, which had been granted by Lord Baltimore to John Welsh who died leaving four daughters, the afsd. Sarah and Elizabeth (above), Mary wife of Josias Toogood and Damaris, wife of Thomas Stockett (BALR TR#A:5).

On 18 June 1720 John Mackwilliam of Philadelphia, with consent of wife Rose, conveyed 500 a. *Upton Court* and 50 a. *Whetstone Point* to John Giles of Anne Arundel Co. The deed included a Letter of Attorney from Mackwilliams to James Stoddard (BALR TR#DS:254). [Whetstone Point is that parcel of land on which Fort McHenry is located- RWB Note]

Colonial Families of Maryland II

On 18 April 1723 John Baldwin of Cecil Co. Gent., conveyed 200 a. *New Town* to John Giles. On 29 October 1724 John Cromwell, with consent of wife Hannah, conveyed 183 a. *Oliver's Range* to John Giles (BALR IS#G:196, 395).

John Giles died leaving a will dated [day and month not given] 1725, proved 6 November 1725. Son John was to have *Upton Court*, and son Jacob was to have *David's Fancy*. Son Nathaniel was to have 250 a. *Newtown*. He left personalty to his daughters Betty Lewis, Sophia Murray, and Anna, Mary, and Sarah, and stated that the last three were to have their portions at age 16 or the day of their marriage. His wife Sarah was to be executrix. Charles Ridgely, Sarah Parish and John Parish witnessed the will (MWB 18:429, abst in *Md. Cal. Wills*, 5:208).

Giles' estate was inventoried on 19 July 1726 by William Parrish, who appraised his personal property at £672.10.8, and signed by Nathaniel Giles and Melchizedek Murray as next of kin. The inventory was filed by the executors, Sarah Giles, and John, Jacob and Nathaniel Giles (INV 11:458).

John and Sarah Giles were the parents of: **10. John; 11. Jacob; 12. Nathaniel; 13. Elizabeth**, m. Richard Lewis on 15 d., 3 mo., 1723; **14. Sophia**, m. Melchizedek Murray on 13 d., 9 mo., 1723; **15. Anna** [**Maria**: stated by Newman in *Anne Arundel Gentry*, 1933, to have married Oliver Cromwell]; **16. Mary;** and **17. Sarah**.

5. Jacob Giles, son of John (1) and Mary, was born b. 11 d., 4 mo., 1673, and died by 28 September 1703 when his widow Elizabeth Giles filed an account, which mentioned John Giles of Anne Arundel Co.; Nathaniel Giles was one of the witnesses (INAC 29:334). Jacob and Elizabeth Arnell or Arnold, daughter of Richard and Martha, were m. on 8 d. 11 m. (commonly called January) 1701 (*AAMR* cites *QRSM*). Elizabeth Arnold Giles m. 2nd, Thomas Hawkins, son of John and Mary, on 30 d. 5 m. 1704 (*AAMR* cites *QRSM*).

8. John Giles, son of Nathaniel (3) and Elizabeth, married 1st, on 16 October 1734 Sarah Butterworth, and 2nd, by 1 September 1752 Hannah, executrix of Daniel Scott.

In November 1736 Nathaniel and John Giles and John's wife Sarah sold 390 a. *Friend's Discovery* to Thomas Taylor (BALR IS#IK: 424).

In September 1752 Giles was summoned before the Vestry of St. John's Parish for marring his deceased wife's sister, as Daniel Scott had married Hannah Butterworth in 1740; John Giles refused to out her way ("Vestry Proceedings of St. John's Parish," MS. at MdHS).

John and Sarah were the parents of: **18. Nathaniel**, b. 29 August 1736; **19. Hester**, b. 9 July 1748, and **20. John**, b. 14 January 1740.

10. John Giles, son of John (4) and Sarah, died about 1736 in Baltimore Co., Md. He married Cassandra Smith on 8 November 1728 in Md. She died about 1754 in Baltimore Co, Md.

On 4 May 1727 Christopher Gardiner and wife Sibrah conveyed 400 a. *Buck Ridge* to John Giles (BALR IS#H:409).

In 1729 John Giles mortgaged *Upton Court*) to William Buckner *et al*. The same year he mortgaged 50 a., part of *Upton Court* and *Whetstone Point* to Daniel Dulany and others. On 15 June 1731 John Giles, innholder, and wife Cassandra, conveyed 400 a. part *Upton Court* to John England and Co., ironmaster; tract is adjacent to land John Giles left by his will to his son Jacob (BALR IS#K:87, 200, IS#L:99).

On 28 February 1732 John Giles and wife Cassandra conveyed *Whetstone Point* to Jacob Giles (BALR IS#L: 363). On 5 November 1736 Nathaniel and John Giles of

Baltimore Co. conveyed 390 a. *Friends' Discovery* to Thomas Taylor. John Giles' wife Sarah consented (BALR IS#1K: 424).

John Giles, Gent., of Baltimore Co., died leaving a will dated 29 March 1736 and proved 28 April 1736. His wife Cassandra, executrix, was to have the tract *Upton Court*, which he had from his father. After his death it was to be divided between his daus. Sarah and Elizabeth. Samuel Richardson, a Quaker, and John and Miriam Croley witnessed the will (MWB 25:147, abst. in *Md. Cal. of Wills* 7:169).

Cassandra Giles of Baltimore Co. died leaving a will dated 30 December 1754 and proved 8 February 1755. She left slaves to her daughter Sarah Hopkins, wife of Samuel Hopkins, certain slaves to her grandson James Slemaker, and certain slaves to her grandson Gerard Hopkins. The remainder of her estate was to go to her two daughters. Sarah Hopkins, and Elizabeth Bankson, wife of Joseph Bankson, Her son-in-law Samuel Hopkins was named executor. Joseph Taylor and Edward Lewis, Jr., witnessed the will (MWB 29:373, abst. in *Md. Cal. of Wills* 11:180).

John and Cassandra were the parents of: **21. Sarah**, m. Samuel Hopkins; and **22. Elizabeth**, m. 1st, James Slemaker, and 2nd, Joseph Bankson.

11. Jacob Giles, son of John (4) and Sarah, was living as late as 1759. He married 1st, on 3 January 1728/9, Hannah Webster, and 2nd, by 19 July 1739, Johannah Phillips, daughter of Col. James Phillips (Third Haven MM; (MDAD 17:181; BALR HWS#1-A:310). Johannah was the widow of George Drew.

In 1750 Jacob Giles owned 220 a. *Johnson's Delay*, 570 a. *Bourne*, 400 a. *Elberton*, 33 a. *Giles Addition*, and 100 a. *Brotherly Love* (Baltimore Co. Debt Book for 1750, MS. at MdHS).

Giles died leaving a will dated 17 January 1784 and proved 11 February 1784. He stated that two granddaughters, daughters of his deceased son Nathaniel, were to have 712 a. *Land Of Promise*. He named his sons James, Jacob (deceased), Thomas, Aquila, Edward (deceased), and his daughters Elizabeth (deceased), wife of William Smith, Sarah (deceased), wife of Nathaniel Rigbie. He named grandchildren William Axtell Giles, eldest son of Aquila Giles, Jacob Giles Smith and Winston Smith, sons of his daughter Elizabeth, a granddaughter Joanna Giles Waters, and a step-daughter Susanna Scott 'by now a widow.' He also named his sons-in-law William Smith and Nathaniel Rigbie, as well as Nathan Sheredine, husband of Cassandra Sheredine (deceased), and Hannah Johns, wife of Skipwith Johns. He mentioned friend Philip Coale, Dr. John Archer, and Samuel Hughes, as well as Negroes Sam, Morea, Poll, Grace, Tom, and Lydia. Sons Thomas and Aquila Giles were named executors. Thomas Boyle, William Evatt, and John Williams witnessed the will (HAWB AJ#2:237).

Jacob and Hannah were the parents of Reamy and Reamy, *St. George's Parish Register:*32, 41): **23. John**, b. 20 October 1729; **24. Jacob**, b. 14 November 1733; and **25. Nathaniel**, b. 2 October 1735.

Jacob and Johanna were the parents of Reamy and Reamy, *St. George's Parish Register:*93): **26. Sarah**, m. Nathaniel Rigby; **27. Eliza**, b. 8 August 1747; **28. James**, b. 2 February 1749/50; **29. Johannah**, b. 29 May 1751; **30. Jacob**, b. 15 March 1753; **31. Thomas**, b. 25 December 1754; **32. Aquila**, b. 29 August 1757; and **33. Edward**, b. 24 April 1759.

24. Jacob Giles, son of Jacob (11) and Hannah was born 14 November 1733. He was named in his father's will as being the father of: **34. Elizabeth**.

25. Nathaniel Giles, son of Jacob (11) and Hannah, was born 2 October 1735. He and Sarah Hammond were married by Rev. Thomas Chase on 7 March 1762 (Reamy and Reamy, *St. George's Parish Register:* 92).

Nathaniel Giles died leaving a will dated 8 May 1775 and proved 5 June 1775. He named Tabitha Richardson, Sarah Coale, and his sister Sarah Rigbie. He named five daughters Hannah, Sarah, Elizabeth, Carolina, and Charlotte, and his brothers William Hammond, Nathan Rigbie, and Thomas Andrews. Larkin Hammond, Daniel Sheredine, and Caroline Sheredine witnessed the will (HAWB AJ#2:219, abst. by Morgan).

At the November 1778 Orphans Court Jacob Giles, Jr., was appointed guardian to Hannah, Sarah, Elizabeth, and Caroline, orphans of Nathaniel Giles, deceased (*HAOC*:2).

Nathaniel and Sarah were the parents of (Reamy and Reamy, *St. George's Parish Register:* 92): **35. Hannah,** b. 6 December 1762, **36. Sarah, 37. Elizabeth, 38. Carolina,** and **39. Charlotte.**

32. Aquila Giles, son of Jacob (11) and Johanna, was born 29 August 1757. He was named in his father's will as being the father of **40. William Axteel.**

Unplaced:
Nathaniel John Giles died by 3 July 1766 when Jacob Giles posted an administration bond for £500.0.0, with Amos Garrett as surety (BAAB 3:168).

== = 0 = =

The Goddard Family of Dorchester County

1. Elias Goddard was registered by Samuel Groome on or after 10 March 1671 (MPL 16:507; Peter Wilson Coldham in *NGSQ* 83:46-48).

Elias Goddard of Dorchester Co., planter, married 1st, on 29 d. 3 m., 1692, Jone (Wright transcribed this as Jane) West, of Talbot Co., spinster, at Tuckahoe Meeting House (Register of Third Haven Meeting, Talbot Co.). He married, 2nd, [-?-], daughter of Thomas Skillington, on whose property Goddard lived (MDTP 16:174).

On 23 March 1671/2 Goddard witnessed the will of Dr. Peter Sharp of Calvert Co. (MWB 1:494 abst. in *Md. Cal. of Wills* 1:68). On 10 January 1692 he was listed as a debtor in the inventory of John Marks of Talbot Co. (INAC 7C:173). On 28 September 1699 he was listed as a debtor in the inventory of Col. George Robotham (INAC 19½A:66).

Elias Goddard died by May 1696 leaving a daughter and executrix (or administratrix) Christian (MDTP 16:174). On 25 November 1696 Sarah, daughter of Elias Goddard, was left a plantation in the will of John Boram of Talbot Co. (MWB 7:239 abst. in *Md. Cal. of Wills* 2:115). On 19 December 1699 Thomas Skillington of Talbot Co. named Sarah Goddard as his granddaughter and left her tracts in Dorchester Co., *Skillington's Right,* or part of *Richardson's Folly* (MWB 6:287 abst. in *Md Cal. of Wills* 2:183).

Elias was the father of: **2. Christian,** m. Moses Alford by 1697 (INAC 15:167); and **3. Sarah,** m. Thomas Berry (See Jourdan, *Early Family of Southern Maryland* 3:44).

== = 0 = =

Colonial Families of Maryland II

The Golding Family of Baltimore County

N.B.: The name is sometimes spelled Golden,

1. Peter Golding died by March 1755. He married Elizabeth Earl on 15 November 1742 (*SJSG:* 50, 121).
Golding was a creditor of Benjamin Cadle on 16 August 1744 (MINV 33:150). On 3 December 1755 he witnessed the will of James Presbury of Baltimore Co. (MWB 24:542, abst. in *Md. Cal. of Wills* 9:96). On 10 March 1753 Golding received a payment from the estate of John Debruler (MDAD 33:357).
Peter and Elizabeth were the parents of (*SJSG:* 60, 67); **2. John**, b. 27 October 1744; **3. Stephen**, b. 10 August 1746; and **4. Elizabeth**, b. 18 August 1749.

2. John Golding, son of Peter (1) and Elizabeth, was born on 27 October 1744. In June 1755, at age 11, orphan of Peter Golding, he was bound to John Hall of Cranberry (BAMI 1755-1763). At the August 1761 Court he was bound to Col. William Young for the remainder of the time he was bound to serve Roger Boyce in March 1759 (Baltimore Co. Court Minutes, 1755-1763). Aged 17 last 1 Nov, formerly bound to John Hall of Cranberry, Roger Boyce, and Col. William Young, in Nov 1763 was bound to Thomas Lucas to age 21 to learn trade of carpenter (BAMI 1755-1763).
In 1773 he was a taxable in Gunpowder Upper Hundred, with Charles Manners and nine Negroes in his household (*IBCP:* 63).
In 1790 he was listed in Baltimore Town with four free white males over 16, three free white males under 16, six free white females, one other free person and one slave (*Heads of Families... 1790... Maryland:* 18).
John Golding and Rachel Demmitt were married on 22 July 1771 (*SJSG:* 137).

== = 0 = ==

The Grant Family of Baltimore County
With Notes on the Haile and Ford Families

1. Alexander Grant, servant of Gerard Hopkins, in January 1703/4 petitioned the court that he be set free (AAJU G:277). He married 1st, Mary Hambleton on 17 November 1709 in All Hallow's Parish (*AACR:*25). He marred, 2nd. Elizabeth Cole on 18 February 1730 (Reamy and Reamy, *St. Paul's Parish Register:* 30). Elizabeth was the mother of Angelica Cole. Elizabeth Grant, aged 68, deposed on May 1760, wife of Alexander Grant (BALR AL#B: 594).
Alexander Grant was a creditor of the estate of David Bowles on 1 October 1712 (INAC 33B:49). Grant was in Baltimore Co. by 4 April 1720 when he witnessed the will of Samuel Hinton (MWB 16:255). William Farfar of Baltimore Co., in a codicil dated 27 December 1721 to his will proved 27 March 1721/2, stated that at the request of his daughter Christian Keith, his sons John and Alexander Keith were to be left to the care of Alexander Grant until they came of age (MWB 17:233).
On 20 May 1724 Grant patented. 50 a. in Baltimore Co. called *Grant's Addition* (MPL PL#5:689, IL#A:341). On 1 March 1727 he patented 114 a. *Gorsuch's Folly* (MPL PL#6: 511, IL#A: 717). This had been conveyed to him by John Gorsuch on 3 January 1721/2 (BALR RM#HS: 669).
Grant's will dated 28 December 1738, proved 31 January 1738/9, stated that he lived in St. Paul's Parish, named his wife Elizabeth, daughter-in-law Angelica Cole, and daus.

76

Mary and Ann (MWB 22:26). An administration bond was posted on 31 January 1738 by Elizabeth Grant, with Richard Gott and John Merryman as sureties (BAAB 3:139). William Bond and Joseph Taylor set a value of £231.13.11 on Grant's personal property when they appraised it on 19 April 1739. Eliza Grant, executrix, filed the inventory on 9 March 1739 (MINV 24:159). Elizabeth Grant had to pay out £41.8.9 from the assets when she admin. Grant's estate on 9 April 1741 (MDAD 18:148).

Alexander and Elizabeth Grant were the parents of: **2. Mary,** b. 10 January 1731 (Reamy and Reamy, *St. Paul's Parish Register:* 7); and **3. Ann,** m. by 31 May 1777, George Hale, (Hall), Jr. (BALR WG#A:362).

2. Mary Grant, daughter of Alexander (1) and Elizabeth, was born 10 January 1731. She married Lloyd Ford, son of Thomas and Leah.

In February 1778, Thomas Ford of Stephen conveyed 50½ a. *Ford's Choice* to Lloyd Ford. In September 1782 Lloyd Ford and Mary sold *Ford's Choice* to John Robert Holliday (BALR WG#A:546, WG#K:168).

Lloyd and Mary were the parents of (Robert T. Nave, unpublished. data on the Ford Family, made available to the author: **4. Lloyd, Jr.,** b. 1748, **5. James,** d. 1845; **6. John,** d. 1838; **7. Thomas,** m. Nancy Wood; and **8. Alexander.**

3. Ann Grant, daughter of Alexander (1), married by 31 May 1777, George Haile, Jr. George was born 16 February 1735 in Baltimore Co. and died 1805 in Washington Co., Tenn.

George and Ann were the parents of (BALR AL#A:208,WG#A:362, WG#Q:362; Robert T. Nave, unpublished data on the Haile Family and made available to the author): **9. Samuel,** m. Caroline Ford in 1789; **10. George,** m. Eleanor Chamberlin in1797; **11. Elizabeth,** and **12. Ann.**

Unplaced:
Alexander Grant died 10 October 1786 when Mary Grant posted an administration bond on his estate for £200.0.0. Thomas Buckingham and Wm. Dunkin were sureties (BAAB 6:367).

== 0 ==

The Haddin Family of Anne Arundel County

1. John Haddin was listed as a servant in the inventory of Edward Parrish of Anne Arundel Co. on 21 August 1723 (MINV 8:282).

John Haddon married Amy (or Naomi) Short in All Hallow's Parish on 24 February 1717 (*AACR:* 197). Amy must have died as John Haddon married 2nd, Sarah Tracey in All Hallow's Parish on 1 February 1721/2 (*AACR:* 33).

John Hadden, mariner, of Anne Arundel Co. died by 26 December 1729 when Ja. Nicholson and William Sellman appraised his personal estate at £24.4.0 (MINV 16:331). On 18 May 1731 Capt. Thomas Gassaway filed an account of the estate. After citing the inventory he listed payments of £22.17.10 (MDAD 11:265). On 23 July 1736 [*sic*] he was listed as a debtor in the estate of James Carroll of Anne Arundel Co. (MDAD 15:41).

John and Naomi Haddon were the parents of (*AACR:* 198, 202): **2. John,** bapt. in All Hallows Parish on 8 October 1718; and **3. Thomas,** bapt. 26 February 1720.

Unplaced:

Thomas Haddon was buried 26 August 1709 in St. Anne's Parish (*AACR:* 67).

William Hadden of Baltimore Town, carpenter, died leaving a will dated 22 June 1762 and proved 20 July 1762. He named his friend and kinsman William Dunlap, and mentioned his good mother Jannett Hadden, his brother John Hadden and his sisters Jannett and Elizabeth. William Dunlap was to be executor. D[aniel] Chamier, J[ames]. Bonfield and Alexander Russell witnessed the will (MWB 31:715, abst. in *Md. Cal. of Wills* 12:145). William Dunlop posted an administration bond on Hadden's estate for £1000.0.0. D. Chamier and Thomas Sick were sureties (BAAB 3:286). Dunlop filed an administration account on 24 October 1763, citing the inventory of £121.1.2, and listing payments of £164.12.1. A second account was filed by Dunlop on 9 June 1766, showing payments of £146.19.2 (MDAD 50:64, 54:239). Dunlop distributed the estate of £376.17,1 on 9 June 1766 to William Haddon's mother Jannet Haddon, and his siblings John, Jannett, and Elizabeth Haddon (BFD 5:6).

== 0 ==

The Hambleton Family of Baltimore County

1. Robert Hambleton and Rebecca Bignall were married on 15 November 1733 (Reamy and Reamy, *St. George's Parish Register:* 47). Rebecca Bignall, daughter of John and Catherine Bignall, was bapt. 24 April 1687 at St. Martin in the Fields, London. She was transported to Maryland as a convict in 1726 (*CBEB).* She settled in Baltimore Co. and in June 1731, as a servant of Ford Barnes, was indicted for bastardy (BACP HWS#7:236).

In 1737 Robert Hambleton was head of a household in Deer Creek Hundred. A Thomas Hambleton and Richard Doyle were in another household in Deer Creek Hundred (*IBCW:* 11).

Robert and Rebecca were the parents of (Reamy and Reamy, St. George's Parish Register: 47, 49, 56): **2. Ann**, b. 26 March 1734; **3. Robert**, b. 3 March 1735; and **4. Thomas**, b. 30 May 1738.

4. Thomas Hambleton, son of Robert and Rebecca, was born 30 May 1738. He may be the Thomas Hambleton who married Esther Samson on 30 January 1753 (*SJSG:* 95). However, he would have only been 15 years old!

Thomas Hambleton was listed as a debtor of Col. Nathan Rigby, in the latter's inventory, appraised 8 December 1752 (MINV 52:63-75).

On 1 Oct 1759 Thomas Hambleton witnessed the will of John Cooper of Baltimore Co. (MWB 30:752 abst. in *Md. Cal. of Wills* 11:248).

Unplaced

Edward Hambleton took the Oath of Allegiance to the State of Maryland in 1778 in Harford Co. (*RPHA:* 102).

Elizabeth Hambleton and William Roach of Harford Co. were married on 27 January 1793 (*SJSG:* 152).

John Hambleton and Phebe Maxwell of Harford Co. were married on 20 May 1790 (*SJSG:* 149).

John Hambleton and Peggy Bond of Harford Co. were married on 17 June 1793 (*SJSG:* 152). John and Margaret were the parents of (*SJSG:* 178, 181): Catherine Sally, b. 10 March 1794, and Mary, b. 5 May 1796.

John Hambleton and Aley Gafford of Harford Co. were married on 26 January 1797 (*SJSG:* 153).

Ralph Hambleton died by 15 September 1785 when James Hamilton (or Hambleton) posted an administration bond for £200.0.0. Hugh Allen and Daniel O'Brien were sureties (BAAB 6:239).

==0==

The Hamill Family of Charles County

1. John Hamill was born 1692 in Charles County, Maryland, and died there on 21 May 1764. He married Sarah, daughter of William Chandler of Charles Co., whose will of 17 November 1735 named among others, his daughter Sarah Hamill (MWB 21:520). Sarah Chandler Hamill died by April 1769.

John Hamill patented several tracts of land. On 4 October 1732 he patented 20 a. of *Hamill's Discovery* (MPL PL#8:609, AM#1:243). On 2 March 1739 he patented 329 a. called *Partner's Purchase* (MPL EI#2:850, EI#5:463). On 21 August 1742 he patented 21 a. *Borough Gammon* (MPL PT#2:277).

Hamill, a schoolmaster, was in Charles Co. by 13 June 1727 when he and his wife Sarah conveyed 50 a. *Wilderness* on 13 June 1727 (CHLR, L#2:361). On 13 June 1733 they conveyed 20 a. *Hamill's Discovery* to Francis Posey (CHLR M#2:345). On 21 June 1739 they conveyed two lots in Charles Town (CHLR O#2:429). On 14 December 1742 John Hamill conveyed 30 a. *Baker's Addition* to Capt. Barton Smoot (CHLR O#2:595). On 7 April 1756 he conveyed to John Hamill 150 *Ashbrook's Rest;* if he should die without heirs the land was to go to his three sons Stephen, Nail, and William (CHLR 1752-1756:491).

He witnessed the will of Jacob Brandt on 27 November 1750 (MWB 28:30, abst. in *Md. Cal. of Wills* 10:145). He witnessed the will of George Thomas on 11 February 1752 (MWB 28:296, abst. in *Md. Cal. of Wills* 10:210).

Hamill died leaving a will dated 21 May 1764 and proved 21 May 1764. He left 164½ a. *Partnership,* and 33 a. *Garnon* to his son Hugh Hamill. He left 150 a. *Ahsbrook's Rest* to his son Stephen Hamill. His son William Chandler Hamill was to have 100 a., part of *Promise,* and 20 a. *Baker's Addition.* His daughter Catherine Shaw was to have Negro woman Jenny and the boy Harry. His three sons, named above, were to have Negroes Deptford, Jacob, Lott, and Charity. His wife Sarah was to have all his moveable estate for life, and then it was to go to his four children. Sam Amery, Mary Amery, and William Brown witnessed the will (MWB 33:290, abst. in *Md. Cal. of Wills* 13:85).

John Hamill's estate was appraised at £181.5.10, by John Wood and John Wilder. John Chandler and Stephen Chandler signed as next of kin. Henry Hamill and William Chandler Hamill, executors filed the inventory on 19 June 1767 (MINV 94:282).

Hugh Hamill and William Chandler filed an account of John Hamill's estate on 17 April 1769, listing payments of £89.4.8. They stated that the widow Sarah Hamill was deceased (MDAD 60:411).

John and Sarah were the parents of: **2. John, Jr., 3. Hugh; 4. Stephen; 5. William Chandler; 6. Neil; 7. Catherine Chandler**, m. [-?-] Shaw; and **8. Sarah**.

2. John Hamill, Jr., son of John (1) and Sarah, died by 1760.

Hamill left a will dated 1 February 1760 and proved 19 [month not given] 1760. He left 150 a. *Ashbrook's Rest* in Durham Parish to his brothers Nail [Neil] and William. If both brothers died without issue the land was to go to his god-son William Groves

Smoot. His sisters Sarah and Katherine were to have one slave each. The residue of his estate was to be divided between his brothers Hugh and Stephen Hamill. His uncles John and Stephen Chandler were named executors. John Fendall, Robert Tates, and Jane Shaw witnessed the will. (MWB 31:42, abst. in *Md. Cal. of Wills* 12:9).

Edward Ford and John Wood appraised John Hamill's estate at £90.6.0. Stephen Hamill, Hugh Hamill, John Chandler, and John Kinsman were mentioned. Stephen Chandler, executor, filed the inventory on 12 October 1760 (MINV 71:75).

Stephen Chandler filed an account of John Hamill's estate on 9 December 1768, listing payments of £44.7.6 (MDAD 60:270).

3. Hugh Hamill, son of John (1) and Sarah, was living as late as March 1786. He married Elizabeth [-?-].

On 7 March 1771 Hugh Hamill conveyed 84 a. *Promise* to Benjamin Douglass. His wife Elizabeth Hamill consented (CHLR S#3:130).

On 13 March 1786 Hugh Hamill of Prince William Co., Va., with the consent of his wife Elizabeth, conveyed 150 a. *Ashbrook's Rest* to William Poston (CHLR 1782-1786:263).

4. Stephen Hamill, son of John (1), died by 3 November 1763. He married Assenal [-?-], who married 2nd, by February 1769 John Shaw.

On 3 November 1763 Jesse Doyne Richard Barns appraised Stephen Hamill's estate at £146.19.5. Hugh Hamill and William Chd. Hamill signed as next of kin. Asinah Hamill filed the inventory on 11 June 1766 (MINV 89:75).

Assenal Shaw, wife of John Shaw filed an account of the estate on 21 February 1769. She listed payments of £24.19.4. The representatives of the deceased were the widow, and two children, John, aged 5, and Sarah, aged 4 (MDAD 61:63). She filed another account on 10 November 1769, listing payments of £1.17.3. Son John was now aged 6, and Sarah was aged 5 (MDAD 62:341).

Stephen and Asinah were the parents of: **9. John,** b. about 1763/4; and **10. Sarah,** b. about 1766/7.

5. William Chandler Hamill, son of John (1) and Sarah, died by 21 April 1770 when his estate was appraised by John Wilder and T. Harris, at £12.19.0. John Smoot and Stephen Chandler signed as next of kin. Hugh Hamill, the administrator, filed the inventory on 11 July 1770 (MINV 103:263).

7. Catherine Chandler Hamill, daughter of John (1) and Sarah, married Joseph Shaw.

==0==

The Harryman Family of Baltimore County

N.B.: For the earlier generations of this family, see *Baltimore Co. Families, 1659-1759.*

1. George Harryman (#5 in *Baltimore County Families*), son of John and Ann, was born about 1702 and died by December 1774 in Baltimore Co. He married Anne Wilkinson, daughter of William and Tamar, on 30 March 1725 (Reamy and Reamy, *St. Paul's Parish Register:* 29). George Harryman, aged 65, deposed in a land commission on 28 September 1767 (BALR WG#A: 123).

On 9 March 1738 Christopher Durbin Shaw, with consent of wife Susannah, conveyed 48½ a. (being one-half of *Swans Delight,* and 50 a. being one-half of *Swans Fancy*) to George Harryman (BALR HWS#1-A: 206).

On 6 December 1742 Robert Boyd and wife Ruth conveyed 97 a. part *Shaw's Delight* 100 a. part *Shaw's Fancy,* and 80 a. *Shaw's Privilege,* in all 257 a., to George Harryman. (BALR TB#C: 223). 5 Oct 1743: John Ingle conveyed to George Harryman all the real estate Christopher Shaw had left to John Ingle and Ruth Bayes, to George Harryman (BALR TB#C: 382).

On 14 May 1745 George Harryman, with the consent of wife Ann, conveyed 50 a. *Harryman's Landing,* 100 a. *Harryman's Range* and 19 a. *K..?.* to Charles Carroll of Annapolis, chirurgeon (BALR TB#D: 155).

George Harryman died leaving a will dated 27 December 1773 and proved 9 December 1774. His son George was to have all his lands and personal estate except as hereafter provided. Daughter Sophia Clark and her husband Samuel were to have 200 a. *Project* and *Harryman's Outlet.* He mentioned Samuel and Sophia's sons William, Samuel, and George. He named his grandsons Thomas and George Jackson, orphans of Thomas Jackson and his daughter Patience. He named his daughter Tamar, his granddaughter Temperance Harryman, and his brother Robert Harryman. His son George was to be executor. John Buck, Benj. Buck, and Henry Frinsham witnessed the will (BAWB 3:285).

George Harryman, the executor, posted an administration bond on his father's estate for £1000.0.0. Edw. Talbott and Elexious Lemmon were sureties (BAAB 3:335).

George Harryman filed an account of his father's estate on 19 December 1774. He cited an inventory of £523.11.7, and listed payments of £27.18.9; he filed another account on 17 June 1776, listing payments of £18.9.10 (MDAD 69:408, 73:418; BAAD 6:359). Harryman administered the estate again on 19 Dece1774 (BAAD 7:254).

George and Anne were the parents of (Reamy and Reamy, *St. Paul's Parish Register:* 4, 8, 11, 15): **2. George,** b. 19 April 1728; **3. Sophia,** m. Samuel Clark; **4. Tamar; 5. Patience,** b. 5 February 1733/4, m. Thomas Jackson on 24 July 1757 (*SJSG:* 101); **6. George; 7. Anne,** b. 2 June 1742; **8. William,** b. 25 September 1746; and **9. Samuel,** d. by 1783 having m. Sophia [-?-].

2. George Harryman, son of George (1) and Anne, was born 19 April 1728, and died by December 1794. He married Sarah Raven on 17 October 1749 (*SJSG:* 91). She was born 1732 in Baltimore Co., and died in 1764. On 5 September 1760 Sarah was named as a daughter in the will of Luke Raven who also named a granddaughter Rachel Harryman (MWB 31:162 abst. by Gibb).

George Harryman, Jr., about 1761 was listed as a debtor in the inventory of Col. Nicholas Rogers (MINV 73:26-44).

There were two George Harrymans who were Non-Jurors to the Oath of Allegiance in 1778 (*BARP:* 122).

Harryman died leaving a will dated 29 November 1794 and proved 20 December 1794. He named his wife Sarah, his son-in-law John Corbin and his wife Rachel, his son-in-law Abel Headington and wife Mary, his son-in-law John Jones and wife Sarah, his son-in-law Luke Brian and wife Eleanor, his son-in-law Joshua Marsh and wife Temperance, and his own sons William and George. So George was to be executor. John Talbott, John Tudor, and Benjamin Talbott witnessed the will (BAWB 5:236, abst. by Burns).

On 12 April 1796 when George Harryman, executor of George Harryman, petitioned the court concerning a certain Negro Toby, and Toby's children Ruth, Ephraim, Abraham, Daniel, and Hannah (Petition of George Harryman, Baltimore Co., 1796).

George and Sarah were the parents of: **10. Sarah,** b. 4 March 1754, m. John Jones; they were the parents of: Rachel, b. 5 October 1782 in Baltimore Co., d. 22 February

1866 in Hamilton Co., Ohio; and Nancy, b. 3 August 1790 in Md, d. 3 September 1871 in Cosby, Hamilton Co., Ohio; **11. Rachel**, m. John Corbin; **12. Mary**, m. Luke Headington; **13. Eleanor**, m. Luke Brian; **14. Temperance**, m. Joshua Marsh; **15. William**; and **16. George**.

Unplaced:
John Harryman died by 12 March 1785 when John Harryman, executor, posted an administration bond for £500.0.0. John Kerbach and Geo. Reese were sureties (BAAB 6:284).

Josias Harryman was a Non-Juror to the Oath of Allegiance in 1778 (*BARP* 122).He died by 25 May 1785 when Sarah Harryman posted an administration bond for £300.0.0, with Daniel Biddison and John Hatton as sureties (BAAB 6:317). On 20 February 1788 his widow and administratrix, now the wife of Barnet Bond, administered the estate. She retained £27.1.10 as her thirds, and John Hatton, guardian of the children, received £74.3.9 (BAAD 9:163).

== 0 ==

The Hatherly Family of Anne Arundel County

1. John Hatherly lived on Elk Ridge Hundred. He married Elizabeth Eyrins (Ewings?) in All Hallows Parish on 21 December 1704 (*AACR:* 18).
On 7 August 1707 he was listed as paying into the estate of Col. Edward Dorsey of Baltimore Co. (INAC 27:59).
On 9 November 1719 William Vines conveyed 60 a. *Vines Fancy* to John Hatherly (BALR TR#DS: 128). John may be the John Hatherly who patented 50 a. in Baltimore Co. called *John's Lot*, on 1 May 1734 (MPL EI#2:27, EI#3:67). On 1 May 1737 as John Hatherly of Anne Arundel Co., carpenter, he conveyed 50 a. *John's Lot*, to Samuel Shipley (BALR IS#IK: 382).
John and Elizabeth were the parents of: **2. John**, bapt. about 1717 in All Hallows Parish; and **3. Ewings**, bapt. about 1717 in All Hallow Parish.

2. John Hatherly, son of John (1) and Elizabeth was bapt. about 1717 in All Hallows Parish. In 1771 he deposed in a land commission giving his age as 63, placing his year of birth at about 1708 (AALC 3:145-176, 170).
On 18 May 1742 he was listed as paying into the estate of Col. Thomas Cockey (MDAD 19:18). Some time after 1748 he joined other inhabitants of the Upper Parts of Anne Arundel Co. in sending a petition to Governor Samuel Ogle and both Houses of the

Assembly, asking for the erection of Elk Ridge into a town (*CMSP Black Books,* document 567).
John Hatherly patented several tracts of land in Anne Arundel Co., 100 a. *Hatherly's Forest* on 12 September 1742 (MPL EI#6:512, LG#E:135), 100 a. *Hatherly's Frest Addition* on 14 April 1744 (MPL LG#E:258, PT#1;108), on the same day, 50 a. *Hatherly's Resolution* (MPL LG#E;254 PT#2:85), and on 16 August 1750 250 a. *Hatherly's Contrivance* (MPL TI#4:522, BY#1:569).
In June 1750 the ship *Tryal,* Capt. John Johnston, from London, arrived in Md. on board was one Jeremiah Swift, from Essex, noted as a runaway (*KPMV:*123).
Swift had become a servant of John Hatherly on Elk Ridge. One day in March 1751, while the parents were at a funeral, Swift quarreled with two of master's sons, aged 11-12 and 9-10. He killed the elder son and Hatherly's 14 or 15 year old daughter, and severely

wounded the younger son. He left three younger children alone (Annapolis *Maryland Gazette* 20 March 1751). At Swift's trial, 9 year old Benedict Leonard Hatherly was a witness, and told how Swift had been working in the field John and Benjamin. Swift got into an argument with John, whom he killed, and then wounded Benjamin. Returning to the house, he stabbed Hatherly's daughter Elizabeth. He left three younger children alone; Elizabeth, aged 14, John, aged 12, and Benjamin, aged 10 (Annapolis *Maryland Gazette* 10 April 1751).

On 15 April 1751 a 'Dead Warrant' was issued to the Sheriff of Ann Arundell County for the Execution of Jeremiah Swift for the murder of Elizabeth Hatherly to be on Wednesday the next and his body is to be hung in chains near the place where the murder was committed (Commission Book 1: 117).

In reporting his execution, the Maryland Gazette stated that Swift had been at Braintree, Essex, of good parents, and that he had been well educated. His execution was scheduled for Elk Ridge on April 24 (Annapolis *Maryland Gazette* 24 April 1751).

On 14 April 1755 John Hatherly, Jr., patented six acres in Frederick Co. called *Hatchery's Adventure* (MPL BC#3:333, BC#5:147).

John Hatherly, Jr., and Robert Davis appraised the estate of Philip Porter on 17 August 1758 (MINV 67:531). John Hatherly, Jr., and Robert Davis appraised the estate of Joseph Walker on 16 November 1758 (MINV 66:130).He received payments from the estates of: John Oliver on 16 September 1764, and William Rolls on 24 September 1765 (MDAD 51:301, 53:114, 124).

John Hatherly, aged about 62 years, deposed in a land commission held 18 April 1773 for a tract of Thomas Cockey's, stating that his brother Ewing Hatherly had shown him the beginning trees of *Yeates Contrivance* and he mentioned other people who had shown him boundary trees (Anne Arundel Co. Land Commissions, 1767-1794, MSA C94-3:168-177). Another land commission was held from 29 September 1780 to October 1782, The commissioners had been waiting for the deposition of John Hatherly, Sr., but they had been informed that he was long indisposed, and then they received word that he had died (Anne Arundel Co. Land Commissions, 1767-1794, MSA C94-3:334-340).

He took the Oath of Allegiance before the Hon Reuben Meriweather on 2 March 1778 (*RPAA:* 91).

John Hatherly, farmer, died leaving a will dated 26 September 1782 and proved 14 October 1782. Son Benjamin Hatherly was to have part of *Hatherly's Contrivance*, 104 a., and one-half of his apple orchard. Son Nathan Hatherly was to have the remainder of *Hatherly's Contrivance* and a Negro woman [Bess?] and her increase. He named his daughter Rachel Keef and her husband Thomas Keef and Stephen West. The two sons were to be executors. Ely Davis, Robert Davis, Jr., Rebecca Davis and [Cosman?] Smith witnessed the will. In a letter dated 15 October 1782 Patience Hatherly stated that her late husband had not mentioned her, so she claimed the part of his estate that the law allowed (AAWB TG#1:76-78).

Benjamin Hatherly and Nathan Hatherly, executors, distributed the estate of John Hatherly, late of Anne Arundel Co., deceased, on 25 August 1785. James Frost and Joshua Brown were sureties. The widow received her thirds after deduction of a legacy to Benjamin and Nathan, each of whom received a Negro and one-half each of the remainder of the balance (Anne Arundel Co. Distributions JG#1:6, abst. by Arps.)

Patience Hatherly was listed in the 1783 Assessment List of Anne Arundel Co. as living in Elkridge Hundred (MSA S 1161-1-3 1/4/5/44).

John Hatherly and his wife Patience were the parents of: **4. Elizabeth**, aged 14, when she was killed in 1751; **5. John,** aged 12 when he was killed in 1751; **6. Benjamin,** b. about 1741; **7. Benedict Leonard,** b. about 1742; testified at Swift's trial in 1751; **8. Nathan;** and **9. Rachel,** m. Thomas Keef.

Colonial Families of Maryland II

6. Benjamin Hatherly, son of John (2) and Patience, was left 104 a. of *Hatherly's Contrivance* by his father's will. He was listed as the owner of the land in the 1783 Assessment List of Anne Arundel Co. (MSA S 1161-1-3 1/4/5/44).

He took the Oath of Allegiance before the Hon Reuben Meriweather on 2 March 1778 (*RPAA:* 91).

8. Nathan Hatherly, son of John (2) and Patience, was left 104 a. of *Hatherly's Contrivance* by his father's will. He was listed as the owner of the land in the 1783 Assessment List of Anne Arundel Co. (MSA S 1161-1-3 1/4/5/44).

He took the Oath of Allegiance before the Hon Thomas Dorsey on 2 March 1778 (*RPAA:* 92).

Unplaced:
John Hatherly was a lieutenant in the militia from 13 April 1813 to 17 May 1813. He joined the 23rd Regiment on 16 August 1813. He was captain of his own company in the 22nd Regiment from 15 October to 3 November 1814 (Wright, *Md. Militia in the War of 1812: Anne Arundel Co.,* pp. 33, 34, 37).

John Hatherly, late Examiner General of the Western Shore of Maryland, died Friday, 28 April 1815 (Annapolis *Maryland Gazette* 4 May 1815).

John Hatherly and Sarah Ann Brown were married by license dated 21 December 1813 (AAML). Sarah Ann Hatherly and Samuel Owings were married by license dated 20 September 1819 (AAML).

Robert Hatherly received a payment from the estate of William Chew Brown of Anne Arundel Co. on 17 January 1771 (MDAD 65:232).

==0==

The Hearn(e) Family of Anne Arundel County

1. Daniel Hearn died after March 1757.

Hearn was living in Prince George's Co. on 10 November 1723 when Timothy Regan of Baltimore Co conveyed him two heifers. By 10 January 1728 he had moved to Anne Arundel Co. when he assigned his interest in the two heifers to John Regan and Timothy Regan, Jr. (PCLR PL#6:310).

Hearn was in Prince George's Co. on 29 September 1726 when Daniel Carroll and his wife Mary, for £35.0.0, conveyed to Hearn 203 a. in Anne Arundel Co. called *Chance* (PCLR PL#6:172). It may be the acquisition of this land that prompted Daniel Hearn to move to Anne Arundel Co. Daniel Hearne conveyed the 203 a. tract to James Ellitt of Prince George's Co. on 16 December 1748 (AALR RB#3:111).

He was listed as living at Mr. Carroll's plantations beyond Elk Ridge (Annapolis *Maryland Gazette* 24 December 1728). He was still living there in July 1761 when he advertised he had a stray mare at his plantation (Annapolis *Maryland Gazette* 2 July 1761).

Daniel Herne was listed as one of the debtors owing the estate of Amos Garrett of Anne Arundel Co. in the latter's inventory filed 15 August 1729 (MINV 15:46-73). On 29 June 1743 Daniel Hearn, Basil Dorsey and James McCollum witnessed the will of Eleanor Herbert of Anne Arundel Co. (MWB 23:232).

On 18 March 1745/6 Richard Warfield and Robert Ridgely of Anne Arundel Co. deposed concerning Daniel Hearn. Warfield states he heard Augustine Gambrill tell of hearing Sylvanus Marriot say that Hearn asked him after the landing of the Pretender's

Son in Scotland, if he had heard of King Charles' or Prince Charles' landing. Hearn spoke in a jesting manner. Ridgely stated he never heard Hearn say anything disrespectful about King George, and Ridgely always took Hearn to be an honest man (*CMSP Black Books*, item 499).

In June 1746 Daniel 'Hern' was indicted as having "drunk The Pretender's Health. John Campbell and Nicholas Gassaway were witnesses. 'Hern' was found guilty and fined 20 lbs, currency (AAJU June 1746 Court: 115). [The Pretender was the young Prince Charles Stuart, who, in 1745, led an abortive attempt to raise a rebellion against King George II. ["Drinking the Pretender's Health" was regarded s an act of disloyalty to the Crown!].

Daniel Hearne, planter, appears in Anne Arundel Judgments between June 1746 and November 1756. At the June 1752 Court he was sued by John Hanbury and Co. (AAJU June 1752:360). In November 1752 and November 1755 two of his slaves were made levy free (AAJU: November 1752:426, and November 1755:335).

Some time after 1748 Daniel Hearn and other inhabitants of the "Upper Parts of Anne Arundel County and Adjacent Places signed a petition to Governor Samuel Ogle and the Upper and Lower Houses of the Assembly, asking that Elk Ridge Landing be erected into a town (*CMSP Black Books*, item 567).

In January 1749 Daniel Hearn, Dr. Joshua Warfield and Za. McDonnell witnessed the will of Henry Rooker of Anne Arundel Co. (MWB 27:268).

In August 1756 he was made levy free and in November 1756 the court made him an allowance and described his house as being distressed (AAJU: August 1756:711, and November 1756:795). In March 1757 it was recorded that the law suit between William Hall and Daniel Hearn had been agreed (AAJU: March 1757:9).

Daniel Hearn was probably the father of: **2. Daniel, Jr.**, who appeared in Anne Arundel Co. Court, March 1749/50, as being sued by Richard Snowden (AAJU: March Court 1749/50:501); **3. Michael;** and **4. John.**

3. Michael Hearn, probably son of Daniel, was b. about 1720 and died 1813. He is the first definitely known progenitor of the Hearn family, but he is probably a son or grandson of Daniel Hearn (#1 above).

Michael Hearn witnessed a deed in 1736 (AALR RD#2:376).In August 1761 he was a defendant against Richard Snowden (AAJU August 1761 Court: 228).

Michael Hearn and John Hearn are listed as debtors in the inventory, filed 18 September 1771, of the estate of William Hall of Anne Arundel Co. (MINV 107:339-355).

On 2 March 1778 Michael Hearn took the Oath of Fidelity to the State of Maryland before Thomas Dorsey (*CMSP Red Books*, Part 3, item 147).

On 26 May 1790 Henry Ridgely conveyed to Michael 'Heron' 75 acres, part of *Grimit's Chance* (AALR NH#5:290). On 26 April 1800 Henry Ridgely, son of Henry Ridgely conveyed 30 more acres of *Grimmith's Chance* to Michael Hearn (AALR NH#10:366).

Michazel Hearn, planter, on 20 December 1805, gave bond he would convey to his sons Isaac, William and John, part of *The Grove* and part *Second Addition to Snowden's Manor* (AALR WSG#2:168).

A deed dated 21 January 1813 stated that Michael Hearn on 9 August 1803 had obtained a conveyance from James Worthington for 300 a. of land, part *The Grove* and part of *Second Addition to Snowden's Manor*. He had also obtained two different conveyances for portions of *Grimmitt's Chance*. He died intestate without conveying the 300 acres to his three sons, and now disputes have arisen among his heirs, so now Edward Iglehart and wife Sophia, Isaac Hearn, John Hearn, Cornelius Iglehart and wife

Anne conveyed all the land by deed of trust to Thomas Worthington (AALR WSG#2:169) [There is a possibility that Sophia was a widow and not a daughter].

Michael Hearn married and was the father of: **5. Isaac; 6. Anne,** m. Cornelius Iglehart in 1802; their son Tilghman m. his first cousin, Ann Hearne; **7. John;** placed as a son of Michael because on 23 August 1815 Isaac Hearn and John Hearn executed a deed of partition for part of *The Grove* and *Second Addition to Snowden's Manor* (AALR WSG#4:40-ff.); in 1813 John Hearn, living near Richard Owings' mills on Elk Ridge, registered a stray (AALR WSG#2:175); **8. Caleb** (possibly); was drafted in Anne Arundel Co. in 1814; in December 1818 was m. in Prince George's Co. to Maria Green; he d. in Howard Co. (then Anne Arundel Co.) in September 1835; his pension application stated that the name was sometimes pronounced Herring; **9. William,** m. by 17 October 1813 Rachel [-?-], and moved to Washington Co., Pa., when he and his wife conveyed their share of his father's estate to Isaac Hearn (AALR WSG#2:631); and **10. (possibly) Sophia,** m. by 1813 Edward Iglehart.

4. John Hearn, prob. son of Daniel (1), may have died by November 1788, leaving a widow Mary. He may be the John Hearn mentioned in the following records: On 20 February 1777 Thomas Dorsey and John Dorsey of Elk Ridge wrote to the Council of Safety recommending that the bearer, John Hearn, should be an officer in the troops being raised; he served with the Elk Ridge Battalion from the first of the disputes with Great Britain, and would have cheerfully marched to reinforce Gen. Washington, at the Council's request, had he been backed by a sufficient number (*CMSP Red Books*, Part 2, item 933).

John Hearn was listed in the 1783 Assessment List of Elk Ridge Hundred, AA Co., but he did not own any land.

John "Harn" was a surety for Jacob Read (AAJU March 1785 Court: 50). In August 1785 he was a "co-recognizer" [prob. surety] for the taverns of John Wayman and Patrick Baxter and for the liquor retailing of Philip Waters (AAJU August 1785 Court:100, 101).

In August 1785 he was a defendant against Jesse Hollingsworth and Amos Lowrey (AAJU August 1785 Court: 111). In August 1786 he was a defendant against Richard Sprigg (AAJU August 1786 Court: 185).

In November 1788 Mary Harn appeared in court for John Harn, deceased (AAJU: 149).

5. Isaac Hearn, son of Michael (3), was b. about 1771, was living in 1853. He married Elizabeth [-?-], b. in the 1770's. She died before 1853, according to a deed dated 16 August 1853 (HOLR WHW#14:35).

On 23 August 1815 Isaac Hearn executed a deed of partition with John Hearn (presumably his brother), for part of The Grove and Second Addition to Snowden's manor (AALR WSG#4:40).

On 23 May 1849 Isaac Hearn and wife Elizabeth conveyed to Tilghman Iglehart part *Second Discovery* and *Howard's Resolution,* 272 acres in all, except for 82 acres conveyed by deed of same date to Rebecca, wife of Richard Hearn, and the said Isaac also reserved a life estate in the said tracts for himself and wife Elizabeth (AALR EPH#9:114).

Maryland Chancery paper # 10079 contained a petition of John Orem of Howard District, stating that Isaac Hearn of Howard District executed two bills of obligation dated 13 May 1848, payable to the petitioner. Hearn then took advantage of the insolvent debtor laws and conveyed all his property to his sons Artemus, Alfred, Richard (with wife Rebecca), and Benjamin Hearn, and to T[ilghman] Iglehart and wife Nancy.

The 1850 Census of Howard District shows Isaac Hearn, Sr., age 79, wife

Elizabeth, age 7-(?), and Isaac, age 35 or 38, living with Trueman Iglehart, 40 and wife Anne, 35 (Census of Howard District, dwelling 1296, family 1313).

Isaac and Elizabeth were the parents of: **11. Artemas**, b. about 1805/7, d. 8 June 1885; **12. Ann**, b. about 1809, d. 17 February 1895 in her 87th year; m. Tilghman H. Iglehart on or about 22 January 1833 (BAML); she was buried at Wavertree, Glenelg, Howard Co. (N:3:48); **13. Alfred C.**, b. about 1812; m. Matilda Carr by Howard Co. Marriage License dated 13 July 1849; on 29 October 1863, Alfred C. Hearn and his two children, Charles E., and Catherine E., mortgaged property to Enoch Selby (HOLR 22 WWW:593); **14. Isaac**, b. about 1812/5, d. leaving a will dated 30 December 1850, proved 20 May 1851, naming the following relatives: brother-in-law Tilghman H. Igelhart, niece Ann Eliza Iglehart, sister Ann Iglehart, brothers Artemus Hearn, Alfred C. Hearn and Benjamin Hearn. (Howard Co. Wills, 1:261); **15. Richard**, b. about 1815, m. Rebecca Ford by Howard Co. Marr. Lic. dated 18 July 1846; **16. Benjamin**, b. about 1816.

Unplaced:

Barnaby Hearne of Nansemond Co., Va., Gent., on 19 July 1711 was in Prince George's Co. when he conveyed to Thomas Greenfield of Prince George's Co. for £32.0.0, tract, part of a greater tract called *Billinsgley,* which had been bequeathed to Barnaby Hearne, by George Billingsley in his will dated 21 December 1681 (PGLR F:97). (The will of George Billingsley of Churcketuck, Upper Norfolk Co., Va. is given in PGLR F: 129).

John Harn, "ye 3rd," on 12 March 1778 took the Oath of Fidelity to the State of Maryland before John Dorsey (*CMSP Red Books*, XXII, item 26-1).

Mary Hearn was mentioned in an Anne Arundel Co. 1774 Court Minute Sheet: 118

Thomas Hearn died leaving a will dated 4 November 1814, proved 24 November 1814, naming wife Priscilla who was to have all his real estate, his mother Sarah who was to have farm on Stoney Creek called *Bachelor's Inheritance*; after death of his wife Priscilla all his property to be divided among his brothers and sisters and his wife's brothers and sisters (AAWB 38:70).

== 0 ==

The Heighe Family of Calvert County

1. Robert Heighe of Calvert Co. died by December 1681. He married 1st, Mary [-?-], and 2nd, by July 1679, Eliza [-?-].

Heighe immigrated to Md. by 1663, transporting his wife Mary at the same time (MPL 5:248). He was in Calvert Co. by 27 March 1671 when he witnessed the will of George Peake (MWB 1:428, abst. in *Md. Cal. of Wills* 1:60). On 15 May 1671 Mary Peake named him as one of her executors (MWB 1:469, abst. in *Md. Cal. of Wills* 1:65).).On 25 September 1676 Robert Heighe and Thomas Stirling were named as executors of James Hume of Calvert Co. (MWB 5:224, abst. in *Md. Cal. of Wills* 1:190).

Robert Heighe died leaving a will dated 26 July 1679, proved 1 December 1681. His wife Eliza, executrix, was to have *Half Woster's Purchase*. Son James and heirs were to have the said plantation and 100 a. *Little Land*. Son Robert and heirs were to have 200 a. at Plum Point. Son Samuel was to have 200 unnamed acres. His daughter Eliza and her heirs were to have *Robert's Chance*. His children were to be of age at 16. Thomas Sterling was named overseer of the will. The will was witnessed by Jno. Cobreath, Peter Browne, and Jno. Troster. In a codicil, Heighe revoked the bequest to his daughter Eliza in favor of his three sons. He left her 200 a. on Hunting Creek (MWB 2:161, abst. in *Md.*

Cal. of Wills 1:101).
Francis Maldin and James Mackall appraised the personal estate of Mr. Robert High on 14 May 1681, at 81,364 lbs. tob. (INAC 7B:161).
Robert Heighe was the father of the following children: **2. James; 3. Robert; 4. Samuel;** and **5. Eliza.**

2. James Heighe of Calvert Co., son of Robert (1), died by 1725. He married Ann [-?-].
On 24 January 1684 James Heighe witnessed the will of Thomas Sterling of Calvert Co. (MWB 4:156, abst. in *Md. Cal. of Wills* 1:156). On 23 March 1699 James Heighe witnessed the will of James "Humbe" of the Clifts, Calvert Co. (MWB 6:213, abst. in *Md. Cal. of Wills* 2:168).
James died leaving a will dated 26 July 1725, proved 12 November 1725. He named his son James (not yet 18), his daughter Althea (not yet 16), his daughters Elizabeth and Mary, his grandsons James Tongue, and James Bourne, as well as his son-in-law Sabrett Sollers. The will was witnessed by Robert Freeland, James Maiden, and Eliza Allen (MWB 18:410, abst. in *Md. Cal. of Wills* 5:203).
Ann Heighe, executrix, administered the estate of James Heighe of Calvert Co. Two inventories, worth £1142.6.1 and £0.18.2, were cited. No heirs were named (MDAD 9:191). Another account was filed on 24 November 1733. Payments were made to children of the deceased: James Heighe, Althea Heighe, Elizabeth Sollers, and Mary Sollers (MDAD 12:116B). Another account was filed on 12 June 1736. Roger Hooper who married Althea Heighe was named (MDAD 14:265).
On 3 November 1732, Samuel Leach of Calvert Co. made a will leaving James, son of Ann Heighe, personalty (MWB 20:572, abst. in *Md. Cal. of Wills* 6:254).
James Heighe was the father of: **6. James,** d. in Calvert Co. by 1757 (MWB 30:404); **7. Althea,** m. by 12 June 1736, Roger Hooper; **8. Elizabeth,** m. 1st, by 1724, Robert Bourne, and 2nd, by November 1733, Robert Sollers; and **9. Mary,** m. 1st, Thomas Tongue, and 2nd, by 24 November 1733, Sabrett Sollers.

3. Robert Heighe of Calvert Co., son of Robert (1), died by May 1721. He married [-?-].
Robert Heighe of Calvert Co. died leaving a will dated 3 June 1720, proved 10 May 1721. His only son Robert was to have the entire [real] estate at age 21. His only daughter Sarah was to have personalty. The testator's brother James and Abraham Downe were named executors. The will was witnessed by Alex. Adair, Richard Stallings, William Hickman, and Thomas Hardesty, Jr. (MWB 16:405, abst. in *Md. Cal. of Wills* 5:50).
Robert Heighe was the father of: **10. Robert;** and **11.Sarah.**

4. Samuel Heighe of Calvert Co. son of Robert (1), died by June 1725.
Samuel Heighe of Calvert Co. died leaving a will dated 31 March 1724/5, proved 22 June 1725, leaving his entire estate to his son Samuel, who was named exec. The will was witnessed by Robert Heighe and Benjamin Newland (MWB 18:395, abst. in Md. Cal. of Wills 5:198).
Samuel Heighe was the father of: **12. Samuel.**

7. James Heighe, son of James (2), died by September 1757. He married Betty Holdsworth
In Nov 1750 James Heighe advertised a sale of the land belonging to Richard Johns of Calvert Co. (Annapolis *Maryland Gazette* 7 November 1750).
James died leaving a will dated 23 November 1756 and proved 12 September 1757. He left his dwelling plantation with all the land on the Bay Side east of the Creek and Branch of Plum Point to his wife and executrix Betty Heighe for life. His son James

Heighe was to have two Negroes: Harry, son of Susy, and Moll, daughter of Maria, and a bed. His son Thomas Holdsworth Heighe was to have four Negroes: Genny, daughter of. Maria, Dick, Dinah, and Lucky, all children. of Maria, and a bed. His daughter Ann, wife of George Gantt, was to have a Negro girl Sophia, daughter of. Lucy. Daughter Betty, wife of Joseph Wilkinson, was to have a Negro girl Amey. Daughter Barbara Heighe, a Negro boy Davey, son of Lucy, a Negro girl Rachel, and a bed. Daughter Mary, a Negro boy Will and a bed. Trustees were George Gantt and Joseph Wilkinson. Joseph Wilson, Edward Wilson, Ellis Slater witnessed the will. The widow stood by the will (MWB 43:404 abst. by Gibb).

Betty Heighe, executrix, advertised she would settle the estate (Annapolis *Maryland Gazette* 3 November 1757). She filed an administration account on his estate on 29 July 1765, citing an inventory of £146.10.1, and listing payments of £1471.0.2 (MDAD 53:14).

Betty Heighe was listed in the 1783 Tax List of the First District, with three whites in her household, and owning 203 a. part *Beakley* (Carothers, *1783 Tax List of Maryland:* 171).

James and Betty were the parents of (order of birth uncertain): **13. James; 14. Thomas Holdsworth; 15. Ann,** m. George Gantt; **16. Betty,** m. Joseph Wilkinson; **17. Barbara;** and **18. Mary.**

13. James Heighe, son of Capt. James (7) and Betty, married Elizabeth Mackall who was born in 1743.

He was First Lieutenant of the 15th Battalion of Calvert Co. Militia from April 1776 through April 1778, and he took the Oath of Fidelity in Calvert Co. in 1778 (*RPCV:* 135).

In 1783 James Heighe was listed n the First District of Calvert Co., with five whites in his household, and owning 67 a. part *Beasley,* 34 a. part *Robert's Chance,* 150 a. *Trostre,* 15 a. *Samuel's Addition,* 19 a. part *Chalk Hill,* 11 a. *Little sound,* 1 a. *Hughes' Addition,* and 21 a. *James Addition* (Carothers, *1783 Tax List of Maryland:* 171). He was also listed in the Third District of Calvert Co. as owning 200a. *Cole Kirby,* 150 a. part *Cole's Gifts,* 30 a. part *Gumby,* 100 a. part of *Theobush Manning,* and 63 a. part of *Preston's Clifts* (Carothers, *1783 Tax List of Maryland:* 193).

James and Elizabeth were probably the parents of: **19. James, Jr.,** listed in the 1783 Tax List of the First District of Calvert Co., with one white in his household, and owning no land (Carothers, *1783 Tax List of Maryland:* 170).

14. Thomas Holdsworth Heighe, son of Capt. James (7) and Betty, died by April 1770. About 1766 he married Mary Wheeler, said to have been born about 1750 in Calvert Co., and died there about March 1799.

On 15 April 1770 his estate was appraised. James Heighe and Betty Heighe signed as next of kin, and Betty Heighe, administratrix, filed the inventory on 1 November 1770 (MINV 105:206). Mary [*sic*] Heighe filed an account on 15 December 1771, citing an inventory of £655.10.4, and listing payments of £73.5.0 (MDAD 66:207).

Thomas and Mary were the parents of: **20. Betty Holdsworth,** b. between 1767 and 1771.

20. Betty Holdsworth Heighe, daughter of Thomas Holdsworth (14) and Mary, was born between 1767 and 1771 in Calvert County. She married James Heighe Blake by 21 May 1792. He died 29 July 1819, aged 51. His obituary gives details of his political career (Washington, D.C. *National Intelligencer* 30 July 1819).

In 1783 Betty Heighe was listed in the Third District if Calvert Co. owning 200 a., part of *Stonerly* and 250 a. part of *Lower Bennett.* There were five white inhabitants in

Colonial Families of Maryland II

her household (Carothers, *1783 Tax List of Maryland:* 188).

Unplaced:
Mary Nichols of Calvert Co. made a will on 22 July 1718 leaving personalty to her daughter Mary Heighe, and £10 to be divided among Mary's children when they were of age (MWB 16:57, abst. in *Md. Cal. of Wills* 5:9).

== 0 ==

The Hennis Family of Baltimore County

1. Miles Hennis of Gloucestershire. glassmaker, on 25 July 1685 bound himself to Thomas Whittop to serve for four years in Md. (*BRCO*: 381). He died in Baltimore Co. on 5 February 1720. He married 1st, Elizabeth [-?-], who was buried at Swan Creek on 4 August 1697, and 2nd, on 24 November 1698, when the banns were published, Elizabeth Kelley (Reamy and Reamy, *St. George's Parish Register:* 3, 4, 21).

Hannis was a creditor of the estate of Thomas Peverill of Baltimore Co. on 15 May 1694 (INAC 12:129). On 27 July 1696 Hannis was listed as a debtor to the estate of Col. George Wells (INAC 15:8). On 4 March 1703/4 Miles Hannis and others were left personalty in the will of James Ines of Baltimore Co. (MWB 3:4, abst. in *Md. Cal. of Wills* 3:30). On 21 March 1702/3 John Elliss conveyed 50 a. *Bedlam,* part of *Expectation,* to Miles 'Hannes.' On 3 February 1706 'Hannis' conveyed the same 50 a. to Tobias Eminson. On 2 March 1708 Eminson conveyed the tract back to Miles Hannis (BALR HW#2:287, RM#HS: 541, 648). On 22 October 1716 John and Martha Hall conveyed 150 a. *Robin Hood's Forest* to Miles Hannis On 26 March 1717 Hannis conveyed two-thirds of the tract, now called *William and Sarah's Inheritance,* to William Robinson (BALR TR#A:450, 522). On 6 December 1718 Samuel Jackson leased *Jackson's Adventure* to Miles Hannis and wife Elizabeth for their lifetimes (BALR TR#A: 10).

Miles Hannes was the father of (by 1st wife) (Reamy and Reamy, *St. George's Parish Register:* 1, 3): **2. Thomas,** b. 23 September 1695 at Rumly Creek; **3. Michael,** b. 20 December, and bur. 28 December 1696 at Rumly Creek; and **4:** (Probably) **William.**

4. William Hannes, is placed as a son of Miles (1) because on 27 August 1720 William Hannis and his wife Elizabeth conveyed Elizabeth conveyed 50 acres of *Robin Hood's Forest* to Benjamin Osborne (BALR IS#G:133).

== 0 ==

The Hickson Family of Baltimore County
With Notes on the Lee Family

1. Joseph Hickson, aged 21, of Grantham, Lincolnshire, grocer, on 3 February 1724 signed his name when he bound himself to serve Christopher Veale of Shoreditch, Co. Middlesex, for five years in Md. (Kaminkow, *List of Emigrants:* 111). He evidently died by June 1735.

Joseph Hickson married Jane Wilson; she married, 2nd, John Lee on 10 June 1735 (Reamy and Reamy. *St. George's Parish Register:* 48).

Joseph and Jane were the parents of the following, born in St. George's Parish, Baltimore (now Harford) Co. (Reamy and Reamy, *St. George's Parish Register:* 44): **2.**

90

Hester, b. August 1727; and **3. Hannah,** b. 2 September 1729.

John and Jane (Wilson) (Hickson) Lee were the parents of (Reamy and Reamy, *St. George's Parish Register:* 49, 57): **4. Johanna,** b. 7 February 1735/6; and **5. Mary,** b. 3 November 1738.

Unplaced:
Anne Hickson and John Crokat were married on 25 December 1744 (*SJSG:* 122).
Thomas Hickson signed the petition for the removal of the county seat to Baltimore Town in 1768 (*IBCP:* 29).

==0==

The Hitchcock Family of Baltimore Co.
With Notes on the Tye Family

1. George Hitchcock, schoolmaster, died by November 1747. Some time prior to 29 July 1713 he married Mary, widow of Teague Tracey (INAC 35B: 29).

On 7 August 1717 Hitchcock and Thomas Hooker appraised the estate of George Picket (INAC 39C:73).
///eyeballed to here

On 1 April 1712 he purchased from Elizabeth Roberts, widow of John, 250 a. called *Hitchcock's Folly,* originally called *Roberts' Forest* (BALR TR#A:184). On 4 November 1724 James Tracey conveyed 100 a. *Tracey's Park* to George Hitchcock (BALR IS#G: 397). On 12 February 1736 Hitchcock conveyed this 100 a. to his daughter Persosha Tye and her husband John Tye, Jr. (BALR IS#IK: 352). On 1 January 1730 George Hitchcock, miller, conveyed 205 a. and 22½ a., parcels of *Hitchcock's Folly* to William Parrish (BALR IS#L: 54). On 1 August 1747 George Hitchcock and John Tye and wife Porsoche [*sic*] conveyed 100 a. *Tracey's Park* to Thomas Foy (BALR TB#E: 506).

George Hitchcock died leaving a will dated 23 d, 8 mo., 1747, proved 4 November 1747, His grandson George Tye was to have his dwelling plantation and house, mills and improvements; if he died for want of heirs, this as to pass to his sister Eleanor Tye. His granddaughter Eleanor Tye was to have the 50 a. conveyed to him by William Knight and called *Knight's Addition.* Grandson George was to have slaves. He also named his granddaughter Susanna Tye, and son and daughter John and Presocia Tye. Wife Mary and son-in-law John Tye were named executors. Henry Saylor, John Cook, and Aquila Carr witnessed the will (MWB 25:164-165, abst. in *Md. Cal. of Wills* 9:124).

The estate of George Hitchcock was inventoried on 21 December 1747 by Samuel Owings and John Willmott, Jr., who appraised his property at £180.3.3. John Bond and Mary Walker signed as creditors, and Mary Hitchcock and Mary Tracey signed as kin.

John Tye, executor, filed the inventory on 13 February 1747 (MINV 35:440).

George and Mary were the parents of: **2. Presiota,** m. John Tye.

2. Presiota Hitchcock, daughter of George (1) and Mary, married John Tye in St, Paul's Parish on 11 December 1735 (Reamy and Reamy, *St. Paul's Parish Register* 1:32).

On 7 June 1732 John Rutledge conveyed *Clay* to John 'Teye;' Rutledge's wife Jane consented (BALR IS#L: 250). On 11 November 1738 John Tye patented 50 a. *Park* (MPL El#2: 834, El#3: 526). On 30 March 1741 John Tye, son of this earlier John Tye, conveyed 50 a. *Clay* and 50 a. *The Park* to Richard Clark. Tye's wife Preciosa consented (BALR HWS#1-A: 492).

Colonial Families of Maryland II

On 1 Aug 1747 George Hitchcock and John Tye and wife Porsoche [*sic*] conveyed 100 a. *Tracey's Park* to Thomas Foy (BALR TB#E: 506).

John Tye died by July 1754 when his widow Presiota conveyed to Thomas Cockey Deye land which George Hitchcock had left to his grandson George Tye (*BCF:* 654).

John and Presiota were the parents of: **3. George; 4. Eleanor;** and **5. Susanna.**

3. George Tye, son of John and Presiota (2), was living in 1763 when he was listed in the tax list of Back River Upper Hundred (*IBCP:*6). He died testate by June1813, having married Ruth [-?-].

In January 1760 he was present at the wedding of Richard Belt to Keturah Price at Gunpowder Monthly Meeting. In January 1772 he was present at the wedding of Mordecai Price to Tabitha Tipton, also at Gunpowder Monthly Meeting (Peden, *QRNM*: 47, 51).

In 1783 George Tye was listed as the owner of 100 a. part *Broad Meadow* in Middle River Upper and Back River Upper Hundred. His household consisted of four white taxables (Carothers, *1783 Tax List of Md.:* 60).

George Tye died leaving a will dated 19 July 1809 and proved 30 June 1813. He left his estate to his wife Ruthy whom he named as executor. Aquila Tipton, Joshua Tipton, John Tipton, and John Bond witnessed the will (BAWB 9:333, abst. by Burns).

==0==

The Joseph Hook Family of Baltimore County

A. [-?-] Hook, probably of Basel, Switzerland, was the father of two sons who came to Maryland: **1. Joseph,** b. c.1720; and **2. Jacob,** b. about 1725.

1. Joseph Hook was born about 1720, probably at Basel, Switzerland and died in Baltimore Co. by 10 May 1773 when his will was probated. He married Barbara [-?-], who was living on 13 March 1775. He was a brother of Jacob Hook.

Joseph Hook and Jacob Hook, Germans, were naturalized in Baltimore Co. on 6 September 1769 when they took communion from Rev. Faber (Provincial Court Judgment Records DD#16:13).

Joseph Hook died leaving a will dated 13 March 1773 and proved 10 May 1773. His son Jacob was to have one acre where he now lives, being part of *Cole's Adventure,* bought from John Dimmitt. His wife 'Barbery' was to have 3½ a. adjoining the above, and all the rest of his estate, to raise his children, now under age. Of this land, Joseph, Margaret and Barbary Hook were to have one acre, Joseph to have first choice, and whoever got the improved acre was to make the others equal. The other one-half acre to daughter Osilla Hook. The rest of his estate was to be divided among all his children Wife Barbary and John Stoler were named executors. Robert Dew, John Demmitt and

Deeter Berger witnessed the will. On 10 May 1773 the widow renounced the division and claimed her legal settlement, but [finally] accepted, (BAWB 3:246).

On 10 May 1774 Barbara Hook and John Stoler, executors, posted an administration bond of £300. Rudolph Hook and Deeter Barger were sureties.

On 25 April 1783 Barbara Hook and John Stoler administered the estate of Joseph Hook (BAAD 8:104). Barbara Hook and John Stoler rendered another account on 26 February 1787. They paid money to Joseph Hook for the use of the representatives of the deceased (BAAD 9:18). On 6 March 1778 they filed another account and paid money to the accounts and mentioned a legacy to Joseph Hook, Jr. (BAAD 9:170).

Joseph and Barbara were the parents of: **3. Joseph; 4. Margaret; 5. Barbara; 6.**

Osilla, who stated that Joseph Hook had d. some 13 years ago, and had left a legacy to his daughter Osilla, who in 1787 petitioned the court that she had not yet received her legacy (Petition of Joseph Hook, 1787, BPET Box 2, Folder 23); 7. **Anne,** daughter of Joseph and Barbara, d. 22 April 1798 and was buried in the Episcopal Cemetery (Reamy and Reamy, *St. Paul's Parish Register:* 117; *Memoirs:* 59); and **8. John,** son of Barbara Hook, died 21 October 1801 and was buried in the Episcopal Cemetery (*Memoirs:* 203).

2. Jacob Hook, almost certainly a brother of Joseph Hook, died prior to January 1801. He married Ursula [-?-].

On 26 April 1746 James Henthorne and his wife Mary, conveyed 100 a. *Providence* to Jacob Hook, weaver (BALR TB#E: 49).

Jacob Hook, a native of Basel, Switzerland, died Friday, 5th inst., at Hookstown in his 76th year. His wife, aged 82, was now separated from the husband with whom she lived in the bonds of union for 53 years (*Federal Gazette and Baltimore* 8 Dec 1800).

Jacob Hook died leaving a will dated 18 December 1795 and proved 10 January 1801. He named his wife Ursula, two children of Arnold Louis: John Jacob, and Ursula (who were to have the land leased from Charles Carroll), and Barbara wife of Arnold Louis. His wife Ursula was named executrix. George Dowig, Peter Beam and Cornelius Howard witnessed the will (BAWB 6:344, abst. by Burns).

Mrs. Ursula Hook, relict of the late Jacob Hook, died last Thurs. at Hookstown, near Baltimore, in her 85th year (*Federal Gazette and Baltimore Advertiser* 25 June 1803).

Ursula Hook died leaving a will dated 19 February 1801 and proved 6 October 1804. All her personal estate was to go to John Jacob Loos, son of Arnold Loos, and to Ursula Oppe, daughter of the said Arnold. John Jacob Loos was named executor. Caleb Merryman, Barbara Loos, and John Hasselbach witnessed the will (BAWB 7:325, abst. by Burns).

On 22 February 1804 it was ordered that Jacob Loos, executor of Jacob Hook, deceased, deliver over the personal estate of the said Jacob Hook, agreeable to the inventory thereof returned to this court, to Jno. Hasselback and John Mumma his securities, the said Jacob Loos refusing and not complying with the order of this court in giving counter security agreeable to the prayer of the petition. (BAOC 5:60)

3. Joseph Hook, son of Joseph (1) married by 3 May 1787 Sophia, daughter of John and Esther Jones, whose will of that date named her daughter Sophia, wife of Joseph Hooke, who was named executor by Hester (Esther) Jones (BAWB 4:254, abst. by Burns; BAAD 10:68).

Cole's Adventure and the Hooks

On 12 February 1774 John Demmitt conveyed to Jacob Hook 4¼ a., 39 sq. p., of *Big Basil* or part *Little Basil*, or part of *Cole's Adventure* (BALR AL#D: 95).

On 12 February 1774 John Demmitt conveyed ¾ a. and 20 sq. p. of *Cole's Adventure* to Jacob Hook, Jr. (BALR AL#1: 95).

13 June 1805: Joseph Hook conveyed one a. part *Cole's Adventure* to Barbara Hennick; land is in Hookstown, adj. Jacob Hook's part (BALR WG#85: 283).

Unplaced:

Andrew Hooke was a Private in Capt. Sheaff's Company on 16 June 1777 when he 'pleaded his age." He was a Non-Juror to the Oath of Allegiance in 1778 (*BARP* 132). He and his wife Margaret stated they had consented to live apart (*Maryland Gazette or Baltimore General Advertiser* 20 February 1784). Andrew Hooke administered the estate of John Summers of Baltimore Co. on 14 April 1786 (BAAD 8:261).

Ann Hook, an orphan girl of the age of six years, came into court on 11 February 1804 and the court appointed Barbara Hook her guardian, who accepts and offers Andrew Bailer and Benjamin Eden as her securities (BAOC 5:49).

Anthony Hook died leaving a will dated 4 September 1795 and proved 19 March 1800. He named his wife Mary, his son Jacob, and sons-in-law John Walton, Benjamin Night (Knight?), and Henry Orban. He named Joseph Hook, and his youngest son George Hook who was to be taught the brick making trade. His wife Mary was named executrix. Wm. Graham and Francis Zeigler witnessed the will (BAWB 6:409, abst. by Burns).

Barenhard Hooke died by 12 February 178[?] when his executors Michael Howke and Peter Gratia posted an administration bond for £3000. John Burns and Geo. Weaver were sureties (BAAB 5:144).

Hetty Hook, daughter of Capt. Joseph Hook, and Peter Hedges, all of Baltimore, were married last Tuesday by Rev. Dashiells (*Baltimore American* 12 December 1805).

Jacob Hook and Elizabeth Campbell were married 23 November 1784. They were the parents of ("Hook Bible: New Testament Printed Edinburgh, 1799," *MGSB* 20 (4) (Fall 1979): 344; Reamy and Reamy, *St. Paul's Parish Register* 2:26): Rebeccah, b. 31 January 1785; Frederick C., b. 3 August 1786, d. 3 January 1823, aged 36 years and 5 mos,; Conrad, b. 25 March 1788, d. 16 December 1830 in his 43rd year; Keturah, b. 3 February 1790; Thomas, b. 20 April 1792; Mary, b. 14 December 1793; Joshua, b. 19 July 1796; Sarah, b. 20 November 1798; Cornelius, b. 3 July 1800 (not shown in the Bible); Jacob Washington, b. 17 June 1802; Elizabeth, b. 8 May 1804; Harriet, b. 20 May 1806, and Marques, b. 14 Dec 1808.

Jacob Hook married by 19 May 1805 Susannah, daughter of Sarah Boone (BAWB 8:156, abst. by Burns).

Joseph Hook married Margaret [-?-]. They were the parents of (Reamy and Reamy, *St. Paul's Parish Register:* 61): James Hervey, b. 19 June 1791, bapt. 23 April 1792.

Capt. Joseph Hook, and Miss Ann Conn, daughter of Capt. Daniel Conn, were married Sat. 11th inst., by Rev. Dr. Roberts (*Baltimore American* 15 November 1815).

Margaret Hook, aged 25, and John M. Glathary, aged 85, stone-cutter, were married last Thurs. eve (*Maryland Journal and Baltimore Advertiser* 28 November 1795).

Michael Hook, and Miss Elizabeth Stagers, all of Baltimore, were m. last Thurs., by Rev. Fenwick (*Baltimore Sun* 16 Oct 1812).

Priscilla Hook, and John Grace, both of Baltimore Co., were m. last eve. at Hookstown by Rev. Ralph (*Federal Gazette and Baltimore Advertiser* 7 October 1811).

==0==

The Rudolph Hook Family of Baltimore County

1. Rudolph Hook died in Baltimore Co. some time before November 1775. He married Ursula [-?-] who was named in the administration account of 1789.

On 7 September 1768 he and Balser Lambert and Felix Seigarsar were naturalized when they took communion from Rev. Chase at St. Paul's Church in Baltimore. (Provincial Court Judgment Records 15:16).

Hook died leaving a will dated 23 September 1775 and proved 2 October 1775. His eldest son Rudolph was to have 100 a. from Charles Carroll, and he was to pay £75.0.0 to his brothers and sisters except Jacob, If he died without issue, his land was to be equally divided among his brothers. Son Jacob was also to have 100 a. from Charles Carroll, and he was to pay £25.0.0 to his brothers and sisters. If he died without issue, his land was to be divided among his brothers. His sons Frederick and Conrad were to have two lots in Baltimore Town. If either died without issue, the land was to go to his brothers. The rest of his personal estate was to go to Frederick and Conrad and his two daughters. Frederick Myers and Jacob Hook were named executors. George Risteau, Mich. Kramer, and John Showers witnessed the will (BAWB 3:309, abst. by Burns).

Frederick Myer and Jacob Hook posted an administration bond for £1000. William Lavely and Jacob Kerns were sureties (BAAB 3:336). On 6 March 1778 Jacob Hook and Frederick Myers administered his estate (BAAD 8:23). The two executors filed another account on 25 April 1789. The deceased had left a widow Ursula, sons Conrad and Frederick, and two daughters Elizabeth, and Margaret wife of John Border. They mentioned money due Joseph Hook (BAAD 9:325).

Richard and Ursula were the parents of ('michellemargraf,' "The Thelen and Margraf Family Tree Web Site," posted on GenForum):

Rudolph was the father of: **2. Rudolph**, b. 1754, d. 4 November 1823; **3. Jacob**. b. 1756, d. 1841; m. Elizabeth Campbell; **4. Conrad**, d. 20 July 1824; **5. Frederick**, b. 1764, d. 1 September 1834; m. Sarah Keyser on 17 September 1794; **6. Elizabeth**, m. William Caploe; and **7. Margaret**, m. John Border.

2. Rudolph Hook, son of Rudolph (1) and Ursula, was born 1754, and died 4 November 1823. He married Catherine Ritter by a license dated 14 Jan 1778, Catherine was a daughter of Anthony and Elizabeth ([-?-]) Ritter, and was b. after 1757 (BAML; 'michellemargraf,' "The Thelen and Margraf Family Tree Web Site," posted on GenForum):

In her will made 18 March 1815 Elizabeth Kitchpole named Rudolph Hook, son of Rudolph Hook, Elizabeth Hackley, and Catherine Hook. She named Rudolph Hook, Sr., as executor. Jonathan Hook was one of the witnesses (BAWB 10:915, abst. by Burns).

Rudolph Hook died leaving a will dated 6 November 1823 and proved 29 November 1823. He named his children, Ann, John, Rudolph, Jonathan, Joseph, Jesse, Josias, and Johns. Sons John and Rudolph and daughter Ann Hook were named executors. Philemon Coale, Solomon Hook, and Henry Ritter witnessed the will (BAWB 11:616, abst.. by Burns).

Rudolph and Catherine were the parents of (Reamy and Reamy, *St. Paul's Parish Register* 1: 59, 61, 122; 'michellemargraf,' "The Thelen and Margraf Family Tree Web Site," posted on GenForum): **8. John**, b. 11 January 1779; m. Nancy Walker about 1801; **9. Jonathan**, b. 8 May 1780; **10. Henry**, b. 29 September 1781; **11. Jesse**, b. 7 May 1783; **12. Joseph**, b. 9 March 1785; **13. Josias**, b. 21 February 1787; m. Sophia Spedden on or about 3 September 1816; **14. Elizabeth**, b. 15 July 1789; m. [-?-] Kitchpool; **15. Ann**, b. 20 December 1791; m. Robert C. Happel in April 1825; **16. Jesse**, b. 7 May 1793; **17. John**, b. 1795; and **16. Rodolph**, b. 1 February 1798; m. Mary Ann Watts.

3. Jacob Hook, son of Rudolph (1), was born about 1747 and died on 19 June 1815 in Baltimore Co. He married Elizabeth Huckin, born about 1749, died 20 June 1815, on 26 December 1769 at the First German Reformed Church in Baltimore,. She was buried at McKendree Methodist Church, Baltimore Co. (Data supplied by Douglas Richardson in a private communication to the author).

In 1763 a Jacob Hook and Samuel Hooke signed a petition for the legislature to levy a tax of three pounds of tobacco on the taxable inhabitants of St. Paul's Parish to hire an organist to play the 'very good organ' at St. Paul's Church (*ARMD* 61:499-500).

Jacob Hook died leaving a will dated 17 March 1815 and proved 8 July 1815. He left his estate, including his property in Hook's Town to his wife Elizabeth. He did not name his children, but a codicil named Mary and John Hook, and John and Ann Taylor. Samuel Billingsley and Priscilla Grace were named executors. Laban Welch, Robert Williams and Mathew Chambs [sic] witnessed the will (BAWB 10:50, abst. by Burns).

Jacob and Elizabeth were the parents of (Data supplied by Douglas Richardson): **17. Jacob**, m. 21 May 1795 at the first Methodist Episcopal Church in Baltimore, Susan Boone; **18. Barbara**, m. 21 May 1795, at the First Methodist Episcopal Church in Baltimore, Thomas Taylor; **19. Mary; 20. Priscilla**, m. 5 October 1811, at the First Methodist Episcopal Church in Baltimore, John Grace (*Federal Gazette and Baltimore Advertiser* 7 October 1811 stated they were m. last evening at Hookstown, by Rev. Ralph); **21 Catherine**, b. about 1785/9, on 19 June 1805 at Trinity Protestant Episcopal Church, m. Samuel Billingsley, and in 1870 was living in Perry Twp., Franklin Co., Ohio; **22. Margaret Ann**, b. 1788, d. about 1850, m. on 16 December 1805 at the Zion German Lutheran Church, Court House Plaza in Baltimore, John Goodshine McClatchie; and **23. Ann**, m. on 29 September 1812 at the First Methodist Episcopal Church in Baltimore, John Taylor.

4. **Conrad Hook**, son of Rudolph (1), was named in his father's will. He was almost certainly the Conrad Hook, native of Baltimore, who died at Charleston, S.C., on 10th March 1805 in his 38th year, leaving a widow and two daughters (*Federal Gazette and Baltimore Advertiser* 4 April 1805).

5. **Frederick Hook**, son of Rudolph (1), was born about 1752 in Baltimore Co. and died in 1814. He is buried in the Hook Family Cemetery at Brooklandville, Baltimore Co. During the Revolutionary War he served as ensign (Henry C. Peden, *Revolutionary Patriots of Maryland, 1775-1783; A Supplement*. Westminster: Willow Bend Books, 2000: 109). He married Sarah Keyser (Darlene Cannon on Gen Forum).

Frederick and Sarah were the parents of (Darlene Cannon on Gen Forum; Reamy and Reamy, *St. Paul's Parish Register* 2:7): **24. Valentine**, b. 14 February 1798; and **25. Isaac O.**, b. 21 January 1801

12. **Joseph Hook**, son of Rudolph (2) and Catherine, was born 9 March 1785 and died before January 1874. On or about 18 December 1811 he married Hannah Alder, born by 1795, died 1869, the daughter of Robert and Mary (Nice) Alder ('michellemargraf,' "The Thelen and Margraf Family Tree Web Site," posted on GenForum).

Joseph and Hannah were the parents of: **26. Robert; 27. Catherine**, m. Joseph McMachen on 16 December 1842; **28. William A.; 29. Emeline**, d. 1839; **30. Rudolph**, b. 1814; m. Eliza A. C. Hobbs on 2 May 1843; **31. Joseph**, b. about 1824; **32. Elizabeth A.**, b. about 1828; and **33. Martha Ellen**; m. [-?-] Lowry.

==()==

The Hughes Family of Baltimore County
With Notes on the Matthews and Rhodes Families.

1. **Joseph Hughes or Hewes**, was transported by 1662 (MPL 5:304). Elizabeth Hewes, wife of Joseph Hewes, had one head right by 1669 (MPL 12:523). Joseph Hughes died by 1700.

In Aug 1669 Hughes surveyed 150 a. *Chance*. It was later in the possession of Thomas Preston who had married the heiress of said Hughes (MRR:62). In April 1671 Hughes made his mark when he sold 100 a. *Red Budd Point* to Thomas Heath (BALR IR#PP: 103). On 28 January 1672/3, Joseph Hughes, carpenter, agreed to pay Thomas

Heath for the land he had recently bought or he would resurvey the land to Heath (BALR IS#IK: 44,45).

Joseph Hewes was mentioned in the administration account of Thomas Carleton of Cecil Co. as being dead (INAC 4:391).

Joseph and Elizabeth were the parents of: **2. Sarah**, m. 1st, Thomas Preston, and 2nd, Henry Matthews.

2. Sarah Hughes, daughter of Joseph (1) Hughes, married 1st, Thomas Preston, and 2nd, Henry Matthews.

Thomas Preston had married some time after 10 August 1669, [-?-], heiress of Joseph Hughes (*Md. Rent Rolls,* 62). Preston died by 6 November 1730 (or 1739) when his estate was administered by Sarah Preston (BAAD 2:252).

Henry Matthews evidently married Sarah, daughter of Joseph Hughes and widow of Thomas Preston.

On 3 Aug 1697 Thomas Heath and wife Sarah conveyed 50 a. *Blocksedge,* 50 a. *Hughes Island,* and 115 a. *Heath's Addition* to Henry Matthews (BALR IS#IK: 154). On 1 March 1702 James Phillips of Baltimore Co., with consent of wife Bethia, conveyed 100 a. *Plumb Point* to Henry Matthews (BALR HW#2: 310).

Henry Matthews died leaving a will dated 6 June 1720 and proved 5 April 1726. His daughter Sarah was to have 100 a. *Hewses Chance* and personalty. He named an orphan boy Abraham Kinsbie. His wife was to have *Matthews Double Purchase* for life and at her death, to daughters Mary and Elizabeth. Daughter Catherine Whaland and her heirs were to have the residue of *Hewses Chance* and *Plumb Point.* Daughters Catherine, Mary, and Sarah were to have 5 s. each. Charles Baker, John and Mary Sumner, and Rachel Smith witnessed the will (MWB 18:490 abst. in *Md. Cal. of Wills* 5:222).

Robert Robeson and William Smith appraised the personal estate of Henry Mathews at £522.8.2. 'Patrick Whayleand' and William Rhoads, who had married daughters of the deceased, signed as next of kin. Sarah Mathews, executrix, filed the inventory on 2 November 1726 (MINV 11:675).

Henry and Sarah were the parents of: **3. Catherine**, m. Patrick Whayland (See The Whayland Family elsewhere in this work); **4. Mary**, m. by 1721 William Rhodes; **5. Sarah**, b. 25 April 1702 (*SJSG:* 3), m. 1st, Thomas Cross, and 2nd, Thomas Price; **6. Elizabeth**, b. 10 July 1708.

4, Mary Matthews, daughter of Henry and Sarah (Hughes) (2) Matthews, m. on 17 January 1717, William Rhodes (*SJSG:* 15).

William Rhodes signed the inventory of Henry Matthews as one of the next of kin. On 11 July 1727 he received a payment from the estate of James Phillips (MDAD 8:297). On 19 March 1742, as the administrator, he filed the inventory of William Beaver's estate (MINV 27:240).

On 24 November 1731 William Rhoades and wife Mary, daughter of Henry Matthews, conveyed one-half of *Matthews Double Purchase* to William Smith (BALR IS#L: 185). On 5 June 1734 Thomas Cross conveyed 10 a. of *Hughes Chance,* out of the 50 a. to which he was entitled to, to William Rhodes; part of 150 a. *Hughes' Chance.* His wife Sarah consented (BALR HWS#M: 67). On 8 Aug 1734 Rhodes conveyed 60 a. *Hughes Chance* to Theophilus Jones and wife Elizabeth; Rhodes had bought 50 a. from Thomas League (who bought it from Patrick Whayland and wife Catherine, who inherited it from her father Henry (Matthews), and 10 a. from Thomas Cross who m. Sarah, daughter of Henry (Matthews?); William's wife Mary consented (BALR HWS#M: 90).

William and Mary were the parents of (*SJSG:* 21, 94, 134): **12. Mary,** b. 2 March 1719; **13. Elizabeth,** b. 30 August 1721; she may be the Elizabeth Rhodes who m. Richard Cosley on 7 July 1752; **14. (prob.)** John, b. 20 September 1738; he may be the John Rhodes who m. Sarah Standiford on 25 October 1769.

5. Sarah Matthews, daughter of Henry and Sarah (2), was born 25 April 1702, and married 1st, by June 1727 Thomas Cross, and 2nd, on 4 May 1743,Thomas Price (BALC HWS#3,#5; BALR IS#:L:77, HWS#M: 67, 90; Reamy and Reamy, *St. George's Parish Register:* 69).

In June 1727 Thomas Cross petitioned the court that he possessed *(Hughes') Chance,* laid out for Joseph Hughes on 1 August 1669, in right of his (Cross') wife Sarah (BALC HWS#3, # 5). On 2 April 1728 Thomas Cross of Baltimore Co., cordwainer, and wife Sarah, conveyed 50 a. of *Hughes' Chance* to James Standiford (BALR IS#1: 77). On 8 March 1731 Cross, with consent of wife Sarah, conveyed 140 a., one-half of *Matthews' Double Purchase,* alias *Heaths Addition,* to Henry Wetherall (BALR IS#L: 198).On 5 June 1734 Cross, with consent of Sarah, conveyed 10 a. out of the 50 a. (part of 150 a.) of *Hughes' Chance* to which he was entitled, to William Rhodes (BALR HWS#M: 67). On 8 March 1731 Cross, cordwainer, and wife Sarah conveyed to Henry Weatherall one-half of *Mathews Double Purchase,* alias *Heath's Addition* 140 a. (BALR IS#L: 198).

On 5 June 1734 Cross, with Sarah's consent, conveyed 10 a. out of the 50 a. (part of 150 a.) of *Hughes' Chance* to which he was entitled, to William Rhodes (BALR HWS#M: 67). On 8 Aug 1734 William Rhodes conveyed 60 a. *Hughes' Chance.* to Theophilus Jones and wife Elizabeth; Rhodes had bought 50 a. from Thomas League (who bought it from Patrick Whayland and wife Catherine, who inherited it from her father Henry (Matthews), and 10 a. from Thomas Cross who had m. Sarah, daughter of Henry Matthews; William's wife Mary consented (BALR HWS#M: 90).

On 14 May 1748 Sarah Price, widow of Thomas Price, conveyed 40 a. part *Chance,* in all a 150 a. tract, to Edward Brucebanks (BALR TR#C: 16).

== 0 ==

The Morgan Jones Family

1. Morgan Jones, of Anne Arundel Co. was buried on 13 September 1718 in St. James Parish (*AACR:* 163). He first appeared in MD when he was listed as a servant in the April 1676 inventory of Jery Sudenant of Anne Arundel Co. (INAC 2:218). Skordas lists several individuals of the name, but Morgan Jones of Anne Arundel Co. was probably the Morgan Jones who was transported by c1674. (MPL 15:431 and 18:121). He married Jane, daughter of John Whipps, whose will of 10 December 1716 named his children, including a daughter Jane Jones. (MWB 14:172; MDTP 38:172). However, a Jane Jones was buried in St. James Parish on 18 April 1711. (AACR: 159).

Morgan Jones may have been illiterate, since, on 26 January 1694, he made his mark on a deed. (AALR WH#4:49). Nevertheless, he prospered. On 26 January 1694, as Morgan Jones, cooper, he purchased 40 a. *Eagle's Nest,* surveyed in 1679 for Nicholas Gross. (AALR WH#4: 52; MRR: 133). On 10 March 1717, as Morgan Jones, carpenter,

he purchased 100 a. from Robert Sollers (AALR IB#2: 504). By about 1707, he had acquired 25 a. of Carter, a 600 a. tract originally surveyed in 1651 for Capt. Edward Carter in Herring Creek Hundred. (*MRR:* 112).

Morgan Jones died leaving a will dated 18 February 1717 (date of probate not given). He left property which had belonged to Jenerate [Jeremiah] Sullivan to his sons William and Morgan. He left *Elgul Island* to his son John, and personalty to his daus.

Colonial Families of Maryland II

The Morgan Jones Family

Jane and Blanch. Son Morgan was executor and residuary legatee. The will was sworn to by his eldest son William, age c23, and John Standforth, age c52. (MWB 15:40, abst. in *Md. Cal. of Wills* 4:195).

Robert Wood and John League appraised the estate of Morgan Jones [date not given] and valued it at £143.6.6. John Jones, Dorothy Powell, and Samuel Chew appraised the inventory. (MINV 1:433). A second inventory was appraised on 15 June 1719 and valued at £25.11.8. William Jones, administrator, filed the inventory on 4 September 1719. (MINV 2:158).

William Jones filed accounts of the estate on 4 and 7 September 1719. Two inventories, worth £143.6.6 and £25.11.8, were mentioned. One of the legatees was daughter Jane Jones" (MDAD 2:201, 215). Another administration account was filed on 10 August 1726 (MDAD 7:486).

Morgan and Jane were the parents of (*AACR* 148, 151, 153, 155, 156, 158): **2. Sybil,** b. 15 December 1691, may have m. [-?-] Wells by about 1730 (MINV 16:25); **3. William,** b. 17 February 1693, bapt. 14 August 1698; **4. Dorothy,** b. 4 May 1696, bapt. 14 August 1698, may have m. 1st, by about 1718, [-?-] Powell, and 2nd, by 1746, [-?-] Wood; **5. John,** b. 7 April 1699, bapt. 7 May 1699; **6. Jane,** b. 12 December 1701, bapt. 5 April 1702; **7. Margery,** b. and d. 18 April 1704; **8. Morgan,** b. 23 August 1706, bapt. 22 September 1706; and **9. Blanche,** bapt. 24 April 1709.

3. William Jones, son of Morgan (1) and Jane, was born 17 February 1693. He gave his age as about 23 in 1717, and died by May 1730. He is probably the William Jones who married Hannah Norris (about 1715, but date not given) in St. James Parish. (*AACR:* 162). William probably married 2nd, Mary [-?-].

William Jones of Anne Arundel Co., planter, conveyed 40 a. of *Eagle's Nest* to William Ford of Anne Arundel Co. (AALR RD#1:14).

The estate of William Jones, of Anne Arundel Co. was appraised by Thomas Wells and George Henderson and valued at £111.3.7. Sebell Wells and Morgan Jones signed as next of kin. Mary Jones, administratrix, filed the inventory on 29 May 1730 (MINV 1:25).

William and Hannah were the parents of (*AACR:* 164): **10. William,** b. 22 October 1718 in St. James Parish.

5. John Jones, son of Morgan (1) and Jane, was born 7 April 1699 and bapt. 7 May 1699 in St. James Parish.

He may be the John Jones who m. Mary [-?-], and had a son (*AACR:* 164): **11. John,** b. 30 July 1719, bapt. 7 June 1720 in St. James Parish.

8. Morgan Jones, son of Morgan (1) and Jane, was born 23 August 1706, bapt. 22 September 1706, and evidently died by 1747. By 1733, he had married Susan [-?-], who married as her second husband John Dowell. (MDAD 41:23).

On 12 March 1738 Morgan Jones was one of the Vestrymen and Church Wardens of St. James Parish who signed a bond concerning the 40 lbs. of tobacco (AALR RD#3:129).

Abraham Birckhead, Sr., of Anne Arundel Co., on 4 January 1744, "for love and affection" conveyed a Negro slave to his cousin Morgan Jones (AALR RB#2:37).

On 6 October 1746, Morgan Jones' personal estate was appraised by Joseph Chew, James Tongue (who died), and John Wood, and valued at £492.13.6. Dorothy Wood signed as next of kin, and Susanna Dowell (lately Susanna Jones), administratrix, filed the inventory on 14 May 1747 (MINV 34:300).

On 13 December 1750, another inventory was taken by Richard Smith and Joseph Chew, and valued at £104.5.9. John Wood and Dorothy Wood were mentioned. Susanna Dowell, wife of John Dowell, administratrix, filed the inventory on 15 March 1750. (MINV 44:437).

Morgan and Susan were the parents of (*AACR:* 165, 167): **12. Morgan**, b. 16 September 1733, bapt. 14 October 1733 in St. James Parish; and **13. Susanna**, b. 24 September 1735.

5. Morgan Jones, son of Morgan (8) and Susan, was born on 16 September 1733, and bapt. 14 October 1733 in St. James Parish. He is probably the Morgan Jones who married Priscilla, daughter of Sarah Wooden. (MDAD 41:135).

In January 1759/60 Joseph Hill and wife Elizabeth, and Morgan Jones and wife Priscilla, filed a petition in the Chancery Court. The Bill of Complaint stated that Solomon Wooden had died leaving three daughters: Elizabeth, wife of Joseph Hill; Priscilla, wife of Morgan Jones; and Sarah, wife of Charles Connant (MCHR 10:25).

Morgan and Susan had issue, all born in St. James Parish (*AACR:* 171): **14. Sarah**, b. 3 November 1757; **15. Priscilla**, b. 10 February 1760; **16. William**, b. 10 April 1763; and **17. Morgan**, b. 10 December 1767.

==0==

The Thomas Jones Family

1. Thomas Jones died after 1696. He married Mary Harrison who was mentioned in the will of Edward Dowse in 1690. She married 2nd, [-?-] Staley (BALR RM#HS: 524; BACP F#1:111).

On 2 September 1671 John Towers conveyed 200 a. *Swan Harbor*; adjacent *Fills Choice* formerly laid out for John Collier, to Thomas Jones (BALR G#J: 44, TR#RA: 33). On 31 October 1687 George Oglesby, tailor, had conveyed 200 a. *Oglesby's Chance* to Edward Dowse. Johanna Oglesby signed with the grantor. (BALR RM#HS: betw. 188 and 240). In 1696 Thomas Jones and wife Mary (formerly Harrison, who was mentioned in the will of Edward Dowse), conveyed *Oglesby's Chance* to Francis Whitehead (BALR RM#HS: 524).

Thomas and Mary were the parents of: **2. Charles**, d. by 1700; **3. Cadwallader**, b, c1670; and **4. Rathvale**, m. Cornelius Harrington.

2. Charles Jones, son of Thomas (1) and Mary, died by 14 June 1701. He married Bridget [-?-], who married 2nd, Edward Smith.

In April 1701 Bridget Jones was paid £11.4.5 as her [husband's] share of the estate of Thomas Jones.

Charles Jones died leaving a will dated and proved 2 June 1701 naming his sons Thomas and Theophilus, and a daughter-in-law Eeula.

Bridget Jones posted an administration bond on 14 June 1701 with William Howard and John Webster as sureties (BAAB 3:370).

Edward Smith held 200 a. *Swan Harbor* for Charles Jones' orphans (*MRR:* 38).

Charles and Bridget were the parents of: **4. Theophilus;** and **5. Thomas**, a minor in 1701.

3. Cadwallader Jones, son of Thomas (1) and Mary, was bon c1670. He married 1st, Mary Ellis, daughter of Peter Ellis (BALR TB#E:157). She died 25 June 1703 (Reamy and Reamy, *St. George's Parish Register*: 9). He married, 2nd, on 30 April 1704 Mary Paywell or Poell.

Jones deposed in 1729 giving his age as 59. On 18 July 1727 Cadwallader Jones conveyed property to Jacob Herrington provided Herrington would maintain Jones and his daughters Avarilla and Frances.

Cadwallader was the father of, by his first wife (Reamy and Reamy, *St. George's Parish Register*: 9): **6. Charles**, b. 25 June 1703; by his second wife: **7. Blanch**, b. 28 January 1706, m. William Dooley on 25 or 21 October 1725; **8. Thomas**,, b. 14 February 1708; **9. Ar'a (Avarilla?)**, b. 22 April 1710; **10 Mary**, b. 13 January 1716; **11. Aquila**, b. 7 June 1721; **12. Frances**, b. 7 May 1722.

4. Theophilus Jones, son of Charles (2) and Bridget, died by 3 March 1735. He married Elizabeth [-?-]. She married 2nd, by 29 September 1737, John Lloyd (BAAB 3:377). He and his wife Elizabeth purchased *Hughes' Chance* (BALR HWS#M:90)..

He died leaving a will dated 15 February 1728/9 and proved 3 March 1735. He named his wife Elizabeth as executrix and left her and her heirs his entire estate provided she should find and provide for his mother, now named Bridget Smith. Thomas Cotrell, William Andrews, Ann Durbin, Thomas Coale (a Quaker), Jos. Middlemore and William Jackson witnessed the will (MWB 21:645, abst. in *Md. Cal. of Wills* 7:169).

John Lloyd, and his wife Elizabeth, executrix on 29 September 1737 posted a bond to administer the estate of Theophilus Jones (BAAB 3:377; MDTP 30:354).

6. Charles Jones, son of Cadwallader (3) and Mary, was born 25 June 1703 and was bapt. 8 August 1703. He married Frances Cobb on 26 December 1727 (Reamy and Reamy, *St. George's Parish Register:* 9, 34). On 1 October 1731 Frances was named as a daughter of James Cobb of Baltimore Co. whose widow Rebecca had m. 2nd, John Hawkins (BAAD 3:155; MDAD 12:476).

Charles and Frances were the parents of (Reamy and Reamy, *St. George's Parish Register:* 34, 53, 68): **13. Benjamin**, b. 4 October 1728; **14. Charles**, b. 12 November 1731; **15. Cadwalader**, b. 11 May1734; **16. Elizabeth**, twin, b. 15 January 1736; **17. Theophilus**, twin, b. 15 January 1736; **17. Frances**, b. 17 July 1739; and **18. Rebecca**, b. 7 February 1741.

11. Aquila Jones, son of Cadwallader (3) and Mary, was born 7 June 1721. He married Elizabeth Brice on 7 May 1741 (Reamy and Reamy, *St. George's Parish Register:* 41).

Aquila and Elizabeth were the parents of (Reamy and Reamy, *St. George's Parish Register:* 41, 72, 73): **18. Mary**, b. 13 April 1741; **19. Charles**, b. 13 April 1744; and **20. Elizabeth**, b. 3 May 1746.

18. Mary Jones, daughter of Aquila (11) and Elizabeth, was born 13 April 1741 (Reamy and Reamy, *St. George's Parish Register:* 41).

In May 1756 she and Thomas Hawkins had been charged with unlawful cohabitation by the Vestry of St. George's Parish; they were admonished and discharged (Reamy and Reamy, *St. George's Parish Register:* 107). She was charged with bastardy at the November 1758 Court (BAMI 1757-1759:164).

Mary Jones was the mother of (Reamy and Reamy, *St. George's Parish Register:* 78): **18a. Aquila**, b. 12 March 1758.

Colonial Families of Maryland II

The Kenley Family of Baltimore and Harford County

1. Daniel Kenley died by May 1796. He married Frances Wells on 6 November 1729 (Reamy and Reamy, *St. George's Parish Register:* 68).

He witnessed a deed in Baltimore County on 20 August 1748 (BALR TR#C: 63). He had moved to York County, Pennsylvania by August 1751 when he and John Wright and George Stevenson advertised that they were to be auditors and an auction of the household goods and effects of Philip Henning (*Pa. Gaz.* 22 August 1751).

Kenly was living in Lancaster Co., Penna. by 23 May 1754 when he was on a grand jury that submitted a complaint to the Justices of the Court of General Quarter Sessions concerning the great abounding Immorality in this borough. One of the complaints was about a Dancing School, "kept for some time in our Court house, and the surprising methods which were taken to obtain it; that some of our magistrates should be so imposed on, when their consent was requested, by desiring the use of the Court house, only as a place to teach the Mathematicks [*sic*]; which, when obtained, was used for a Dancing school; and that when our commissioners understand what use it was put to, and demanded the key, were answered they should not have it, but that they would make use of it, for that they had the consent of the justices (*Pa. Gaz.* 23 May 1754).

Kenly seems to have been teaching in Lancaster Co. himself in 1755, when his son ran away from his master (*Pa. Gaz.* 1 May 1755).

Kenly had returned to Baltimore County by July 1764 when he and Aug. Hartt, at Mount Pleasant (where John Giles resided), in Baltimore County, advertised they would open a school where they would teach Latin and Greek, Logic, Philosophy, Euclid's Elements of Geometry, Trigonometry, Construction of Logarithms, Algebra and bookkeeping after the Italian method, Navigation, Dialing, Mensuration, Extraction of the roots...Computation of Time according to the Julian and Gregorian Account, Elements of Astronomy, Projection of the Spheres...Conic Sections, the Planetary Worlds, or the System of the Sun, according to Ptolemy and Copernicus, the English Language, Grammatically, Composition, pronouncing Orations, Writing, and Arithmetic, both Vulgar and Decimal (Annapolis *Maryland Gazette* 12 July 1764).

In 1768 he signed a petition protesting the removal of the county seat from Joppa to Baltimore Town (*ARMD* 61:577).

In 1790 Daniel Kenly was head of a family in Harford Co., with one white male over 16, one white female, and one slave. Next to him was Richard Kenly, with one white male over 16, two white males under 16, three white females, and two slaves (*1790 Census of Md.:* 77). Samuel Kenly was also head of a family in Harford Co. in 1790 (*1790 Census of Md.:* 78).

Daniel Kenly died by 19 May 1796 when Harford Co. Estate File # 168 (indexed as pertaining to Edward Mitchell) contained a bill of sale, and Samuel Kenly was the administrator. Another Estate File, no. 668, dated 5 April 1796, also indexed as belonging to Edward Mitchell, shows that 'Lemuel' Kenly was the administrator, and the next of kin were Richard and Mary Kenly (Peden, *Heirs and Legatees of Harford County, Maryland, 1774-1802:* 12, 48).

Daniel and Frances were the parents of (Reamy and Reamy, *St. George's Parish Register:* 68; Mrs. Robert Bishop (Peggy) "The Church Register of Churchville Presbyterian Church of Churchville, Roll of Infant Church Members," Maryland, *Maryland Genealogical Society Bulletin* 31 (3) 241): **2. William**, b. 17 March 1741; **3. Elizabeth**, b. March 1743; **4. Susanna**, b. 9 November 1745; **5. Letitia**, b. 11 April 1749, m John Willson by license dated 27 August 1779 (HAML); **6. Sarah**, b. 8 June 1753; **7. Mary**, b. 23 April 1756; **8. Samuel** [Sometimes read as Lemuel], b. 22 August

1758, m. Jane Willson by license dated 5 September 1779 (HAML);   **9. Richard,** b. 3 November 1761, m. Avis Ward by license dated 25 March 1781 (HAML).

2. William Kenly, son of Daniel (1) and Frances, was born 7 March 1741 in St. George's Parish (Reamy and Reamy, *St. George's Parish Register:* 68).

William Kenly..."ran away, on the 21st of April, from the subscriber, living in the Borough of Lancaster, an apprentice lad, named William Kenly, about 15 years of age, of a fresh complexion, and has brown hair: He had on when he went away, a felt hat, half worn bearskin coat, green 'napt' jacket, buckskin breeches, white shirt, worsted stockings, and good shoes. Whoever takes up and secures said apprentice, so that his master may have him again, shall have Forty Shillings reward, and reasonable charges, paid by William Dunlap.N.B. It is supposed he is sent off by his Father Daniel Kenly, schoolmaster in Lancaster, to his grandfather, ---- Wells, in Baltimore County, Maryland, and is harboring him, or some one of that family." (*Pa. Gaz.* 1 May 1755).

== 0 ==

The Henry King Family of Baltimore County

1. Henry King married Tabitha Long, daughter of Thomas and Jane, by 15 April 1698 (MDTP 17: 87). Tabitha may have married, 2nd, by November 1718, but definitely January 1721 Major Thomas Sheredine.

On 24 June 1702 Tabitha King received a payment from Jane Long's estate (INAC 21:377). On 31 Aug 1698 as '...itha' King she received another payment from her mother's estate (INAC 16:208).

The tax lists for Baltimore Co. from 1699 through 1706 show only one Henry King (Raymond B. Clark *Baltimore County Tax Lists, 1699-1706*).

On 3 June 1696 James Todd and wife Elizabeth sold 187 a. *The Plains* (or *Todd's Plains*) to Henry King (BALR IS#IK: 8). on 4 August 1698 Charles Calvert, Lord Baltimore, granted 124 a. *Kingsberry* to Henry King (BALR HW#2: 58).

Henry King died leaving a will dated 18 January 1717 and proved 30 April 1718. His son William and heirs were to have the dwelling plantation of 187 a. *Todd's Plains.* Daughter Mary and her heirs were to have *Kingsberry,* totaling 130 a. The residue of his estate was to be divided among his son and daughter. However the great still was not to be moved or sold. William Tibbs and John Wilmott, Jr., were named joint executors and guardian of the children during their minority. Nich. Rogers, Thomas Sheredine, Sam Maxwell and William Reeves witnessed the will (MWB 14:600, abst. in *Md. Cal. of Wills* 4:161).

Charles Merryman and Benjamin Bowen appraised the personal estate of Henry King at £243.19.5. Thomas Long and John Talbott approved the inventory (MINV 1:381). Mary Maxwell, wife of Samuel Maxwell, administrator, filed an account of the estate of Henry King on 29 September 1720. She cited the inventory cited above and listed payments of £18.3.3 (MDAD 3:356).

Tabitha Long King almost certainly married 2nd Thomas Sheredine. Her son William chose Sheredine as his guardian in November 1718.

Henry and Tabitha were the parents of: **2. William,** minor in January 1717; **3. Mary,** a minor in January 1717, m. Samuel Maxwell by 29 September 1720.

2. William King, son of Henry (1) and Tabitha, was a minor in January 1717. He died by 1750. He married by 10 November 1724 Susanna [-?-] who married, 2nd, Edmond Baxter.

In November 1718 William chose Thomas Sheredine as his guardian (BACP IS#C: 4). He patented 100 a. *King's Adventure* on 7 Feb 1739 (MPL El#5:437, El#6:157. On 10 November 1724 King conv. 124 a. *Kingsbury* and 500 a. *Maiden's Oute* to Thomas Sheredine. His wife Susanna signed (BALR IS#H: 14). In Aug 1726 William King conveyed 187 a. *The Plains* (or *Todd's Plains*) to Thomas Sheredine, but no wife signed (BALR IS#H: 279).

In 1763 William King was a taxable in Back River Upper Hundred (*IBCP:* 5).

On 8 May 1767 Edmond Baxter and wife Susannah, widow of William King, conveyed *King's Adventure,* and *Susannah's Addition to King's Adventure,* in all 20 a., being Susannah's one-third right of dower, to Andrew Buchanan (BALR B#P: 567).

William and Susanna were probably the parents of: **4. Henry.**

4. Henry King, son of William (8) and Susanna, was living on 4 May 1767 when he conveyed 100 a. *King's Adventure* to Andrew Buchanan (BALR B#P:525).

In 1763 King was a taxable in Back River Upper Hundred (*IBCP:* 5).

== 0 ==

The Richard King Families of Maryland

1. Richard King, b. about 1655, d. about 1720

Richard King was born about 1655 and died by 4 August 1720.

He was in Baltimore Co. by 1701 as a taxable in the N. side of Patapsco Hundred and by 1704 he had moved to Elk Ridge Hundred. On 24 January 1707/8 he witnessed the will of Thomas Brown (MWB 12:300, abst. in *Md. Cal. of Wills* 3:114).

On 1 January 1710 Anthony Drew and wife Margaret conveyed 400 a. *Stop Lying* to Richard King. On 6 January 1710 Richard King conveyed the 400 a. *Stopp* [?] to Anthony Drew (BALR TR#A: 103, 104).

Thomas Knight deposed that Richard King was living on 1 May 1719. King died by 4 August 1720 when an administration bond was posted by John Hall and Thomas Randall, with Roger Matthews and Christopher Randall as sureties (MDTP 24:304). His personal property was appraised on 6 March 1720/1 by Roger Matthews and John Clark and valued at £235.11.9. John Hall administered his estate. He is *not known [so far]* to have had any children (BAAD 1:82).

2. Richard King, living 1716 - 1727

He is probably the Richard King who on 3 October 1716 conveyed various movable property to John March, surgeon of Kent Co. (*BCF:* 387).

On 14 October 1727 Richard King conveyed 50 a., part of 100 a. *White Hall* to his daughter Ann Marsh. On 13 June 1728: Richard King, with consent of his wife Mary, conveyed 100 a. *White Hall* to Hyde Hoxton and Lloyd Harris (BALR IS#I: 20, 137.).

Richard King had at least one child: **Ann,** m. by 14 October 1727 John Marsh (For their descendants, see *BCF:* 413).

3. Richard King, died by 1754

C. John King of Merton College, Oxford, matriculated 17 October 1589 as a son of a Gentleman of Norfolk. He was granted his D.D. on 9 July 1615. He was Rector of Stourton, and a Prebendary of Westminster, as of 18 September 1613; he was Canon of Windsor on 23 November 1615, and was later Rector of Islip. He died 7 August 1638 and was buried at St. George's Chapel, Windsor. He married Elizabeth, daughter of Richard Foxcroft of Cambridge by his wife Alice Hodson.

John and Elizabeth were the parents of the following children (Reginald Ames, *The Ames Genealogy:* 12-13): **Nicholas** of Seville, Merchant, b. at Stourton, and d. s.p., 1649; **John**, matriculated at Oxford, and was living 1648/9, m. Judith [-?-] and had issue; **Rachel**, d. 30 March 1664, m. by 27 July 1636 Nathaniel Fields; and **B. Richard**.

B. Richard King, of Upham, son of John (A) and Elizabeth, was Sheriff of London in 1657. He died by May 1668, and was buried at Aldhouse. He left a will dated 6 February 1667, proved 27 May 1668. He married, 1st, Martha, daughter of Edward and Priscilla (Doyley) Goddard. He married 2nd, Mary, daughter of John Marsh of Shenley, Co. Herts., widow, of St. Michaels Queenhithe, Surrey.

By his first wife Richard was the father of (*Ames Genealogy:* 12, 13). **A. Thomas**.

A. Thomas King, son of Richard (B) and Martha (Goddard), resided in St. Dionis Backchurch, where he was buried on 19 December 1728 at the entrance to the South Aisle (Joseph Lemuel Chester, ed. *The Register Booke of Saynte De'nis Backchurch Parishe for Maryages, Chrystenynges and Buryalles Begynnyng in the Yeare of O'r Lord God 1638.* London: the Harleian Society, 1878: 297). A woolen draper, he was age 24 on 10 February 1671/2, when he married at St. Helen Bishopsgate, Anne, daughter of Rev. Richard Roberts of Watford, Co. Herts. She died 9 August 1726 and was buried 13 August at St. Dionis Backchurch.

Thomas and Anne were the parents of *Ames Genealogy:* 12-13): **1. Richard; Samuel**, bur. 10 June 1687 in the S. Aisle (Chester: 254); **Thomas**, bur. 22 August 1682 in the South Aisle (Chester: 248); **Elizabeth**, b. 1675, d. 1688, bur. 20 November 1688 in the South Aisle (Chester: 255); **2.Ann** (see below); **Elizabeth**, m. Jasper Mauduit (brother of William Mauduit of Maryland); and **Martha**, bur. 21 May 1698 in the South Aisle (Chester: 266).

1. Richard King, son of Thomas (A) and Anne, settled in Baltimore Co., Md., where he died by 27 April 1754.

On 9 August 1716 Thomas Chamberlain and wife Mary conveyed 20 a. *Adams' Addition* and 140 a. *God's Providence* to Richard King, being the property mortgaged to him on 2 October 1713 (BALR TR#A: 402).

On 27 April 1754 Richard King's heirs, Thomas Philibrown, Jr., of Devonshire St., London, cooper, and Thomas Wright, and wife Elizabeth of Cullum St., London, woolen draper, conveyed *God's Providence* to William York (BALR BB#1:295).

5. Ann King, daughter of Thomas (A) and Anne, married 20 February 1710/11 at St. Dionis Backchurch, (where she was buried on 6 February 1721/7, aged 42, in the South Aisle), as his first wife Thomas Phillibrun of St. Botolph Bishopsgate, who was buried 13 June 1764 at St. Dionis Backchurch, age 81 (*Ames Genealogy:* 12-13; Chester: 55, 295).

On 27 April 1754 Thomas Phillibrown, Jr., of Devonshire St., London, cooper, and

Colonial Families of Maryland II

Thomas Wright of Cullum Street, woolen draper, and w. Elizabeth, being the heirs of Richard King of BA Co., conveyed 147 a. *God's Providence* to William York (BALR BB#1:295).

RWB Comment: I can find no proof that any of these Richard Kings were the father or the brother of Mary, wife of Edward Stevenson.

== 0 ==

The Knight Family of Baltimore County

1. Thomas Knight married Susanna Simpson on 28 November 1718 (Reamy and Reamy, *St. George's Parish Register:* 19).

Susanna Simpson had been charged with bastardy at the March 1710/11 Court and named Garret Close as the father. She was charged again at the Aug 1716 Court and named James Collins as the father (BACP IS#B: 305, 210, IS#IA: 56). Susanna's daughter, Sarah Collins Simpson, was born 27 Feb 1715 (Reamy and Reamy, *St. George's Parish Register:* 18).

Thomas Knight patented *Knight's Increase* on 24 June 1728 (MPL BC#24:627, IL#B: 205). On 24 June 1724 he sold it to Isaac Butterworth, who sold it to Samuel Hughes (BALR HWS#M: 412). On 15 February 1727, Thomas Knight, schoolmaster, and wife Susanna, of Baltimore Co. conveyed 100 a. *Knight's Increase* on Deer Run to Isaac Butterworth (BALR IS#1:133).

On 22 November 1720 Thomas Knight witnessed the will of William Jenkins of Baltimore Co. (MWB 16:382, abst. in *Md. Cal. of Wills* 5:48). On 28 May 1735 he was a creditor of Richard Jenkins of Baltimore Co. (MINV 22:331).

On 27 April 1723 the vestry agreed that Thomas Knight's allowance for officiating as reader should be 500 pounds per quarter (Reamy and Reamy, *St. George's Parish Register:* 102).

In 1737 Thomas Knight was head of a household in Spesutia Upper Hundred (*IBCW:* 13).

Thomas and Susanna were the parents of the following children, born in St. George's Parish (Reamy and Reamy, *St. George's Parish Register:* 19, 20, 23, 25, 26, 92): **2. Light**, b. 8 June 1719, bapt. 20 April 1720; **3. Elizabeth**, b. 20 February 1720, bapt. 22 July 1722; **4. Thomas**, b. 12 September 1723, bapt. 3 December 1724; and **5. David**, b. 6 May 1726.

2. Light Knight, son of Thomas (1) and Susanna, was born 8 June 1719, and bapt. 20 April 1720. He married Rachel Ruse on 12 October 1743 (Reamy and Reamy, St. George's Parish Register: 19, 26, 92).

In 1776 Light Knight, aged 59; Rachel, 46; and their children were listed in the Census of Susquehanna Hundred, Harford Co. (Carothers, *1776 Census of Maryland:* 116). In 1783 he was a taxable in Susquehanna Hundred, with no whites in his household (Carothers, *1783 Tax List of Maryland:* 142).

Light and Rachel were the parents of (Reamy and Reamy, *St. George's Parish Register:* 92): **6. Thomas**, b. 9 February 1746; **7. Mary**, b. 10 February 1748, was aged 26 in 1776; **8. Elizabeth**, b. 12 July 1751; **9. Ann**, b. 7 January 1753; **10. William**, b. 29

Colonial Families of Maryland II

July 1756, was aged 20 in 1776; **11. Sarah,** b. 8 April 1758; **12. Rachel,** b. 28 January 1760, was aged 16 in 1776; **13. Isaac,** b. about 1764, age 12 in 1776; **14. Sarah,** b. about 1765, aged 9 in 1776; and **15. Hannah,** b. about 1771, aged 5 in 1776.

4. Thomas Knight, son of Thomas (1) and Susanna, was born 12 September 1723, and bapt, 3 December 1724. He married Margaret [-?-], born about 1751.

In 1776, Thomas Knight, 30, and Margaret Knight, 25, were listed in the Census of Susquehanna Hundred, with the children listed below (Carothers, *1776 Census of Maryland:* 115).

In 1783 a Thomas Knight was listed as a 'pauper' in Susquehanna Hundred with one taxable in his household was a taxable in Susquehanna Hundred, with no whites in his household (Carothers, *1783 Tax List of Maryland:* 145).

Thomas and Margaret were the parents of: **16. William,** b. about 1770; **17. Mary,** b. about 1771; **18. Elizabeth,** b. about 1773; and **19. Light,** b. about 1774.

5. David Knight, son of Thomas (1) and Susanna, was born 6 May 1726. He married, but his wife may have died before 1776.

William Hughes of Baltimore Co. died leaving a will dated 14 February 1765 and proved 26 March 1776. He named his wife Amy, several children, and 'David Knight's children' (unnamed) (HAWB AJ#2:271).

In 1776 David Knight, age 49, was listed in the Census of Susquehanna Hundred, with an Elizabeth Green, age 30, and the children listed below (Carothers, *1776 Census of Maryland:* 117). In 1783 David Knight was a taxable in Susquehanna Hundred, with seven whites in his household (Carothers, *1783 Tax List of Maryland:* 142). About 1777 David Knight had volunteered into Baltimore Co. Regiment # 36 (*BARP:* 152).

David Knight was the father of: **20. David,** b. about 1755, age 21 in 1776; he is prob. the David Knight who in 1783 was a taxable in Susquehanna Hundred, with no whites in his household (Carothers, *1783 Tax List of Maryland:* 142); **21. Mary,** b. about 1763, age 13 in 1776; **22. John,** b. about 1767, age 9 in 1776; and **23. Ezekiel,** b. about 1769, age 7 in 1776.

10. William Knight, son of Light (2) and Rachel, was born 29 July 1756, and was aged 20 in 1776.

He may be the William Knight listed in the 1783 Assessment List of Harford Lower Hundred with four taxables in his household (Carothers, *1783 Tax List of Maryland:* 127).

He may be the William Knight whose estate was distributed on 29 January 1822 by Abraham Jarrett, admin. The heirs and legatees were William's widow Sarah, and his children Charlotte, Ann Maria, George, Elizabeth, William and John (Peden, *Heirs and Legatees of Harford County, Maryland, 1802-1846:* 27).

William's children were: **24. Charlotte; 25.Ann Maria; 26. George; 27. Elizabeth; 28.William;** and **29. John**

19. Light Knight, son of Thomas (4) and Margaret, was born about 1774.

He may be the Light Knight who in April 1813 was in the 42nd Regiment of Maryland Militia, which rendezvoused in Harford County, and mustered in Annapolis (Wright, *Maryland Militia in the War of 1812. Vol. 3, Harford and Cecil Counties:* 25).

Unplaced:
Charles Knight died by 4 Aug 1784 when Michael Donnelly administered the estate (BAAD 8:134).

== 0 ==

The Knowlman Family of Kent County

1. Anthony Knowlman was transported to Md. about 1674 (MPL 18:150). He died in Kent Co. by March 1714/5. He married Mary [-?-], who was buried January --- [prob. between 1710 and 1712 (St. Paul's Parish Register, Kent Co., *Maryland Eastern Shore Vital Records*, accessed on CD-ROM FTM CD#178; hereafter cited as SPKE).

By 1698 Anthony and his wife Mary were living in St. Paul's Parish, as can be seen by the births of their children.

Mary Knowlman (Knoleman) was examined in Cecil Co. Court concerning several salacious words she had uttered against Justice William Potts. Anthony Knoleman and Morgan Seyney were her sureties (*CMSP Black Books*, documents 42, 43, 44, and 56).

Anthony Knolman of Kent Co. died leaving a will dated 21 December 1714 and proved 9 March 1714. He left his dwelling plantation to his son Anthony. If Anthony did without heirs, it was to pass to his son Richard and then to his son John, and then to his daughter Rachel. Son Richard and his heirs were to have the plantation *Knave's Choice* on Farloe Creek. Eleanor Cole and Richard Cole at their day of freedom were to have personalty. His children aforesaid were to have the residue of his estate. Son Anthony was named exec., and was to be of age at 18. Nobody witnessed the will (MWB14:45, abst. in *Md. Cal. of Wills* 4:29).

Edward Skidmore and Hans Hanson appraised the estate of Anthony Noleman on 29 March 1716. His personal property was worth £102.9.3. Anthony Knoulman, Jr, heir of the deceased was one of the creditors. Joseph Kid and John Burk were debtors (INAC 37A:59).

Josias Crouch filed an account of Anthony Knowlman's estate on 16 June 1716. Payments came to £4.4.11. On 20 March 1716 Joseph Crouch filed an account of Anthony Knolman's estate totaling £6.6.1. Josias [sic] Crouch, administrator, filed an account of Anthony Knoulman of Kent Co. on 21 April 1716. He listed payments of £38.15.6. One payment was to Rachel Knoulman for her part of her unnamed father's estate. Crouch filed another account on Anthony Knoulman's estate on 14 June 1716, listing payments of £4.14.11. Croutch [sic] filed an account for Knowlman's estate on 15 June 1717. Payments totaling ¢19.5.1 were made to Thomas Browne and to Anthony Knowlman, a son of the deceased (INAC 37A:1111, 39B:53, 70).

Anthony and Mary were the parents of the following children, not all of whom were named in their father's will, but may have been living anyhow (SPKE); **2. Anthony; 3. Rachel**, b. 3 December 1698, bapt. 28 May 1699; m. Vincent Hatcheson on 22 April 1716 (SPKE); **4. Robert**, bapt. 30 March 1701, bur. 5 November 1702; **5. Rebecca**, b. 24 August 1702, bapt. 27 September 1702; **6. Richard**, bapt. 27 July 1707; **7. John**, bapt. 2 October 1710.

2. Anthony Knowlman, son of Anthony, married Mary [-?-].

Anthony Knoleman was listed in the Kent Co. Debt Books as owning *Bluntville* and *Neif's* Choice from 1733 to 1735, and *Neif's Choice,* between 1736 and 1769 *INKE:* 22).

Knowlman received a payment from the estate of Benjamin Griffith of Kent Co. on 17 March 1738 (MDAD 17:116). In September 1745 he received a payments from the estate of Mary Freestone (MDAD 22:17).

On 15 Sep 1747 Knowlman witnessed the will of John James of Kent Co. (MWB 24:488, abst. in *Md. Cal. of Wills* 9:87).

Anthony and Mary were the parents of (SPKE): **8. Anthony**, b. August 1727; **9. Mary**, b. June 1728.

6. Richard Knowlman, son of Anthony (1) and Mary, was bapt. on 27 July 1707 and may have died by 1738. He married Jane Hanson in St. Paul's Parish on 27 July 1729. She was the widow of George Hanson, who had married Jane Hynson on 17 September 1713 in St. Paul's Parish, Kent Co. (*ESVR* 1:24).

On 23 February 1730 Richard Knolman (Knoulman) of Kent Co., and his wife Jane, conveyed land to Frederick Hanson: whereas George Hanson, deceased, former husband to said Jane, was possessed of part of a tract called *Tolchester and Tomb*, 150 acres, which was by George Hanson in his last will devised to his son William Hanson, under the care of said Frederick Hanson until William Hanson arrived at the age of 21; the said Richard hath married afsd. Jane, widow of afsd. George Hanson, and they claimed the third part of afsd. tract for her dower (KELR JS#16:120).

On 20 September 1733, Richard Knowlman, administrator of William Hanson, filed the inventory (MINV 17:406).

Jane Knoleman is listed in the Kent Co. Debt Books as owning *Tolchester* and *Tomb* in 1738 and 1739 (*INKE:* 22).

Mr. Morgan Hurd of Kent Co., died by 22 September 1748, when his estate was appraised by W. Hynson and Jo. Wickes, and valued at £571.0.1. Hans Hanson and James Anderson signed as creditors. John Hurd and Joannah Knowlman signed as next of kin. Martha Hurd, administratrix, filed the inventory on 27 October 1748 (MINV 37:158).

Unplaced
Knowlman, Theophilus, was transported to Md. about 1674 with his wife Abigail and son Theophilus, Jr. (MPL 18:150).

==0==

The Leeke Family of Baltimore County

The Leeke Family in England

Nicholas Leeke of Yaxley Hall died by 11 April 1760. He married Christian, daughter of Commander Edward Vaughan, who was killed in the Russian Service. Nicholas and Christian had one surviving legitimate son: Seymour Leeke, Nicholas also had an illegitimate son: Francis Gilbert Yaxley Leeke, bapt. 12 September 1715 ("Yaxley Hall," *Proceedings of the Suffolk Institute of Archaeology and History.* pp. 152-153).

The Leeke Family in Maryland

1. Richard Leeke, married Lucy [-?-]. Research to date has failed to reveal any additional data on the existence of Richard or Lucy.

Colonial Families of Maryland II

Richard and Lucy were the parents of (Francis B. Culver, ed. *Society of Colonial Wars in the State of Maryland, Genealogies of the Members and Services of the Ancestors. Volume II.* Baltimore, 1940: 48): **2. Nicholas**, b. 28 September 1740.

2. Nicholas Leeke, son of Richard (1) and Lucy, was born 29 September 1749 at London, England. He came to America in 1769, and settled at Annapolis. He died in Baltimore Co. on 31 January 1824. As Nicholas 'Lecke' he and Mary Farrell were married by license dated 22 October 1778 (AAML). Mary, wife of Nicholas Leeke, was born about 1756 and was buried 4 May 1802 (Culver: 48; Reamy and Reamy, *St. Paul's Parish Register:* 2:13). He married 2nd, on 22 July 1802 Hannah Busk (Marr. Register of Rev. Lewis Richards, MS.690 at MdHS).

In March 1778 Nicholas Leeke took the Oath of Fidelity before the Hon. Samuel Harrison (*AARP:* 120). During the Revolutionary War, he was a sergeant of marines on the ship *Virginia.* Later he was pensioned at $8.00 a month beginning 3 April 1818. He died by April 1829. "Marked Dead. See letter to G G. Belt, 18 April 1829 to 4 March 1820 [*sic*]." (Revolutionary War Pension Application of Nicholas Leeke).

Nicholas Leeke was called on by his neighbors. On 2 November 1781 he witnessed the will of Benjamin Norman of the Swamp (AAWB TG#1:42-44). In February 1785 he informed the attorney acting for Mrs. Ann Pemberton, administratrix of Joseph Pemberton, that he had not yet been paid the money due him (Annapolis *Maryland Gazette* 24 February 1785). He was foreman of a coroner's jury that met on 18 November 1788 Anne Arundel County Court (Coroner's Inquests, 1787-1790), MdSA C 58.

Leeke advertised "an English School to be opened in the city of Annapolis, next door to Mr. Petty's store, Cornhill Street, on the first week in July next, for the instruction of youth, by the public's most humble servant, Nicholas Leeke" (Annapolis *Maryland Gazette* 26 June 1788).

In 1789 he moved to Southeast Street, next door to Mr. Hyde's large house, one year later (*Adomanis:* 49). "Nicholas Leek, School-Master. removed from Cornhill-Street to South-East Street, next door to Mr. Thomas Hyde's large house, teaches youth reading after the best and most approved method, *i.e.,* one t a time, in any proper book--writing the Round and Italian hands, after the most modern methods--Arithmetic in all its branches and dependencies--Book keeping, etc.--Likewise some of the most useful branches of the Mathematics, as Navigation and Surveying, etc., both instrumentally and practically, and the use of the plain and sliding Gunter, and the Sector, in the aforementioned branches of the Mathematics and Arithmetic. A diligent discharge of his duty may be depended on, and am the Public's most humble servant. Nicholas Leeke. Young Gentlemen boarded." (Annapolis *Maryland Gazette* 24 September 1789).

By 1790 he had moved to Baltimore Town where he was listed as head of a family with one white male over 16, and two white females (*Heads of Families, 1790, Maryland:* 17). In 1796 he was listed in the Baltimore City Directory as a schoolmaster at 22 Alisanna St., Fell's Point. He did not appear in the Directory for 1799, but in 1807 he was again listed in the Baltimore City Directory at 25 Alisanna St., Fell's Point.

Leeke's school in Fell's Point in 1794 was known as Leeke's Academy. The 1804 Baltimore City Directory listed Elizabeth Parker, a widow, as the resident of the building, which may indicate the site was rented, as were many houses in that era (*Early Wooden Houses in Fell's Point,* accessed at <www.baltimoreheritage.org>).

On 5 June 1799 Aquila Johns of Prince George's Co. deeded to Nicholas Leeke for 50 dollars and seven shillings part of lot # 153 in Fells Point on the north side of Lancaster St. (BALR WG#59:11).

Leeke was obviously trusted by his neighbors to assist them. In March 1794 he witnessed the will of George Campbell, and on 8 September 1794 as Nicholas Leeke,

Colonial Families of Maryland II

schoolmaster of Fell's Point, he witnessed the will John Burney. He witnessed many other wills from this period on. On 29 October 1794 he was named sole executor of Jordan Nicholas Wastman (who left his entire estate, real and personal, to Leeke's daughter Mary (BAWB 5:152, 364. 408; abst. by Burns). On 24 December 1794 Elizabeth Wilson, orphan, aged 10 on 1 February 1795, was bound to Nicholas Leeke to learn to learn to knit, spin, and sew (BOCP 3:125). Throughout the first three decades of the 19th century Leeke witnessed many wills. In April 1808 he was named executor of the will of Samuel Toon (BAWB 8:320, abst. by Burns). On 10 December 1813 his wife Hannah joined him and John Bush [Busk?] in witnessing the will of Charles Howell Weems (BAWB 11:281, abst. by Burns).

Nicholas Leeke was evidently closely associated with the Busk family. On 11 March 1801 Nicholas Leeke was appointed guardian to Hannah Busk, who accepted. He offered Isaac Atkinson and John Boyer as his securities (BOCP 4:153). [He later married her.] In July 1802, Leeke witnessed the will of Ann Davis, mother-in-law of Greenbury Busk (BAWB 7:167; abst. by Burns). Mrs. Barbara Busk died last Wed. evening; her funeral was from the house of Nicholas Leake, Ann St., Fell's Point (*Baltimore American* 28 July 1813). In May 1813 James Busk (Bush) made a will leaving his estate to Nicholas Leeke in trust for James' daughter-in-law Rhoda and her children (BAWB 10:413, abst. by Burns).

Leeke's life was not without conflict. On 27 May 1812 Nicholas Leeke, guardian of Alice Cockey, stated that under the "direction of his Counsel" he took a slave named Perry that belonged to the estate of his ward "from out of the street near your petitioner's house without noise or tumult." Later, Perry was "quietly sitting in a Back room," when Catharine Pearce, the wife of John Pearce, former guardian of Alice Cockey, "broke open the Street door of your petitioner's house and ... seized the said Negro Perry and took him away." Leeke "strove to keep the said Negro for his ward, and received a violent blow from the said Catharine Pearce." Leeke failed miserably in his row with Pearce, and Perry is currently in the custody of John Pearce. Leeke asks the court to issue an attachment against John Pearce and compel him to return the slave (Baltimore City Register of Wills (Petitions) [MSA T621-179]; MSA SC 4239-14-50; Petition 20981213).

Nicholas Leake died Saturday, 31 January 1824, aged 76, an old inhabitant of Fell's Point. He had taken part in the great struggle for American independence (*Baltimore Patriot & Mercantile Advertiser* 2 Febr 1824). As Nicholas Leeke, scrivener, he died leaving a will dated 18 September 1823 and proved 7 February 1824. He named his wife Hannah, who was named executrix, and his daughter Mary, wife of Henry Dashiell. Elizabeth Wilson and Jane Wilson witnessed the will (BAWB 11:631, abst. by Burns).

On 30 March 1837 Henry W. Gray wrote a letter stating he had been requested by the widow of Nicholas Leeke who wished to know the proper vouchers that will be necessary for her to file (Revolutionary War Pension Application of Nicholas Leeke).

Nicholas and Mary were the parents of: **3. Mary,** who m. Capt. Henry Dashiell "last Thursday" by Rev. Mr. Ireland (*Federal Gazette and Baltimore Advertiser* 26 Jan 1799).

Nicholas and Hannah were the parents of (Reamy, *St. Paul's Parish Register* 2:48):
4. Francis Gilbert Yaxley, b. 24 April 1806, bapt. 12 April 1807 (prob. d. young, as he was not mentioned in Nicholas Leeke's will).

3. Mary Leeke, daughter of Nicholas (2) and Mary, was born 17 April 1780 and died 9 May 1869. She married Capt. Henry Dashiell "last Thursday" by Rev. Mr. Ireland. (Culver: 48; *Federal Gazette and Baltimore Advertiser* 26 January 1799).

She was named as sole legatee in the will of Jordan Nicholas Wastman (BAWB 5:408, abst. by Burns).

Capt. **Henry Dashiell** was born on 8 February 1769, son of Thomas and Janes (Renshaw) Dashiell of Somerset County. He went to sea at an early age, and was commander of a ship at age 21 (Scharf, *History of Baltimore City and County:* 744). His mansion stood on the other corner of Aliceanna Street, at its intersection with Broadway. (*Early Wooden Houses in Fell's Point,* accessed at <www.baltimoreheritage.org>).

Henry Dashiell died leaving a will dated 24 September 1830 and proved 7 December 1830. He named his wife Mary as executrix. He named his daughter Jane Clendinen, her husband Dr. William H. Clendinen, and their son Henry Dashiell Clendinen. He named his other children Louisa Maria Dashiell, Nicholas Leeke Dashiell, Alice Ann Dashiell, and a daughter Mary Leeke Robinson. Nathaniel Knight, George Smith, and Charles Johnson witnessed the will (BAWB 13:481, abst. by Burns).

Henry and Mary (Leeke) Dashiell were the parents of (Scharf: 744): **5. Levin**, b. 26 June and bapt. 14 November 1802 (Reamy and Reamy, *St. Paul's Parish Register:* 2:17). He probably d. young as he was not named in his father's will); **6. Jane**, as Mrs. Clendinen, died of consumption at age 48, and was buried in second Presbyterian Church Cemetery the week ending 25 May 1835. She m Dr. William Haslett Clendinen, who died at age 67 on 6 November 1839 from an inflammation of the bladder, and was buried in Second Presbyterian Cemetery (Peden, *Baltimore City Deaths and Burials:* 65); **7. Mary**, b. 28 November 1807, bapt. 18 June 1809 at Trinity Episcopal Church (*MGSB* 30 (3) (Summer 1989) 200); m. 1st, Matthew Robinson, Esq., master of the Brig *Mary* of Baltimore, and d. 7 January 1833 at Kingston, Jamaica, leaving a wife and two children (from the Kingston, Jamaica *Chronicle* of 8 January 1833; *Baltimore American* 8 February 1833; she m. 2nd, on 21 May 1835 Dr. Moreau Forrest of Chateau Blanc, Montgomery Co., Md. (*Baltimore American* 23 May 1835); **8. Louisa Maria**, m. Thruston M. Taylor of the U.S. Navy on 21 May 1835 (*Baltimore American* 23 May 1835). He was a nephew of President Zachary Taylor, and of Gov. Clark of Ky; **9. Nicholas Leeke**, b. 1 July 1814; **10. Alice Anne**, late of 207 Broadway, d. 14 July 1854 (Baltimore *Sun* 17 July 1854); **11. Eleanor Virginia**, d. in early childhood.

9. Nicholas Leeke Dashiell, son of Henry and Mary (3) (Leeke) Dashiell, was born 1 July 1814 and died 28 February 1895. On 20 December 1855 he married Louisa Turpin Wright, born 17 November 1832, died 15 October 1919 (Culver: 40).

Nicholas Leeke and Louisa were the parents of: **12. Nicholas Leeke Dashiell**, b. 23 February 1860.

Unplaced:
Mary Leeke of Baltimore City bound herself on 21 May 1800 to John Dulany of Baltimore City until 21 May 1809, when she will be 16 years old, to learn sewing, washing and housework. (BA IND 2:525).

==0==

The Levely Family of Baltimore County.
With Notes on the Grangett, Morton, Sweeting, and Wineman Families.

N.B.: The name sometimes appears as Lably or Lavely.

1. George Levely, died by 26 November 1777 when his son William ["Lably" in German], exec., posted a bond for £3000. Frederic Myer and Andrew Schranhat

(Grangett) (both signed in German) were sureties (BAAB 3:343). He married Catherine Whistler, widow and executrix of John Rohra. On 13 June 1769 Catherine wife of George Levely was named as a daughter in the administration account of Esther Whistler, widow of Ulrick Whistler (BAAD 7:30, 33).

He may be the George 'Loble', German speaking, who April 1767 petitioned the Governor that Baltimore Co. Justices were overcharging him (*ARMD* 32:194-195).

George Levely, watch and clockmaker from Philadelphia, in July 1774 advertised he had opened a shop in Baltimore *(Maryland Journal and Baltimore Advertiser* 16 July 1774).

William Loveley, executor, advertised he would settle the estate of George Loveley [*sic*] of Baltimore (*Dunlap's Maryland Gazette* 10 February 1778).

William Lavely filed an account of the estate on 10 March 1779 (BAAD 8:47). He filed a second account on 17 February 1786, when portions of £47.5.2½ each were paid to Ludwick Little, George Levely, Andrew Levely, a son of the deceased, who received a double portion, Peter Littig, and Henry Wineman (BAAD 8:246). George Lavely is presumed to have had three married daughters, who received a share of their George's estate. The children of George Lavely or Levely may be tentatively identified as: **2. William; 3. George; 4. Andrew; 5.** [-?-], daughter, m. Ludwick Little; **6.** [-?-], daughter, m. Peter Littig; and **7:** [-?-], perhaps Anna Barbara, who m. Henry Wineman.

2. William Levely, son of George (1), was a German, in September 1760 who was naturalized when he took communion from Rev. Kirchner in Baltimore Co. (Wyand, *Colonial Maryland Naturalizations*: 25). He died in September 1787, having married by 9 September 1767, Catherine, daughter of Andrew Harrier (YOLR C: 495).

William 'Lobley,' German speaking, April 1767 petitioned the Governor that the Baltimore Co. Justices were overcharging him (*ARMD* 32:194-195).

William and Catherine Levely were godparents of Johann Wolff, bapt. 1 August 1779, son of Michael and Salome Wolff (Records of First Reformed Church of Baltimore, MS at MdHS: 5).

William Lavely was a private in Capt. Howell's Company on 30 Dec 1775 (*BARP:* 155).

Levely was listed as an innkeeper on Gay Street (*Maryland Journal and Baltimore Advertiser* 18 February 1785).

Wiliam Levely, tavernkeeper, died a few days ago (*Maryland Journal and Baltimore Advertiser* 14 September 1787). He died leaving a will dated 19 September 1780 and proved 15 September 1787. His wife Catherine was to have one-third of his personal estate and one-third of the rents and profits from his real estate for her widowhood. The residue of his estate was to be divided among his seven children: Mary Eve, wife of Andrew Grenshed, George, Catherine, Barbara, Susanna, Salome, and William, His sons George and William are to have his two brick houses on Gay St. where I have kept tavern, and to have the choice of others to live in. His wife, son-in-law Andrew Grandhed and John Leypold were named executors, but Leypold renounced. William Levely signed the will in German. Philip Yeiser, Engelhard Yeiser, and John Siegfried Gerock witnessed the will. Wife Catherine renounced the will and claimed her thirds. (BAWB 4:263, abst. by Burns).

Catherine Levely, executrix, advertised she would settle the estate (*Maryland Journal and Baltimore Advertiser* 26 January 1790). Catherine had administered the estate on 17 June 1789 and she administered it again on 4 September 1790 (BAAD 10:18, 196).

Catherine Lavely or Levely died leaving a will dated 23 February 1803 and proved 20 April 1803. She named her daus. Mary Gorsuch and Catherine Thompson, the two children of her deceased daughter Susanna Harrison, her daughter Sarah Milburn, the children of her daughter Susanna, her son William and grandson William Lavely. James McCannon, Owen Dorsey and George Gouldsmith Presbury witnessed the will (BAWB 7:174, abst. by Burns).

William and Catherine were the parents of: **8. Mary Eve**, m. 1st, Andrew Grenshed or Grangett, and 2nd, Nicholas Gorsuch; **9. George; 10. Catherine**, m. [-?-] Thompson; **11. Barbara; 12. Susanna;** may be the; **13. Salome** (possibly the 'Sarah' who m. [-?-] Milburn; and **14. William.**

3. George Levely, son of George (1) and Catherine, was born about 1750 and died 29 April 1796, in his 47th year. He may have been married three times. A George Levly and Chartine Mull were married on 1 January 1770 (Reamy and Reamy, *St. Paul's Parish Register:* 36). George 'Lavely' and Sarah Rees were married by license dated 9 Nov 1780 (BAML). He married Elizabeth [-?-] who administered his estate. George Allen, father of Mrs. Levely, died yesterday morning at the house of George Levely (*Baltimore Daily Intelligencer* 11 February 1794).

George Levely was a member of the Sons of Liberty in Baltimore in 1776. He took the Oath of Fidelity before the Hon. William Spear in 1778, He may be the George Leably" who was a private in Capt. McClellan's Company, Baltimore Town Militia in 1780 (*BARP:* 159).

George Levely conveyed property on the northeast side of Exeter St., between Pollack and York Sts., to George Hussey on 8 February 1782. The city commissioners were to meet to establish the boundary line of the property (*Baltimore Patriot* 18 September 1815).

George Levely, watch-maker of Baltimore, died yesterday in his 47th year. His funeral would be today (*Federal Gazette and Baltimore Daily Advertiser* 30 April 1796). Elizabeth Levely, administratrix, advertised she would settle the estate (Annapolis *Maryland Gazette* 16 June 1796).

On 17 April 1799 Susannah, Mary, Elizabeth, George, Henry, Catharine, Sophia, John and William Levely (Lavely), orphan children of George Lavely, came into court and the court appointed Catharine Lavely as their guardian, who accepted and offered Peter Littig and Henry Dukehart as her securities (BAOC 4:49).

George Levely was the father of: **15. Susannah; 16. Mary; 17. Elizabeth; 18. George; 19. Henry; 20. Catharine; 21. Sophia;** on 17 November 1810 she was mentioned in the will of Henry Wineman (BAWB 9:85); **22. John;** and **23. William.**

7. Anna Barbara Levely, probably daughter of George (1), married Henry Wineman.

Henry Wineman died leaving a will dated 17 November 1810 and proved 23 Janu1811. His legatees were the children of Catherine Sweetng, deceased, formerly the wife of Thomas Sweeting, his wife Ann Barbara, and Sophia Levely, daughter of George Levely, deceased His wife was executrix. Thomas Spiers, Edward Stapleton and Alexander McCain witnessed the will (BAWB 9:85, abst. by Burns).

Henry and Anna Barbara were the parents of: **24. Catherine**, m. Thomas Sweeting on 14 November 1799 at the First Presbyterian Church in Baltimore (Register of First Presbyterian Church, MS. At MdHS).

8. Mary Eve Levely, daughter of William (2) and Catherine, married, 1st, Andrew Grangett, and, 2nd, Nicholas Gorsuch.

Andrew Grangett died leaving a will dated 5 February 1785 and proved 5 March 1785. His brother Peter Grangett and his sisters Catherine and Susanna were to have all the estate now possessed in the Duchy of Wurtemburg, Germany. He named his wife

Mary and a daughter Mary. George Levely and John Laybold were execs. Philip Miller, James Davidson and Jacob Brown witnessed the will. A codicil dated 6 Feb 1785 named Jacob Greenawald (BAWB 4:57, 58, abst. by Burns).

Geo. Lavely and John Laypold posted an administration bond for £1000.0.0 on 5 March 1785. Jacob Brown and Valentine Snider were sureties (BAAB 6:286).

Laypold and Levely, a watchmaker, executors, advertised they would settle the estate (*Maryland Gazette or Baltimore General Advertiser* 22 April 1785). Leybold [*sic*] and Levely administered the estate on 27 March 1787, 15 April 1790, and 20 Sep 1790 (BAAD 9:28, 10:128, 201).

Mary Eve and Andrew were the parents of: **25. Mary**, b. earlier than 14 February 1785; poss. the Mary Grandget who m. John Andrew Morton on 26 January 1795 (Marr. Register of Rev. Lewis Richards, MS.690 at MdHS).

24. Catherine Wineman, daughter of Henry and Anna Barbara (7) Levely, died Monday, [-?-] September 1806 in her 25th year (*Federal Gazette and Baltimore Daily Advertiser* 19 September 1806). She married Thomas Sweeting on 14 November 1799 at the First Presbyterian Church in Baltimore (Register of First Presbyterian Church, Baltimore, MS at MdHS: 13). Thomas Sweeting married, 2nd, Caroline Phillips on 26 March 1809 (Reamy and Reamy, *St. Paul's Parish Register:* 2:60). She was a daughter of Isaac Phillips (*Federal Gazette and Baltimore Daily Advertiser* 27 March 1809), Mrs. Caroline Sweeting, wife of Thomas Sweeting and daughter of Isaac Phillips, died this morning She resided in King Tammany St. (*Federal Gazette and Baltimore Daily Advertiser 19* August 1813).

Thomas and Catherine were the parents of (Peden, *Presbyterian Records of Baltimore:* 63): **26. Anna Barbara**, b. 26 October 1800, bapt. 24 February 1801.

25. Mary Grangett, daughter of Andrew and Mary Eve (8) (Levely) Grangett, was born much earlier than 14 February 1785. She married John Andrew Morton on 26 January 1795 (Marriage Register of Rev. Lewis Richards, Pastor of First Baptist Church, MS. 690 at MdHS). John Andrew Morten [*sic*] was married last Mon. eve. by Rev. Richards, to Miss Mary Grangett, both of this town (*Federal Intelligencer and Baltimore Daily Gazette* 28 January 1795).

John Andrew and Mary (Grangett) Morton were the parents of (Reamy and Reamy, *St. Paul's Parish Register:* 2:29, 34): **27. Mary**, b. 12 December 1800, bapt. 23 July 1804, buried 15 July 1804.

26. Anna Barbara Sweeting, daughter of Thomas and Catherine (24) (Wineman) Sweeting, was born. 26 October 1800, bapt. 24 February 1801. Miss Ann B. Sweeting, was married last eve. [Tues.] by Rev. John Mason Duncan, to Isaac Phillips, Jr, all of Baltimore (*Federal Gazette and Baltimore Advertiser* 14 May 1817; *Baltimore Patriot* 14 May 1817).

Unplaced:
Catherine Levely and Col. Peter Little were married last Sunday by Rev. the Rev. Mr. Hargrove (*Federal Gazette and Baltimore Daily Advertiser* 21 May 1816).
Catherine Lavely and Job Merryman, all of Baltimore, were m. last Thurs. eve. by Rev. George Roberts (*Federal Gazette and Baltimore Advertiser* 2 April 1819; *Baltimore Patriot* 3 April 1819 gives the bride's name as Margaret Lavely).
Elizabeth Levely and Capt. Joseph Hall were married on Thursday evening by Rev. Bend (*Federal Gazette and Baltimore Daily Advertiser* 4 October 1806).

George Levely died by March 1819, leaving a house and lot at 140 Market St., next door to Littig's Brush Manufactory. The "very valuable" property was being sold by Susannah Louisa Weise, executrix of Augustus Weise, deceased (*Baltimore Patriot* 10 March 1818).

John L. Levely, formerly of Baltimore, died at Annapolis (*Baltimore Patriot* 26 October 1821).

John S. Levely and Miss Phebe Ann Skelton, all of Baltimore Co., were m. last Thurs. (*Baltimore Evening Post* 17 November 1811).

Philip Levely formerly resided on the road leading from Baltimore to Liberty Town, within 20 miles of the latter and within one mile of the place where he formerly kept tavern (*Federal Intelligencer and Baltimore Daily Gazette* 28 March 1795).

Susan Levely and Robert Herring were married yesterday eve. by Rev. Mr. Kurtz (*Baltimore Daily Intelligencer* 5 September 1794)

Mr. William Levely died 17th inst., in his 38th year (*Baltimore Patriot 23* July 1818; *Federal Gazette and Baltimore Advertiser* 23 July 1818).

Mr. William Levely, of Baltimore, and Mrs. Mary Holtzman of Georgetown, were m. at Washington Thurs., 13th Aug (*Baltimore Patriot* 20 August 1818; *Federal Gazette and Baltimore Advertiser* 19 August 1818; *Baltimore American* 20 August 1818).

== 0 ==

The Litton Family of Baltimore County
With Notes on the Cole and Vine Families

1. Thomas Litton was in Baltimore Co. by 1694 as a taxable in South Side of Gunpowder Hundred. He died by 1700. He married Mary [poss. a sister of John Webster]. She married 2nd, [-?-] Miles.

On 28 April 1695 Robert Gates by his last will and testament devised 50 a. *Fall Hill* to Sarah Spinks and 50 a. *Fall Hill* to Thomas Litton, Sr. (BALR TB#E: 675).

Thomas Litrton was mentioned in a deposition as having helped John Indrell hide in the woods about 1697.

Thomas Litton died leaving a will dated 29 October 1700 and proved 7 November 1700, naming his wife Mary, his brother John Webster and his children Thomas and Sarah.

By 1707 May Litton held 50 a. *Tall Hill* for the Thomas Litton's orphans, who also owned *Speedwell* (*MRR:*58, 70).

Thomas and Mary were the parents of two children who were minors in 1700: **2. Thomas;** and **3. Sarah**

2. Thomas Litten, son of Thomas (1) and Mary, was stated in a deposition Made by Antill Deaver on 12 May 1730 that about 23 years earlier Litten had lived with John Webster as an apprentice (BALR HWS#3, #21). He married by April 1715, Ann, daughter of John Hawkins, Sr., by an unidentified first wife.

On 15 September 1716 John and Mary Miles conveyed 62 a. *Father-in-Law's Bounty,* being one-half of *Margaret's Mount,* to Thomas Litton (BALR TR#A: 449). On 2 November 1720: John Miles' wife Mary conveyed 60 a., being one-half of *Litton's Adventure* to Thomas Litton (BALR TR#DS: 284).

On 1 May 1739 Isaac Webster and Jacob Giles conveyed 100 a. *Arabia Petrea* to Thomas Litten (BALR HWS#1-A:222). 28 January 1741 Litton and his wife Ann conveyed 100 a. *Bare Hills* to James Rowland (BALR TB#A: 97). On 23 February 1747 Litton, son and heir of Thomas Litton, the Elder, deceased, conveyed 50 a. *Fall Hill,* which Robert Gates had devised to the grantor's father, to Nicholas Ruxton Gay. Litton's wife Ann consented (BALR TB#E: 675).

In 1750 Litton owned 112 a. *Margaret's Mount.* 80 a. *Litton's Fancy,* 50 a. *Aim's Delight,* and 100 a. *Arabia Petrea* (Baltimore Co. Debt Book for 1750: 33).

On 5 February 1754 Thomas Litton made a deed of gift to his granddaughter Ann Litton, the sole surviving heiress of his son Thomas Litton, deceased (BACT TR#E:120).

Litton died leaving a will dated 29 Jan 1756 and proved 21 April 1751. His wife Ann was to have part of his dwelling plantation, *Margaret's Mount.* He named his son Samuel, and his son James, who was to have 40 a. part of *New Design.* His son Michael was to have *Spencer's Neighbors* and *Falling Branch.* Son Isaac was to have *Litten's Fancy* and son John was to have part of *Arabia Petrea.* His named his daughter Mary, his deceased son Thomas and his daughter Ann; he also named his grandchildren Samuel and Ann Pritchard. Jacob Giles, William Smith, and John Rigbie witnessed the will (BAWB 2:342). Samuel Litton, administered the estate on 23 August 1762, citing an inventory of £79.10.6 and listing payments of £37.19.2 (MDAD 48:181).

Thomas Litten married Ann [-?-]. They were the parents of (Reamy and Reamy, *St. George's Parish Register*: 17, 23, 24, 34, 39, 47, 60, 62): **4. Elizabeth,** b. 6 April 1715; **5. Mary,** b. 1 April 1717; **6. Hannah,** b. 10 March 1719; **7. Thomas,** b. 30 January 1721; **8. John,** b. 10 March 1722/3; **9. Isaac,** b. 13 February 1724/5; **10. Michael,** b. 14 April 1730; **11. Elizabeth,** b. 4 November 1732; **12, Samuel,** b. 10 August 1735; **13. Ann,** d. 25 April 1740;she may have been the Ann Litton indicted for bastardy at the Aug 1765 Court (Court Minutes and Criminal Docket, 1765, p. 17); and **14. James,** b. 5 February 1740 [1740/1?]; in 1769 he signed a petition protesting the removal of the county seat from Joppa to Baltimore (*IBCP:*20).

3. Sarah Litton, daughter of Thomas (1) and Ann, was a minor in 1700. In November 1718 Thomas Miles was charged with begetting a bastard on the body of Sarah Litton (BACP IS#C:31). Sarah's daughter, Martha Litton, was b. 27 April 1718 (Reamy and Reamy, *St. George's Parish Register:* 19). Sarah Litten married 1st, John Beddoe on 3 December 1724, and 2nd, on 14 February 1733, Godfrey Vine (Reamy and Reamy, *St. George's Parish Register:* 24, 103).

On 11 April 1737 George Farmer, Church Warden, was ordered by the vestry of St. George's Parish to inquire whether Godfrey Vine and Sarah Beddo cohabited together still. On 6 June 1737 Vine and Beddo were summoned to appear at the next vestry and answer their contempt. On 5 July 1737 Vine and Beddo appeared, but could not prove their marriage. The vestry was pleased to give them until the last Saturday of the month to produce a certificate. On 4 October 1737 Godfrey Vine and Sarah Beddo produced a certificate to show they had been married on 14 February 1733 by Rev. James Cox, minister of St. Paul's Parish in Queen Anne's Co. (Reamy and Reamy, *St. George's Parish Register:* 104).

Sarah Litton and Thomas Miles were the parents of: **15. Martha Litten,** b. 27 April 1718, m. George Cole on 2 March 1732 (Reamy and Reamy *St. George's Parish Register:* 26).

Sarah Litton and Godfrey Vine were the parents of (Reamy and Reamy, *St. George's Parish Register:* 49, 60): **16. Godfrey,** b. 5 July 1733; **17. Sarah,** b. 6 September 1736; and **18. John,** b. 1 March 1738.

6. Hannah Litton, daughter of Thomas (2) and Ann, was born 10 March 1719. She was charged with bastardy at the Aug 1742 Court and a bill was presented against her at the March 1743/4 Court; she was indicted again at the Nov 1746 Court (BACP TB#D:8, Liber 1743-1745:154, and TB&TR#1:220).

7. Thomas Litton, son of Thomas (2) and Ann, was born 30 January 1721and died by 15 February 1745. He married by 31 July 1742, Margaret, administratrix of Seaborn Tucker of Baltimore Co. (MDTP 31:295; MDAD 19:193).

On 15 February 1745 Jacob Giles posted an administration bond with Jonathan Jones and John Kemp as sureties, the widow Margaret having renounced the right to administer (BAAB 2:82).

Thomas and Margaret were the parents of: **19. Ann** (named in the will of her grandfather).

8. John Litton, son of Thomas (2) and Ann, born 10 March 1722/3 and died by 9 April 1793. He married Mary [-?-], mother of a son John Richey.

On 7 June 1758 John Litton assigned 30 a. of *Hickory Hollow* to James Clarke (BALR B#G: 61).

He may be the John Litton, with three whites in his household, listed in the 1783 Assessment List of Broad Creek Hundred as owning 104 a. part *Maiden's Mount*, 60 a. *James' Portion*, and 30 a. of *Litton's Vein* (Carothers, *1783 Tax List of Maryland:* 148).

In 1783 he was on the Harford Co. War Committee (*RPHA:* 139).

John Litton died leaving a will dated 4 June 1785 and proved 9 April 1793. He named his daughter Mary Ely, and John Ely, son of Mary. He named his wife Elizabeth, a boy William James, his wife's son John Richey, who was to have a tract of 34 a. He named his daughter Hannah, who was to be executrix. Stephen Norton, Robert Morgan, and John Cook witnessed the will (HAWB AJ#2:402).

John Litton was the father of: **20. Mary,** m. [-?-] Ely; and **21. Hannah.**

9. Isaac Litton, son of Thomas (2) and Ann, was born 13 February 1724/5 and married by 12 May 1746, Mary, executrix of Thomas Jones of Baltimore Co. (MDAD 22:336). On 11 Jan 1750/1 Isaac Litton stated he would not be responsible for wife Mary Litton (BACT TR#E:21).

In 1750 he owned 50 a. *Arabia Petrea*, and part of *Neighborhood* ((BADB for 1750:69).

12. Samuel Litton, son of Thomas (2) and Ann, was born 10 August 1735. He married Ann [-?-], born about 1742.

In 1769 he signed a petition protesting the removal of the county seat from Joppa to Baltimore (*IBCP:*20). In 1773 he served on a jury in the trial of the Lord Proprietary vs. the Negro Hercules (*IBCP:* 49).

In 1776 Samuel, aged 39, Ann Litten, aged 35, Mary Fulk, aged 72, and John Craford, aged 72, were listed in the 1776 Census of Susquehanna Hundred Harford Co., with the children listed below (Carothers, *1776 Census of Maryland:* 111).

Samuel Linton, with 12 whites in his household, but owning no land, was listed in the 1783 Assessment List of Susqueanna Hundred. He was also security for Peter Donovan (Carothers, *1783 Tax List of Maryland:* 142, 146). In 1783 he was on the Grand Jury in Harford Co. (*RPHA:* 139).

Samuel and Ann were the parents of: **22. Clemency,** b. about 1759; **23. Sarah,** b. about 1761; **24. Elisabeth,** b. about 1763; **25. Mary,** b. about 1765; **26. Susannah,** b. about 1765; **27. Samuel,** b. about 1767; **28. Ruth,** b. about 1772; and **29. Ann,** b. about 1774.

15. Martha Litten, daughter of Sarah Litton (3) and Thomas Miles, was born 27 April 1718, and married George Cole on 2 March 1732 (Reamy and Reamy, *St. George's Parish Register:* 36).

In 1722 John Miles made his will, leaving his entire estate to his wife Mary for life, who had the power to make over the estate to his well beloved son, but if she did not the land was to go to his son, and if he died, then to Martha Litton (BALR IS#G:136).

George and Martha were the parents of (Reamy and Reamy, *St. George's Parish Register:* 49): **26. Henry Cole**, b. 25 March 1736.

Unplaced:
Thomas Litten, aged 58, was listed in the 1776 Census of Broad Creek Hundred, Harford Co. With him were Mary, aged 44, and Mary, 13, Hannah, 10, and John Lee, aged 11 (Carothers, *1776 Census of Maryland:* 88).

==0==

The Lomax Family of Baltimore County

1. Thomas Lomax, aged 18, of St. Leonard's, Shoreditch, Co. Middlesex, made his mark on 1 February 1719 when he bound himself for seven years service in Md. (Kaminkow, *List of Emigrants:* 143). Thomas Lomax and Ann Hakman were married in January 1726 (*SJSG:* 37).

In 1737 Thomas Lomax was head of a household on the Lower Side of North Gunpowder Hundred. He appeared in the Baltimore Co. Levy List for 1739 (*IBCW:*15, 32).

Daniel Dulany of Annapolis, on 9 March 1732 conveyed to Thomas Lomax 250 a. which John Dorsey had lately conveyed to Dulany (BALR IS#L:337).

On 4 June 1740 William Dallam posted an administration bond on Thomas Lomax' estate, with John Paca and James Phillips as sureties (BAAB 2:99). On 6 June 1740 Nicholas Ruxton, Jr., and John Holloway appraised his personal estate at £48.13.3. Lomax's 'young children' were designated as the next of kin. William Dallam , admin., filed the inventory on 15 Oct 1741 (MINV 26:205).

Thomas and Ann were the parents of (*SJSG:* 37): **2. Thomas,** b. 22 February 1731; and **3. Theophilas,** b. 25 December 1737.

2. Thomas Lomax, son of Thomas (1) and Ann, was born on 22 February 1731. He was aged 9 as of February 1740/1 and in November 1740 he was bound to Charles Baker (BACP HWS#TR: 353).

Thomas and Sarah Downey were m. 11 February 1735 (*SJSG:* 98).

3. Theophilus Lomax, son of Thomas (1) and Ann, was born 25 December 1737. He was bound to John Morris in Nov 1740, and was aged 7 in November 1745 when he was bound to Capt. William Young (BACP HWS#TR:351, Liber for 1743-1745:740).

==0==

The Mahan Family of Baltimore County
With Notes on the Brogden, Gray, and Towson Families.

1. John Mahan (Mahonn, Mahones), of Co Wicklow, Ireland, on 10 November 1698 bound himself as apprentice to John Smith of Biddeford, merchant to serve him for in

Va., or Md. for 7 years; the document mentioned the good ship *The Tacktor* that came to anchor in Chester River on 4 February 1698 (BALR TR#RA:354). He married a woman named Mary [-?-].

In November 1722 Ann Brogden named John Mahonn as the father of her two children (BACP IS#TW#2:21). In 1737 John 'Marhorue' was head of a household in Lower Hundred of Back River. John Brogdon was in his household (*IBCW:* 22).

In August 1736 John 'Mahorn' was a surety for Cornelius Angling, admin. of Robert Gardner (BAAB 4:18).

On 21 November 1734 Thomas and Tabitha Sheredine conveyed 150 a. *Long's Addition* to John Mahorne (BALR HWS#M: 175).

John 'Mahone' died leaving a will dated 5 March 1741 and proved 23 October 1742. He named his wife Mary; he left 150 a. *Long's* Addition to his youngest daughter Isabel. To his grandsons Mathias Gray and John James, daughter Frances Carback, and John Brogden, he left personalty, Christopher Duke, John Bays and Walter Dallas witnessed the will (MWB 22:533 abst. in *Md. Cal. of Wills* 8:92).

Mary Mahone posted an administration bond with Thomas Sligh and Christopher Duke as sureties (BAAB 2:180). William Polton, a servant with six years and two mos. to serve was listed in Mahone's inventory, posted in 1746 (BINV 6:260). Mary Mahone posted an administration account on 18 July 1746. She cited an inventory of £124.10.10, and listed payments of £45.8.4. The legatees were daughters Isabel Mahone and Frances Carback and grandsons John James and Mathias Gray All of the representatives were of age. William Polton, the servant, was now deceased. Mary Mahone administered the estate on 18 July 1746 (MDAD 22:207; BAAD 4:138).

By Anne Brogden John Mahone was probably the father of: **2. John Brogden;** and **3. [-?-] Brogden.**

John and Mary were the parents of: **4.** [-?-], m. [-?-] James [possibly Watkins James]; **5.** [-?-], m. [-?-] Gray, and had a son Mathias Gray; **6. Frances,** m. 14 July 1734 John Martin Carback (Reamy and Reamy, *St. Paul's Parish Register:* 31); **7. poss. Elizabeth,** m. Abraham Towson on 1 January 1745 (Reamy and Reamy, *St. Paul's Parish Register:* 34); and **8. Isabel,** the youngest daughter.

2. John Brogden, probably son of John (1) and Ann Brogden, was named in Mahone's will on 5 March 1741. He was a servant to John Mahone when he was indicted for a felony on 16 March 1736 (BACP HWS#1A:1). He died by 8 September 1749 or 1769 [illegible] when Wm. Hopham posted an administration bond (BAAB).

4. [-?-] Mahone, daughter of John (1) and Mary, married [-?-] James [possibly Watkins James who signed the inventory of John Mahone as next of kin; Watkins James married Mary [-?-] and had a son John].

In 1778 Watkins James was a Non-Juror to the Oath of Allegiance (*BARP:* 142).

[-?-] and her husband were the parents of: **9. John;** named as a grandson in the will of John Mahone.

5. [-?-] Mahone, daughter of John (1) and Mary, married [-?-] Gray. She and her husband were the parents of: **10. Mathias;** named as a grandson in the will of John Mahone.

6. Frances Mahone, daughter of John (1) and Mary, married on 14 July 1734 John Martin Carback. (Reamy and Reamy, *St. Paul's Parish Register:* 31). She or another Frances Carback married Francis Wilkins on 18 February 1762 (*SJSG:* 108). (See **The Carback Family,** elsewhere in this work).

7. Elizabeth Mahone, possibly a daughter of John and Mary, married Abraham Towson on 1 January 1745 (Reamy and Reamy, *St. Paul's Parish Register:* 34). Abraham Towson died by 9 June 1752 when James Carey posted an administration bond, with Thomas Norris.

James Carey administered Towson's estate on 18 September and 21 November 1754. The first account listed 'expenses for burying the wife of the deceased' (MDAD 36:437).

Abraham and Elizabeth were the parents of two daughters who chose their uncle William Towson as their guardian (Balto. Co. Court Minutes, 1755-1763). The daughters were: **11. Mary Towson**; and **12. Dorcas Towson**.

8. Isabel Mahone, youngest daughter of John (1) and Mary, on 5 March 1741was left 100 a. *Long's Addition* in her father's will (MWB 22:533).

== 0 ==

The Mallonee Family of Baltimore County

N.B: The name has sometimes been transcribed as Mallence, but in the compiler's opinion, the name was actually Malonee. The "nee" ending has been misread as "nce."

1. Peter Mallonee died in Baltimore Co. by March 1750.

In August 1724, as the "late servant of John Rawlings," he was ordered to receive his freedom dues. In November 1724 he petitioned the court for freedom from Eleanor Presbury but his petition was denied. Again in March 1724/5 he petitioned to for his freedom from the estate of Joseph Presbury (BACP IS&TW#3:441, IS&TW#4:34)

On 38 January 1722/3 Peter Mallonee witnessed the will of John Rawlings of Anne Arundel Co. (MWB 18:90, abst. in *Md. Cal. of Wills* 5:135). He witnessed the will of Benjamin Tayman, planter of St. John's Parish, Baltimore Co. (MWB 20:259, abst. in *Md. Cal. of Wills* 6:200). On 16 August 1734 Mallonee was a creditor of the estate of James Hicks of Baltimore Co. (MDAD 12:394).

Mallonee died by 5 December 1749, when an administration bond on his estate was posted by Talbot Risteau, with John Roberts as surety (BAAB 2:206).

N. Ruxton Gay and James Moore, Jr., appraised the personal estate of Peter Mallonee at £58.15.9. John Mallonee and Emanuel Mallonee signed as next of kin. Talbot Risteau, administrator, filed the account of 28 July 1750 (MINV 44:161).

On 16 February 1750/1 Talbot Risteau, administrator, filed an account of Mallonee's estate. He cited the inventory as given, and cited payments of £69.3.6. (MDAD 29:161).

Peter Mallonee was the father of: **2. John**; and **3. Emanuel**.

2. John Mallonee, son of Peter (1), died by June 1783 when his will was proven. He married Edith Cole on 6 or 8 November 1748 (*SJSG:* 89. 126). Edith was named as a daughter of Dennis Garrett Cole in his will made December 1772 (BAWB 3:252). She was born 8 August 1728. Mallonee married 2nd, Rebecca [-?-] [possibly Brown], in September 1766] This second marriage is probably what resulted on 24 d., 9 m., 1766, when John Maleney (Mallonee) was charged with having been "married by a priest, and suffering [allowing] music, and dancing, and gaming in his house (*QRNM*:45).

In 1750 John Mallonee owned *Timber Ridge* (Baltimore Co. Debt Book for 1750: 95). On 15 October 1764 Edmund Deadman assigned to John Malonee (Malone) 74 a. of *Deadman's Venture*, being part of the lands leased to Deadman on 10 August 1752 for 99 years, and Deadman now assigned the land to Malloney for the rest of the time in the lease (BALR B#O:227). In 1769 John'Malloonee' signed a petition for the removal of the county seat from Joppa to Baltimore Town. On 18 July 1773 he was listed by Joshua Boreing as a taxable in North Hundred (*IBCP:* 29, 76).

Peden placed this John Mallonee as a private in Capt. John McGuire's Company of Col. William Grayson's Regiment of the Maryland Line (*BARP:* 169).

In 1783 John Mallone owned 91 a., part of *James Prospect,* in Middle River and Back River Upper Hundreds. Elizabeth Ensor also owned 92 a. of the same tract (along with other lands) (Carothers, *1783 Tax List of Baltimore Co.*). Middle River and Back River Upper Hundreds took in the areas of Shawan, Brooklandvile, Cockeysville, and Towson.

John Mallonee, farmer, died leaving a will dated 19 February 1780, proved 5 June 1783. He named his sons Leonard, William, James, and Thomas, and his wife Rebecca who was appointed executrix. She was to have the residue of his estate for her life, and then it was to go to all his children. Christopher and Benjamin Vaughan witnessed the will (BAWB 3:536. abst. by Burns).

Rebecca Mallonee posted an administration bond on 2 August 1783. Francis Daws and John Miller were sureties (BAAB 6:53).

John and Edith (Cole) Mallonee were the parents of (Fred M. Chilcoat, Mallonee Notes sent to the compiler in a private communication): **4, Rachel**, b. 24 February 1754, m. 28 d., 9 m., 1775, Mordecai Price of John and Mary (*QRNM*:53); **5. Leonard**, b. 1760; **6. William**, b. about 1756/60; **7. Thomas; 8. Dennis**, m. by 15 February 1792 [-?-] , who received an equal share of the estate of Richard Bond (BAAD 10:544); and **9. John**, m. by 23 September 1773, Sarah Bond.

John and Rebecca may have been the parents of: **11. James**, b. after 1772; and **12. Peter**, b. after 1772.

3. Emanuel Mallonee (sometimes styled Malance, Mallane, or Mallence), son of Peter (1), and Margaret Reeves were married on 11 February 1749/50 (*SJSG:* 127). On 26 September 1760 Margaret was named as a daughter of William Reaves.

Emanuel and Margaret were the parents of (BAWB 2:174): **13. Elizabeth** 'Malance.'

5. Leonard Mallonee, son of John (2) and Edith, was born 27 February 1763 in Baltimore Co. and died in Anne Arundel Co. in 1854. He and Achsah Sewell (born 1768, died 1859), were married by license dated 18 January 1791 (AAML). She was a daughter of John and Mary (Marriott) Sewell (Warfield, *Founders*: 142):

Leonard Mallonee died leaving a will dated 24 November 1853 and proved 20 September 1854. His daughter Anne S. Kirby was to have a Negro girl Henny, which he had given her many years ago. His wife Achsah is to have the farm on which I now reside and all my personal estate for the rest of her natural life, and after her death, son Brice Mallonee was to have the notes he held for him and no more, as he had done a great deal for him. The children of his deceased daughter [Sarah?] Welsh were to have $60.00 dollars and no more. Granddaughter Achsah Ann Mallonee was to have $50.00 and no more. His two great-grandchildren, George Mallonee and Ann E. Mallonee were each to have ten dollars and no more. His grandson Leonard M. Disney was to have fifty dollars and no more. After the death of his wife he bequeathed the rest and residue of his estate real and personal, to his five children: John Mallonee, William Mallonee, Mary Bradford, Achsah Fairall, and Ann T. Kirby, with the proviso that his son John Mallonee, because he has had to pay him a considerable sum of money, was to have two hundred and fifty dollars less] than William, Mary, Achsah, and Ann. and his Negroes were to be free as they arrived at the age of thirty-five, the females, and thirty-eight, the males. If any of his representatives attempted to prevent any of his Negroes from enjoying their freedom, they were to receive one dollar and no more. George Bradford and Ann S. Kirby were to be executors. Wm. H. Baldwin, James Rawlings, and William Hammond witnessed the will (AAWB BEG#41:231-232).

Leonard and Achsah were the parents of: **14.Edith**, m. Joshua Disney by license dated 3 December 1827 (AAML); **15. John**, b. 1791, m. Rachel Lyon; **16. Denton**, b. 1798 (not mentioned in his father's will), m. Ann Kirby; **17. William**, b. 1801; **18. Brice**, b. 1805, m. Eliza Louisa Fairall; **19. Achsah**, m. Alfred Fairall by license dated 26 May 1825 (AAML); (He or another Alfred Fairall and Mary Jane Disney were married by license dated 28 January 1851 (AAML); **20. Ann Sewell**, b. 1815; **21. Mary**, m. by license dated 20 December 1819 (AAML) George Bradford, who was b. about 1789, and d. 1867 in Howard Co. (Warfield mistakenly names her as Mary Edith Mallonee); and **22. Sarah**, d. before her father, m Robert Welch by license dated 10 November 1806 (AAML).

6. William Mallonee, son of John (2) and Edith, could be the William Mallonee b. about 1756, who married about 1778 Sarah Johnson.

In 1798 William Malonee was listed as owning 35 a. *Mallonee's Habitation*, in North Hundred (Horvath, *Particular Assessment Lists:* 24). The family settled in Jefferson Co., Ohio about 1808,

William was the father of: **23. Emanuel**, b. 3 November 1779; **24. Mary**, b. about 1781; and **25. Jared**, b. about 1783.

8. Dennis Mallonee, son of John (2), married some time before 15 February 1782 a daughter of Richard Bond, who received an equal share of her father's estate (BAAD 10:544).

On 18 February 1781 John Bond of Richard made over to Dennis Mallonee all the land leased to him by Henry Cole (BALR WG#O: 141).

Mallonee was living in Baltimore Co. on 11 January 1817 when he joined Benjamin Busby of Harrison Co., Ohio, in conveying to Joshua Kemp all that land called *Deer Park* and *Chance*, granted to John Busby, deceased, and heirs (BALR WG#140:539).

Dennis Mallonee was the father of: **26. Dennis**, who on 11 July 1799 bound himself to James Griffith, tailor, for 11 years (BAOC WB#B: 105); **27. John**; Stephen Gill, died by 30 November 1811 when his heirs and legal representatives William Gill, Joshua Gill, Elizabeth Gill, John Mallonee of Dennis, Cooper Gill, and Nicholas Gill, renounced the right to administer in favor of John Gill (Baltimore Co. Renunciations, 1822).

9. John Mallonee, son of John (2) and Edith, married by 23 September 1773, [Sarah?], daughter of Mary Brown (BALR AL#1: 246).

In 1798 he was living on 91¼ a. called *Mallonee's Habitation*, which contained five old houses. This tract was in Middle River Upper Hundred, and was probably the same land as *James Prospect* (Horvath, *Particular Assessment Lists:* 30).

John and Sarah were the parents of ten children, including (Mallick, *Sketches:* 43): **28. Shade (Shadrach)**; **29. Lewis**; **30. Josiah**; **31. John**; and **32. Hezekiah**, b. 24 July 1799; and perhaps others.

15. John Mallonee, son of Leonard (5) and Achsah, was born in 1791, and married Rachel Lyon on 18 April 1833 (*Baltimore American* 23 April 1833). She was a niece of Moses Sheppard, the founder of Moses Sheppard Asylum. They were the parents of

(Warfield, *Founders*: 142): **28. William; 29. John; 30. Rachel; 31. Leonard; 32. James;** and **33. Benjamin.**

16. Denton Mallonee, son of Leonard (5) and Achsah, was born in 1798, and married Ann. daughter of George and Anna (Randall) Kirby, by license dated 8 November 1821 (AAML).
He is not mentioned in his father's will, so he probably died before 1854.
Denton and Ann were the parents of: **34. George; 35. Leonard;** and **36. Achsah Ann.**

17. William Mallonee, son of Leonard (5) and Achsah, was born in 1801. He married Thomasine Keirle, daughter of John W Keirle, a prominent business man (Warfield, *Founders*: 142).
John W. Keirle, died by 14 February 1840 when his widow Ann Keirle, and his daughters Maria Farinholt, Eliza M. Redding, and Emily J. Walker, Washington T. Keirle, and William H. Keirle, his sons, and William Mallonee, his son-in-law, renounced the right to administer and recommended that letters be granted to John W. Walker. Henry Howard Burgess witnessed. Matthew M. Keirle died by 23 December 1840 when his next of kin, Wm. H. Keirle, William Mallonee, Emily J. Walker, Eliza A. Redding, Ann Keirle, and W. T. Keirle, renounced the right to administer and recommended that letters be granted to John W. Walker. S. J. Joice witnessed (MdSA: Baltimore Co. Renunciations, 1840).
William Mallonee was a dry-goods merchant in Baltimore, and was located at the corner of Baltimore and Hanover Sts.
William and Thomazine were the parents of (Warfield, *Founders:* 142): **37. John; 38. Leonard; 39. William; 40. Matthew; 41. Mark;** and **42. Achsah.**

18. Brice Mallonee, son of Leonard (5) and Achsah, was born in 1805, and married Eliza Louisa Fairall by AAML dated 17 November 1824.
Brice and Louisa were the parents of (Warfield, *Founders*: 142): **43. John Stephen; 44. William; 45. Alexander; 46. Brice; 47. Martin Van Buren; 48. Achsah; 49. Edith; 50. Maryland;** and **51. Virginia.**

30. Hezekiah Mallonee, son of John (9) and Sarah was born 24 July 1799.He married Keturah Tipton (Mallick, *Sketches:* 43).
A wheelwright, Hezekiah and Keturah were the parents of ten children (Mallick. *Sketches:* 43): **52. Sarah Ann,** d. 1862; **53. Mary Jane,** m. John C. Kelly; **54. John T.,** b. 22 September 1827; **55. William,** d. 1890; **56. Lewis,** also a wheelwright; **57. Hezekiah,** d. young; **58. George,** a builder and contractor in Baltimore **59. Ephraim,** a farmer in Baltimore Co.; **60. Thomas W.,** a blacksmith; **61. -?-|,** d. in infancy.

Unplaced:
Eliza Mallonee has been granted a personal discharge and she will have a final hearing as an insolvent debtor on the first Saturday in next September term of The Baltimore County court (*Baltimore Patriot and Mercantile Adviser* 31 March 1823).
Emmanuel Mallonee and Rachel Matthews were married on 25 May 1806 ((Marr. Register of Rev. Lewis Richards, MS.690 at MdHS).

Frewilliam [*sic*] **Mallonee**, age 12 next 9 November, on 10 April 1811, with the consent of his father [unnamed], bound himself to Michael Porter for nine years (BIND WB#H: 71).

George Mallonee, with the consent of his father, John Mallonee, on 21 December 1799 bound himself to Benjamin Wooden for one year (BAOC WB#B:355). George Mallonee and Mary Marsh were married on 11 January 1806 (Marr. Register of Rev. Lewis Richards, MS.690 at MdHS). John Everett died by 15 March 1834 when his widow Eliza Everett renounced the right to administer due to her ill health and in the interest of her children believed that her husband's property should be properly administered; she recommended her father George Mallonee. John Philpot witnessed (Baltimore Co, Renunciations, 1834).

Henry Maloney, orphan, aged 15 yrs., was bound with consent of his brother John Vanroson on 6 October 1821 to Pall Placid of Baltimore City for 6 yrs. to learn the trade of cooper. /s/ Henry Maloney, Pall Plassed, John Van Rossum (BIND 11:410)

James Maloney, orphan, aged 13 yrs. was bound by Justices of the Peace on 2 May 1803 to William Kennard of Baltimore City until 21 yrs. old to learn the trade of cooper. (BIND 4:360)

James Mallonee and Delilah Cullison were married on 13 February 1795 in Baltimore Co., Md. They lived in Bedford Co., Pa., before moving to Ohio (Norma L. Cullison Myers, "Cullison Family: Elusive Ancestors." *Maryland Genealogical Society Bulletin* 35 (3) (Summer 1994): 373).

John Mallonee, orphan, aged 19 yrs. on March 1 last, was bound with consent of Jacob King, his former master, on 12 April 1803 to Philip Littig for an unstated term to learn the trade of comb maker. (BIND 4:335)

John Mallonee died by 2 October 1821 when George Mallonee stated that he had obtained letters of administration on the estate of John Mallonee, and anyone with claims against the estate had until 29 March 1822 to present their claims.(*Baltimore Patriot and Mercantile Adviser* 2 Oct 1821).

William Mallonee and Martha Tudor were married on 17 October 1807 ("Register of the First Methodist Episcopal Church, Baltimore; MF701 at MdHS: 11).

==0==

Matriarch Ann [-?-] Vickory Plowman of Baltimore County
With Notes on the Haile, Merryman, Plowman, Stevenson, and Vickory Families.

Introduction: There is a theory that Ann was a daughter of Edward and Mary ([-?-]) Stevenson, and that Mary was a daughter of Henry and Mary (Haile) King. Edward and Mary did name their third son Richard King Stevenson, which might have shown the use of Mary's maiden name, King (Robert Barnes, *Descendants of Edward and Mary Stevenson*, hereinafter cited as Barnes: 3, 24).

Edward Stevenson is said to have owned land, surveyed in 1689 for Nicholas Haile who was the uncle of Mary King. Mary (King?) Stevenson married 2nd, by 1718, Henry Sater who owned *Haile's Discovery*, which he patented in 1724 (BACP IS#IA: 316; MDAD 2:2).

Mary Haile, the mother of Mary King, is said to have been the daughter of Nicholas Haile, the First. Mary Haile married first Henry King and second Charles Merryman, Sr. [*Colonial Abstracts of Lancaster County, Virginia:* 241, dated 13 March 1671/2, record the order to George Haile administrator of the estate of Mary Haile who was the administrator of the estate of Nicholas Haile, to give to "Henry King married Mary, daughter of Nicholas Haile one-third of two thirds part of the estate of Nicholas Haile, deceased and deliver it to her. He was ordered to deliver one-third part of the estate of Mary Haile, widow, deceased, to her (*Virginia Colonial Court Records for Lancaster County:* 84; Elsie Howlett Tracy. *Merrymans (Merrimans) and Tracys (Traceys): Pioneer Community Builders,* La Jolla [CA]: E. H. Tracy, 1976: 2).

The 1695 Tax List for Baltimore Co, of taxables on the North Side of Patapsco Hundred showed that living next to each other were Nicholas Haile, uncle of Mary; Henry King, brother of Mary; Edward Stevenson [possibly the future husband of Mary]. Ten households away was Charles Merryman, Sr., the step father of Mary King (Baltimore Co. Tax Lists Years 1692, 1694, 1695, compiled by the Ida Charles Wilkins Foundation. typescript at the MdHS).

In 1717 John Merryman was listed as "nearest relation" in the estate administration of Edward Stevenson, the husband of Mary King. John Merryman, as the son of Charles Merryman, Sr., and Mary Haile, was the half-brother of Mary King (Testamentary Proceedings, Box 4, folder 26; Maryland State Archives).

Mary King Stevenson's son Edward Stevenson along with her son-in-law George Brown(e) and half-brother John Merryman and his wife Mary Merryman witnessed the will of Charles Merryman, Jr. (half-brother of Mary King Stevenson) in 1722 (MWB 22:297).

Edward Stevenson, the husband of Mary King Stevenson, witnessed the will of Thomas Long in 1716. Thomas Long was the father of Jane Long who married in 1702, Charles Merryman, Jr., the half-brother of Mary King Stevenson.

Edward Stevenson, husband of Mary King Stevenson, was transported by Thomas Todd to Maryland in 1671 along with John Merryman, the father of Charles Merryman, Sr., who was the step-father of Mary King Stevenson (MPL 16: 394).

Charles Merryman, Jr., and Jane Long's daughter Jemima Merryman married 1735, Baltimore Co., MD, Henry Stevenson. Charles Merryman, Jr., was the half-brother of Mary King Stevenson and his daughter Jemima would have been her niece. Henry Stevenson was the son of Edward Stevenson and Mary King Stevenson (Barnes:12). **[RWB Note:** More work needs to be done to confirm this theory].

1. Matriarch Ann married 1st, by 4 February 1710/11 John Vickory when they witnessed the will of John Harryman (MWB 13:158 abst. in *Md. Cal. of Wills* 3:184). She married 2nd, John Plowman.

On 3 December 1710 Francis Thornbury of Baltimore Co. conveyed 200 a. *Jack's Double Purchase* (part of *Selsed*) to John Vickory; the deed stated that Roland Thornborough had left his youngest son 300 a. *Selsed* (BALR TR#A: 95).

John and Ann Vickory witnessed the will of John Harriman on 4 February 1710/11 (MWB 13:158, abst. in *Md. Cal. of Wills* 3:184).

John Vickory died leaving a will dated 5 November 1711 and proved 12 January 1711/2. He left *Jack's Double Purchase* to his son Richard Stevenson Vickory and his heirs. His wife Ann was named executrix, and was left his personal estate for life. If his son should die without issue, the land was to pass at his wife's death to Richard King Stevenson, son of Edward and Mary Stevenson. Samuel Merryman, William Welsh and Samuel Hinton witnessed the will (MWB 13:244, abst. in *Md. Cal. of Wills* 3:216).

On 27 January 1700/1 at Liverpool, Eng., 12 year old Jonathan Plowman of Yorkshire, Eng., as bound as an indentured servant ("Emigrants from America to Liverpool," *NEHG Register:* 1911: 44). He served his time and then married Ann [-?-], widow of John Vickory.

Jonathan Plowman and his wife Ann on 13 February 1714 conveyed a cow to their son Richard Vickory (BALR TR#A: 359).

Jonathan Plowman died by 1747, for on 30 March 1747 Ann Plowman, Jonathan Plowman, and John Plowman conveyed to Thomas Ford 50 a. of *Selsed* called *Jack's Double Purchase*. Eliza Plowman wife of Jonathan Plowman released her right of dower (BALR TB#E:386).

John and Ann ([-?-]) Vickory were the parents of: **2. Richard Stevenson Vickory**. Jonathan and Ann ([-?-]) Plowman were the parents of (Reamy and Reamy, *St. Paul's Parish Register:* 1): **3. Rachel**, b. 22 February 1715 (she may have m. Richard King Stevenson; **4. Jonathan**, b. 25 February 1717; and **5. John**.

2. Richard Stevenson Vickory, son of John and Ann (1), died by 2 March 1735/6 when George Buchanan, administrator, posted bond to administer his estate (BAAB 4:195). On 25 April 1736 his brother of the half-blood, John Plowman renounced his right of administration (MDTP 30:147).

On 12 August 1735 Richard Stevenson Vickory conveyed 100 a. *Jack's Double Purchase* to George Buchanan of Baltimore Co., surgeon, and would defend the sale against all except the heirs of Roland Thornborough who had taken up *Selsed* (BALR HWS#M: 258).

Buchanan filed the inventory of Richard Stevenson Vickory on 10 November 1736. Nicholas Haile and Thomas Tipton had appraised the estate on 10 November 1736 at £38.6.10. John Plowman and Ann Plowman signed as next of kin (MINV 22:109). On 11 November 1736 Buchanan administered Vickory's estate, and cited the inventory as given above, and listed payments of £29.20.10, to Sarah Chambers (MDAD 15:235).

4. Jonathan Plowman, son of Jonathan (1) and Anne, was born 25 February 1716/7 and died at age 78 by November 1795. In August 1740 Jonathan Plowman married a woman named Elizabeth [-?-] at St. Paul's Church in Baltimore. At about age 42, and as a brother of John Plowman, as heirs of their mother by Richard King Stevenson, he deposed on 9 September 1762 (BAEJ: Charles Ridgely, *Ridgely's Goodwill*). At age 62, he deposed on 3 March 1785 (BALR WG#V: 642).

On 30 August 1740 Richard King Stevenson conveyed 50 a. *Jack's Double Purchase,* part of *Selsed,* to his cousins John and Jonathan Plowman (BALR HWS#1-A: 438). Ann Plowman, mother of Jonathan and John, was still living on 30 March 1747 when, Jonathan Plowman and John Plowman conveyed 50 a. of *Selsed,* called *Jack's Double Purchase.* to Thomas Ford. Eliza, wife of Jonathan Plowman, relinquished her right of dower (BALR TB#E: 386).

Jonathan Plowman took the Oath of Allegiance in 1778 before the Hon. James Calhoun (*BARP:* 212).

In 1783 Jonathan Plowman was listed in Pipe Creek Hundred as owning 339 a. *Plowman's Park.* His household consisted of one white male and five white inhabitants (Carothers, *1783 Tax List of Baltimore Co.:* 94).

Plowman died leaving a will dated 8 April 1794 and proved 3 November 1795. He named his children James, Edward, and Jonathan, and a granddaughter, daughter of his deceased son Richard as well as Ruth Plowman, widow of Richard. He mentioned tracts *Jonathan's Meadow, Plowman's Meadow, Buck's Thicket* (a portion of which was to be reserved for a burying ground), *Plowman's Second Adventure, Timber Bottom, and Jacob's Beginning.* His son James was named executor. Absalom Butler, Zachariah Loveall, and Micajah Corbin witnessed the will (BAWB 5:333, abst. by Burns).

Jonathan and Eliza were the parents of (Reamy and Reamy, *St. Thomas' Parish Register:* 8, 10, 11, 13): **6. Stevenson**, b. 24 June 1749; **7. James**, b. 24 September 1751; **8. Jonathan**, b. 13 February 1754; **9. Richard**, b. 23 December 1754; **10. Edward**, b. 12 March 1759; and **11. Sarah**.

5. John Plowman, son of Jonathan and Ann (1), and Sarah Chambers were married on 3 May 1736 (Reamy and Reamy, *St. Paul's Parish Register:* 32). John was a brother of the half-blood of Richard Stevenson Vickory (*q.v.*) (BAAB 4:195).

Richard King Stevenson had inherited *Jack's Double Purchase*, or *Selset*, which descended to him by the death of Richard Stevenson Vickory, and on 3 Aug 1740 he conveyed 50 a. of *Jack's Double Purchase* to his cousins John and Jonathan Plowman (BALR HWS#1-A:438).

7. James Plowman, son of Jonathan (4) and Eliza, was born 24 September 1751. In 1778 he was a Non-Juror to the Oath of Allegiance (*BARP:* 212). He married Tabitha Green in 1774. They were the parents of (undocumented source on the internet): **11. Catherine Margaret; 12. Elizabeth; 13. Ephraim; 14. Henry; 15. James, Jr.; 16. Joshua; 17. Mary; 18. Jonathan; 19. Charles;** and **20. Nicholas.**

9. Richard Plowman, son of Jonathan (4) and Eliza, was born 23 December 1754 and died by 8 April 1794. He married Ruth [-?-].

In 1778 he took the Oath of Allegiance before the Hon. James Calhoun, and on 7 February 1782 was listed as an ensign in Capt. Kelly's Co., Soldier's Delight Battalion of Militia (*BARP:* 212).

Richard left at least one child: **21. Jantha.**

10. Edward Plowman, son of Jonathan (4) and Eliza, was born 12 March 1759. In 1778 he took the Oath of Allegiance before the Hon. James Calhoun (*BARP:* 212).

21. Jantha Plowman, daughter of Richard, on 25 July 1798, came into court and the court appointed Zachariah Loveall as her guardian, who accepted and offered Elijah Corbin and Ely Oursler as his securities (BAOC 4:25). On 9 August 1798 Henry Brawn and Henry Epaugh, at the request of Zachariah Loveall, entered into the lands and plantation of Jantha Plowman, an orphan and viewed the same with the improvements, which consist of a dwelling house and kitchen, the latter wants a new roof, one old barn almost useless, one old corn house, a spring house wanting a new cover, a small house covered with straw, the land mostly cleared, an apple orchard of about 200 trees which appears to be old and not thriving, all which we estimate at the annual value of £13, and agreed that the guardian should be further permitted to clear three acres at the east end of the said plantation for keeping the houses and fences in repair (BAOC 4:30-31)

A Second Jonathan Plowman Family

Jonathan Plowman died leaving a will dated 22 May 1776 and proved 28 October 1776. He named his wife Rebecca, and her brother David Arnold of Calvert Co. as executors, with [the advice?] of his friend Walter Tolley, Jr. His son Jonathan was to have 14 a., part of *Mountenay's Neck;* a lot on Fell's Point, opposite the tobacco Warehouse; a lot in Baltimore Town on the west side of the Falls; part of *United Friendship*, purchased of Clara Yung (and other tracts as well). He named Edward Johnson, son of Dr. Edward Johnson., and his brother James Plowman, now in England. Charles Gorsuch of Charles was to have £20. He named his daughters Rebecca, Mary, Sarah, and Ann Plowman, all under 18. R. Moale, Harry Dorsey Gough, and Eliz. Barney witnessed the will, David Arnold renounced as executor (BAWB 3:318).

Robert Ballard, administrator, posted a bond for £100,000, on 9 August 1780, with Wm Smith and Sam'l Young as sureties (BAAB 5:83). Ballard, the administrator *de bonis non* filed an account on 17 February 1785 and 17 June 1786 (BAAD 8:234, 277).

Ballard filed accounts again on 2 April 1787, 18 April 1787, 29 June 1787, and 31 October 1787 (BAAD 9:31, 44, 77, and 113).

Plowman was the owner of a dwelling house and lot on the east side of Jones Falls as well as other assorted tracts of land, and he left a son Jonathan. Edward Johnson and William M'Laughlin, trustees, advertised the sale of the land (*Maryland Journal and Baltimore Advertiser* 26 October 1787).

Rebecca Plowman, widow of Jonathan died leaving a will dated 24 August 1777 and proved 25 July 1778. She left personalty to her eldest daughter Rebecca and her daughter Nancy. The rest of her personal estate was left equally to her daughters Rebecca, Mary, and Nancy. Her brother David Arnold was named executor. Charles Frederick Wiesenthal, and Thomas Logan and Rebecca Arnold witnessed the will (BAWB 3:374).

David Arnold posted an administration bond for £10,000 on 1 August 1778. Thomas Russell and Nathaniel Smith were sureties (BAAB 3:35). David Arnold was deceased, so Dr. Edward Johnson administered the estate on 17 February 1785. Robert Ballard swore to the account (BAAD 8:227).

Rebecca died possessed of a considerable estate. David Arnold was named executor in her will. Robert Ballard married the eldest daughter of the said Rebecca. A certain Rebecca Arnold has some of the property of the deceased (Plowman, Rebecca, 1785, BPET Box 1, Folder 15). In April 1787 Dr. Edward Johnson, guardian of Jonathan Plowman, heir and devisee of Jonathan Plowman, petitioned the court, stating that Jonathan Plowman's eldest daughter Rebecca had married Robert Ballard (BPET: Plowman, Jonathan, 1787; Box 1, Folder 46).

Jonathan and Rebecca were the parents of (Peden, *Presbyterian Records of Baltimore:* 45): **Rebecca,** the eldest daughter, m. by April 1787, Robert Ballard; **Mary,** b. 13 August 1765, bapt. 2 October 1766; She and William M'Laughlin were married by Rev. Dr. West (*Maryland Journal and Baltimore Advertiser* 21 January 1787; *Maryland Gazette or Baltimore General Advertiser* January 1787); **Jonathan,** b. 28 August 1766, bapt. 2 October 1766; **Sarah,** b. 19 October 1770, bapt. 10 November 1770; and **Ann,** b. 3 October 1773, bapt. 8 August 1774; She and Edward Johnson, Jr., both of Baltimore, were married last evening by Rev. John Robinson (*Maryland Journal and Baltimore Advertiser* 1 April 1791). On 14 April 1791 she was paid a legacy from the estate of Rebecca Arnold (BAAD 10:347).

==0==

Matriarch Deborah [-?-] Johnson Benger
With Notes on the Benger, Johnson and Scott Families

1. Deborah [-?-], died by 5 August 1700, having married 1st, John Johnson, and 2nd, some time after 6 March 1682/3 and by 6 November 1691, as his second wife Robert Benger, who had married as his first wife Katherine Therrell, relict and administratrix of John Chadwell (Shadwell) (INAC 4:631, 632, 7A:9; BAAD 2:41; MDTP 9:335)..

On 2 June 1674 Mary Harmar, widow, conveyed 150 a. *Oliver's Reserve* to Robert Benger and John Johnson, being the same land formerly taken up by Oliver Spry, deceased, and then by the grantor's deceased husband Godfrey Harmer (BALR G#J: 242).

Robert 'Benjar' on 6 March 1676 was named as a son-in-law in the will of Margaret Therrell (Thurrrold) of Back River, Baltimore Co. (MWB 5:347, abst. in *Md. Cal. of Wills* 1:201; MDTP 10:36). Margaret was the widow of Richard Thurroll. Robert Benjar, executor of Margaret Therrell, exhibited her will. John Waterton was to prove said will. Said Benjar was granted administration. The appraisers were John Arden, John

Boaring. Said Waterton was to administer oath (MDTP 9A:336). On 13 April 1678 Robert Benjar, executor of estate of his wife's mother, Margaret Therrell, exhibited her inventory (MDTP 10:36).

On 9 October 1677 Robert Benjar, who married Katharine relict and administratrix of John Shadwell, petitioned for John Waterton, Gent., to take the oath of said Katharine as she Could not travel to the Office, because of great sickness. (MDTP 9A:335). On 15 April 1680 Robert Benjar, who married the relict and administratrix of John Shadwell, exhibited accounts. On 4 October 1688 Robert Benjar and wife, administratrix of John Chadwell, exhibited additional accounts, proved before Francis Watkins, Gent. (MDTP 12A:18, 14:101).

On 31 May 1681 Robert Benger of Gunpowder R. gave bond to Thomas Harris of Herring Creek, Anne Arundel Co. that he would convey 30 a. *Benger's Addition* and 150 a. *Oliver's Reserve* to said Harris (BALR IR#AM: 134). On 15 August 1688 58 a. *Benger's Addition to Privilege* was surveyed for Robert Benger (BALR TR#A: 278). On 6 March 1682/3 Robert Benger, shoemaker, and wife Katherine, conveyed 150 a. *Oliver's Reserve* and 30 a. *Jenifers Kindness*, to Daniel Scott (BALR RM#HS: 33). On 20 May 1688 John Fuller and wife Easter of Baltimore Co. conveyed 100 a. *Fuller's Outlet* to Robert Benger, cordwainer (BALR RM#HS: 276).

On 6 November 1691 Robert Benger and wife Deborah of Baltimore Co. conveyed *Fuller's Outlet* to William Wright (BALR RM#HS: 333). In 1699 Robert Benger left 70 a. *Witherington* to his wife Deborah (MWB 6:314, abst. in *Md. Cal. of Wills* 2:188).

As Deborah Benger, she died leaving an undated will, proved 5 August 1700. Her son Benjamin Johnson was to have 50 a. on Back Creek. Her daughter Eliza Shaw was named executrix and residuary legatee, and was to have *Benjar's Privilege*, 100 a. *Addition to Privilege*, and her 100 a. dwelling plantation at the head of Gunpowder River. Francis Dallahide, Charles Adams, and Ellinor Brittnell witnessed the will (MWB 6:374 abst. in *Md. Cal. of Wills* 2:197). Deborah was the mother of Jane Johnson (who m. Daniel Scott), and of Elizabeth Shaw (BALR TB#C: 471).

By John Johnson, Deborah was the mother of: **2. Benjamin; 3. Elizabeth**, m. John Shaw; and **4. Jane**, m. Daniel Scott.

3. Elizabeth Johnson, daughter of John and Deborah (1), married John Shaw. On 15 January 1700 John Shaw of Cecil Co. conveyed 180 a. *Benger's Privilege*, 100 a. *Hopewell*, 100 a. being one-half of *Salisbury Plains*, 70 a. *Witherington*, 80 a. *Shadwell's Range*. and 100 a. *Smith's Range* to Alexander Graves (BALR HW#2: 53).

4. Jane Johnson, daughter of John and Deborah (1), died 23 December 1732. She married, 1st, Daniel Scott (BALR TB#C: 471). She married, 2nd, on 12 May 1729, John Watson, who married, 2nd, Mary Chennerworth, spinster, on 24 May 1733 (*SJSG:* 26, 40).

On 3 Aug 1703 Daniel Scott and wife Jane conveyed 150 A. *Oliver's Reserve* and 30 a. Jenifer's Kindness to William Galloway (HW#2: 334).

Daniel and Jane were the parents of: **5. Daniel**, d. 1745; **6. Ann**, m. Thomas Smithson; **7. Nathaniel; 8. Jane**, m. 1st, Francis Watkins and 2nd, Samuel Hughes; **9. Sarah**, m. James Preston; and **10. Avarilla**, m. John Durbin on 1 March 1715.

==0==

Matriarch Dinah [-?-] Nuthead Devoran Oley Assa
With Notes on the Devoran, Nuthead, and Oley Families

1. Dinah [-?-] married 1st, William Nuthead. William Nuthead, printer, of St. Mary's City, was 39 when he deposed in 1693 mentioning Richard Smith (*Archives of Maryland*, hereafter cited as *ARMD*, 20:33, abst by Henry C. Peden in *Maryland Deponents, 1634-1699*, Westminster: Family Line Publications 1991).

Dinah married 2nd, Manus Devoran, who died on 14 December 1700 in St. Margaret's Parish (*AACR*: 136.).

Manus Devoran died leaving a will dated 10 December 1700 and proved 20 December 1700. He left personalty to his daughter Catherine, his son-in-law William Nuthead and daughter-in-law Susan Nuthead. His wife, unnamed, was named executrix and she and her heirs were to have the residue of his estate, real ad personal. William Pennington, William Anderson, and An [*sic*] Smith witnessed the will (MWB 11:36, abst. in *Md. Cal. of Wills* 2:210).

On 14 January1700, George Eager, planter, conveyed to Dinah Deaveran or Devoran, of Anne Arundel Co., widow, 90 a. of *The Heirs Purchase*, on the north side of Severn River. On 27 January 1700 Edward Lunn conveyed to the widow Devoran, his dwelling house and appurtures [*sic:* appurtenances] at the ferry landing across the Severeigne [Severn] River in the town of Annapolis, lately built by Lunn (AALR WT#1:127, 130).

Dinah married 3rd, on 28 April 1701 in St. Margaret's Parish, Sebastian Oley (*AACR*: 81).

Oley was prosperous enough that on 22 January 1705 he as listed as a creditor of the estate of Thomas Ryder of Anne Arundel Co. (INAC 25:56).

Sebastian Oley died in March 1706 in St. Margaret's Parish (*AACR*: 137). He left an undated will that was proved 3 April 1707. He left personally to his children Sebastian and Margaret, his daughter-in-law Susanna Mathace, and Robert Job. His wife Dinah was named executrix. J. Brice, Sarah Pure, Michael Singclear and Thos. Holmes witnessed the will (MWB 12:96, abst. In *Md. Cal. Of Wills*).

On 7 February 1708 Dinah Oley, widow, conveyed to William Taylor, trustee for Wm. Nuthead, Susannah Nuthead, and Sebastian Oley, children of the said Dinah Oley, lately called Dinah Devoran, the tract *Heirs Purchase* on the north side of Severn River, cont. 90 a. Taylor was to hold the tract for one year. At the end of the year Dinah Oley was to be paid one pepper corn rent if demanded. On the following day, Dinah Oley, widow, conveyed to Taylor, in consideration of the love and affection she bore her children, as named above, the tract *Heirs Purchase*. After the death of Dinah, the property was to go first to her eldest son William Nuthead; if he has no lawful issue, to her eldest daughter Susannah Nuthead, and if she has no lawful issue, to Sebastian Oley, her second son (AALR WT#2:684, 687).

Dinah "Olle," administratrix of Sebastian "Olle" filed an account of his estate on 16 June 1708. A list of his debts was filed in the Prerogative Court on 14 July 1708 (MDTP 21:24, 47).

Dinah married 4th, by 21 February1710, Samuel Assa (AALR PK: 364). In June 1711, he left a great silver cup and spoon, weight £1.14.0 to Sebastian Oley. He left a small silver cup worth £0.20.0 and cash to buy a small ring to Margaret Oley. The cups and things were committed to the care of Robert Jubb for the use of the said children (AAJU TB#2:281-282). On 31 November 1711 Samuel Assa was noted as a creditor to the estate of Richard Horner of Baltimore Co. (INAC 33A:68).

By William Nuthead, Dinah was the mother of: **2 William Nuthead**, living in 17101 and **3. Susannah Nuthead**, living in 1708, m. [-?-] Matheace.

Dinah and Manerus Devoran were the parents of: **4. Catherine.**

By Sebastian Oelly, Dinah was the mother of two children; **5. Sebastian Oelly**, b. 25 Dec 1704 in St. Margaret's Parish (*AACR*: 108).and **6. Marget [Margaret?]**, b.

March 1706 in St. Margaret's Parish (*AACR:* 109); in March 1709/1710, Margaret Oley, aged about three years, was bound to Robert Jubb to serve him according to the law (AAJU TB#2:118).

2. William Nuthead, son of William and Dinah, was living on 21 February1710, when as William Nuthead, son and heir of Dinah Asa, wife of devisee of Manus Devoren, late of Anne Arundel Co., carpenter, deceased, he conveyed to William Bladen, for £21.0.0 current money, a lot in the City of Annapolis, with a house thereon erected by Manus 'Devron' (AALR PK: 40). He seems to have died without heirs by September 1726 when his half-brother sold *Heirs Purchase.*

4. Catherine Devoran, daughter of Manerus and Dinah, was born about 1698. In 1705 she was the ward of 'Seb.' Oley in Town Neck Hundred. On 14 March 17109/10, Robert Jubb undertook to be the guardian of Catherine 'Devorian.' On 14 March 1709/10, Katherine 'Devouria,' aged about 11 years, was bound to Robert Jubb to serve him according to the law (AAJU TB#1:353-354, TB#2:116, 119).

5. Sebastian Oley, son of Sebastian and Dinah (1), was born 25 December 1704 in St. Margaret's Parish, Anne Arundel Co. and died there on 10 March 1749. He married Elizabeth Hall in St. Margaret's Parish on 9 February 1725 (*AACR:* 131, 139).

In 1705 'Seb.' Oley, living in Town Neck Hundred was listed as the guardian of William and Susan Nuthead, orphans of William Nuthead, and of [-?-] Duarne, orphan of Menass Deuourne [Devoren] (AAJU TB#1:354). On 14 March 17109/10, Robert Jubb undertook to be the guardian of Catherine Devorian, and Sebastian and Margaret Oley, orphans of Dinah Asa. On 14 March 1709/10, Sebastian Oley, aged about five years, was bound to Robert Jubb to serve him according to the law (AAJU TB#2:116, 119).

Sebastian Oley evidently inherited *Heirs Purchase,* for on 17 September 1726 as Sebastian Oley of Baltimore Co., planter, he conveyed 90 a. of *Heirs Purchase,* on the north side of Severn River, to William Worthington of Anne Arundel Co., Gent., in exchange for £60 and a 200 a. tract in Baltimore Co. called *Locust Thicket.* His wife Elizabeth released her dower (AALR SY#1:241).

An agrrement dated 4 August 1746 was made between Charles Conaway and Sebastian Oley [evidently for the conveyance of 100 a. *Lucky Hole*] (AALR RB#3:209).

'Sabastan' Oley of Anne Arundel Co. died leaving a will dated 10 March 1748 and proved 22 June 1749. His eldest son 'Sebaston' Oley was to have his dwelling plantation after his mother's decease. Son Vachel Oley was to have his plantation called *Lucky Hole.* Son Mordecai Oley was to have 15 pounds money. His daughters Elizabeth Grimes, Constant Oley, Susannah Oley, Bethier Oley, Hannah Oley, and Anis Oley were to have cattle. His eldest daughter Dinah Conaway was to have [shillings]. His wife Elizabeth was executrix. Thomas Joyce, Elliner Joyce, and Peter Johnson witnessed the will (MWB 26:145, abst. in *Md. Cal. Of Wills* 10:33).

Elizabeth Oley, the widow and executrix, filed an account of her husband's estate on 25 June 1750. She cited an inventory of £152.14.9, and listed payments coming to £13.6.4. The legatees were two daughters; Elizabeth Grimes, and Constant, wife of Jacob Merriken (MDAD 28:161).Elizabeth Oley was listed as a creditor of the estate of Peter Johnston of Anne Arundel Co. on 21 January 1755 (MDAD 37:35).

Sebastian "Owly/Owley" and Elizabeth were the parents of the following children, born in St. Margaret's Parish (*AACR:*114, 118, 119, 123, 132): **7. Dianah,** b. 11 January

1726, m. Charles Conaway on 8 February 1743 in St. Margaret's Parish; **8. Elizabeth**, b. 2 November 1728, m. George Grimes; **9. Constant**, b. 27 January 1730; m. Jacob Merriken; Constant Merriken, widow of Jacob, died 17 September 1779 in St. Margaret's Parish (*AACR:* 140). **10. Sebastian**, b. 20 December 1732; **11. Susanna**, b. 6 February 1736; **12. Bethiah**, b. 15 September 1739; **13. Vachel**, b. 16 November 1741; **14. Mordecai**, b. 6 July 1744; **15. Hannah**, b. 9 September 1746; and **16. Anice**, b. 4 February 1748/9.

10. Sebastian Oley, son of Sebastian (4) and Elizabeth, was born 20 December 1732.

On 22 August 1760 Sebastian Oley, waterman, son of Sebastian, deceased, conveyed to George Page, planter, 90 a. *Heirs Purchase* (AALR RB#2:376).

On 11 April 1771 he was listed as a creditor of the estate of Jacob Merriken (MDAD 63:273). On 6 March 1773 he was a surety for Samuel Jacobs, administrator of John Jackson (MDAD 68:255).

13. Vachel Oley, son of Sebastian (4) and Elizabeth, was born 16 November 1741.

On 12 November 1749 John Conaway of Baltimore Co., planter, brother of Charles Conaway, deceased and Sophia Conaway, wife of the late Charles Conaway, conveyed to Vachel Oley, son of the late Sebastian Oley, 100 a. *Lucky Hole,* near Swan Gut, and adjacent to *Locust Thicket.* Elizabeth Oley, widow of Sebastian, paid the alienation fine on behalf of Vachel Oley [who was only eight years old at the time] (AALR RB#3:209).

== 0 ==

Matriarch Elizabeth [-?-] Cogell Dorman Swindell
With notes on the Dorman Family

Elizabeth [-?-] married 1st James Cogell who was transported about 1664 as a servant by John Dixon (MPL 8:129). She married 2nd, Robert Dorman, who was transported by 1663 (MPL 6:125). Her third husband was Daniel Swindell, who was transported to Maryland in 1663 and who died by 1 July1701 (MPL AA: 509).

Cogell did not buy or sell any land in Baltimore Co. On 12 March 1668/9 he made his mark when he and John Roads witnessed a deed from John Dixon to Richard Ellinsworth (Scisco, *Baltimore Co. Land Records:* 12. He witnessed the will of John Dixon on 20 October 1669 (MWB 1:396, abst. in *Md. Cal. of Wills* 1:55). On 8 October 1675 Cogell was listed as debtor to the estate of Thomas Salmon (INAC 2:160). In April 1676 he and John Channell appraised the estate of Samuel Trasey (INAC 2:67).

James Phillips posted an administration bond on Cogell's estate on 14 March 1676 [1676/7?] with Thomas Long and Richard Ball as sureties (BAAB 1:282). On 5 February 1676/7 James Phillips of Baltimore Co. was granted administration on estate of James Cogell, as the greatest creditor, even though the said Phillips lived remote from the Office. The appraisers were John Harden, Giles Stephens. (MDTP 8:411).

On 7 February 1676/7 Giles Stevens, for Elisabeth Dorman, executrix of James Cogill (also known as James Covill) of Baltimore Co. exhibited his will, proved by said Stevens, one of the witnesses. Giles Stevens signed as 'Joyles Steavens.' Another witness, who was the author of the will, was Oliver Haile. Richard Ball, Gent., was to summon said Haile to testify. Said Elisabeth was granted administration, revoking the admin granted to James Phillips. The appraisers were John Arden and Giles Stevens, and Ball was to administer the oath (MDTP 8A:412-3).

John Arden and Giles Stevens appraised Cogell's personal estate on 11 May 1677. They listed the following property: one chest; three cows three calves, one steer, and two yearlings, They valued his personal property at 3270 lbs. tobacco (INAC 4:498).

On 20 October 1677 it was exhibited that Richard Ball of Baltimore Co. had sworn James Phillips as administrator of James Cogill on 14 March 1676. There was a bond on said estate with securities: Thomas Long said Ball had sworn Elisabeth Dorman as executrix. Said Cogill [Phillips?] refused to execute said will, since the debts exceed the credits. On 28 February 1676 the said will had been declared void. James Phillips, administrator of James Cogill exhibited the inventory (MDTP 9A:377-8).

James Phillips filed an account of his estate on 11 April 1678. He cited the inventory as given above and listed payments coming to the same amount. Payments were made to Thomas Long in behalf of Nicholas Greenberry, Richard Ball, and Mr. Mills (INAC 5:17).

Robert Dorman had been transported by 1663. In October 1670 he had surveyed 120 a. *Selah's Point* on the north side of Back River. This tract was later held by Selah Dorman (*MRR:* 78-9).

Daniel Swindell was in Baltimore Co. by 1694 as a taxable in the North Side Patapsco Hundred, and in 1695 he was in the same Hundred with Selah Dorman listed next to him (*IBCW:* 6, 10). On 10 December 1695 he patented 100 a. *Daniel's Plains* (MPL 37:276). Daniel Swindell and William Harper appraised the estate of Isaac Waskell on 19 November 1688 (BINV 1:69).

On 1 July 1701 Elizabeth posted an administration bond on the estate of Swindell, with Selah Dorman and William Wright as sureties (MDTP 18B:98). Elizabeth Saunders administered the estate on 2 June 1702 (INAC 21:369).

Elizabeth Swindell conveyed half of her estate to her granddaughter Sarah Dorman on 6 August 1701.

Elizabeth died leaving a will dated 23 February 1704/5 and proved 18 May 1705. She left personalty to her daughter Judith Gorman, and the residue of her estate to her son Selah, who was named executor. Edward Hoale, Bolit Gardiner, George Hoppam, and Andrew Anderson witnessed the will (MWB 3:436, abst. in *Md. Cal. of Wills* 3:46).

Dorman posted an administration bond on 18 May 1705 with John Oldton and Thomas Long. Her estate was inventoried by Oldton and Long on 19 May 1708 and valued at £23.5.4. Dorman administered the estate on 16 August 1706 (INAC 25:416).

Benjamin Roberts, aged 50, deposed on 13 January 1784 that he had heard his father John Roberts or Camel (who was over 90 when he died), say that one of Daniel Swindell's daughters had married Michael Gorman, and that Selah Dorman had married the other daughter (BACT 1773-1784:401).

Robert and Elizabeth Dorman were the parents of: **2. Selah;** and **3. Judith.**

2. Selah Dorman, almost certainly the son of Robert and Elizabeth (1), was of age in 1682 to be a taxable in the North Side of Patapsco Hundred. He died by 14 February 1717 when an administration bond on his estate was posted by John Ensor with James Durham and James Watkins.

In 1710 he bought 100 a. *Inloes Loin* from Thomas and John Boring (BALR TR#A: 82).

Selah was the father of: **4. Sarah**, m. Lewis Barton (See The Barton Family of Baltimore County, elsewhere in this work).

3. Judith Dorman, daughter of Robert and Elizabeth, may have married 1st, Andrew Peterson. On 16 May 1692, Judith Dorman, spinster, posted an administration bond on Andrew Peterson's estate with John Hayes and Selah Dorman (BAAB 2:429, 430; MDTP 16:173). Judith married, 2nd, by May 1696 Michael [-?-] Gorman (sometimes transcribed as Gormacon, Gormack, or Garmaton). About May1696 Gormack and his wife Judith, administratrix of Andrew Peterson, exhibited their accounts (MDTP 16:170). Michael Gormacon married 2nd, Ann [-?-]. It is almost certainly another Judith who married a Lewis Barton, and William Farfarr.

== 0 ==

Matriarch Elizabeth [-?-] Sampson Bagford Hinton Stone

See also: George Ely Russell, "Elizabeth (-?-) (Sampson) (Bagford) (Hinton) Stone of Patapsco Hundred," *MGSB* 40 (3) (Summer 1999) 301-310.

1. **Elizabeth [-?-]** married, 1st, Richard Sampson, 2nd, James Bagford, 3rd, Samuel Hinton, and, 4th, Thomas Stone (MWB 14:43, abst. in *Md. Cal. of Wills* 4:29; BACP IS#C:4; BALR IS#H:328, 385; HWS#M:163; MWB 21:768, abst. in *Md. Cal. of Wills* 7:212).

John Gay and Charles Merryman appraised Richard Sampson's estate on 20 June 1709. They cited an inventory of £115.9.6. Richard and Isaac Samson approved the inventory (INAC 30:216). On 9 August 1713 Isaac Sampson administered Richard Sampson's estate, listing payments of £13.5.0 (INAC 34:35).

James Bagford first appeared in Baltimore Co. when he and John Downes were sureties for Elizabeth Sampson's administration bond (MDTP 22:475). On 26 May 1735 Sarah James, aged about 64 years, deposed that 18 or 19 years earlier Bagford had married Elizabeth (now the widow of Thomas Stone, deceased), and that she (Sarah James) had been sent for as a midwife to Elizabeth Bagford, and had delivered her of a son James Bagford, now living with his mother, and that James Bagford, Sr., was present at the birth (BALR HWS#M: 237). (See The Bagford Family of Baltimore County elsewhere in this work)

Samuel Hinton was first taxed on the North Side of Patapsco Hundred in 1705 (Clark, *Baltimore Co. Tax Lists, 1699-1706:* 54). On 4 November 1710 he purchased 260 a. *Bachelor's Delight* from Samuel Arden (BALR TR#A: 122).

Between 1711 and 1719 Hinton was often called upon to approve estates (BINV 1, 3, 5).

Samuel Hinton died leaving a will dated 4 April 1720 and proved 15 December 1720. He left his dwelling plantation to his wife Elizabeth, then to his son Timothy Hinton and to Sarah Hinton Olive; he hoped his son Timothy Hinton and his daughter Sary Hinton Olive shall live along with their step-mother until they have a right to the land by law; he also named his son-in-law James Bagford; he gave detailed instructions on who should inherit the land should his children should die without heirs. His wife Elizabeth was to be the sole executrix. Alexander Grant, Robert Mungumorer [Montgomery?], and John Eager witnessed the will (MWB 16:255, abst. in *Md. Cal. of Wills* 5:32).

John Eager and John Eaglestone appraised Hinton's personal estate on 27 March 1721 at £67.15.2½ (MINV 5:88).

On 14 February 1725/6 Thomas Stone conveyed *Arden's Adventure* to his son-in-law Richard Sampson (BALR IS#H:385). He also conveyed property to his son-in-law James Bagford. On 17 December 1726 Thomas Stone and wife Elizabeth conveyed 80 a. *Bagford's Fortune* to Luke Stansbury (BALR IS#H: 328). On 12 June 1733 Thomas Stone and wife Elizabeth conveyed 100 a. *Olive Yard* to Philip Jones (BALR IS#L:399).

Elizabeth Stone died leaving a will dated 28 January 1736 and proved 13 June 1737. She named her son John Sampson, who was to maintain Sarah Hinton Olive in accordance with the contract. She named her son James Bagford and daughter Constant Rowles (MWB 21:268, abst. in *Md. Cal. of Wills* 7:212).

Richard and Elizabeth ([-?-]) Sampson were the parents of: **2. Isaac,** b. about 1669/73; and **3. Richard,** b. about 1677.

James and Elizabeth ([-?-]) Bagford were the parents of: **4. James** (See the Bagford Family of Baltimore County elsewhere in this work).

Samuel Hinton, possibly by an earlier wife than Elizabeth, or by Elizabeth ([-?-]) Hinton were the parents of: **5. Timothy,** a minor in 1720, may have d. young; and **6. Sarah Hinton Olive,** who is last heard from on 11 February 1734 when she conveyed 325 a., being one-half of *Bachelor's Delight*, which she had inherited from Samuel Hinton, to Elizabeth Stone (BALR HWS#M:163).

== = 0 == =

Matriarch Jane [-?-] Waites Dixon Long
With Notes on the Dixon, Hayes, Scudamore, and Long Families

1. Jane [-?-] Waites Dixon Long died testate in Baltimore County by 3 June 1696. She married, 1st, in England. [-?-] Waites or Wright who had died before 1650, leaving a daughter Christiana who came to Maryland and married Francis Watkins. Jane married, 2nd, John Dixon, and 3rd Thomas Long.

In 1664 Mr. John Dixon immigrated to Maryland, bringing his wife Jane, and Jane's daughter by a previous marriage, Christiana Waites, and ten servants: James Cogell, Edward Walder, Hugh Broadwater, Michael Shadwell, John Shadwell, Edward Horton, Richard Anderson, James Abell, and Anne Bohemont (MPL DD:155, 8:129).

On 19 August 1664 Daniel Jones conveyed 420 a. *Dickenston* to John Dixon (BALR IS#I:1). Dixon had surveyed 450 a. *Dixon's Neck* on 7 June 1667 (*MRR:*59). On 1 November 1669 John Dixon gave a power of attorney to Richard Thurrell to convey 300 a. *Dixon's* Chance to Richard Ellingsworth. John Dixon signed his name, but Jane Dixon only made her mark. On 1 August 1671 Jane Dixon conveyed the entire 450 a. tract to Joseph Hawkins (BALR IR#PP: 74, 107).

John Dixon was a Justice of the Baltimore Co. Court in 1665 and he witnessed deeds on 17 August 1664, 12 March 1665/6 and 14 August 1666. On 1 April 1667 John Dixon and Lewis Bayne appraised the estate of Paul Kinsey (Scisco. *Baltimore Co. Land Records:* 3, 5, 9; MDTP 2:120).

Dixon died leaving a will dated 20 October 1669 and proved 3 September 1670. Christiana Waites and Eliza Southard were to have personalty. Wife Jane was named executrix and was to have the plantation, 2510 a. *Dickinston* during her life and 450 a. *Dixon's Neck* on Back River absolutely. Daughter Abigail and her heirs were to have the aforesaid plantation after the death of said wife. Capt. Thomas Howell and Nath. Stiles were overseers. Jas. Cogell, John Stevens, and John Clough witnessed the will (MWB 1:396, abst. in *Md. Cal. Wills* 1:55).

The inventory of Mr. John Dixon's estate was appraised by Capt. John Collier and Mr. Godfrey Harman on 31 December 1670. His inventory listed the following property: one old writing trunk, one-half ounce of silver; a parcel of skills [scales?] and waits, one old saddle and bridle, twelve old tubs, one hand mill, one mortar and pestle, a set of wedges, a ... saw, set of stilyards, a parcel of old iron, one small bote [boat?]; one iron pestle; one old feather bed and the rods belonging to it; two old feather beds and furniture, one old bed; bed hangings or furniture: four old chairs; six old leather chairs; one old table; one parcel of linen napkins, table cloths, goods; one small chest; two old iron pots; two brass kettles; skillet?, two spits, one milling pan, one pudding pan, two pot hooks and five racks; one parcel of earthenware; 14 pewter dishes, other pewter ware;

two brass candlesticks; a remnant of stuff and a remnant of linsey-woolsey; eight yards of motheaten kersey; one lame mare, nine cows and part of one?, two three-year –old heifers, and one four year-old heifer, eight two-year-old steers and ...?, three three-year-old steers, seven yearling calves, one young bull, six sows and their pigs, four barrow hogs, eight shoats; a parcel of lumber: two men servants: two old muskets, one old gun, one small carbine; one old cupboard; three monmouth ???, three pounds of [???]. The estimated value of his estate was 115,698 lbs. of tobacco (INAC 5:77-79).

On 11 November 1670 George Uty swore in Jane Dixon relict as administratrix of John Dixon (MDTP 6:259).

Jane married as her third husband, Thomas Long, who died by April 1693.

On 23 March 1671/2 Joseph Hawkins, Gent., of Back River, appointed his kinsman Richard Thurell his attorney to convey *Dixon's Neck* to Thomas Long, if Long should surrender a bill made by Hawkins (BALR G#J:15, TR#RA:11,13).

In July 1674 Thomas Long, Gent., with consent of his wife Jane, of Back R., conveyed 74 a. *Rich Neck*, on the south side of Middle River, to John Leakins (BALR G#J: 308).

On 4 May 1675 Thomas Long, Gent., was to prove the will of Johanna Spry of Baltimore County (MDTP 6:446). He was called Capt. Thomas Long on 23 March 1675 when he was a security for Giles Stevens (MDTP 7:359). He was the High Sheriff of Baltimore Co. in November 1676 when he was to administer the oath to Miles Gibson, admin. of Abraham Clarke (MDTP 8A:267). In November 1677 he was styled Major Thomas Long when he exhibited the bond of Col. William Ball, as administrator of Richard Ball (MDTP 9A:290).

Long testified on 25 August 1679 that Ralph Gearth had made a nuncupative will at Long's house, leaving everything to Long's wife. Long was appointed administrator (MDTP 11:178).

On 6 May 1680 Long and Jane of Back River conveyed 200 a. *Northwick* (part of 450 a. patented to Thomas Long) to Thomas Gibson (BALR IR#PP: 51). On 3 June 1682 the Longs conveyed 100 a. *Northwick* to Thomas Peart (BALR IR#AM: 170). On 6 June 1682 Thomas and Jane conveyed 100 a. of 450 a. *Northwick* to Thomas Gibson of Charles County (BALR IR#AM: 183).

On 1 June 1682 Thomas Scudamore and wife Abigail of Back River conveyed to Thomas Long, Gent., 136 a. of 420 a. *Dickenston*, being the plantation where Long now lives in right of his wife (BALR IR#AM: 187).

On 4 August 1684 Thomas Long, Gent., signed his name and wife Jane of Back River made her mark when they conveyed to Richard Enoch and Francis Freeman, planters of same place, 111 a., *Long Point*, adjacent to the tract *Hopewell*; on 5 August Long acknowledged the sale, and John Boring certified Long's wife's consent (BALR RM#HS: 95).

On 28 May 1689 John Hayes of Back River, planter, and wife Abigail, conveyed 136 a. *Dickenston* to Thomas Long, Gent. (BALR RM#HS:296).

In 1693 Thomas Long was indicted for threatening to burn this old courthouse [For this reference and much about the second courthouse I am indebted to the Reverend George B. Scriven for the use of his manuscript article, "Baltimore County's Second Court-house"].

On 16 August 1675 a commission was issued to Thomas Long of Baltimore County, Gent., to be Coroner of and in the Lower Parts of the same County. In 1689 Mr.

Thomas Long was chosen Major of the Baltimore County Militia in the room of Col. Wells, and he was appointed Sheriff (*ARMD* 15:46, 13:1143).

On 13 April 1693 Jane Long, administratrix of Thomas Long of Baltimore County, petitioned the court to allow Col. Nicholas Greenbury to examine her accounts. She stated she lived "150 miles from this city [St. Mary's City, at that time the capital of Maryland]." (MDTP 15A:21).

Thomas Heath, aged 50, deposed on 13 September 1693 that he had kept a house of entertainment and a ferry in Baltimore Co. for Major Thomas Long. He mentioned Mr. Mark Richardson, and Jane Long, widow and administratrix of said Thomas (MDTP 15A:47).

In October 1694 Jane administered the estate of Major Thomas Long, citing an inventory of £104.10.0 and listing payments in the same amount (INAC 13A:226).

Jane Long died leaving a will dated 19 May 1696 and proved 3 June 1696. She left personalty to her daughter Jane Peake, and said she was to have charge of the plantation for the benefit of her son Thomas Long. Daughter Tabitha was to have personalty *provided she did not marry George Chancy*. Lettice Robinson was to have personalty and if she died during her minority, it was to pass to Jane's granddaughter Penelope Scudamore. She named her grandchildren George and Joseph Peake, as well as Susanna Robinson, and John Wilkinson Robert Phillips, Isaac Martin, Thomas Durbin, and Mary Whaylum witnessed the will (MWB 7:125, abst. in *Md. Cal. of Wills* 2:100).

The will of Madam Jane Long, of Baltimore Co. was brought into the Prerogative Court. It constituted her daughter Jane Peek overseer for the benefit of her son, who was under the age of 19. The will had been proved by three witnesses (MDTP 16:183).

William Williamson and William Farfare appraised the estate of Mrs. Jane Long at £166.14.6. The inventory showed that she owned: one old horn comb and one small tooth comb of ivory; a silver seal; one old looking glass; two pair of horse harness, one old still, three pair old andirons, one hand mill and frame, one old spinning wheel: one feather bed and furniture: in the hall, a feather bed and furniture; a feather bed; an old flock bed; a little feather bed; two a feather beds, an old bed; one old couch; had furniture, valence and curtains; one bolster, sheets and three blankets, three old coarse sheets; four old turkey worked chairs, two old wooden chairs; 12 old leather chairs; a black walnut table 7½ feet long, four old tables; an old knife; one diaper table cloth , one old coarse table cloth, six coarse napkins; four old chests; two old trunks; two old cupboards; two old rugs; one four gallon iron pot, three old broken iron pots; two old brass kettles, one iron kettle, a parcel of old earthenware; a parcel of old pewter; two old pewter candle sticks, one old lanthorn; country cloth, harne, a parcel of wool, buckram, dowlas, painted linen, seven raw hides; Mrs. Jane Long's wearing apparel and linen, a pair of old stays; 13 barrels of Indian corn, two bushels winter wheat, one bushel summer wheat, seven pecks of oats, one bushel of barley; livestock (not enumerated); servants enumerated were:Thomas Gellett, orphan, aged 19, come next August, Mary Phipps with five years to serve the first of last March, and Mary Whalle with five years to serve the latter end of last February; one old broken barrel of a gun, an old gun lock, one old carbine without a lock, one old gun, one old pistol barrel and lock; three forty gallon casks, one seven gallon cask, and one small cask, and 40 oz. of plate. The value of her estate was £166.14.6, plus £136.4.3 in debts (INAC 15:16-19).

On 23 August 1697 Joseph Peake who had married Jane, executrix of her mother, Jane Long, exhibited accounts of the estate of said Jane Long. Henry King and his wife were among those mentioned as receiving payments (INAC 15:137; MDTP 17:33).

On 31 August 1698 an account was filed by Joseph and Jane Peake, executors of Jane Long. They cited an inventory of £166.14.6, and listed payments of £62.4.3. A "...itha" King was mentioned as a daughter. [There was a tear in the page which deleted the first part of the name]. The legatees were: Blithe King, Jane Baker, Catherine Peake and George Peake (grandchildren), Penelope Skidmore, Susannah Robinson, Joseph Peake, John Wilkinson, John Hedge, Jr. (who was the exec. of Thomas Hedge, Sr., and

Joseph Wells (INAC 16:208). An account filed on 26 October 1698, citing an inventory of £116.14.0, and listing payments of £73.1.9, named legatees Susannah Robertson and James Todd (INAC 17:67).

On 24 June 1702 Jane Merryman, lately Jane Peake, filed an additional account showing an inventory of £166.14.0, and a second inventory of £40.1.0. Payments amounted to £463.8.11. Tabitha King was mentioned as a daughter (INAC 21:377).

By [-?-] Waites or Wright, Jane was the mother of: **2. Christiana**, m. Francis Watkins: See the Watkins Family elsewhere in this work.

By John Dixon, Jane was the mother of: **3. Abigail**, m. 1st, Thomas Scudamore; and 2nd, John Hayes.

Thomas and Jane Long were the parents of: **4. Jane**, m. 1st, Joseph Peake, 2nd, Charles Merryman, and 3rd, Benjamin Knight; **5.Tabitha**, m. 1st, Henry King by 15 April 1698 (MDTP 17:87): See The King Family of Baltimore County elsewhere in this work; she may have m. 2nd, Thomas Sheredine; **6. Lettice**, m. [-?-] Robinson (or Robertson); and **7. Thomas**, d. by 1720, having m. Susanna Mead.

3. Abigail Dixon, daughter of John and Jane (1), died by 3 August 1705. She married 1st, Thomas Scudamore and, 2nd, John Hayes, who married as his third wife, Mary, administratrix of Philip Johnson.

On 1 June 1682 Thomas Scudamore and wife Abigail of Back River conveyed to Thomas Long, Gent., 136 a. of 420 a. *Dickenston*, being the plantation where Long was now living in right of his wife (BALR IR#AM: 187).

On 9 May 1687 130 a. of *Scudamore's Last* was surveyed for Thomas Scudamore on Stony Run; on 10 October 1704 the tract was patented to John Hayes (*MRR*: 95).

On 27 February 1687/8 Abigail Scudamore posted a bond to administer Thomas Scudamore's estate (BAAB 3:445). She administered his estate on 6 March [1687/8] (INAC 9:481).

On 28 May 1689 John Hayes of Back River, planter, and wife Abigail, conveyed 136 a. *Dickenston* to Thomas Long, Gent. (BALR RM#HS:296). On 6 January 1699 John Hayes conveyed *Dickenston* to James Todd (who had married Penelope Scudamore, daughter of John Hayes' wife Abigail by her first husband Thomas Scudamore); Hayes' daughter Jane was mentioned in the deed (BALR TR#RA: 418).

On 2 July 1695, 317 a. of *Mount Hayes* was surveyed for John Hayes on the north side of Back River (*MRR:* 54). On 11 November 1719 Hayes conveyed 370 [sic] a. *Mount Hayes* to Thomas Harris, with the agreement that the dower rights of Hayes' wife Mary Ann be excepted; on 1 December 1719 Hayes gave a power of attorney to Mary Ann to acknowledge the sale of said 370 a. (BALR TR#DS:12-13).

On 3 August 1705 John Hayes gave a power of attorney to his wife Elizabeth to make over *Longland's Purchase* to Richard Longland; also to sell another 209 a. of land (BALR IR#AM:15). On 5 September 1705 John Hayes and Elizabeth conveyed 100 a. *Longland's Purchase*, a part of *Privilege*, to Richard Longland (BALR IR#PP:187).

John Hayes married 2nd, by 3 August 1705 Elizabeth [-?-].

Thomas Scudamore and Abigail were the parents of: **8. Penelope**, m. James Todd

John Hayes and Abigail were the parents of: **9. Jane**, b. about 1688, m. Thomas Stansbury.

John Hayes was also the father of the following, but the mother has not definitely been identified: **10. Elizabeth**, m. 1st. John Lenox and, 2nd, Luke Trotten; **11. Avarilla**, and **12. Jemima**.

7. Thomas Long, son of Thomas and Jane (1), died in Baltimore Co. by March 1720. He married Susanna Mead, who married 2nd, Stephen Body on 3 April 1722 (Reamy and Reamy, *St. Paul's Parish Register:* 119).

On 5 September 1706 Thomas Long and wife Susanna deeded to James Crooke, 733 a. *Jacob's Chase (Choice)* (BALR RM#HS: 544).

Henry Dunard of Patapsco Hundred, on 20 August 1713 bound himself to Thomas Long, to serve him for five years, until August 1718 (BALR TR#A:306).

Thomas Long died by 28 January 1720 when Susanna Long signed over all rights of administration on the estate of her deceased husband to Thomas Sheredine (MWB 16: 500, abst. in *Md. Cal. of Wills* 5:63). Thomas Sheredine posted a bond on 20 March 1720 he would administer the estate of Thomas Long (MDTP 24:322).

On 31 May 1721 the Sheriff of Baltimore Co. was directed to summon Susanna, widow of Thomas Long (MDTP 34:384). She deposed that Thomas Long sold *Dixon's Neck* and *Long's Addition* to Thomas Sheredine, but died before the sale was complete (MDTP 24:449).

Thomas and Susanna were the parents of: **13. John**; and **14. (poss.) Ann**, m. Nicholas Haile 25 Dec 1723 (Reamy and Reamy, *St. Paul's Parish Register:* 29).

13. John Long, son of Thomas (7) and Susanna, married Eleanor Owens on 8 March 1735. He died by 22 September 1761. Eleanor married John McConikin on 20 September 1762 (Reamy and Reamy, *St. Paul's Parish Register:* 32, 36).

On 6 March 1733 John Long of Baltimore Co. conveyed 2510 a. *Ballestone* to Stephen Body (BALR HWS#M: 119). On 6 June 1733 he conveyed part *Ballestone* to Joseph Ward (BALR IS#L: 378). In September 1740 John Long, with the consent of his wife Eleanor, conveyed part *Ballestone* to Buckler Partridge (BALR HWS#1-A: 449). On 8 January 1743 John Long and wife Eleanor convey 450 a. *Dixon's Neck* to Thomas Stansbury, Jr. (BALR TB#C: 402). On 6 October 1758 John Stinchcomb conveyed to John Long that tract called *Privilege* which Nathaniel Stinchcomb, father of said John, gave a bond to Thomas Long, father of afsd. John Long for conveyance in 1703 (BALR B#G: 240).

Long was a vestryman of St. Paul's Parish in 1751 and 1752 (Reamy and Reamy, *St. Paul's Parish Register:* 155).

John Long died leaving a will dated 30 May 1759 and proved 25 July 1759. His sons John Long and Joshua Long were to have all his lands where he lived, divided by a line of *Ballistone,* or part of *Ballistone,* now in possession of 'Domine' Buckner Partridge, till it intersected a line of the land where William Savory had lately died. His daughter, Susannah Trotten, was to have £5. Of the residue of his personal estate, one-third was to go to his wife and executrix, Eleanor, and the other two-thirds were to be equally divided to his 5 youngest children [not named]. Christopher Duke, Dixon Brown, and Richardson Stansbury witnessed the will (MWB 30:717, abst. by Gibb).

Eleanor Long administered John Long's estate on 22 September 1761 citing an inventory of £306.8.1 and listing payments of £135.7.11. Besides the daughter Susanna Trotten, and the wife of John Murray, the account mentioned four unnamed children (MDAD 47:19).

John and Eleanor were the parents of (order of some births uncertain; Reamy and Reamy, *St. Paul's Parish Register:* 17, 19, 20, 21, 42, 166): **15. Susanna**, m. Luke Trotten on 10 February 1754; **16. [-?-]**, m. John Murray by 22 September 1761; **17. Elenor,** b. 15 September 1749, d. 22 November 1764; **18. John,** b. 13 January 1753; **19. Jeane,** b. 17 October 1756; and **20. Joshua,** b. 13 May 1759, d. 11 November 1764.

18. John Long, son of John (13) and Eleanor, was born 13 January 1753.

In May 1776 John (or Jonathan) Long was a 1st Lieutenant in Capt. Garretson's Company in Back River Lower Hundred (*BARP:*163).

He was listed in 1783 as a taxable in Back River Lower hundred as owning 136 a.

part *Dixons*, 11½ a. *Rocky Point*, and 250 a. part *Privilege*. His household consisted on four free males and eight white inhabitants (Carothers, *1783 Tax List of Baltimore Co.*, p. 4).

John Long and his daughter Jane were named in the 1798 will of Thomas Hamm of Back River Neck (BAWB 6:247).

He may have died by 7 May 1801 leaving at least three children, **21. Thomas; 22. Eleanor;** and **23, Jane**, m. Thomas Raven.

21. Thomas Long, son of John (18), was named as a nephew on 6 April 1787, in the will of Richard Stansbury (BAWB 4:233). on 7 May 1801 Thomas and Eleanor Long, legal representatives of John Long, deceased, conveyed *Walter Dickson's Land*, which James Stansbury had died owning, to Richard Stansbury (BALR WG#69:363).

23. Jane Long, the legal representative of John (18) Long, married by 7 February 1807 Thomas Raven when she and Thomas Raven conveyed the tract *Walter Dickson* to Isaac Stansbury, the land James Stansbury died owning (BALR WG#93:320).

Unplaced:

|-?-| **Long** m. by 1 May 1723, Jane, formerly Tealle, accountant of John Tealle of Baltimore Co. (MINV 8:207).

|-?-| **Long** m. by 18 December 1781 Ann, daughter of John Stansbury (BAWB 4:102).

Abraham Long on 22 August 1794 was named as one of the children in the nuncupative will of Christopher Curtz (BAWB 5:163).

Elizabeth Long on 19 August 1801 came into court and the court appointed Thomas Long as her guardian, who accepted and offered Robert Porter and Alexis Lemmon as his securities. On 3 March 1802 it was ordered that Benjamin Buck and Alexis Lemmon, Jr., be appointed to estimate the annual value of the real estate of Elizabeth Long, orphan daughter of John Long. (BAOC 4:187, 230). On 24 April 1802, the subscribers reported that they had viewed the real estate of Elizabeth Long, orphan daughter of John Long and have estimated the annual value thereof: There are about 180 acres of arable land and about 100 acres of timbered land, in all, about 288 acres of land; two old dwelling houses, three old out houses, 20 cherry trees, 20 peach trees, and seven apple trees. They allowed the annual value of the said real estate to be $133.33. Also there is one lot of ground on the Federal Hill near the Observatory, it fronts the street 48 feet and runs back to the water 425 feet, then fronts the water 35 feet; there is one old frame dwelling house on said lot and we allow the annual value thereof to be $25 (/s/ Benjamin Buck, Alexise Lemmon). (BAOC 4:252)

James Long and Robert Slater administered the estate of Mones Moody on 17 February 1786, 3 March 1786, and 13 January 1787 (BAAD 8:247, 252, 351). On 15 December 1787 and in 1788 Long administered the estate of James Boyd (BAAD 9:136, 202).

James Long m. by 7 January 1794 Patience, widow of Roger Horace Pratt of Baltimore Co. (BALR WG#NN:594).

James Long on 10 June 1778 bought land in Baltimore Town from James Moore and his wife Cassandra of Kent Co. Cassandra was sister and heir at law of Robert Adair of Baltimore Co. (BALR WG#B:294).

James Long was on the 1774 Levy List for suppressing the tumultuous meeting of Negroes. On 10 July 1781 James Long and Catherine Long gave sworn testimony that they were present at the marriage of Thomas Lowry and Catherine Bryan, performed by Rev. Thomas Chase on or about 27 July 1784 (Reamy and Reamy, *St. Paul's Parish Register*, p. 38).

James Long's child was buried on 26 July 1790 (Reamy and Reamy, *St. Paul's Parish Register* p. 49).

John Long in November 1760 paid a criminal fine (BAMI 1755-1763).

John Long d. by 2 December 1772 when Margaret Long, administratrix, posted a bond for £300, with Francis Sanderson and James Long as sureties (BAAB 2:49). On 12 July 1774 Margaret Long was summoned to render accounts (MDTP 46:127-128).

John Long m. by 20 April 1780, Eleanor, formerly Eleanor Moore (BALR WG#E:264).

John Long m. by 18 November 1783 Elizabeth Sittlemeyer, who was a granddaughter of Mary [-?-], the widow of Sebastian Sittlemeyer (BALR WG#T:8-9).

John Long was paid a legacy from the estate of John Stansbury on 10 November 1790 (BAAD 10:221). He m. by 16 February 1793 Ann Stansbury, who was mentioned in the administration account of John Stansbury (BAAD 11:206).

John Long and Elizabeth Partridge were married by license dated 9 November 1791 (BAML). On 6 March 1793 Elizabeth was named as the administratrix of Danbury B. Partridge (BAAD 11: 225).

Robert Long m. 28 January 1768 Elizabeth Edwards 1772 ("The Nicholas Dorsey Bible," *The Notebook* 10 (3) (Sep 1994; *MBR* 3:67-69).

Robert Long was charged with bastardy at the March 1768 Court (BAMI 1768-1769:9). Robert Long, in his will, made 13 January 1779, named his natural son Robert Carey Long, and his bros. Andrew and James Long, and a sister Jane Parkhill (BAWB 3:389).

Robert Long by 4 September 1782 had a marriage contract with Mary [-?-], who named her children John and Mary Norwood in her will (BAWB 3:526).

Samuel Long and Mary Cummins were married by December 1799, when Margaret Cummins, in her will made 6 December 1799 named her granddaughter Jane Long (BAWB 6:238).

Sewell Long m. by 31 August 1747 Margaret, daughter of Richard Acton MDTP 32:116, 132).

Thomas Long died by 5 October 1781 when Jane Long, administratrix, with John Parks and John Tinges, sureties, posted a bond for £1000.0.0 (BAAB 5:103).

Thomas Long and Elizabeth Johnston were m. by lic. on 18 October 1792, at St. Peter's Catholic Church, Baltimore (*Piet*:138). (BAML gives her name as Elizabeth Inkston).

==0==

Matriarch Rebecca [-?-] Daniell Emson Cobb Hawkins
With Notes on the Emson, Hawkins, Paulson, and Whitaker Families

See also: Robert Barnes, "The Em(er)son-Cobb-Hawkins Connection," *Maryland Magazine of Genealogy* 4 (2) (Fall 1981) 67-73; and Ruby Whitaker-Buck. *Mark Whitaker, Baltimore County, Maryland (about 1670-1729) and Allied Families*. Sacramento, CA: Privately Printed, 1992.

1. Rebecca [-?-], married 1st, John Daniell, who died in Calvert Co. about 1685. Rebecca married, 2nd, by 9 July 1686 James Em(p)son (INAC 9:27). By 9 October 1710 she had married, 3rd, James Cobb (INAC 32A:23; BAAD 2:147). She married 4th, John Hawkins.

John Daniell's inventory was appraised by William Turner and James Dossey at £14.0.6 (INAC 8:324). On 9 July 1686 his relict and administratrix, Rebecca, now the wife of James Emson, filed an account of the estate citing an inventory of 2805 lbs. tob. (INAC 9:27).

On 2 November 1703 Thomas Thurston of Baltimore Co., planter, son and heir of Col. Thomas Thurston, deceased, conveyed *Elburton* to James Empson of Calvert Co. (BALR HW#2: 307).

James Emison or Emson of Baltimore Co. died leaving a will dated 5 January 1707 and proved 31 January 1707. He named his wife Rebecca and left her all his personal estate. Son James was to have his 150 a. dwelling plantation and was to be of age at 16. His daughters Eliza, Rebecca, and Anne, and the unborn child and their heirs were to have the residue of his lands, and the dwelling plantation if James died during his minority. John Roberts, Thomas Taylor and Grace Roberts witnessed the will (MWB 12:229 abst. in *Md. Cal. of Wills* 3:104).

James Cobb and Rebecca Ernston [*sic*] were married on 30 October 1709 (Reamy and Reamy, *St. George's Parish Register:* 14). James Cobb was probably the son of James Cobb who had been born about 1651, transported to Md. about 1676 and moved to Baltimore Co. by Nov 1721 when at age 70 he had petitioned the court to be levy free (*BCF:*117).

James Cobb died 12 March 1718 (Reamy and Reamy, *St. George's Parish Register:* 19). His executrix and relict Rebecca, widow of John Hawkins, filed an account of his estate on 1 Oct 1734. She cited an inventory of £121.6.6, and a second inventory of £22.18.4. The estate was distributed with one-third going to the widow, and the balance in equal shares to the children, all of whom were of age: daughter Priscilla Cobb, daughter Frances wife of Charles Jones, daughter Charity, wife of Zachariah Spencer, daughter Margaret wife of Seaborn Tucker, and son James Cobb (MDAD 12:476). Another account was filed on 22 July 1737; an inventory of £13.8.0 was cited and daughter Priscilla was now the wife of John White (MDAD 15:354).

Rebecca married, 4th, John Hawkins. John Hawkins died leaving a will dated 19 November 1732 and proved 8 August 1733. His son John, daughter Ann Litton, and son-in-law James Cobb were to have his portion of his father's estate when he arrived at the age of 21. Wife Rebecca was to be the executrix, and have his dwelling plantation for life; it was then to be divided between his son John and daughter Ann Litton. Nathan Rigbie, Seaborne Tucker, and William Duley (or Daley) witnessed the will (MWB 20:750 abst. in *Md. Cal. of Wills* 7:33).

On 22 July 1737 Rebecca filed an account of his estate, citing an inventory of £8.6.0 (MDAD 15:353).

John and Rebecca ([-?-]) Daniell are not known to have had any children.

James and Rebecca ([-?-]) Emson were the parents of: **2. James,** under age in 1707, d. 21 February 1719/20 (Reamy and Reamy, *St. George's Parish Register:* 20); **3. Elizabeth,** m. 1st, Mark Whitaker, and, 2nd, Francis Taylor; **4. Rebecca,** m. John Hawkins; **5. Anne,** m. Cornelius Poulson; **6. Rachel,** b. 7 June 1708 (Reamy and Reamy, *St. George's:* 18).

James and Rebecca ([-?-]) Cobb were the parents of: **7. Rebecca,** b. 26 March 1710 (Reamy and Reamy, *St. George's Parish Register:* 18), m. John Hawkins, Jr.; **8. Priscilla,** m. John White on 18 May 1726; **9. Frances,** m. Charles Jones on 26 December 1727; **10. Charity** (or Christiana), b. 15 April 1712, m. Zachariah Spencer on 2 February 1728 (Reamy and Reamy, *St. George's Parish Register:* 18, 33); **11. Margaret,** b. 15 May 1714, m. Seaborn Tucker on 2 April 1730 (Reamy and Reamy, *St. George's Parish Register:* 18, 34); and **12. James,** b. 16 September 1716 (Reamy and Reamy, *St. George's Parish Register:* 19).

3. Elizabeth Emson, daughter of James and Rebecca (1), married 1st, Mark Whitaker on 13 February 1717 [prob. 1717/8]. She married, 2nd, on 6 October 1729 Francis Taylor (Reamy and Reamy, *St. George's Parish Register:* 19, 33).

Mark Whitaker's first wife, Catherine, died 15 November 1717. He died 1 May 1729 (Reamy and Reamy, *St. George's:* 19, 32).

On 3 March 1713/4 Robert West and wife Sarah conveyed. 100 a. *Westwood* to Mark Whitaker (BALR TR#A: 266).

Francis Taylor, about 1729, had a prenuptial contract with Elizabeth Whitacre, administratrix of Mark Whitecar (Whitseer) of Baltimore Co. As part of this contract in 1729 Elizabeth Whiteacre conveyed 250 a. part of *Elburton* to Francis Taylor (BALR IS#K: 109; MDTP 29:89; MDAD 11:433). On 24 November 1735 Taylor and his wife Elizabeth, conveyed 200 a. part of *Elburton* to Jacob Giles (BALR HWS#M: 339). On 23 July 1746 Francis and Elizabeth conveyed 50 a. *Taylor's Delight* to John Risteau (BALR TB#E: 131).

Mark and Elizabeth (Emson) Whitaker were the parents of (Reamy and Reamy, *St. George's Parish Register:* 19, 21, 24, 32): **13. Charity Whitaker,** b. 8 December 1718; **14. James Whitaker,** b. 8 February 1720/1; **15. Empson Whitaker,** b. 30 September 1724; and **16. Elizabeth Whitaker,** b. 28 August 1726

Francis and Elizabeth (Emson) Taylor were the parents of (Reamy and Reamy, *St. George's Parish Register:* 33, 39): **17. Grace Taylor,** b. 5 August 1730; and **18. Rachel Taylor,** b. 16 November 1732.

4. Rebecca Emson, daughter of James (1) and Rebecca, married John Hawkins on 23 December 1718 (Reamy and Reamy, *St. George's Parish Register:* 19). John Hawkins died between December 1743 and September 1744.

On 20 October 1737 Isaac Webster and Jacob Giles conveyed 100 a. *Arabia Petrea* to Rebecca Hawkins (BALR HWS#1-A:10). On 7 June 1742 Gregory Farmer, Jr., and wife Rachel conveyed 102 a. *Arabia Petrea* to Rebecca Hawkins (BALR TB#A:177). On 3 September 1744 Rebecca Hawkins, widow, conveyed two 100 a. parcels of *Arabia Petrea* to Michael Montgomery of Pa. (BALR TB#C:570).

On 19 July 1725 Nathan Rigbie, with consent of wife Cassandra, conveyed 100 a. of land to Hawkins (BALR IS#K: 174). On 9 December 1743 John Hawkins, with the consent of his wife, Rebecca, conveyed 100 a. *Hawkins Change* to Michael Hodgkins (BALR TB#C: 399). On 9 December 1743 John Hawkins and wife Rebecca conveyed 100 a. part of *Elburton* to Jacob Giles (BALR TB#C: 396).

John and Rebecca (Emson) Hawkins were the parents of (Reamy and Reamy, *St. George's Parish Register:* 22, 26, 34, 39, 43, 56): **19. John Hawkins,** b. 16 July 1721, may have died young; **20. Ann Hawkins,** b. 29 March 1724; **21. John Hawkins,** b. 23 May 1726; **22. Joseph Hawkins,** b. 23 April 1728; **23. Rebecca Hawkins,** b. 23 February 1729; **24. James Hawkins,** b. 31 July 1733; **25. Elizabeth Hawkins,** b. 6 February 1735; and **26. Rachel Hawkins,** b. 21 March 1737.

5. Ann Emson, daughter of James and Rebecca (1), married Cornelius Poulson (Poleson, Polson, Powlson) on 23 December 1720 (Reamy and Reamy, *St. George's Parish Register:* 21).

On 16 July 1757 Ann was named as a daughter and coheiress of James Empson (BALR B#G:22).

Paulson later moved to Frederick Co.

Cornelius and Ann were the parents of (Reamy and Reamy, *St. George's Parish Register:* 22, 24, 47): **27. Elizabeth Paulson,** b. 6 January 1721/1; **28. Rebecca Paulson,**

b. 5 October 1724; as Rebecca Polson she was charged with bastardy at the August 1742 Court and again at the March 1750/1 Court (BACP TB#D:1, 73, TR#6: 270); and **29. Andrew Paulson**, b. 18 February 1734.

6. Rachel Emison, daughter of James and Rebecca (1), was born 7 June 1708. She married Gregory Farmer on 14 June 1723 (Reamy and Reamy, *St. George's Parish Register:* 18, 23).

On 25 March 1737 Gregory Farmer and wife Rachel conveyed 100 a. part *Elburton* to Jacob Giles (BALR IS#IK: 371). In September 1754 Gregory and Rachel conveyed part of *New Westwood* to William Cox (BALR BB#I:288).

Gregory and Rachel do not appear to have had any children.

29. Andrew Paulson, son of Cornelius and Ann (Emson) (5) Paulson, was born b. 18 February 1734, and died testate in Frederick Co. in 1807. He married by 27 November 1758, Prudence, daughter of John Evans (MDAD 44:227).

On 20 July 1775 he was one of the appraisers of the estate of Jacob Myers (Miers) of Frederick Co. (MINV 122:43).

Andrew and Prudence were the parents of the following children, named in his will (Query posted by Brian Bovey in *MGSB* 23 (1982) 266): **32. John Paulson; 33. James Paulson; 34: Cornelius Paulson; 35. Betsy Paulson; and 36.** and **37.**, two unnamed daughters.

== 0 ==

The Maxwell Family of Baltimore County

1. Samuel Maxwell married, 1st, by 29 September 1720. Mary King, daughter of Henry and Tabitha (Long), who was a daughter of Thomas and Jane Long (MDAD 3:356; BAAD 2:13). Samuel Maxwell married 2nd, Jane [-?-]. Mary Maxwell, wife of Samuel Maxwell, administrator, filed an account of the estate of Henry King on 29 September 1720. She cited the inventory and listed payments of £18.3.3 (MDAD 3:356).

In 1719 Maxwell was licensed to keep an ordinary at his house (BACP IS#C: 240).

On 9 December 1724 he bought *Westwood* from William and Judith Houchings (BALR IS#H:89). On 5 June 1733 Maxwell conveyed 200 a. *Westwood* and 100 a. *Addition to Westwood* to Luke Stansbury (BALR IS#L: 374). On 9 June 1737 Maxwell conveyed 240 a. *Maxwell,* which he had surveyed on 20 December 1735 to William Maccubbin (BALR IS#IK: 446). On 24 November 1737 he patented 240 a. *Maxwell's Habitation* (MPL El#2: 650, El#5: 228). On 17 March 1738 Maxwell, with the consent of his wife Jane, conveyed 240 a. *Maxwell's Habitation,*, made up of *The Forest* and *Addition,* to William Maccubbin (BALR HWS#1-A: 248).

On 18 June 1737 Nicholas Gostwick, with consent of wife Avarilla, conveyed 52 a. *Shure's Inheritance* to Samuel Maxwell (BALR IS#IK: between folios 454-461). On 1 December 1738 Maxwell, with the consent of his wife Jane, conveyed the 52 a. back to Nicholas Gostwick (BALR HWS#1-A: 158).

On 19 June 1738 Edward Pigg of Spottsylvania Co., Va., conveyed *Black Wolf Neck,* 200 a. *Felks Range* and 200 a. *Good Hope* to Samuel Maxwell (BALR HWS#1-A: 104). On 15 October 1738 Maxwell conveyed 150 a. *Black Wolf Neck* and other tracts, to Buckler Partridge of Baltimore Co., surgeon (BALR HWS#1-A: 184). On 14 June 1740 Maxwell conveyed 150 a. *Black Wolf Neck* to Walter James; Maxwell's wife Jane consents (BALR HWS#1-A: 396).

Maxwell died by 28 April 1744 [sic] when Jane Maxwell posted an administration bond with Joseph Thomas and Nicholas Day as sureties (MDTP 31:493). Another bond was posted on 13 December 1744 [sic] by Nicholas Day with George Brown and Robert Dutton as sureties (MDTP 31:558; BAAB 2:189, 292). Day administered the estate on 20 Oct 1745 (BAAB 5:44).

The following deed suggests that Samuel may have died later. On 3 September 1745 Thomas Baxter of Bucks Co., PA, with consent of wife Mary, conveyed 100 a. of *Spring Neck* to Samuel Maxwell (BALR TB#D: 351).

In August 1746 Joseph Thomas was chosen guardian for Samuel's two sons, Samuel and James (BACP TB#TR#1:120).

Samuel and Mary were the parents of: **2. Joseph**, b. about 1729; **3. Samuel; 4. James;** and **6. Moses.**

2. Joseph Maxwell, son of Samuel (1) and Mary (3), was born about 1729. In June 1744 he was bound to Joseph Thomas (BACP 1743-1745/6:229). In 1750 Joseph Thomas owned 100 a. *Spring Neck*, and 100 a. *Maxwell's Hope* (Baltimore Co. Debt Book for 1750: 80).

On 8 August 1750 Joseph Maxwell, the only surviving son of Samuel Maxwell, and brother of James Maxwell, deceased, conveyed to Nicholas Ruxton Gay, 100 a. *Spring Neck* and 100 a. *Maxwell's Hope* (BALR TR#C: 555).

4. James Maxwell, son of Samuel (1) and Mary, died by 4 August 1748 when administration bond was posted by Nicholas Ruxton Gay with John Paca and Isaac Risteau as sureties (MDTP 32:186; BAAB 2:106). Walter James and Benjamin Baxter appraised the personal estate of James Maxwell, son of Samuel on 4 December 1748, and valued it at £27.0.4, Joseph Maxwell and Moses Maxwell, signed as next of kin (MINV 43:489). Gay administered the estate on 9 November 1750 (BAAB 2:196; BAAD 5:108).

6. Moses Maxwell, son of Samuel (1) and Mary, signed the inventory of Joseph Thomas as next of kin on 30 January 1748 (MINV 38:197). He signed the inventory of James Maxwell as next of kin on 4 December 1748 (MINV 43:489). He received a payment from the estate of Joseph Thomas on 23 May 1752 as his portion of the estate of his father James Maxwell (MDAD 32:248).

Unplaced:
Robert Maxwell signed the inventory of Joseph Thomas as next of kin on 30 January 1748 (MINV 38:197).

== 0 ==

The McClain Family of Baltimore County

N.B.: The name also appears as MacClan, Mackland, Macklane, McClane, McLane, McClean, and McLean,

1. Hector McClain was in Baltimore Co. by 1692 as a taxable in N. Side of Patapsco Hundred in the same household as Joseph Heathcote (*IBCW:*1). He married by 9 June 1697 Sarah, daughter of Capt. Thomas Morgan (MWB 7:392)/ Morgan's daughter

Martha married 1st, Joseph Heathcote, and 2nd, by 2 September 1693 Nicholas Fitzsimmons (BACP G#1:116, 152; MWB 7:392; MDTP 17:69).

On 25 July 1694 McClain surveyed 300 a. *Hector's Hopyard,* and 100 a. *Hector's*

Fancy on 22 March 1695. He patented *Hector's Hopyard* on 9 November 1695 (MPL 34:109, 40:69), and *Hector's Fancy* on 10 March 1696 (MPL 40:549). He patented 40 a. *Bought Witt* in 1700 (MPL DD#5: 100).

On 8 April 1698 James Murray conveyed 100 a. *Athol* to Hector Maclane, in exchange for *MacLane's Hope* (BALR IS#L: 254).

McClain witnessed the will of John Carrington on 22 March 1695 (MWB 7:168, abst. in *Md. Cal. of Wills* 2:105).

No death or probate records have been found for this Hector McClain.

Hector and Sarah were the parents of: **2. Hector,** d. by 1 October 1722 in Baltimore Co., MD.

2. Hector McClain, son of Hector (1) and Sarah, died by 1 October 1722 in Baltimore Co., MD. He married 1st, Ann [-?-], and 2nd, Amy Norman, daughter of George and Johanna ([-?-]) Norman. Amy married 2nd, John Townsend.

On 28 March 1702 James Carroll conveyed 200 a. part of *Hector's Hopyard* to Hector Maclane (BALR HW#2:132).

In 1703 Hector 'Macklane' patented 46 a. *Boughtwitt* (MPL CD#4"147, DD#5:100). Sometime in 1719 he patented 300 a. *Hector's Chance* (MPL CD#4:147, IL#B: 284).

Macclain was one of the appraisers of the estate of John Wealls (or Wells) of Baltimore Co. on 11 August 1721 (MINV 6:190).

Hector Macclain of Baltimore Co. died by 9 October 1722 when Christopher Randall and Richard Owens (Owings) appraised his estate at £261.2.3. George Baley (Bailey) and John Macclaine signed as next of kin (MINV 8:157).

John and Amy Townsend filed an account of Maclane's estate on 19 November 1724. After citing the inventory as given above, they listed payments of £53.10.8 (MDAD 6:223). On 26 May 1723 they filed a final account and listed payments of £263.3.1. John Maclane was listed as a son and legatee, and the balance was paid to the widow and three children: William, Katherine, and Sarah (MDAD 12:1).

On 22 February 1742 Charles Carroll of Annapolis petitioned the Court that Hector Maccclane of Baltimore County made his will in 1722 appointing his wife Amy as executrix, and later died possessed of several tracts of land and other chattels of considerable value. Said Amy acquired letters testamentary on 1 October 1722 and later married John Townsend, surgeon, who by virtue of his marriage possessed the personal estate of said McLane, Townsend has been indebted to Carroll for £81.3.2, and in spite of Carroll's requests has 'combined and confederated' with one William Macclain, son of the said Hector. John Townsend died by 5 May 1739 (MCHR JK#4: 359).

Hector and Ann were the parents of: **3. John; 4. William,** d. by 18 January 1751/52, m. Mary [-?-]; **5. Nathaniel; 6. Sarah,** m. George Bailey, who d. by 27 August 1763 (BALR B#L:468); **7. Mary;** and **8. Catherine,** m. John Stinchcomb.

3. John McClain, son of Hector (2) and Ann, married Margaret Taylor on 14 January 1732/33 (Reamy and Reamy, *St. Paul's Parish Register:* 30).

John 'Macklane' and [his sister] Katherine patented 300 a. *Hector's Chance* on 29 September 1730 (MPL PL#7:609, IL#A:53).

In 1736 John Stinchcomb gave a bond to John McClaine to carry out agreement they made to divide *Hector's Chance*, which Hector McLane had devised to his son John and daughter Katherine, now wife of Stinchcomb (BALR HWS#M:382; HWS#M: 122).

On 30 June 1744 John Maclain conveyed 150 a., being one-half of *Hector's Chance*, to John Stinchcomb. His wife consented (BALR TB#C: 544).

John Maclain patented 25 a. *Macklaine's Hills* in 1745 (MPL LG#C: 465, LG#E:

147

517). He patented 575 a. *Addition to McClains Hills,* on 31 August 1752 (MPL BY#5: 632). On 5 October 1753 he conveyed 74 a. part *McLane's Hills* and *Addition to Maclanes Hills* to Solomon Stocksdale. His wife Margaret consented (BALR BB#1:139).

He may be the John McClane who administered the estate of Abraham Durham on 6 November 1770 (BAAD 6:224).

John and Margaret were the parents of (Reamy and Reamy, *St. Paul's Parish Register:* 9, 12, 13) ; **9. Sarah**, b. 16 November 1734; **10. Hector**, b. 14 September 1736; and **11. John**, b. 4 February 1738/39.

4. William McClain, son of Hector (2), died by 18 January 1752. He married Mary [-?-].

In 1750 he owned 40 A. *Bought Well,* 40 a. *Hector's Fancy,* and 20 a. *Athol* (Baltimore Co. Debt Book for 1750:29).

McClain died leaving a will dated 26 January 1749/50 and proved 18 January 1751. To his wife and executrix, Mary Macclan, he left *Athol* 20 a., *Bought Witt* 40 a., and part of *Hectors Fancy* 40 a., for life, and on her death to his sister Catherine Stinchcomb; also *Macclans Venture* 50 a. and his personal estate. John Bailey, Jabez Bailey, and Bazel Ragon witnessed the will (MWB 28:220, abst. by Gibb).

Mary 'McLane' posted an administration bond on 8 January 1752 with Thomas Johnson and Emanuel Teal (BAAB 2:219). On 29 July 1752 Mary filed an inventory of William's personal estate appraised on 20 March 1752 by Joshua Owings and Chris Randall, who valued McLane's personal estate at £56.4.5. Amy Townsend and Katherine Stinchcomb signed as next of kin (MINV 49:54).

By 17 October 1754 Mary had married 2nd William Williams, when she filed an account of William's estate, citing the inventory as given, and listing payments of £75.8.7 (MDTP 36:56; MDAD 36:434).

Unplaced:
Alexander McClane married by 8 August 1786 Kezia, administratrix of Samuel Haslet (BAAD 8:289).
Hector McLane died intestate in York Co., Penna., prior to 27 May 1761, leaving a widow Elizabeth and an orphan daughter Elizabeth, aged 5 years (YOCD A: 177).
Hector 'McLane' married Mary Rebecca [-?-] who died by 3 April 1761; their daughter Margaret was b. January 1760 and baptized 30 April 1761("Christ Evang. Lutheran Church, York"). Rebecca McLain, wife of Hector, died 4 July at York ("Records of St. James Church, Lancaster, Pa.")
John McClean of York Co., Penna. died leaving a will dated 18 February 1754 and proved 26 May 1755 (YOWB A: 106). His son John was to have the plantation the testator now lives on; son James was to have one cow and one heifer; daughter Ceteran was to have two cows and four sheep; he left money to his son William, and his son-in-law Henry Black. His son John was to be sole executor. Andrew Hart and David Hart witnessed the will.
John McClain on 15 August 1769 stated he would not pay the debts of his wife Sarah (BACT B#G:298).
William McLane was listed as a pauper in the 1783 Assessment List of Delaware Upper Hundred, with one male and a total of six inhabitants (Carothers, *1783 Tax List of Baltimore Co.:*20).
William 'McLane' was at Springfield Twp., Huntingdon Co., Penna. on 20 June 1797 when he deeded to Thomas Stocksdale all of *McClain's Hills* and *Addition to McClains Hills* that had not been previously conveyed to anyone by the grantor's father John 'McLane' (BALR WG#51:248).

The McQueen Family

1. Dugal McQueen was born 1690 in Corybrough, on the Findhorn River, Inverness Shire, Scotland (Woody Young. "Our Genealogy, Young, Hodge, Davis, Swicegood, and many more. . ." Undocumented material posted on Ancestry World Tree). He died 1747 in Baltimore Co., Md., having married Grace [-?-].

Dugal was captured after the Jacobite Uprising in 1715, and was taken prisoner at Preston, Lancs., Eng., and shipped to Maryland in *The Friendship,* Michael Mankin, master. In Maryland he was purchased for seven years by William Holland (Smith, Transported Jacobite Rebels, 1716," *National Genealogical Society Quarterly,* 64:31; Stein, *History of Calvert Co.,* p. 375).

'Dugle McQueen" and Hector McQueen [possibly a brother?] were listed as debtors in the administration account, filed 27 May 1725, of Robert Eade of Anne Arundel Co. (MDAD 6:397.). By 1732 he was a taxable in the Upper Hundred of the Clifts, Calvert Co. In 1739 McQueen was listed as a debtor in the inventory of John Smith of Calvert Co. (MINV 24:80-88).

On 2 September 1740 Dougal Macqueen "of Prince George's Co." patented 72 a. in Baltimore Co. called *Cranberry Plains* (MPL EI#5: 506, LG#B: 183.).

Dugal MacQuain [*sic*] of Baltimore Co., died leaving a will dated 26 March 1746 and proved 4 March 1746/7. The land he lived on was equally divided between his sons William and Francis. To son William, he left his 'fear nothing' coat and his new jacket. To son Thomas he left the rest of his clothes except his white coat, which he gave to his son-in-law John Brown. The bond he had from John Kees was to be signed over to Mr. Alexander Lawson. Wife Grace Macquaine was named executrix. William Hall, Edward Logsden, and Richard Stevens witnessed the will.

Dugal and Grace were the parents of: **2. Ruth,** b. 1725, m. John Brown, d. 1810 in Baltimore Co., Md.; **3. William; 4. Francis,** b. 1 August 1741 in St. Paul's Parish (Reamy and Reamy, *St. Paul's Parish Register* 1:14); and **5. Thomas.**

3. William McQueen, son of Dugal (1), in 1754 was listed as owning '*Cranbury Plains.''* In March 1761 he surveyed 35½ a. *McQueen's Choice*; on 2 February 1796, William, now of Washington Co., PA, sold 35½ a. *McQueen's Choice* to Elias Raughter of Baltimore Co. (BALR WG#VV:460). In 1763 William McQueen was a taxable in Pipe Creek Hundred (*IBCW:* 60). In 1768 he signed a petition for the removal of the county seat from Joppa to Baltimore Town (*IBCP:* 3, 37.

5. Thomas McQueen, son of Dugal (1) is probably the Thomas Macqueen of Baltimore Co., who, on 22 January 1760, patented 29 a. *Foxes' Thicket* (MPL BC#12: 312, BC#13: 434). In 1763 McQueen was a taxable in Pipe Creek Hundred. (*IBCP:* 3).

Unplaced:
Joshua McQueen, of Ohio Co, Va., on 11 February 1786 deeded to George Brown of Baltimore Co. 29 a. *Foxes Thicket Enlarged,* 115 a of *Wee Bit Enlarged,* and 63 a., *Newfoundland Bottom* (BALR WG#Y:398).
Thomas McQueen was b. 2 December 1761 in Baltimore Co., MD, and d. 1838 In Bartholomew Co., Ind. In 1785 he m. Sarah Vaughan. He was a private in the Rev. War under Capt. Hogan.

The Merryman Family of Baltimore County

1. Charles Merryman married Jane Long, daughter of Major Thomas and Jane ([-?-]) Waites Dixon Long (See Matriarch Jane [-?-] Waites Dixon Long).
Charles and Jane were the parents of: **2. William;** and **3. John Charles.**

2. William Merryman, son of Charles (1) and Jane, was born 1707 in Baltimore County, Maryland, and died there in 1803. He married Margaret Lane in 1725 in Baltimore County, daughter of Dutton and Pretiosa (Tydings) Lane. Margaret was born 1709 in Baltimore County, Maryland.
William Merryman of Charles and Jane, was a Non-juror to the Oath of Allegiance in 1778 (*BARP:* 183).
William and Margaret were the parents of (Reamy and Reamy, *St. Paul's Parish Register:* 6, 9, 11, 14, 42): **4. Jemima,** b. 24 November 1726 and d. 13 August 1736; **5. Margaret,** b. 24 February 1728, and d. 5 August 1736; **6: William,** b. 11 April 1729, d. 1790; **7. George,** b. 25 October 1734; **8. Joanna,** b. 15 October 1736; and **9. Chloe,** b. 28 February 1741, m. Basil Tracy in 1765.

3. John Charles Merryman, son of Charles (1) and Jane (4), was born in Baltimore County, and married Millicent Haile on 20 February 1730 in Baltimore County, Md. (Reamy and Reamy, *St. Paul's Parish Register:* 30). She was a daughter of Nicholas and Frances (Broad) Haile.
John Charles and Millicent were the parents of (Reamy and Reamy, *St. Paul's Parish Register:* 7, 9, 11): **10. Charles,** b. 22 May 1733; **11. Mary,** b. 28 January 1735; and **12. Millicent,** b. 7 December 1736.

6. William Merryman, son of William (2) and Margaret, was born 11 April 1729 and died in 1790.
William Merryman of William and Margaret was a Non-juror to the Oath of Allegiance in 1778 (*BARP:*183).
William was the father of: **13. Micajah,** b. 25 April 1775 in Baltimore Co., and d. 1847 in Tuscarawas Co., Ohio, having m. by 1793 Mary, daughter of John Ensor (MCHP# 2029); **14. Nicholas,** b. 5 May 1779 in Baltimore Co., and d. 1 July 1855 in Wayne Township, Jefferson Co., Ohio; **15. George,** d. January 1864 in Indiana; **16. Delilah; 17. Keziah,** d. in Wayne Co., m. [-?-] Tracy; and **18, William,** b. 1756 in Baltimore Co., and d. 3 January 1844 in Wayne Co., Ohio, m. Elizabeth Goodin.

7. George Merryman, son of William (2) and Margaret, was born 25 October 1734.
George Merryman was a Non-juror to the Oath of Allegiance in 1778 (*BARP:*182).
He may have been the father of: **19. William,** who was also a Non-juror to the Oath of Allegiance in 1778 (*BARP:*183).

==0==

The Mohler Family of Baltimore County

1. Ludwig Mohler was born 4 April 1696 in Swiss-Germany, and died 6 January 1754 in Ephrata, Lancaster Co., Pa., where he was buried. He married [-?-], born 22 May 1698 in Swiss-Germany, and died 23 December 1772. She was buried in Ephrata, Lancaster Co.

Ludwig and his wife were the parents of: **2. Ludwig Jr.; 3. George Adam**, d. November 1783; and **4. Jacob**, b. after 1714.

2. Ludwig Mohler, Jr., son of Ludwig (1), married Anna [-?-]. They were the parents of: **5. Henry; 6. John;** and **7. Jacob**, b. 17 April 1745, d. 12 September 1773; and **8 Solomon**, b. 1763, d. 12 May 1852.

7. Jacob Mohler, silversmith, clock and watch maker, d. last Sun., in his 29th year (*Maryland Journal and Baltimore Advertiser* 18 September 1773; Cox, "Preliminary List," *MGSB* 21:223). He was born on 5 April 1745, son of Ludwig (Lewis) and Ann (Huntzinger) Mohler. He married on 4 April 1768, Elizabeth Tschudy, b. 17 March 1743, daughter of Winbert and Elizabeth (Rover) Tschudy (Tschudy Family Register in *Register of First Reformed Church of Baltimore*, Westminster: Family Line Publications: 53).

Jacob Mohler died leaving a will dated 10 September 1773 and proved 27 September 1773. He named his wife Elizabeth who was to bring up the children until they were of age and they were to be bound out to trades. His three sons, Jacob, Wimbert, and Peter, were to have his entire estate, real and personal. The executors were to be his wife and brother-in-law Peter Schitz of York Co., Pa. He signed his name in German. Wm. Spencer, Wingbert Judy and Conrad Markell witnessed the will (BAWB 3:272).

Elizabeth Mohler and Peter Schitz posted an administration bond for £1500.0.0 on 27 September 1773. Wingbert Judy and Peter Keener signed in German as the sureties. Elizabeth Mohler and Peter Schitz administered the estate on 12 February 1778 (BAAD 7:359).

Elizabeth Mohler of Baltimore Town died leaving a will dated 8 August 1787 and proved 15 September 1787. Her three sons, Jacob, Wimbert, and Peter were to have her entire estate, real and personal when they were of age. She named James Calhoun and her son Jacob execs. She signed her name in German. James Gordon, James McCullough, and Thomas B. Usher witnessed the will (BAWB 4:265, abst. by Burns). On 12 October 1787 James Calhoun and Jacob Mohler advertised they would settle the estate (*Maryland Journal and Baltimore Advertiser* 12 October 1787).

On 13 December 1787 the executors petitioned the court that they proposed to apprentice the second son Wimbert to learn the art of navigation; the youngest son Peter, age 15, wanted to learn the trade of silver smith and watchmaker, but the executors would have to pay an apprentice fee of 12 guineas (BAOC Petition of Elizabeth Mohler, 1787, BPET Box 2, Folder 15).

On 15 April 1788 Elizabeth Mohler's estate was administered by James Calhoun and Jacob Mohler. They filed another account on 12 June 1799 (BAAD 9:192, 10:10)>

Jacob and Elizabeth were the parents of the following [arranged roughly by age as to whether they chose a guardian or had one appointed (*Register of First Reformed Church of Baltimore:* 53, 54). **9. Jacob**, b. 27 January 1769; on 2 September 1797 he was made a ward of Nicholas Tschudy (BAOC 3:229); he died by October 1795 when Nicholas Tschudy advertised he would settle the estate (*Federal Intelligencer and Baltimore Daily Gazette* 17 October 1795); **10. Wimbert**, b. 24 February 1771; at age 18, on 21 February 1789, he chose James Calhoun to be his guardian and was bound to David Shields to be a hatter (BAOC 2:100); **11. Peter**, b. 7 April 1773, aged 15 on 9 April 1788.

9. Jacob Mohler, son of Jacob (7) and Elizabeth, was born 27 January 1769 and died on 11 March 1795, aged 26 years. He married Sarah [-?-], who died 7 August 1795 and was buried 18 August 1795 (*Register of First Reformed Church of Baltimore:* 53, 65, 66). In October 1795 when Nicholas Tschudy advertised he would settle Jacob Mohler's estate (*Federal Intelligencer and Baltimore Daily Gazette* 17 October 1795).

The births of the first three children of Jacob and Sarah were recorded in the Register of the First Reformed Church, with the notation that both parents 'died early.' Nicholas and Barbara Tschudi were witnesses and foster parents (*Register of First Reformed Church of Baltimore:* 29): **12. Anna Mariah**, b. 20 April 1792, bapt. 30 August 1795; on 2 September 1797 was made a ward of Nicholas Tschudy (BAOC 3:229); **13. Katherine** (read as Ruth), b. 30 August 1794, bapt. 30 August 1795, David Mohler a witness; on 2 September 1797 she was made a ward of Nicholas Tschudy (BAOC 3:229); **14. Jacob**, b. 23 July, bapt. 30 August 1795, Peter Mohler a witness; on 2 September 1797 was made a ward of Nicholas Tschudy (BAOC 3:229); **15. (possibly) Sarah Eliza**, on 2 September 1797 was made a ward of Nicholas Tschudy (BAOC 3:229). She may be the Sarah Mohler of Baltimore who was m. last eve. by Rev. Kurtz to George Bowersox (*Baltimore Telegraphe* 11 January 1804). However, she may be the Eliza Sarah Mohler of Hanover who was married at York, Pa., to Michael M. Maslin (or Mastik) of Baltimore on 13th inst. by Rev. Armstrong (*Federal Gazette and Baltimore Daily Advertiser* 15 September 1810).

11. Peter Mohler, son of Jacob (7) and Elizabeth, was born on 7 April 1773 (*Register of First Reformed Church of Baltimore:* 54). He died in February 1827. He married Barbara Lutz, who died 11 August 1849 (Baltimore *Sun* 13 August 1849).

Peter Mohler, aged 15 on 9 April 1788, son of Jacob and Elizabeth, was bound by the court to a certain Matthew Atkinson to learn the trade of a clock and watch maker, and as of 1790, had left this place and was said to be imprisoned in South Carolina, and not able to discharge his duty to the petitioner (BAOC Petition of Peter Mohler, 1790). On 21 February 1789 he chose James Calhoun to be his guardian and the court approved him; he had been discharged from Atkinson on 17 February 1790, and at age 19 on 12 April 1792 he was bound to Henry Aubern to learn the trade of a gunsmith (BAOC 3:229).

He may be the Peter Mohler listed as a brass founder on Harrison near Baltimore St. (BCD 1809).

Peter and Barbara were the parents of: **16. Jacob**, d. 1869; **17. Peter**, d. 1829; **18. Alonzo**, d. 12 February 1829 at Cincinnati, Ohio (*Baltimore Patriot* 23 February 1829) ; **19. Wilber [Wimbert]**; **20. Ann Maria**, d. 1879; **21. Cora**, d. 1858; **22. Edward**, d. 1857; **23. Mary**; **24. Barbara**; and **25. Isaac Wimbert**, b. 3 August 1823, d. 18 February 1906.

Unplaced:
Peter Mohlar, in his will made 10 September 1773 named his brother-in-law Peter Schels of York, Penna., as co-exec. (BAWB 3:272, abst. by Jean K. Brandau in *MGSB* 28 (2) (Spring 1987) 222-223).
Wimbert T. Mohler died 19 July 1821 in the 21st year of his age (*Baltimore Patriot* 20 June 1821),

==0==

The Moran Family of Charles and St. Mary's Counties

1. Gabriel Moran died in Charles Co. prior to July 1734. He married 1st, Elizabeth [-?-], who married 2nd, Meverell Hulse.

On 8 October 1720 Gabriel Moran and John Anderson appraised the estate of Thomas Polson of Prince George's Co. (MINV 5:56).

Moran was in Charles Co. by 10 October 1722 when he patented 250 a. *Cattle Grave* (MPL PL#5:214, IL#A:25). On 26 June 1727 he patented 333 a. called *Cattle Grave Addition* (MPL PL#6:608, IL#A:704).

Colonial Families of Maryland II

Gabriel died leaving a will dated 15 March 1733 and proved 3 July 1734. He left his dwelling plantation first to his wife Elizabeth, during her life and then to his son John. He also left 150 a. of *Addition to Cattle's Grave*. He left the residue of his estate to his sons John, Peter, Andrew and William. His wife and son John were named executors. John Anderson, Jonathan Wilson, Thomas Farrand, and Hugh Stone witnessed the will. In a codicil Moran left his wife one-third of the personal estate, and mentioned an unborn child. (MWB 21:137, abst. in *Md. Cal. of Wills* 7:93).

On 25 July 1734 John Anderson and John Willson appraised the personal estate of Gabriel Moran at £211.1.11. Elizabeth Moran and John Moran, executors, filed the inventory on 13 August 1734 (MINV 18:501).

John Moran and Meverell Hulse and his wife Elizabeth, executors, administered Gabriel Moran's estate on 2 March 1737. They cited the inventory as above, and listed payments of £61.9.11 (MDAD 16:46).

Gabriel and Elizabeth were the parents of: **2. John; 3. Peter; 4. Andrew;** and **5. William.**

2. John Moran, son of Gabriel (1), died in Charles Co. by December 1791. He married by 23 February 1748/9, Rebecca [-?-].

John Moran, Elizabeth [Hulse?], and William Cantar signed the undated inventory (filed on 24 September 1739) of Peter Villett of Charles Co. as next of kin (MINV 24:313).

John, Peter, Andrew, and William Moran, all of St. Mary's Co., patented 858 a. *Four Brothers* on 16 September 1747 (MPL B#T:202, T#11:12). John Moran had moved to Charles Co. by 2 June 1774 when he patented 108 a. *Dear Bought* (MPL BC#45:475, BC#46:410).

On 23 February 1748/9, Peter Villett of Charles Co. made his will. He named his sister Rebecca Villett, and then left £3.19.6 to John Moran, and various legacies to these children of John and Rebecca Moran: William, Gabriel, John, and Meverell Hulse Moran (MWB 26:114, abst. in *Md. Cal. of Wills* 10:26).

John Moran died leaving a will dated 29 December 1788, and proved 24 December 1791. He named his sons John (who was to have the testator's claim to a lease of land called *Calverton Manor*, originally granted to Mary Stone, and 108 a. of *Dear Bought*. Meveral Hulse, Gabriel, and William. John Moran and Meveral H. Moran were executors. John Morton, Jonathan Anderson, and Jesse Davis witnessed the will (CHWB 11:55).

John and Rebecca were the parents of: **6. John; 7. Meveral Hulse; 8. Gabriel;** and **9. William.**

3. Peter Moran, son of Gabriel (1), was living in St. Mary's Co. by 19 November 1743 when he and William Elliott and Cornelius Barber witnessed the will of Meverell Hulls of St. Mary's Co. (MWB 23:317, abst. In *Md. Cal, of Wills*). On 24 December 1743 he witnessed the will of Elias Barber of St. Mary's Co. (MWB 23:458, abst. in *Md. Cal. of Wills*).

On 30 June 1761 Peter Moran signed the inventory of John Herbert of St. Mary's Co. as one of the next of kin (MINV 79:268).

Peter Moran was listed in the St. Mary's Co. Debt Books as owning 86 a. *Good Yielding,* and 67 a. *Addition Resurveyed* in 1768, 1769, 1770, 1773, and 1774 (Skinner, *St. Mary's Co. Debt Books Volume III*: 71,. 110, 150, 224, 265).

4. Andrew Moran, son of Gabriel (1), died in Charles Co. by February 1791. He married

Colonial Families of Maryland II

Mary [-?-], who died by April 1798.

Andrew Moran patented 60 a. *Four Brothers Addition* on 26 November 1756 (MPL BC#8:16, BC#9:192).

Andrew Moran, Sr., took the Oath of Allegiance in 1778, and in November 18782 provided wheat for the use of the military (*RPCH:*208).

He died leaving a will dated 25 February 1790 and proved 7 February 1791. His wife and son Robert were to be executors. He named his children Zachariah, Benjamin, Jonathan, Andrew, Mary, and Sarah Barber Moran. Gabriel Moran, Josias Smoot and George Morton witnessed the will (CHWB 11:21).

Mary Moran died leaving a will dated 26 February 1798, and proved 10 April 1798. She named her children, Andrew, Zachariah, Mary Cartwright, Robert, and Sarah Barber Ward. She also named a grandson William Andrew Cartwright. Son Zachariah was to be the executor. Merverel and Mary Moran, and John Monro witnessed the will (CHWB 11:447).

Andrew and Mary were the parents of: **10. Zachariah; 11. Benjamin; 12. Jonathan; 13. Andrew; 14. Mary,** m. [-?-] Cartwright; and **15. Sarah Barber,** m. [-?-] Ward.

6. John Moran, Sr., son of John (2) and Rebecca, died by March 1812 in Charles County. He married Elizabeth [-?].

John Moran, of Charles Co., died leaving a will dated 26 April 1809 and proved 17 March 1812. He named his wife Elizabeth, who was to have the plantation *Dear Bought.* He also named children Ann Davis, Mary Canter, John Moran, and son Charles (who was to be administrator). Samuel Smoot, James Robey, and Gustavus Gill witnessed the will (CHWB 13:162).

John and Elizabeth were the parents of: **16. Ann,** m. [-?-] Davis; **17. Mary,** m. [-?-] Canter; **18. John;** and **19. Charles.**

7. Meveral Hulse Moran, son of John (2) and Rebecca, died by February 1825 in Charles County.

Meveral Hulse Moran was a private in the 12th Battalion of Militia in Capt. Peter Wood's Co., in 1777, and took the Oath of Allegiance in 1778 (*RPCH:*209)

Moran died leaving a will dated 2 August 1821 and proved February 1825. He named a son Thomas Alfred Moran as sole executor, his nieces Mary Wood, Susan Wood, Ann Wood, and Jane Wood. William Morton, Clement Billinglsey, and Henry Canter witnessed the will (CHWB 14:347).

Meveral Moran was the father of: **20. Thomas Alfred Moran.**

8. Gabriel Moran, son of John (2) and Margaret was born 30 June 1730 and died after 20 September 1810, having married Margaret Wood (*RPCH:*208).

In 1777 he was a private in the 12th Battalion of Militia, in Capt. Alexander McPherson's Company, and in 1778 he took the Oath of Allegiance (*RPCH:*1208).

13. Andrew Moran, son of Andrew (4) and Mary, was a private in the 12th Battalion of Militia in Capt. Peter Wood's Co., in 1777, and took the Oath of Allegiance in 1778 (*RPCH:*208).

Unplaced:

[-?-] Moran m. by 2 November 1777 Mary, daughter of Henry Lyon (CHWB 7:153).

Gabriel Moran of Charles Co. patented 400a. *Blue Bank* on 6 July 1739 (MPL EI#5:458,EI#6:199).

John P. Moran died leaving a will dated 9 February 1807 and proved 17 March 1812. He named his wife Nancy Moran, and a daughter Henrietta M. Moran, who were his sole heirs and executors. Cleon Clements, Wm. Farrand, and George Smoot witnessed the will (CHWB 13:158).

Rebecca Moran and Elizabeth Hulse signed the inventory of Luke Barber Houls [Hulls] of St. Mary's Co. as the next of kin on 10 January 1763 (MINV 81:227).

Rinaldo J. Moran of Charles Co. died leaving an undated will which was proved on 21 September 1880. He named his wife Annie and his only son Nicholas Sidney Greer [sic] who was not yet 21. Arthur H. Lawrence was appointed his executor and guardian of Nicholas Greer. M. R. Latimer, E. H. Swann, and George L. Murray witnessed the will (CHWB 18:152-153).

== 0 ==

The Morris Family of Baltimore County

1. Thomas Morris was born about 1670 and was living at least as late as September 1721. On 27 June 1730 he gave his age as c60 and stated that that 40 years earlier he had been a servant of Lodowick Martin who owned part of *Carter's Rest* (BALC HWS#3, # 23). He deposed again on 20 Jan 1730/1 stating he had heard old Richard [Perkins] speak of a tract named *Contest* (BALC HWS#3, # 26).

As Thomas Morris, living on *The Level*, he married Elizabeth Jackson on 14 July 1698 (Reamy and Reamy, *St. George's Parish Register:* 1). She was a widow of Simeon Jackson and a daughter of John and Katherine Shadwell. Thomas married 2nd by 1708, Mary [-?-].

On 20 October 1703 Thomas Edmonds conveyed 100 a. *Perkington* to Thomas Morris (BALR HW#2: 293).

On 10 March 1704 Thomas Morris of Baltimore Co. and wife Eliza made their marks when they conveyed to William Stevens 100 a. part *Expectation*, now called *Morris' Folly* (BALR IR#PP: 146). On 2 March 1720 Thomas Morris with consent of wife Mary conveyed to Edward Parks 100 a. *Expectation*, adjacent *The Grove;* the land had formerly been held by William Stevens of Kent Co. (BALR RM#HS: 678, 679). On 13 May 1721 Oliver Hickinbotham of Kent Co., carpenter, gave a power of attorney to Edward Hall of Baltimore Co. to sell his interest in *Expectation* and the interest of the heirs of William Stevens, to Thomas Morris, and *The Grove* (BALR RM#HS: 679). On 3 Jan 1708 Thomas Morris and wife Mary conveyed 100 a. *Perkington* to Rowland Kimble (BALR RM#HS: 627).

Thomas and Elizabeth were the parents of (Reamy and Reamy, *St. George's Parish Register:* 4, 12, 17, 35): **2. Sarah,** b. 12 January 1698/9, bapt. 2 July 1699, may be the Sarah Morris who m. Daniel Maccarty on 20 January 1714; **3. Elizabeth,** b. 1 October 1701; **4. Mary,** b. 10 July 1703; **5. Susanna,** b. 2 April 1705/6; **6. Thomas,** b. 1 August 1701 or 1707; may be the Thomas Morris who m. Mary Murphy on 19 January 1731.

Thomas and Mary were the parents of (Reamy and Reamy, *St. George's Parish Register:* 19, 20): **7. Richard,** b. 1 February 1709; and **8. Henry,** b. 20 Oct 1713.

7. Richard Morris, son of Thomas and Mary, was born 1 February 1709. He was aged 11, on 2 September 1721 when he was indentured by his father, Thomas Morris, to serve

7. Richard Morris, son of Thomas and Mary, was born 1 February 1709. He was aged 11, on 2 September 1721 when he was indentured by his father, Thomas Morris, to serve Rowland Kemble to the age of 21 (BALR TR#DS:315).

He married 1st, Mary Murphy on 25 December 1734 (Reamy and Reamy, *St. George's Parish Register:* 44). He married, 2nd, Jane [-?-].

About 1770 Richard Morris, Tim Murphy, William Murphy, and others, held pew no, 23 in St. George's Parish (Reamy and Reamy, *St. George's:* 115).

In 1776 he lived in Spesutia Lower Hundred. He was aged 64, and living with him was Jane, aged 30, Giles, aged 8, Susanna, aged 4, and [Frances], aged 2½ (Carothers, *1776 Census of Maryland:* 103).

Richard Morris died leaving a will dated 18 July 1775 and proved in Harford Co. on 18 November 1777. He named his son Thomas and his wife Jane. He named his daughters Elizabeth Grant, Sarah Young, and Mary Yoakley. He named his sons Richard, Edward, John, Michael, and William, and his three youngest children, Giles, Susannah, and Frances. His wife Jane was named executrix. Frances Holland, James Taylor, and John Perry witnessed the will (HAWB AJ#2:413).

Richard and Mary were the parents of (Reamy and Reamy, *St. George's Parish Register:* 58, 63, 69, 79): **9. Elizabeth,** b. 6 August 1736, m. James Grant on 1 February 1753; they had a son David, b. 31 January 1756; **10. John,** b. 28 May 1736; **11. Sarah,** b. 3 January 1740, m. [-?-] Morris; **12. Mary,** b. 3 March 1742, m. [-?-] Yoakley; **13. Thomas,** b. 15 January 1745; **14. Richard,** b. 1 March 1749; **15. Edward,** b. 1 March 1753; **16. Michael,** b. 1 February 1755; **17. John,** b. 3 June 1758; **18. Giles,** b. about 1769, aged 8 in 1776; **19. Susanna,** b. about 1773. aged 4 in 1776; and **20. Frances,** b. about 1774/5. aged 2½ in 1776.

==0==

The Nichols Family

1. Humphrey Nichols was transported c1664. He was in Baltimore Co. by 1 March 1669/70 when Gabriel Brown conveyed him 150 a. *Hemley* (or *Homley*) (BALR IR#PP: 78).

On 14 May 1672 Nichols was listed as a debtor in the inventory of John Hawkins (MDTP 5:316-317). On 6 April 1676 he was listed as one of the appraisers of the estate of Richard Blunt of Cecil Co. (MDTP 8A:17).

As Humphrey Nicholas [sic] he died leaving a will dated 8 February 1685/6 and proved 4 July 1687 in Cecil Co. His son Thomas was to have all his land, including his plantation, and one-third of his personalty at age 21. Daughter Sarah at age 16 was to have the residue of his personalty. Jacob Devilyard [sic] was named executor and guardian of the children. If the children died during their minority he was to inherit the estate. Andrew Clemounce, Andrew Poulson and Edw. Bynn witnessed the will (MWB 6:24, abst. in *Md. Cal. of Wills* 2: 34). On 24 July 1688 his executor Jacob Haviland filed an account of the estate showing an inventory of £12.16.6 (INAC 10:167).

Humphrey was the father of: **2. Thomas,** not yet 21 in 1686; and **3. Sarah,** not yet 16 in 1686.

==0==

Colonial Families of Maryland II

The Norrington Family
With Notes on the Hayes and Norris Families

1. John Norrington was transported by 1681 (MPL WC#4:152). He was born c1664 and gave his age as 60 in March 1724 when he petitioned to be levy free. He married Elizabeth [-?-].

John Norrington was listed as a taxable in North Side Gunpowder Hundred in 1700, 1702, 1703, 1704, and 1706 (Clark, *Baltimore Co. Tax Lists, 1699-1706:* 9, 24, 32, 41, 59).

In March 1703 he purchased 106 a. *Webster's Enlargement* from John and Hannah Webster (BALR IR#AM: 5). In August 1714 John made his mark when he and his wife Elizabeth conveyed this tract to Peter Overard (BALR TR#A: 302). On 4 November 1714, John McComas conveyed 92 a. *Littleton* to John Norrington (BALR TR#A: 30). In 1729 Norrington conveyed 76 a. *Hopewell* to William Davis. At the same time Davis conveyed 92 a. *Littleton* to Norrington (BALR IS#K: 25, 28).

About 1716./7 he delivered tobacco to John Crockett (*IBCW:* 33).

John and Elizabeth were the parents of (*SJSG:* 9, 25, 63): **2. John**, m. and had issue; **3. Mary**, b. March 1711, m. Thomas Hayes on 11 August 1735; **4. Jane**, b. 25 December 1712; **5. Elizabeth**, b. 1714; and **6. Francis**, b. June 1718.

2. John Norrington, son of John (1) and Elizabeth, married Mary Hays on 1 August 1737 (*SJSG:* 41).

On 6 November 1745 John Norrington, cordwainer, made his mark when he conveyed 76 a. *Hopewell*, which had been patented on 24 June 1726 by William Davis, to Abraham Jarrett. His wife Mary consented (BALR TB#D:358). John Norrington leased *Lew's Den*, and *Wadle's Good Luck* from Lord Baltimore or his agents in 1745 ("Lease Agreements in the Scharf Collection," *MGSB* 32 (2) (Spring 1991), p. 161).

In 1790 Mary Norrington was listed as head of a household in Harford Co., with one free white male and four white females in her household (*Heads of Families... .1790... Maryland:* 75).

Mary Norrington died leaving a will dated 29 December 1791 and proved 17 April 1792. She named her daughters Mary Poteet and Hannah and Sarah Norris, Ann Thompson, Frances Thompson, Cassandra Thompson, Priscilla Lion (Lyon) and Temperance Long, and sons John, Isaac, and Abraham Norrington, and three daughters Rachel, Martha, and Susanna Norrington. John Lyon was the executor. Elijah Norris, William Sinclair, and Aaron Norris witnessed the will (HAWB AJ#2:488).

John and Mary were the parents of: **7. Mary**, m. [-?-] Poteet; **8. Hannah**; **9. Sarah**, m. [-?-] Norris; **10. Ann**, m. [-?-] Thompson; **11. Frances**, m. [-?-] Thompson; **12. Cassandra**, m. [-?-] Thompson; **13. Priscilla**, m. John Lyon; **14. Temperance**, m. [-?-] Long; **15. John**; **16. Isaac**; **17. Abraham**; **18. Rachel**; **19. Martha**; and **20. Susanna**.

3. Mary Norrington, daughter of John (1) and Elizabeth, was born in March 1711. She was indicted for bastardy in March 1733/4 and tried in June (BACP IS&TW#4:121).

Colonial Families of Maryland II

Mary Norrington married Thomas Hayes on 11 August 1735 (*SJSG:* 63).

Thomas and Mary were the parents of (*SJSG:* 63, 65): 21. James, b. 21 October 1738; **22. Edmund,** b. 21 or 22 November 1739; **23. Elizabeth,** b. 12 February 1745; and **24. Mary,** b. 15 July 1747.

6. Francis Norrington, son of John (1) and Elizabeth, was born in June 1718. He married Mary Everett on 19 February 1749/50 (*SJSG:* 92, 127). As a daughter of John and Rebecca (Poteet) Everett, Mary was conveyed property by her uncle John Poteet in March 1732 (See BALR IS#L: 337)

In 1783 Francis Norrington, with eight white inhabitants in his household, was listed in Gunpowder Upper and Lower Hundreds, Harford Co. Joshua Norrington, a single man with James Poteet as his security, was listed in the same hundred (Carothers, *1783 Tax List of Md.:* 109, 115).

Francis Norringon was listed as head of a family in Harford Co. in 1790 with one white free male and four white females in his household (*Heads of Families...1790... Maryland:* 74).

8. Hannah Norrington, daughter of John (2) and Mary, married Thomas Norris on 4 May 1762 (*SJSG:* 108).

They were the parents of at least one son: **16: Abraham Norris.**

15. John Norrington, son of John (2) and Mary is probably the John Norrington who signed the Association of Freemen at Bush River in 1776 and took the Oath of Fidelity in 1778 (*RPHA;* 167).

In 1783 John Norrington was listed in Bush River Upper and Eden Hundreds, Harford Co., with seven white inhabitants in his household. Mary Norrington was listed with eight white inhabitants and owning 120 a. *Lion's Den* (Carothers, *1783 Tax List of Md.:* 88).

16: Abraham Norris, son of Thomas and Hannah (8) (Norrington) Norris, was born 1770 in Baltimore Co, Maryland, and married Ellen Anna Lamb, daughter of William and Sarah (Wood) Lamb.

In 1790 he was living in Mine Run Hundred, Baltimore County, but by 1820 he was in the 5th Election District of Harford County. They eventually moved to Brown County, Ohio.

Abraham and Ellen Ann had at least one daughter: **17. Rachel Norris,** b. 12 August 1803 in Brown County.

Unplaced:
Drucilla Norrington had a bastard child by Aaron Norris; on 11 October 1793 Thomas Norris and James Monholland posted bond that Aaron was to provide for the child (Harford Co. Court Papers 18.08.1). She evidently also had a child by John Smith (tanner) some time before 26 April 1801 (Harford Co. Court Minutes, 1798-1809:

52; both cases are in Peden, *Bastardy Cases in Harford County, Maryland, 1774-1844*).
Elizabeth Norrington and William Ewing were m. on 21 November 1805 (*SJSG:* 164).

==0==

The Oakley Family.

1. Thomas Oakley, felon, was transported from London by the *Patapsco Merchant*, Darby Lux, Capt., in March 1730, and registered at Annapolis in September 1730 (*KPMV*:44). He married 1st, Prudence [-?-], and 2nd, Susanna [-?-].

He may have been the Thomas Oakey [*sic*], servant, listed in the 1732 inventory of Thomas Hutchins (BINV 5:244).

On 22 February 1742 Thomas Oakley, age about30, leased 205 a. part of *My Lady's Manor*, the lease to run for the lifetimes of Thomas, his wife Prudence, aged c27, and son Thomas, Jr., age c1 (BALR TB#C:135). On 30 September 1744, Oakley, still 30, leased two lots in *Charlotte Town* land for his lifetime and that of his wife Prudence, age about 28, and son Thomas, Jr., age about 2 (BALR TB#C:603).

On 12 August 1746 Oakley sold two servants, William Perry, with two years to serve, and Manas Oakan, with four years to serve, to Charles *Ridgely* (BALR TB#E: 171).

Thomas and Prudence were the parents of (*SJSG:* 54): **2.Thomas**, age about 1 in February 1742, may have d. young; **3. Thomas**, b. 4 April 1742

Thomas and Susanna were the parents of (*SJSG:* 39): **3. William**, b. 16 June 1744.

Unplaced;
Elizabeth Oakley married Joseph Franklin on 15 January 1756 (*SJSG:* 100).
Esau Oakley and Jane Smith were married on 15 October 1774 (Reamy and Reamy, *St. Paul's Parish Register:* 36).
Mary Oakley married George Ward on 24 August 1760 (*SJSG:* 1065).

==0==

The Ogg Family

1. William Ogg was born by 1648. He married Barbara Hume who was born c1650.
William and Barbara were the parents of (James Ogg. "My Ancestral Lineage." Undocumented material posted on Ancestry World Tree): **2. George**, b. 1667.

2. George Ogg, possibly son of William (1) and Barbara, was born 1667 in Baltimore Co., MD, and died there in November 1713. He married Elizabeth Bagley in June 1691 in All Hallows Parish, Anne Arundel Co., Md. (Register of All Hallow's Parish, Anne Arundel Co., In F. Edward Wright, *Anne Arundel County Church Records of the 17th and*

18th Centuries. Westminster: Family Line Publications, 1989, hereafter cited as AACR, 7). She was born c1670 in Anne Arundel Co., MD, and died 1723 in Baltimore Co., Maryland.

On 25 August 1693 Edward Parrish of Anne Arundel Co. planter, conveyed 300 a. *Parrishes Range* to George Ogg; tract had been patented to Edward Parish, father of grantor. Parrish's wife Mary consented (BALR IR#AM: 76).

Ogg acquired other lands as well. On 1 November 1710 he patented 150 a. *Ogg's Bashan* (MPL DD#5:676; PL#3:234). He patented 100 a. *George's Beginning* on 10 Aug 1717 (MPL EE#6:324, PL#4:275).

On 15 May 1704 Ogg was listed as a creditor of George Hollingsworth of Baltimore Co. (MWB 5:361, abst. in *Md. Cal. of Wills*).

George and Elizabeth were the parents of: **3. John**, b. 24 September 1691, and d. after 1723 (*AACR:* 4); **4. Katherine**, b. 1 January 1694 in Anne Arundel Co., MD and d. 22 February 1762 in Baltimore Co., m. 1st, William Talbot, and 2nd, John Risteau; and **5. George**, b. 30 April 1696 in All Hallows Parish, Anne Arundel Co. (*AACR:* 3).

5. George Ogg, son of George (2) and Elizabeth, was born 30 April 1696 in All Hallows Parish, Anne Arundel Co., MD, and died 1759 in Baltimore Co., Md. He married Mary Potee on 22 August 1722 in St. Paul's Parish, Baltimore Co., Md. (Reamy and Reamy, *St. Paul's Parish Register:* 33). She was a daughter of Francis and Lucy ([-?-]) Potee and was born after 1691 in Green Spring Valley, Baltimore Co. and died 1735.

As George Ogg, Jr., he patented 50 a. *Security* on 10 July 1725 (MPL PL#6: 317; IL#A: 551).

On 20 November 1756, George Ogg conveyed property to his daughters Rebecca, wife of William Shipley, Katherine wife of George Shipley, Sarah wife of [-?-] Whips, Ruth Ogg, Rachel Ogg, and to grandchild Mary, daughter of Philemon Barnes (Baltimore County Court Chattel Records, hereafter cited as BACT, 1:228, 229, 230, 231, 232).

1754: George Ogg conv. 238 a. *Morgan's Tent Resurveyed*, 30 a. *Plumb Tree Bottom*, and 60 a. *Mount Pleasant* to Lovelace Gorsuch (BALR BB#1: 458).

George and Mary were the parents of (Reamy and Reamy, *St. Paul's Parish Register:* 10): **7.** (Possibly) **Duncan**, b. 1723 in Baltimore Co., d. after November 1756 in Anne Arundel Co.; **8. George**, b. 12 April 1724 in Baltimore Co., MD, d. there in 1770. **9. Sarah Lucerne**, b. 5 September 1726 in Anne Arundel Co., MD, d. 1782 in Baltimore Co., m. John Whips by November 1756; **10. Katherine**, b. 15 July 1728 in Baltimore, Co., d. 1804 in Anne Arundel Co., m. by 1756, George Shipley; **11. Mary**, b. 10 October 1730, m. Philemon Barnes; **12. Ruth**, b. c1725 in Baltimore Co., d. after 1756; **13. Rebecca**, b. 20 October 1732 in St. Paul's Parish, Baltimore Co., MD, m. by 1756, William Shipley; **14. William**, b. c1725 in Baltimore, Co., d. there c1820, m. Sarah Beasman, b. 2 January 1743/44 in Baltimore Co.; **15.** (Possibly) **Mary**, b. 10 October 1730 in All Hallows Parish, Anne Arundel Co., d. after 1800 in Frederick Co.; **16.** (Possibly) **Rachel**, b. 20 Sep 1735 in Baltimore Co., MD, d. after 1756.

8. George Ogg, son of George (5) and Mary, was born 12 April 1724 in Baltimore Co., and died there in 1770. He married Helen Hamilton 1746 in Baltimore Co. a daughter of William Hamilton and Sarah Benedict. She was born c 1730 in the Green Spring Valley, Baltimore Co., and died c March 1798 in Baltimore Co.

George Ogg died leaving a will dated 13 August 1767 and proved 23 Augu1770. He named his wife Helen (to be executrix), sons Benjamin, George and William Hamilton, and daus. Rachel and Mary. William Lux, Daniel Bowly, and Philip Allingham witnessed the will (BAWB 3:121).

Helen Ogg, executrix, posted an administration bond on 6 December 1770 with Geo. Risteau and Mordecai Hammond as sureties (BAAB 2:399). She administered the estate on 6 August 1772. The deceased left six children (BAAD 7:169). She administered the estate again on 12 Oct 1790. She retained her thirds; William Hamilton Ogg received £50.9.81/2, and other heirs were the wife of Charles Sater, George, James, and Benjamin Ogg, and the wife of John Jacobs (BAAD 10:209).

Helen Ogg died leaving a will dated 2 April 1798 and proved 29 April 1798. She named her sons George, his daughter Helen; her son James, and James' daughter Helen; her grandchildren George and Helen Sater, children of Charles Sater; her daughter Rachel Jacobs; her sons Benjamin, George, William Hambleton, and James were to have the residue of her estate. Her son William Hambleton Ogg was named executor. Elias Brown, John Cross, Nicholas Merryman, and Anthony Hoke witnessed the will (BAWB 6:92, abst. by Burns).

Helen Ogg died by March 1799. Her estate was administered by William H. Ogg, exec. The inventory and assets totaled £1118.10.9. The balance due the estate was £1077.18.0. The account was filed on 13 March 1799. (BAAD 13:4).

George and Helen were the parents of: **17. George**, b. July 1746; **18. Benjamin**, b. 29 April 1748; **19. Rachel**, b. 1754, m. [-?-] Jacobs by 2 April 1798; **20. Mary**, b. c1758, m. Charles Sater by BAML Dated 27 June 1781; **21. William Hamilton**, b. 1767; **22. Vachel**, b. c1774, d. 22 November 1825 in Deerfield Twp., Morgan Co., Ohio; **23 James**.

14. William Ogg, son of George (5) and Mary, was born c1725 in Baltimore, Co. and died there c1820. He married Sarah Beasman, who had been born 2 January 1743/44 in Baltimore Co.

In 1742 he was granted 25 a. *William's Delight.* 1742: on 5 October 1767, with the consent of wife Sarah, he conveyed the entire tract to William Lux, William Lyon, Charles Graham and James Dock (BALR B#Q: 202).

He was a Non-Juror to the Oath of Fidelity in 1778 (*BARP:* 199).

17. George Ogg, son of George (8) and Helen, was born July 1746, and died 13 November 1847 in Carroll County.

He was a Non-Juror to the Oath of Fidelity in 1778 (*BARP:* 199).

He was the father of (Carroll Co. Chancery Book 5:489-510, Carroll Co. Equity Case #371, filed 1849): **24. George**; **25. John**; **26. Sarah**, m. Charles Shockney and moved to Indiana; **27. Moses**, moved to Ohio; **28. Nicholas**; **29. Helen**, m. William Jordan; **30. William**; **31. James**; **32. Susan**; **33. Henrietta**; **34. Laban**; **35. Richard**; **36. Catherine**, m. Lloyd Shipley; **37. William Hamilton**; and **38. Mary**.

==0==

The Peale Family of Maryland
With Notes on the Polk, Robinson, and Simes Families

N.B.: Unless otherwise noted much of this material is from *Four Generations of Commissions: The Peale Collection of the Maryland Historical Society, March 3, 1975 – June 29, 1975.* Catalogue and Exhibition Prepared by Eugenia Calvert Holland, Romaine Stec Somerville, Stiles Cuttle Colwill, and K. Beverly Whiting Young. Baltimore: Maryland Historical Society, © 1975 by the Maryland Historical Society.

C. William Peale, carpenter, of Great Dalby, Rutlandshire, was the father of (*Alumni Cantabrigensis,* hereafter cited as *ALCA*): **B. Thomas.**

B. Thomas Peale, son of William (A), was b. 1658, and buried 2 August 1717. On 25 May 1677, age 18, he was admitted sizar of St. John's, Cambridge; he matriculated in 1677, and took his B.A. in 1680/1. He was Archdeacon at Peterborough on 29 May 1681, and Vicar of Great Dalby from 1681 to 1717. From 1687 he was Rector of Edith Weston Parish (*ALCA*). He married Jane (possibly Wilson). Jane Peale witnessed the will of Charles Wilson in 1723.

Thomas and Jane were the parents of: **A. Charles**, b. 21 October 1688; **i. Ann; ii. Jane; iii. Thomas; iv. Richard; v. Catherine; vi. Elizabeth; vii. William;** and **viii. George.**

A. Charles Peale, son of Thomas (B) and Jane, was b. 21 October 1688 in Co. Rutland, Eng. He married Elizabeth (Digby?).

Undocumented data on the Internet states that he was born 21 October 1688 in Edith Weston, Rutlandshire, England, and died there on 12 October 1734. He married Elizabeth Camparl on 22 July 1708 in Edith Weston. She was born 1692 in Newark-Upon-Trent, Nottinghamshire, and died at Edith Weston on 10 September 1735.

Charles and Elizabeth were the parents of: **1. Charles**, b. 22 December 1709 in Edith Weston; and **2. Jane**, b. about 1710 in Edith Weston, d. 3 March 1766; m. Joseph Digby at Edith Weston.

1. Charles Peale, son of Charles (A) and Elizabeth, was b. 22 December 1709 and died in Kent Co. Md., in December 1750. He came to Md..and in 1736 and married Margaret Trigg at St. Margaret's, Westminster, Anne Arundel Co. In 1742 he moved to Chestertown, Md., where he was Master of the Kent Co. School, and where he remained until his de0ath.

Charles Peale of London, in February 1736 was transported 'for life' on the '*Dorsetshire*,' Capt. William Loney (*KPMV:* 66).

He advertised: "At Kent County School, in Kent Co. Md.., in December 1750, near Chester Town, Maryland, young Gentleear Chester Town, Maryland, young Gentlemen are boarded and taught the Greek and Latin Tongues, Writing, Arithmetick, Merchants Accounts, Surveying, Navigation, the Use of the Globes, by the largest and most accurate Pair in America: Also any other Parts of the Mathematicks, by Charles Peale. N.B. Young Gentlemen may be instructed in Fencing and Dancing by very good Masters (*Pennsylvania Gazette* 12 March 1744/5)."

The marriage of Charles Peale to Margaret Triggs was not found in this author's *Maryland Marriages 1634-1777,* or in F. Edward Wright's *Anne Arundel County Church Records of the 17th and 18th Centuries,* but it is found in the following deposition: [On 11 September 1762] Elizabeth Bennett of the City of Annapolis, in the Province of Maryland, aged sixty years ..., "deposeth and sayeth that she had constantly resided in the City of Annapolis aforesaid, and in St. Marg't's Westminster Parish in the neighborhood of the City for these thirty years last past, and that she was well acquainted with, and personally knew, Charles Peale, formerly of the City of Annapolis aforesaid, that her knowledge and acquaintance with him began upon his first coming to reside in Annapolis upwards of twenty two years ago, that she always understood and from his speech and pronunciation of his words believes he was an Englishman, and that the said Charles Peale for some time past and chiefly during his stay in Annapolis was Master of and taught school in the Publick School in Annapolis aforesaid, and that in the time of teaching school in Annapolis... and as this deponent thinks twenty two years ago, the said Charles Peale and Margaret Peale, now of the City of Annapolis, widow (a person then and still well known to this deponent) came to the then dwelling house of the deponent in St. Margaret's Westminster Parish aforesaid, where they both stayed all night and requested this deponent to go with them the next day to the Rev. Mr. Vaughan, then Minister of the said Parish to see them married, and on such request this deponent did go with the said Charles and Margaret to the said Mr. Vaughan (PCLR DD#2:236-238)."

The *Maryland Gazette* reported that 'Mr. Charles Peale died last week in Chestertown. He was formerly Deputy Secretary of the General Post Office in London (Annapolis *Maryland Gazette* 5 December 1750).

The personal property of Charles Peale, schoolmaster, of Kent County, was appraised by James McClean, Jr., and James Piner, Jr., on 17 July 1751 and valued at £59.6.10. The next of kin were described as children (under age and very young), and a widow who lived at Annapolis. Solomon Wright and John Bordley, administrators, filed the inventory on 17 April 1752 (MINV 48:369). An undated list of debts owed the estate totaling £111.9.8 was filed some time later (MINV 51:81).

Wright and Bordley administered the estate of Charles Peale on 1 June 1752, when payments came to £69.10.2 (MDAD 33:49).

The children of Charles and Margaret included: **3. Charles Wilson**, b. 15 April 1741, d. 1827; **4. Margaret Jane**, b. 1743 in Charlestown, Cecil Co., Md.., d. 1788; **5. St George**, b. 23 April 1745 in Charlestown, Cecil Co., Md., d. 3 July 1778; **6. Elizabeth Digby**, b. 20 January 1746/7 and d. 1776; and **7. James**, b. 1749, d. 1831, m. Mary Chambers Claypoole, b. 1753, d. 1829.

3. Charles Wilson Peale, son of Charles (1) and Margaret, was born 15 April 1741 and died 1827. He married, 1st, on 12 January 1762 Rachel Brewer in Annapolis, daughter of John Brewer. Rachel was born 14 May 1744 in Annapolis, and died on 12 April 1790 in Philadelphia, Pennsylvania. He married, 2nd, about 1791, Elizabeth De Peyster, daughter of William de Peyster, merchant of New York (*Maryland Journal and Baltimore Advertiser* 10 June 1791). Elizabeth was born 10 July 1765, and died 19 February 1804 in Philosophical Hall, Philadelphia (*Baltimore Telegraphe* 23 February 1804). His third marriage was to Hannah Moore on 1794 in Philadelphia. She was born 10 July 1755 in Montgomery Co., Penna., and died 22 February 1827 in Philadelphia. Peale advertised his business of clock making and repair, watch cleaning, and also the saddler's business (Annapolis *Maryland Gazette* 9 February 1764).

Charles Wilson and Rachel Brewer were the parents of: **8. Margaret Jane,** b. and d. 1763 in Annapolis; **9. James Willson,** b. 1765 in Tuckahoe, Queen Anne's Co., Md.., and d. 1767; **10. Clara E.**, b. about 1767; **11. Eleanor,** b. 20 May 1770 in Annapolis; **12. Margaret Van Bordley,** b. 13 January 1772 in Annapolis, d. 1773; **13 Raphaelle,** b. 17 February 1774 in Annapolis, d. 5 March 1825 in Philadelphia; **14. Angelica Kauffman,** b. 22 December 1775 in Charles Town, Cecil Co., Maryland, and d. 1853; **15. Rembrandt,** b. 22 February 1778 in Bucks Co., Penna., d. 3 October 1860 in Philadelphia; m. Eleanor [-?-], who died 5 April 1836 (*Baltimore American* 11 April 1836); **16. Titian Ramsey,** b. 1 August 1780 in Philadelphia, and d. 19 September 1798; m. Eliza Cecilia Laforgue on 10 October 1822; she d. 1846; **17. Rubens,** b. 4 May 1784 in Philadelphia, d. 17 July 1865 in Holmesburg, Pennsylvania; **18. Sophonisba Angusciola,** b. 24 April 1786 in Philadelphia, d. 26 October 1859 in Upper Darby, Chester County, Pennsylvania; and **19. Rosalba Carriera,** b. 25 October 1788 in Philadelphia, and d. there on 3 October 1790.

Charles Willson and Elizabeth (de Peyster) were the parents of; **20. Vandyke**, b. 19 September 1792 in Philadelphia; **21. Charles Linnaeus**, b. 20 March 1794 in Philadelphia; **22. Sybilla Miriam**, b. 27 October 1797 in Philadelphia; **23. Titian Ramsey**, b. 1800 in Philadelphia, d. 1885; and **24. Elizabeth De Peyster**, b. 16 April 1802 in Philadelphia, d. 25 July 1857 in Upper Gwynedd, Pennsylvania.

Charles Willson and Hannah were the parents of: **27. Benjamin Franklin**, b. 15 October 1795 in Philadelphia, d. there on 5 May 1870, m. Caroline E. Haslam on 4 May 1839. She died 1875.

5. St George Peale, son of Charles (1) and Margaret, was born 23 April 1745 in Charlestown, Cecil Co., Md., and died 3 July 1778 in Baltimore (*Maryland Journal and Baltimore Advertiser* 7 July 1778). He married about 1769 Elizabeth Emerson Callister.

St. George Peale was a Clerk in the Land Office of Maryland, and eventually became Chief Clerk, and then Register on 21 April 1777. On 6 March 1776 he was commissioned 1st Lieutenant Capt. James Brice's Independent Company of Militia of Annapolis. He also served as Commissary of Military Supplies. He died of exposure (*RPAA*: 149).

St. George Peale died leaving a will dated 22 June 1778 and proved 11 July 1788. He left his nephews Charles Peale Polk and Raphael Peale 331½ a. *The Granary* and 159 a. *Sancha Pancha*. His nieces Margaret Jane Polk, Elizabeth Polk, and Angeline Peale were each to have £1000 at age 21 or marriage. He left £100 and personalty to each of the following: his friend Margaret Durgan, sister-in-law Sarah Callister, and his mother-in-law Sarah Callister. He named his wife's sisters Margaret, Harriet, and Callista, his friends Col. Nathaniel Ramsay and John Kennedy. He left the rest of his estate to his wife His brothers Col. Nathaniel Ramsay and Charles Peale, and his wife were executors. James Nicholson, James Smith of William, and George Turnbull witnessed the will (BAWB 3:362).

Elizabeth Peale, Charles Wilson Peale, and Nathaniel Ramsay posted an administration bond for £5000 on 11 July 1778. James Nicholson and John McLure were sureties (BAAB 3:353).

Elizabeth Peale died leaving a will dated 31 December 1785 and proved 22 June 1786. She mentioned two tracts now in the possession of George French of Frederick Co. She had put her papers in the hands of Luther Martin. She left one-fourth of her three quarters, and personalty, to her mother Sarah Callister, sisters Margaret Kennedy and Mary Harriott Callister, and her nephew Henry Callister Kennedy. Her mother was to have the house and lot in Chestertown adjoining the Club House Green. William Gibson, Lyde Goodwin and Jacob H. Levy witnessed the will (BAWB 4:15, abst. by Burns).

Sarah Callister. executrix, posted an administration bond for £1000 on 22 July 1786, with William Gibson, and Nathaniel Smith as sureties (BAAB 6:403).

St George and Elizabeth were the parents of: **28. |-?-|**, daughter, b. about 1772.

6. Elizabeth Digby Peale, daughter of Charles (1), and Margaret, was born 1747 and died 1776. She married Capt. Robert Polk of Va., who was born about 1744 and died 1777.

Robert and Elizabeth were the parents of: **29. Charles Peale Polk**, b. 1767; **30. Elizabeth Bordley Polk**, b. 1770; m. Rev. Joseph Grove John Bend, for many years the Rector of St. Paul's Episcopal Parish in Baltimore; and **31. Margaret Jane**.

7. James Peale, son of Charles (1) and Margaret, was born 1749 in Annapolis and died in Philadelphia on 24 May 1831. He married, 1st. Ellen Bordley Polk. He married 2nd, Mary Chambers Claypoole, born 27 July 1753 in Philadelphia and died there on 27 July 1829.

James Peale was commissioned an Ensign in Col. Smallwood's Regiment in July 1775, and fought at the Battles of Long Island, Trenton, Princeton, and Monmouth. he was at Valley Forge, was Commissioned a Captain in the Maryland Regiment on 27 March 1779, resigning on 2 June 1778 (*RPAA:*149).

James and Mary were the parents of the following, all said to have been born in Philadelphia: **32. Jane Ramsey**, b. 1785, d. 9 April 1812 in Baltimore; **33. Maria**, b. 1787, d. 27 March 1866; **34. James**, b. 6 March 1789, d. 27 October 1876; **35. Anna Claypoole**, b. 9 March 1791, d. in Philadelphia on 25 December 1878; m. 1st, on 27 August 1829 William Straughton, b. 4 January 1770 in Philadelphia, and d. there on 12 December 1829. She m. 2nd, on 10 June 1841 William Duncan, b. 14 October 1772 in Philadelphia, and d. there on 16 February 1864; **36. Margaretta Angelica**, b. 1 October 1795, d. 17 January 1882; and **37. Sarah Miriam**, b. 19 May 1800, d. 4 February 1885 in Philadelphia.

13. Raphaelle Peale, son of Charles Wilson (3) and Rachel, was born 17 February 1774 in Annapolis and died 5 March 1825 in Philadelphia. Raphaelle and Miss M. McGlathery, both of Baltimore, were married Thurs. eve. by Rev. J. B, Smith (*Federal Gazette and Baltimore Daily Advertiser* 31 May 1797). She was a daughter of Matthew McGlathery, and was born 19 Aug 1775, and died 17 January 1852 in Philadelphia.

Raphaelle and Mary were the parents of the following, all said to have been born in Philadelphia: **38. [-?-]**, b. 1798, d. 4 November 1798; **39. Eliza Ferguson**, b. 6 August 1799, d. 30 August 1876 in Mt Vernon, Knox Co., Ohio;.**40. Sophonisba**, b. 15 May 1801, d. 3 August 1878 in Philadelphia; m. her cousin James Peale (see below); **41. Charles Willson**, b. 4 August 1802, d. 4 August 1829; **42. Edmund**, b. 8 December 1805 in Philadelphia, d. 25 September 1851; **43. St George**, b. 27 April 1807 in Philadelphia, d. 19 January 1850; **44. Rubens**, b. 15 September 1808 in Philadelphia, d. 23 December 1891; and **45. Margaret**, b. 15 October 1810 in Philadelphia, d. 26 October 1847.

13. Angelica Kauffman Peale, daughter of Charles Wilson (3) and Rachel, was born in 1775 and died 1853. She married as his 2nd wife Alexander Robinson, born 1751, died 1845, a Baltimore merchant and ship-owner.

"Citizen" Alexander Robinson, of Baltimore, and Miss Angelica Peale, daughter of Mr. Peale of Philadelphia, were m. there on Tues., 15h inst. (*Maryland Journal and Baltimore Advertiser* 18 July 1794).

Alexander and Angelica were the parents of: **46. Priscilla**, b. 1797, d. 1820, m. Dr. Henry Boteler of Shepherdstown, Va. (now W. Va.); they were the parents of: **Alexander Robinson Boteler,** b. 1815, d. 1892.

18. Sophonisba Angusciola Peale, daughter of Charles Wilson (3) and Rachel, was born 1786 and died 1859. She married Coleman Sellers, born 1781, died 1834.

Coleman and Sophonisba were the parents of: **47. Anna**, b. 30 September 1824 in Philadelphia, and d. 4 March 1905 in Chattanooga, Tenn.

19. Charles Peale Polk, son of Capt. Robert and Elizabeth Digby (Peale) (6) Polk, was born 1767, and died in Washington, D.C., on 6 May 1822. He married 1st, about 1785 Ruth Ellison of N. J.; Mrs. R. Polk, consort of Charles P. Polk, died in Washington, D.C., on died 24 November 1810 aged 44 years. He married 2nd, on 14 June 1811, Mrs. Lucy Brockenbrough of Port Royal, Va.; she died 17 March 1816, aged 34; and 3$^{rd.}$ Ellen B. Downman (Washington D.C., *National Intelligencer* 27 November 1810, 15 June 1811, and 19 March 1816).

31. Jane Ramsay Peale, daughter of James (7) and Mary, was born 1785 and died 1834. She married Samuel Simes, who died 1813.

Jane R. Simes, aged 49, consort of the late Samuel Simes of Philadelphia, died 20 April 1834 (*Baltimore American* 24 April 1834).

Samuel and Jane were the parents of; **48. Mary Jane**, b. 1 April 1807 in Baltimore, d. 26 May 1972; on 6 July 1836 she married John Lloyd Yeats, M.D. (*Baltimore American* 8 July 1836). He was born 1802 and died 1875.

33. James Peale, son of James (7) and Mary, was born 6 March 1789 in Philadelphia, where he died on 27 October 1876. He married, 1st, Anna Dunn on 18 December 1813 in Philadelphia. She was born 1793 in Chestertown. Md.., and died 1814 in Philadelphia, Pa. He married, 2nd, his cousin, Sophonisba Peale on 11 May 1822 in Philadelphia. She was a daughter of Raphaelle and Martha 'Patty' McGlathery, and was born 15 May 1801 in Philadelphia, where she died on 3 August 1878.

James and Sophonisba were the parents of: **49. James Godman**, b. 11 February 1823 in Philadelphia, d. 1891; m.. Ellen Q. Field; **50. Washington**, b. 9 February 1825 in Philadelphia, d. 1868; m. Margaret Briggs; **51. Virginia**, b. 1 October 1828 in Philadelphia; **52. Howard**, b. 5 October 1830 in Philadelphia; and **53. Henry 'Harry,'** b. 15 October 1839 in Philadelphia.

34. Anna Claypoole Peale, daughter of James (7) and Mary, was born 1791 and died in Philadelphia, on 25 December 1878. She married 1st, on 27 August 1829, Rev. Dr. William Straughton, born 1770, died 1829. She married 2nd, as his third wife, General William Duncan, born 1772, died 1864. She had no children by either marriage.

41. Edmund Peale, son of Raphaelle (13), was born 8 December 1805 in Philadelphia, and died 25 September 1851. Edmund was the father of: **54. Sophonisba**, d. 13 March 1844; and **55. Raphaelle J.**, d. 6 July 1849 (Baltimore *Sun* 14 March 1844, and 7 July 1849).

== 0 ==

The Pickering Family of Anne Arundel County
With Notes on the Purnall and Scrivener Families

1. |-?-| Pickering was the father of: **2. James**; and **3. Stephen**.

2. James Pickering, son of [-?-] (1), was teaching in 1750, and died by August 1759. James "Pickerell" married, 1st, Elizabeth Simmons in St. James Parish on 8 May 1735 (*AACR:*166). He married, 2nd, by 1743, Elizabeth daughter of John Eliot Brown of St. James Parish (AALR RB#1:283, RB#3:278). Pickering married, 3rd, Anne [-?-].

On 5 October 1738 he and Stephen Pickering witnessed the will of Roger Crudgenton of Anne Arundel Co. (MWB 22:271). On 3 March 1739 he witnessed the will of Thomas Trott of Anne Arundel Co. (MWB 24:439).

On 24 October 1739 Elizabeth Brown, widow of John Eliot Brown, conveyed a Negro girls named Sarah and clothing to her daughter Elizabeth, wife of James Pickering. Elizabeth Brown also mentioned James and Elizabeth's daughter Elizabeth Pickering (AALR RD#3:204; see also AALR RB#1:283, 397). On 5 July 1744 a "release of a deed of gift" was recorded. Elizabeth Brown, widow, repented of her deeds of gift, and charged her daughter Elizabeth to return the items, and the document released Elizabeth

Brown from her deeds of gifts (AALR RB#1:398). The Widow Brown had another change of heart, and on 3 July 1750 conveyed a Negro child named Nell to her granddaughter Mary Pickering, daughter of James Pickering by his late wife Elizabeth (AALR RB#3:278).

In November 1740, James Pickering, schoolmaster, was sued by Richard Chew for £3.15.0. Pickering was ordered to pay (AAJU November 1740 Court:740; see also AAJU IB#2:740). On 3 April 1745 James Pickering conveyed household goods and livestock to George Simmons (AALR RB#2:15).

On 1 October 1755 Stephen Pickering of Anne Arundel Co., Gent., made his will, leaving his brother James Pickering, five shillings (MWB 29:479).

George Simmons, administrator, filed an account of James Pickering's estate on 17 August 1759. He cited assets worth £0.0.0, and made payments of £65.2.10 (MDAD 44:46). Simmons filed a second account on 11 March 1762 and listed a second inventory in the amount of £6.0.0, and made payments of £28.16.1 (MDAD 47:318).

James and Elizabeth Pickering were the parents of the following children, born in St. James Parish (*AACR:* 166): **3. Mary,** b. 2 March 1733/4, bapt. 7 April 1734, m. Richard Purnall, Jr., on 16 April 1751 (*AACR:* 170).

By a 3rd wife, Anne, James Pickering was the father of (*AACR:* 170): **4. Elizabeth,** b. 6 March 1753.

3. Stephen Pickering, Gent., of Anne Arundel Co., son of [-?-] (1), died by May 1755. He was in Prince George's Co. on 13 December 1744 when he witnessed the will of Zachariah Wade (MWB 24:51-53).

Stephen Pickering died leaving a will dated 10 January 1753 and proved 10 May 1755. To his niece, the wife of Richard Purnall, Jr., he left a silver tankard, now in the possession of John Philpot of London, merchant. To Rev. Charles Lake, Samuel Keene and James Dick, he left each a guinea to buy a ring; to George Simmons, Jr., stock; to brother James Pickering, 5 s. sterling; and to George Simmons, Sr., the other half of his estate. Archibald Spence and Vachel Keene witnessed the will (MWB 29:479).

3. Mary Pickering, daughter of James (2) and Elizabeth, was born 2 March 1733/4, and bapt. 7 April 1734. She married Richard Purnall, Jr., on 16 April 1751, in St. James Parish. (Wright, "St. James Parish," in *AACR:*170).

Richard and Mary were the parents of: **5. Elizabeth Purnall,** b. 20 February 1752; and **6. Rachel Purnall,** b. 15 October 1753.

3. Elizabeth Purnell, daughter of Richard and Mary(3) (Pickering) Purnall, was born 20 February 1752 in Anne Arundel Co., and died 1801. She married John Scrivener about 1775 in Ann Arundel Co. He was a son of William and Elizabeth (Clark) Scrivener, and was born about 1745/50 in Anne Arundel Co. and died 1812 in Edwards Ferry, Montgomery Co., Md.

John and Elizabeth were the parents of: **7. Elizabeth; 8. Mary A. (Polly),** b. 11 May 1776 in Montgomery Co., and d. in Georgetown, Washington, D. C.; **9. Margaret; 10. Rezin; 11. Sarah; 12. William;** and **13. Levi.**

==0==

The Piper Family of Anne Arundel County
With Notes on the Auld, Goldsborough, and Harrington Families

1. Michael Piper married Rosanna Button in Ireland. Rose Piper, wife of Michael Piper, Register of St. Anne's Parish, died 29 November 1724 in her 35th year (*AACR*:92).

Michael and his wife came to the colonies about 1717, and by 23 October 1718 he was in Philadelphia (V. L. Auld cites W. Edwin Auld Remly, *Ten Generations in America*, and Lambeth Palace Library Papers; see also the *Pennsylvania Magazine of History and Biography* 61:370n).

On 7 November 1720 Michael Piper was chosen Register of St. Anne's Parish in place of John Talbot. On 5 December 1721 Michael Piper, the Register and Schoolmaster of Annapolis, petitioned the vestry for a small quantity of ground at the east end of the church where his dead could lie. The petition was allowed and he was allowed seven square feet of ground. The Minister, vestry, and church wardens decided that the schoolmaster of Annapolis and the charity boys on the foundation of the school in Annapolis, be permitted, during the vacancy of the Assembly, constantly to sit in the front seat joining to the back door until such time as further provision can be made for them. On 2 July 1723 Mrs. Piper and Elizabeth Piper were allowed to sit in the Second Public Pew ("St. Anne's Parish, Vestry Proceedings," *MdHM* 7:74, 79, 80, 172).

On 23 April 1723 Edward Smith of Annapolis, named Michael Piper as one of his executors. In May 1723 Mary Smith, widow of Edward Smith, innholder of Annapolis, sued Michael Piper (MDTP 26:147). On 16 May 1723 Piper declined to serve as executor, but claimed the right to see that Smith's children were brought up in the Protestant Religion (MWB 18:147; abst. in *Md. Cal. of Wills* 5:144). On 2 September 1724 Henry Carter left him one pistole for writing his will. Piper was one of the witnesses (MWB 18:356; abst. in *Md. Cal. of Wills* 5:188).

On 5 October 1723 Piper received a payment from the estate of Margaret Slater of Anne Arundel Co. On 12 October 1723 he received a payment from the estate of Thomas Holmes. (MDAD 5:23, 334).

On 10 January 1724 Michael Piper was to be allowed 500 lbs. tobacco for last year's service as clerk of the vestry 50 lbs. for transcribing the new act of the Assembly against profaning the Sabbath, and another 150 lbs. for transcribing the two tables hanging in the Church: one was to be the Table of Marriages, and the other the Table of Donations of several gentlemen towards the public buildings of the city ("St. Anne's Parish, Vestry Proceedings," *MdHM* 7:178). Michael Piper made a payment to the estate of Daniel Thompson, innholder of Anne Arundel Co., in the account filed 7 July 1726 (MDAD 7:388). He was a debtor of Edward Smith, listed in the administration account filed 19 July 1726 (MDAD 8:474). He was also listed as a debtor in the account filed 20 December 1729 of Hugh Kennedy (MDAD 10:125).

Rosanna Piper witnessed a deed of 7 December 1720 from Thomas Cross to Thomas Larkin (AALR CW#1: 414).

Michael Piper witnessed a deed of 13 April 1724 from Daniel Dulany to Robert Gordon (AALR SY#1: 33).

No record of death or settling of an estate has been found for Michael Piper; he may have moved away from Maryland.

Michael and Rose were the parents of (*AACR*: 88, 91, 92): **2. John,** b. about 1711, d. 8 September 1721; and **3. Rose Anna,** b. 22 December 1723, bapt. 29 December 1723; her godparents were Capt. Thomas Larkin, Elizabeth Beale, and Mrs. Transum.

3. Rosanna Piper, daughter of Michael (1) and Rosanna, was born 22 December 1723 and bapt. 29 December 1723 (*AACR:* 91). She married, 1st, in 1745, Howes Goldsborough, who was born 14 November 1715 and died in 1746, the son of Robert Goldsborough of Ashby, (Roberta Bolling Henry, "Robert Goldsborough of Ashby and His Six Sons," *Maryland Genealogies* 2:22, 23). Rosanna Piper Goldsborough married,

Colonial Families of Maryland II

2nd, in 1747, James Auld. They lived in Dorchester Co., and then moved to Halifax Co., N. C. (Letter from V. L. Auld).

Mr. Howes Goldsborough, Clerk of Dorchester Co., died there last week. He was succeeded in office by Mr. John Caile (Annapolis *Maryland Gazette* 8 April 1746). John Stevens and Francis Howell appraised the personal estate of Mr. Howes Goldsborough on 2 August 1746 at £386.19.10. Charles Goldsborough and William Goldsborough signed as next of kin. Rosanna Goldsborough, administratrix, filed the inventory on 4 November1746 (MINV 34:29).

Rosannah Piper Goldsborough married 2nd, in 1747, James Auld, , son of John and Mary (Sherwood) Auld. Rosannah Auld, wife of James Auld, filed an account of the estate of Howes Goldsborough on 18 May 1754. After citing the inventory as given above she listed payments of £335.2.4 (MDAD 36:205).

In 1765 James Auld and his family moved to Halifax, North Carolina, where on 21 September 1773, he conveyed 258 a. *Newport Glasgow* to Matthew Tilghman. His wife Rosanna released her dower, and his son John was mentioned in the deed (Peden, *More Marylanders to Carolina:* 6-7).

Howes and Rosanna (Piper) Goldsborough were the parents of: **4. Caroline,** b. 1744, d. 10 March 1816.

James and Rosanna (Piper) Auld were the parents of: **5. Nancy; 6. Betsey,** d. 1850 in Fayetteville, N. C., buried at the Auld Plantation in Anson Co., N. C.; **7. Rosanna,** b. 1754, widowed at age 45, d. 13 October 1828 in Wadesboro, NC (See *History of the Old Cheraws:* 104-105); **8. Michael Piper,** b. 3 March 1757 in Dorchester Co., Md., d. 18 Sep 1788 in Anson Co., N. C.; and **9. John,** b. 17 April 1763 (See *History of the Old Cheraws:* 330).

8. Michael Piper Auld, son of James and Rosanna (3) (Piper) Auld, was born 3 March 1757 in Dorchester Co., Md.., and died 18 September 1788 in Anson Co. N. C. He married Sidney Fields, some time before 1788 in Guilford or Anson County N. C. She was a daughter of J. Smith and Elizabeth ([-?-]) Fields, and was born 1756 in Guilford Co., N. C, and died some time between 1820 and 1826 in Anson Co. N. C.

Michael Piper and Sidney were the parents of: **19. John Field,** b. 6 May 1788 in Anson Co., N, C., d. 28 August 1859 in Union Parish, La.; m. Mary Kendricks Jackson in 1806 in Anson County N. C., who was b. 1790 in Anson Co. and d. 28 August 1859 in Union Parish, La.

== = 0 = =

The Popejoy Family of Baltimore County

Sources: A: Charles Luther Popejoy. *The Popejoy Family in America, 1700-1976.* Juneau [AL]: Privately Printed, 1976.

1. William Popejoy was bound for Md.. on the *Comfort* on 10 August 1680; his agent was Thomas Lawrence (*BRCO*:359).

In August 1714 William Summers complained to the county court about Popejoy. On 21 April 1715 Popejoy was a debtor to the estate of William Bosworth, chirurgeon, of Baltimore Co. (INAC 37A:144). In August 1719 neighbors complained that Popejoy had blocked a road (William B. Marye, "The Baltimore County 'Garrison,' and the Old Garrison Road," *MdHM* 16:117).

William Popejoy was the father of: **2. William,** bapt. in 1689 in Baltimore Co.

2. William Popejoy, son of William (1), was bapt. 1689 in Baltimore Co. and died 1762 in Stafford Co., Va. He married Cassandra Smith about 1710 in Stafford Co., Va. (Data posted by Jessy Santee Shepherd on the internet; undocumented statements in the LDS Ancestral File).

William and Cassandra were said to have been the parents of: **3. Nathaniel Smith,** b. about 1711; **4. Edward B.,** b. about 1713; **5. John,** b. about 1717; and **6. Terrence,** b. about 1717.

3. Nathaniel Smith Popejoy, son of William (2) and Cassandra, was born about 1711.

He may have married Ann Tarrence, and have been the father of: **7. Edward,** b. about 1748 in Stafford Co., Va.

4. Edward Popejoy, son of Nathaniel Smith (3) and Ann, was born about 1748 in Stafford Co., Va. An Edward Popejoy appears in Stafford Co., Va., in 1782 (AIS *Pre-1790 Census Index*).

= = 0 = =

The Prebble Family of Baltimore County

N.B: The name appears as Prebbel, Prebble, Preble, Pribble, and Prible.

1. Thomas Prebble died by 1704. He was over 21 on 29 August 1684 when he bound himself to Robert Shanks of Wapping, Co. Middlesex, to serve him for 4 years after his arrival in Md.. Robert Shanks, mariner, promised to provide Thomas Pribble with meals, apparel, lodging and other necessities and that he would be paid according to the customs of this country after four years service. (BACP D: 222).

On 24 June 1681 100 a. *Hazard* had been surveyed for John Yeo; it was later regranted to Thomas Preble; still later possessed by Mary Preble for Thomas' orphans; Archibald Buchanan had m. the widow (*MRR:* 21).

Prebble married Mary Bucknell about 1686 in Baltimore County, daughter of Thomas Bucknell and Mary. Mary Preble, administratrix of Thomas Preble posted an administration bond on 19 July 1704 (MDTP 19B:11). Mary married 2nd, Archibald Buchanan by 1706 when she administered John Preble's estate. The funeral expenses were $500. Debts were paid to John Hall, James Phillips, Aquila Paca, and Charles Carroll (INAC 25:415-416).

In 1733 Archibald Buchanan named Sarah and Thomas Prebble as his grandchildren.

Thomas and Mary were the parents of (Reamy and Reamy, *St. George's Parish Register:* 1, 3, 4, 5, 7, 9, 17): **2. Ann,** b. 28 November 1689 at Swan Creek, m. Robert Hawkins on 15 November 1709 in St. George's Parish, son of John Hawkins; **3. Thomas,** b. 7 July 1691 at Musketo Creek; **4. Mary,** b. 6 June 1695, Musketo Creek, d. 16 October 1729; m. Samuel Brown; **5. John Stephen,** b. 21 June 1697 at Musketo Creek, bapt.2 July 1699; **6. Elizabeth,** b. 27 December 1699 at Duck Creek; she died 17 January 1731/32, having m. William Simpson; and **7. Sarah,** b. 12 August 1702 at the Head of Duck Creek, bapt. 4 October 1702; m. John Poloke.

5. John (or John Stephen) Prebble, son of Thomas (1) and Mary, was born 21 June 1697 at Musketon Creek, Baltimore Co., Md., and died 1776. He married Ann Gallion by 1719, probably in St. George's Parish. In 1730 Ann was named as a daughter of John

Gallion (MWB 20:263, abst. in *Md. Cal. of Wills* 6:201).

On 17 January 1732 John was named as a son, and Sarah and Thomas Pribble were named as grandchildren, in the will of Mary Buchannan, widow of Archibald Buchannan (MWB 30:698 abst. in *Md.. Cal. of Wills* 7:23).

John Preble was paid for wine by the vestry of St. George's Parish on 3 May 1748 (Reamy and Reamy, *St. George's Parish Register:* 106).

On 3 September 1738 William Allein, with the consent of his wife Mary, conveyed 80 a. *Neighbor's Good Will* to John 'Prible' (BALR HWS#1-A: 273). On 28 August 1739 Richard Butts, carpenter, with the consent of his wife Mary conveyed 50 A. *West's Favour* to John Prible (BALR HWS#1-A: 269). He still owed both these tracts in 1750 (Baltimore Co. Debt Book, 1750). On 8 June 1759 John Prebble conveyed property to his son Stephen (BACT 2:30).

As John Pribble he was listed in Sheriff Aquila Hall's Assessment Ledger of 1762-4. In 1764 John Pribell was a creditor of Samuel Hyde of London to the sum of £0.12.0 (*IBCP:* 11, 21).

John and Ann were the parents of (Reamy and Reamy, *St. George's Parish Register:* 24, 27, 37, 51, 59): **8. Sarah,** b. 22 December 1719; **9. Thomas,** b. 25 March 1724, Baltimore County, d. after 1796; **10. Mary,** b. 3 October 1726; **11. Sophia,** b. 25 March 1733; **12. John Stephen,** b. 15 August 1736, Baltimore County, d. 1804; and **13. James,** b. 21 January 1739.

9. Thomas Prebble, son of John (5) and Ann, was born 5 March 1724, and died after 1796. He married Elizabeth Teegarden.

Thomas Pribble was listed in Sheriff Aquila Hall's Assessment Ledger of 1762-4 (*IBCP:*21).. On 1 May 1766 Thomas Pribble advertised he would settle the estate of Joseph Smith, nailer (BAAD 7:181).

Thomas and Elizabeth were the parents of: **14. Thomas, Jr.,** b. 1760; m. Hannah Enoch; **15. Rachel;** m. George Teegarden in 1763; **16. Job;** and **17. Reuben.**

12. John Stephen Preble, son of John (5) and Ann, was born 15 August 1736, and died in 1804. He may be the John Preble who married [-?-], a daughter of James Low(e) or Laws by 12 July 1758 (BAAD 4:312, 6:2½).

In 1768 Stephen Prebble signed a petition against the removal of the county seat from Joppa to Baltimore Town (*IBCP:*44).

Stephen Preble was the father of at least one son: **18. James,** b. 1762.

14. Thomas Preble, Jr., son of Thomas (9) and Elizabeth, was born 1760 in Baltimore Co., Md.., and died 20 December 1836 in Wood Co., Va. He married in 1784 at Red Stone Fork, Green Co, Pa., Hannah Enoch, born 1766, died 1846, a daughter of Col. Henry and Sarah ([-?-]) Enoch (*BARP:* 216).

Thomas, Jr. and his wife moved to Virginia from Pa. in 1796. He served in the Revolutionary War and in the War against the Indians (Peden, *Marylanders to Kentucky:* 118).

Thomas and Hannah were the parents of (*BARP:* 216): **19. Elizabeth,** b. 1785, m. James Fought; **20. Abram,** b. 1788, m. Ann Butcher; **21. Mary,** b. 1791, m. Joshua Darnell; **22. Hiram,** b. 1793, m. Debora Butcher; **23. Hugh,** b. 1796, m. Elizabeth Permelia Jackson; **23. Armanelah,** b. 1798, m. John Foster; **24. Nancy,** b. 1800, m. Thomas Pickering; **25. Hedgeman,** b. 1802, m. Priscilla Devaughn; **26. Daniel,** b. 1804, m. Amanda M. Jackson; and **27. Thomas,** b. 1806, m. Delilah Walker.

16. Job Preble, son of Thomas (9) and Elizabeth, served in the Revolutionary War and in the War against the Indians (Peden, *Marylanders to Kentucky:* 118).

17. Reuben Preble, son of Thomas (9) and Elizabeth, served in the Revolutionary War and in the War against the Indians (Peden, *Marylanders to Kentucky:* 118).

18. James Pribble, son of Stephen (12), was born 1762 in Baltimore Co., Md.., and died in Pendleton Co., Ky. In 1783 he was living in Washington Co., Penna., where he married Margaret [-?-].

He served in the Revolutionary War as a spy, and then in 1789 moved to Bourbon Co., Ky. (Peden, *Marylanders to Kentucky:* 118, cites an article written by Mrs. Robert J. Burton in *Kentucky Ancestor* 12 (1) (July 1976) 19-23).

Unplaced:
John Pribble, Jr., in November 1756 was charged with begetting a bastard on the body of Mary Lee (BACP BB#C:312, TR#6:1, 41).
John Pribble m. by 23 August 1769, [-?-], daughter of James Preston (BAAD 7:314).
Stephen Pribble m. by 14 June 1794, Clemency, daughter of Clemency Billingslea (HAWB AJ#2:57).

== 0 ==

The Rathell Family

1. John Rathell died in Talbot Co. by January 1735/6. He married, 1ˢᵗ, by 21 September 1708, Sarah, daughter of Michael Kerby of Talbot Co. (TALR RF#11:50). He married, 2ⁿᵈ, Elizabeth Russum on 26 August 1725 in St. Peter's Parish, TA Co. (*ESVR* 1:71). She survived him.

In June 1707 John Rathell, tailor, was named as having committed fornication and begotten a child on the body of Catherine Noble, servant of John Emerson. She was ordered to receive 25 lashes. In March 1714 he was again charged with fornication, with Bridget Penny, and begotten a child (Wright, *Talbot Co. Judgment Records,* pp. 154, 162). In his will dated 23 September 1718, Michael Kirby, planter of Talbot Co., entrusted the care of his youngest son Richard to John Rathell until he should reach the age of 18 (MWB 18:277). Rathell received payments from the estates of Michael Kirby of Talbot Co. on 17 August 1725 and Paul Roux of Talbot Co. on 9 August 1727 (MDAD 7:73, 8:304).

John Rathell patented 50 a. *Rathell's Chance* on 6 August 1719 (MPL FF#7:252, PL#4:368).

As John "Rathrell," tailor, of Talbot Co., he died leaving a will dated 17 August 1735, proved 22 January 1735. He named his wife Lidia, sons Thomas and Richard, neither of whom were yet 18, and he mentioned his eight children. His wife and son John were named executors. David Kerby, Isaac Dobson, and Richard Kirby witnessed the will (MWB 21:503).

Elizabeth Rathell, executrix, filed an administration account of John Rathell's estate on 16 September 1747. She cited assets of £61.76.3, and made payments coming to £42.14.10. The representatives of the deceased were the widow, and children: John, David, Thomas, Mary, Elizabeth, Samuel, and Joseph (MDAD 14:446).

On 11 Aug 1743 Elizabeth Russum conveyed various livestock and household furnishings to Elizabeth Rathell in consideration that Elizabeth Rathell would find and provide all necessities for her during her natural life (TALR 15:368).

On 9 March 1765 Elizabeth Rathell, spinster, for £32 current money of Maryland, conveyed 52 a. of *Elizabeth's Enlargement* to Michael Kirby (TALR 19:306). She had patented this tract for 196 a. on 29 September 1762 (MPL BC#18:653, BC #21:200).

Elizabeth Rathell of Talbot Co. died leaving a will dated 28 November 1766 proved 23 December 1766. She named her son Samuel Rathell and her daughter Elizabeth Baly, who were each to have 1 s. sterling. Her son Joseph, executor, was to have her lands. Ambrose Kinnimont, John Garey, and Michael Kirby witnessed her will (MWB 35:61).John Rathell was the father of eight children, including: **2. John; 3. David; 4. Thomas,** under 18 in 1735; **5. Mary; 6. Elizabeth,** m. [-?-] Baly by 28 November 1766; on 11 August 1743 Elizabeth Russum conveyed to Elizabeth Rathell, her granddaughter, one bed, two blankets, one sheet, her best ruff [rugg?], a bolster, and two pillows (TALR 15:369); **7. Samuel,** b. about 1733, under 18 in 1735; in 1786 at age 55 he made a deposition (Talbot Co. Land commissions 4:200-201); by 5 July 1763 he was in Dorchester Co. when he patented 54 a. of *Rathell's Chance* (MPL BC #18:95, BC #21:200); and **8. Joseph,** b. about 1736.

2. John Rathell, son of John (1), was living on 4 July 1732 when he conveyed livestock to John Eustace, who was to pay William Warren 1800 lbs. of tobacco (TALR 13:716).

3. David Rathell, son of John (1) and Elizabeth, died in Dorchester Co. by 18 May 1761. He married by 4 August 1746 Ann, representative of Lotan West, planter of Talbot Co. (MDAD 22:282). David and Ann witnessed the will of Lotan West of Talbot Co. on 21 May 1745 (MWB 24:121).

George West administered the estate of David Rathell of Dorchester Co. on 18 May 1761. He listed assets of £23.18.10, and payments of £3.7.6 (MDAD 47:40). West filed a second administration account on 6 November 1764. He cited payments of £14.0.11, and named the following representatives: the widow (unnamed), and the children named below (MDAD 52:108).

David and Ann were the parents of: **9. Rebecca; 10. David;** he may be the David Rathell who received a payment from the estate of David McQuinney of Dorchester Co. on 12 November 1765 (MDAD 38:326); **11: John; 12. William;** and **13. Ann.**

4. Thomas Rathell, son of John (1) and Elizabeth, died in Talbot Co. by June 1762. He married Mary [-?-], who married 2nd, John Warren or Warron of Dorchester Co.

On 28 November 1757 the house where he lived was mentioned in the valuation of the lands of Charles Bullen, son and heir of Thomas Bullen, made by Samuel Abbott and Matthew Jenkins (TALR 18:442).

Mary Rathell, now Mary Warren, administered the estate of Thomas Rathell on 2 June 1762. Out of assets totaling £53.6.7, she made payments of £33.7.3. The deceased left six children named below (MDAD 48:27).

Thomas and Mary Rathell were the parents of: **14. Richard,** age 12, was b. about 1750; on 5 January 1768, as one of the representatives of Thomas Rathell, deceased, he received a payment from the estate of John Warren of Dorchester Co., deceased (MDAD 58:96); **15. Kirby,** aged 10, was b. about 1752; **16. Pritchard,** aged 8, b. about 1754; **17. Mary,** aged 6, b. about 1756; **18. Elizabeth,** aged 4, b. about 1758; **19. Thomas,** aged 3, b. about 1759.

8. Joseph Rathell, son of John (1) and Elizabeth, was born about 1736 (perhaps posthumously), giving his age as 49 in 1784 and 50 in 1786 depositions (Talbot Co. Land Commissions 4:101, 201). He was living as late as 1790. He married by November 1768 Rachel [-?-].

On 4 November 1768 Joseph Rathell and his wife Rachel conveyed to John Garey, for £10.12.6 of current money of Maryland, 4½ a. part of *Elizabeth's Enlargement*, adjoining *Strawberry Hill's Addition,* and another 4 a. of *Elizabeth's Enlargement* (TALR 19:532). On the same day, John Carey and his wife Susanna, for £18.15.0, conveyed 15 a. *Partner's Hazard,* adjoining *Bowes' Range* (TALR 19:534).

Joseph moved to Annapolis for a short time and advertised that he intended to open a school in town, and would teach reading, true pronunciation, proper delivery, writing, and arithmetic at Mr. Lyttleton's (Annapolis *Maryland Gazette* 18 April 1765). In September 1765 he advertised he would open an evening school (Annapolis *Maryland Gazette* 26 September 1765).

On 3 February 1773 Thomas Dickinson Richardson, of the Parish of St. Bartholomew the Little, London, clerk, and second and posthumous son of Anthony Richardson, through James Dickinson, his attorney, conveyed to Joseph Rathell 200 a. *Parker's Park, Brown's Lott, Widow's Lot,* an part of *Hazely,* and *Partner's Hazard,* and all of *Brown's Lot* on the east side of the main branch of King's Creek (TALR 20:278-280, 337, 338). Joseph Rathell, planter, and his wife Rachel conveyed 6 a. *Buck's Range* and 13 a. *Elizabeth's Enlargement* to George Garey, for £38.5.0 (TALR 20:423).

Joseph and William Rathell witnessed the will of Ann Sherwood on 17 October 1775 (MWB 40:723).

Joseph Rathell took the Oath of Fidelity in Talbot Co., before John Bracco some time prior to 10 April 1778 (*CMSP Red Book#5:* 130).

Joseph Rathell was listed in the 1790 Census of Talbot Co., with 2 white males over 16, 1 white male under 16, 2 white females, and 8 slaves (*Heads of Families, Md., 1790:* 111).

He is probably the Joseph Rathell who was in Talbot Co. by 1759 when he and his wife Rachel had the following children whose births were recorded in St. Peter's Parish (**ESVR** 3:56): **20. Elizabeth,** b. 21 October 1759; **21. Mary,** b. 17 November 17--; **22, David,** b. 8 December 17--; **23. Nancy,** b. 29 August 17--; and **24. Isaiah,** b. 4 April 17--.

Unplaced:

David Rathell m. Sarah [-?-]. Mrs. Sarah Rathell, wife of David Rathell in Tuckahoe, about eight miles from Easton was murdered last Friday (Easton *Maryland Herald* 26 July 1791). She was far advanced in pregnancy. Her husband was arrested on suspicion of murder and committed to gaol for trial (Easton *Maryland Herald* 27 July 1791).

Thomas Rathell administered the estate of William Love (whose widow he had married) of Talbot Co. on 20 April 1730 (MDAD 10:255).

== 0 ==

The Rogers Family

See also:
Various Articles on the Rogers Family, *NEHG Reg,* repr. in *Eng. Origins of New Eng. Families from the NEHG Register,* 2nd ser., 3:19-41; Shirley V. Baltz, *The Quays of the*

City: An Account of the Bustling 18th Century Port of Annapolis. Annapolis: The Liberty Tree, Ltd. 1975; Mrs, Nathaniel G. Gee, "William Rogers of Annapolis, Maryland," *NGSQ* 51 (2) 100-102.

A. Rev. John Rogers of Dedham, Essex, Eng., is stated to have been a grandson of John Rogers, the noted martyr, but the Publishing Committee of the NEHG Society in 1851 felt that this was based solely on conjecture (C:19). Rev. John married about 1595, as his first wife, Bridget, bapt. 5 January 1576, daughter of Richard and Mary [-?-] Ray. Her ancestry is given in Elizabeth French, "Genealogical Research in England," repr. in *Eng. Origins of New Eng. Families from the NEHG Reg.*, 1st ser., 1:56-66, hereafter cited as French: 56-66.

Rev. John and Bridget were the parents of (Abraham Hammatt, *The Hammatt Papers: Early Inhabitants of Ipswich, Massachusetts, 1633-1700*, Repr.: Baltimore: Genealogical Publishing Co., 1980, hereafter cited as *Hammatt*: 290; French: 65): **a. John; 1. Rev. Nathaniel; b. Samuel; c. Daniel; d. Bridget; e. Abigail;** and **f. Martha**.

1. Rev. Nathaniel Rogers, son of Rev. John (A), was b. 1598 at Haverhill, Eng., and d. 3 July 1655 aged 57 years. He married Margaret Crane, daughter of Robert Crane of Coggeshall, Essex (Hammatt: 290-291).

Nathaniel Rogers entered Emmanuel College at the age of 14. He became a curate at Bocking, Essex, and later came to Boston, Mass., in November 1636. He was ordained Pastor at the Church at Ipswich, Mass. (Hammatt: 290-291).

Rev. Nathaniel and Margaret had: **2. Rev. Dr. John.**

2. Rev. Dr. John Rogers, son of Rev. Nathaniel (1) and Margaret, 5th President of Harvard, was born January 1630 at Coggeshall, Essex, Eng., and died 2 July 1684 at Ipswich, Mass. (Hammatt: 292-293). He married on 14 November 1660, Elizabeth Denison, daughter of Maj. Gen. Daniel Denison and his wife Patience Dudley (a daughter of Gov. Thomas Dudley). Elizabeth Denison Rogers died at Ipswich 13 July 1723 in her 82nd year (Hammatt: 293). For the Royal Descent of Gov. Thomas Dudley from Edward I, see *PASC*: 90-93.

Rev. Dr. John and Elizabeth were the parents of (Hammatt: 293-293): **3. Elizabeth,** b. 3 February 1661, m. Hon. John Appleton; **4. Margaret,** b. 18 February 1664, m. 1st, Thomas Berry, and 2nd, Hon. John Leverett; **5. Rev. John,** b. 7 July 1666; **6. Daniel; 7. Nathaniel,** b. 21 February 1669; and **8. Patience,** b. 13 May 1676.

5. Rev. John Rogers, son of Rev. Dr. John (2) and Elizabeth (Denison) Rogers, was born 7 July 1666 and died 26 December 1745. He married on 4 March 1690, Martha Whittingham, died 9 March 1759, daughter of John Whittingham. John Rogers graduated at Harvard College, 1684, and was ordained on 12 October 1692 (Hammatt: 298)

John and Martha were the parents of (Hammatt: 298): **9. John,** b. 27 January 1692, m. Susanna Whipple; **10. Martha,** b. 2 November 1694; **11. Capt. William,** b. 19 June 1699; **12. Richard,** b. 2 December 1703; **13. Daniel,** b. 28 July 1707; **14. Elizabeth,** b. 28 July 1707; **15. Samuel,** b. 31 August 1709; and **16. Mary.**

11. Capt. William Rogers, son of Rev. John (5) and Martha, was b. 19 August 1699 at Ipswich, Mass., and died 29 July 1749 at Annapolis, Md., in his 50th year. He married, 1st, Mary (poss. Townley), cousin of Gov. John Seymour, and widow of 1) John Contee and 2) Philemon Hemsley. Rogers and Mary had no children, and Mary died in St. Anne's Parish on 24 May 1725 (*AACR*:93); Mrs. Nathaniel G. Gee, "William Rogers of

Annapolis, Maryland," *NGSQ* 51 (2), 100-101). On 18 Aug 1726 in All Hallows' Parish, AA Co. He married 2nd, Lucinda, daughter of Daniel (died 1724) and Mary (([-?-]) Thompson (*AACR*:41).

William Rogers' obituary stated that "He was very much lamented, and was a gentlemen born and bred in New England, but had long been a worthy inhabitant of this place [Annapolis]. He enjoyed many posts of honor and trust. He left a widow and three children" (Annapolis *Maryland Gazette* 2 August 1749).

Lucinda Rogers of Annapolis, widow, had died leaving a will dated 10 October 1755 and proved 30 October 1755, naming her children John, William, and Martha, and naming Martha Rogers as her executrix. William Lux, Susannah Read and Katherine Read witnessed the will. Martha Rogers gave up the administration of her mother's estate to her brother William Rogers (MWB 30:3, 108).

William and Lucinda (Thompson) Rogers were the parents of: **17. John**, b. 1726; **18. William**; and **19. Martha**.

17. John Rogers, son of Capt. William (11) and Lucinda, was b. 1726 and d. 23 September 1789 in Annapolis, Md. In 1776 he married Margaret Lee Clark, b. 1755, d. 1794, daughter of Thomas and Alice (Lee) Clark.

Rogers represented Prince George's Co. in the Conventions of 1774, 1775, and 1776 (*BDML* 2:703-704).

John and Margaret were the parents of: **20. Margaret**, m. Walter Story Chandler on 19 September 1799.

19. Martha Rogers, daughter of Capt. William (11) and Lucinda, was forced to open a school of dancing on Northeast Street after her mother, Lucinda Rogers, died (Adomanis 43).

In 1755 she advertised she would open a dancing school for children; she will also sell furniture at the house where Mrs. Lucinda Rogers lately lived in North East St. (Annapolis *Maryland Gazette* 13 November 1755).

==0==

The Rowles Family

N.B.: This account corrects and expands accounts of the family as given in Barnes *Colonial Families of Anne Arundel Count*, and Barnes, *Baltimore County Families, 1659-1759*.

1. Christopher Rowles was transported to Md. about 1649 (MPL 6:84), and died about 1691 in Anne Arundel Co., Md. He married Elizabeth [-?-] who married 2nd, Joseph Hawkins (INAC 18:194). Elizabeth may have been Elizabeth Ricaud (Richard), daughter of Benjamin Ricaud or Richand (MWB 4:80, abst. in *Md. Cal. of Wills* 1:140). She was living as late as February 1695.

On 1 November 1652 John Brown, 'Xtop' (Christopher) Rowles, and John Mosey surveyed 260 a. *Northwest River* (later called *Poplar Knowles*, on the north side of West River. Later Edward Talbott and John Talbott each owned 130 a. of the land (*MRR*: 140). On or about 24 December 1653 he was conveyed 60 a. *Brownton* by Jno. Browne and John Clark (AALR IH#1: 312, WH#4:46). In August 1662 Edward Lloyd conveyed 100 a., part of *Swan Neck*, to Christopher Rowles (*MRR*: 230). In December 1663 Rowles sold one-half of the land to John Browne who signed it over to Henry Catlin who sold it to Abraham Dawson, father of Thomas Dawson who sold it to Thomas Rowles (See below), 'grandson' [most likely a mistake for 'son'] of Christopher Rowles, who some time before 18 April 1702 sold it to William Taylard (AALR WT#1:281).

Rowles surveyed 150 a. *Addition* on 21 March 1665. Later John Harwood held 50 a. for John Cusin, and still later John Gadsby held 50 a. and R'd Hampton held 100 a. (*MRR:* 249). Rowles surveyed 11 a. *Rowles Chance* on the south side of Magothy River on 9 August 1681. This was later held by his orphans (*MRR:* 255). Rowles also surveyed 150 a. *Addition* on the east side of Eagle Nest Bay, North of Severn, on 21 March 1665. By about 1707 this was held by John Harwood for John Cusin (*MRR:* 249). In Aug 1681 he surveyed 11 a. *Rowles Chance,* on the South Side of Magothy River, which by about 1707 was held by his orphans (*MRR:* 255).

On 18 December 1669 William Crouch and Christopher Rowles were authorized to appraise the estate of John Browne (MDTP 3:335). In May 1674 he was called cousin in the will of Thomas Meares (MDTP 6:278).

On 14 February 1695 Elisabeth Hawkins, wife of Joseph Hawkins, relict and administratrix of Christopher Rolls exhibited accounts. The residue was distributed to the orphans (MDTP 16:129).

Christopher was the father of: **2. John,** d. by 1700; **3. Thomas; 4. William; 5. Jacob,** b. about 1683; **6. Christopher.,** poss. b. by 1683; and **7. (poss.) Martha.**

2. John Rowles, son of Christopher (2), died by 1700. He married Mary, widow of James Crouch and daughter of William Hill. She married 3rd, Philip Jones by 16 October 1701 at St. Margaret's, Westminster Parish (*AACR:* 109).

On 20 May 1713 Rowles, with his wife Mary, daughter of William Hill, conveyed part of *North Crutchfield* to Jams Crouch and John 'Rolls' [sic], sons of Mary Jones by her former husbands (AALR IB#2:93).

John and Mary were the parents of: **8. John,** b. 25 May 1698 at St. Margaret's Parish (*AACR:* 109).

3. Thomas Rowles, son of Christopher (1) and Elizabeth, died in Anne Arundel Co. by 8 May 1743. He married Sarah Fisher who died in 1756.

On 12 September 1701 Joseph Hawkins, who had married the widow of 'Charles' [sic] (Christopher) Rowles, conveyed 40 a. *Burton's Hope* to Thomas Rolls, one of the son of 'Charles ,' deceased.' On the same day Thomas 'Rolls' conveyed to Charles Stevens 40 a. *Burton's Hope* (AALR WT#1:201, 202). Thomas Rowles, cooper, on 12 September 1704 conveyed to Edward Hall 40 a. *Burton's Hope.* Rowles' wife Sara released her dower (AALR WT#2:166). On 29 December 1701 Thomas Rowles, planter, conveyed 100 a. *Swan Neck* to William Taylard (AALR WT#1:41). On 18 November 1720 Thomas Rowles of Baltimore Co., planter, and his wife Sarah conveyed to John Mills of Dorchester County 50 a. *Oyster Point[?;]*50 a. *Addition to Oyster Point,* and 50 a. *Mulberry Point,* all lands in Dorchester Co. which had been devised by Philip Griffin, late of Anne Arundel Co., deceased, to his wife's daughter, Sarah Fisher, now wife of Thomas Rowles, and which had belonged to her mother, the wife of said Griffin (DOLR 8 Old:1).

In May 1705 400 a. *The Stones,* in Baltimore Co., was surveyed for Thomas Rowles and patented on 10 Jan 1705 (MPL CD#4: 268). On 10 August 1738 John Wilmot, schoolmaster, conveyed 356 a. *Gray's Luck* to Thomas Rowles, innholder (AALR RD#3:81).

Thomas Rowles of Anne Arundel Co. died leaving a will dated 20 October 1738 and proved 18 May 1743. Son Thomas was to have *Gray's Luck*. Son John was to have the dwelling plantation, *The Stones*. His daughter Elizabeth Bell was left £10. Daughter Ruth Whitham was left *Solomon's Hills* provided she lived there. Wife Sarah was named executrix. Thomas Wright, Jonas Slade, and Elizabeth Coverly witnessed the will (MWB 23:258 abst. in *Md. Cal. of Wills* 8:233).

Sarah Rowles of Anne Arundel Co., widow, died leaving a will dated 17 September 1754 and proved 13 September 1756. Daughter Elizabeth Graham, was to have 40 sh. if she survived Sarah; if she did not, to her son Thomas Bell. Daughter Sarah Smith was to have 10 sh. Daughter Rachel Kitten was to have Sarah's best bed, Negro fellow Jockey, his bed and chest and all belonging to him, and one pair spoon moulds. Granddaughter Sarah Kitten was to have a Negro girl Pamela. Daughter Susanna Stewart was to have Sarah's second best bed, Sarah's clothes, her best side saddle, a wooden spinning wheel, a five-gal. iron pot, and an iron pestle. Daughter Mary Cheney was to have a Negro girl Betty, her bed, chest, gray mare Bonny and her bell, a side saddle, household furniture, and the rest of her clothes equally divided between her and daughter Ruth Graham. Granddaughter Sarah Cheney was to have Sarah's third best bed, a Negro child Hannah, a bell-metal skillet, and an eight gallon iron pot. Daughter Ruth Graham was to have a bed, a large chest with lock and key, one-half of Sarah's clothes, and a two-year-old heifer. Daughter Constant Yieldhall was to have 10 sh. Son Thomas Rowles was to have 1 sh. Her son & executor, John Rowles, was to have all he livestock and a pair of pocket stillards. Grandson Thomas Kitten was to have a mare Coone. The residue was to be divided between son John Rowles and daughter Comfort Robinson. John Dorsey, Robert Caples, and J[ames] Walker witnessed the will (MWB 30:294, abst. by Gibb).

Thomas and Sarah were the parents of: **9. Comfort,** m. Oneall Robeson on 13 Nov 1740 in St Margaret's Parish (*AACR:*132); **10. Thomas; 11. John; 12. Elizabeth,** m. 1st, Jacob Bell on 18 February 1727 in St Paul's Parish (Reamy and Reamy, *St. Paul's Parish Register:* 29); she m. 2nd, [-?-] Graham; **13. Ruth,** m. 1st, [-?-] Witham, and, 2nd, [-?-] Graham; **14. Mary,** m. [-?-] Cheney; **15. Rachel,** m. Edward Kitten; **16. Constant,** m. Robert Yieldhall; **17. Sarah,** m. John Smith on 3 August 1736 in St Margaret's Parish (*AACR:*132); and m. [-?-] Stewart

4. William Rowles, son of Christopher (1) and Elizabeth, died by 1 Dec 1750 in Baltimore Co. He married Martha Smith about 1707 in St. Margaret's Parish (*AACR:*130). She was the widow of John Smith 'lately deceased' (AALR PK:208). In her will dated 10 August 1703 Eliza Baker of Anne Arundel Co. named her daughter Martha Smith (MWB 11:394, abst. in *Md. Cal. of Wills* 3:25).William m. 2nd, by 3 December 1720, Ann Davice, daughter of John Davice (AALR CW#1:293).

William Smith, son of John Smith, on 9 August 1709 of his own free will was bound out to Susanna Crouch until he was 18., as his mother, Martha Rowles, was not able to keep him (AAJU TB#2:73).

William Smith, son of John, conveyed 125 a. *Swan Neck* to William Rowles on 19 April 1720 (AALR CW#1:160, 168). On 3 December 1720 Rowles and his wife joined Eliza Harpe, widow, and Thomas and Mary Robinson in conveying 50 a. *North Crutchfield* to William Anderson (AALR CW#1:293). On 14 January 1720/1 William and Anne conveyed 125 a. *Swan Neck* to Amos Garrett (AALR C#1:300). In 1729 William Gosnell conveyed 100 a. *Leafe's Chance* to William Rowles (BALR IS#K: 224).

William Rowles, of Baltimore Co., planter, died leaving a will dated 31 January 1748/9 and proved 1 December 1750. His son and executor, Jacob Rowles, was to have *Jacobs Delight*, 72 a. Son David Rowles was to have *James Adventure*, 200 a, *William the Conqueror*, 100 a, and *Rowles Contrivance*, 25 a. Son John Rowles was to have a

Negro boy Bowson and a bed. Son William Rowles was to have a Negro man Sango, a Negro girl Uiner and a bed. Wife Ann Rowles was to have for life, *Jones* [sic] *Adventure* 200 a., eight Negroes, and all his personal estate. Robert Davis, son of Thomas, John Sellman, Jr., and Jason Frizell witnessed the will (MWB 27:427, abst. by Gibb).

Jacob Rowles filed an account of the estate on 24 September 1765. He cited an inventory of £261.6.3, and listed payments of £47.0.0. The account also included 328 lbs. tob. (MDAD 53:124; BAAD 6:170).

William and Martha were the parents of (*AACR:* 110): **18. Christopher**, b. 9 May 1708; **19. William**, twin, b. 1 August 1710; and **20. Mary**, twin, b. 1 August 1710.

William and Ann were the parents of; **21. John**, b. 11 April 1734; **22. Jacob**, b. 1740; and **23. David**, b. 1740, d. about 1780.

5. Jacob Rowles, son of Christopher (2), was born about 1683, giving his age as about 47 in 1734 (BALC 1:14). He died by 3 August 1768. He married, 1st, on 27 January 1723 Ann Lynch, who died 30 April 1727.Jacob married, 2nd, on 4 January 1727/8, Constance Sampson. She was a daughter of Richard and Elizabeth Sampson. Rowles married, 3rd, on 28 September 1746, Mary Scarf (Reamy and Reamy, *St. Paul's Parish Register:29*, 34, 41). Jacob Rowles married, 4th, on 16 June 1750, Patience, widow and administratrix of Nathaniel Stinchcomb (MDAD 28:127; BALR AL#D: 257). Nathaniel Stinchcomb and Patience Rowles [sic] had been m. on 15 January 1733 (Reamy and Reamy, *St. Paul's Parish Register:* 31).

Nathaniel and Patience (Rowles) Stinchcomb had been the parents of (Reamy and Reamy, *St. Paul's Parish Register*: 14, 15): Nathaniel, b. 7 November 1734, Patience, b. 22 September 1736, John, b. 25 January 1738/9, Sarah, b. 24 September 1741, and Mary, b. 5 September 1743.

Jacob and Mary administered the estate of James Scarfe on 8 August 1749 and 21 January 1750 (MDAD 27:1, 29:137).

On 14 January 1772 Jacob Rowles and his wife Patience, widow of Nathaniel Stinchcomb, sold to John Stinchcomb 1/2 of *Pistole*, and *Addition to Pistole*, which had formerly been owned by Nathaniel Stinchcomb (BALR AL#D:257).

On 3 March 1739 Philip Jones, Jr., conveyed 40 a. part *Johnston* (or) *Johnson* to Jacob Rowles. Jones' wife Ann consented (BALR HWS#1-A: 378). On 3 July 1746 Jones, with the consent of his wife Ann, again conveyed 40 a. part *Johnston* to Jacob Rowles (BALR TB#E: 194).On 22 July 1746 Jacob Rowles conveyed 40 a. part *Johnston* back to Philip Jones, Jr. (BALR TB#E: 133). On 18 March 1739 Richard Gist conveyed 100 a. part *Triple Union* to Jacob Rowles (BALR HWS#1-A: 369).

On 20 March 1754 Rowles conveyed 100 a. *Jones' Venture* and other lands to David Rowles (BALR BB#I:302). On the same day he conveyed *Jacob's Delight* to John Chapman (BALR BB#I:301)

Jacob 'Rolles' died leaving a will dated 26 August 1760 and proved 5 August 1768.He named his children William, Christopher, Ruth, and Richard, and his grandchildren Jacob, Elizabeth, and Rachel Rolles, and Anne Rolles, daughter of Ruth. He stated that his friends George Harryman and Jarvis Bidderson would divide the estate, including the tracts *Johnson* and *Triple Union*. Edward and Robert Sweeting, John Lloyd, and George Bramwell witnessed the will (MWB 36:551. abst. in *Md. Cal. of Wills* 14:55).

Jacob and Constance were the parents of **24. Richard**, b. 25 September 1728 (Reamy and Reamy, *St. Paul's Parish Register:"* 4); **25. William; 26. Christopher;** and **27. Ruth.**

8. John Rowles, son of John (2), was born 25 May 1698 at St. Margaret's Parish (*AACR:*109). He died by 15 September 1736 in Queen Anne's Co., Md., having married Martha [-?-], who died by 25 May 1738 in Queen Anne's Co.

In 1724 400 a. *Eagle's Nest* was surveyed for John Rowles, On 25 August 1733 John Rowles of Queen Anne's Co., and wife Martha, conveyed 400 a. part *Eagle's Nest* to Philip Jones of Anne Arundel Co. (BALR IS#L: 427).

On 25 September 1736 Martha Rowles exhibited the will, dated 15 July 1736, of John Rowles to the Prerogative Court and was granted administration, with Joseph Wickes and John Elliott as sureties (MDTP 30:205). Joseph Wickes, now the administrator, exhibited accounts on 8 August 1738 (MDTP 30:438).

Martha Rowles, 'spinster,' of Kent Island, Queen Anne's Co., died leaving a will dated 29 March 1738 and proved 25 May 1738. Her children Levin and 'Reason' to have her estate, real and personal, divided equally, but they were to be under the care of her sister Elizabeth and her husband Joseph Wickes (named as the executor) until they reached the age of 21. Mary Elliott, Quaker, Susanna Elliott, and Thomas Williams, Jr., witnessed the will (MWB 21:902, abst. in *Md. Cal. of Wills* 7:254). On 11 September 1738 Joseph Wickes, the exec., was granted administration with Samuel Blunt and John Elliott as sureties (MDTP 30:443).

John and Martha were the parents of: **28. Levin,** d. by 4 October 1745 when Rezin Rowles was listed in the administration account of Joseph Wickes (MDAD 22:1); and **29. Rezin (Reason).**

10. Thomas Rowles, son of Thomas (3) and Sarah, married Sarah Joyce on 16 October 1740 in St. Margaret's Parish (*AACR:*132).

Thomas Rowles conveyed 100 a., part of *Swan Neck,* to John Marsh on 23 April 1748. His wife Sarah released her dower (AALR RB#3:116). On 1 September 1750 Rowles conveyed 100 a. *Stewart's Lot,* part of *Gray's Luck,* to David Stewart. Sarah released her dower (AALR RB#3:293).

Thomas and Sarah were the parents of the following children, born at St. Margaret's Parish (*AACR:*109, 120, 122): **30. Sarah,** b. 17 March 1742; **31. Thomas,** b. 21 April 1746; **32. Jacob,** b. 31 January 1747, d. 17 March 1748; **33. Susanna,** b. 7 December 1749; and **34. Nance** (daughter), b. 20 April 1752.

23. David Rowles, son of William (4), died in Baltimore Co. by September 1780. His wife has not been identified.

Rowles left a will dated 8 January 1780, proved 9 September 1780. Son Thomas was to have 206 a. *Arnold's Desire.* Son David was to have 200 a. *Jones Venture,* 25 a. *Rowles' Care,* 92 a. part *William the Conqueror,* and 45 a. part *Stinchcomb's Hills.* If David died without male heirs, land was to go to testator's son Ely, who otherwise was to have personalty. Wife, unnamed, was to have one-third of his estate. The rest of his personal estate was to go to his seven children: Thomas, David, Ely, Ann, Elizabeth, Sarah, and Ruth. The will was witnessed by Benj. Wells, Charles Wells, and Francis McDaniel (BAWB 3:408).

David Rowles, executor, posted an administration bond on 9 September 1780, with Benj. Wells, and Nathaniel Stinchcomb (BAAB 5:72). Rowles administered the estate on 5 February 1781 (BAAD 8:70). Thomas Rowles, administrator, posted another administration bond on 15 December 1784, with John Stinchcomb and Ely Rowles as sureties (BAAB 6:133). Thomas Rowles administered the estate on 29 July 1785 and on 25 Jan 1790 (BAAD 8:197, 10:95).

David Rowles was the father of: **35. Thomas; 36. David; 37. Ely; 38. Ann; 39. Elizabeth; 40. Sarah;** and **41. Ruth.**

24. Richard Rowles, son of Jacob (6) and Constance, was born 25 September 1728. He married Anne Gorswick on 30 January 1753 (Reamy and Reamy, *St. Paul's Parish Register:* 4, 35).

Richard and Anne were the parents of (Reamy and Reamy, *St. Paul's Parish Register:* 21): **42. Elizabeth,** b. 3 November 1753; **43. Jacob,** b. 21 July 1756; **44. Rachel,** b. 6 March 1759; and **45. Anne,** b. 6 March 1761.

25. William Rowles, son of Jacob (6) and Constance, died by October 1773. He married Mary [-?-].

Rowles died leaving a will dated 24 April 1772, proved 21 October 1773. He left his wife Mary his entire estate real and personal. His brother Richard Rowles was exec. The will was witnessed by William Lynch, William Wilkinson, and Edw. Sweeting (BAWB 3:237).

Richard Rowles, executor, posted an administration bond on 3 November 1773, with Edw. Sweeting and Thomas Shaw (in preamble) or Thomas Gash (in signature) as sureties (BAAB 5:264).

27. Ruth Rowles (Roles), daughter of Jacob (6) and Constant, was charged with bastardy in November 1757 and Jethro Lynch Wilkinson was named as father. In November 1760 Ruth Rowles (Roles) and George Stansbury were charged with bastardy and each was fined 30 shillings. Ruth had had a daughter Ann Rowles born in August 1760. In 1762 another bastard child was born but Ruth did not name the father (BAAD 5:54; Baltimore Co. Rough Court Minutes, 1755-1763:42; Baltimore Co. Criminal Proceedings, 1757-1759, p. 74; Balto. Co. Court Minutes, 1768-1769).

Ruth was the mother of: **42: Ann,** b. August 1760; **43. [-?-],** almost certainly William; and **44. [-?-],** name unknown.

Unplaced:
Elizabeth Rowles and Aquila Jarvis were married on 9 December 1787 (Reamy and Reamy, *St. Paul's Parish Register:* 51).
Jacob Rowles and Elizabeth Dungan were married on 20 July 1794 (Reamy and Reamy, *St. Paul's Parish Register:* 81).
Joseph Rowles, b. about 1747, Mary Rowles, b. about 1756, and Matthew Rowles, b. about 1775, were listed in the 1776 Census of Susquehannah Hundred, Harford Co. (Carothers, *1776 Census of Maryland:*113). On 15 July 1779 John Coen [Cowan], with consent of wife Elizabeth conveyed 18 a., part *Coens' Meadows,* to Joseph Rowles (HALR JLG#C:160). In 1783 Joseph Rowles, with 7 whites, was listed in Susquehannah Hundred, Harford Co., owning 100 a. *Cowans Meadows* (Carothers, *1783 Tax List of Maryland:* 143).
Prudence Rowles and Maurice Reading were married on 14 January 1796 by banns (Reamy and Reamy, *St. Paul's Parish Register:* 95).
Rezin Rowles married Sophia [-?-], who was buried 22 April 1806 (Reamy and Reamy, *St. Paul's Parish Register* 2:47).
Sarah Rowles and Ralph Gaither were married on 30 Nov 1788 (Reamy and Reamy, *St. Paul's Parish Register:* 52).

Colonial Families of Maryland II

Thomas Rowles married Ann [-?-]. They were the parents of: Arianna b. 22 October 1764 in St. Margaret's Parish (*AACR:*128). She is probably the Airy Rolls who married Christopher Hanson on 28 October 1781 (Reamy and Reamy, *St. Paul's Parish Register:* 39).
Thomas Rowles, and Christiana [-?-] were married by 13 July 1792 when their son Davie was born. David was bapt. on 19 October 1792 (Reamy and Reamy, *St. Paul's Parish Register;* 63).
William Rowles may be the "William Row" who was a taxable (free male over 16) in 1778 in Eden Hundred (HA78:24). William Roles, with 2 white inhabitants was listed as a Pauper in Bush River Lower Hundred (Carothers, *1783 Census of Maryland*).
William Rowles, a minor in 1795, came into court in June 1795 and chose William Mitchell, Sr., as his guardian (HAOC: 55).

== 0 ==

The Sickelmore Family
With Notes on the Peacock and Ward Families

N.B: The name is also written as Sicklemore.

1. Samuel Sickelmore was born about 1659 and was in Baltimore Co. by September 1683. He married. 1ˢᵗ, by 7 June 1693, Martha [-?-]. He married, 2ⁿᵈ, by 5 November 1707 Sarah [-?-].

On 28 April 1687 Samuel Sicklemore surveyed 100 a. *Rama* (*MRR:* 69). On 6 June 1693 he and his wife Sarah conveyed the land to Thomas Smith (RM#HS: 382). In 1688 Thomas Richardson assigned 10 a. *Arthurs's Delay* to Samuel Sickelmore (Archer Notes).

In June 1689 Samuel Sicklemore surveyed 318 *Wolf's Harbor* on the north side of Gunpowder River, on the west side of the mouth of Custer's Creek (or Foster's Creek); this was later described as having been taken away by a survey of *Fosters Neck* (*MRR:* 69). On 7 June 1693 John Taylor conveyed 53½ a. *George's Hill* to Samuel Sickelmore (BALR RM#HS: 387). On 7 January 1694 Sicklemore and his wife Martha conveyed the land back to Taylor (BALR RM#HS: 450).

On 1 January 1695 Sicklemore surveyed 226 a. *Turkey Hill,* on the east side of the Little Falls of Gunpowder; this was later owned by William Hitchcock (*MRR:* 69; BALR TR#C: 194). On 6 March 1699 Anthony Demondidier conveyed 50 a. *Cold Comfort,* 100 a. *Rich Level,* and 145 a. *Roper's Range* to Samuel Sicklemore and Henry Wriothesley in trust for Margaret and Hance Kiersted (BALR HW#2: 29).

On 6 November 1702 Sicklemore conveyed *The Dock* to Robert Cutcheon; his wife Sarah gave consent (BALR HW#2: 181). On 3 March 1702/3: Robert Cutchin and wife Dorothy conveyed 158 a. *The Dock* to Sicklemore (BALR HW#2: 213). On 10 October 1704 Sicklemore patented 150 a. *The Dock* (MPL DS#F: 536, DD#5:133).

On 5 November 1703 Samuel Sicklemore and his wife Sarah conveyed 400 a. of *Neighbor's Affinity* to William Jones of Upper End of Cliffs, Calvert Co. (BALR HW#2: 302). In November 1709 Samuel Sicklemore conveyed one-half of 400 a. *Neighbor's Affinity* to Benjamin Braine of London; the tract had been granted to Samuel Sicklemore by Lord Baltimore on 1 June 1701; Sarah Sicklemore signed as attorney in fact for Samuel Sicklemore (BALR TR#A: 22). On 27 October 1706 Sicklemore of Baltimore Co., gave power of attorney to his wife Sarah to collect debts, pay debts, and sell all land except land where she lived called *Wolf Harbor* (BALR R#HS: 560). On 5 November 1707 Sickelmore and his wife Sarah conveyed 14 a. *Arthur's Delay* to John Ewings (BALR RM#HS: 616).On 14 June 1711 Sickelmore conveyed *Wolves' Harbor* to his son Samuel; he gave 200 a., part 400 a. *Neighbor's Affinity* to his son Sutton Sickelmore; his daughter Hannah was to have *Sicklemore's Dock;* they were all to live together until they marry, and to teach Thomas Wriothesley Sickelmore to read and write (BALR TR#A: 244). In 1720 Samuel Sickelmore patented 400 a. *Ipswich* (MPL FF#7, 294, 300).

Samuel and Sarah were the parents of: **2. Samuel; 3. Sutton; 4. Hannah;** and **5. (poss.) Thomas Wriothesley.**

2. Samuel Sickelmore, son of Samuel (1) and Sarah, married 1st, Ruth Cammel on 8 December 1713 (*SJSG:* 4), and 2nd, Katherine Herrington on 12 September 1716.

On 10 March 1713 Samuel Sickelmore and wife Ruth conveyed part *Wolf's Harbor* to Robert Cutchin. On 13 April 1714 Sicklemore and his wife Ruth conveyed part *Wolf's Harbor* to John Roberts (BALR TR#A: 263, 297). On 18 February 1719 Sickelmore conveyed 200 a. *Drysdale's Habitation* to Roger Matthews (BALR TR#DS: 98). On 7 August 1723 he conveyed 300 [actually 200 a.?], one-half of *Neighbor's Affinity* (deeded to him by his father) to George [Read?] (BALR IS#G: 187).

Samuel and Ruth were the parents of (*SJSG:* 7, 11): **6. Ruth Sarah,** b. 23 December 1715, d. 22 September 1716.

3. Sutton Sickelmore, son of Samuel (1) and Sarah, died in Baltimore Co. by 23 August 1765. He married, 1st, Constant Love, daughter of John Love. She died after 9 April 1751 and he married 2nd on 29 July 1762, Prudence Hendon. Prudence Sickelmore married 2nd on 20 May 1773 Isaac Phillips (*SJSG:* 109, 142).

On 2 November 1737 Robert and Sarah Love conveyed the residue of 150 a. *Jamaica* to Sutton Sickelmore (BALR HWS#M: 54). On 8 March 1744/5 Sutton and wife Constance conveyed 107 a. pt. *Jamaica* to William Young (BALR TB#D: 67). On 8 August 1746 Sutton Sickelmore conveyed 200 a. *Ann's Delight,* originally granted to Henry Wriothesley and 318 a. *Jerusalem* to Stephen Onion (BALR TB#E: 159).

On 20 November 1740 Constant Sickelmore signed the inventory of Robert Love as next of kin (MINV 26:336). On 9 April 1751 Sutton and Constant Sickelmore witnessed the will of William Demmitt (MWB 28:209, abst. in *Md. Cal. of Wills* 10:189).

Samuel Sickelmore died leaving a will dated 9 July 1762 and proved 23 August 1765. He named his wife Prudence and his children Sarah Burk, Constant Love Peacock, Elizabeth Holland, and Hannah Ward. He also named his grandchildren Samuel Sicklemore Peacock and Sutton Sickelmore Ward. His wife Prudence was named executrix. James and Mary Bain witnessed the will (MWB 33:344, abst. in *Md. Cal. of Wills* 13:90).

On 20 September 1765 Henry Bennett Darnall, executor, was granted letters of administration on Sickelmore's estate. John Hilton and Richard Hendon, Jr., were sureties (MDTP 41:187).

Sutton and Constant were the parents of (*SJSG:* 4, 35, 40, 96, 99): **7. Sarah,** b. 21 March 1717, m. Thomas Burke on 14 April 1737; **8. Constant Love,** m. Luke Peacock on 26 July 1753; **9. Elizabeth,** b. 17 December 1738, m. John Holland on 23 December 1735; and **10. Hannah,** m. [-?-] Ward.

5. Thomas Wriothesley Sickelmore, possibly a son of Samuel (1) and Sarah, was living as late as 1711. He was named in the will of Henry Wrothesley. He was mentioned in a 1711 deed of Samuel Sickelmore.

8. Constant Love Sickelmore, daughter of Sutton (3) and Constant, married Luke Peacock on 26 July 1753 (*SJSG:* 96).

Luke Peacock was a corporal in Capt. Rigdon's Company, No. 12, on 2 Dec 1775. He assigned the Association of Freemen in Deer Creek Upper Hundred in 1776 (*RPHA:* 177).

In 1783 Luke Peacock was listed in Deer Creek Middle Hundred, Harford Co., as owning 113 a. *Andrews Choice,* and 43 a *James' Meadows.* His household consisted of nine whites. He was a surety for Samuel Peacock, a single man (Carothers, *1783 Tax List of Maryland:* 164, 166).

Constant Love and Luke were the parents of at least one son: **11. Samuel Sickelmore Peacock**, on 9 July 1762 named as a grandson of Sutton Sickelmore (BAAD 5:304).

10. Hannah Sickelmore, daughter of Sutton (3) and Constant, married [-?-] Ward.

On 31 July 1714 Hannah Sickelmore, spinster, conveyed 150 a. *Sicklemore's Dock* to William Demmitt (BALR TR#A: 304).

Hannah and her husband had at least one son: **12. Sutton Sicklemore Ward**, on 9 July 1762 named as a grandson of Sutton Sickelmore (BAAD 5:304).

11. Samuel Sickelmore Peacock, son of Luke and Hannah, on 9 July 1762 named as a grandson of Sutton Sickelmore (BAAD 5:304).

He was a corporal in Capt. Rigdon's Company, No. 12, on 2 Dec 1775 and a Private in Capt. Bussey's Company on 25 July 1776. He assigned the Association of Freemen in Deer Creek Upper Hundred in 1776 (*RPHA:* 177).

Unplaced:
Elizabeth Sickelmore married John Brown of Thomas on 18 November 1705 (Reamy and Reamy, *St. George's Parish Register:* 13). Brown was a son of Thomas and Margaret ([-?-]) Brown, and Margaret had m. 2nd, Anthony Drew. On 15 January 1721 John Brown was named as the father of Margaret Drew's grandsons Thomas Brown Augustine and Gabriel (Gambrall) Brown (MWB 17:217 abst. in *Md. Cal. of Wills* 5:102).

== 0 ==

The Simmons Family

1. George Simmons of Anne Arundel Co. died by May 1679. He may be the George Simonds who was transported to Maryland c1650 (MPL AB7&H: 193). He married by October 1671 Sarah [-?-].

George Simmons was in Anne Arundel Co. by 11 February 1667 when Stephen Benson of Calvert Co. conveyed him 300 a. called *Keighotan Choice,* to be divided equally between George Simmons, planter and Faith Wilson, *alias* Gongo, spinster (AALR WT#1:236). On 22 July 1678 he witnessed a deed (AALR WH#4:119).

Simmons died leaving a will dated 2 April 1679, proved 4 May 1679, naming his brother William, and his own children: George, Abraham, Isaac, Sarah, and Mary. His lands were to pass in natural succession. The residue of estate was to pass to his children, when the last four were of age. Maj. Samuel Lane and Nathan Smith were named execs. The will was witnessed by Thomas Merridale, Thomas Sutton, and Abraham Bird (MWB 10:45).

On 23 April 1679 Major Lane exhibited the will of George Simmons. Mr. John Welsh was to prove said will. The appraisers were Charles Beavan, Richard Deavors (MDTP 11:27).

On 3 May 1679 Charles Beavan and Richard Deaver appraised George Simmons' personal estate at 25,168 lbs. tob. The inventory named several servants: Thomas Gant, Francis Priestly, George Lee, and Benjamin Simmons (INAC 6:113). A second inventory was filed on 1 November 1679, showing a value of 3662 lbs. tob., and listing payments of 27,830 lbs. of tob. (INAC 7B:207, 208).

Mrs. Margaret Evans, executrix of Samuel Lane (Simmons' original executor), and Nathan Smith filed an account of Simmons' estate on 17 July 1682 (INAC 8:262).

George and Sarah were the parents of the following, baptized at St. James Parish (*AACR:* 149): **2. George,** b. 2 October 1671, and bapt. 25 September 1698; **3. Abraham,** b. 11 December 1673, and bapt. 25 September 1698; **4. Isaac,** b. 10 August 1676, bapt. 25 September 1698; **5. Sarah,** under age in April 1679; **6. Mary,** under age in April 1679; she may have m. 1st, Thomas Lee; Mary Simmons and Philip Scrivener were m. on 18 September 1703 in St. James Parish (*AACR:* 154).

2. George Simmons, son of George (1) and Sarah, was born 2 October 1671, and bapt. 25 September 1698. He was buried at St. James Parish on 18 June 1720 (*AACR:* 164). He was married by 10 October 1702 Elizabeth, daughter of Thomas Knighton, when he conveyed 140 a. *Gadshill* to John Hall of Baltimore Co. (AALR WT#1:315).

On 3 January 1701/2 George 'Simons' was appointed one of the appraisers of the estate of Thomas Thompson ((MDTP 19A:37).

On 21 October 1702 George Simonds (Simmonds) and his wife Eliza conveyed 140 a. *Gadshill* to John Hall of Baltimore Co. (AALR WT#1:315).

Simmons died leaving a will dated 14 June 1720 and proved 15 August 1720. His daughter Diana, wife of Roger Crudgington was to have 10 sh. His wife Elizabeth was to have her thirds, £10. The residue of his estate was to go to his children, Mary, Elizabeth, George, and Sophia, equally. The girls were to receive their portions at age 16 or marriage; the boys were to have theirs at age 21. Samuel Guichard, William Vernon, and Wm. Wotton witnessed the will (MWB 16:182, abst. in *Md. Cal. of Wills* 5:24).

On 15 August 1720 Elizabeth Simmons, executrix, posted bond to administer the estate of George Simmons. Her sureties were Roger Crudgenton and Samuel Guichard (MDTP 24:262).

On 3 October 1720 Alexander Rosenquist and Robert Wood appraised George Simmons' estate at £213.17.6. Abraham and Isaac Simmons approved the inventory (MINV 4:207).

George and Elizabeth Simmons (Simonds, Symmons) were the parents of the following children, baptized in St. James Parish (*AACR:* 153, 156, 159, 160, 162, 163, 201): **7. Diana,** b. 29 April 1701, bapt. 3 Aug 1701; m. Roger Crudgington on 24 November 1718; **8. Mary,** b. 19 February 1705, bapt. 5 May 1706; **9. Elizabeth,** b. 25 Xber 1709; she may be the Elizabeth 'Simson' who m. John Elliot Brown on 17 January 1720/1 at All Hallow's Parish; **10. George,** b. 6 December 1711, bapt. 11 May 1712; **11. Sarah,** b. 9 Xber 1713, bapt. 11 February 1713/4, and bur. 28 February 1713/4; and **12. Sophia,** b. 3 October 1716, bapt. 23 December 1716.

3. Abraham Simmons, son of George (1), and Sarah, was born 11 December 1673 and bapt. 25 September 1698. He gave his age as 71 in 1745. He died by October 1750 having married 1st, Martha [-?-], and 2nd, by 1735 Eleanor [-?-].

On 26 April 1703 Teague Tracy of Anne Arundel Co., with wife Mary, conveyed 100 a. *James His Chance* to Simmons (AALR WT#2:60). On 11 June 1706 Thomas

Tench, Mathias Clarke, millwright, and Clarke's wife Eliza conveyed 100 a. *Warburton Square,* being part of *The Forest of Dann,* to Abraham 'Symons' (AALR WT#2:411).

On 7 February 1731/2 Abraham Simmons conveyed Negroes to his sons Benjamin, Isaac, William and Samuel, and daughters Eleanor Fisher, Martha, and Sarah (AALR IH&TI#1:358-363). On 7 February 1744/5 he again conveyed Negroes to his daughters Eleanor Ryan and Martha Tillard (AALR RB#2:51, 52).

On 12 April 1735 Abraham Simmons of Anne Arundel Co., planter, conveyed 100 a., being one-half of *Simmons' Choice,* which he had originally patented, to James Lee. His wife Ellinor consented (BALR IS#IK:289). On 31 May 1742 Abraham 'Symonds' [sic] conveyed 84 a. *Simmons Choice* to his son-in-law William Taylard, and 100 a. to his son-in-law Edward Morgan (BALR TB#A:173, 175).

Simmons died leaving a will dated 3 January 1748, proved 13 October 1750. He named his son William, and the latter's son James, grandson William Fisher, granddaughter, Martha Fisher, daughters Eleanor Ryan, Sarah Morgan, and Martha Tillard, son Samuel's son Samuel Simmons. William Simmons and son-in-law William Tillard were named execs. The will was witnessed by Lewis Jones, Sarah Jones, and James Trotter (MWB 27:405).

Abraham and Martha were the parents of the following children born in St. James Parish (*AACR:*149, 152, 154, 158, 160, 162, 164, 168): **13. William,** b.10 November 1698, bapt. 10 April 1699; **14. Abraham,** bapt. 5 January 1700, d. by April 1745, leaving a will in which he named his two bros.-in-law, Charles Drury and William Tillard as trustees (MWB 24:368); **15. George,** b. 29 October 1703 [*sic;* prob. 1702], bapt. 13 February 1703; **16. Isaac,** b. 2 June 1703, bapt. 1 August 1703, d. by 10 June 1741, leaving a will in which he named his bros. and sisters (MWB 22:395); John Franklin, Jacob Franklin appraised the estate of Isaac Simmons at £317.1.9 on 3 March 1741. Abraham Simmons and Eleanor Fisher signed as next of kin. Abraham Simmons, Jr., the executor, filed the inventory of 18 June 1742 (MINV 26:561); **17. James,** b. 28 April 1709, bapt. 26 June 1709; **18. Samuel,** b. 11 January 1711, bapt. 29 May 1712; **19. Benjamin,** b. 1 September 1714, bapt. 16 October 1714; **20. Martha,** b. 8 November 1720, m. William Tillard on 22 December 1741 in St. James Parish; **21. Sarah,** m. Edward Morgan; and **22. Eleanor,** m. 1st, Martin Fisher, and 2nd, Dennis Ryan; on 3 May 1744 Eleanor Ryan, wife of Dennis Ryan, administered the estate of Martin Fisher as his executrix. (MDAD 20:131).

4. Isaac Simmons, son of George (1) and Sarah, was born 10 August 1676 and bapt. 25 September 1698. He married Deborah [-?-]. He died by 5 October 1734 when his estate was appraised at £132.7.0, by D. Weems and Edward (Nanchit?). John Watkins and R. Rosenquist signed as creditors, while 'Isaak' Simmons, Jr., and Richard Simmons signed as next of kin. George Simmons, administrator, filed the inventory (MINV 20:140).

Isaac and Deborah were the parents of the following children, bapt. in St. James Parish (*AACR:* 156, 157, 159, 161, 163, 164): **23. Isaac,** b. 5 February 1705, bapt. 21 April 1706; **24. Eleanor,** b. 21 September 1708, bapt. 17 October 1708; **25. Richard,** b. 14 9ber 1710, bapt. 30 March 1711; **26. Deborah** ('Debrugh'), b. 1713; **27. Rachel,** b. 25 December 1717; and **28. Margaret,** b. 16 October 1720.

10. George Simmons, son of George (2) and Elizabeth, was born 6 December 1711 and bapt. 11 May 1712. He married Margaret [-?-].

Simmons died leaving a will dated 1 February 1765 and proved 10 February 1769. He named his wife Margaret, and his children George, Knighton, John, Isaac, and Elizabeth, as well as a god-son James Simmons. He mentioned the tracts *Burridge* and *Hopell.* His sons George and Knighton were named executors. John Franklin, Henry

Sanders, and Robert Lewis witnessed the will (MWB 37:3, abst. in *Md. Cal. of Wills* 14:70).

George Simmons died by 27 February 1769, when his estate was appraised by Isaac Hall and Richard Green at £740.19.4. Henry Darnall of *Portland Manor*, and Stephen West signed as creditors, while John and Abraham Simmons approved the inventory as the next of kin. Knighton Simmons, the surviving exec., filed the inventory on 17 August 1769 (MINV 100:.214).

Knighton Simons filed an account on 13 October 1771. After citing the inventory as given above he listed payments of £27.19.2 (MDAD 66:131).

George 'Simmonds' estate was distributed on 13 October 1771. The sureties were Richard Llewellen of St. Mary's Co., and John Carty. The legatees were his children John, Isaac, and Elisabeth, and godson James Simmons. The balance was distributed to the widow, who received her thirds, and to the five children (equally); George, Knighton, John, Isaac, Elisabeth. The surviving executor was Knighton 'Simmonds' (BFD 6.96).

George and Margaret were the parents of the following children, born in St, James Parish (*AACR:* 168, 169, 170, 175): **29. George**, b. 22 January 1743/4 at Herring Creek; **30. Knighton,** b. 1 March 1745/6; m. Elizabeth Saunders on 31 --- 1772 in St. James Parish; **31. John,** b. 27 December 1749; **32. Samuel,** b. 13 April 1751 [may have d. young as he was not mentioned in his father's will]; **33. Elizabeth;** and **34. Isaac** birth date not found].

13. William Simmons, son of Abraham (3) and Martha, was born 10 November 1698, and bapt. 10 April 1699. He married Margaret [-?-].

William and Margaret were the parents of the following children, bapt. in St. James Parish (*AACR:*165, 166, 167): **34. Chapman,** b. 8 March 1724/5; **35. William,** b. 28 April 1728; **36. James,** b. 29 September 1729; **37. Jeremiah Chapman,** b. 13 December 1732; **38. Ann,** b. 17 April 1735, bapt. 8 May 1735; **39. Isaac,** b. 12 February 1726/7, bapt. 8 May 1737; and **40. Samuel,** b. 11 February 1739/40, bapt. 1 June 1740.

14. Abraham Simmons, son of Abraham (3) and Martha, was bapt. 5 January 1700 and died by April 1745. He married Sarah [-?-], who married 2nd, Abel Hill.

He left a will in which he named his two brothers-in-law, Charles Drury and William Tillard as trustees (MWB 24:368).

On 6 Aug 1746 'Abraham Simons" estate was appraised by John Franklin and Jacob Franklin. Thomas Lloyd and Thomas Sharbutt signed as next of kin. William Simmons and Elinor Ryan also signed as next of kin. Sarah Simmons, the executrix, filed the inventory on 7 August 1746 (MINV 33.137).

Sarah Hill, now the wife of Abell Hill, Jr., filed a second inventory on 13 June 1750, citing an inventory of £241.76, which had been appraised by Jacob Franklin and James Deal. Abraham Simmons and Eleanor Ryan signed as next of kin. Sarah Hill (the widow), the wife of Abell Hill, Jr. (MINV 42:235).

Abraham and Sarah were the parents of the following children, born in St, James Parish (*AACR:* 169): **41. Betridge,** b. 18 July 1742 [or 1744].

17. James Simmons, son of Abraham (3) and Martha, was born 28 April 1709, bapt. 26 June 1709. He may be the James Simmons who married Mary [-?-], who married 2nd, Joseph Chew on 15 September 1771 in All Hallow's Parish (*AAMR*:214).

Mary Chew, wife of Joseph Chew, administratrix, filed an account of James Simmons' estate on 28 March 1772, listing payments of £261.10.8. No heirs were named (MDAD 67:74).

18. Samuel Simmons, son of Abraham and Martha, was born 11 January 1711 and bapt. 29 May 1712. He died by 25 August 1752 when John Cheney posted a bond that he would pay the sum of £38.8.7, and 342.11.8 current money to Samuel Simmons' three orphans, Mary, Sarah, and Samuel, when they should come of age (AALRRB#3:507).

Samuel was the father of at least three children, all of whom were under age in 1752: **42. Mary; 43. Sarah;** under age in 1752; and **44. Samuel.**

Unplaced:

Abigail Symons and John Draper were married on 17 November 1709 at St. James Parish (*AACR:* 158).

Abraham Simmons and Priscilla Liles were married on 19 December 1773 in St. James Parish (*AACR:* 175). They were the parents of the following children, born in St. James Parish (*AACR:* 172): **Thomas,** b. 19 January 1775, and **William West,** b. 19 August 1776.

Basil Simmons and Mary Lawrence were married on 15 May 1783 in St. James Parish (*AACR:* 181).

Isaac Simmons and Mary Child were married on 22 February 1784 in St. James Parish (*AACR:* 181).

James Simmons and Rebecca Sheckells were married on 2 June 1772 in St. James Parish (*AACR:* 175).

Richard Simmons and Sarah Thornbury were married in 8br 1713 in St. James Parish (*AACR:* 162).

Sarah Simmons and Richard Sheckels were married on 10 February 1774 in St. James Parish (*AACR:* 175).

Van Simmons and Mary Drury were married on 5 May 1774 in St. James Parish (*AACR:* 175).

== 0 ==

The Simpson Family

N.B.: The name is sometimes spelled Simson or Symson.

1. Richard Simpson, died by 7 June 1711. He married Ann [-?-]. He was in Baltimore County by 15 July 1688 when he patented 53 a. *Simson's Choice* (MPL 25:441).

In 1692, 1694, and 1695, Richard Simpson (Symson) was head of a household in Spesutia Hundred (*IBCW:*3, 4, 8).

On 22 April 1693 Richard Simpson was listed as a debtor in the administration account of John Walston (INAC 10:27C). About the same time he received a payment from the estate of Samuel Brand (INAC 10:339).

On 24 January 1707/8 Richard Simpson witnessed the will of Thomas Browne (MWB 12:300, abst. in *Md. Cal. of Wills* 3:114).

Richard Simpson died leaving a will dated 9 March 1710 and proved 6 June 1711. He left 12 pence to the boy Richard (Simpson). To the seven children by his 'last wife' Ann, he left his entire estate, real and personal. His son Thomas was named executor, and was to take care of the said small children during their minority. Thomas Gilbert, John Brown, and Garrett Garrettson witnessed the will (MWB 13:283, abst. in *Md. Cal. of Wills* 3:206).

Richard and Ann were the parents of (Reamy and Reamy, *St. George's Parish Register:* 2, 4, 5, 13, 18, 19, 23, 27): **2. Thomas,** b. 1 November 1691 near to the Susquehanna River; **3. Susanna,** b. 5 April 1693 near to the Susquehanna River.; she was aged 15 on 2 April 1707; in March 1710/11 she was indicted for bastardy, and on 15 June

1711 named Garrett Close as the father. In August 1716 she named James Colllins as the father of Sarah Collins Simpson, b. 27 February 1715; m. Thomas Knight on 28 November 1718; **4. William**, b. 14 February 1695; **5. Elizabeth**, b. 5 April 1697 near Susquehanna River., bur. 30 September 1698 at the head of Swan Creek;   **6. Jonathan**, b. 12 November 1699 at the Bay Side near to the mouth of the Susquehanna River; **7. Matthew [?], or Martha [?]**, aged 8 on 27 August 1708; Martha Simpson and William Hamby were m. on 25 December 1722; **8. Ann**, aged 3 on 25 January 1708; may have m. Samuel Smith on 28 August 1726; and **9. Elizabeth**, aged 7 mos. on 27 February 1708.

2. Thomas Simpson, son of Richard (1), was born 1 November 1701 and was aged 17 on 7 November 1706, and he gave his age as 31 in 1732, and as 41 in 1736 when he stated his father Richard had been living 28 years earlier. He married 1st, Eleanor [-?-], and 2nd, on 13 February 1717 Mary Smith (Reamy and Reamy, *St. George's Parish Register*: 25). She was a daughter of Emanuel Smith.

On 13 June 1722 Thomas Simpson and wife Mary conveyed 120 [sic] a. *Sisters Dowry*, which Gideon Gamble had conveyed to Emanuel Smith on 4 March 1699, to Joshua Wood (BALR IS#G: 72).

Thomas Simpson witnessed the will of Richard Jenkins of Baltimore Co. on 17 November 1734 (MWB 21:318, abst. in *Md. Cal. of Wills* 7:126).

Thomas and Eleanor were the parents of (Reamy and Reamy, *St. George's Parish Register*: 24): **10. Richard**, b. 26 December 1714.

Thomas and Mary were the parents of (Reamy, *St. George's Parish Register*: 24, 27, 33, 41, 53, 57): **12. William**, b. 28 January 1718; **13, Eleanor**, b. 11 July 1721; **14. Gilbert**, b. 21 July 1724, d. 22 July 1725; **15. Mary**, b. 7 March 1726/7; **17. Thomas**, b. 3 February 1729; **18. Samuel**, b. 4 January 1731/2; **19. Martha**, b. 7 December 1736; and **20. Joshua**, b. 6 January 1737.

4. William Simpson, son of Richard (1), was b. 14 February 1695. He was aged 14 on 14 February 1707. He was aged 31 in 1732, and aged 41 in 1736 when he named his uncle Gilbert. He married Elizabeth, daughter of Mary Buchanan, who named a granddaughter Hannah Simpson (MWB 30:698 abst. in *Md. Cal. of Wills* 7:23).

Elizabeth Buchanan Simpson died about 1732/3, and he married 2nd, Ann [-?-]. He married 3rd, on 12 November 1739 Mary Larrissee (Reamy and Reamy, *St. George's Parish Register:* 59).

Simpson patented 100 a. *Simpson's Hazard* on 10 July 1724 (MPL PL#6:50, IL#A: 203). He patented 100 a. *Simpson's Second Hazard* on 26 June 1730 (MPL PL#7:526, II.#B: 389).

On 24 Aug 1726 William Simpson conveyed 100 a. *Simpson's Hazard* to John Stokes (BALR IS#H: 301). On 4 October 1730 (or 1736) William Simpson, carpenter, conveyed 100 a. *Simpson's Second Hazard* to Jacob Giles (BALR IS#IK: 304).

William and Elizabeth were the parents of (Reamy and Reamy, *St. George's Parish Register:* 21, 33). **22. Mary**, b. 4 February 1714; **23. William**, b. 31 March 1721;   **24. Hannah**, b. 31 January 1722; and   **25. Sarah**, b. 16 February 1729.

William and Ann were the parents of (Reamy, *St. George's Parish Register:* 41, 54): **26. Ann**, b. 19 April 1734; and **27. John**, b. 29 June 1737 (His mother's name is given as Elizabeth).

William and Mary were the parents of (Reamy and Reamy, *St. George's Parish Register:* 59): **28. Anna**, b. 2 February 1739; and **29. Thomas**, b. 23 September 1739.

10. Richard Simpson, son of Richard (1) and Elizabeth, was born 26 December 1714. He married Elizabeth [-?-].

Richard and Elizabeth were the parents of (Reamy and Reamy, *St. George's Parish Register:* 74): **30. Thomas,** b. 23 September 1739; and **31. Nathaniel,** b. 11 July 1745.

18. Samuel Simpson, son of Thomas (2) and Mary, was born 4 January 1731/2. He may be the Samuel Simpson who signed a petition for the removal of the county seat to Baltimore Town in 1768 (*IBCP:* 29).

23. William Simpson, son of William (4) and Elizabeth, was born 31 March 1721. He married Avarilla Perkins on 18 August 1742 (Reamy and Reamy, *St. George's Parish Register:* 68).

William and Avarilla were the parents of (Reamy and Reamy, *St. George's Parish Register:* 70): **32. Reuben,** b. 6 Oct 1743.

27. John Simpson, son of William and Ann, was born 29 June 1737. He may be the John Simpson who signed a petition for the removal of the county seat to Baltimore Town in 1768 (*IBCP:* 29).

John Simpson married Elizabeth [-?-], by whom he was the father of (Reamy and Reamy, *St. Paul's Parish Register:* 22): **33. Hannah,** b. 2 March 1763.

Unplaced:
Ann Simson received a share of £6.3.0¾ from the estate of Basil Lucas on 21 February 1786 (BAAD 8:250).
Elizabeth Simpson and Thomas Osborn were married on 3 August 1751 (Reamy and Reamy, *St. George's Parish Register:* 91).
James Simpson, merchant of Baltimore, was m. Thurs. eve., 21st inst. at Mt. Serenity, Lancaster Co., Pa. to Miss Clingan, daughter of the late James Clingan (*Maryland Journal and Baltimore Advertiser* 29 Jan 1790).
John Simpson died by 20 May 1742 when his estate was administered by Priscilla, wife of Charles Motherby (BAAD 3:282).
John Simpson married Elizabeth [-?-], by whom he was the father of: Hannah, b. 2 March 1763 (Reamy and Reamy, *St. Paul's Parish Register:* 22).
Dr. John Simpson, and Elizabeth Durbin William Andrew were m. on 13 February 1794 (Marr. Register of Rev. Lewis Richards, MS.690 at MdHS). John Simpson entered into a marriage contract with Elizabeth Durbin William Andrew on 13 Feb 1794. She was a sister of Abarilla Andrew and Abraham Andrew. Abraham George Hammond had m. Mary Andrew, widow of William Andrew who had d. testate, and mother of Elizabeth Durbin William Andrew (BALR WG#NN: 286). In Feb 1794 Elizabeth Durbin William Simpson, formerly Andrew, orphan daughter of William Andrew, chose her husband Dr. John Simpson as her guardian (BAOC 3:81).
Jonathan Simpson died leaving a will dated 27 September 1784 and proved 25 April 1786. He named his wife Charlotta Elizabeth his executrix, and left her his entire estate real and personal. Adam Rohrbach, Thomas Bidwell, and Margaret Magan witnessed the will (BAWB 4:167, abst. by Burns). On 25 April 1786 Mayberry Helm, administrator. with will annexed, posted a bond for £300. John Martin and Caleb Arnest were sureties (BAAB 6:395).
Mary Simpson and Samuel Hamby were m. on 18 August 1738 (Reamy and Reamy, *St. George's Parish Register:* 50).

Colonial Families of Maryland II

Sarah Simpson was charged with bastardy at the August 1743 Court (BACP 1743-1745L 395). Sarah Simpson was the mother of Thomas Simpson, b. 11 June 1737 (Reamy, *St. George's Parish Register:* 55).

Richard Simpson: in May 1793 Prudence Kelly brought a Bible in which his age was listed, showing he was of full age; in October 1793 he was discharged from Samuel Owings (BAOC 3:64).

Walter Simpson administered the estate of Walter Pickett on 22 August 1785 (BAAD 8:222).

==0==

The Sligh Family of Baltimore County

1. Thomas Sligh married Sophia Wilkinson, daughter of William and Tamar, on 17 April 1734 (Reamy and Reamy, *St. Paul's Parish Register:* 31).

Thomas Sligh (or Slye) patented a number of tracts in Baltimore Co.: 100 a. *Sophia's Garden* on 13 October 1733; 440 a. *Privilege* on 6 August 1736; 30 a. *Find Me Out* on 4 November 1737; 50 a. *Sligh's Discovery* on 28 August 1743; 250 a. *Mill's Angles* on 14 February 1745; 785 a. *Sophia's Garden* on 18 May 1757; 1,145 a. *Sophia's Garden* on 5 April 1758; 570 a. *Cub Hill* on 14 March 1758; and 400 a. *Spring Garden* on 24 November 1763 (Coldham, *Settlers of Maryland, 1679-1783:*609).

Sligh not only patented land, he bought and sold many tracts. On 25 November 1731 Thomas Sheredine and his wife Tabitha conveyed 100 a. *Longland's Purchase*, part *Privilege*, to Sligh (BALR IS#L: 279). On 10 September 1737 Thomas Sligh and wife Sophia conveyed 100 a. *Cumberland* to Edward Corbin (BALR HWS#M: 16). In 1753 Sligh conveyed 100 a. *Tower Hill.* 56 a. *Knaves Foresight*[?], and 90 a. *Bosley's Expectation* to Jacob Anseller and Jno. Summer. Sligh's wife Sophia consented (BALR BB#1:45).

On 2 January 1741 Dutton Lane, with consent of his wife Dianah, conveyed 100 a. *The Landing* to Thomas Sligh (BALR TB#A:109).

In June 1752 Thomas Sligh advertised a brigantine for sale at William Rogers' house in Baltimore Town (Annapolis *Maryland Gazette* 4 June 1752). Sligh and John More, both of Baltimore Town, advertised a lot for sale in that town, and also a lot "on the other side of the Falls," belonging to John Sheppard (Annapolis *Maryland Gazette* 26 June 1755). Sligh also advertised the sale of part of *Cole's Harbor* at the house of Mr. Cary in Baltimore Town (Annapolis *Maryland Gazette* 23 June 1757).

On 5 February 1762 Thomas Sligh was named as one of the executors of Thomas Clendenning (BAWB 2:149).

Thomas Sligh died leaving a will dated 27 July 1774 and proved 11 August 1774. His executors were to settled debts owing to Charles Croxall, and the administrators of Robert Adair and Daniel Chamier. The residue of his estate was to be paid to his granddaughter Elizabeth 'Slye.' Mrs. Ann Flanagan was to have a part of his estate. Thomas Jennings, Esq., of Annapolis, and Charles Frederick Wiesenthal were named execs. William Augustine Dashiell, Morice Wersler, and George Gale, Sr., witnessed the will (MWB ; abst. in *Md. Cal. of Wills* 15:151).

On 14 February 1774 [*sic*] Charles Frederick Wiesenthal, executor, exhibited a bond to administer Thomas Sligh's estate. Jacob Myers and George Gale were sureties (MDTP 46:91).

Thomas and Sophia were the parents of (Reamy and Reamy, *St. Paul's Parish Register:* 9): **2. William**, b. 9 January 1734/5.

2. William Sligh, son of Thomas (1) and Sophia, was born 9 January 1734/5. He was Clerk of the Provincial Court and of Annapolis, when he died of small pox, leaving a widow and one infant (Annapolis *Maryland Gazette* 10 March 1757). He married Ann [-?-]. She may have been Anne, daughter of Robert and Elizabeth McLeod, born 10 December 1736, since on 15 January 1759 Ann Sligh and Hugh McLeod signed the inventory of Mrs. Elizabeth McLeod of Anne Arundel Co. as next of kin (MINV 71:52). (*AACR:*97).

William Jones and his wife Anne, on 29 June 1741 conveyed to William Sligh, son of Thomas and Sophia, and godson of the said Ann Jones, 640 a. *Tibbs United Inheritance* on Middle River, after the death of Ann Jones; if William Sligh should die, the land was to go to his parents (BALR (BACP HWS#1A:530).

On 2 July 1759 R. Boyce, Sheriff of Baltimore Co. was ordered to summon Thomas Sligh of Baltimore, merchant to show why he refused to deliver the estate of William Sligh, Jr., to the administratrix. At the same time Ann Sligh, administratrix of William Sligh, was summoned to show why she did not render an inventory (MDTP 37:278, 305). She exhibited the inventory on 6 May 1760 (MDTP 37:370).

On 14 May 1760 Ann Sligh filed an account of William Sligh's estate citing an inventory of £157.7.10 and listing payments of £44.5.7 (MDAD 45:28).

Anne Sligh evidently kept a tavern for a while, but on 26 February 1761 Robert Swan advertised a sale at her house, she having "declined keeping tavern" (Annapolis *Maryland Gazette* 26 February 1761).

In her will made 20 January 1765 Rebecca Gladman of Annapolis named Samuel Sligh, son of Ann Sligh (MWB 33:263; abst. in *Md. Cal. of Wills* 13:82). On 26 Feb 1767 Ann Sligh was named as a legatee in the account of Rebecca Gladman's estate (MDAD 55:342).

William and Ann were the parents of (Wright, "St. Anne's Parish Register:" 103).
3. Elizabeth Sophia, b. 20 December 1756.: and **4. Samuel**, living 20 January 1765.

Unplaced:
William Sligh (or Slye) was a disabled soldier who was paid in Anne Arundel Co. on 20 May 1783, and at other times through 17 December 1784 (*RPAA*).

== 0 ==

The Anthony Smith Family of Anne Arundel County

1. Anthony Smith was listed as a servant in July 1683 inventory of Richard Bedworth of AA Co. (INAC 8:99). He died 21 June 1711 (*AACR:* 159). He married, 1st, by 16 May 1696, Dinah, widow and administratrix, of Thomas Knighton of Anne Arundel Co., and daughter of Ferdinand Battee (INAC 13B:15; *BDML* 2:749). Dinah, wife of Anthony Smith died 13 October 1698, and was buried on 15 October 1698 in St. James Parish (*AACR:* 147). Anthony married, 2nd, Johanna Hull on 9 January 1700 in All Hallows Parish (*AACR:* 13). Alexander Rozenquest and "Hanna" Smith were m. 22 Dec 1712 in St. James Parish (AACR:360).

On 6 August 1695 he was a creditor of Luke Gregory (INAC 10:442). On 21 December 1705 he was named overseer of the will of Ferdinando Battee (MWB 3:744). On 7 August 1703 he signed as one of a panel of Jurors (AALR WT#2:64).

On 13 October 1701 he paid £175 for one sixteenth of the ship called *Anne Arundell*, Walter Norton, master (AALR WT#2:376). On 8 May 1710 John Trundle of PG Co., joiner sold 250 a. Pagget's land to William Lock of AA Co., chirurgeon, and Anthony Smith of Anne Arundel Co., Gent., being the land where Lock and Smith were now living (AALR PK:278).

Anthony Smith died leaving a will dated 6 May 1711, proved 2 August 1711. He left his estate to his only son and heir; Samuel. If his son died s.p., his estate was to go to his sister Mary Hunter of London and her children. He also named his kinfolk Benjamin, Ferdinando and Eliza Battee, mother-in-law Eliza H[ar]wood, William son of Thomas H[ar]wood, Daniel son of William Richardson, and his own servants Richard Green and Hezekiah Williams. Wife Johanna was named executrix, and left personalty. William Richardson was named overseer and Thomas Harwood, Jno. Brewer and Jas. Wanthand witnessed the will (MWB 13:333).

Josias Towgood and John Batie appraised the personal estate of Anthony Smith, Gent., on 9 Augu1711 and valued his property at £411.3.9 (INAC 33A:149).

Johanna Roszenquest, the relict, administered Anthony Smith's estate on 22 September 1713. In addition to assets of £470.3.2, a second inventory was cited in the amount of £51.8.2 (INAC 35B:73).

Anthony and Dinah were the parents of: **2. Samuel.**

2. Samuel Smith, son of Anthony (1), was born in 1695 and died in 1748. He married, 1st, Elizabeth Watkins on 27 January 1714 in All Hallows Parish (*AACR:* 26).Elizabeth was a daughter of John and Ann Watkins (*BDML* 2:749). Elizabeth, wife of Samuel, was buried in All Hallows Parish on 14 November 1733 (*AACR:*47). Samuel Smith married, 2nd, by 3 June 1734 Elizabeth [-?-] (*AACR:* 168). Samuel Smith gave his age as 36 when he deposed in 1732 (MCHR IR#2:384).

On 21 May 1716 Elizabeth Smith granted release of dower when Smith sold to Dr. William Lock 150 a. *Pagget,* which Samuel Smith had inherited (AALR IB#2:314).

Samuel Smith was the clerk of St. James Parish Vestry, and an overseer of the highways. He represented Anne Arundel Co. in the Legislature in 1738 and was a Justice of Anne Arundel Co. (*BDML* 2:749).

Smith died leaving a will dated 16 October 1747 and proved 23 May 1748. His two sons, John and Anthony, were to have two adjacent tracts on the north side of the Susquehanna in Cecil Co.: *Heaths Adventure,* 200 a., and *Holland* 650 a., but if his son Anthony should die before age 21, the land was to be equally divided between sons Samuel and John. Son Samuel was to have a Negro man Jack. Son John was to have negro man Harry. Son Anthony was to have Negro man Jemm, Negro boy George, a watch, wearing apparel, and £50 at age of 21. Daughter Ann was to have a Negro woman Sarah and her child, Cassey. Daughter Dinah was to have a Negro woman Young Bess, Negro girl Pegg, a riding horse Rock, and a sidesaddle to be sent for from England. Daughter Jane was to have Negro woman Jenny and Negro boy Tom. Daughter Elizabeth was to have a young Negro wench Sarah, Negro boy Will, and Negro girl Chloe. Cousin Dinah Hanchett was to have £5. Granddaughters Mary and Elizabeth Smith, at age 16 or marriage were to have two cows and calves each. Grandson Samuel Smith was to have two cows and calves. Wife Elizabeth Smith, if she did not marry, was to have Negro men Bacon and Bob, Negroes Clemming, Moll, and Great Bess, and residue. Wife Elizabeth Smith, and son Samuel Smith were named execs. Joseph Ward, Margaret Watkins, Thomas Ijams, and Elizabeth Ijams witnessed the will (MWB 25:324).

Samuel and his first wife Elizabeth were the parents of (*AACR:* 42, 147, 163, 166, 197): **3. Ann,** b. 3 November 1717 in St. James Parish, bapt. 25 April 1718 in All Hallows Parish; **4. Samuel,** b. 11 August 1722 in St. James Parish; he m. his cousin Ann Watkins; **5. John,** b. 3 February 1726 in St. James; **6. Anthony,** bapt. 6 March 1727 in St. James or All Hallows Parish, m. his cousin Jane Watkins; and **7. Dinah,** b. 25 September 1730 in St. James.

Samuel and his second wife Elizabeth were the parents of *AACR:* 168): **8. Jane,** b. 3 June 1734 [*sic*] in St. James; and **9. Eliza,** b. 5 April 1738.

4. Samuel Smith, son of Samuel (2), was born 11 August 1722 in St. James Parish. He married his cousin Ann Watkins, daughter of John and Margaret Watkins.

On 18 March 1768 Margaret Watkins made her will naming her granddaughter Ann, daughter of her daughter Ann and Samuel Smith (MWB 36:307 abst. in *Md. Cal. of Wills* 13:30).

Samuel and Ann were the parents of **10. Ann**, b. by 18 March 1768

6. Anthony Smith, son of Samuel (2) was bapt. 6 March 1727 in St. James or All Hallows Parish. He married by 1749 Jane, daughter of John Watkins (*AAMR* lists *BDML* 2:749, and MDAD 26:134). He died by July 1754.

In January 1752 Anthony Smith advertised he now kept a tavern at the house lately kept by John Conner, about seven miles from London Town, on the road to We3dst River in Calvert County (Annapolis *Maryland Gazette* 9 January 1752). In September 1753 he gave notice about a horse race to held at the Race Ground near his house (Annapolis *Maryland Gazette* 20 September 1753). In February 1754 he advertised for the return of a runaway indented servant, a Scotchman James Roberson, aged about 25 years (Annapolis *Maryland Gazette* 7 February 1754).

Samuel Smith in July 1754 advertised the sale of *Anthony's Purchase*, near the plantation of Mrs. Elizabeth Smith. He also advertised the sale of various household goods, late the property of Anthony Smith, as well as the houses where Anthony Smith and John Conner kept tavern (Annapolis *Maryland Gazette* 11 July 1754).

On 18 March 1768 Margaret Watkins made her will naming her grandchildren John, Anthony and Mary Smith, children of daughter Jane and Anthony Smith: John, Anthony, and Mary Smith (MWB 36:307 abst. in *Md. Cal. of Wills* 14:30).

Anthony and Jane were the parents of: **11. John**, b. by 18 March 1768; **12. Anthony**, b. by 18 March 1768; and **13. Mary**, b. by 18 March 1768.

11. John Smith, son of Anthony (6), of Anne Arundel Co., died by February 1794. Margaret Smith, administratrix, advertised she would settle the estate (Annapolis *Maryland Gazette* 20 February 1794).

==0==

The James Smith Family of Anne Arundel County

1. James Smith was listed as a servant in September 1674 in the inventory of Thomas Mears of Anne Arundel Co. (INAC 1:67). He died by December 1696. He married Ann [-?-].

On 16 May 1674 he witnessed the will of Thomas Meers of Anne Arundel Co. (MWB 2:3). On 1 August 1662 Edward Lloyd of Severn conveyed 100 a. *Swan Neck* to James Smith. Later Philemon Smith, brother and heir of James Smith [son of James (1) Smith] requested the deed to be recorded (AALR IH#1:122). On 23 May 1668 William Crouch conveyed a parcel of land to James Smith (AAL IH#1:124). Peter Bond conveyed a parcel of *Swan Point* to James Smith on 12 July 1673 (AALR IH#1:123). On 10 November 1676 Smith patented 21 a. *Jacob's Point* in Anne Arundel Co. (SMC 1)

James Smith died leaving a will dated 13 September 1695 and proved 1 December 1696. He named his wife Ann as executrix, and left her an interest in all his real estate during her widowhood. He named his sons James, John, Samuel, and Philemon, and daughters Mary and Eliza. If his son Philemon should die, his wife Eliza was not have any portion of the estate left him by the testator (MWB 7:213).

Anne Smith administered the estate of James Smith on 14 October 1697. Assets of £88.10.0 were cited and payments were made to daughter Mary, wife of Edward Gibbs, and daughter Eliza, wife of George Norman (INAC 15:180).

The inventory of Edward Topp of Anne Arundel Co., filed 1 September 1702 mentioned "old Mrs. Ann Smith," and her sons John and Philemon (INAC 25:97). Topp's administration account, filed 12 March 1705 listed payments to Mrs. Alice Smith and Mr. Philemon Smith (INAC 25:155).

On 9 March 1705/6 Anne Smith, widow of James Smith, sold 463 a. *Timberneck* t William Bladen in order to relieve her great necessity (AALR WT#2:332)..

James and Ann were the parents of: **2. James**; **3. John**; **4. Samuel**; **5. Philemon**; **6. Mary**, m. Edward Gibbs; and **7. Eliza**, m. George Norman.

3. John Smith, son of James (1) and Ann, died 29 June 1705 (*AACR:*137). He married Martha [-?-], who married 2nd, by 14 June 1710 William Rowles (AALR PK: 22).

John Smith died leaving a will dated 20 June 1705 and proved 18 July 1705. His sons James and William were to have personalty and dwelling plantation at the decease of their mother. His son John and daughters Elizabeth and Cassandra were to have personalty. His sons were to be of age at 16 if their mother remarried. Wife Martha was named executrix and residuary legatee. Philip Jones, Sarah Carter and Mary Jones witnessed the will (MWB 3:446, abst. in *Md. Cal. of Wills* 3:48).

John and Martha Smith were the parents of the following children, bapt. at St. Margaret's, Westminster Parish (*AACR:*107): **8. James**, b. 16 November 1688; **9. Elizabeth**, b 16 February 1691; **10. John**, b. 1 November 1696; **11. William**, b. 8 April 1699; and **12. Cassandra**, b. 11 November 1704.

4. Samuel Smith, son of James (1) and Ann, died leaving a will dated 18 February 1700 and proved 9 December 1701. His mother Ann Smith was to be executrix and sole legatee of his estate real and personal, for life. At her death, his cousin William Norman was to have 260 a. *Timber Neck,* and if he died without heirs, the land was to pass to cousin, William Smith. Cousin John Smith and heirs were to have the residue of *Timber Neck.* Cousins Ann and William Gibbs wee to have personalty. Brothers John and Philip [Philemon?] were executors after the death of his mother, and his 'brother' Edward Gibbs was named overseer. Jno. Charbars, William Pepper, and Mary Dalling witnessed the will (MWB 11:142, abst. in *Md. Cal. of Wills* 2:227).

5. Philemon Smith, son of James (1) and Ann Smith, died by 1 April 1713.

He was married to Eliza [-?-] at the time his father made his will, but at the time of his death Anne Smith was his executrix.

He was mentioned in the inventory and administration account of Edward Topp (INAC 25: 97. 155). On 30 January 1705 Philemon Smith and William Anderson appraised the estate of Charles 'Greyham,' planter of Anne Arundel Co. (NAC 25:283).

On 12 August 1700 Philemon Smith conveyed 200 a. *Smith's Forest* to Ambrose Nelson. Wife Anne released her dower (AALR WT#1:95). On 21 August 1708 Philemon and Ann conveyed 250 a., one-half of *Swan Neck,* and 25 a. *Addition* to Amos Garrett (AALR WT#2:677).

Philemon Smith died leaving a will dated 6 March 1712/3 and proved 27 March 1713. He left his entire estate to his wife Anne, whom he named executrix. William Rowles, Sarah Maynard, and Eliz Crouch witnessed the will (MWB 15:92, abst. in *Md. Cal. of Wills* 4:201).

Robert Jub and William Pennington appraised Philemon Smith's estate at £30.12.5 on 1 April 1713. James Smith approved the inventory (INAC 34:116). Anne Smith, executrix, filed an account of Philemon Smith's estate on 8 March 1713 [1713/4?]. She cited assets worth £38.11.2 (INAC 35A:7).

Philemon Smith and his wife were the parents of two daughters bapt. in St. Margaret's, Westminster Parish (*AACR:* 107, 108): **13. Ann,** b. 8 October 1703; and **14. Comfort,** b. 17 February 1704.

8. James Smith, son of John (3) and Martha, was born, 16 November 1688 and died by 9 October 1713. On 4 May 1710 in All Hallow's Parish he married Mrs. Susannah Crouch (*AACR:* 25). She was the widow of William Crouch and John Howard, and daughter of John Rockhold (*AAMR:*217).

On 14 June 1710 James Smith conveyed 250 a., half of *Swan Neck* and 25 a. *Addition to Amos Garrett*. The deed mentioned John Smith [his father] and his widow, who has since married William Rowles. James Smith's wife Susannah released her dower (AALR PK:208).

11. William Smith, son of John (3) and Martha, was born 8 April 1699.

On 19 April 1720 William Smith conveyed to William Rowles 125 a., part of *Swan Neck,* which William had inherited by his father's will (AALR CW#1:160, 168).

==0==

The Sweeting Family of Baltimore County
With Notes on the Marchant Family

1. Edward Sweeting died by 8 October 1716. He married Mary Pearle, daughter of William and Ann Pearle. Mary was born about 1681. In November 1692 she was bound to William Wilkinson (BACP F#1:300, 307, 333).

Sweeting was one of the appraisers of William Demment's estate on 25 April 1711 (INAC 33A:68).

On 12 December 1713 Ralph Winter of Dorchester Co. made a will leaving his entire estate to Edward Sweeting, who administered his estate on 30 December 1714 (MWB 13:611, abst. in *Md. Cal. of Wills* 3:255; INAC 36A:23, 36B:8).

On 8 October 1716 Francis Whitehead posted bond that he would administer Sweeting's estate. John Thomas and George Walker were sureties (BAAB 3:423). It was the widow's prerogative to administer her husband's estate. That she did not do so is a strong indication that she may have died, and yet she was alive on 21 June 1716 when she sold land.

On 21 June 1716 Mary Sweeting, widow, conveyed *Upper Spring Neck* to Philip Washington; in the deed she mentions property due her by inheritance in Md. (BALR TR#A: 408).

On 13 November 1716 Sweeting's personal estate was appraised by S. Hinton and Henry Jones at £15.7.3. His debts included money due the estate of William Pearle (INAC 39C:199).

Edward and Mary (Pearle) Sweeting were probably the parents of: **2. Mary,** b. about 1707; **3. Edward,** b. about 1709; and **4. Robert,** b. about 1710.

2. Mary Sweeting, daughter of Edward (1) and Mary, was born about 1707, She was age 11 in November 1718 when she was bound to Sarah Spink until she should reach the age of 16 (*BCF:*618). She married Richard Marchant on 28 July 1723 (Reamy and Reamy, *St. Paul's Parish Register:* 29).

On 3 August 1725 Richard Marchant of Baltimore Co., weaver, and wife Mary, conveyed 50 a. of *John's Interest,* on the south side of Back River, on the south side of

Hog Branch, to Samuel Harryman (BALR IS#H:150).
Richard and Mary (Sweeting) Marchant were the parents of (Reamy and Reamy, *St. Paul's Parish Register:* 4; Additional data from Joyce McGehee Bockemuehl): **5. William,** b. 15 September 1725; **6. Ellinor,** b. 12 March 1727; **7. Mary,** b. 27 March 1734; **8. Richard, Jr.,** b. 1744 in Opequon, Va.; and **9. Rosannah,** b. 1748 in Opequon, Va.

3. Edward Sweeting, son of Edward (1) and Mary, married Mary Watts on 21 December 1732 by license (Reamy and Reamy, *St. Paul's Parish Register:* 30).

John Francis Holland, in his will made 23 February 1731, leaving personalty to Edward Sweeting and two others, and the rest of his estate to Frances Holland Watts, daughter of Edward and Mary Watts (MWB 20:565, abst. in *Md. Cal. of Wills* 6:253).

On 23 April 1733 Edward and Mary Sweeting were creditors of John Francis Holland of Baltimore Co. (MINV 17:197). On 13 March 1734 Sweeting was named as a legatee in Holland's administration account (MDAD 12:753).

In 1737 Sweeting was head of a household in Patapsco Lower Hundred. In 1739 he was on the Levy List for squirrels' heads (*IBCW:* 24, 29). In 1750 he received a payment from the estate of Benjamin Bowen (MDAD 29:217).

Edward Sweeting in 1762 paid a criminal fine for fornication and bastardy (BAMI 1755-1763). Sweeting was a surety for Sarah Watts, administratrix of John Watts on 21 June 1768 (MDAD 58:218). In 1769 an Edward Sweeting signed the petition favoring the removal of the county seat from Joppa to Baltimore Town (*ARMD* 69).

On 20 August 1771 Edward Sweeting leased *Barney's Inheritance* from John Beale Bordley (BALR AL#D: 93).

He was a surety for Mrs. Ann Legate when she distributed the estate of John Legate (BFD 6:348).

Edward and Mary were the parents of (Reamy and Reamy, *St. Paul's Parish Register:* 11): **10. William,** b. 8 November 1746.

4. Robert Sweeting, son of Edward (1) and Mary, married Sarah Laine on 5 December 1731 (Reamy and Reamy, *St. Paul's Parish Register:* 30). He died in Wilkes Co, N.C.

On 26 August 1760 Robert and Edward Sweeting witnessed the will of Jacob Rolles [Rowles?] of Baltimore Co. (MWB 36:551, abst. in *Md. Cal. of Wills* 14:55).

Robert Sweeting moved to Carolina by 25 March 1777 when he deeded 150 a. *Upper Spring Neck,* originally surveyed for Walter Dickinson on 4 Aug 1659, to William Wilkinson of Baltimore Co. (BALR AL#O:288).

Robert and Sarah were the parents of (Reamy and Reamy, *St. Paul's Parish Register:* 10, 11): **11. Edward,** b. 23 October 1732; and **12. Elizabeth,** b. 25 August 1734.

11. Edward Sweeting, son of Robert (4) and Sarah, was born on 23 October 1732. He married Ruth Trotten on 6 June 1756 (Reamy and Reamy, *St. Paul's Parish Register:* 10, 35).

He is probably the Edward Sweeting, aged 80 years who died 16 June 1809 at his residence on Patapsco Neck (*Federal Gazette and Baltimore Daily Advertiser* 19 June 1809). Sweeting died leaving a will dated 25 June 1808 and proved 21 June 1809. He named his sons Thomas and Benjamin. and his daughter Mary Odell. Thomas Jones and Josias Stansbury witnessed the will (BAWB 8:417, abst. by Burns).

They were the parents of (Reamy and Reamy, *St. Paul's Parish Register:* 22): **13. Elizabeth,** b. 28 February 1757 (St. Paul's, p. 22); **14. Thomas; 15. Benjamin;** and **16. Mary,** m. [-?-] Odell.

Colonial Families of Maryland II

Unplaced:

[-?-] **Sweetin** m. by 7 October 1778, Ann, daughter of Mary Bowen (BAWB 4:355).

Robert Sweeting married Elizabeth [-?-]. They were the parents of (Reamy and Reamy, *St. Paul's Parish Register:* 22): William, b. 22 October 1761.

Thomas Sweeting of this city, and Miss Catherine Wineman of the county, were m. last eve. by Rev. Dr. Allison (*Federal Gazette and Baltimore Daily Advertiser* 15 November 1799).

==0==

The Tanzey Family

1. Alexander Tanzey was transported by 1680 (MPL WC#2:406). He was in Anne Arundel Co. by August 1704 when he took the Oath in order to be licensed to teach, as ordered by the Governor and Council (AAJU: August 1704). He was buried in September 1713.

Alexander Tanzey married 1st, by 1698, Mary [-?-], and 2nd, Mary Parsons on 20 January 1704 in St. James Parish. Mary Tansey married, 2nd, Daniel Osborn in St. James Parish on 2 February 1715/6 (*AACR:* 155, 162).

On 16 August 1705 he was a creditor of John Stockdon of Anne Arundel Co. (INAC 25:62). On 9 May 1711 he witnessed the will of Benjamin Capell of Anne Arundel Co. (MWB 13:333, abst. in *Md. Cal. of Wills* 3:213).

Alexander and Mary were the parents of the following children, whose births were recorded in St. James' Parish (*AACR:* 150, 160, 161):

By 1st wife Mary [-?-]: **2. Ann**, b. 26 October 1696; and **3. Rebecca**, b. 28 December 1698.

By 2nd wife Mary Parsons: **4. Martha**, b. 9 February 1705; **5. Abraham**, b. 12 July 1711; **6. Alexander**, b. 10 August 1707; and **7. Mary**, b. 8 May 1713.

6. Alexander Tansey, son of Alexander (1) and Mary, was born 10 August 1707, and was probably the Alexander who moved to Baltimore Co., and married Katherine [-?-].

In 1737 Tansey was on the Baltimore Co. Levy List for bringing in squirrels' heads. In 1739 Alexander Tansey was head of a household in Back River Upper Hundred (*IBCW:* 20, 29). On 30 November 1747 Alexander Tansey was a creditor of the estate of Capt. John Cockey of Baltimore Co. (MDAD 24:189).

On 21 March 1741/2 Alexander was granted a certificate to Monocacy Meeting (Records of Gunpowder Meeting). On 10 March 1746 he witnessed the will of Isaac Wells of Prince George's Co. (MWB 25:61).

It was reported that Alexander 'abused his family when in anger.' He was disowned at Fairfax on 27 d., 9 m., 1745. He acknowledged his fault, and was reinstated on 30 d., 5 m., 1752. On 27 d., 1 m., 1756, he was reported to have removed to North Carolina without paying his debts, and was disowned at Fairfax Monthly Meetng (*EAQG:* 6:570).

He and Katherine moved to Cane Creek, N.C. On 9 d., 7 m, 1757 Catharina 'Tanzy' was received in Cane Creek Meeting, by Certificate from 'Monaqucy' Monthly Meeting; Alexander 'Tanzy' was received by certificate on 7 d., 4 m. 1761 (*EAQG* 1:422).

Alexander and Katherine were the parents of the following children, born in St. Paul's Parish (Reamy and Reamy, *St. Paul's Parish Register:* 7; *EAQG* 1: 422): **8. Ann**, b. 18 January 1729; **9. Mary**, b. 25 January 1731; and **10. Abraham**, b. 10 January 1733/4; he may be the 'Abram 'Tansey who was a debtor to the estate of Jacob Toop of

Frederick Co. on 12 January 1774 (MDAD 71: 96); and **11. Leah,** m. William Wright at Cane Creek Monthly Meeting on 15 d., 5 m., 1758; **12. Alexander, Jr.; 13. Catherine; 13. Edward;** and **14. Abraham.**

5. Abraham Tanzey, son of Alexander (1) and Mary, was born on 12 July 1711. On 19 May 1722 Daniel Osbon [sic] of St. James Parish, for love and affection, gave his son-in-law Abraham Tansey a cow and a calf (AALR RCW#2:16).

13. Edward Tanzey, son of Alexander (6) and Catherine, was disowned at Fairfax in 1757 for joining the army. He was granted a certificate from Fairfax to Cane Creek, N.C. in 1755. There is no record of the receipt of this certificate by Cane Creek Monthly Meeting, nor of Edward's return to Fairfax Monthly Meeting (*EAQG:* 6:570). About 1766 Edward Tansey was a creditor of the estate of Richard Richardson of Frederick Co., Md. (MDAD 54:145).

14. Abraham Tanzey, son of Alexander (6) and Catherine married Mary Pugh.

He was granted a certificate from Fairfax to Cane Creek Monthly Meeting, N. C. on 25 d. 5 m., 1755, and transferred to New Garden Monthly Meeting by which meeting he was granted certificate to Cane Creek in 1761 to marry (*EAQG:* 6:570).

Unplaced:
Alexander Tansey married Rebecca [-?-]. They were the parents of one daughter, born in St. George's Parish (Reamy and Reamy, *St. George's Parish Register:* 8): Rebecca, bapt. 12 July 1702.

== 0 ==

The Taylor Family
With Notes on the Sing and Wiley Families

1. Richard Taylor was born about 1667 and died by 18 May 1729. He married Anne Tracey on 7 d., 6 m., 1687.

Richard and Ann Taylor, then living in Prince George's Co., sold 600 a. *Denton* to William Bladen on 5 September 1699. In December 1713 Taylor purchased *Friendship,* part of *Darley Hall,* from John Ensor (BALR TR#A: 277). On 28 March 1713 John Roberts, planter, conveyed to Taylor two tracts: 464 a. *Roberts Forest,* and also a plantation in Anne Arundel Co., where Henry Roberts was living, and which said John inherited from his father John Roberts. On 8 August 1717 Roberts of Baltimore Co. conveyed 496 a. *Roberts Choice* to Richard Taylor (BALR TR#A: 496, 236).

Richard Taylor of Baltimore Co. died leaving a will dated 1726 and proved 18 May 1729. His daughter Frances was to have 275 a. *Taylor's Discovery* and personalty. If she died without issue, the land was to pass to his son Joseph and then to his son Thomas. Son Thomas and heirs was to have 300 a. *Taylor's String,* 125 a. *Addition to Taylor's String,* and 30 a. *Taylor' Discovery.* Son Joseph was to have 860 a. *Taylor's Range,* 70 a. *Addition to Taylor's Range,* and 99 a. *Addition to Shoemaker's Hall.* His granddaughter Margaret Sing was to have 150 a. *Taylor's Discovery.* If she died without heirs it was to pass to his son Thomas, and then to son Joseph. Son Richard was to have 5 s. Son Joseph was to have 1 acre bought from John Ensor for a meeting house and burying place for Friends. His wife Ann was to have the use of dwelling plantation for life and one-third of his personal estate. Executors were to be sons Joseph and Thomas. John Cross, Benjamin

Colonial Families of Maryland II

Price, Edward Fell and George Hitchcock witnessed the will (MWB 19:781 abst. in *Md. Cal. of Wills* 6:130).
Richard and Ann were the parents of: **2. Frances; 3. Richard**, b. about 1688; **4. Thomas**, b. about 1704; and **5. Joseph**, b. about 1705.

2. Frances Taylor, daughter of Richard (1) and Anne, was to have 275 a. *Taylor's Discovery* by the terms of her father's will. She may have married [-?-] Sing by whom she may have been the mother of: **6. Margaret Sing.**

3. Richard Taylor, son of Richard (1) and Anne, was born about 1688 and was living in 1739 when he made a deposition.
On 7 April 1716 *Stone's* Delight was surveyed for Richard Taylor, Jr., adjacent land formerly surveyed for Job Evans, on Western Run and a branch of Herring Run; pat. 25 April 1717 for 100 a. (MPL FF#7: 180, PL#4: 3). In 1721 Richard Taylor, Jr., with consent of wife Mary, conveyed *Stone's Delight*, on Little Britain Ridge to William Lyell (BALR IS#G: 402). On 16 April 1723 Richard Taylor, Jr., now of Stafford Co., Va., gave a power of attorney to his father, Richard Taylor, to sell *Stone;s Delight*, Richard, Jr.'s, wife Mary agreed (BALR IS#G: 400).
By September 1739 he was living in Goochland Co, Va., when he deposed again, giving his age as 51 and stating that his father Richard had died (See BALR (BACP HWS#1A:279).

4. Thomas Taylor, son of Richard (1) and Anne, was born c1704 and died 20 April 1788. He married Sarah Price, born April 1705, daughter of Mordecai and Mary (Parsons) Price.
He was left 300 a. *Taylor's String*, 125 a. *Addition to Taylor's String*, and 30 a. *Taylor' Discovery* in his father's will.
On 5 November 1736 Nathaniel and John Giles of Baltimore Co. conveyed 390 a. *Friends' Discovery* to Thomas Taylor. Giles' wife Sarah consented (BALR IS#1K: 424).
On 14 June 1737 Thomas Taylor, with consent of his wife Sarah, conveyed 400 a. *Bachelor's Fancy*, being part of *Friend's Discovery*, to Henry Morgan (BALR HWS#1-A: 20).
On 2 March 1744 Taylor conveyed 50 a. *Smallwood*, and 80 a. *Taylor's Discovery* to Nicholas Haile (BALR TB#D: 63).
Thomas and Sarah were the parents of: **7. Rachel**, m. Solomon Wheeler in 11 m. 1745 (Records of Gunpowder Meeting); **8. Jemima**, m. Samuel Meredith on 2 February 1748 (Reamy and Reamy, *St. Paul's Parish Register:* 34); **9. Joseph Neal**, d. 1762. unm.; **10. John**, m. Susanna [-?-], and by 1749 was living in Penna; **11. Richard**, b. 1738; **12. Mary**, m. Moses Lawson; **13. Samuel**, b. 1740; and **14. Sarah**, m. John Head.

5. Joseph Taylor, son of Richard (1) and Anne, was born c1705. He died leaving a will dated 19 April 1788 and proved 9 March 1789. He named his 'cousins' [*i.e.,* nephews] Richard and Samuel Taylor, sons of Thomas Taylor, Joseph Daughaday, and Johns Hopkins. He mentioned one acre of land called *Friendship,* on which the meeting house was built for the use of 'Friends' for public worship. His cousins Joseph, Abraham, John, and Thomas Daughaday were to have the plantation where they now lived, reserving to their mother Katherine Daughaday her thirds of the said land for the rest of her natural life. His cousins John and Joseph Floyd were to have the land they lived on called *Taylor's Addition*. His cousin John Taylor, son of Sarah Taylor was to have *The Forest*. He also mentioned his cousins Jemima Meredith and Mary Lawson. His cousins Richard and Samuel Taylor were named executors. Henry Stevenson, Nicholas Stevenson and Thomas Hillen witnessed the will (BAWB 4:346, abst. by Burns). In a codicil dated 15 January 1789 he stated that since Samuel Taylor had died since the execution of the testator's last will, all the property formerly given to Samuel Taylor should be equally divided between Joseph, Samuel, Isaac, Jacob, and Elijah Taylor, and all personal estate devised to Samuel to be equally divided between his children Joseph, Samuel, Richard, Isaac, Jacob, Elijah, Mary, Sarah, and Hannah Taylor. Patience Taylor, widow of Samuel was to have all the lands and personal estate devised to her late husband. Henry Stevenson, William Sixsmith, and Joshua Stevenson witnessed the codicil (BAWB 3:438).

Richard Taylor administered his estate on 15 May 1790 and paid legacies to Joseph, Richard, and Catherine Daughaday, and to Joseph Floyd (BAAD 10:144). A second account was filed on 14 June 1791 (BAAD 10:379).

6. Margaret Sing, was possibly a daughter of [-?-] and Frances (2) (Taylor) Sing, but was definitely named as a granddaughter in the will of of her grandfather, Richard Taylor, was to have 150 a. *Taylor's Discovery* in her grandfather's will, She married William Wiley on 23 December 1734 (Reamy and Reamy, *St. Paul's Parish Register:* 31).

She might possibly have married a Daughaday before she married William Wiley.

In October 1745 Margaret Wiley gave consent for John Daughaday (Daugherty) to be bound to Samuel Collier to learn the trade of blacksmith (BALR TB#D:331).

William and Margaret were the parents of: **15. Richard Wiley,** died without issue before 14 October 1781; he had inherited the 150 a. of *Taylor's Discovery,* which descended to his sisters, Edith, wife of John Cross, living in York Co., Penna., and Ann, wife of Thomas Hunt. On that day the sisters and their husbands sold the land to William Hunter (BALR WG#G:496-497); **16. Edith,** m. John Cross; and **17. Ann,** m. Thomas Hunt.

11. Richard Taylor, son of Thomas (4) and Sarah, was born 16th d., 12th m., 1738 ("Gunpowder Monthly Meeting," *QRNM*:33) and died 1821 in Baltimore Co. He married Ann Stevenson.

In 1754 Richard Taylor, born on the date given above, and his 'cousin' Joseph Taylor were accepted into membership in Gunpowder Meeting (*QRNM*:33).

On 10 September 1810 Richard Taylor and wife Anne, and the children of Samuel Taylor, deeded part of *Taylor's Addition* to John E. Stansbury (BALR WG#110:391). On 4 September 817 he conveyed 12½ a. *Ill Will* to his daughter Mary Pickett (BALR WG#112:410).

Richard Taylor died leaving a will dated 22 May 1816 and proved 15 February 1821, naming sons Thomas and Joshua as executors, son Richard, daughters Ruth Gatch, Rachel Welsh, granddaughter Lora Poteet (daughter of Ann Poteet), daughter Mary Pickett, granddaughters Mary Sindall, Ann Smith, Rachel Daughaday, Elizabeth Taylor (daughter of son Richard), Martha Taylor and Sarah Ann Taylor; his son-in-law Aquila Carroll, and granddaughters Juliann and Sarah Taylor, daughters of Samuel Taylor. The witnesses were: Thomas Hillen, Jno. E. Stansbury, and Solomon Carter (BAWB 11:217, abst. by Burns).

On 25 April 1822 Thomas, Richard, Samuel, and Joshua Taylor, and Sarah wife of Joseph Daughaday, Ruth Gatch, Rachel wife of Laban Welch and Mary wife of John Pickett, all heirs at law of Richard Taylor, released to Joshua Richards *Taylor's Discovery* (BALR WG#163:688).

Richard and Ann were the parents of: **18. Richard**, b. 26 March 1768; **19. Sarah**, b. 9 April 1749, d. 6 August 1849, m. Joseph Daughaday; **20. Mary**, m. John Pickett on 8 June 1808 (*Federal Gazette and Baltimore Daily Advertiser* 11 June 1808); **21. Rachel**, who m. Laban Welch by license dated 17 December 1804 (BAML); **22. Thomas Wilkinson**, d. 1834, m. Ruth Stansbury on 31 January 1799; **23. Joshua**, b. about 1779, d. 12 November 1866; **24. Ruth**, b. about 1779, m. Benjamin Gatch; **25. Samuel**; **26. Ann**, m. Jesse Poteet by license dated 16 November 1811 (BAML); and **27. Jemima**, m. Aquila Carroll by license dated 23 January 1806 (BAML).

13. Samuel Taylor, son of Thomas (4) and Sarah, was born 1740 and died by 15 Jan 1789. He married Patience, daughter of Samuel and Mary ([-?-]) Tipton (BALR WG#65: 161, 194).

Patience Taylor, administratrix, filed an account of Samuel Taylor's estate on 15 December 1790 (BAAD 10:252).

Patience Taylor died leaving a will dated 19 June 1793 and proved 27 August 1793. She named her daughters Sarah, Hannah, and Anney Taylor, and mentioned her husband Samuel Taylor's estate. Her son Joseph Taylor was executor. Richard Taylor and Henry Stephenson witnessed the will (BAWB 5:117, abst. by Burns).

In February 1794 Taylor's orphan children Jacob, Ann, Hannah and Elijah Taylor chose Joseph Taylor to be their guardian (BAOC 3:78).

Patience Taylor died intestate by 1794. Joseph Taylor, administrator, petitioned the court for permission to sell the personal estate (Baltimore Co. Petition of Joseph Taylor, 1794). Joseph Taylor filed an account on 13 March 1799. He retained the balance as guardian of the children of the deceased (BAAD 13:5).

Samuel and Patience were the parents of (Will of Joseph Taylor, BAWB 4:346, 348, abst. by Burns): **28. Joseph**, b. 1764, d. 1830, m. Sarah Gatch, b. 1761; **29. Samuel**; **30. Isaac**, b. 1772, m. Elizabeth Thompson; **31. Richard**; **32. Mary**, b. 1774; **33. Rebecca**, b. [1776?]; **34. Sarah**, b. 1778, m. [-?-] Baxter; **35. Hannah**, b. 1779, m. William Scarfe by licesne dated 30 December 1794 (BAML); **36. Jacob**, b. 18 February 1782; **37. Anna**, b. 1784, m. [-?-] Hale; and **38. Elijah**, b. 1796.

18. Richard Taylor, son of Richard (11) and Anne, was born 26 March 1768 and died in Baltimore County on 14 July 1853. He married on 24 May 1806 Catherine, daughter of Luke and Catherine [-?-] Stansbury, Catherine Stansbury Taylor died 7 July 1827, aged 59 (She may be the Catherine Stansbury who married William Welsh on 17 February 1798). Richard and Catherine are both buried at Govanstown Presbyterian Church.

Catherine Welsh of Baltimore City, on 30 August 1802, deeded to Nancy Hobbs part of *Cole's Harbor and Todd's Range* (BALR WG#71:564). On 14 June 1802 John Liggett deeded to Richard Taylor part of *Cole's Harbor and Todd's Range* (BALR WG#73:13). On 14 June 1804 George Leggett of Baltimore Co. conveyed part of the same tracts to Richard Taylor (BALR WG#81:287).

A deed found in BALR TK#264:267, stated that Thomas Stansbury by his will dated [1793?], left part of *Long's Addition* to Catherine, late the wife of his son Luke Stansbury, deceased. If she remarried the land was to go to her two eldest daughters: Hannah and Catherine. The widow Catherine had died and her daughter Catherine had married Richard Taylor and died leaving the following children: Richard, Jr., who m. Eleanor, Mary Anne Taylor, Hannah wife of Lloyd Donovan, Nelson and Lorenzo Taylor, who now deeded part of *Long's Addition* to Elijah Taylor (BALR TK#264:267).

On 21 March 1825 Richard Taylor, for the love he bore his daughter Martha Riley, wife of John Riley, conveyed her part of *Taylor's Range* (BALR WG#177:86). On 8 May

1837 he conveyed part of *contrivance* to [his son] Richard Taylor (BALR TK#269:400). Richard and Catherine were the parents of: **39. Richard,** b. about 1809; **40. Hannah Eugenie,** b. about 1811, m. 1st, on 21 October 1833, Lloyd Donovan, and 2nd, by BAML dated 26 August 1853, John Taylor; **41. Nelson,** b. about 1814, m. Sarah [-?-]; **42. Lorenzo D.,** b. about 1815, m. Elizabeth [-?-]; **43. Mary Ann,** b. 15 November 1817, d. 28 May 1866, buried at Govanstown Presbyterian Church; **44. Catherine,** b. 3 February 1818, d. 2 October 1895, bur. at Govanstown Presbyterian Church; m. 18 April 1839 John Hall (BAML); **45. Elizabeth,** m. Wilkes Bowen on or about 17 November 1830 (BAML); **46. Henry;** and **47. Martha,** m. by 21 March 1825 John Riley. **22. Thomas Wilkinson Taylor,** son of Richard (11) and Anne, married Ruth Stansbury on 31 January 1799. They were the parents of: **48. Thomas; 49. Wilkerson,** m. Rebecca Stansbury on 28 July 1836 (*Baltimore American* 3 August 1836); and **50. Eliza S.,** m. [-?-] Marsh.

23. Joshua Taylor, son of Richard (11) and Anne, was b. about 1779 and died 12 November 1866. He married Lydia Richards by license dated 16 March 1811 (BAML). She was a daughter of John and Rebecca (Scar-borough) Richards. They were the parents of: **51. Dr. Milton N.; 52. Sarah Rebecca,** m. [-?-] Jones and moved to Louisiana; **53. Elmira G.,** m. [-?-] Dulaney of Anne Arundel Co.; **54. Lydian,** m. [-?-] Buell of Baltimore Co.; **55. Eliza S.,** m. [-?-] Hall; and **56. Harriet W.,** m. [-?-] Murray.

29. Samuel Taylor, son of Samuel (13) and Patience, was born 1765. He m. [-?-] Thompson.

On 22 August 1801 Samuel Taylor, with consent of his wife Ann, deeded parts of *Robert's Choice, Ill Will, Taylor's Range,* and *Taylor's Addition* to Richard Taylor of Joseph (BALR WG#68:544).

31. Richard Taylor, son of Samuel (13) and Patience, died by March 1808. He married Clemency Thompson on 2 February 1789 (Reamy and Reamy, *St. James Parish Register:* 1). She and Benjamin Hart were married on 4 December 1806 by Rev. Lewis Richards (BAML)..

A legal dispute was settled on 5 March 1808 when it was ordered that all matters in dispute between Benjamin Hart and Clemency his wife, administrators of Richard Taylor deceased, and Wm. Scarf and Hannah his wife, Randel Hales and Anne his wife, and Elijah Taylor be referred to John Hambleton and Thos. Hillen, and they return an account of their proceedings to this court, and if they cannot agree to choose a third person. (BAOC 6:309). On 22 March 1808 in the case of Wm. Scarf and Hannah his wife, Randall Hales and Anne his wife, and Elijah Taylor against Benjamin Hart and Clemency his wife, administratrix, and Isaac Taylor, administrator of Richard Taylor, the court ordered and determined that Benjamin Hart and Clemency his wife and Isaac Taylor, the defendants, were to sell at public sale after giving ten days' notice for cash all the estate, right and title of Richard Taylor which he had at the time of his death in and to a lot of ground with a frame house thereon erected, appraised and returned in the inventory of the deceased's estate at $800; also in and to two Negroes called Betty and Night appraised at $280, and return the sales to this court. The court also ordered and determined that the said defendants account in their administration account for the sum of $110, being the difference between the sales and appraisement of a house and lot on Bridge Street continued, and also for the sum of $18, being the amount of the prizes drawn by the five lottery tickets. (BAOC 6:314)

Colonial Families of Maryland II

36. **Jacob Taylor,** son of Samuel (13) and Patience, was born 18 February 1782. Jacob Taylor, orphan, aged 13, on 18 February 1795, in April 1795 was bound to Alexander Bradburn, blacksmith (BAOC 3:146). Jacob Taylor and Sarah Thompson were married 21 March 1799 and were the parents of (Burnham Bible, Filing Case A, MHS): **57. Ann,** b. 27 December 1799, d. 27 October 1800, aged 10 mos; **58. Richard,** b. 12 May 1802; **59. Elizabeth,** b. 14 December 1803; and **60. Sarah Ann,** b. 14 August 1809.

39. **Richard Taylor,** son of Richard (18) and Catherine, was born about 1809, and died 1 April 1877 in his 68th year, at Rockland, Baltimore. Co. On or about 22 December 1834 he married by license Eleanor Norris BAML). She was born about 1809 and died 7 July 1870. Richard and Eleanor are buried at Govanstown Presbyterian Church.

Richard Taylor died at noon on Sunday, 1 April, in his 68th year. The funeral was to be from the residence of his son Dorsey on Falls Road, near Rockland on 3 April. Carriages will leave his brother Nelson's, corner of Chase and Gay (Baltimore *Sun,* 2 April 1877). The Towson *Maryland Gazette* of 7 April 1877, stated that he died near Rockland, and he was a member of the Towson Lodge, I. O. O. F.

Ellen V., consort of Richard Taylor, died 7 July, 1870. Her funeral was from the Govanstown Presbyterian Church (Baltimore *Sun,* 8 July 1870).

Richard and Eleanor (Norris) Taylor were the parents of: **61. Christieanne,** m. Michael Denton Barnes; **62. Thomas Dorsey,** m. 13 August 1872 by Rev. W. A. Koontz at the M. E. Parsonage in Govanstown Eliza Bell (*Baltimore County Union,* 17 August 1872); **63. Richardanna,** m. 6 June 1872 at the Methodist Episcopal Parsonage, Govanstown, Charles Townsend; **64. Isaac;** and **65. Catherine.**

== 0 ==

The Tebedo Family
The name also appears as Tepedo and Tibbido.

1. **Peter Tebedo (Tibbido)** married Mary, widow of Robert Trevitt, who died by 1698. She was a daughter of Anthony Gongo (*AAMR:* 236 cites MWB 25:326, and Barnes' *Colonial Families of Anne Arundel Co.,* 124).

By about 1707 Peter 'Tibedan' possessed 50 a. *Kequotan's Choice,* which had been surveyed for Stephen Benson on 5 May 1663 in right of his wife the daughter of Ann Gongoe (*Maryland Rent Rolls:* 115).

About 1716 Peter "Teppodoe' administered the estate of William Trevis of Anne Arundel Co. (INAC 37A:94).

Peter Tepedo and Jos. Tepedo were in Anne Arundel Co. by 9 November 1733 when they signed the inventory of Samuel Guichard as next of kin (MINV 18:186). Guichard had also married a daughter of Anthony Gongo.

Mary Tepedo of Anne Arundel Co., widow, died leaving a will dated 17 April 1744 and proved 18 June 1748. Her son Joseph Tepedo was to have *Knighton's Choice,* 50 a. near Herring Creek., where she lived, but if he died without issue, the land was to go to her grandson Joseph Mumford. Son Joseph Tepedo was named executor. James Trott, Thomas Borer, and John Gardner witnessed the will (MWB 25:326, abst. by Gibb).

Peter and Mary were the parents of (*AACR:* 154, 156, 158): **2. Mary,** b. 14 March 1703, bapt. 14 May 1704; **3. Joseph,** b. 5 January 1705, bapt. 25 March 1706; and **4. Faith,** b. 12 July 1708, bapt. 25 April 1709.

3. Joseph Tebedo, son of Peter (1) and Mary, was born 5 January 1705 and was baptized at St. James Parish on 25 March 1756.

As Joseph "Tibbets' some time after March 1755 he testified that Mark Guishard was an honest man (*CMSP Black Books*, document 830).

Joseph Tippeto of St. James Parish was taxed as a bachelor worth between £100 and £300 at the vestry meetings of 7 June 1756, 5 July 1757, 11 July 1758, 8 July 1760, 14 July 1761, 13 July 1762, and 12 July 1763.

== 0 ==

The Temple Family
With Notes on the Munday and Powell Families

1. Thomas Temple was in Baltimore Co. by March 1693/4 when he absented himself from his master Thomas Brown (BACP G#1:217). He died in May 1710 and his wife had died in April He had married 1st, on 17 April 1699 Eleanor Laurenson who died in April 1709 (Reamy and Reamy. *St. George' Parish Registers:* 4, 14).

In November 1695 he was listed in Spesutia Hundred in the household of Samuel Brown (*IBCW:* 7).

On 4 March 1704 John Wattes of Patapsco River conveyed 50 a. *Temple's Claim,* part of *Waterford,* to Thomas Temple (BALR IR#PP: 131).

Thomas Temple died leaving a will dated 4 May 1710 and proved 8 June 1710. He left personalty to his daughters Ellinor and Johannah, and land to his daughter Susanna and her heirs. Aquila Paca and John Deavor witnessed the will. (MWB 13:51, abst. in *Md. Cal. of Wills* 3:170).

On 9 August 1711 John Webster filed an account of Temple's estate. He cited an inventory of £19.14.8, including 900 lbs. tob. He listed payments of £14.4.5 (INAC 33A:8).

Thomas was the father of (Reamy and Reamy, *St. George's Parish Register:* 5, 33): **2. Susanna,** b. 21 August 1699, m. Henry Munday; **3. Philissana,** m. John Powell; **4. Johanna,** b. 31 August 1707; and **5. Elinor,** b. 1 October 1709, m. Sherwood Lee on 3 November 1729 (For more on The Lee Family, see *Colonial Families of Maryland I*).

2. Susanna Temple, daughter of Thomas (1), was born 21 August 1699 at Rumley Creek (Reamy and Reamy, *St. George's Parish Register:* 5). As a servant of Daniel Scott, she was charged with bastardy at the August Court 1724, and was indicted at the November Court 1724, naming Abraham Whitaker as the father of her child; she was ordered to receive 15 lashes on her bare back (BACP IS B:17; IS&TW:438, IS&TW#4:42).

Susanna Temple married Henry Munday on 25 November 1725 (Reamy and Reamy, *St. George's Parish Register:* 35)

Abraham Whitaker and Susanna Temple were the parents of (Reamy, *St. George's Parish Register:* 35): **6. Michael Temple,** b. 11 July 1724.

Henry Munday and Susanna Temple were the parents of (Reamy and Reamy, *St. George's Parish Register:* 35, 41, 43, 45, 58): **7. John,** b. 25 October 1726; **8. Henry,** b. 28 April 1729; **9. Thomas,** b. 7 October 1730; **10. Sarah,** b. 2 May 1734 [*sic*], d. 26 March 1735; **11. John,** b. 29 September 1734 [*sic*]; and **12. James,** b. 2 March 1738.

3. Philissana Temple, daughter of Thomas (1), was not named in her father's will, but in June 1710 she was bound to John Webster (BACP IS#B: 137). She married John Powell in September 1725 (*SJSG:* 16). Powell married 2nd, by 7 August 1733, Elizabeth, widow of John Poteet, Sr.

Edward Wild, by his last will and testament, left *The Fork* to Phillis Temple who had married John Powell (BALR IS#L:110). On 29 October 1725 John Powell and his wife Phillis conveyed 150 a. *The Fork* to Solomon Armstrong (BALR IS#H: between 196 and 200). On 3 June 1731 Powell made good the deed to Solomon Armstrong dated 29 October 1725 (BALR IS#L: 108).

On 29 October 1725 Solomon Armstrong, with consent of his wife Mary, conveyed 125 a., being one-half of *Whitacre's Ridge* to John Powell (BALR IS#H: 196). On 2 June 1726 John Powell, tailor, with consent of his wife Phillis, conveyed 50 a., part of *Whitacre's Ridge* now called Whitaker's Venture, to Peter Whitaker (BALR IS#H: 390). On 18 March 1727/8 John Powell, staymaker, with consent of his wife Phillis, conveyed 75 a. part of *Whitacre's Ridge* to Charles Whitaker (BALR IS#I: 88).

On 5 March 1727/8 Charles Whitaker and wife Mary conveyed to John Powell 70 a. of *Jones' Addition* (BALR IS#I: 95). On 6 April 1731 Powell, a ropemaker, with the consent of his wife Phillis, conveyed the 70 a. to Sherwood Lee (BALR IS#L: 97).

On 8 November 1732 John Powell, planter, conveyed 100 a. being one-half of (*God's Providence* to Thomas Denbow (BALR IS#L: 303). On 7 August 1733 John Powell conveyed 100 a. part *Powell's Choice* to Jacob Bull. Powell's wife Elizabeth consented (BALR IS#I: 408). On 15 May 1734 John Powell and his wife Elizabeth, relict and widow of John Poteet, Sr., deceased, conveyed 179 a. *Hereford* to John Poteet, Jr. (BALR HWS#M: 55).

John and Phillisanna were the parents of (Reamy and Reamy, *St. George's Parish Register:* 27, 30, 83): **10. Hannah Penina Winifred,** b. 7 March 1722; **11. Eleanor** (Elioannah), b. 3 November 1726/7; **12. poss. Sarah,** who m. William Harman on 24 June 1744 (*SJSG:* 85, 122); **13. poss. Elizabeth,** who m. John Symonds on 30 March 1755 (*SJSG:* 98); and **14. poss. Patience,** who m. Moses Collins on 6 January 1749/50 (Reamy and Reamy, *St. George's Parish Register*: 83).

4. Johanna Temple, daughter of Thomas (1), was born 31 Aug 1707.

In June 1710, at age 3 she was bound to Mary, wife of Christopher Cox, and to Mary's daughter, Elizabeth, wife of Nicholas Day (BACP IS#B:137).

== 0 ==

The Tolley Family

1. Walter Tolley, Sr., was born about 1670 and died in Kent Co. in 1699. He married Elizabeth [-?-], who was born about 1673.

On 3 April 1685 Robert Chapman of Kent Co. made his will, leaving 220 a., part of *Hinchingham,* which he had bought from Edward Lloyd, to Thomas and William, children of Walter and Eliza Tally [*sic*]. If the brothers should die without issue the land was to go to their brother, Walter, Jr. He left personalty to John, George, and Mary Tally. Walter Tally, Sr., was name executor. M. Miller, Ebeneze Blackistone, Rich'd Louder, and Jno. Persifull witnessed the will (MWB 4:128, abst. in *Md. Cal. of Wills* 1:151).

As Walter Tally [*sic*] of Kent Co. he died leaving a will dated 23 April 1699 and proved 29 June 1699. To his two daughters Mary and Eliza he left land bought out of *Hyntingham Haven* equally. Son Thomas and his two daughters aforesaid were to have the residue of his estate equally. Hans Hanson, George Sturtun, Edward Skidmore, and Geo. Lumley witnessed the will (MWB 6:313, abst. in *Md. Cal. of Wills* 2:187.)

Colonial Families of Maryland II

William Smith and Benjamin Ricaud appraised the personal estate of Walter Tolley on 12 December 1699, and valued it at £259.12.6 (INAC 21:99). An undated administration account of Walter Tolley's estate was filed some time in 1702 or 1703 by Thomas Tolley, executor. His wife was deceased. Payments of £164.12.6 were deducted from the inventory and the balance was distributed among Mary Tolley, wife of Alexander Graves, Elizabeth Tolley, and Thomas Tolley (INAC 23:17).

Walter and Elizabeth were the parents of: **2. Thomas**, not yet 21 in 1685, d. 1732; **3. William**, not yet 21 in 1685, not mentioned in 1699; **4. Walter, Jr.**, b. by 1685, not mentioned in 1699; **5. John**, b. by 1685, not mentioned in 1699; **6. George**, b. by 1685, not mentioned in 1699; **7. Mary**, b. by 1685, m. by 1703, Alexander Graves; Mary died without issue by 9 March 1709, and her share of *Hinchingham* descended to her sister Elizabeth, wife of James Wessells (INAC 23:17; Kent Co. Court Land Records, hereafter cited as KELR, JSN#10:169); and **8. Elizabeth**, b. by 1685, m. in All Hallows Parish, Anne Arundel Co., on 10 September 1707, James Wessels (*AACR:*24).

2. Thomas Tolley, Sr., son of Walter (1), died in 1732 in Baltimore Co. He married Mary Freeborn, daughter of Thomas and Sarah (Howard) Freeborn. Mary was born about 1698 and died 1733.

Thomas Tolley was living with, but not married to Mary Freeborn between 1709 and 1716 and was repeatedly admonished for this by the Vestry of St. Paul's Parish, Kent Co. Various deponents testified that all of the children of Thomas and Mary were born out of wedlock except for the youngest child, James (*BDML* 2:836-837).

Tolley held a number of public offices. He represented Baltimore Co. in the Lower house of the Assembly, 1722-1724, and 1728-1731, Justice of Baltimore Co. 1729-1732, Commissioner of Joppa Town in 1724, and was appointed to purchase the land on which Baltimore Town was to be built (*BDML*: 2: 836).

Thomas Tolley, Gent., of Baltimore Co. died leaving a will dated 13 September 1732 and proved 9 October 1732. His wife Mary was named executrix, and was to have the use of the lot and house in Joppa for her life; then the rents and profits were to be divided among his three sons until Michael Miller, son of Michael and Elizabeth Miller arrived at the age of 21. Son Walter was to have one moiety of *Collins' Lot, Tracey's Level*, and part of *Long Point*. Son James was to have part of *Collins' Lot* and my dwelling plantation. Son Thomas was to have part of *Richardson's' Outlet*. The parson of St. John's Parish, Garrett Garrettson, and John Scott personalty. The residue of his personal estate was to be divided among his three sons. Edward Day, Elizabeth Goodwin, and Joseph Perry witnessed the will. The widow claimed her thirds (MWB 20:447, abst. in *Md. Cal. of Wills* 6:233).

At the time of his death, the total estimated value of his estate was £759.18.7 current money, including eight slaves, one servant, and books. He owned 1885 acres in Baltimore Co. including a house and lot in Joppa (*BDML* 2:837).

Mary Tolley, widow, of Baltimore Co. died leaving an undated will, which was filed 15 January 1733. She left personalty to her sons James, Thomas, and Walter, and daughter Elizabeth, wife of Michael Miller. John Scott, executor, was to have charge of son James. Jos. Middlemore, Will Cawthren, and Thomas Gittings witnessed the will (MWB 21:34, abst. in *Md. Cal. of Wills* 7:74).

Thomas and Mary were the parents of: **9. Walter**, d. 1782; **10. Thomas**, died leaving a will dated 17 January 1733 and proved 10 August 1734. He left his brother James, son and heir of Thomas Tolley, deceased, his entire estate. If James died without issue, his estate was to pass to his brother Walter. He mentioned personalty left by the will of his mother. He also mentioned his sister Elizabeth, wife of Michael Miller. Richard

207

Caswell, Joseph Perry, William Powell and Joshua Starkey witnessed the will (MWB 21:193, abst. in Md. Cal. of Wills 7:104); **11. Elizabeth**, m. Michael Miller; and **12. James**, d. 17 October 1744 (*SJSG:* 62), m. Mary Watkins.

9. Walter Tolley, son of Thomas (2), and Mary (Freeborn) Tolley, died by 6 June 1783. He married, 1st, Mary Garrettson on 20 December 1735. Mary died 19 July 1749. He married 2nd, Martha Hall in St. George's Parish on 22 December 1751 (*SJSG:* 29, 52, 53, 7).

Walter Tolley represented Baltimore County in the General Assembly in 1751 and from 1754 to1757; he was a member of the 5th Convention of Maryland in 1775. He was on the vestry and was a Churchwarden of St. John's Parish, Baltimore County (*BDML* 2: 837).

Walter Tolley died leaving a will dated 26 February 1781 and proved 6 June 1783. He named his son Edward Carvill Tolley who was to have *Saint George's*, which was then to pass to Edward Carvill Tolley's son James Tolley. He named his daughter Ann wife of Aquila Hall and his grandson Walter Tolley Hall. He named his grandsons Walter Goldsmith Presbury and Walter Worthington. He named his daughter Sophia, wife of William Allender; his granddaughters Martha Tolley; Martha Susanna Hall, Martha Worthington, Mary Allender, Eliz. Allender; his grandsons Thomas Tolley Worthington, James Tolley Worthington. Josias Hall, James Phillips, Henry Hart, and Mark Brown Sappington witnessed the will. He added a codicil dated 22 December 1782. There was a second undated codicil. Edwd. Green, Richard Jones, and Mary Hart witnessed this codicil (BAWB 3:507).

Martha Tolley posted an administration bond for £10,000 on 6 June 1783. Benj. Rumsey, Edw. C. Tolley, and Aquila Hall were sureties (BAAB 6:63).

Walter and Mary (Garrettson) were the parents of: (*SJSG*: 22, 52, 79, 100, 103): **13. Elizabeth**, b. 16 November 1736, d. 1786, m. George Gouldsmith Presbury on 10 June 1756 or 1 July 1758; **14. Thomas**, b. 15 October 1738, d. 15 April 1743; **15. Mary**, b. 21 March 1740, d. 1777, m. Samuel Worthington on 17 January 1759; **16. Sophia**, b. 3 March 1742, m. William Allender; **17. Walter**, b. 10 May 1744, d. 1776; **18. James**, b. 20 June 1746, d. 1768, a student at law; **19. Thomas Garrettson**, b. 29 June 1748.

Walter and Martha were the parents of (*SJSG:* 74): **20. Edward Carvil**, born 14 October 1753 (Reamy and Reamy, *St. George's Parish Register*: 76); married 1st, Cordelia Hall, and 2nd, in 1784 Elizabeth Worthington; **21. Martha**, b. 21 May 1755, d. 3 June 1755; **22. Ann**, b. 7 July 1756, d. 1830, m. Aquila Hall; and **23. Martha**, b 17 September 1758.

== 0 ==

The Tongue Family

1. Thomas Tongue died by May 1748. He married Mary, daughter of James Heighe. She married, 2nd, Sabrett Sollers.

On 26 July 1725 James Heighe of Calvert Co. made a will naming his daughter Althea, and his grandsons James Tongue and James Bourne, as well as his son-in-law Sabritt Sollers (MWB 18:419).

On 5 May 1748 Thomas Tongue's estate was administered by Mary Tongue, now wife of Sabrett Sollers of Baltimore Co. Payments came to £464.6.11. The account mentioned Thomas Tongue, "the only and legal representative" (MDAD 24:299).

Thomas and Mary were the parents of: **2. James**, d. before 1748; and **3. Thomas**, "the only legal" (or living) heir of his father in 1748.

2. James Tongue, son of Thomas (1) and Mary (Heighe), was born by July 1725, and died by November 1746. He married Anne [-?-], who evidently married, 2nd, on 29 August 1747, in St. James Parish, Nathaniel Dare (*AACR:* 169).

James Tongue appraised the estate of Morgan Jones on 6 October 1746 and was dead by 26 November 1746 (MINV 34:300).

James Tongue's own estate was appraised by Jacob Franklin and James Deale on 3 June 1747 and valued at £529.0.3 Nathaniel and Joshua Chew signed as next of kin. Mrs. Ann Dare, formerly Ann Tongue, did not file the inventory until 29 October 1765 (MINV 88:268B). A second inventory totaling £143.1.8 was appraised on 26 October 1765 by James Deale and James Franklin, and valued at £143.1.8. Richard and Joseph Chew signed as kin, and Mrs. Ann Dare, the administratrix, filed the inventory on 9 September 1766 (MINV 90:246).

Mrs. Ann Dare administered James Tongue's estate on 10 September 1766. She cited the two inventories, appraised in 1747 and 1765 (proving that both inventories, 18 years apart, pertained to the same James Tongue), and made payments totaling £105.11.7. The representatives were the widow and Thomas Tongue (MDAD 54:303).

The estate of "Thomas Tongue" [almost certainly an erroneous transcription for James Tongue] of Anne Arundel Co. was distributed in December 1766, with a balance of £672.1.11 by Mrs. Ann Dare, administratrix. The representatives were unknown to the Prerogative Court Office (BFD 4:169).

One wonders why James' widow Ann waited so long to file the inventory and distribute the balance. Could it have been because the children were minors for part of the time? Did her second husband, Nathaniel Dare have a part to play? Nathaniel Dare died by 31 August 1766 when Benjamin Harrison and John Weems appraised his estate at £1089.3.8. Samuel and P. Chew signed as next of kin, and Ann Dare, the executrix, filed the inventory on 17 November 1766 (MINV 89:209).

James Tongue and Anne were the parents of at least two children, born in St. James Parish, AA Co. (*AACR:* 169): **4. Mary**, b. 14 February 1743/4; and **5. Thomas**, b. 29 May 1746.

5. Thomas Tongue, son of James (3) and Anne Tongue, was b. 29 May 1746 (*AARP:* 169), and died 6 February 1823, aged 76 years, 8 mos., 28 days. He was buried at St. James Church, Herring Creek. He married, 1st, Elizabeth Roberts on 1 September 1769 (*AARP:* 200). Thomas Tongue of Anne Arundel Co. deposed in 1785, giving his age as 39 (MCIIR 14:505). Elizabeth Roberts was born 5 October 1748, and died 12 June 1821, aged 72 years, 8 days and 7 mos. She was also buried at Herring Creek. Thomas Tongue married, 2nd, by 1771 Elizabeth, daughter of Thomas Morgan of Calvert Co. (MDTP 44:37). [**Author's comment:** Is it possible that Elizabeth Morgan m. 1st, [-?-] Roberts, and 2nd, Thomas Tongue?]

A Thomas Tongue was commissioned First Lieutenant in the South River Battalion on 15 February 1776 and served in Col. John Weems' Battalion of Militia in 1778. He or another Thomas Tongue was drafted in October 1780 to serve until 10 December 1780 (*AARP:* 200).

On 10 November 1825 Thomas Tongue, executor, distributed the estate of Thomas Tongue. Thirds of the balance were distributed to Ann Collinson, Harriet Waters, and Elizabeth Allein (Anne Arundel Co. Distribution Book TH#1:81).

Thomas Tongue and Elizabeth were the parents of: **6. Elizabeth**, m. by AAML dated 8 January 1790 Benjamin Allein, who died by 8 July 1816 when Elizabeth Allein, and Thomas Tongue, Jr., execs., distributed the estate (Anne Arundel Co., Distribution Book JG#3:38); **7. Mary**, m. by AAML of 20 April 1795 Thomas McPherson; **8. Harriet**, m. by AAML of 23 March 1809 Jacob F. Waters; **9. James Tongue**, M.D., m. by AAML of 9 June 1803, Anne Cowman; **10. Ann**, m. by AAML of 20 June 1819 John Collison; and **11. Thomas**, m. by AAML of 3 January 1809 Anne Harrison.

11. Thomas Tongue, son of Thomas (5), was buried 3 January 1826. He married by AAML dated 3 January 1809 Anne, daughter of Benjamin Harrison. She may have been the Mrs. Anne Tongue, adult, who was baptized 11 November 1831 ("St. James Parish Register, 1663-1886).

In July 1826 William and Richard Simmons, James Owens, and John Sellman filed the following petition in the Court of Chancery, citing Thomas I. Hall, administrator of Thomas Tongue, Benjamin Tongue, Elizabeth Tongue, Sarah Tongue, Thomas Tongue, John N. Watkins, and William Ennis. The complainants stated that before his death, Thomas Tongue was indebted to them. Thomas Tongue left the following children: Benjamin Tongue, Elizabeth Tongue, Sarah Tongue, and Thomas Tongue, who were all infants under the age of 21 (MCHP 11300, folder no. 1).

On 18 October 1826 Anna Tongue, widow of Thomas Tongue, filed a petition admitting the truth of the petition of the claimants. She mentioned her four helpless and dependent children, and that a short time prior to the death of her husband, she lost her father, Benjamin Harrison, who had devised various property to her, by his will. She asked that her friend Robert Garner be appointed trustee to oversee the sale of the real estate (MCHP 11300, folder no. 19).

On 24 January 1827 Anna Tongue, widow of Thomas Tongue, Jr., petitioned that the real estate of her husband should be sold subject to her dower, and she asked that a commission be issued to lay out her dower land (MCHP 1130, folder no. 6).

Thomas Tongue was the father of: **12. Benjamin H.; 13. Elizabeth; 14. Sarah**, baptized as an adult at St, James on 30 July 1833; and **15. Thomas**.

12. Benjamin H. Tongue, son of Thomas, Jr. (11) and Anne (Harrison), was born 10 July 1810, and died 27 April 1888. He was buried at St. James Parish.

The wife of Benjamin Tongue has not been identified but could she be the Ellen Tongue, adult, baptized 11 November 1831 (St. James Parish Register).

A search of published newspaper and marriage records for Anne Arundel, Baltimore, Frederick, Montgomery, and Prince George's Counties has failed to reveal a marriage for a Benjamin Tongue. A search of Anne Arundel County Land Records, 1839 to 1851 has failed to reveal any land sales by Benjamin Tongue and wife.

In 1850 Benjamin Tongue, are 37, farmer, owning $6000.00 real estate lived in the 8th District of Anne Arundel Co., with Mrs. Tongue, b. c1816, his (mother?) Annie and (bro.?) Thomas R., as well as the three children listed below.

Mrs. Ben Tongue was buried 29 March 1852 (St. James Parish Burial Register).

Benjamin Tongue and his wife were the parents of: **16. Henry**, b. about 1844; **17. Mary**, b. about 1846; and **18. James**, b. about 1848.

Unplaced:
John Tonge was in Maryland by 12 January 1664 when Bartholomew Phillips made a will naming his wife Margaret, daughter Eliza Phillips, and son in law John Tonge (MWB 1:236).

John Tonge of St. Clement's Manor, St. Mary's Co., died leaving a will dated 16 August 1686 and proved 1 September 1688. He named Penelope Hayden, daughter of Francis Hayden, who was to have his entire estate. Thomas Aude, Ellianor Chester, and Owen Bradee witnessed the will (MWB 6:9).

Thomas Tonge was listed as a creditor of John Greeniffe of Baltimore Co. in the administration account of the latter's estate filed 11 July 1710 (INAC 31:271).

Thomas Tonng [sic] of Calvert Co. died by 10 May 1721 when his personal property was appraised at £159.10.0 by Thomas Billingsley and Abraham Downe (MINV 5:67).

Thomas Tinge (Tongue), of Calvert Co. died by 10 May 1722 when his estate was administered by Mary Tinge. An inventory of £597.6.2 was mentioned and payments came to £48.4.10 (MDAD 3:340).

William Tongue was in Talbot Co. by 6 January 1685/6 when he witnessed the will of Roger Wedill (MWB 4:300).

==0==

The Tucker Family

1. Seaborn Tucker, was born c1672, bapt. 25 September 1698 in St. James' Parish, and died about 1753 (*AACR:*150; *AAMR:*237). He married by 1695 Dorothy [-?-], administratrix of Charles Harrington of Calvert Co. (INAC 10:447; 17:74).

On 17 September 1703 Seaborn Tucker made his mark as one of those signing a warrant of resurvey granted to Christopher Vernon (AALR WT#2:71). On 24 August 1703 he and Richard Tucker both made their marks on another warrant of survey (AALR WT#2:98).

On 15 April 1703 John Thomas and wife Jane conveyed 200 a. *Chevy Chase* to Seaborn Tucker; Jane Thomas gave power of attorney to William Reid to acknowledge above sale as her "infirmity, impotence, and old age" made it impossible for her to travel to the county court (BALR HW#2: 227, 229). On 1 July 1712 Tucker, of Anne Arundel Co. planter, conveyed 200 a., being one-half of *Chevy Chase*, to Samuel Groom of London, merchant (BALR TR#A: 217).

On 29 September 1728 Isaac Webster and Jacob Giles conveyed 183 a. *Arabia Petrea* to Seaborn Tucker (BALR HWS#1-A: 126). On 6 June 1734 John White, carpenter, conveyed 100 a. *Bachelor's Beginning* to Seaborn Tucker; White's wife Priscilla consented (BALR HWS#M: 69).

Tucker purchased 100 a. *Herring Creek* and 25 a. *Connant's Chance* from Francis Holland, planter, on 1 September 1735 (AALR RD#2:279).

Seaborn Tucker of Anne Arundel Co. died leaving a will dated 22 June 1752 and proved 12 March 1753. His daughter Ann Birckhead was to have his dwelling plantation, and all his lands. Son John was to have the sterling money in John Buchanan hands to buy him a piece of land, and on his death to grandson Seaborn Tucker. Son Jacob was to have a Negro girl Dighder. Granddaughter Ann Birckhead was to have a Negro girl Love. The residue was to be equally divided to John Tucker, Mary Car[?], and Ann Birckhead. His son-in-law Samuel Birckhead was named executor Neh[emiah] Birckhead, Alexander Frazer, and Elender Fowler witnessed the will, on 12 March 1753, affirmed by Birckhead. one of the people called Quaker, and sworn to by Fraizer. (MWB 28:434 abst. by Gibb).

Robert Ward and Lewis Lewin appraised the estate of Seaborn Tucker at £605.2.9 on 25 May 1753. John Tucker and Jacob Tucker signed as next of kin. Samuel Birckhead, a Quaker, and the executor, filed the inventory on 18 June 1753 (MINV 54:38).

Seaborn and Dorothy were the parents of the following born in St, James Parish, Anne Arundel Co. (*AACR:*146, 149, 150, 152, 155, 157, 183): **2. Ann,** b. 12 February 1695, bur. 17 August 1699; **3. John,** twin, b. 17 August 1698, bapt. 25 September 1698; **4. Jacob,** twin, b. 17 August 1698, bapt. 25 September 1698; **5. Robert,** twin, b. 4 December 1700, not named in the will; **6. Mary,** twin, b. 4 December 1700; **7.Seaborn,** b. 2 October 1704, bapt. 24 May 1713; **8. Susanna,** b. 19 June 1707, not named in the will; and **9. Margaret,** bapt. 24 May 1713, not named in the will.

3. John Tucker, twin son of Seaborn (1) and Dorothy, was born 17 August 1698, and bapt. 25 September 1698. He died by 14 June 1757.

Tucker died leaving a will dated 4 February 1757 and proved 14 June 1757. He named his children John, Seaborn, Mary, Ann, Jacob, and Charles Tucker. John was to have land in Calvert Co. called *Hambleton's Park.* Son Seaborn was to have land in Anne Arundel Co. called *Edmonton's Range.* John Tucker was named executor. John Griffis, Samuel Stone, and Samuel Robertson witnessed the will (MWB 30:300, abst. in *Md. Cal. of Wills* 11:167).

Robert Ward and Lewis Lewin appraised the estate at £118.19.4. Seaborn Tucker and Isaac Tucker signed as next of kin, and John Tucker filed the inventory on 18 October 1758 (MINV 64:506.

John Tucker administered the estate on 25 May 1758. After citing the inventory of £119.19.4, he listed payments of £76.2.11, including 2200 lbs. tobacco (MDAD 42:197).

John Tucker, executor, distributed the estate, worth £118.19.4, on 25 May 1758. Seaborn Tucker and Mary Tucker were legatees. The balance was distributed equally to Ann, Jacob, Charles, Isaac, and Mary Tucker (Distributions 2:104).

John Tucker was the father of: **10. John, 11. Seaborn, 12. Mary, 13. Ann, 14. Jacob,** and **15. Charles.**

4. Jacob Tucker, twin son of Seaborn (1) and Dorothy, was born 17 August 1698, and bapt. 25 September 1698. He may be the Jacob who died in Calvert Co. by 9 February 1764. He married Cassandra [-?-].

Tucker died leaving a will dated 15 December 1763 and proved 9 February 1764. His son Benjamin was to have certain slaves. His grandson Benjamin Tucker was to have land after the decease of the testator's wife. Granddaughter Elizabeth Tucker was to have slaves. The balance of his estate was to go to his two grandchildren. His wife was to be executrix. Daniel Tibbens, William Hickman, and Francis Woolfe witnessed the will (MWB 32:49, abst. in *Md. Cal. of Wills* 13:9).

In 1764 William Allnutt and William Hickman appraised the estate of Jacob Tucker at £354.7.2. Joseph Parker and Jacob Tucker signed as next of kin. Cassandra Tucker, the executrix, filed the inventory (MINV 84:137). Cassandra Tucker, executrix, filed an account of the estate on 16 October 164. She cited the inventory as given and listed payments of £28.17.0 MDAD 51:326).

Jacob and Cassandra were the parents of: **16. Benjamin.**

7. Seaborn Tucker, son of Seaborn (1) and Dorothy, was born 2 October 1704, bapt. 24 May 1713, and died 1740. On 2 April 1730 he married Margaret Cobb, daughter of James and Rebecca (Reamy, and Reamy, *St. George's Parish Register:* 34). Margaret married, 2nd. Thomas Litton, Jr. (See **The Litton Family** elsewhere in this work).

Colonial Families of Maryland II

On 29 September 1728 Isaac Webster and Jacob Giles conveyed 183 a. *Arabia Petrea* to Seaborn Tucker (BALR HWS#1-A: 126).

Seaborne Tucker witnessed the will of John Hawkins of Baltimore Co. on 19 November 1732 (MWB 20:750).

Margaret Tucker, administratrix, filed an inventory of Seaborn Tucker's personal estate on 7 November 1740. Richard Dallam and Thomas Litton appraised his goods and chattels on 6 October 1740, and valued them at £99.5.3. Gregory Farmer, Sr., and Charles Jones signed as next of kin (MINV 25:332).

Thomas Litton, Jr., and his wife Margaret, filed an account of Seaborn Tucker's estate on 30 September 1742. They cited an inventory of £74.16.2, and listed payments of £99.5.3 (MDAD 19:193).

Seaborn and Margaret were the parents of (Reamy and Reamy, *St. George's Parish Register*, pp. 34, 47, 53): **17. Jacob,** b. 22 May 1731; **18. Susanna,** b. 15 April 1734; m. Mordecai Crawford on 16 September 1750 (*SJSG:* 92); and **19. Margaret,** b. 28 August 1736.

11. Seaborn Tucker, son of John (3) is believed to be the John Tucker who died in Rowan Co, N.C., in 1805, as Seaborn 'Tacker.' As Seaborn 'Tuckin' he married Elizabeth Hitchcock in Baltimore Co. in 1762 (*SJSG:* 109).

Seaborn and Elizabeth were the parents of the following children named Tacker (Henry C. Peden, Jr. *Marylanders to Carolina, Westminster: Family Line Publications:* 185): **20. William; 21. Susannah,** b. 1770 in Baltimore Co., m. Isaac Morris in 1790 in N.C.; **22. John,** m. Elizabeth [-?-]; **23. Hannah,** b. in Rowan Co., N.C., m. William English; **24. Joshua,** m. Susannah Kernut; **25. Nancy,** m. William H. McCreery; and **26. Jacob Fisher,** m. Anna English Tomlinson.

Unplaced:
John Tucker of the Swamp died leaving a will dated 21 January 1782 and proved 4 June 1783. His wife Rebecca was to have all his lands and tenements for her widowhood, and then to his son Thomas Tucker and his heirs and assigns. Wife Rebecca was to have all of his personal estate during her widowhood, and after then to my younger children: James Sole[?], John, William, and Richard and daughters Elizabeth, Mary, Ann, Rebecca, and Margaret. Wife Rebecca was to be sole executrix. J. Hamilton, Thomas Tucker, Richard Bryant, and Matthew Beard witnessed the will (AAWB TG#1: 117-118)
John Tucker, of Elk Ridge advertised that his wife Sarah had eloped (*Maryland Journal and Baltimore Advertiser* 24 February 1784).
Richard Tucker, a young man, aged 24, was lost in his own schooner on Thus., 17th inst. Susanna Tucker, his mother, living in The Swamp, near the Mouth of the West River, offered a reward for the return of his body (Annapolis *Maryland Gazette* 8 December 1774).
William Tucker and Ann Palmer were married on 26 December 1769. William and Clement Beck were married on 9 Feb 1762 (*SJSG:* 105, 108).

==0==

The Turner Family

NB: Unless otherwise noted, the material in this report is from William W. Turner, 1251 CR 305, East Bayshore Drive, Palacios, TX, 77465.

1. Matthew Turner was born about 1710, giving his age as about 23 in 1733. From Sussex, he was transported from Newgate Prison, and arrived in Maryland on 19 April 1733, on the ship *Patapscoe,* Capt Darby Lux (*KPMV:* 56-58).

Matthew and Sarah Maybury were married on 14 (or 15) August 1734 in St. Mary Ann's Parish, Cecil Co. (*CECH:* 58, 61).

Turner died by 14 October 1757 in Baltimore Co., when Sarah Turner, administrator, filed an account of his estate. She cited an inventory of £146.14.10 and cited payments to Nicholas Rogers, Joseph Ensor, Dr. William Lyon and John Ensor, Jr. Matthew left four children: Frances, of age, Joseph, aged 15, Matthew, aged 7, and Sarah, aged 5 (MDAD 41:243).

Matthew and Sarah were the parents of the following children (*CECH:*60; Reamy and Reamy, *St. Paul's Parish Register:* 17): **2. Francis**, b. 24 Dec 1735 in St. Mary Ann's Parish, Cecil Co. **3, Joseph**, b; 8 June 1742; **4. Rachel**, b. 16 January 1744: was not mentioned in 1757; **5. Jacob**, b. 14 November 1747: as not mentioned in 1757; **6. Matthew**, b. 11 April 1750; and **7. Sarah**, b. about 1752.

2. Francis Turner, son of Matthew (1) and Sarah, was born 24 December 1735 in St. Mary Ann's Parish, Cecil Co. (*CECH:* 60). At age 36 he deposed on 5 September 1772, naming his father Matthew Turner (BAEJ:OS: Long, Robert). He married by 1758 Sarah [-?-]. He may have married 2nd, by 1796, Ann [-?-].

In 1768 he signed a petition in favor of moving the county seat to Baltimore Town (*IBCP:* 27). In 1773 he and Matthew Turner were taxables in Back River Lower Hundred. Francis was listed there again in 1776 (*IBCP:* 55, 101). He or another Francis Turner was listed as a taxable in Patapsco Hundred, St. Paul's Parish, in 1774 (*IBCP:* 105).

Francis Turner was a Non-juror to the Oath of allegiance in 1778 (*BARP:* 277).

In 1783 Francis Turner was listed in Patapsco Lower Hundred with nine white inhabitants in his household. He did not own land (Carothers, *1783 Tax List of Baltimore County:* 86).

In 1790 A Francis Turner was listed as head of a family in Baltimore Town with two free white males over 16, one free white male under 16, two free white females, and two slaves. Another Francis Turner was listed as head of a family in Baltimore Town, with one free white male over 16, two free white males under 16, and one free white female (*1790 Census of Maryland:* 21, 22).

Francis Turner died by 5 Dec 1794 leaving an estate unsettled and in the possession of Ann Turner and Robert Turner. Francis Turner, son of the deceased, petitioned the court to attach the two people, who are living on the Philadelphia Road about two miles from town (BPET, Francis Turner, 1795).

Francis Turner died by 15 September 1796 when Ann Turner administered the estate. She retained £10.7.6 as her widow's thirds, and shares of £2.11.10½ each were paid to Francis Turner, Joshua Turner, John Murray, Nathaniel Turner, Caleb Turner, William Futz, George Wilson, and Robert Turner (BAAD 12:189).

Francis and Sarah were the parents of (Reamy and Reamy, *St. Paul's Parish Register:* 21): **8. Sarah**, b. 28 ---1758, m. John Murray by license dated 13 November 1779 (BAML); **9. Elizabeth**, b. 20 April 1761; m. William Fitch by license dated 9 January 1790 (BAML); **10. Ann**, m. George Wilson by license dated 6 October 1792 (BAML); **11. Francis; 12. Joshua; 13. Nathaniel; 14. Caleb;** and **15. Robert**.

3. Joseph Turner, son of Matthew (1) and Sarah, was born 8 June 1742 in St. Paul's Parish, Baltimore Co. He married Chloe [-?-]. She may well have been a Durham.

On 12 March 1770 Cloey Turner and Peter Brunts signed the inventory of Abraham Durham of Baltimore Co. as two of the next of kin (MINV 103:55). In 1773 and again in 1776 Joseph Turner was a taxable in Back River Lower Hundred (*IBCP:* 55,101).

Joseph may be the Joseph Turner who did not take the Oath of Fidelity to the State of Maryland in 1778 (*BARP:* 277).

After the Revolutionary War Joseph and Chloe moved to Nelson or Hardin Co., Kentucky. Seven of their children went with them, but their daughter Rachel and her husband did not make the trip.

Joseph and Chloe were the parents of he following children, only one of whom, Rachel, had her birth recorded (Reamy and Reamy, *St. Paul's Parish Register:* 23): **16. Rachel**, b. 14 June 1765; **17. Matthew**, b. 1770; **18. Durham**, b. 1773; **19. Nancy Jane**, b. 1777; **20. Mary (Polly)**, b. 1779; **21. Joseph, Jr.**, b. 1782; **22. Francis**, b. 1785; and **23. Sally**, b. 1787.

6. Matthew Turner, son of Matthew (1) and Sarah, was born 11 April 1750.

In 1773 he was listed with Francis Turner as a taxable in Back River Lower Hundred (*IBCP:* 55).

He may be the Matthew Turner who was a private in Capt. Deems' Company, 7th Md. Regiment, on 10 December 1776. However, he was a Non-Juror to the Oath of Allegiance in 1778 (*BARP:* 277).

In 1783 Matthew Turner, with five white persons was listed in the tax list for Middle River Upper and Back River Upper hundreds, but he did not own any land (Carothers, *1783 Tax List of Baltimore County:* 60).

In 1790 a Matthew Turner was listed in Baltimore Co. as head of a family with one white male over 16, two white males under 16, and three free white females (*1790 Census of Maryland:* 32).

== 0 ==

The Ward Family of Anne Arundel County

1. Robert Ward died in Anne Arundel Co. by November 1709. He is probably the Robert Ward who married Susannah [-?-]. She was buried in All Hallows Parish on 6 February 1698/9. He was buried there on 8 September 1709 (*AACR:* 8, 30).

A Robert Ward was transported about 1663 (MPL 7:491). He or another one was transported about 1670 (MPL 16:79, 190). Yet another Robert Ward was transported to MD by 1665 (MPL DD: 281, 8:243). [Since there is only one Robert Ward appearing in seventeenth century Maryland, these events may all pertain to the same individual--RWB].

Robert was in Anne Arundel Co. by 15 October 1677 when he witnessed the will of Thomas Besson, Sr. (MWB 10:42, abst. in *Md. Cal. of Wills* 1:214). On 8 January 1677 Edward Cox, son of Edward Cox, deceased, conveyed him 100 a. called *Coxby Land* (AALR IH#3:33). On 6 February 1682 Edward Selby the Elder conveyed Ward 492 a. of land near *Selby's Marsh* (AALR IH#3:47).

On 30 May 1692 Ward was left personalty by the will of John Wagstaffe of Anne Arundel Co. (MWB 2:221, abst. in *Md. Cal. of Wills* 2:47).

Robert Ward of Anne Arundel Co. died leaving a will dated 25 July 1709 and proved 3 November 1709. His second son Robert was to have the dwelling plantation *Coxby* and 50 a. *Selby's Marsh*. Sons William, Allen, Samuel, and Edward, and daughters Ann Ward and Eliza Leeke were left personalty. Son John was named executor Son

Robert and daughter Eliza Leeke were left the residue of his estate. Thomas and Susanna Gassaway witnessed the will (MWB 12, pt. 2:193, abst. in *Md. Cal. of Wills* 5:9).

Stephen Warman and Jesse Lewis appraised on his personal estate at £221.14.6, on 3 December 1709; Robert Ward and Henry Leeke signed as next of kin. The inventory was filed on 15 February 1709/10. Warman and Lewis appraised a second inventory on 29 June 1711, showing a value of £123.0.5 (INAC 31:48, 32B:150).

John Ward filed an administration account on 4 June 1709 [*sic*]. He showed payments totaling £32.18.3 (INAC 32C:54).

In an undated document John Ward, Robert Ward, and Henry Leeke, planters posted bond that they would pay Edward Ward, one of the orphans of Edward Ward, deceased, the sum of £20.0.0 when he became 21 years of age (AALR IB#2:272).

Robert Ward was the father of [by which wife has not been determined] (*AACR:* 10, 11, 30): **2. John; 3. Robert; 4. William**, son of Robert, was buried 3 September 1709; **5. Allen; 6. Samuel; 7. Edward**, bapt. 20 February 1700 in All Hallows Parish; **8. Sarah**, bur. 13 January 1700 in All Hallows Parish; **9. Ann**, m. James Disney, b. 1695, d. 1731; and **10. Eliza**, m. [Henry?] Leeke.

2. John Ward, son of Robert (1), was probably the eldest son as he was named executor. He married 1st, Elizabeth Gover on 20 February 1700 in All Hallows Parish. He married 2nd, Elizabeth Phillips in All Hallows Parish on 5 Xber [December] 1706 (*AACR:* 13, 22).

On 14 August 1707 John Ward, with Robert and Edward Ward [his father and brother?] posted bond that he would pay Rachel Gover, daughter of Robert Gover, the sum of £243.17 when she came of age (AALR WT#2:521).

Robert Grundy of Oxford, Talbot Co., for £140 sold 200 a. *Broughton Ashley* to John Ward on 10 October 1702 (AALR WT#1:57). John Ward, eldest son and heir of Robert Ward conveyed to Robert Ward, the younger son of Robert Ward 100 a. *Coxby,* and 50 a. *Selby Marsh*, for the sum of £80 (AALR IB#2:191). On 4 March 1730/1, John Ward, for love and affection, conveyed to his son John, *Ward's Care.* Elizabeth, wife of John, released her dower rights (AALR IH#TI#1:119).

Elizabeth Ward, Quaker, filed an administration account on 8 July 1745. She cited an inventory of £576.2.9 and listed payments of £9.16.8. The unnamed representatives were all of age (MDAD 21:300).

John and Elizabeth (Phillips) were the parents of the following children, whose births are recorded in All Hallows Parish (*AACR:* 27, 30, 201): **11. Phillizanna**, b. 29 9ber [October] 1707; **12. John**, bapt. 8 June 1712; and **13. Robert**, bapt. 24 July 1720.

3. Robert Ward, Jr., son of Robert (1), married Rebecca Cox on 5 May 1706 in All Hallow's Parish (*AACR:* 22).

Robert Ward was buried on 18 March 1719 in All Hallows Parish (*AACR*: 201). He left a will dated 8 February 1719/20 and proved 19 May 1720. He named his wife Rebecca executrix and left her the dwelling plantation of *Coxbie* and parts of *Selby's Marsh*. Son Robert was to have *Coxbie,* part of *Selby's Marsh*, and after wife Rebecca's decease he was to pay his brothers and sisters (unnamed) £12.0.0. His wife and children (unnamed) were to have the residue of his estate equally. James Monat [Mouat?], William Copland, and George Miller witnessed the will (MWB 16:59, abst. in *Md. Cal. of Wills* 5:9).

John Watkins and John Brewer appraised the personal estate of Robert Ward on 8 May 1720, valuing his goods and chattels at £364.13.11. Samuel Ward and Edward Ward signed as next of kin (MINV 4:262).

Rebecca Ward filed an administration account on 19 June 1721, citing an inventory of £364.13.11, and listing payments of £46.16.4 (MDAD 3:378).

Robert and Rebecca were the parents of the following children, born in All Hallows Parish, AA Co. (*AACR*::23, 27, 29, 32, 33, 39, 46, 200): **14. Robert**, b. 13 February 1706, bapt. 20 April 1707; **15. Edward**, b. 8 January 1708, bapt. 22 April 1709; **16. Avice**, b. 22 April 1711, bapt. 29 May 1711; **17. John**, bapt. 8 October 1713, bur. 8 December 1713; **18. Avis**, b. 28 November 1714, bapt. 18 January 1714/5; m. Francis Day, son of Francis, Sr., on 5 February 1732/2 in All Hallows Parish; **19. John**, b. 9 April 1717; **20. Rebecca**, twin, b. 5 August 1719, bapt. 29 September 1719; and **21. Elizabeth**, twin, b. 5 August 1719, bapt. 29 September 1719.

6, Samuel Ward, son of Robert (1), was the subject of bond for £24 posted by John Ward, Robert Ward, and Henry Leeke, on 11 March 1712 that John Ward promised to pay to Samuel the sum of ?12 left him by Robert Ward when he attained the age of 21 (AALR IB#2:272).

7. Edward Ward, son of Robert (1), was bapt. 20 February 1700 in All Hallows Parish. In an undated bond for £40 John Ward, Robert Ward, and Henry Leeke promised that John Ward wold pay to Edward, one of the orphans of Robert Ward, the sum of ?20 left him by Robert Ward when he arrived at the age of 21 (AALR IB#2:271).

13. Robert Ward, son of John Ward (2), was born 14 July 1720 in All Hallows Parish, Anne Arundel, Maryland, and died by 12 June 1781. He married Elizabeth [-?-], who died about 12 January 1790.

On 29 September 1746, Ephraim Gover of Anne Arundel Co. conveyed 50 a. of *Broughton Ashley* to Robert Ward (AALR RB#2:280).

Robert Ward died leaving a will dated 31 May 1774 and proved 12 June 1781. His wife was to have his dwelling house, land, and one-third clear of his personal estate including a Negro girl named Suck. Son John was to have 400 a. in Baltimore Co. called *The New Tavern*, and a Negro boy named Dick. After John's death his son Robert was to have 200 a. of the aforesaid land. Sons Robert and William to have all other lands, called *Broughton Ashley*. Son Robert to have a Negro boy named Ted Crobe. Son William to have a Negro boy named Sambo. Daughter Sarah Plummer to have a Negro girl named Doll; daughter Eliza Talbott to have a Negro girl named Grace; daughter Mary Ward to have a Negro girl named Tamer; and daughter Ann Ward to have a Negro girl named Rachel. The remainder of his personal estate was to go to his second son Robert, third son William, his eldest daughter Sarah Plummer, second daughter Eliz'th Talbott, third daughter Eleanor Robertson, fourth daughter Mary Ward, and fifth daughter Ann Ward. Morgan Jones, Nehemiah Birckhead, and Francis Birckhead witnessed the will (AAWB TG#1:20-21).

Robert and Elizabeth were the parents of: **22. William; 23. Sarah**, m. Abraham Plummer; they declared their intention to marry on 29 d., 1 m., 1762 (*AAMR:* 185). **24. Mary; 25. Ann; 26. Robert; 27. Eleanor**, m. [-?-] Robertson; **28. Elizabeth**, b. about 1742 in of Calvert Co., Md., m. Daniel Talbott on 23 February 1764 in Calvert Co., Md.; and **29. John**, m. Rachel Talbott on 27 July 1764, daughter of Joseph Talbott and Mary Birckhead (*AAMR*: 240).

14. Robert Ward, son of Robert (3) and Elizabeth, was born b. 13 February 1706, bapt. 20 April 1707.He had inherited *Coxby* and *Selby's Marsh* from his father, and on 17 March 1749 as Robert Ward of Frederick Co., planter and grazier, for £72 currency he sold the two tracts to Alice and Elizabeth Nicholson of Anne Arundel Co. No wife joined him (AALR RB#3:269).

26. Robert Ward, prob. son of Robert (13), married Sarah [-?-].
Robert and Sarah were the parents of the following children whose births were recorded in St. James' Parish Register; all were bapt. on 7 June 1795. (AACR: 182): **30. Elizabeth,** b. 25 April 1775; **31. William,** b. 30 March 1777; **32. Robert,** b. 27 October 1779; **33. John,** b. 15 April 1782; **34. Sarah,** b. 14 October 1784; **35. Eleanor,** b. 4 July 1788; **36. Richard,** b. 22 December 1790; and **37. Samuel,** b. 24 January 1793.

Unplaced:
John Ward married Elizabeth [-?-]. They were the parents of the following children, born in St. James Parish (*AACR:*154, 161): Eleanor, b. 16 May 1703; and Richard, b. February 1711.
Elizabeth Ward of Anne Arundel Co., widow, died leaving a will dated 7 July 1748 and proved 27 October 1749. Her son Robert Ward was to have household furniture. Her daughter Eleanor Franklin was to have her clothes and side saddle. The residue of her estate was to pass to her children, Eleanor Franklin, Richard Ward, Samuel Ward, Joseph Ward, and Benjamin Ward. Son Richard Ward was named as executor. Richd. Stallinges, William Tucker, and Elizabeth Keys witnessed the will (MWB 27:89, abst. by Gibb).

== 0 ==

The Ward Family of Baltimore County

1. Joseph Ward was listed as a servant in the December 1700 inventory of Thomas Blackwell, Gentleman, of Anne Arundel County (INAC 20:159). He died testate by March 1754. He married Bridget [-?-].
On 9 February 1721 he was listed as a creditor of the estate of John Henderson of Baltimore Co. On 8 November 1723 he was listed as a creditor in the account of Rev. Dr. Evan Evans (MDAD 4:95, 5:276). In 1737 Joseph Ward was listed in the Upper Hundred, North of Gunpowder. Ward was on the levy list for that year, but Richard Gist was his assignee for criminal fees and for the annual allowance for beating the drum. Ward also appeared in the levy list for 1739. At the time Old Joppa was founded, Joseph Ward, was listed as an inn-holder (*IBCW:* 16, 29, 22, 38).
On 15 November 1724 Joseph Ward conveyed 50 a. *Ward's Adventure* to Jacob Roberts or Robinson. His wife Bridget consented. He purchased part of *Ballestone* in Baltimore Co. from John Long on 6 June 1733 (BALR IS#C: 415, IS#L: 378).
Joseph Ward of Back River, Baltimore Co., house carpenter, died leaving a will dated 7 February 1748/9 and proved 7 March 1754. His granddaughter Mary Stansbury, wife of

Richardson Stansbury, and second daughter of Isaac and Letitia Raven, was to have *Ballston,* where the testator now lived upon, and then the land was to descend to Elizabeth Raven, sister of said Mary Stansbury. If Mary Stansbury should die without heirs, then her husband Richardson Stansbury should enjoy the land for seven years. His grandson Luke Raven was to have money to buy tools. His grandchildren, Elizabeth, Letitia, Hester, Maria, Avarilla, and Drusilla Raven were each to have 4 lbs. money, which amounted to 24 lbs. Daughter Letitia Raven was to have his riding horse and five chairs. Christopher Duke was to have his tools in Kent Co. Nancy Harryman, daughter of Prudence Harryman, was to have cattle. His son Isaac Raven was to have £5.0.0. Richardson Stansbury was named executor. Elizabeth Brown, Dixon Brown, Francis Coleman, and Walter Dallas witnessed the will (MWB 29:70, abst. in *Md. Cal. of Wills* 11:15).

On 6 June 1754 Richardson Stansbury, with Thomas Sligh and Christopher Duke as sureties, posted an administration bond (BAAB 4:178). Stansbury administered the estate on 28 July 1755 and cited an inventory of £62.6.3. He listed payments of £47.10.7. The legatees were the wife of Robert Dow, an unnamed daughter of Isaac Raven, the wife of Charles Harryman, Isaac Raven, Luke Raven, and Ann Harryman (BAAD 5:351; MDAD 38:51).

Joseph and Bridget were the parents of (*SJSG:* 4, 6, 23, 26): **2. Elizabeth**, b. 1 May 1707; **3. John**, b. 22 November 1711; **4. Richard**, b. 15 March 1713 or 1 March 1714; **5. Joseph**, b. and d. last day of June 1717; **6. Mary**, b. 1 July 1717; may have d. young; **7. Mary**, b. July 1719; **8. Joseph**, b. 22 January 1720/1, may have d. young; **9. Joseph**, b. 1 April 1722; **10. Sarah**, b. September 1724; and **11. Letitia**, m. Isaac Raven.

3. John Ward, son of Joseph (1) and Bridget, was born 22 November 1711. He married Sarah Burrough on 17 December 1737 (*SJSG:* 42).

In 1737 John Ward was head of a household in Upper Hundred North of Gunpowder (*IBCW:* 16).

He purchased 50 a. *Ward's Adventure* from Jacob and Mary Robinson on 7 March 1728/9. On 9 June 1738 Ward conveyed 50 a. of the tract to Stephen Onion. Ward's wife Sarah consented (BALR IS#1: 271, HWS#1-A: 82).

John and Sarah were the parents of (*SJSG:* 103, 113): **12. William**, b. 10 March 1738; **13. Elizabeth**, b. 21 June 1741; **14. John**, b. November 1742; and **15. Sarah**, b. 1745.

4. Richard Ward, son of Joseph (1) and Bridget, was born 15 March 1713 or 1 March 1714. He married Mary Gross on15 August 1739 (*SJSG:* 149).

In 1737 Richard Ward was at his father's household in Upper Hundred North of Gunpowder (*IBCW:* 16).

Richard and Mary were the parents of (*SJSG:* 63): **16. John**, b. 1 August 1740; **17. Mary Gross**, b. 17 May 1742; **18. Richard**, b. 28 May 1742; and **19. Bridget**, b. 18 December 1746.

9. Joseph Ward, son of Joseph (1) and Bridget, was born on 1 April 1722. He married, 1st, on 24 August 1743 Hannah Lee. He married, 2nd, on 13 February 1748, Mary Parkinson (*SJSG:* 52. 90).

He may be the Joseph Ward, Jr., who was tried in March 1736 (when he was 14 at the time!) only for fathering an illegitimate child on the body of Prudence Harryman, who had been charged with bastardy at March Court, 1736/7, and named Joseph Ward as the father of her child; she confessed to having another child at the November 1739 Court (BACP HWS#1A:90, HWS&TR38). Her daughter Elizabeth was born on 2 November 1736 (Reamy and Reamy, *St. Paul's Parish Register:* 12).

Joseph and Prudence were the parents of: **20. Nancy** (left cattle by her grandfather Joseph Ward).

Joseph and Hannah were the parents of (*SJSG:* 60): **21. Rachael**, b. 6 November 1745.

Joseph and Mary were the parents of (*SJSG:* 80, 81): **22. Sarah**, twin, b. 8 October 1761; **23. Elizabeth**, twin, b. 8 October 1761; **24. Joseph**, b. 8 April 1764; and **25. Stephen**, b. 17 March 1768.

11. Letitia Ward, daughter of Joseph (1) and Bridget, married Isaac Raven, who died by November 1760, leaving orphans Elizabeth, Mary, Letticia, Esther, Keziah, Avarilla, Drusilla, William, and Millla Raven (BACP A:37).

Lettice Raven died by 1 June 1772, when William Raven, with Richardson Stansbury and Luke Raven posted an administration bond (BAAB 5:226).

Charles Harryman, administrtor d*de bonis non*, posted bond on 13 May 1770, with Robert Day and Thomas Davis. Lettice Raven had been the original administratrix (BAAB 5:221).

Isaac and Letitia were the parents of: **26. Luke**, d. 1770 in Baltimore Co.; **27. Mary**, m. Richardson Stansbury; **28. Elizabeth; 29. Letitia Raven; 30. Avarilla; 31. Esther; 32. Keziah; 33. Drusilla; 34. Averilla; 35. Millicent;** and **36. William.**

Unplaced:
Edward Ward died by 18 July 1783 when an administration bond for £500 on his estate was posted by administratrix Mary Ward with Abraham Stansbury and Luke League as sureties (BAAB 6:60). The estate was administered on 12 June 1792 by Thomas Hatton who had m. the administratrix Mary Ward. Hatton retained his wife's thirds, and the heirs were (BAAD 11:66): **Mary,** may have m. David Tucker, by November 1799; **John; Sarah,** ward of George Franciscus; **Edward,** ward of George Franciscus; aged 13 on 15 January 1788 was bound to James Cooper, shoemaker, on 14 October 1788 (BAOC 2:85); he may be the Edward Ward who died leaving a will, dated November 1799, proved 6 April 1800, naming his sister Mary Tucker, and also naming David Tucker (BAWB 6:256; abst. by Burns); **William,** ward of George Franciscus; Franciscus died by October 1792 and William was ward of John Mackenheimer (BAOC 3:14); he may be the William Ward, aged 14 or 16 on 27 October; in October 1793 he was bound to William Murphy, tailor (BAOC 3:63); **Elizabeth,** ward of George Franciscus; **Talbot,** ward of George Franciscus; **James,** ward of George Franciscus; aged 15 on 30 June 1792, was bound to John Mackenheimer, house carpenter and joiner, in October 1792 (BAOC 3:15).

John Ward died by 3 March 1785 when Thomas Randall posted an administration bond for £500, with Isaac Hammond and Geo. Tanner as sureties (BAAB 6:293). On 12 April 1790 his estate was administered by Thomas Randall; he left a widow Catherine (BAAD 10:124).

Colonial Families of Maryland II

Mary Ann Ward, daughter of Joseph Ward, deceased, died leaving a will dated 14 March 1783 and proved 8 April 17884. She named her sister Elizabeth, wife of William Spencer; her mother, now wife of Elisha Orsbourne [*sic*]; her brothers Benjamin, Joseph, and John, and her sister Ann wife of James Wimsett. Her brother Benjamin and brother-in-law William Spencer were named executors. Hugh Finlay and John Hinds witnessed the will (BAWB 3:547).

==0==

The Watkins Family of Baltimore County

N.B.: The material on the Welsh and English generations of the Watkins Family has been generously made available to the author by David Watkins. I have modernized some of the spelling.

C. John Watkins of Llangattock Vibon Abell, Monmouth County, Wales, had a son named **B. William,** prob. b. before 1589.

B. William Watkins, son of John (C) was probably born by 1589 and died in Shrewsbury in 1650. He married Margaret [-?-]. William was buried on 10 August 1650 and Margaret was buried on 21 May 1651, both at St. Chad's Church in Shrewsbury, Shropshire, England.

William moved to Tewkesbury, Glos., probably sometime between 1614 and 1629. By 1629 he had moved to Shrewsbury.

The will of William Watkins reads thus: In the name of God Amen The first Day of August in the year of our Lord one thousand six hundred and fifty, I, William Watkins of the Town of Shrewsbury in the County of Salop [Shropshire], maulster [maltster], being weak of body but of perfect mind and memory (Thanks be to God), do make and ordain this my last Will and Testament in manner and form following: viz., First, I bequeath my Soul into the hand of Almighty God my Creator and Redeemer And my body to be buried in St Chad's Churchyard in decent manner according to the discretion of my Executrix. Item I give and bequeath unto the poor of St Chad's Parish the sum of Forty shilling to be bestowed as my Executrix Shall think fit.

Item I. devise and bequeath unto Margaret, my wife, all that dwelling house with the appurtenances situate lying and being in Franckewell, one of the suburbs of the Town of Shrewsbury in the County of Salop, together with all Tables, Boards, Cupboards, Stools, and bedsteads thereunto belonging for and during the term of her natural life And after her decease My will is, that my three daughters, Frances Martha, and Mary, shall enjoy the said house with all things as aforesaid for and during the space of six months, and at the end of the said six months My will is that my said daughters Shall quietly yield and deliver up the said house with the things aforesaid according as it is hereafter by me bequeathed.

Item I devise and bequeath the said house with all the things before mentioned after my said wife's decease and the expiration of the six months (according as is before sett forth and expressed) unto William Watkins my son and the heirs of his body, lawfully begotten for ever; the Said William Watkins and his heirs yielding and paying unto

Item I devise and bequeath the said house with all the things before mentioned after my said wife's decease and the expiration of the six months (according as is before sett forth and expressed) unto William Watkins my son and the heirs of his body, lawfully begotten for ever; the Said William Watkins and his heirs yielding and paying unto Samuel Watkins, my second son, the sum of five pounds yearly during his natural life at two several payments (viz.) fifty shillings at the Feast of St Michael The Archangel which shall first happen after the death of my said wife and the expiration of the said term of six months, And if it happens that either of the said payments, being lawfully demanded, be behind or unpaid in part or in all for six weeks after either of the said days upon the which the same ought to be paid, that then it shall and may be lawful for the said Samuel or his assigns to enter and distrain for the said sum then due and for twenty shillings more for the non payment and default thereof.

Item: I give and bequeath unto my grandchildren eight pounds apiece four pounds of which to be paid to them within one year after my decease, and the other four pounds to be paid to them when they shall accomplish the age of Eighteen years or the Death of my said wife whether shall happen first, and further I bequeath unto my three grandchildren viz., Elizabeth Watkins, Margaret Hunt, and Margaret Hale five pounds a year more to be paid as aforesaid because of their several infirmities And my will is That if it happen that any of my Said Grandchildren shall *die* before the death of my Said wife or accomplishing the age of eighteen years as aforesaid, that then the legacy or legacies to him her or them so bequeathed shall equally be divided amongst the survivor or survivors of them.

Item I give and bequeath unto my three sons-in-law Phillip Ellis, John Hale, and Robert Hunt twenty shillings a year in full of their portions, and to be paid unto them within one year after my decease.

Item I give and bequeath unto my grandchild Samuel Hale five pounds more for his service to me, to be paid within one year after my decease. Item I give and bequeath unto my grandchild William Watkins five pounds besides my former gift to get him Pr[?], and to be paid as before.

Item I give and bequeath unto my wife all my debts by bond, bills or otherwise that are due to me and all my malt and household stuff heretofore not bequeathed, she discharging my funeral expenses, debts, and legacies. And my will is that after my wife's decease, my household stuff which is not otherwise bequeathed shall be equally divided between Margaret Hale, Martha Hunt, and Marie Hunt if my wife shall think fitting. And of this my will and Testament I do make and ordain Margaret, my wife, my sole executrix, and for the due execution of the same I do make and ordain my friend Mr. Francis Hinkes and my Son-in-Law Phillip Ellis my overseers to see this my last will performed And I doe hereby utterly revoke and annul all and every other former Testament, wills, legacies, bequeaths [bequests], executors and overseers by me at any time heretofore made. In witness whereof I have hereunto put my hand [and] seal the Day and year first above written. William Watkins. Signed sealed and published In the presence of --William Bonaston Sign-- Richard Smyth, Francis Hynckes.

Shortly after William Watkins died his wife also died, leaving a will that was dated March 10, 1650, and proved on June 16, 1651. If the wishes of William were carried out, then the house would pass to his son William six months after the death of his wife.

Roughly this would have been about November 1651. The items bequeathed by Margaret were mainly household and personal items that belonged to her. Her will reads as follows: In the name of God Amen: the tenth day of March in the year of our Lord God One thousand six hundred and fifty, I, Margaret Watkins of Frankwell, one of the suburbs of the Town of Shrewsbury in the County of Salop, widow being sick and weak in body but of perfect mind and memory, thanks be given to Almighty God, do make this my last will and Testament in manner and form following: first, I bequeath my soul to Almighty God, my Maker, and to Jesus Christ, my Redeemer, by whose means and merits I hope for salvation, and my body to be buried in St. Chad's Church by my beloved husband And whereas I have of my husband's estate which he lately by his last will and Testament to me bequeathed, and all the rest of my goods, Chattels real and personal estate I bequeath as followeth viz.: I bequeath to the poor of Frankwell twenty shillings immediately after my Death to be distributed amongst them.

Item I give and bequeath unto my son William Watkins twenty shillings.

Item I give and bequeath unto my son Samuel Watkins fifty pounds to be paid him within one month after my Decease; also one good feather bed, two pair shoes, one pair of blankets, one blue Rugg with the curtains and pillows thereunto belonging.

Item I give and bequeath unto my Frances Hale one feather bed, one pair of blankets, one green Rugg, two pair of shoes with the green curtains thereunto belonging.

Item I give and bequeath unto my grandchild Martha Hunt one green Ousted Rugg one featherbed, and my biggest brass kettle. Item I give and bequeath unto my kinswoman Elizabeth Clarkson one bed and forty shillings in money. I give to the widow Colley twenty shillings.

Item I bequeath more to my said son Samuel, one fair gilt silver saltcellar. Item I give to my grandchild William Watkins one silver bowl. Item I give and bequeath unto my grandchild Mary Hunt one silver beaker. Item I give and bequeath unto my grandchild Margaret Hayle one broken silver bowl. Item I give and bequeath more to my grandchildren Margaret Watkins, Margaret Hayle and Margaret Hunt to each of them a silver spoon.

Item I give and bequeath more to Margaret Hayle my second great kettle. Item I give and bequeath more to my said son Samuel one great brass pot. Item I bequeath more: Margaret Hunt my Warming pan Item I bequeath to Mary Hunt more my booking kettle. Item I give and bequeath more to my said son Samuel my husband's best cloak and best black worked cap.

Item I leave and bequeath to my Daughter Mary Ellis twenty shillings to buy her a ring, and to her daughter which she now lieth *item* of eight pounds to be paid according to the *time* as the legacies which are left to the rest of grandchildren by my deceased husband ought to be paid. Item all my pewter and linen with all the rest of my household stuff which is mine and not bequeathed, I bequeath to my three grandchildren Margaret Hayle Martha Hunt and Mary Hunt equally to be divided amongst them according to my husbands will.

Item I leave and bequeath all my wearing apparel equally to be divided between my two daughters Frances Hayle and Martha Hunt. Item I give to my grandchild Israel Hayle one great brass pot. And of this my last will and testament I hereby constitute make and appoint my son William Watkins to be my sole executor, and do hereby revoke all former wills by me made. In witness whereof I have hereunto put my hand and seal the day and year first above written, signed Margarett Watkins. Memorandum that Israel Hayles legacy was interlined before the sealing and publishing hereof sealed and published in the presence of Roger Cripps, Humphrey Fawkener ,Ad Hinkes. The Will above written was Proved in London before Thomas Walters M. of Arts and --- the sixteenth day of June one thousand six hundred fifty and one by the oath of William Watkins son and executor in this will named to whom was committed administration of all and singular the goods he being first sworn faithfully to administer the same.

William and Margaret were the parents of: **Frances**, b. 1606, and died 29 July 1666; married John Hale, died 30 June 1675; both are buried at St. Chad's, Shrewsbury; they were the parents of: Richard, Israel, Margaret, and William; **A. William**, b. 1608; **Martha**, b. 1610; married Robert Hunt and had the following children: Martha, Robert, Mary, Margaret; **Samuel**, b. 1612, and d. after about 1650; and **Mary**, b. about 1618, d. after 1650, and married Phillip Ellis.

A. William Watkins, Jr., son of William (B) and Margaret, was born 1608. He married 1st, Frances [-?-]. probably in Tewkesbury about 1635. Frances was buried on 17 September 1658 at St. Chad's Church in Shrewsbury. William married second Allies Dicker (Ditcher, Dicher) on 29 October 1660. William was buried on 19 July 1669 at St. Chad's Church in Shrewsbury.

William and Frances were the parents of: **William**, bapt. on 30 April 1637 in Tewkesbury, Glos.; and was bur. at St. Chad's 23 October 1681; m. Eleanor [-?-], who was buried in Augu1681 at St. Chad's; William and Eleanor had the following children: Elinor, bapt. 2 February 1662; Marie, bapt. 27 May 1664; William, bapt. 16 December 1666; and Sara, bapt. 5 October 1670; **Elizabeth**, b. c1639, d. December 1672; **Thomas**, b. about 1641, d. after 1670; **Margaret**, b. about 1643, d. after 1670; **Samuel**, b. about 1645, at Tewkesbury, attended Cambridge University in 1664, d. after 1670; **1. Francis**, b. about 1647 (see below); **John**, b. about 1649, d. after 1670; **Joseph**, b. about 1651, d. after 1670; **Mary**, born and died in December 1653; and **James**, bapt. 1655 at St. Chad's, d. after 1670.

1. Francis Watkins, son of William (A), in 1680 claimed land for immigrating to Md. (MPL WC#2:150), He died by April 1696. He married, 1st, by 7 June 1681, Christiana Waites, or Wright, daughter (by an earlier marriage) of Jane, wife of Thomas Long. Watkins m., 2nd, Mary [-?-], who survived him. She married, 2nd, by 1698, William Barker (MDTP 17:202; INAC 16:209).

Marrying so soon after his arrival in Maryland would indicate that Francis Watkins was probably a man of some substance. If he had arrived as an indentured servant, he would have had to wait for at least four years to complete his service, before he could marry.

Skordas lists one other Francis Watkins: one transported to Md., probably as an indentured servant in 1671 (MPL 16:175). The only Francis Watkins listed in the *Bristol Registers* was a Francis Watkins of Henbury, Gloucestershire, Eng., who on 7 July 1659 was bound to serve Gabriel Blike for five years in Virginia. He was too early to be the settler in Baltimore County (Peter Wilson Coldham. *The Bristol Registers of Servants*

Sent to Foreign Plantations, 1654-1686. Baltimore: Genealogical Publishing Co., 1988:101).

Francis Watkins and Thomas Fenn appraised the estate of John Grange of Baltimore County on 14 April 1677 (INAC 4:448). Watkins and Roland Nance appraised the estate of Robert Wilson of Baltimore County in November 1678 (INAC 5:369). Appraisers were men of status and integrity in the community. In March 1687 Mr. Francis Watkins was referred to as a Judge in the administration account of Thomas Scudamore of Baltimore County (INAC 9:481).

Francis Watkins, Gent., patented three tracts of land in Baltimore County: 74 a. *Better Hopes* on 6 February 1686 (MPL 25:288, 33:519); 65 a. *Barnsbury* on 12 June 1688 (MPL 33:670); and 200 a. *Sister's Hope* on 13 September 1681 (MPL 40:501). (*A Genealogical Gazetteer of England,* by Frank Smith [Baltimore: Genealogical Publishing Co.], does not list a Barnsbury, but it does list a Banbury, parish and borough in Oxfordshire).

On 7 June 1681 Thomas Long, for natural affection and through the intercession of his wife, conveyed to Francis Watkins the 185 a. tract *Hopewell,* said Watkins having m. Christiana Wright (or Waites), daughter of Long's wife (BALR IR#AM:121).

On 17 March 1691 Christopher Bembridge conveyed 111 a. *Long Port,* adjacent to *Hopewell,* formerly taken up by Maj. Thomas Long, to Francis Watkins (BALR RM#HS:611).

Watkins died leaving a nuncupative will proved 11 April 1696, naming wife Mary, who was to have his plantation for her lifetime. After her death it was to go to his son Francis. Son Samuel was to have unnamed land on the Gunpowder River Daughters Margaret and Christiana were to have land on the Back River. No executor was named. Edward Cantwell, Lidia Handen, and John Haws witnessed the will (MWB 7:197, abst. in *Md. Cal. of Wills* 2:110). An administration bond was posted 27 June 1696 by Mary Watkins and William Barker, and with John Hayes and Nicholas Fitzsimmons as sureties (BAAB 4:69).

John Hayes and Nicholas Fitzsimmons appraised Watkins' personal estate on 12 May 1696. His inventory showed that he owned a parcel of old books, one old bed pan, two silver spoons, one looking glass, two pair of andirons, a fire shovel, a pair of shears, a box of iron, a pair of spring tongs, a parcel of old iron, a hand saw, one mill, one grindstone, two pair of old stilyards, one bellmettle mortar and pestle, nine [oz?] of yarn, eight oz? of wool, eleven sickles, two spinning wheels, a drawing knife, a trowel, a tien [ton?] of caske, one awl, three grubbing [?], three axes, and trays.

Household furnishings included two featherbeds with furniture and a feather bed with no furniture, and a parcel of old bedding, six old chairs, six leather chairs, one couch wainscoted, one grouning [?] chair, two tables, one old chest, one chest of drawers, three old chests, and an old cupboard.

Kitchen utensils included five old pots, three pair pothooks, one flesh fork, one frying pan, one spit, one dripping pan, one brass ladle, one skimmer, one iron ladle, two brass kettles, two pair pot hooks, a pair tongs, two pots, and one chafing dish.

Other property included a iron candlestick, a parcel of old linning [linen], five and a half yards of kersey, two ordinary deer skins, three and a half tanned hides, a parcel of old clothes, two pair old shoes, three pair of old stockings, two old hats, and one old belt, and 4576 lbs. tob.

Watkins' livestock included 32 head of sheep, two horses, one mare, three cows and calves, seven cows and calves, four six-year-old steers, two2 four-year-old steers, six two-year-old steers, four yearlings, one five-year-old bull, one four-year-old heifer, one four-year-old steer, 21 head of hogs.

Other assets included a man servant, Edward Cantwell with nine months to serve, a 1 boy servant, James Isum, with four years to serve, a boy, Richard [ffroston?], with six years to serve, a woman, Leddy Hendon, with years to serve, one old pistol, one old blunderbuss, one old sword, one gun, 71 oz[?] of powder, 6,782 lbs. tobacco in debts; and two old trunks. The total value was £169.11.4 (INAC 14:25-26).

Mary Barker, wife of [-?-] Barker, administered the estate of Francis Watkins on 5 September 1698. She cited the inventory of £169.11.4; payments came to £39.11.8 (BAAD 2:86).

Mary [-?-] Watkins Barker Oldton died by 10 December 1709 when her inventory was signed by her son-in-law (i.e., stepson) Francis Watkins (INAC 39:86).

Francis Watkins was the father of the following children) the first two of whom were definitely by his first wife) (*BCF*:666): **2. Christiana**, d. by November 1703, evidently unm.; the estate of Christiana Watkins, spinster, with an inventory of ?26.5.0 and payments of ?6.18.4, was administered by Mary Oldton on 6 August 1707 (INAC 27:56); 3. **Francis**, d. by 11 May 1713; **4. Samuel**, d. 1743; and **5. Margaret**.

3. Francis Watkins, son of Francis (1) and Christiana, died by May 1713. He married Jane, daughter of Daniel Scott. She died about 1765, having married as her second husband, Samuel Hughes, on 4 November 1714 (Reamy and Reamy, *St. George's Parish Register:* 16). On 9 July 1725 Jane was named as a daughter of Daniel Scott of Baltimore Co. (MDAD 6:406).

Francis Watkins surveyed a tract named *Shrewsbury* on 9 February 1697 (*MRR:*77). On 28 May 1707 Watkins conveyed *Better Hope, Hopewell* and *Surplus*, to James Crooke, yeoman (BALR RM#HS:559).

On 11 May 1713 an administration bond on Francis Watkins' estate was posted by Jane Watkins with Daniel Scott, Jr., and Thomas Biddison as sureties (BAAB 4:47). The estate of Francis Watkins, with an inventory appraised at £21.1.8 and payments coming to £20.2.11, was administered by Jane Watkins, administratrix, on 19 March 1714 (INAC 35A:111).

Jane Scott Watkins Hughes died leaving a will dated 14 April 1762 and proved 31 October 1765, naming the children of her son Francis Watkins: Daniel Scott, Francis, Jane, Elizabeth, and Nathaniel Watkins (BAWB 3:27).

Francis and Jane were the parents of: **6. Francis**, d. by 1757.

4. Samuel Watkins, son of Francis (1) and Christiana, died y August 1743. He married Mary, probably the daughter of William Wright whose will of 25 February 1723/4 named a daughter Mary Watkins (MWB 18:263 abst. in *Md. Cal. of Wills* 5:166).

On 7 June 1721 Oliver Harriott and wife Susanna conveyed 196 a. *Harriott's Fancy* to Samuel Watkins (BALR TR#RA:318). In 1739 Samuel Watkins, with consent of his wife Mary, conveyed the tract to William Bond (BALR IS#K:259).

Samuel died leaving a will dated 2 April 1743 and proved 22 August 1743, naming his son Samuel, daughter Mary Anne, and "other children." An unnamed servant was given her freedom (MWB 23:202 abst. in *Md. Cal. of Wills* 8:225).

Thomas Gittings and Darby Henley appraised his estate at £113.0.0, on 25 November 1743. Abraham Enlow, Martha Standiford, and William Watkins signed as next of kin. Samuel Watkins filed the inventory on 27 January 1745 (MINV 28:421).

Samuel Watkins filed an account of his father's estate on 13 October 1744. He cited an inventory of £113.8.0, and a second inventory of £30.6.2. Payments came to £75.0.4 (MDAD 20:514).

Samuel and Mary were the parents of (BACP TB&TR#1:208; *SJSG*:25, 42, 94): **7. Martha**, b. 15 January 1715, m. James Standiford on 6 October 1737; **8. Samuel**, b. 15 November 1717; **9. William**, b. 10 December 1720, d. by June 1754; m. Ann Barkabee on 9 December 1741; d. leaving a will dated 16 August 1753 and recorded 4 September 1753, naming his wife Ann as his executrix, and his brothers and sisters, Samuel Watkins, John Watkins, sister Mary Watkins, and Martha Standifer, and Solomon (?). Richard Bodington, W. Slade, and James [?] Pocock witnessed the will. (MWB 29:154 abst. in *Md. Cal. of Wills* 11:33); **11. John; 12. Mary;** and **13. Solomon.**

6. Francis Watkins, son of Francis (3), died by May 1757. He married Elizabeth Mead on 19 January 1738/9 (*SJSG:* 53, where Francis' name is given as Thomas Watkins).

Elizabeth Watkins administered his estate on 17 May 1757. She cited an inventory of £209.12.11, and listed payments totaling £51.8.7 (MDAD 41:21).

Elizabeth Mead, widow of Francis Watkins, may be the Elizabeth who died by 10 March 1764 when 10 March 1764 when Daniel Watkins posted an administration bond for ?100, with John Bick and John Hatton as sureties (BAAB 4:135).

Francis and Elizabeth were the parents of (*SJSG:* 53, 59): **14. Daniel Scott,** b. 5 December 1739, was aged 18 in 1757; **15. Francis,** b. 27 September 1741, was aged 16 in 1757; **16. Jane,** b. 17 November 1743, was aged 14 in 1757; she may be the Jane Watkins who m. James White on 7 August 1766 (*SJSG:* 114); **17. Benjamin,** b. 10 August, and d. 18 October 1745; **18. Elizabeth,** aged 9 in 1757; **19. Nathaniel,** aged 8 in 1757; and **20. Mary** aged 8 in 1757.

8. Samuel Watkins, son of Samuel (4) and Mary, was born c1717, and died by November 1795 in Baltimore Co. He may have married 1st, Margaret [-?-]. He married Frances Hardesty on 11 June 1757 (*BCF:* 667; *SJSG:* 101).

In 1783 Samuel Watkins, with 11 free males, and 5 white inhabitants, lived in Gunpowder Upper Hundred. He owned 175 a. *Bachelor Hall*. Another Samuel Watkins was listed as a "Pauper" (*i.e.,* he owned property worth less than £10.0.0) in Patapsco Lower Hundred (Carothers, *1783 Tax List of Baltimore Co*:36, 87).

Samuel Watkins died leaving a will dated 20 November 1793, proved 4 November 1795. He named his wife Frances, elder son John, second son Samuel, eldest daughter Martha Chance, younger daughter Sarah Guyton, granddaughter Elizabeth Chance, daughter of John, and granddaughter Frances Guyton. Sons John and Samuel were named executors. The will was witnessed by Benjamin Guyton, Jr., John Lindsay, and James Rice (BAWB 5:336, abst. by Burns).

Samuel and Margaret were the parents of: **21. Mary,** b. April 1753 (*SJGS:* 164).

Samuel and Frances were the parents of: **22. John Watkins II; 23. Samuel; 24. Martha,** m. [-?-] Chance; and **25. Sarah,** m. John Holt Guyton on 30 October 1787 (*SJSG:* 148).

14. Daniel Scott Watkins, son of Francis (6) and Elizabeth, was born 5 December 1739 and was aged 18 in 1757. He married Elizabeth Hatten on 29 December 1761. He may be the Daniel Watkins who married Sosia [Sophia?] Biddison on 3 May 1770 (*SJSG:* 108, 137).

15. Francis Watkins, son of Francis (6) and Elizabeth, was born 27 September 1741 and was aged 16 in 1757. He married Elizabeth Pines on 25 September 1769 (*SJGS:* 135).

22. John Watkins II, son of Samuel (8) and Frances, was born 1758, and died 3 May 1847, aged 90. He married Ruth Guyton on 11 June 1796 (*SJSG:* 153, 174).

He was a private during the Revolutionary War (*BARP*).

John Watkins died leaving a will dated October 1844, and proved 3 June 1847. He named his sons John, Samuel, and Isaiah, the tract *Brown's Farm,* wife Ruth, grandson John Burton (son of his daughter Eleanor), grandson William Henry Watkins (son of son Samuel). Sons Samuel and Isaiah were executors. John Riddle, J. Hillen Jenkins, and Coleman Yellott were witnesses (BAWB 21:464, abst. by Burns).

John and Ruth were the parents of: **26. Ellen,** m. John Burton; **27. Samuel; 28. Isaiah,** b. 1800, d. 1801; **29. John III,** b. 1803, d. 1878, m. Minerva Slade, and was buried at Fork M. E. Church.

Unplaced:
Ann Watkins and William Wood were married on 3 October 1754 (*SJSG:* 98).
Frances Watkins and John Hammond Dorsey were married on 12 February 1744 (*SJSG:* 17).
James Watkins married Mary [-?-]. They were the parents of (*SJSG:* 61): Benjamin, b. 11 January 1745.
James Watkins married Unity Green on 4 May 1758 (*SJSG:* 52).
John Watkins and Elizabeth James were married on 25 June 1730 (*SJSG:* 92).
John Watkins and Elizabeth Jones were married on 10 February 1747 (*SJSG:* 85).
John Watkins married Purify, daughter of William Greenfield, 9 October 1754 (Reamy and Reamy, *St. George's Parish Register:*79; BAAD 6:94). John and Purify were the parents of (Reamy and Reamy, *St. George's Parish Register:*79, 91): Margaret, b. 14 October 1754 Elizabeth, b. 11 December 1757; Susanna, b. 23 February 1758; John, b. 14 January 1760; and William, b. 22 November 1762).
Margaret Watkins and Ralph Rench were married on 21 December 1755 (*SJSG:* 99).

Nicholas Watkins died by 15 June 1763 when his widow, now the wife of John Ijams, administered the estate (BAAD 6:49).
Sarah Watkins and John Holt Guyton were married on 30 October 1787 (*SJSG:* 148).

== 0 ==

The West Family of Anne Arundel County

1. **Stephen West** was born about 1682 and died 5 January 1751/2 and was buried 11 Jan 1752 at All Hallows Church Yard (*AACR:*53). He married 1st, on 21 August 1712 in St. James Parish Elizabeth, daughter of Samuel Maccubbin (*AACR:* 165; *AAMR* cites *BDML* 1:384, 2:378). He married, 2nd, Martha Hall on 28 April 1726 in All Hallow's Parish (AACR:42). She was the daughter of Rev. Henry and Mary (Duvall) Hall. Martha was born 27 October 1708 in Anne Arundel Co., Md., and died 8 April 1752; she was buried 10 April 1752 (*AACR:*53)..

Stephen West died leaving a will dated 3 January 1751 and proved 14 August 1752. He named his daughters Priscilla Smith wife of Richard Smith, Eleanor Lyles, Mary West, Martha West, Ann West, and Elizabeth West, and his grandchildren: Eleanor Austin, Henry Austin and Priscilla Smith, Martha Lyles, Barbara Lyles, Priscilla Lyles, and William Lyles, his son Stephen West, and a cousin Ann Caton. His wife Martha West and son Stephen West were named executors.

Stephen and Elizabeth were the parents of the following children, born in All Hallows; Parish (*AACR:*32, 36, 200): **2, Mary**, b. 30 May 1714, b. 20 June 1716, may have d. young; **3. Priscilla**, b. 12 April 1716, bapt.20 June 1716; m. Richard Smith by 3 January 1751; **4. Robert**, bapt. 16 September 1719; **5. Elizabeth**, b. 15 April 1721, m. by 1743, Anthony Beck (AALR RB#1:305); **6. Elianor**, b. 22 May 1723, bapt. 25 July 1723, m. [-?-] Lyle by 1751 (*AAMR* cites MWB 28:353)..

Stephen and Martha were the parents of the following, bapt. in All Hallows Parish (*AACR:* 41, 43, 45, 47, 48, 51): **7. Stephen**, 23 July 1727, bapt. 2 August 1727; **8. Mary**, 6 July 1729, bapt. 20 August 1729, may have d. young; **9. Mary Magdalene**, b. 19 September 1731, bapt. 5 November 1731; **10. John Henry**, b. 2 September 1733, bapt. 23 October 1733; **11. Rebecca Ann**, b. 20 February 1735/6, bapt. 15 July 1736; **12. Martha**, b. 13 December 1738, m. on 20 April 1766 John Dorsey Lawrence; **13. Ann**, b. 19 August 1741; and **14. John,** b. February [year not given].

7. **Stephen West**, son of Stephen (1) and Martha, was born 23 July 1727, and died 1790. On 5 March 1753 he married Hannah Williams. She was born c1735 in Prince Georges, Maryland, and died 1815.

Stephen West of *the Woodyard* advertised that he taught Latin, Greek, English, and arithmetic, and was advertising for a new place (Annapolis *Maryland Gazette* 14 November 1771).

In 1783 Stephen West owned 587 a. *Talbots Resolution Manor*, in Elkridge Hundred (1783 Assessment List, p. 7. MSA S 1161-1-3 1/4/5/44).

Stephen West advertised he had conveyances from Elizabeth Hopkins, widow of Philip, Gerard Hopkins, 1st son, Richard Hopkins, 2nd son, a daughter who m. Richard

Dowell, and a daughter who m. William Hatton for their right to certain land (Annapolis *Maryland Gazette* 30 July 1789).

Stephen West and his wife advertised that they would petition for a restoration of the tract called *Black Acre*, formerly the property of William Black, merchant, of London, to whom he subscribers are heir (Annapolis *Maryland Gazette* 3 Dec 1789).

Stephen West of *The Woodyard*, died by September 1792 when Hannah West, the executrix, advertised the sale of twenty Negroes (Annapolis *Maryland Gazette* 20 September 1792).

Stephen and Hannah had issue: **15. Stephen**, b. about 1755; **16. Richard Williams**, b. about 1762 in Prince Georges Co., d. by 1850; and **17. Rachel Sophia**, b. about 1764 in Prince Georges Co., d. by 1813; m. Benjamin Oden on 25 January 1791 in Prince Georges, MD. He was b. 1762 in Prince Georges Co., Maryland, and d. 1829.

15. Stephen West, son of Stephen (7) and Hannah, was born about 1755. On 26 September 1794 he married Anna Pue, daughter of Michael and Mary (Dorsey) Pue. Anna was born about 1772 in Anne Arundel Co., Md.

Stephen and Anna were the parents of: **18. Harriett Black**, b. 1795 in Prince George's Co.; and **19. Arthur Pue**, b. about 1799; m. Eleanor 'Ellen' Oden on 29 May 1821 in Prince Georges Co., daughter of Benjamin Oden and Rachel Sophia West.

16. Richard Williams West, son of Stephen (7) and Hannah, was born about 1762 in Prince Georges, Co., and died by 1850. He married Maria Lloyd on 9 October 1798 in Anne Arundel Co., Maryland, daughter of Edward Lloyd and Elizabeth Gwynn Tayloe.

Richard Williams and Maria were the parents of: **20. Mary Lloyd**, b. May 1818 in Prince George's Co., and d. 1901 in Mellwood, Prince George's Co.

== 0 ==

The Whayland Family of Baltimore County

N.B: The name is sometimes spelled Wayland or Wealand.

1. Patrick 'Whalan' in August 1711 petitioned the court for his freedom, saying that he had served his time with Abraham Inloes, deceased. His petition was granted (BACP IS#A: 252). He married by 2 November 1726 Catherine, daughter of Henry Matthews.

In August 1715 or 1716 he and Henry Matthews were sureties for Mary Smith when she posted bond for the estate of her husband Thomas Smith (BCF:593). On 2 September 1724 he received a payment from the estate of John Rawlings (MDAD 6:118). On 14 June 1726 he was a surety for Sarah Matthews when she posted an administration bond for her husband Henry Matthews. On 2 November 1726 he signed Henry Matthews' inventory as one of the next of kin because he had married one of the daughters. (MINV 11:675).

Henry Matthews died leaving a will dated 6 June 1720 in which he stipulated that daughter Catherine Whaland and her heirs were to have the residue of *Hewses Chance* and *Plumb Point*. (MWB 18:490 abst. in *Md. Cal. of Wills* 5:222).

On 9 March 1731 Catherine Whayland, daughter of Henry Matthews, conveyed 50

a. *Chance* to Thomas Lego, which Henry Matthews had by his last will and testament devised 100 a. *Chance* to his daughter Sarah Matthews, and 50 a. to his daughter Catherine (BALR IS#L: 208).

Patrick and Catherine had issue (*SJSG:* 5, 22, 26, 89): **2, Henry,** b. 6 August 1712; **3. Margaret,** b. 17 November 1715; **4. William,** b. 10 May 1717; **5. Sarah,** b. 13 February 1720; m. Francis Flanner on 2 October 1748; and **6. Patrick,** b. 29 April 1722.

2, Henry Whayland, son of Patrick (1) and Catherine, was born 6 Aug 1712. He married 1st, Catherine Lego, on 27 January 1746, and 2nd, by July 1741 Rebecca [-?-] (*SJSG:* 45, 48).

On 28 May 1748 Henry, his wife Catherine, and his mother Catherine, widow, conveyed 100 a. *Plumb Point* to Edward Brucebanks (BALR TR#C:25). On 10 August 1752 he received a payment from the estate of Robert Muckilvain (MDAD 33:12).

Henry and Catherine were the parents of (*SJSG:* 45): **7. Solomon,** b. 26 October 1738.

Henry and Rebecca were the parents of (*SJSG:* 48): **8. Elizabeth,** b. 19 July 1741.

4. William Whayland, son of Patrick (12) and Catherine, was born 10 May 1717. He married 1st, by August 1745, Martha [-?-], and 2nd, Mary Legoe on 21 April 1751 or 1752 (*SJSG:* 94, 124).

William and Martha were the parents of (*SJSG:* 60, 65): **9. Mary,** b. 30 August 1745; and **10. Martha,** b. 14 September 1747.

6. Patrick Whayland, son of Patrick (2) and Catherine, was b. 29 April 1722. He married Mary Cowdrey or Caudrey on 26 January 1749. He may be the Patrick Whealand who married Phoebe Tunis on 6 August 1767 (*SJSG:* 91,115, 127).

In 1737 he had been bound to Aquila Massey to age 21 (BACP HWS#1A:134).

7. Solomon Whayland, son of Henry (2) and Catherine, was born 26 October 1738. He married 1st, Elizabeth Copeland, on 18 January 1756, and, 2nd, Elizabeth Ward on 22 February 1726 (*SJSG:* 114).

In October 1763 he received a payment from the estate of Jane Copland (MDAD 50:73).

Unplaced:
Ann Whayland was charged with bastardy at the November 1750 Court and Stephen White confessed to being the father (BACP TR#6:40, 60).
Elizabeth Whayland and Henry Kersey were married on 21 July 1746 (*SJSG:* 88).
Henry Whayland and Isabel Wilson were married on 21 July 1764 (*SJSG:* 111).
James Whayland (Whealand) died 14 August 1740 (*SJSG:* 70).
Sarah Whealand and Francis Flannan (or Flannel) were m. on 4 September or 2 October 1748 (*SJSG:* 99, 125).
Stephen Mathews Whealand, son of Ann Whealand and Stephen White, "as she says" was born 17 September 1749 (*SJSG:* 35).

Thomas Whayland and Martha Dorney were married on 21 July 1767 (*SJSG*: 115).

== 0 ==

The Whipps Family

B. John Whipp(s) or Whyppe, of Thirsk, Yorkshire, was the father of the following children, bapt. at Thirsk (*Parish Registers of Thirsk, Yorkshire. YASP* 42: 102, 104, 105, 106, 107, 110): **Fraunces**, bapt. 28 July 1592; **John**, bapt. 5 February 1594; **William**, bapt. 13 April 1596; **Robert**, bapt. 13 April 1600; **Jane**, bapt. 10 Jan 1601/2; and **A. Thomas**, bapt. 22 February 1606.

A. Thomas Whipp(s), son of John (B), was bapt. 22 February 1606 at Thirsk, Yorkshire, where he married Sybil Hodge on 3 August 1628. They were the parents of at least four of the following children, bapt. at Thirsk; the last five may have been children of a second marriage, or may not have been baptized until some years after their birth (*Parish Registers of Thirsk, Yorkshire. YASP* 42: 38, 86, 110, 129, 132, 136, 138, 141, 143, 144, 146, 148): **Jane**, bapt. 26 July 1629; **1. John**, bapt. 8 December 1631; **Francis**, bapt. 6 March 1635/6; **Christopher**, bapt. 7 November 1637, bur. 16 December 1638; **Anne**, bapt. 1 May 1642; **Roger**, bapt. 6 October 1643; **Cicelie**, bapt. 15 July 1645; **Ellen**, bapt. 11 Dec 1646; and **Elizabeth**, bapt. 21 March 1648.

1. John Whipps, son of Thomas (A), was bapt. 18 December 1631, although the Whips Bibles, printed in 1816, stated that "John Whipps of Calvert Co. was born in the year of Our Lord in 1622, within 16 miles of York City, in a town commonly called Thursk [sic]" ("Whips Family Bibles," *MGSB* 17:165). He was probably the John who came to Md., and died by 26 December 1716, and who married Elizabeth Medcaff, who died 1729.

John Whipps was in Anne Arundel Co. by 19 April 1672 when he was listed as a debtor to the estate of Richard Wells of Herring Creek, Anne Arundel Co. On 2 December 1675 he was listed as a debtor in the estate of Thomas Chandler, innholder of Anne Arundel Co. He was a debtor in the undated inventory of Nathan Smith of Anne Arundel Co. (MDTP 5:267).

On 3 October 1685 he and William Lyle appraised the estate of Paule Bensee [Paul Busey?] (INAC 8:498). On 15 June 1687 he was listed as a creditor in the administration account of Philip Jones of Calvert Co. (INAC 9:298). On 5 June 1697 he was a debtor in the inventory of Richard Wells of Anne Arundel Co. (INAC 15:274; see also INAC 22:42, 31:271, 32A:98).

On or before 10 November 1707, John Whipps conveyed a cow called Guift to his granddaughter Phylothia Standforth, daughter of John Standforth of Herring Creek (AALR IH#3:27).

John Whipps of Calvert Co. died leaving a will dated 10 December 1716 and proved 26 December 1716. He left his wife Eliza one-third of his dwelling plantation and one-third of his personal estate. He named his children Abigail Evans, Jane Jones, Sarah Busey, Susannah Stanford and John Whipps, Jr., who were to have 20 s. each. Daughter

Eliza was also to have 20 s. when she came of age. Son John was named executor and residuary legatee. Mary Chew, Henry Johnson, and William Preston witnessed the will (MWB 14:172, abst. in *Md. Cal. of Wills* 4:156; MDTP 30:172).

The estate of John Whipps, Sr., of Calvert Co. was appraised on 22 January 1716 by Samuel Griffith, Jr., and Charles Busey, who set a value of £191.0.0 on his personal property. Joseph Jackson and John Whipps, Jr., signed (INAC 37C:103).

John Whipps, the executor, filed an administration account of John Whipps' estate on 14 Dec 1717. Out of the inventory cited above, payments of £80.0.1 were made to a number of people including Elizabeth Whipps. The legatees were Sarah Busey, Susannah Standforth, Abigail Evans, and Morgan Jones (INAC 39C:113). A second account was filed by John Whipps on 9 December 1718. Out of assets totaling £196.5.3, payments totaling £85.12.2 were made to Elizabeth Whipps and John Sheredine. Of the balance, one-third was paid to Elizabeth, and the balance was paid to the accountant (MDAD 1:297).

Elizabeth Whips, widow, of Calvert Co., died leaving a will dated 11 November 1729 and proved 5 December 1729. She left her entire estate, except legacies to Thomas Vernon, Rachel Griffith, and Eliza Foudry, to her younger brother and sister William and Jane Medcaff, living near Askridge, in Yorkshire. Roger Crudgington was named executor, and was to sell the estate and send the proceeds to Philip Smith, merchant in London, who was to pay the same to her brother and sister aforesaid. William Phillips, Eliza Fadry, and Rachel Griffith witnessed the will (MWB 19:855, abst. in *Md. Cal. of Wills* 6:142).

On 29 December 1729 Henry Austin and William Austin of Halls Creek appraised her personal estate at £81.11.9. Roger Crudgington, executor, filed the inventory on 15 March 1729 (MINV 15:471).

John and Elizabeth were the parents of ("Whips Family Bibles," *Maryland Genealogical Society Bulletin* 17:165 gives birth dates of Jane, Susanna, John, and Abigail only): **2. Jane**, b. 1 February 1670, m. by 1716, Morgan Jones (MWB 14:173; MDTP 30:172); **3. Susanna**, b. 29 May 1677, m. by 1716, John Standford (MWB 14:172; MDTP 30:172; AALR WT#1:213); **4. John**, b. 30 April 1680; **5. Abigail**, b. 28 July 1687, m. by 1716, Edmond Evans (MWB 14:172, 173; MDTP 30:172); **6. Sarah**, m. by 1716, Paul Busey (MWB 14:172, 173; MDTP 30:172); and **7. Eliza**.

2. Jane Whipps, daughter of John (1) and Elizabeth, was born 1 February 1670, and married by 1716, Morgan Jones, who was buried 13 September 1718 in St. James Parish, Anne Arundel Co. Their descendants are traced in Robert Barnes, *Colonial Families of Anne Arundel County* (Westminster: Family Line Publications).

4. John Whipps, son of John (1) and Eliza, was born 30 April 1680, and died by 6 August 1735. He married Margaret Thurston on 14 November 1702 in St. James Parish, Anne Arundel Co. She died by 4 April 1764.

John Whipps was listed as a creditor in the estates of John Fitzredmond on 19 October 1721 and Thomas Randall on 26 October 1723 (MDAD 5:271, 273).

On 10 May 1704 Thomas Bale of Baltimore Co., merchant, conveyed 200 a. part *Stout*, in all 529 a. to John Whips, Jr., Bale's wife Sarah consented (BALR IR#PP:137).

Colonial Families of Maryland II

On 25 July 1724 John Whips and his wife Margaret mortgaged *Stout* to Philip Smith of London (BALR IS#G:348). On 19 January 1733 Whips conveyed to Richard Gist 200 a. part of *Stout*, which he had bought from Thomas Bale. His wife Margaret consented (BALR HWS#M:26).

On 6 Aug 1735 John Hammond, son of Charles, and Edward Dorsey exhibited an inventory of the personal estate of John Whips, showing a value of £36.14.2. Margaret and John Whips signed as next of kin. Adam Shipley, administrator, filed the inventory on 16 Aug 1735 (MINV 21:187).

Margaret Whips of Baltimore Co. died leaving a will dated 4 May 1769 and proved 4 April 1764. She left her personal estate to her daughter Susanna Whips, and named her son-in-law Adam Shipley, Sr., her executor. Robert and Helen Gilcrest and John and Bryan Avery witnessed the will (MWB 32:99, abst. in *Md. Cal. of Wills* 13:16).

John and Margaret were the parents of ("Whips Family Bibles," *MGSB* 17:165, gives birth dates of John, Samuel, Benjamin and Mary only); **8. Susanna**, b. 1711, d. 1764; **9. Uroth**, b. 1713, d. 1764, m. 1737 Adam Shipley; **10. John**, b. 9 July 1719; **11. Samuel**, b. 21 July 1721, d. 1764, m. Mary McComas on 22 January 1742 in St. Johns Parish (*SJSG:* 51); **12. Benjamin**, b. 3 October 1723, d. leaving an undated will proven on 7 February 1757. He named his mother Margaret Whipps and his sister Susanna. Nicholas Dorsey, Robert Gilcrist, and John Glover witnessed the will (MWB 30:243, abst. in *Md. Cal. of Wills* 11:157); and **13. Mary**, b. 27 March 1726, d. 1778, m. Adam Shipley in 1750 (He was possibly the widower of Uroth Whipps (#9 above)).

10. John Whipps, son of John (19) and Margaret, was born 1719 and died 1778. He married Sarah Lucretia Ogg, daughter of George and Mary (Potee) Ogg. She was born. 1726 and died 1794.

On 2 November 1754 John Whips of Anne Arundel Co. conveyed part of *Progress* to Benjamin Whips of Baltimore Co. (BALR BB#I:334). On 6 November 1758 he conveyed 100 a. part *Progress* to Edward Dorsey of John (BALR B#G:256).

Sarah Lucrese Whips of Anne Arundel Co. died leaving a will dated 1 January 1781 and proved 6 July 1782. Negro girl Hannah and her increase to be equally divided amongst her three grandchildren: John Whips, son of George, John Whips Poole, son of Peter, and Sarah Lucrese Whips, daughter of Benjamin Whips. Grandson John Whips Poole also to have a Negro boy Caleb. Negro man Tone to her sons George and Benjamin. Negro woman Hardy to be free at my death, and her future increase to be equally divided among her three grandchildren (named above). The residue of her estate was to be equally divided between her sons George and Benjamin, who were also named her sole executors. John Hood, Benjamin Shipley, and Benjamin Hood witnessed the will (AAWB TG#1:52-53).

In December 1783 a newspaper notice stated that John Whips of Anne Arundel Co. had died leaving a son Samuel (*Maryland Journal and Baltimore Advertiser* 16 December 1783).

John and Sarah were the parents of ("Whips Family Bibles," *MGSB* 17:165; Data from genforum, posted by leahm@columbus.rr.com): **14. Usley [Ursula?]**, b. 9 April 1740, d. 1780; **15. Rachel**, b. 15 June 1747, d. 1820, m. Adam Shipley; **16. Ruth**, b. 13 February 1748/49, d. 1780, m. Peter Poole; **17. Katherine** (twin), b. 31 July 1751, d.

1780; **18. Valite** (twin), b. 31 July 1751, d. 1780; **19. Samuel**, b. 20 Jan 1753, d. 1780, m. Henrietta Pool; in March 1780 Samuel Whips advertised that he would not be responsible for the debts of his wife Henrietta, who had misbehaved herself with Robert Brown (*Maryland Journal and Baltimore Advertiser* 7 March 1780); **20. Sarah Lucretia**, b. 2 July 1754, d. 1780; **21. Benjamin**, b. 5 August 1750 (or 1758), d. 1840, m. 1st, Sara H. Lewis, and 2nd, Susanna Rebecca Pierce; and **22. George**, b. 15 January 1761, d. 1762, m, Elizabeth Pierce

19. Samuel Whipps, son of John (10) and Margaret, was born 1721, and died 1764. He married Mary McComas.

On 1 August 1745 Samuel Whips, with consent of wife Mary, for brotherly love, conveyed 125 a. *Whipps Purchase* to his brother Benjamin Whips (BALR TB#D:255).

On 3 March 1747 Samuel Whipps and wife Mary conveyed *Long Valley* to William Gosnell (BALR TB#E:670).

== = 0 = =

The Wilkinson Family

1. William Wilkinson was in Baltimore Co. by 1681 when he claimed land for service (MPL WC#4:123). On 5 March 1681 he surveyed 50 a. *Wilkinson's Spring*. He married, 1st, by September 1694 Elizabeth, heir of Abraham and Sarah Clark. He married, 2nd, by 1705, Tamar, daughter of Robert Love. Tamar married, 2nd, Richard Lenox.

In November 1684 he was made an allowance for accommodating the jury for the laying out of (an early) Baltimore Town. In 1695 he was a vestryman of St. Paul's Parish (Reamy and Reamy, *St. Paul's Parish Register:* 152).

In March 1693 he was named by Martha Cage as the father of her child (BACP G#1:175-176).

On 7 March 1693 Wilkinson made his mark when he conveyed to John Smith of Biteford [Biddiford?], County Devon, England, Lot #3 in the Town of Absolute on the Patapsco River (BALR RM#HS:414).

On 11 June 1694 William Hollis and wife Mary, daughter of Abraham and Sarah Clarke, conveyed *Landisell* (which formerly belonged to Mary) to William Wilkinson (BALR RM#HS:401). On 16 June 1705 William and his wife Tamar conveyed. 89 a. *Wilkinson's Folly* to Moses Edwards (BALR TR#A:284).

In 1708 John Love made a will naming William Wilkinson as his brother-in-law. Wilkinson stated on 6 June 1711 that he knew Hannah Keon, alias Dictus Keon of N.C., and she was reputed and taken to be the wife of Lodowick Williams, 'formerly a liver [*i.e.,* resident] in Baltimore Co.' (BALR TR#A:135).

Wilkinson died leaving a will dated 21 April 1718 and proved 16 June 1718, He left his dwelling plantation to his son Robert, *Cumberland* to his daughters Jane Corbin, Ann, Philisanna, and Sophia. He named his wife Tamar as executrix. The estate of William Wilkinson was inventoried on 28 June 1718 by John Norton and S. Hinton, and valued at £162.3.9. His estate was administered on 4 June 1725 and 4 July 1725 by Tamar, now wife of Richard Lenox. On 27 Jan 1724 Tamar was named as the, executrix of William Wilkinson of Baltimore Co. and administratrix of Frances Keys (BAAD 1:94, BAAD 2:335; MDAD 6:296; 7:103; MDTP 27:1258).

William Wilkinson was the father of: (By Elizabeth): **2. Robert**; and **3. William**, who died leaving a nuncupative will dated 28 March 1715 and proved 31 March 1715, He left his brother Robert land given him by his mother. Edward Mahun, Mary Lynch, and William Wilkinson and 'Tamor' his wife witnessed the will. James Wilkinson, the executor, requested that the will be recorded (MWB 14:680 abst. in *Md. Cal. of Wills* 4:179). (By Tamar): **4. Jane**, m. by 21 April 1718 Edward Corbin (See The Corbin Family elsewhere in this work); **5. Anne**, m. George Harryman by 30 March 1725 (See The Harryman Family elsewhere in this work); **6. Sophia**, m. Thomas Sligh on 17 April 1734 (See The Sligh Family elsewhere in this work; and **7. Philisanna**.

2. Robert Wilkinson, son of William (1) and Elizabeth, died 1760 in Baltimore County. He married Rachel Lenox on 8 June 1736 (Reamy and Reamy, *St. Paul's Parish Register:* 33, gives her name as Rachel Lenore [*sic*])

In June 1733 he chose his mother [step-mother?] as his guardian. He died leaving a will dated 13 August 1759 and proved 6 March 1760.

On 22 May 1758 Edward Corbin and wife Jane conveyed to Robert Wilkinson *Landisell*, which they had already conveyed to his mother, Tamar Wilkinson (BALR B#G:157).

Robert and Rachel were the parents of (Reamy and Reamy, *St. Paul's Parish Register:*12): **8. William**, b. 10 August 1736; and **9. Sarah**, m. Thomas Todd.

6. Philisanna Wilkinson, daughter of William (1) and Tamar, was fined for bastardy in June 1733 and again June 1738.

On 7 July 1740 Phillis Wilkinson for love she bore her son Jethro Lynch Wilkinson, conveyed him 100 a. *Cumberland*. Robert Wilkinson witnessed the deed (BALR HWS#1-A: 398).

Philisanna was the mother of: **10. Jethro Lynch Wilkinson**.

8. William Wilkinson, son of Robert (2) and Rachel, was born 10 August 1736. He died by 16 May 1783. He married Sarah [-?-].

On 22 December 1763 Edward Ward conveyed to William Wilkinson the land where he was now living, being part of the land that formerly belonged to Edward ward (BALR B#M:379). On 2 April 1779 Wilkinson, with the consent of his wife Sarah conveyed to Samuel Owings and his wife Deborah, and to Samuel Owings of Stephen and his wife Nelly, the said William and Sarah's third of an undivided half of two lots of and bequeathed to Joshua Lynch, now deceased, by his mother Eleanor Lynch (BALR WG#D:8).

William Wilkinson witnessed the will of William Jenkins on 4 September 1760 (MWB 31:316). He was listed in the 1783 Assessment List of Patapsco Lower Hundred as owning 487 a. of land [not named]. His household consisted of eight white inhabitants (Carothers, *1783 Tax List of Baltimore Co.:* 87).

William Wilkinson died leaving a will dated 28 March 1783 and proved 16 May 1783. His two eldest sons William and Robert were to have all the lands on Patapsco

Colonial Families of Maryland II

Neck he held at his decease, by descent or purchase; such a division of land was to take place after Robert had reached the age of 21. He named his daughters Sarah and Rachel. He left 500 a. of unpatented land in Washington Co. that he had bought from Thomas Jones to his third and fourth sons Joshua and Thomas. He named his son Caleb. His friends Samuel Owings and Samuel Owings of Stephen were to be executors. Thomas Jones, Josias Bowen and Thomas Hamm witnessed the will (BAWB 3:542).

On 14 February 1792 his estate was administered by Samuel Owings and Samuel Owings of Stephen, executors. (BAAD 10:533).

William Wilkinson was the father of: **11. William,** d. by 6 January 1789; **12. Robert,** not yet 21 on 28 March 1783; **13. Joshua;** may have been the Joshua Wilkinson hatter, who was married to Miss Ann Patrick last Sat, eve. by Rev. William Lynch (*Maryland Journal and Baltimore Advertiser* 28 February 1792); **14. Thomas,** b. 4 December 1773; **15. Samuel; 16. Richard; 17. Caleb; 18. Rachel;** and 19. **Sarah,** who may have been the Sarah Wilkinson who was m. to Mr. Caleb Hewie 'last eve.' by Rev. William Lynch (*Baltimore Daily Intelligencer* 16 May 1794).

10. Jethro Lynch Wilkinson, son of Phillisanna (6), was born about 1733. He married Elizabeth Harryman on 29 January 1761 (*SJSG:* 106).

Jethro Lynch Wilkinson was named as the father of Ruth Rowles' child in November 1757 (Baltimore Co. Rough Court Minutes, 1755-1763; Baltimore Co. Criminal Proceedings, 1757-1759: 74).

Jethro and Elizabeth were probably the parents of: **20. Moses.**

11. William Wilkinson, son of William (8), died leaving a will dated 10 November 1788 and proved 6 January 1789. He mentioned the will of his father William, and stated that his brother Robert was to have all of the lands on Patapsco Neck. His brother Joshua was to have all the lands not before given to Robert. He named his brothers Thomas, Samuel, Richard, and Caleb, and his sisters Sarah and Rachel. His friends Samuel Owings of Stephen and Samuel Owings were named executors. Junus Ogleter and Thomas Risteau witnessed the will (BAWB 4:323, abst. by Burns).

In September 1789 Samuel Owings advertised that Wilkinson's plantation on Patapsco Neck was to be sold (*Maryland Journal and Baltimore Advertiser* 8 September 1789).

12. Robert Wilkinson, son of William (7), was not yet 21 on 28 March 1783. On 11 August 1795 Robert Wilkinson and Joshua Wilkinson, deeded to Philip Rogers 499 a. of land, all their right to *Nashes Rest, Landisell, Upper Spring Neck,* and *Wilkinson's Spring (*BALR WG#TT:111).

20. Moses Wilkinson, son of Jethro Lynch (10) and Elizabeth, was living as late as 20 May 1784, when as a grandson of Phyllis Wilkinson, deceased, he deeded to Vincent Corbin all that part of *Cumberland* which William Wilkinson had left to Phyllis Wilkinson n his will (BALR WG#T:63).

Unplaced:

John Wilkinson, m. by 10 March 1769 Barbara, administratrix of George Pickett (BAAD7:61). George Pickett had m. Barbara Gorsuch on 16 February 1751 (*SJSG:* 93). John and Barbara were the parents of (Reamy and Reamy, *St. Paul's Parish Register:* 24): Rebecca, b. 11 September 1770

John Wilkinson died by 13 April 1772 when his estate was administered by Eliza Wilkinson. She cited an inventory of ?11.18.3, and listed payments of ?11.14.9 (BAAD 7:157; MDAD 66:327).

Richard Wilkinson and Miss Fanny Perriage [Peregoy?] of Baltimore Co. were m. last Thurs. by Rev. McCain (*Baltimore American* 2 December 1813).

==0==

Index

Abbott, Samuel 173
Abell, James 136
Acton, Margaret 142; Richard 142
Adair, Alex 88; Cassandra 141; Robert 11, 59, 191
Adder, Robert 26
Adkinson, Levina Ann 7
Airey, David 1, 2; Deborah 1, 2; Easter 2; Elizabeth [-?-] 2; Elizabeth Cook 1; Esther 1, 2, 3; Hannah Jadwyn 1; Jane Parrott 3; Jane [-?-] Parrott 2; Jonathan 1, 2, 3; Joseph 1, 2, 3; Mary 2, 3
Aisquith, William 19
Alder, Hannah 96; Mary Nice 96; Robert 96
Alford, Christian Goddard 75; Moses 75
Allbuy, John 15
Allein, Benjamin 209; Elizabeth Tongue 209, 210; Mary [-?-] 171; William 171
Allen, Eliza 88; Elizabeth 114; George 114; Hugh 79; John 22; Margaret 48
Allender, Eliz. 208; Mary 208; Sophia Tolley 208; William 208
Allingham, Philip 160
Allison, [-?-] (Rev.) 198
Allnutt, William 212
Amery, Mary 79; Sam 79
Amos, James 18; Martha Bradford 18
Anderrson, Peter John 36
Anderson, Andrew 10, 134; Daniel 46; Elizabeth Edwards 64, 65; John 152, 153; Jonathan 153; Richard 136; Sarah Edwards 65; Susannah Meek 65; William 64, 65, 131, 178, 195
Andrew(s), Abarilla 190; Abraham 11, 190; Elizabeth Durbin William 190; Mary [-?-] 3, 190; Samuel 3, 4; Thomas 75; William 101, 190
Angling, Cornelius 10, 120
Anseller, Jacob 191
Appleton, Elizabeth Rogers 175; John 175
Archer, John 74, 129, 133; Samuel 135
Arey. See Airey.
Armstrong, James 34; John 206; Mary [-?-] 206
Arnest, Caleb 190
Arnold, David 128, 129; Elizabeth 73; Hannah Debruler 60; John 60; Martha [-?-] 73; Rebecca 128; Rebecca [-?-] 129;
Richard 73
Ashley, Abraham 4, 5, 6; Ann 5, 6; Ann Emerich 7; Benjamin 6, 7; Charles 4; Daniel 6, 7; David 7; David C. 7; Eliza Ann 7; Elizabeth 4, 5, 6; Elizabeth [-?-] 6; Hannah 5; Isaac 5, 6; Isaiah 7; Jacob 6; James 6; James David 7; Jane Cooper 4; John 4, 5, 6, 7; John Dudley 7; John Jones 5, 7; Joseph 7; Joshua 5; Joshua Jones 5; Lemuel Washington 7; Levina Ann Adkinson 7; Margaret 6; Martha 5; Martha Wroth 5; Mary 4, 5; Mary [-?-] 6; Mary Dudley 7; Mary Wroth 5; Milcah 6, 7; Nancy 6, 7; Phebe 6; Rachel 6; Sarah 6; Sophia 6, 7; Thomas 4, 5, 6; Thomas Wroth 7; William 4, 5, 6, 7
Ashman, George 31
Assa, Dinah [-?-] Nuthead Devoran Oley 130, 131, 132; Samuel 131
Atkinson, Ann 8; Ann Maria Leroy 8; Ann Wilton 7, 8; Anna Leroy 9; Elizabeth 8; Hannah 8; Isaac 24, 111; Jane 8; Joshua 8; Leroy 8; Margaret 8; Margaret Thornborough 8; Mary Leroy 8; Matthew 8, 152; Matthew Abraham 8; Samuel 8; Sarah 8; Stephen 7, 8; Thomas 8; Thomas Wilton 8; William 8, 9; William Benjamin 8; Wilton 8
Aubern, Henry 152
Aude, Thomas 211
Auld, Betsy 169; James 169; John 169; John Field 169; Mary Kendricks Jackson 169; Michael Piper 169; Nancy 169; Rosanna 169; Rosanna Piper Goldsborough 169; Sidney Fields 169
Austin, Eleanor 229; Henry 229, 233; William 233
Ayres, Thomas 16
Babson, Amory 52
Backford, [-?-] 9
Bacon, Elizabeth 68; Martin 68; Mary [-?-] 68
Bagford, Comfort [-?-] 9; Elizabeth [-?-] Sampson 9, 135, 136; James 9, 135, 136; William 9
Bagley, Elizabeth 159
Bagshaw, William 5
Bailer, Andrew 94
Bailey, George 147; Jabez 148; John 148;

239

Index

Sarah McClain 147
Bailey: See also Baily, Baly.
Baily, Lucy Ann 25
Baily: See also Bailey, Baly.
Bain, James 183; Mary [-?-] 183
Baker, Charles 97, 119; Eliza 178; Jane 138; Martha 178
Baldwin, John 73; William H. 123
Bale, Sarah [-?-] 233; Thomas 233, 234
Baley. See Bailey.
Baly: See also Bailey, Baily.
Bandell, George 13
Banks, Elizabeth Cleverly 51
Bankson, Elizabeth Giles Slemaker 74; Joseph 74
Barber, Cornelius 153; Elias 153
Barkabee, Ann 227
Barker, Mary [-?-] Watkins 224, 226; William 224
Barkey, Margaret 57
Barklie, Eliza McCalmont 45
Barnard, Charles 13
Barn(e)s, Christieanne Taylor 204; Ford 78; John 1; Mary 160; Mary Ogg 160; Michael Denton 204; Barnes, Philemon 160; Richard 64, 80
Barney, Benjamin 50; Delilah [-?-] 50; Eliz. 128; Francis 58, 60
Barrett, Alice [-?-] 62; Alice [-?-] Corbin 41; John 41, 42, 62
Barton, Ann [-?-] 11, 12; Ann Barton 13; Ann Hitchcock 13; Ann Holt 12; Aquila 12; Barton, Asael 11, 12; Cathender 12; Celia 12; Comfort Roberts 10, 11; Dorothy Nice 13; Elizabeth 12, 13; Greenbury 10, 11, 12; James 11, 13; Joan [-?-] 10; Johanna Simmons 11; John 13; Joshua 11, 12; Judith [-?-] 10; Judith Dorman 135; Lewis 10, 11, 26, 134, 135; Mary 12; Nicholas 12; Priscilla 12; Rachel 12; Rebecca Biddison 10; Sally Maxwell 13; Sarah 12; Sarah [-?-] 12; Sarah Dorman 10, 134; Sarah Everett 13; Selah 11, 12; Selah Dorman 10; Seth 14; Sillis 12; Susanna [-?-] 12; Susanna Sharp 13; Temperance Rollo 13; Thomas 12
Batee, Eliza 193
Batie, John 193
Battee, Benjamin 193; Ferdinando 192, 193

Battson, [-?-] 51; Amy 52; Amy Dare 51, 52
Baxter, [-?-] 31; Benjamin 146; Edmond 104; Mary [-?-] 146; Patrick 86; Sarah Taylor 202; Susanna [-?-] King 104; Thomas 146
Baxton, Mary 28
Bayes, Ruth 81
Bayly, Lucy Ann 26
Bayly: See also Bailey, Baly.
Bayne, Lewis 136
Bays, John 120
Beale, Elizabeth 168
Beall, Verlinda Ferguson 66; Zephaniah 66
Beam, Peter 93
Beard, Matthew 213; Susannah 64
Beasman, Sarah 160, 161
Beavan, Charles 185
Beaver, William 97
Beck, Anthony 229; Clement 213; Elizabeth West 229; John 4; Mary 4
Beddoe, John 117; Sarah Litton, 117
Bedworth, Richard 192
Bell, Eliza 204; Rowles 178; Jacob 178; Thomas 178
Belt, Keturah Price 92; Richard 92
Bembridge, Christopher 225
Bend, Elizabeth Bordley Polk 164; Joseph Grove John 164
Benedict, Sarah 160
Benger, Deborah [-?-] Johnson 129, 130; Robert 34, 35, 129, 130; Katherine Therrell Chadwell 34, 35, 129, 130
Benjar. See Benger.
Benjer. See Benger.
Bennett, Elizabeth 162; John 66
Bensee, Paul 232
Benson, Stephen 184, 204
Berger, Deeter 92
Berry, Joseph 39, 40; Margaret Rogers 175; Sarah Cockayne 40; Sarah Goddard 75; Thomas 75, 175; William 65
Besson, Thomas 215
Beswick, Thomas 38
Bick, John 227
Bicknell, Thomas 64
Bidderson. See Biddison.
Biddison, Daniel 82; Jarvis 179; Rebecca 10; Sophia 228; Sosia 228; Thomas 26, 226

240

Index

Biddle, Ann 13; Jesse 13
Bidwell, Thomas 190
Bignall, John 78; Rebecca 78
Billingslea, Clemency 172
Billingsley, Catherine Hook 96; Clement 154; George 87; Samuel 96; Thomas 211
Birckhead, Abraham 99; Ann Tucker 211; Francis 217; Nehemiah 211, 217; Samuel 211, 212
Bird, Abraham 184
Birens, John 35
Black, Henry 148
Black, William 230
Blackistone, Ebenezer 206
Blackwell, Thomas 218
Bladen, Thomas 21; William 132, 195, 199
Blake, Betty Holdsworth Heighe 89; James Heighe 89
Blike, Gabriel 224
Blunt, Richard 156; Samuel 180
Boaring, John, 129, 130
Boaring. See also Boreing, Boring.
Bodington, Richard 227
Body, Martha 5; Martha Ashley 5, 6; Stephen 139, 140; Susanna Mead Long 139
Bohemont, Anne 136
Bonaday, Francis Mahorne Carback 29; James 29
Bond, Abraham 15; Ali 14; Alice 15; Alice [-?-] 13, 14; Ann 14, 15; Barnet 13, 14, 15, 82; Barnett 13; Barzilla 15, 16; Bazil 16; Bernard 14; Charles 15, 16; Edward 15, 16; Eleanor 15; Eliz. 16; Elizabeth 14, 15, 16, 46; Ellonor 15; George 15, 16; James 15; Jane 18; John 15, 91, 123; Joshua 14, 48; Julia McCord 15; Margaret 78; Maria [-?-] 15; Mary 13, 14, 15, 16; Peggy 78; Peter 194; Richard 122, 123; Ruth Hughes 15; Ruth Sampson 16; Samuel 39; Sarah 14, 122; Sarah [-?-] 15, 16; Sarah [-?-] Harryman 82; Sarah Bond 14, 15; Sarah Jordan 14, 15; Susanna 15; Thomas 13, 14; Tobias 14, 15; William 13, 14, 15, 77, 227
Bonfield, James 78; Margaret 18
Bonner, Henry 71
Bonsaton, William 222
Boone, Sarah [-?-] 94; Susannah 94

Boothby, Edward 26, 67
Boram, John 75
Borck, Henry 69
Border, John 95; Margaret Hook 95
Bordley, John 163; John Beale 197
Boreing, James 50; Joshua 122
Boreing. See also Boaring, Boring.
Borer, Thomas 204
Boring, John 134, 137; Rebecca Cox 50; Thomas 134
Boring. See also Boaring, Boreing.
Bosley, Charles 50; Elizabeth 51; Elizabeth Cox 50; James 50; Joseph 51; Ruth 51; William 21
Bosman, Edw. 69
Boston, [-?-]; 34; Samuel 67
Bosworth, William 169
Boteler, Alexander Robinson 165
Boteler, Henry 165; Priscilla Robinson 165
Bourne, Barbara Burke 22; Catherine [-?-] 63; Henry 63; James 88, 208; John 22; Robert 88
Bowen, Ann 198; Benjamin 103, 197; Elizabeth Taylor 203; John 41; Josias 237; Mary 198; Wilkes 203
Bowers, Thomas 60
Bowersox, George 152; Sarah Eliza Mohler 152
Bowes, George 1
Bowle, James 51
Bowles, David 76
Bowly, Daniel 16
Bowyer, Elizabeth Ashley 6
Boyce, R. 192; Roger 76
Boyd, James 141; Robert 81; Ruth [-?-] 81
Boyer, John 24, 111
Boyle, Thomas 74
Boyls, Mary 48; Thomas 48
Bracco, John 174
Bradburn, Alexander 204
Bradbury, Procello 3
Bradee, Owen 211
Bradford, Catherine Rhodes Osborne 17; Elizabeth 18; Elizabeth Lightbody 17, 18; George 17, 18, 123; Hannah 17; Jane Bond 18; John 16, 17; John George 17, 18; Joseph 18; Margaret Bonfield 18; Margaret Talbot 18; Martha 18; Mary 18; Mary Mallonee 122, 123; Mary Skinner

241

Index

17; Samuel 17, 18; Sarah 18; Sarah McComas 18; Susanna 18; Susanna McComas 18; William 16, 17, 18
Brady, James 12; Mary Barton 12
Braine, Benjamin 182
Bramwell, George 179
Brand, Samuel 188
Brandt, Jacob 79
Brannon, Mary 48
Brawn, Henry 128
Brerewood, Thomas 68
Brewer, John 163, 193, John 216; Rachel 163
Brian, Eleanor Harryman 81, 82; Luke 81, 82
Brice, Elizabeth 101; J. 131; James 164
Briggs, Margaret 166
Broad, Frances 150
Broadwater, Hugh 34, 136
Brockenbrough, Lucy [-?-] 165
Brockshaw, James 34
Brogden, Ann 120; John 120
Brogdon. See Brogden.
Broome, [-?-] 53; Kezia Dare 52; Regia Dare 53;
Brown, Abel 71; Abel 72; Augustine 184; Blanch 47; Dixon 140, 219; Elias 161; Elizabeth 48, 166, 167, 219; Elizabeth [-?-] 166; Elizabeth Sickelmore 184; Elizabeth Simmons 185; Gabriel 156, 184; Gambrall 184; George 126, 146, 149; Hannah Atkinson 8; Jacob 115; James 8, 10; John 149, 176, 184, 188; John Eliot 166; John Elliot 85; Joshua 83; Margaret [-?-] 184; Martha 57; Mary Prebble 170; Rebecca 121; Robert 234; Ruth McQueen 149; Samuel 170, 205; Sarah 123; Sarah Ann 84; Thomas 104, 184, 205; William 79; William Chew 84
Browne, John 177; Peter 87; Thomas 108, 188
Browning, John 6; William 6
Brucebanks, Edward 98, 231
Brunts, Peter 215
Bryan, Catherine 142; Lewis 41; Richard 213
Buchanan, Andrew 104; Archibald 170, 171; Elizabeth 189; George 38, 127; John 211; Mary [-?-] 189; Mary Bucknell Prebble 170, 171
Buck, Benjamin 24, 81, 141; John 36, 81
Buck. See also Busk.
Buckingham, Thomas 77
Bucknal, Blanch Brown 47; Francis 47; Judith 47
Bucknell, Mary 170; Mary [-?-] 170; Thomas 170
Buckner, William 73
Bulger, Martin 22
Bull, Catherine 19; Catherine Walker 19; Constantine 19; Constantine Cooke 19; Deborah 19; Edward 19; Jacob 206; John 19; Margaret 19; Mary 19; Mary [-?-] 19; Peter 19; Stephen 19; William Horatio 19
Bullen, Charles 173; Thomas 173
Burchfield, Joan [-?-] Chattam Cantwell 26; Mary 27; Thomas 26, 56, 70
Buredy, Frances 59
Burges, Henry Howard 124
Burk(e), Ann Ryland 23; Barbara 22; Cealia 22; Delilah Peacock 22; Edward 22; Elisia Elizabeth 22; Eliza 32; Eliza [-?-] 22; Elizabeth 21; Elizabeth [-?-] 20, 21, 22; Ellick 21; Greenbury 24; John 22, 108; John James 22; Margaret 21, 22, 23; Mary 21; Mary Leekings 20, 21; Mary Lemmon 22; Muck 21; Richard 21, 23; Sarah 21, 23; Sarah Sickelmore 183; Sarah Sicklemore 21, 22; Susanna Templeton 22; Thomas 20, 21, 22, 23, 183; Ulick 20, 21, 22; William 23; William Goldsmith 22
Burke. See also Busk.
Burney, John 111
Burns, John 94
Burridge, Frances 59
Burrough, Sarah 219
Burton, Eleanor Watkins 228; Ellen Watkins 228; John 228
Busby, Benjamin 123; John 123
Busey, Charles 63, 233; Elizabeth [-?-] Eastwood 63; Paul 232, 233; Sarah 233; Sarah Whipps 232, 233
Bush, James 111; John 111
Bush, Ruth. See Busk, Ruth [-?-].
Bush. See also Busk.
Busk, Anna 24; Barbara 24; Barbara [-?-] 111; Darby 24; David 24; Eleanor (Helen) Ridden Gash 24; Elenor 24; Elizabeth 23;

Index

Greenbury 23, 24, 111; Hannah 24, 110, 111; Hester 23; Hester Dobbin [-?-] 25; James 23, 24, 111; John 23, 24, 25, 111; Rhoda 111; Rhoda Davis 23, 24; Ruth [-?-] 23; Thomas 24; William 23, 24, 25
Bussey, [-?-] 184
Butcher, Ann 171; Debora 171; Elizabeth [-?-] Eastwood 63; James 63; Mary 63
Butler, Absalom 127
Butterworth, Hannah 73; Isaac 106; Sarah 73
Button, Robert 37; Rosanna 168
Butts, Mary [-?-] 171; Richard 171
Bynn, Edw. 156
Cadle, Benjamin 76
Cage, Martha 235
Caile, John 169
Caine, William 34
Calhoun, James 127, 128
Calhoun, James 151, 152
Callister, Elizabeth Emerson 164; Harriet 164; Margaret 164; Mary Harriott 164; Sarah 164; Sarah [-?-] 164; Vallista 164
Calvert, Charles 103
Camel, John 11, 134
Cammel, Ruth 183
Camp, James 8
Camparl, Elizabeth 162
Campbell, Elizabeth 94, 95; James 16, 44; John 85; Nicholas 110; Samuel 43; Sarah Coulter 43
Canaday, Rachel 6; Rachel Ashley 6
Cannon, Henrietta [-?-] 25; Thomas 10, 25, 26
Cantar, William 153
Canter, Henry 154; Mary Moran 154
Cantwell, Adam 26, 27; Blanch Jackson 26; Catherine Goff 28; Edmond 27; Edmund 26, 27; Edward 26, 225, 226; Elizabeth 26; Elizabeth M'Kim 27; Francis 26; Hannah 26; Hugh 27; James Smith 28; Jane 26; Joan [-?-] Chattam 26; Johanna 26, 27; Johanna [-?-] 26; John 26, 27; Lucian 26; Lucy 26, 27; Malley 27; Mary 26; Mary [-?-] 26; Mary Ann 26; Mary Burchfield 27; Mary Cantwell 28; Mary Debaes 27; Mary Vincent 27; Matthew 27; Nathaniel 26; Nicholas 27; Pattison 26; Peter 27; Richard 26; Ruth 26, 27; Sallie Woody 26; Sally Smith 28; Sarah 26, 28; Sarah [-?-] 26; Thomas 26, 28; William 26, 28
Capell, Benjamin 198
Caples, Robert 178
Caploe, Elizabeth Hook 95; William 95
Carback, [-?-] 29; Ann 29; Anne 28; Anne [-?-] 30; Avarilla 29; Cassie Wilkinson 29; E. 29; Elizabeth 29; Frances Mahon 120; Frances Mahorne 29; Henry 28, 29; Isabella [-?-] 29; Jane Rawlings 29; Jane Wright 29; John 5, 28, 29; John Martin 29, 120; John Valentine 28, 29; Margaret Harryman 28; Mary 28; Mary [-?-] 28, 29; Mary Harryman 28; Philip 29; Ruth Jones 29; Temperance 29; Thomas 28, 30; Valentine 28, 29; William 20, 28, 29
Carey, Abarilla [-?-] 30; Andrew 31; Anne [-?-] 31; Dorothy [-?-] 30; Eleanor 30; Is. 30; James 30, 31, 121; John 30, 174; Margaret 30; Susanna [-?-] 174
Carey. See also Garey.
Cark, George 81
Carleton, Thomas 96
Carr, Aquila 91; Matilda 87
Carrington, Ann 31, 32; Catherine 32; Catherine [-?-] 31; Daniel 31, 32; George 31, 32; Henry 31, 32, 33; John 31, 32, 147; Katherine [-?-] 31; Margaret 31, 32; Mary 31, 32
Carroll, Aquila 201, 202; Charles 55, 64, 81 93, 94, 95, 170; Daniel 84; Isabella Cowan 48; James 77, 147; Jemima Taylor 202; John 48; Mary [-?-] 84
Carter, Anne 38; Edward 98; Edward F. 15; Henry 168; Mary 38; Richard 38; Sarah 195; Solomon 201; Thomas 15, 38; William 38
Cartwright, Mary Moran 154; William Andrew 154
Carty John 187
Cary, [-?-] 191
Cary. See Carey
Casdrop, John 36
Caswell, Christian [-?-] 37; Richard 207, 208
Cathling, William 5
Catlin(e), Henry 177; Thomas 5, 6
Caton, Ann 229
Caudrey, Mary 231

243

Index

Cawthren, Will 207
Chadwell, Elizabeth 35; John 34, 35, 129, 130; Katherine [-?-] 34; Katherine Therell 129; Margaret 35; Mary [-?-] 35
Chadwell, See also Shadwell.
Chadwill. See Chadwell.
Chainy, Sarah 37
Chalmers, Ann 65
Chalmers, Sarah 65
Chamberlain, Mary [-?-] 105; Thomas 105
Chamberlin, Eleanor 77
Chambers, Sarah 127, 128
Chambs, Matthew 96
Chamier, Daniel 78, 191
Chance, Elizabeth 228; John 228; Martha Watkins 228
Chanc(e)y, George 70, 138
Chandler, John 79, 80; Chandler, Margaret Rogers 176; Sarah 79; Stephen 79, 80; Thomas 232; Walter Story 176; William 79
Channell, John 133
Chapman, John 179; Robert 206
Charbars, John 195
Chase, [-?-] 94; Thomas 75, 142
Chattam, Francis 26; Joan [-?-] 26
Cheney, John 188; Mary Rowles 178; Sarah 178
Chenoweth, Keziah 56; Mary 130; Richard 56
Chester, Ellianor 211
Chetham, Edward 3
Chew, Joseph 99, 100, 187, 209; Joshua 209; Mary 233; Mary [-?-] Simmons 187; Nathaniel 209; P. 53, 209; Richard 167, 209; Samuel 53, 99; 209
Cheyn(e), Chloe 37; Christian 36; Elizabeth 36, 37; Elizabeth [-?-] 36; Frederick 36; James W. 36; Jean Walker 36; Pamela 37; Roderick 35, 36. 37; Rodericus 36; Sarah 37
Chilcoat, Joshua 22; Sarah [-?-] 22
Child, Mary 188
Chilton, Elizabeth 64
Chine, Elizabeth 36; Mary 36
Chine. See also Cheyne
Chltton, Eleanor 64
Chnnerworth. See under Chenoweth.
Christopher, Elizabeth 14; Elizabeth [-?-] 15; James 15
Clagett, Charles 52; Diana Dare 52; Diannah Dare 52; Nathaniel 52
Clare, John 52
Clark, Abraham 235; Alice Lee 176; Edward 1; Elizabeth 167, 235; James 51; John 56, 104, 176; Margaret Lee 176; Richard 91; Samuel 81; Sarah [-?-] 235; Sophia Harryman 81; Thomas 176; William 81
Clark. See also Clarke.
Clarke, Abraham 137; Ann 45; Eliza [-?-] 186; James 118; Mathias 186
Clarke. See also Clark
Clarkson, Elizabeth 223
Clayland, James 40
Claypoole, Mary Chambers 163, 164
Clayton, William 38
Clements, Cleon 155
Clemounce, Andrew 156
Clendenin, Henry Dashiell 112; Jane Dashiell 112; William H. 112
Clendenning, Thomas 191
Cleverly, Ann [-?-] 51; Thomas 51
Clingan, [-?-] Simpson 190; James 190
Clinton. See Chilton.
Close, Garrett 106, 189
Clough, John 136
Coale, Philemon 95; Philip 74; Sarah 75; Thomas 101
Cobb, Charity 37, 38, 143; Christiana 38, 143; Frances 37, 38, 101, 143; James 37, 38, 101, 142, 143, 212; Joseph 38; Margaret 37, 39, 143, 212; Mary Poge 38; Priscilla 28, 37, 143; Rebecca 37. 143; Rebecca [-?-] 101, 212; Rebecca Daniell 37, 142, 143; Ruth Elledge 48
Cobreath, Jno. 87
Cockayne, Anne Carter 38, 39, 40; Carter 40; Catherine 39; Christopher 39, 40; James 40; Mary 39, 40; Rebecca 40; Samuel 38, 39. 40; Sarah 39, 40; Sarah [-?-] 40; Sarah Harwood 39; Sarah Kemp 40; Sarah Scales 39; Thomas 38, 39, 40; William 38. 39
Cockey, Alice 111; John 55, 198; Thomas 82, 83, 92
Coen. See Cowan.
Cogell, Elizabeth [-?-] 133; James 34, 133,

134, 136
Coin. See Cowan.
Cole, Angelica 76; Dennis Garrett 121; Edith 121; Eleanor 108; Elizabeth 76; George 31, 117, 119; Henry 119, 123; Martha Litton 117, 19; Richard 108; William 39, 70
Coleman, Francis 219
Colley, [-?-] 223
Collier, John 34. 100, 136; Samuel 56, 201
Collins, James 34, 106, James 189; Johanna Cantwell 26; Moses 206; Patience Powell 206
Collinson, Ann 209
Collison, Ann Tongue 210; John 210
Collnns, William 26
Collyer. See Collier.
Combest, Jacob 26; John 67
Conaway, Charles 132, 133; Dianah Oley 132; John 133
Condrin, John 71
Conn, Ann 94; Daniel 94
Connant, Charles 100; Sarah Wooden 100
Conner, John 194
Conner, Robert 34
Connor, Eleanor 32, 33; Margaret [-?-] 33; Margaret Carrington 32; Philip 32, 33
Contee, John 175; Mary [-?-] 175
Conway, Amelia 8; Charles William Augustus 8; Maria Cecilia 8; Philip 32; Robert 22; Sarah Atkinson 8; Thomas 8; William 8
Cook, Elizabeth 1; John 91, 118; William 26
Cooke, Alethua Dare Smith 52; George 52
Cooper, Jane 4; John 4, 23; Richard 4; Thomas 78
Copeland, Elizabeth 231; Jane 231
Copland, William 216
Copley, Abigail [-?-] 47; Thomas 47
Corbin, Abraham 42, 43; Alice [-?-] 41; Catharine Maryann Leary 43; Edward 41, 42, 43, 191, 236; Eleanor 42; Eleanor [-?-] 42; Eliakim 42; Elijah 128; Elizabeth 41; Elizabeth [-?-] 41; Jane Wilkinson 41, 42, 235, 236; John 42, 43, 81, 82; Leah 42; Mary 41, 42; Mary [-?-] 42, 43; Micajah 127; Nathan 42; Nicholas 41, 42; Phyllisann 42; Providence 42; Rachel 42; Rachel Harryman 43, 81, 82; Rachel Marshall 42; Sarah 42; Thomas 42; Unity 42; Vincent 237; Vincent 43; William 43; William Wilkinson 41; Zany 43
Corbitt, Daniel 61 Rachel 61
Cord, Thomas 67
Cosley, Elizabeth Rhodes 98; John 71; Richard 98
Cotrel, Thomas 101
Cotter, John 70
Cotton, John 53
Coulter, Alexander 43, 44, 45; Andrew 43, 44, 45; Ann 44; Ann Clarke 45; Deborah Symington 45; Delia 45; Eliza 45; Eliza McCalmont Barklie 45; Elizabeth 43, 44; Elizabeth [-?-] 45; Esther 44, 45; Esther Coulter 44, 45; Hannah 44; Hannah Kilpatrick 43, 45; Henry 45; Henry Stevenson 44, 45; Hetty McCaskey 45; James 44; Jane 45; Jane [-?-] 45; John 44, 45; John Alexander 44; John Thomas 45; Joseph 44; Louisa 44; Margaret [-?-] 45; Margaret McElroy 45; Mary 44, 45; Mary McCaskey 44; Mifflin 45; Samuel 44; Sarah 44; Sarah Foster 44; Sarah Hall 43, 44; Susan 44; Susanna 44
Coulthred. Thomas 13
Coursey, John 3
Coverly, Elizabeth 178
Covill, James 133
Covington, John 3; Mary Airey 3
Cowan, Ann 48; Benjamin 46; Edward 46, 47, 48; Elias 46; Elizabeth 46, 48; Elizabeth [-?-] 181; Elizabeth Bond 46; Elizabeth Wood 46; George 48; Hannah 46; Isabella 48; James 48; John 46, 48, 181; Josiah 48; Judith [-?-] 47, 48; Judy [-?-] 46; Juliana de Courcy 46; Mark 48; Martha 46; Mary 46, 47, 48; Mary Richardson 48; Rachel 47, 48; Sarah 46; Sarah [-?-] 48; Stephen 47, 48; Susanna 46; Susanna Teague 46; Susannah 47, 48; Thomas 46, 47, 48; William 46, 47, 48, 49
Cowdrey. See under Caudrey.
Cowen. See Cowan.
Cowin. See Cowan.
Cowing, See Cowan.
Cowman, Anne 210

Index

Cox, [-?-] Vaughn 50; rabella Wheeler, 51; Casiah [-?-] 50; Christopher 206; Dinah 50; Edward 20, 50, 215; Elijah 50, 51; Elizabeth 50, 206; Elizabeth [-?-] 49; Elizabeth Gain 50; Elizabeth Merryman 49; Honour Hall 49; Jacob 49, 50, 51; James 117 ; Jane [-?-] 20, 50; John 50, 51; Joseph 50; Keziah Peregoy 50; Mary 50; Mary [-?-] 49, 50, 206; Merryman 49; Providence 50; Rachel 50; Rebecca 216; Richard 50; Ruth Bosley 51; Sarah 50; Susannah 50; William 48, 49, 50, 51, 145; Zebediah 50
Crane, Margaret 175; Robert 175
Crawford, Mordecai 213; Susanna Tucker 213
Cretin, John 20
Cripps. Roger 224
Crockett, George 58; John 157
Crokat, Ann Hickson 91; John 91
Croley, John 74; Miriam [-?-] 74
Cromwell, Alex 67; Anna Maria Giles 73; [-?-] 73; John 73; Oliver 73l Richard 66; Sarah 67
Crook, James 30
Crooke, James 140, 226
Cross, Edith Wiley 201; John 161, 199, 201; Sarah Matthews 97, 98; Thomas 97, 98, 168
Crouch, Eliz. 196; James 177; Joseph 108; Josias 108; Mary Hill 177; Susanna 178; Susannah Rockhold Howard 196; William 177. 194, 196
Crow, John 47
Crowley, Daniel 32, 33; Dennis 32, 33
Crown, Judith [-?-] 47
Croxall, Charles 191; R. 30
Crudgenton. See Crudgington.
Crudgington, Diana Simmons 185; Roger 166, 185, 233
Cullison, Delilah 125
Culver, Benjamin 63
Cumber, John 72
Cummins, Margaret [-?-] 142; Mary 142
Curtz, Christopher 141
Cusin, John 176
Cutchin, Dorothy [-?-] 182; Robert 163, 182
Daley, William 143
Dallam, Richard 213; W. 59; William 119

Dallas, Walter 120, Walter 219
Dalling, Mary 195
Dandell, George 13; John 37, 142, 143
Daniell, Rebecca [-?-] 37, 142, 143
Dare, Alethia 52, 53; Amy 51; Ann 53; Ann [-?-] 54; Anne [-?-] Tongue 53, 209; Cleverly 52; Diana 52, 53; Elizabeth 54; Elizabeth [-?-] 54; Elizabeth Cleverly Banks 51; Elizabeth Parrott 53; Elizabeth Wilson 54; Gideon 52, 53, 54
Dare, Henry 54; James 51; Jean Gray 54; John 52, 53; Mary 53; Mary [-?-] 52; Nathaniel 51, 52, 53, 54, 209; Parrott 52; Priscilla 54; Rachel 54; Regia 53; Richard 53; Samuel 52, 53; Sarah 52, 53, 54; Sarah [-?-] Taylor 53; Susanna 53; Susanna [-?-] 53; Susanna Parker 52; Thomas Cle(a)verly 52, 53, 54; William 52, 53, 54
Darnall, Henry 187; Henry Bennett 183; Joshua 171; Mary Prebble 171
Dashiell, Alice Ann 112; Eleanor Virginia 112; Henry 111, 112; Jane 112; Janes Renshaw 112; Levin 112; Louisa Maria 112; Louisa Turpin Wright 112; Mary Leeke 111, 112; Mary Leeke Robinson 112; Nicholas Leeke 112; Thomas 112; William Augustine 191
Dashiells, [-?-] (Rev) 94
Daughaday, [-?-] 54; Abraham 55, 200; Caleb 55; Caleb Owings 55; Catherine 201; Constantine 57; Eleanor 56; George 56, 57; Helen 55; Helen Maria 55; Hollin 55; John 55, 56, 57, 200, 201; Johnza 55; Joseph 54, 55, 200, 201, 202; Katherine 55; Katherine [-?-] 200; Margaret 56, 57; Margaret Sing 55; Mary Ann 57; Rachel 54.201; Rachel Hamilton Sater 55; Richard 54, 55, 56, 201; Samuel 57; Sarah Taylor 202; Thomas 55, 200; Usen 56; William 56; William Hamilton 55
Daugharday. See Daughaday.
Daugherday. See Daughaday.
Daugherterey. See Daughaday
Daugherty. See Daughaday.
Daughtery. See Daughaday.
Davice, Ann 178; John 178
Davidson, James 115
Davis, Ann [-?-] 111; Davis, Ann Atkinson

Index

8; Ann Moran 154; Anna 24; Archibald 29; Elizabeth Carback 29; Elizabeth Cox 50; Ely 83; Esther Fugate 67; George 57; Jesse 153; John 67; Mary 27; Rebecca 83; Rhoda 23; Robert 83, 179; Thomas 29, 179, 220; William 157
Daws, Francis 122
Dawson, Abraham 177; Thomas 177
Dawtridge, William 58
Day, Avis Ward 217; Edward 11, 36, 59, 207; Elizabeth Cox 206; Francis 217; John 59; Nicholas 146, 206; Robert 220
Days, Edward 39
Deadman, Edmund 121, 1211
Deal(e), James 187, 209
Dean, Hugh 11
Deans, Christian [-?-] 37
Deaver, Antil(l) 63, 116; John 205; Richard 185; Sarah [-?-] 63
Deaveran. See Devoran
Deavor. See Deaver.
Deavors, Richard 185
Debaes, Gurturie Jacobsen 26; Mary 27
Debaes, Roelff 2
Debrewah. See Debruler.
Debrulear. See Debruler.
Debruler, Ann 58; Ann [-?-] 58; Anthony 57, 58, 59, 60; Benjamin 58, 59; Cordelia 59; Delila 59; Diana Greenfield 59; Eliza 57; Elizabeth 58, 59, 60; Elizabeth [-?-] 57, 58, 59; Enohan 59; Esther Lewis 58, 59; Euphan 59; Frances Burridge 59; Francis 58, 59, 60; George 57, 58, 59; Hannah 58, 60; Hester Lewis 58; James 58, 59; Jane 57; John 57, 58, 59, 60, 76; Margaret 58, 60; Margaret Skidmore 58, 59, 60; Mary 57, 59; Mary Greenfield Drunkord 57, 58; Micajah 59; Peter 57, 58, 59, 60; Rosamond 57; Sarah 59; Sarah Watters 59; Semelia Jackson 59; Ufaan 59; William 57, 58, 59, 60
Debrulo. See under Debruler.
Debruly. See under Debruler.
deCourcy, Juliana 46
Deems, [-?-] 215
Delahunt, Abraham 3
Demment, William 196
Demmitt, John 92, 93; Rachel 76; William 184
Demondidier, Anthony 182
Denbow, Thomas 206
Denison, Daniel 175; Elizabeth 175; Patience Dudley 175
Denson, Elizabeth Cowan 46; John 46
DePeyster, Elizabeth 163; William 163
Devaughn, Priscilla 171
Devilyard, Jacob 156
Devoran, Catherine 131, 132; Dinah [-?-] Nuthead 131; Manus 131, 132
Devorian. See Devoran.
Devouria. See Devoran.
Devron. See Devoran.
Dew, Robert 92
Dewhattway. See Duhadaway.
Dexter, John 28; Mary Ann [-?-] 28
Dicher. See Dicker.
Dick, James 167
Dicker, Allies 224
Dickinson, James 174; Walter 197
Digby, Elizabeth 162; Jane Peale 162; Joseph 162
Dimmitt, John 92; William 183
Disney, Ann Ward 216; Edith Mallonee 123; James 216; Joshua 123; Leonard M. 122; Mary Jane 123; Solomon 14
Ditcher. See Dicker.
Ditto, Abraham 62
Dixon, Abigail 136; Ella 52; Ellis 52 , 53; Jane [-?-] Waites 136, 137; John 34, 133, 136, 137; Robert 51
Dnnelly, Michael 108
Doan, James 40
Dobbin, George 24; Hester [-?-] 25; Isaac 172
Dock, James 161
Dockins, Simon 67
Docwra, Thomas 64
Dollerhead. Mary Ashley 5
Donovan, Lloyd 202, 203; Hannah Eugenie Taylor 202, 203
Dooley, William 101
Dorman, Elizabeth [-?-] Cogell 133, 134; Judith 134, 135; Robert 133, 134; Sarah 10, 134; Selah 10, 11, 134
Dorney, Martha 232
Dorsey, Basil 84; Edward 82, 234; Flora Fitzsimmons 67; Frances Watkins 228; Greenbury 27; J. M. 12; John 84, 86, 119,

247

Index

178, 234; John Hammond 228; Joshua 67;
  Mary 230; Owen 114; Thomas 85, 86
Dossey, James 143
Douglass, Benjamin 80
Dow, Robert 219
Dowell, John 99; Richard 229, 230;
  Susan[na] [-?-] Jones 99, 100
Dowig, George 93
Downe, Abraham 88, 211
Downes, John 9, 135
Downey, Sarah 119
Downman, Ellen B. 165
Dowse, Edward 100
Doyle, Elizabeth Atkinson 8; Richard 78;
  Thomas 8
Doyley, Priscilla 105
Doyne, Jesse 80
Draper, Abigail, Simmons 188; John 188
Drew, Anthony 104, 184; George 70, 74;
  Johannah Phillips 74; Margaret [-?-] 104;
  Margaret [-?-] Brown 184
Drunkord, James 57; Mary Greenfield 57
Drury, Charles 186, 187; Mary 188
Duarne. See Devoran.
Dudley, Eleanor [-?-] 1; Mary 7; Richard 1;
  Thomas 175
Duehataway. See Duhadaway.
Duff, Simon 64
Duhadaway, Alice [-?-] 61; Daniel 62;
  Edward 61; Elizabeth Parish 61; Jacob 60,
  61; Margaret 61; Margaret [-?-] 60, 61;
  Mary 61; Rachel Corbitt 61; Thomas 61
Duhaddaway. See Duhadaway.
Duhadwy. See Duhadaway.
Duhataway. See Duhadaway.
Duhattes. See Duhadaway.
Duhattoway. See Duhadaway.
Duke, Christopher 120, 140, 219
Dukehart, Peter 114
Dulancy, Elmira G. Taylor 203
Dulany, Daniel 22, 75, 119, 168; Dennis 68;
  Easter Fugate 68; John 112 ; Thomas 29
Duley, William 143
Dunard, Henry 140
Duncan, Anna Claypoole Peale Straughton
  165, 166; John Mason 115; William 165,
  166
Dungan, Elizabeth 181
Dunlap, William 78, 103

Dunlop. William. See Dunlap, William.
Dunn, Anna 166
Durbin, Ann 101; Avarilla Scott 130; John
  130; Thomas 138; William 47
Durgam Margaret 164
Durham, Abraham 15, 148; Chloe 314;
  James 134
Duskin, Daniel 62; Dennis 62; Mary [-?-]
  62; Michael 62; Sarah Johnson 62
Duskins. See Duskin.
Dutton, Robert 146
Duvall, Mary 229
Eade, Robert 149
Eager, George 131; John 135
Eagleston, Thomas 29
Eaglestone, John 49, 135
Earl, Elizabeth 76
Eastwood, Elizabeth 63; Elizabeth [-?-]
  63; Hannah 63; James 63; John 63;
  Mary 63; Michael 63
Ebden, William 25, 34
Eden, Benjamin 94
Edmonds, Thomas 155
Edmondson, Archibald 43; Jane [-?-] 43;
  Susanna [-?-] 39; William 39
Edwards, Alice 41; Ann [-?-] 64; Ann
  Chalmers 65; Anne [-?-] 63, 64, 65;
  Aquila 64, 65; Cadwallader 63, 64, 65;
  Catherine 65; Catherine [-?-] Bourne 63,
  64; Edward 64, 65; Eleanor Chilton 64;
  Elizabeth 64, 65, 142; Elizabeth Chilton
  64; Jemima Welsh 64 ; Jonathan 64, 65;
  Mary 64, 65; Moses 235; Sarah 64, 65;
  William 64, 65
Egleston, Thomas 29
Elledge, Ruth 38
Ellingsworth, Richard 133, 136
Elliot(t), John 180; Mary 180; Robert 25;
  Susanna 180; Thomas 43; William 153
Ellis(s), Ann 24; John 90; Mary 100; Mary
  Watkins 223, 224; Peter 25, 100; Philip
  222, 224
Ellison, Ruth 165
Ellitt, James 84
Ely, John 118; Mary Litton 118
Emerich. Ann 7
Emerson, John 172
Eminson,. See Emson.
Emison. See Emson.

Index

Empson. See Emson.
Emson, Ann 143, 144; Anne 143; Eliza 143; Elizabeth 143; James 37, 142, 143, 144; Rachel 145; Rebecca 143, 144; Rebecca [-?-] Daniell 37, 142, 143, 144, 145
England, John 73
English, Anna English Tomlinson 213; Hannah Tucker 213; William 213
Enlow, Abraham 227
Ennis, William 210
Enoch, Hannah 171; Henry 171; Richard 137; Sarah [-?-] 171
Ensor, Elizabeth 10, 122; John 10, 42, 134, 150, 199, 214; Joseph 214; Luke 55; Mary 150
Epaugh, Henry 128
Eustace, John 173
Evans, Abigail 233; Abigail Whipps 232, 233; Amos 41; Edmond 233; Evan 218; Jemima [-?-] 64; Jemima Edwards 65; John 200; John 145; Margaret [-?-] 185; Prudence 145
Evatt, William 74
Everett, Eliza [-?-] 125; John 125, 158; Mary 158; Rebecca Poteet 158; Sarah 13
Ewing, Elizabeth Norrington 159; William 159
Ewings, Elizabeth 82; John 183
Eyrins, Elizabeth 82
Faber, [-?-] 92
Fadry, Eliza 233
Fairall, Achsah Mallonee 122, 123; Alfred 123; Eliza Louisa 123, 124; Mary Jane D Disney 123
Fairbank, John 40
Farand, Thomas 153
Farfar, William 76
Farfarr, Joan [-?-] Barton 10; Johanna [-?-] 66; Judith [-?-] Barton 10; Judith Dorman Berton 135; William 10, 66. 135, 138
Farguson. See under Ferguson,
Farinholt, Maria Keirle 124
Faris, William 20
Farmer, George 117, 144 ; Gregory 37, 46, 145; 213; Rachel [-?-] 144; Rachel Emson 145; Rebecca [-?-] Daniel Cobb Emson Hawkins 37
Farrand, William 155
Farrell, Mary 110

Faurgeson. See under Ferguson.
Fawkener, hunphrey 224
Fell, Edward 200
Fendall, John 80
Fenn, Thomas 225
Fenwick, [-?-] (Rev.) 94
Ferguson, Ann Skinner 65, 66; Bathsheba Ferguson 65; Bersheba Griffith 65; Bethsheba 66; Catherine 65, 66; Catherine [-?-] 65; Duncan 65; Elizabeth 65; John 65, 66; Mary 65; Rebecca 66; Susannah 66; Thomas 65; Verlinda 66; Vialindo 66
Fewgate. See Fugate.
Fews, Dorothy Nice Barton 13; Philip 13
Fews. See also Foos.
ffroston, Richard 226
Field, Ann 66; Catherine Hogg 66; Ellen Q. 166; Jo. 66; John 66
Fields, Elizabeth 66, 169; J. Smith 169; Nathaniel 105; Rachel King 105; Sidney 169
Filredman. See Fitzredmond.
Finlay, Hugh 220, 221
Finley, Hugh 31
Finney, William 2
Fisher, Eleanor 186; Eleanor Simmons 186; Martha Simmons 186; Martin 186; Sarah 177; Thomas 70; William 186
Fitch, Elizabeth Turner 214; William 214
Fitzredmond, John 233
Fitzsimmons, Flora 67; Martha Morgan Heathcote 66, 146; Mary 67; Nicholas 66. 67, 146, 225
Flanagam. Ann [-?-] 191; Francis 231; Sarah Whayland 231
Flannel. See under Flannan.
Flanner, Francis 231; Sarah Whayland 231
Floyd, Anne [-?-] 55; John 200; Joseph 55, 200, 201; Rachel Daughaday 54; Richard 55; Thomas 54
Fogleman, George 44; Susanna Coulter 44
Fonerden, John 65; Margaret Edwards 65
Fookit. See Fugate.
Foos, Dorothy Nice Barton 13; Philip 13
Foos. See aso Fews.
Forbes, William 36
Ford, Alexander 77; Ann 77; Caroline 77; Edward 80; Elizabeth 77; James 77; John

Index

77; Leah [-?-] 77; Lloyd 77; Mary Grant 77; Nancy Wood 77; Rebecca 87; Stephen 77; Thomas 77, 127; William 99
Forrest, Mary Dashiell Robinson 112; Moreau 112
Forwood, Jacob 71
Foster, [-?-] 13; Armanelah Prebble 171; John 171; Sarah 44
Foudry, Eliza 233
Fought, Elizabeth [-?-] 171; James 171
Fowcate. See Fugate.
Fowler, Catherine Garland 70, 71; Eleneder 211; William 70, 71
Foxcroft, Elizabeth 105; Richard 105
Foy, Thomas 91
Franciscus, George 220
Frank, Peter 50
Franklin, Artridge Giles 72; Eleanor Ward 218; Elizabeth Oakley 159; Jacob 53, 186, 187, 209; James 209; John 186, 187; Joseph 159; Robert 72; Thomas 21
Fraser, John 62; Mary [-?-] Duskin 61; Richard 62
Frasher. See Fraser.
Frazer, Alexander 211
Freeborn, Mary 207, 208; Sarah Howard 207; Thomas 207
Freeland, Mary 16; Robert 88
Freeman, Francs 137; Mary 109
French, George 164
Frinsham, Henry 81
Frisby, Richard 6
Frizell, Jason 179
Frost, James 83
Ftzredmond, John 10
Fucat. See Fugate.
Fuckett. See Fugate.
Fugate, Ann 67, 68; Ann [-?-] 68; Cassandra [-?-] 69; Dorothy [-?-] 68; Easter 68; Edward 68, 69; Elizabeth Bacon 68, 69; Esther 67; Frances Mould 67, 68; James 67, 68; John 67, 68; Martin 69; Mary 67, 68; Mary Watson 68; Peter 67, 68; Sarah 68
Fulk, Mary 118
Fuller, Easter [-?-] 130; John 130
Fullerton, James 18
Futz, William 214
Gadds, Jane 70

Gadsby, John 177
Gafford, Aley 79
Gain, Elizabeth 50
Gaither, John 31
Gaither, Ralph 181; Sarah Rowles 181
Gale, George 191
Gallion, Ann 170; John 170, 171
Galloway, James 12, 37; John 37; Joseph 61; Moses 37; Pamela Cheyne 37; Pamelia Cheyne Owings 37; Priscilla Barton 12; Richard 61; Robert Christie 37; William 37, 51, 130
Gamble, Gideon 189
Gambrill, Augustine 84
Gant, Thomas 185
Gantt, Ann Heighe 89; George 89
Gardiner, Sibrah 73
Gardner, Christopher 73; John 204; Robert 10, 34, 120, 134
Garey, George 174; John 173, 174
Garey. See also Carey.
Garland, Bethia Ogg 70; Catherine 70, 71; Elizabeth 69, 71; Francis 70, 71; Henry 69, 70, 71; James 70, 71; Jane 71; Jane Gadds 70; Lydia [-?-] 69, 70; Lydia: See also as Garland, Bethia Ogg; Nicholas 71; Sarah 69; Sarah [-?-] 71; Sarah Herrington 70; Susanna 70; William 69, 70, 71
Garmaton. See under Gorman.
Garner, Robert 210
Garrett, Amos 48, 56, 75, 84, 178, 195, 196, Bennett 56
Garrettson, [-?-] 140; Garrett 188, 207; James 27; Mary 208
Gash, Basil 24; Daniel 24; Eleanor (Helen) Ridden 24; Rachel 24; Thomas 181
Gassaway, Nicholas 85; Susannah [-?-] 16; Thomas 37, 77, 216
Gatch, Benjamin 202; Ruth Taylor 201, 202; Sarah 202
Gates, Robert 116, 117
Gay, John 135; Nichiolas Ruxton 37, 117, 121, 146
Gayne, Timothy 32
Gearth, Ralph 137
Gellett, Thomas 138
Gibbons, Thomas 10

Index

Gibbs, Ann 195; Edward 195; Mary Smith 195; William 195
Gibson, Miles 68, 137; Thomas 137; William 164
Gilbert, Michael 46' Thomas 188
Gilc(h)rest, Robert 30, 234; Helen [-?-] 234
Gilcrist. See Gilcrest.
Giles, Anna 73; Anna Maria 73; Aquila 74, 75; Artridge 72; Betty 73; Carolina 75; Cassandra Smith 73, 74; Charlotte 75; Edward 74; Elizabeth 71, 72, 73, 74, 75; Elizabeth Arnold 73; Elizabeth Harris 72; Hannah 75; Hannah [-?-] Scott 73; Hannah Webster 74, 75; Hester 73; Jacob 72, 73, 74, 75, 116, 117, 118, 144, 145, 189, 211, 213; Johanna Phillips Drew 74, 75; John 33, 71, 72, 73, 74, 102, 200; Louis F. 71; Mary 72, 73; Mary [-?-] 71, 72, 73; Nathaniel 71, 72, 73, 75, 200; Nathaniel John 75; Sarah 73 74, 75; Sarah [-?-] 200; Sarah Butterworth 73, 74; Sarah Welsh 72, 73; Sophia 73; Thomas 74; William Axteel 75; William Axtell 74
Gill, Cooper 123; Elizabeth 123; Gustavus 154; John 123; Joshua 123; Nicholas 123; Stephen 123; William 123
Gist, David 51; Richard 33, 179, 218, 234
Gittings, Thomas 207, 227
Gladman, Rebecca 192
Glathary, John M. 94; Margaret Hook 94
Glendy, [-?-] 44
Glover, John 234
Goddard, [-?-] Skillington 75; Christian 75; Edward 105; Elias 75; Jane West 75; Jone West 75; Martha 105; Priscilla Doyley 105; Sarah 75
Godding, Sarah Ashley 6
Golden. See Golding.
Golding, Elizabeth 76; Elizabeth Earl 76; John 76; Peter 76; Rachel Golding 76; Stephen 76
Goldsborough, Caroline 169; Charles 169; Howes 168, 169; Robert 168; Rosanna Piper 168, 169; William 169
Golt, George 3
Gongo, Ann [-?-] 204; Anthony 204; Faith 184; Mary 204
Gongoe. See Gongo.
Goodin, Elizabeth 150
Goodwin, Elizabeth 207; Lyde 164
Gordon, James 151; Robert 168
Gormack. See Gorman.
Gormacon, Ann [-?-] 135; Michael 10, 135
Gormacon. See also Gorman.
Gorman, [-?-] Barton 10; [-?-] Swindell 11, 134; Judith [-?-] 134; Michael 10, 11, 134
Gorsuch, Barbara 238; Charles 128 ; John 76; Lovelace 160; Mary Eve Levely Grangett 114; Mary Levely 113; Nicholas 114
Gorswick, Anne 181
Gosnell, William 178, 235
Gostwick, Avarilla [-?-] 145; Joseph 41; Mary Corbin 41; Nicholas 145
Gott, Richard 77
Gough, Harry Dorsey 128
Gouldsmith, George 67
Gover, Elizabeth 216; Ephraim 217; Philip 48; Rachel 216; Robert 216
Grace, John 94, 96; Priscilla Hook 94, 96
Grafflin, Jacob 24
Grafton, John 63
Graham Charles 161; Elizabeth Rowles Bell 178; Ruth Rowles 178; Ruth Rowles Witham 17; William 94
Graham. Charles 195
Grange, John 225
Grangett, Andrew 112, 113, 114; Catherine 114; ; Mary 115; Mary Eve Levely 114, 115; Peter 114; Susanna 114
Grant, Alexander 76, 77, 135; Ann 77; David 156; Elizabeth Cole 76, 77; Elizabeth Morris 156; James 156; Mary 77; Mary [-?-] 77; Mary Hambleton 76
Gratia, Peter 94
Graves, [-?-] 53; Alexander 130, 207; Mary Tolley 207
Gray, Adam 5; Blanch Jackson Cantwell 26; Henry W. 111; Jean 54; John 26, 52; Mathias 120
Grayson, Alfred 44; Elizabeth Coulter 44; William 122
Green, Abraham 29; Edward 208; Elizabeth 107; John 6; Maria 86; Michael 3; Richard 187, 193; Robert 42; Ruth Jones Carback 29; Tabitha 128; Unity 228; Unity Corbin 42
Greenawald, Jacob 115

Index

Greenbury, Nicholas 134, 138
Greenfield, Diana 59; Mary 57; Micajah 59; Purify 228; Sophia 49; Thomas 58, 87
Greeniffe, John 66, 211
Greer, Elizabeth Barton Wright 13; James 13; Nicholas Sidney 155
Gregory, James 14; Luke 192; Sarah 15; Sarah Jordan Bond 14
Grenshed, Andrew 113; Mary Eve Levely 113
Grenshed. See also Grangett.
Grey, Elizabeth 39; Joseph 39
Greyham. See Graham.
Griffin, John 28; Joseph 14; Mary Harryman Carback 28; Philip 177; Rufus 45
Griffis, John 212
Griffith, Anne Skinner 65; Bathsheba 65; Benjamin 109; Bersheba 65; James 123; Luke 26; Rachel 233; Samuel 65, 70, 233
Grimes, Alice [-?-] Bond 13; Elizabeh Oley 132, 133; George 133; William 13, 14
Groom(e), Samuel 5, 75, 211
Gross, Mary 219; Nicholas 98
Grover, Benj. 16; Joshua 16; Thomas 53
Grundervil, [-?-] 22
Grundy, George 33; Robert 2, 216
Guichard, Samuel 185, 204
Guishard, Mark 11, 205
Gunnell, Edward 25; George 25
Guyton, Benjamin 228; Frances 228; John Holt 228, 229; Ruth 228; Sarah Watkins 228, 229
Gwynn, William 45
Hackley, Elizabeth 95
Hadden. See Haddin.
Haddin, Ann Short 77; Elizabeth 78; Janet 78; Jannett 78; John 77 78; Naomi Short 77; Sarah Tracey 77; Thomas 77, 78; William 78
Haddon,. See Haddin.
Hagan, David 32, 33; Margaret Carrington Connor 32, 33
Hagg, William 40
Hail, Matthew 50
Haile, Ann Grant 77; Ann Long 140; Caroline Ford 77; Eleanor Chamberlin 77; Frances Broad 150; George 77, 125; Mary 125, 126; Millicent 150; Nicholas 50, 125, 126, 127, 140, 150, 200; Oliver 133; Samuel 77
Haile. See also Hale.
Hakman, Ann 119
Hale, Ann Grant 77; Anna Taylor 202; Frances Watkins 223, 224; George 77; Israel 224; 222, 224; Margaret 222, 223, 224; Margaret Watkins 221; Richard 224; Samuel 222; Thomas 42; William 224
Hale. See also Haile.
Hales, Anne Taylor 203; Randel 203
Halett. James 8
Hall, Ann Tolley 208; Aquila 26, 63, 171, 208; Catherine Taylor 203; Cordelia 208; Edward 3, 4, 155, 177; Eliza S. Taylor 203; Elizabeth 132; Elizabeth Levely 115; George. See George Hale; Henry 229; Honour 49; Isaac 187; James 4, 23; John 76, 90, 104, 170, 185, 203; Joseph 115; Josias 208; Martha 208, 229; Martha [-?-] 90; Martha Andrews 3, 4; Martha Susanna 208; Mary 4; Mary Ann Andrews 3, 4; Mary Duvall 229; Michael 3, 4; Samuel 4; Sarah 4, 43; Sarah Burke 23; homas I. 210; William 85, 149
Hambleton, Aley Gafford 79; Ann 78; Catherine Sally 78; Edward 78; Elizabeth 78; Esther Samson 78; James 79; John 78, 79, 203; Margaret Bond 78; Mary 76, 78; Phoebe Maxwell 78; Ralph 79; Rebecca Bignall 78; Robert 78; Thomas 78; William 32
Hambleton. See also Hamilton 161
Hamby, Martha Simpson 189; Mary Simpson 190; Samuel 190; William 189
Hamill, Asinah. See Hamill, Assemal; Assenal [-?-] 80; Catherine 79; Catherine Chandler 79. 80; Elizabeth [-?-] 80; Henry 79; Hugh 79, 80; John 79, 80; Katherine 80; Nail 79; Neil 79; Sarah 79. 80; Sarah Chandler 79, 80; Stephen 79, 80; William 79; William Chandler 79, 80; William Chd. 80
Hamilton, Helen 160; J. 213; James 79; Rachel 55; Sarah [-?-] 55; Sarah Benedict 60; William 24, 55, 160
Hamilton. See also Hambleton.
Hamm, Thomas 141, 237
Hammond, Abraham George 190; Charles

234; Isaac 220; John 234; Larkin 75; Mary [-?-] Andrew 190; Mordecai 161; Philip 64; Sarah 75; William 75, 123
Hampton, R'd 177
Hanbury, John 85
Hanchett, Dinah 193
Handen, Lidia 225
Handland, John 26; Mary Cantwell 26
Hankin, John 2
Hannis. See Hennis.
Hanson, Airy Rowles 182; Christopher 182; Frederick 109; George 109; Hans 108, 109, 206; Jane [-?-] 109; Jane Hynson, 109; William 109
Happel, Ann Hook 95; Robert C. 95
Harden, John 133
Hardesty, Frances 227; Thomas 88
Harding, Elias 65
Hargrave, [-?-] Carter 38
Hargrave, Nathaniel 28
Hargrove, [-?-] (Rev.) 115
Harman, Godfrey 136; Sarah Powell 206; William 206
Harmar. See Harmer.
Harmer, Godfrey 34, 35, 129; Mary [-?-] 34, 129
Harn. See under Hearn.
Harpe, Eliza [-?-] 178
Harper, William 134
Harrier, Andrew 113; Catherine 113
Harrington, Charles 211; Cornelius 100; David 1; Dorothy [-?-] 211; Katherine 1 82; Rathvale Jones 100
Harriott, Oliver 227; Susanna [-?-] 227
Harris, Benjamin 65; Elizabeth 72; Lloyd 32, 104; Sarah 61; T. 80; Thomas 130
Harrison, Anne 210; Benjamin 53, 209, 210; Jonathan 12; Mary 100; Samuel 110; Susanna Levely 114
Harryman, Ann; Ann [-?-] 80; Anne 81; Anne Wilkinson 80, 236; Charles 219, 220; Eleanor 81, 82; Elizabeth 219, 220, 237; George 42, 43, 80, 81, 82, 179, 236; John 28, 80, 81, 126; Josias 82; Mary 28, 81, 82; Nancy 219; Patience 81; Prudence 219, 220; Prudence [-?-] 219; Rachel 43, 81, 82; Robert 81; Samuel 81, 197; Sarah 81, 82; Sarah [-?-] 82; Sarah Raven 81; Sophia 81; Tamar 81; Temperance 81, 82; William 81, 82
Hart, Andrew 148; Benjamin 203; Clemency Thompson Taylor 203; David 148; Henry 208; Mary 208
Hartt, Aug. 102
Harvey, William 24
Harwood, Eliza 193; Grace 39; John 177; Mary Cockayne 40; Peter 39, 40; Richard 72; Robert 39; Samuel 72; Sarah 39; Thomas 193; William 193
Haslam, Caroline E 164
Haslet, Kezia [-?-] 148; Samuel 148
Hasselbach, John 93
Hatcheson, Rachel Knowlman 108; Vincent 108
Hatherly, Benedict Leonard 83; Benjamin 83, 84; Elizabeth 83; Elizabeth Ewings 82; Elizabeth Eyrins 82; Ewings 82; John 82, 83, 84; Nathan 83; Patience [-?-] 83, 84; Rachel 83, 84; Sarah Ann Brown 84
Hatten, Elizabeth 228
Hatton, John 81, 227; Mary [-?-] Ward 220; Thomas 220; William 230
Haviland, Jacob 156
Hawkins, Ann 116, 143, 144; Ann Prebble 170; Elizabeyth 144; Elizabeth [-?-] Giles 72; Elizabeth [-?-] Rowles 176, 177; Elizabeth Arnold Giles 73; James 144; John 37, 73, 101, 116, 137, 142, 143, 144, 156, 170, 113; Joseph 136, 144, 176, 177; Mary [-?-] 73; Rachel 144; Rebecca 144; Rebecca [-?-] Daniel Cobb Emson 37, 101, 142, 143, 144; Robert 170; Thomas 72, 73, 101
Haws, John 225
Hayden, Francis 211; Penelope 211
Hayes, Abigail Dixon Scudamore 137, 139; Avarila 139; Edmund 158; Elizabeth 139, 158; Elizabeth [-?-] 139; James 168; Jemima 139; John 10, 49, 134, 137, 139, 225; Mary 158; Mary Anne [-?-] Johnson 139; Mary Norrington 157, 158; Thomas 157, 158
Hayes. See also Hays.
Hayle. See Hale.
Hayles. See Hale.
Hays, Mary 157
Hays. See also Hayes.
Hazlewood, [-?-] 34

253

Index

Head, John 200; Sarah Taylor 200
Headington, Abel 81, 82; Mary Harryman 81, 82
Hearn, Alfred 86; Alfred C. 87; Ann 87; Anne 85, 86; Artemas 87; Artemus 86; Barbary 87; Benjamin 86; Caleb 86; Catherine E. 87; Charles E. 87; Daniel 84, 85; Elizabeth [-?-] 86, 87; Isaac 85, 86; John 85, 86; Maria Green 86; Mary 87; Mary [-?-] 86; Matilda Carr 87; Michael 85, 86; Priscilla [-?-] 87; Rebecca [-?-] 86; Rebecca Ford 87; Richard 86; Sarah [-?-] 87; Sophia 85, 86; Thomas 87; William 85
Hearne. See Hearn.
Heath, James 72; Sarah [-?-] 97; Thomas 96, 97, 138
Heathcote, Joseph 66, 146; Martha Morgan 66, 146; Joseph 41
Hedge, John 138; Thomas 138
Hedges, Hetty Hook 94; Peter 94
Heighe, Althea 88, 208; Ann 89; Ann [-?-] 88; Athea 88; Barbara 89; Betty 89; Betty Holdsworth 88, 89; Eliza 87, 88; Elizabeth 88; Elizabeth Mackall 89; James 87, 88, 89, 208, 209; Mary 88, 89, 90, 208; Mary [-?-] 87; Mary Tongue Sollers 88; Mary Wheeler, 89; Robert 87, 88; Samuel 87, 88; Sarah 88; Thomas Holdsworth 89
Helm, Mayberry 190
Helmkin(g), Aaron 14, 15; Elizabeth [-?-] 14; Mary Bond 15
Hemsley, Mary [-?-] Contee 175; Philemon 175; William 1
Henderson, George 99; James 56; John 218; Robert 63; Thomas 30
Hendle, Elizabeth 8
Hendon, Leddy 226; Prudence 183; Richard 183
Hendricks, [-?-] 22
Hendrix, Eliza 16; William 16
Henley, Darby 227; Joseph 57
Henning Philip 101
Hennis, Elizabeth [-?-] 90; Elizabeth Kelley 90; Michael 90; Miles 90; Thomas 90; William 90
Henthorne, James 93; Mary [-?-] 93
Herbert, Eleanor 84; John 153; William 66
Hern. See Hearn.

Herne. See Hearn.
Heron. See Hearn.
Herring, Robert 116; Susan Levely 116
Herring. See also Hearn.
Herrington, Jacob 101; Sarah 70
Hewes. See Hughes.
Hewie, Caleb 237; Sarah Wilkinson 237
Hewitt, Ann Coulter 44; Eli 44
Hickinbotham, Oliver 155
Hickman, William 88, 212
Hicks, James 121
Hickson, Ann 91; Hannah 91; Hester 91; Jane Wilson 90; Joseph 90; Thomas 91
High. See Heighe.
Hill, Abel 187; Elizabeth Wooden 100; Joseph 100; Mary 177; Samuel 31; Sarah [-?-] Simmons 187; William 10, 177
Hillen, Elizabeth 18; John 26, 203; Solomon 55; Thomas 201
Hilton, John 183
Hinckley, Chris 4
Hinds, John 220, John 221
Hinkes, Ad. 224; Francis 222
Hinton, Elizabeth [-?-] Sampson Bagford 9, 135, 136; S. 196, 235; Samuel 76, 126, 135, 136; Timothy 135, 136
Hiser, Richard 9
Hitchcock, Ann 13, 70; Elizabeth 213; George 91, 92, 200; Henry 70; Josiah 70; Mary [-?-] Tracey 91; Nancy Ann 70; Persosha 91; Presiota 91; Randal 70; Susanna Garland 70, 71; William 13, 182
Hoale, Edward 134
Hobbs, Elizabeth A. C. 96; Nancy 202
Hodge, Sybil 232
Hodgkins, Michael 144
Hogan, [-?-] 149
Hogg, Catherine 66
Hoke, Anthony 161
Holdsworth, Betty 88
Holland, Elizabeth Sickelmore 183; Frances 156, 211; John 183; John Francis 197; John T. 55; William 149
Holliday, John Robert 77
Hollingsworth, George 160; Jesse 86
Hollis, Amos 17; Mary Clark 235; William 70, 235
Holloway, John 119
Holmes, Thomas 131, 168

254

Index

Holt, Ann 12
Holtzman, Mary [-?-] 116
Hood, Benjamin 234; John 234
Hook, Andrew 93; Ann 94, 95, 96; Ann Conn 94; Anne 93; Anthony 94; Barbara 92, 94, 96; Barbara [-?-] 92, 93; Barenhard 94; Catharine 95, 96; Catherine Ritter 95; Conrad 94, 95, 96; Cornelius 94; Elizabeth 94, 95; Elizabeth A. 96; Elizabeth A. C. 96; Elizabeth Campbell 94, 95; Elizabeth Huckin 95; Elizabeth Stagers 94; Emeline 96; Frederick 95; Frederick C. 94; George 94; Hannah Alder 96; Harriet 94; Hetty 94; Jacob 92, 93. 94, 95, 96; Jacob Washington 94; James Hervey 94; Jesse 95; John 93, 95, 96; Johns 95; Jonathan 95; Joseph 92, 93, 94, 95, 96; Josias 95; Keturah 94; Margaret 92, 94, 95; Margaret [-?-] 93, 94; Margaret Ann 96; Marques 94; Martha Ellen 96; Mary 94, 96; Mary [-?-] 94; Mary Ann Watts 95; Michael 94; Nancy Walker 95; Osilla 92, 93; Priscilla 94, 96; Rebeccah 94; Robert 96; Rudolph 92, 94, 95; Samuel 95; Sarah 94; Sarah Keyser 95, 96; Solomon 95; Sophia Jones 93; Sophia Spedden 95; Susannah Boone 94; Ursula [-?-] 93, 94, 95; Valentine 96; William A. 96
Hooke. See Hook.
Hooker, Sarah [-?-] 66; Thomas 66, 91
Hooper, Althea Heighe 88; John 68; Roger 88; William 10
Hopham, William 120
Hopkins, Eliza Debruler 57; Elizabeth [-?-] 229; Gerard 65, 72, 74, 229; Johns 200; Philip 229; Rebecca 40; Rebecca Cockayne 40; Richard 229; Samuel 74; Sarah Giles 74; William 4, 39, 40
Hoppam, George 134
Horner, Richard 131
Horton, Edward 136
Houchings, William 145
Houcihngs, Judith 145
Houls. See Hulse.
Howard, Anne [-?-] Edwards 64; Cornelius 93; John 196; Joshua 31; Sarah 207; Susannah Rockhold 196; Thomas 64; William 100

Howell, [-?-] 113; Francis 169; Thomas 136
Howen, [-?-] 32; Turla Michael 32
Howke, Miahcel 94
Hoxton, Hyde 104
Hubert, William 4
Huckin, Elizabeth 95
Hudson, John 3, 4
Huggins, William 48
Hughes, [-?-] 31; Amy [-?-] 107; Ann Bond 14, 15; Elizabeth [-?-] 96, 97; Elizabeth Carback 29; Henry 29; Hugh 14, 15; Jane Scott Watkins 130, 226; John 14, 15; Joseph 96, 97; Ruth 5; Samuel 74, 106, 130, 226; Sarah 97; William 47, 107
Hughs, Thomas 44
Hull. Johanna 192
Hulls. See Hulse.
Hulse, Elizabeth 155; Elizabeth [-?-] Moran 152, 153; Luke Barber 155; Meverell 152, 153
Humbe, James 88
Hume, Barbara 159; James 87
Hunking, John 25
Hunt, Ann Wiley 201; Margaret 222, 223, 224; Margaret Watkins 221; Marie 222; Martha 222, 223, 224; Martha Watkins 223, 224; Mary 223, 224; Robert 222, 224; Thomas 201
Hunter, Mary Smith 194; William 201
Hunton, Samuel 9
Huntzinger, Ann 151
Hurd, John 109; Martha [-?-] 109; Morgan 109
Hussey, George 114
Hutchins, Nicholas 62; Thomas 159
Hutton, Robert 37
Hyde, Samuel 171; Thomas 110
Hynson, Jane 109; W. 109; William 60
Iamp, Benj. 31
Igelhart. See Iglehart.
Iglehart, Ann Eliza 87; Ann Hearn 87; Anne [-?-] 87; Anne Hearn 85, 86; Cornelius 85, 86; Edward 85, 86; Sophia Hearn 85, 86; ilghman 86; Tilghman H. 87; Trueman 87
Ijams, Elizabeth 193; John 229; Mary 65; Thomas 193
Indrell, John 116
Ines, James 90

Index

Ingle, Catherine [-?-] 30; John 81; William 30
Inglish, John 27
Ingram, Arthur 48
Inkston. Elizabeth 142
Inloes, Abraham 230
Inoes, Henry 34
Ireland, [-?-] 53, 111; Mary Dare 52, 53
Israel, John 33
Isum, James 226
Jackson, Amanda M. 171; Blanch 26; Elizabeth Chadwell 35; Elizabeth Debruler 58, 60; Elizabeth Permelia 171; Elizabeth Shadwell 155; Emanuel 1; George 81; Henry 26; Isaac 32; John 133; Joseph 233; Mary Kendricks 169; Patience Harryman 81; Samuel 90; Semelia 59; Simeon 155; Simon 35; Thomas 58, 60, 81; william 101
Jacob, Rachel Ogg 161
Jacobs, John 161; Samuel 133
Jacobsen, Gurturie 27
Jadwin, John 1
Jadwyn, Hannah 1
James, Elizabeth 228; John 109, 120; Mary [-?-] 120; Sarah 9, 135; Sarah [-?-] 10; Thomas 10, 35; Walter 145, 146; Watkins 29, 120; William 118
Janney, Isabella [-?-] Carback 29
Janney, P. 29
Jarman, Mary Barton 12; Thomas 12
Jarrett, Abraham 107, 157
Jarvis, [-?-] 44; Aquila 181; Elizabeth Rowles 181
Jenkins, J. Hillen 228; Matthew 173; Richard 106; William 106,236
Jennick, Barbara 93
Jennngs, Thomas 191
Job, Robert 131; Thomas 33
Johns, Aquila 110; Hannah [-?-] 74; Richard 88; Skipwith 74
Johnson, [-?-] 25; Ann Plowman 129; Benjamin 130; Charles 112; Deborah [-?-] 129; Edward 128, 129; Elizabeth 130; Henry 233; Jacob 21, 51; Jane 130; John 129; Luke 62; Mary 70; Mary [-?-] 139; Nathan 51; Peter 132; Philip 139; Sarah 62, 123; Susanna 52; Thomas 148; William 20

Johnston, Elizabeth 142; John 82; Peter 132
Joice, S. J. 124
Jones, Ann [-?-] 179; Anne 192; Aquila 101; Avarilla 101; Benjamin 17, 101; Blanch 99, 101; Bridget [-?-] 100; Cadwallader 100, 101; Charles 37, 100, 101; 143, 213; Daniel 136; Diana [-?-] 17; Dorothy 99; Eeula [-?-] 100; Elizabeth 101, 228; Elizabeth [-?-] 97, 98, 101; Elizabeth Brice 101; Esther [-?-] 93; Frances 101; Frances Cobb 3, 48, 101, 143; Hannah Norris 99; Henry 196; Jane 98, 99; Jane Whipps 98, 232, 233; John 5, 35, 81, 82, 93. 98, 99; Jonathan 118; Judith 47; Lewis 186; Margaret Chadwell 35; Margery 99; Mary 101, 195; Mary [-?-] 99, 118; Mary Ellis 100; Mary Harrison 100; Mary Hill Crouch Rowles 177; Mary Paywel 100; Mary Poell 100; Morgan 98, 99, 100, 209, 217, 233; Nancy 81; Philip 49, 135, 177, 179, 180, 195, 232; Priscilla 100; Priscilla Wooden 100; Rachel 81; Rathvale 100; Rebecca 101; Rebecca Taylor 203; Richard 29, 208; Ruth 29; Sarah 100, 186; Sarah Harryman 81, 82; Susan[na] [-?-] 99, 100; Sybil 99; Theophilus 97, 98, 100, 101; Thomas 5, 34, 38, 64, 100, 101, 118, 197, 237; William 99, 100, 182, 192; William Dooley 101
Jordan, Helen Ogg 161; Sarah 14; William 161
Jouse, Jane [-?-] 25
Joyce, Elliner 132; Sarah 180; Thomas 132
Jub, Robert 196
Jubb, Robert 131, 132.
Judd, Jane [-?-] 25; Michael 25
Judy. See under Tschudy
Keef, Rachel Hatherly 83; Thomas 83
Keene, Samuel 167; Vachel 167
Keener, Peter 151
Kees, John 149
Keirle, Ann [-?-] 124; Eliza M. 124; Emily J. 124; John W. 124; Maria 124; Matthew M. 124; Thomasine 124; Washington T. 124; William H. 124
Keith, Alexander 76; Christian 76; John 76
Kelley, Elizabeth 90
Kelly, [-?-] 128; John C. 124; Mary Jane

Index

Mallonee 124; Prudence 191
Kemble, Rowland 155
Kemp, John 40, 118, 123; Sarah 40
Kenley, Avis Ward 103; Daniel 102, 103; Elizabeth 102; Frances Wells 102, 103; Jane Willson 103; Letitia 102; Mary 102; Richard 103; Samuel 102; Sarah 102; Susanna 102; William 102, 103
Kenly, Lemuel 102; Richard 102; Samuel 102
Kennard, William 125
Kennedy, Henry Callister 164; Hugh 168; John 164; Margaret Callister 164
Kenslaugh, Dominick 3
Keon, Dictus 235; Hannah 235
Kerbach, John 81
Kerby, David 172; Michael 172; Sarah 172
Kerby. See also Kirby.
Kerns, Jacob 95
Kernut, Susannah 213
Kersey, Elizabeth Whayland 231; Henry 231
Keys, Elizabeth 218; Francis 236
Keyser, Sarah 95, 96
Kid, Joseph 108
Kiersted, Hance 182; Margaret 172
Kilpatrick, Hannah 43; Samuel 44
Kimble, Margaret Daughaday 57; Rowland 155; Stephen 56, 57
Kindred, Sarah 1
King, Ann 104, 105; Anne Roberts 105; Blithe 38; Elizabeth 105; Elizabeth Foxcroft 105; Henry 103, 104, 124, 126, 138, 139, 145; Jacob 125; John 104, 105; Judith [-?-] 105; Martha 105; Martha Goddard 105; Mary 103, 125, 145; Mary [-?-] 104; Mary Haile 125, 126; Mary Marsh 105; Nicholas 105; Rachel 105; Richard 33, 104, 105, 106; Samuel 105; Susanna [-?-] 104; Tabitha 139; Tabitha Long 103, 104, 139, 145; Thomas 105; William 103, 104
Kinnard, Richard 5
Kinnimont, Ambrose 173
Kinsbie, Abraham 97
Kinsey, Paul 136
Kinsman, John 80
Kinword, Richard 6
Kirby, Ann 123, 124; Ann S. 123; Ann S.

Mallonee 122; Anna Randall 124; George 124; Michael 172, 173; Richard 172
Kirby. See also Kerby.
Kirchner, [-?-] (Rev.) 113
Kitchpole, Elizabeth 95; Elizabeth Hook 95
Kitten, Edward 178; Rachel Rowles 178; Sarah 178; Thomas 178
Knight, Ann 106; Ann Maria 107; Benjamin 30, 56, 94, 139; Charles 108; Charlotte 107; David 106, 107; Elizabeth 106, 107; Elizabeth [-?-] 30, 56; Ezekiel 107; George 107; Hannah 107; Isaac 107; Jane Long Peake Merryman 139; John 107; Light 106, 107; Margaret [-?-] 107; Mary 106, 107; Nathaniel 112; Rachel 106, 107; Rachel Ruse 107; Sarah 107; Sarah [-?-] 107; Susanna Simpson 106, 107, 189; Thomas 104, 106, 107, 189; William 91, 106, 107
Knighton, Dinah [-?-] 192; Dorothy [-?-] 66; Elizabeth 185; Thomas 25, 66, 185, 192
Knoleman. See Knowlman.
Knolman. See Knowlman.
Knoulman. See Knowlman.
Knowles, Henry 32; Mary Fugate 68; Peter 68
Knowlman, Abigail [-?-] 109; Anthony 108, 109; Jane Hynson Hanson 109; Joannah 109; John 108; Mary 109; Mary [-?-] 108, 109; Rachel 108; Rebecca 108; Richard 108, 109; Robert 108; Theophilus 19
Kramer, Mivh. 95
Kune, William 53
Kurtz, [-?-] 116, 152
Lably. See Levely.
Lackie, Hans 49
Lacklen, John 65
Laforgue, Eliza Cecilia 163
Laine, Sarah 197
Lake, Charles 167
Lamb, Ellen Anna 158; Sarah Wood 158; William 158
Lambert, Balser 94
Lane, [-?-] 185; Dianah [-?-] 191; Dutton 150, 191; Margaret 150; Pretiosa Tydings 150; Samuel 184, 185
Lanham, Catherine 65; Catherine Ferguson 66; William 66
Larkin, Thomas 168

Index

Larrissee, Mary 189
Latimer, M. R. 155
Lauder, Francis 54
Laughan, Richard 50
Laurence, Jacob 31
Laurenson, Eleanor 205
Lavely. See Levely.
Lawrence, Arthur H. 155; John 25; John Dorsey 229; Martha West 229; Mary 188; Thomas 169
Laws, James 171
Lawson, Alexander 149; Mary Taylor 200; Moses 200
Laybold, John 115
Laypold, John 115
Leach, Samuel 88
League, John 99; Luke 220; Thomas 97, 98
Leakins, John 137
Leary, Catharine Maryann 43
Lecke. See Leeke.
Lee, Alice 176; Elinor Temple 205; George 185; Hannah 219; James 186; Jane Wilson Hickson 90, 91; Johanna 91; John 90, 91; Mary 91, 172; Mary Simmons 185; Sherwood 205; Thomas 185
Leeke, Christian Vaughan 109; Eliza Ward 215, 216; Francis Gilbert Yaxley 109, 111; Hannah Busk 110, 111; Henry 216, 217; Lucy [-?-] 109, 110; Mary 111, 112; Mary Farrell 110; Nicholas 23, 24, 109, 110, 111; Richard 109, 110; Seymour 109
Leekings, Elizabeth 20; Mary 20
Legate, Ann [-?-] 197
Legatt, Elizabeth Burke 21; Jos. 21
Leggett. George 202
Lego, Catherine 231; Thomas 231
Legoe, Mary 231
Lemmon, Alexis 22, 141; Elexious 81; Elexus 22; John 22; Mary 22; Moses 22; Nicholas 43
Lenore, Rachel 236
Len(n)ox, Elizabeth Hayes 139; John 139; Mary Richardson; Rachel 236; Richard 66, 235; Tamar Love Wilkinson 235, 236
Leroy, Abraham 8; Ann Maria 8; Anna 9; Anna Maria 9; Elizabeth 9; Salome 9; Samuel 52
Levely, Andrew 113; Anna Barbara 113, 114; Barbara 113; Catharine 114; Catherine 113, 114, 115; Catherine Harrier 113; Catherine Whistler Rohra 113; Chartine Mull 114; Elizabeth 114, 115; Elizabeth [Allen?] 114; George 112, 113, 114, 115, 116; Henry 114; John 114; John L. 116; John S. 116; Mary 113, 114; Mary [-?-] Holtzman 116; Mary Eve 113, 114; Phebe Ann Skelton 116; Philip 116; Salome 113; Sarah 114; Sarah Rees 114; Sophia 114; Susan 116; Susanna 113, 114; Susannah 114; William 95, 112, 113, 114, 116
Leverett, Margaret Rogers Berry 175; John 175
Levy, Jacob H. 164
Lewin, Lewis 212
Lewis, Betty Giles 73; Catherine 64; Elizabeth Giles 73; Esther 58; Jesse 216; Richard 73; Robert 187; Sara H. 235
Leypold, John 113
Liggett. John 202
Lightbody, Elizabeth 17
Liles, Priscilla 188
Lindsay, John 65, 228; Mary [-?-] 65; Thomas 64
Lion. See Lyon.
Litten, Margaret Cobb Tucker 212
Litten. See also Litton.
Littig, [-?-] Levely 113; Lewis 45; Peter 113, 114, 115; Phlip 125
Little, [-?-] Levely 113; Catherine Levely 115; Guy 26; Ludwick 113
Litton, Ann 117, 118; Ann [-?-] 118; Ann Hawkins 116, 117, 118, 143; Clemency 118; Elizabeth 117; Hannah 117, 118, 119; Isaac 117, 118; James 117; John 118; John Lee 119; Margaret [-?-] Tucker 118; Martha 117, 119; Mary 117, 118; Mary [-?-] 119; Mary [-?-] Jones 118; Mary Richey 118; Mary Webster 116; Michael 117; Ruth 118; Samuel 117 118; Sarah 116, 117, 118, 119; Susannah 118; Thomas 116, 117. 118. 119, 212; 212, 213
Llewellen, Richard 187
Lloyd, Edward 6, 176, 194, Edward 206, 230; Elizabeth [-?-] 101; Elizabeth Gwynn Tayloe 230; John 101, 179; Maria 230; Thomas 187

Index

Loble. See Levely/
Lock, William 192, 193
Lockard, Francis 33; Jean 33
Lockwood, Robert 71
Logan, [-?-] 7; Thomas 129
Logsden, Edward 149
Lomax, Ann Hakman 119; Sarah Downey 119;Theophilas 119; Thomas 119
Loney, William 162
Long, Abraham 141, 142; Andrew 142; Ann 140; Ann Stansbury 141, 142; Benjamin 56; Catherine 142; Eleanor 141; Eleanor Moore 142; Eleanor Owens 140; Elenor 140; Elizabeth 141; Elizabeth Edwards 142; Elizabeth Inkston 142; Elizabeth Johnston 142; Elizabeth Partridge [-?-] 142; Elizabeth Sittlemyer 142; James 141, 142; Jane 126, 139, 141, 142, 150; Jane [-?-] 103, 134, 142; Jane [-?-] Tealle 141; Jane [-?-] Waites Dixon 136, 137, 138, 139, 150, 224, 225; Jeane 140; John 140, 14, 142, 218; Jonathan 140; Joshua 140; Lettice 139; Margaret [-?-] 142; Margaret Acton 142; Mary Cummins 142; Mary Norwood [-?-] 142; Patience [-?-] Pratt 141; Robert 31, 142; Robert Carey 142; Samuel 142; Sewell 142; Susanna 140; Susanna Mead 139, 140; Tabitha 103, 138, 145; Temperance Norrington 157; Thomas 103, 126, 134, 134, 136, 137, 138, 139, 140, 141, 142, 145, 150, 224, 225
Longland, Richard 139
Loos. See Louis.
Losey, Elizabeth Barton 12; Samuel 12
Louder, Rich'd 206
Louis, Arnold 93; Barbara [-?-] 93; John Jacob 93; Ursula 93
Love, Constant 21, 183; John 235; Robert 183, 235; Sarah [-?-] 183; Tamar 235; William 174
Loveall, Zachariah 127, 128
Loveday, John 2
Lovelace, Katherine 65
Low, James 171
Lowe, James 171
Lowrey, Amos 86
Lowry, [-?-] 96; Catherine Bryan 142; Martha Ellen Hook 96; Thomas 142

Lucas, Basil 190; Thomas 76
Lugg, John 13
Lumley, Geo. 206
Lunn, Edward 131
Lusby, Catherine [-?-] 64; Catherine Edwards 65; Edward 65
Lutz, Barbara 152
Lux, Darby 159, 214; William 160, 161, 176
Lyle, Elianor West 229; William 323
Lyles, Barbara 229; Eleanor West 229; Martha 229; Priscilla 229; William 229
Lyn, Rachel 123
Lynch, Ann 179; Comfort Roberts Barton 10, 11; Eleanor [-?-] 236; James 10; Joshua 236; Mary 236; Patrick 9; Robuck 9; William 181, 237
Lyon, John 157; Mary 154; Priscilla [-?-] 157; Rachel 123; William 161, 214
Lyttleton, [-?-] 174
M'Kim, Elizabeth 27
M'Laughlin, Mary Plowman 129
M'Laughlin, William 129
Macarty, Samuel 56
Maccarty, Daniel 155; Sarah Morris 155
MacClan. See McClain.
Maccubbin, Elizabeth 229; Mary 61; Samuel 229; William 145
Mackall, Elizabeth 89; James 88; John 52, 53
Mackarny, Ann 32
Mackelfish, David 31
Mackelfresh, David 31
Mackenheimer, John 220
Mackery, Daniel 26
Mackland. See McClain.
Macklane. See McClain.
Macklove, James 32
Mackwilliam, John 72; Rose [-?-] 72
MacQuain See McQueen
Magan, Margaret 190
Mahan, Elizabeth 121; Isabel 121; John 121; Mary [-?-] 121
Mahon(e), Elizabeth 120; Frances 29, 120; Isabel 120; John 119, 120; Mary 120; Mary [-?-] 120
Mahon(e). See Mahorne.
Mahones. See Mahan.
Mahonn. See Mahan.

Index

Mahun, Edward 236
Maiden, James 88
Mail, John 40
Malance. See Mallonee.
Maldin, Francis 88
Maleney. See Mallonee.
Mallane. See Mallonee
Mallence. See Mallonee.
Mallonee, [-?-] Bond 123; Achsah 122, 123, 124 ; Achsah Ann 122, 124; Achsah Sewell 122, 123 124; Alexander 124; Ann E. 122; Ann Kirby 123, 124; Ann S, 122; Ann Sewell 123; Benjamin 124; Brice 122, 123, 124; Delilah Cullison 125; Denton 123, 125; Edith 123; Edith Cole 121, 122; Eliza 124; Eliza Louisa Fairall 123, 124; Elizabeth 122; Em(m)anuel 121, 122, 123, 124; Ephraim 124; Frewilliam 125; George 122, 124, 125; Henry 125; Hezekiah 123, 124; James 122, 124, 125; Jared 123; John 121, 122, 123, 124, 125; John Stephen 124; John T. 124; Josiah 123; Keturah Tipton 124; Leonard 122, 123, 124; Lewis 123, 124; Margaret Reeves 122; Mark 124; Martha Tudor 125; Martin Van Buren 124; Mary 122, 124; Mary Jane 124; Mary Marsh 25; Maryland 124; Matthew 124; Peter 121, 122; Rachel 122, 124; Rachel Lyon 123; Rachel Matthews 124; Rebecca [-?-] 11, 122; Sarah 122, 123; Sarah Ann 124; Sarah Bond 123; Sarah Brown 124; Sarah Johnson 123; Sarah Mallonee 122; Shade 123; Shadrach 123; Thomas 122; Thomas W. 124; Thomasine Keirle 124; Virginia 124; William 122, 123, 124, 125
Maloney. See Mallonee.
Mankin, Michael 149
Manners, Charles 76
March, John 104; Temperance Harryman 81, 82
Marchant, Ellinor 197; Mary 197; Mary Sweeting 196, 197; Richard 196, 197; Rosannah 197; William 197
Marhorne. See Mahon.
Markell, Conrad 151
Marks, John 75
Marriott, Mary 122; Sylvanus 84
Marryman. See Merryman.
Marsh, Ann King 104; Beale 42; Eleanor Beale 42; Eliza S. Taylor 203; John 104, 105; Joshua 42, 43, 81; Mary 105, 122; Sarah Corbin 42; Thomas 42
Marshal(l), [-?-] 51; Rachel 42; Rachel Cox 50, 51; Thomas 16
Martin, Isaac 138; John 190; Lodowick 155; Luther 164
Marton, Mary 41
Marywell, James 47
Maslin, Eliza Sarah Mohler 152; Michael M. 152
Massey, Aquila 231
Mastik. See under Maslin.
Mathace, Susanna 131
Matheace, [-?-] 131; Susannah Nuthead 131
Matthews, Catherine 97, 230; Elizabeth 97; Henry 97, 230, 231; John 70; Mary 97; Rachel 124; Roger 104, 183; Sarah 97, 231; Sarah [-?-] 230; Sarah Hughes Preston 97
Mauduit, Elizabeth King 105; Jasper 105; William 105
Mauldin, James 72, 146
Maxwell, Jane [-?-] 145, 146; Joseph 146; Mary King 103, 145; Moses 146; Phoebe 78; Robert 146; Sally 13; Sam 103; Samuel 145, 146
Maybury, Sarah 214
Maynard, Sarah 196
McCan, Alexander 114
McCannon, James 114
McCaskey, Alexander 45; Esther 45; Hetty 45; Mary 44
McClain, Alexander 148; Amy Norman 147; Ann [-?-] 147; Catherine 147; Ceteran 148; Elizabeth 148; Elizabeth [-?-] 148; Elizabeth 148; Hector 30, 146, 147, 148; James 148, 163; John 147, 148; Katherine 147; Kezia [-?-] Haslet 148; Margaret 148; Margaret McClain 147, 148; Mary 147; Mary [-?-] 148; Mary Rebecca [-?-] 148; Nathanel 147; Rebecca [-?-] 148; Sarah 147, 148; Sarah [-?-] 148; Sarah Morgan 146, 147; William 147, 148
McClane. See McClain.
McClatchie, John Goodshine 96; Margaret

Index

Ann Hook 96
McClean. See McClain.
McClellan, [-?-] 114
McClone, James 32
McCollum, James 84
McComas, Aaron 17; Alexander 17; Anne [-?-] 17; Daniel 18; Elizabeth Hillen 18; James 18; John 17, 157; Mary 234, 235; Sarah 18; Susanna 18
McConikin, Eleanor Owens Long 140; John 140
McCord, Julia 15
McCreery, Nancy Tucker 213; William H. 213
McCullough, James 151
McDaniel, Francis 180
McDonnell, Za. 85
McElroy, Margaret 45
McGlathery, M. 165; Matthew 165
McGuire, John 122
McKenney, [-?-] 69
McLane. See McClain.
McLean. See McClain.
McLeod, Ann 192; Elizabeth [-?-] 192; Hugh 192; Robert 192
McLure, John 164
McMachen, Catherine Hook 96; Joseph 96
McPherson, Alexander 154; Mary Tongue 210; Thomas 210
McQuaine. See McQueen.
McQueen, Dugal 149; Francis 149; Grace [-?-] 149; Hector 149; Joshua 149; Ruth 159; Sarah Vaughan 149; Thomas 149; William 149
McQuinney, David 173
Mead, Edward 58; Elizabeth 227; ; James 58; Susanna 139
Meares, Thomas 177
Mears, Thomas 194
Medcaff, Elizabeth 232; Jane 233; William 233
Meek, Susannah 65
Meers. See under Mears.
Meredith, Jemima Taylor 200; Samuel 200
Merridale, Thomas 184
Merriken, Constant Oley 132, 133; Jacob 132, 133
Merriweather, Reuben 83
Merryman, Caleb 93; Catherine Levely 115;
Charles 49, 103, 125, 126, 135,. 139, 150; Chloe 150; Delilah 150; Elizabeth 48; Elizabeth Goodin 150; George 150; Jane [-?-] Peake 139; Jane Long 126, 150; Jemima 126, 150; Joanna 150; Job 115; John 77, 126; John Charles 150; Keziah 150; Margaret 150; Margaret Lane 150; Mary 49, 150; Mary Ensor 150; Mary Haile 125; Micajah 150; Millicent 150; Millicent Haile 150; Nicholas 161; Samuel 126; William 150
Middlemore, Jos. 101, Jos. 207; Josias 47
Miers. See Myers.
Milburn, Sarah Levely 114
Miler, Elizabeth [-?-] 207
Miles, John 116, 119; Margaret [-?-] 21; Margaret Burke Taylor 21; Mary [-?-] 119; Mary Webster Litton 116; Peter 21; Thomas 11, 21, 62, 117, 119
Mill, Chartine 114
Miller, Elizabeth Tolley 207, 208; G. W. 8; George 216; John 122; M. 206; Michael 207, 208; Nicholas 16; Philip 115; Sarah [-?-] Bond 16; Sarah Burke 23; Thomas 23
Mills, [-?-] 134; John 177
Minshall, Jane Atkinson 8; Joshua 8
Mitchell, Edward 46, 102; Elizabeth 43; James 46; Kent 46; William 46, 182
Moale, R. 128
Mohler, Alonzo 152; Ann Huntzinger 151; Ann Maria 152; Anna [-?-] 151; Anna Mariah 152; Barbara 152; Barbara Lutz 152; Cora 152; David 152; Edward 152; Eliza Sarah 152; Elizabeth Tschudy 151; George Adam 151; Henry 151; Isaac Wimbert 152; Jacob 151, 152; John 151; Katherine 152; Lewis 151; Ludwig 150; Mary 152; Peter 151, 152; Ruth 152; Sarah [-?-] 151, 152; Sarah Eliza 152; Solomon 151; Wilber 152; Wimbert 151, 152; Wimbert T. 152
Monat, James 16
Money, Ann Ashley 6
Monholland, James 158
Montgomery, Michael 144; Robert 135
Moody, Mones 141
Moore, Cassandra Adair 141; Eleanor 142; Hannah 163; James 121, 141

Index

Moran, Andrew 153, 154; Ann 154; Annie [-?-] 155; Benjamin 154; Charles 154; Elizabeth [-?-] 152, 153, 154; Gabriel 152, 153, 154, 155; Henrietta M. 155; John 153, 154; John P. 155; Jonathan 154; Margaret [-?-] 154; Margaret Wood 154; Mary 154; Mary [-?-] 154; Mary Lyon 154; Meveral 154; Meverel Hulse, 153, 154; Nancy [-?-] 155; Peter 153; Rebecca [-?-] 153, 154, 155; Rinaldo J. 155; Robert 154; Sarah Barber 154; Thomas Alfred 154; William 153; Zachariah 154
More, John 191
Morgan, [-?-] 7; Abraham 1; Edward 186; Elizabeth 209; Henry 200; Martha 66, 146; Philip 1; Robert 118; Sarah 146; Sarah Simmons 186; Thomas 66, 146, 209
Morris, Edward 156; Elizabeth 155, 156; Elizabeth Chadwell Jackson 35; Elizabeth Shadwell Jackson 155; Frances 156; Giles 156; Henry 155; Isaac 213; Jane [-?-] 155; John 156; Mary 155, 156; Mary [-?-] 155; Mary Murphy 155; Michael 156; Richard 155, 156; Sarah 155, 156; Susanna 155 156; Susannah Tucker 213; Thomas 35, 155, 156; William 156
Morton, George 154; John 153; John Andrew 115; Mary 115; Mary Grangett 115; William 154
Mosey, John 176
Motherly, Charles 190; Priscilla [-?-] 190
Mouat, James 216
Mould, Frances 67; John 67
Muckilvain, Robert 231
Mumford, Joseph 204
Mumma, John 93
Munday, Henry 205; James 205; John 205; Sarah 205; Susanna Temple 205; Thomas 205
Mungumorer. See Montgomery.
Murdagh, Daniel 46; Martha Cowan 46
Murphy, James 37; Mary 155; Patrick 33; Sarah Cheyne 37; Thomas 24; Tim 156; William 156, William 220
Murray, [-?-] Long 140; Dinah 50; Dinah Cox 50; George L. 155; Harriet W. Taylor 203; James 147; John 50, 140, 214;

Melchizedek 72, 73; Sarah Turner 214; Sophia Giles 73
Mutsey, Mary 6
Myer(s), Francis 112; Frederick 95; Jacob 145
Nance, Roland 225
Nauchit, Edward 186
Nedels, Edward 2, 3
Negro Abraham 39, 81
Negro Amey 89
Negro Bacon 193
Negro Bess 83
Negro Betty 178, 203
Negro Bob 193
Negro Bows 40
Negro Bowson 179
Negro Caleb 234
Negro Cassey 193
Negro Charity 79
Negro Chloe 193
Negro Clemming 193
Negro Daniel 81
Negro Davey 89
Negro Deptford 79
Negro Dick 89, 217
Negro Dighder 211
Negro Dinah 89
Negro Doll 217
Negro Esther 39
Negro Genny 89
Negro George 21, 193
Negro Grace 74, 217
Negro Gteat Bess 193
Negro Hannah 81, 178, 234
Negro Hardy 234
Negro Harry 79, 89. 193
Negro Henny 122
Negro Hercules 118
Negro Jack 193
Negro Jacob 53, 79
Negro Jemm 193
Negro Jenny 39, 79, 193
Negro Jockey 178
Negro Lott 79
Negro Lucky 89
Negro Lucy 89
Negro Lydia. 74
Negro Maria 89
Negro Moll 89, 193

Index

Negro Morea 74
Negro Nan 52
Negro Nell 167
Negro Night 203
Negro Pamela 178
Negro Peg 52
Negro Pegg 193
Negro Perry 111
Negro Peter 39
Negro Phill 39
Negro Poll 74
Negro Rachel 89, 217
Negro Ruth 39, 81
Negro Sam 74
Negro Sambo 217
Negro Sango 179
Negro Sarah 193
Negro Sophia 89
Negro Suck 217
Negro Susy 89
Negro Tamer 217
Negro Ted 217
Negro Tim 39
Negro Toby 81
Negro Tom 74, 193
Negro Tone 234
Negro Uiner 179
Negro Will 193
Negro Youjg Bess 193
Nelson, Ambrose 195
Newland, Benjamin 88
Newman, Joane [-?-] 38; John 38
Nice, Dorothy 13; Mary 96
Nicholas. See Nichols.
Nichols, Humphrey 156; Mary 90; Sarah 156; Thomas 156
Nicholson, Alice 218; Elizabeth 218; Ja. 77; James 164; Nathan 29
Night. See Knight.
Noble, Catherine 172; Richard 39; Robert 39, 40
Noleman. See Knowlman.
Norman, Amy 147; Benjamin 110; Eliza Smith 195; George 147, 195; Johanna [-?-] 147; William 195
Norrington, Abraham 157; Ann 157; Cassandra 157; Drucilla 158; Elizabeth 157, 159; Elizabeth [-?-] 157, 158; Frances 157, 158; Hannah 157, 158; Isaac 157; Jane 157; John 157, 158; Joshua 158; Martha 157; Mary 157, 158; Mary [-?-] 158; Mary Everett 158; Mary Hays 157; Priscilla 157; Rachel 157; Sarah 157; Susanna 157; Temperance 157
Norris, Aaron 157, 158; Abraham 158; Benjamin 28; Eleanor 204; Elijah 157; Ellen Anna Lamb 158; Hannah 99; Hannah Norrington 158; John 18; Rachel 158; Sarah Norrington 157; Susanna Bradford 18; Thomas 121, 158
Norten, Elizabeth 6
North, Robert 28
Norton, John 235; Stephen 118; Walter 192
Norvil, William 26
Norwood, Edwad 67; John 142; Mary 142; Mary [-?-] 142; Mary Fitzsimmons 67; Nicholas 49; Samuel 55
Nuthead, Dinah [-?-] 131, 132; Susan 132; Susan [-?-] 131; William 131, 132
Oakan, Manus 159
Oakley, Elizabeth 159; Esau 159; Jane Smith 159; Mary 159; Prudence [-?-] 159; Susanna 159; Thomas 159; William 159
Obrien, Daniel 79
Odell, Mary Sweeting 197
Oden, Benjamin 230; Eleanor "Ellen" 230; Rachel Sophia West 230
Oely. See Oley.
Ogg, Barbara Hume 159; Benjamin 160, 161; Catherine 161; Duncan 160; Elizabeth Bagley 159; George 159, 160, 161, 234; Helen 161; Helen Hamilton 160, 161; Henrietta 161; James 161; John 160, 161; Katherine 160; Laban 161; Mary 116, 160; Mary Potee 160, 234; Moses 161; Nicholas 161; Rachel 160, 161; Rebecca 160; Richard 161; Ruth 160; Sarah 160, 161; Sarah Beasman 160, 161; Sarah Lucretia 234; Susan 161; Vachel 161; William 159, 160, 161; William Hambelton 161; illiam Hamilton 160, 161
Ogle, [-?-] 65; Samuel 82, 85
Oglesby, George 100; Johanna [-?-] 100
Ogleter, Junius 237
Oldton, John 134; Mary [-?-] Watkins Barker 226

263

Index

Oley, Anice 133; Ans 312; Bethiah 133; Bethier 132; Constant 132, 133; Dianah 132; Dinah [-?-] Nuthead Devoran 131; Dinah 132; Elizabeth 132, 133; Elizabeth Hall 132; Hannah 132, 133; Margaret 131; Mordecai 132, 133; Sebastian 131, 132, 133; Susanna 133; Susannah 132; Vachel 132, 133
Olive, Sarah Hinton 135, 136
Oliver, James 71; William 83
Olle. See Oley,
Onion, Stephen 36, 60, 183,219
Oppe, Ursula Louis 93
Orban, Henry 94
Orem, John 86
Organ, Catherine [-?-] Carrington Scutt 31, 32; Matthew 3, 31, 32
Orrice, James 44
Orrick, John 45, 56; Nicholas 45
Orsbourne, Elisha 220, 221
Osbon. See Osborn.
Osborn, [-?-] 36; Daniel 198, 199; Elizabeth Simpson 190; Mary Parsons Tanzey 198; Thomas 190; William 70
Osborne, Benjamin 17, 90; Catherine Rhodes 17; William 25
Oursler, Ely 128
Overard, Peter 157
Owen, John 37; Pamela Cheyne 37
Owens, Eleanor 140; James 210; Richard 147
Owings, Caleb 55; Deborah [-?-] 236; Elijah 30; John 37; Joshua 30, 148; Nelly [-?-] 236; Pamelia [sic] Cheyne 37; Richard 33, 86, 147; Samuel 91, 191, 236, 237; Sarah 21; Stephen 236, 237
Oxford, John 118
Paca, Aquila 170, 205; John 119, 146
Page, George 133; James 44; Mary Coulter 44
Palmer, Ann 213; Thomas 43, 44
Parker, Elizabeth [-?-] 110; Elizabeth Carback 29; George 52; John 29; Joseph 212; Robert 32; Susanna 52; Susanna [-?-] 52
Parkhill, Jane Long 142
Parkinson, Mary 219
Parks, Edward 155; John 142; Peter 55
Parran, Samuel 52
Parratt, Benjamin 1, 3; Deborah Airey 1; Eliazer 2; William 2
Parratt. See also Parrott.
Par(r)ish, Edward 61, 77, 160; Elizabeth 61; John 33, John 73; Mary 33; Mary [-?-] 61, 160; Sarah 73; William 21, 73, 91
Parrott, Benjamin 1, 2, 3; Hannah 2; Jane 3; Jane [-?-] 2
Parrott. See also Parratt.
Parsons, Mary 198, Mary 200
Partridge, Buckler 140, 145; Danbury B. 142; Domine Buckler 140; Elizabeth [-?-] 142
Patrick, Ann 237
Paulson. See Poulson.
Paywell, Mary 100
Peacock, Constant Love Sickelmore 183 ; Delilah 22; Luke 183 , 194; Samuel 184; Samuel Sickelmore 183, 184
Peake, Catherine 138; George 87, 138; Jane [-?-] 138; Joseph 138, 139; Mary [-?-] 87
Peal, Joseph 35
Peale, Angelica Kauffman, 163 165; Angeline 164; Ann 162; Anna Claypoole 165; Anna Dunn 166; Benjamin Franklin 164; Caroline E. Haslam 164; Catherine 162; Charles 162, 163, 164; Charles Linnaeus 164; Charles Willson 163, 164, 165; Clara E. 163; Edmnd 166; Edmund 165; Eleanor 163; Eleanor [-?-] 163; Eliza Cecilia Laforgue 163; Eliza Ferguson 165; Elizabeth 162; Elizabeth Camparl 162; Elizabeth DePeyster 163, 164; Elizabeth Digby 162, 163, 164; Elizabeth Emerson Callister 164; Ellen Bordley Polk 164; Ellen Q. Field 166; George 162; Hannah Moore 163, 164; Harry 166; Henry 166; Howard 166; James 163, 164, 165, 166; James Godman 166; James Willson 163; Jane 162; Jane Ramsay, 165 166; Jane Wilson 162; M. McGlathery 165; Margaret 165; Margaret Jane 163, 173; Margaret Trigg 162, 163, 164; Margaret Van Bordley 163; Margaretta Angelica 165; Maria 165; Martha McGlathery 166; Mary Chambers Claypoole 163, 164, 165, 166; Rachel Brewer 163, 165; Raphael 164; Raphaelle 163, 165, 166; Raphaelle J. 166;

264

Index

Rembrandt 163; Richard 162; Rosalba Carriera 163; Rubens 163, 166; Sarah Miriam 165; Sophonisba 165, 166; Sophonisba Angusciola 163, 165; St. George 164, 165; Sybilla Miriam 164; Thomas 162; Titian Ramsey 163, 164; Vandyke 164; Virginia 166; Washington 166; William 162, William 162
Pearce, Catherine [-?-] 111; John 111
Pearle, Ann [-?-] 196; Mary 196; William 196
Peart, Thomas 137
Peek. See Peake.
Peirpoint, Amos 31
Pemberton, Ann [-?-] 110; Joseph 110
Pennington, William 131, 196
Penny, Bridget 172
Pepper, William 195
Peragoy. See Peregoy.
Peregoy, Fanny 238; Henry 42, 50; John 50; Keziah 50; Providence Corbin 42
Perkins, Avarilla 190; Mary 40; Richard 155; Samuel 40; Sarah [-?-] 40; Thomas 39, 40; William 40
Perriage. See Peregoy.
Perry, John 156; Joseph 207, 208; William 159
Persifull, Jno. 206
Peter, John 23
Peterson, Andrew 134, 135; Judith Dorman 134
Pettibone, Philip 11
Petty, [-?-] 110
Philibrown, Ann King 105; Thomas 105
Philibrum. See Philbrown.
Philips. See Phillips.
Phillips, Anna Barbara Sweeting 115; Bartholomew 210; Bethia [-?-] 97; Caroline 115; Elizabeth 216; Isaac 115, 183 ; James 25, 74, 119, 133, 134, 170, 208; Johannah 74; Margaret [-?-] 210; Prudence Hendon Sickelmore 183; Robert 138; Thomas 97; William 233
Philpot, John 125, 167
Phipps, Mary 138
Pickerell. See Pickering.
Pickering, Anne [-?-] 166; Elizabeth 166, 167; Elizabeth Brown 166, 167; Elizabeth Simmons 166; James 166, 167; Mary 167; Nancy Prebble 171; Stephen 166, 167; Thomas 171
Picket(t), Barbara Gorsuch 238; Elizabeth Barton Wright Greer 13; George 91; Heathcote 13; Mary 201; Mary Taylor 201; Walter 191
Pierce, Elizabeth 235; Susanna Rebecca 235
Pigg, Edward 145
Pilott, Wm. 12
Piner, James 163
Pines, Elizabeth 228
Pipen, Milcah Ashley 7; Richard 7
Piper, John 168; Michael 168; Rosanna 168; Rosanna Button 168; Rose Anna 168
Pitts, Josiah 12; Sarah Barton 12
Placid, Pall 125
Plased, Paul, 125
Plowman, Ann 127, 128; Ann [-?-] Vickory Plowman 125, 127; Catherine Margaret 128; Charles 128 ; Edward 127, 128; Eliza [-?-] 127, 128 ; Elizabeth 128; Elizabeth [-?-] 127;Ephraim 128; Henry 128; James 127, 128; Jantha 128 ; John 126, 127; Jonathan 126, 127, 128, 129; Joshua 128; Mary 128, 129; Nancy 129; Nicholas 128; Rachel 127; Rebecca Arnold 128, 129; Richard 127, 128; Ruth [-?-] 127, 128; Sarah 127, 128,129; Sarah Chambers 128; Stevenson 127; Tabitha Green 128; Rebecca 128, 129
Plummer, Abraham 217; Sarah Ward 217
Pocock, James 227
Poell, Mary 100
Poge, Mary 38
Polk, Charles Peale 164, 165; Elizabeth 164; Elizabeth Bordley 164; Elizabeth Digby Peale 165; Ellen B. Downman 165; Ellen Bordley 164; Lucy Brockenbrough [-?-] 165; Margaret Jane 164; Robert 164, 165; Ruth Ellison 165
Poloke, John 170; Sarah Prebble 170
Polson, Thomas 152
Polton, William 120
Pool(e), Henrietta 235; John Whips 234; Laurence 34; Peter 234; Ruth Whipps 234
Popejoy, Ann Tarrence 170; Cassandra Smith 170; Edward 170; Edward B. 170; John 170; Nathaniel Smith 170; Terrence 170; William 169, 170

Porter, Eleanor Connor 33, 34; Elizabeth 33; Greenbury 33; Mary [-?-] 33; Mary Parrish 33, 34; Michael 125; Philip 33, 34; Richard 33; Robert 141; Shadrack 33; Thomas 33, 34
Posey, Francis 79
Poston, William 80
Potee(t), Ann Taylor 201, 202; Elizabeth [-?-] 206; Francis 160; James 158; Jesse 202; John 158, 206; Lora 201; Lucy [-?-] 160; Mary 160, 234; Mary Norrington 157; Rebecca 158
Potts, William 107
Poulson, Andrew 145, 156; Ann Emson 143, 144, 145; Betsy 145; Cornelius 143, 144, 145; Elizabeth 144; James 145; John 145; Prudence Evans 145; Rebecca 144
Powell, [-?-] 99; Dorothy Jones 99; Eleanor 206; Elioannah 206; Elizabeth 206; Elizabeth [-?-] Poteet 206; Hannah Peninah Winifred 206; James 2; John 205, 206; Patience 206; Philissana Temple 205; Phillis Temple 206; Sarah 206; William 208
Pratt, Patience [-?-] 141; Roger Horace 141
Prebbel. See Prebble.
Prebble, Abram 171; Amanda M. Jackson 171; Ann 170; Ann Butcher 171; Ann Gallion 170; Armanelah 171; Clemency Billingslea 172; Daniel 171; Debora Butcher 171; Delilah Walker 171; Elizabeth 170, 171; Elizabeth Permelia Jackson 171; Elizabeth Teegarden 171, 172; Hannah Enoch 171; Hedgeman 171; Hiram 171; ; James 171, 172; Job 171, 172; John 171, 172; John Stephen 170, 171; Margaret [-?-] 172; Mary 170, 171; Mary Bucknell 170; Nancy 171; Priscilla Devaughn 171; Rachel 171; Reuben 171, 172; Sarah 170, 171; Stephen 171, 172; Thomas 170, 172, 172
Preble. See Prebble.
Presbury, Cordelia Debruler 59; Eleanor 121; Elizabeth Tolley 208; George Gouldsmith 37, 114, 208; Hannah Bradford 16; James 76; Joseph 121; Walter Goldsmith 208; William 59; William Robinson 59
Preston, James 130, 172; Sarah Hughes 97; Sarah Scott 130; Thomas 96, 97; William 233
Pribble. See Prebble.
Prible. See Prebble.
Price, Benjamin 199, 200; Keturah 92; Mary Parsons 200; Mordecai 92, 122, 200; Rachel Mallonee 122; Sarah 200; Sarah Matthews Cross 97, 98; Tabitha Tipton 92; Thomas 97, 98; William 26
Prichard, Elizabeth [-?-] 63; James 63; Margaret [-?-] 63
Prichard. See also Prickett, Pritchard, Pritchett.
Prickett, George 62
Prickett. See also Prichard, Pritchard, Pritchett
Priesty, Francis 185
Pritchard, Ann 117; Samuel 117
Pritchard. See also Prichard, Prickett, Pritchett.
Pritchett, Obadiah 63
Pritchett. See also Prichard, Prickett, Pritchard.
Pue, Anna 230; Mary Dorsey 230; Michael 230
Pugh, Mary 199
Pure, Sarah 131
Purnall, Elizabeth 167; Mary Pickering 167; Rachel 167; Richard 167
Quail, James 43
Rabbling, Joseph 61
Ragon, Bazel 148
Rallence. See Mallonee.
Ralph, [-?-] (Rev.) 94
Ramsay, Nathaniel 164
Randall, Anna 124; Bale 30; Christopher 30, 104, 147, 148; Eleanor Carey 30; James Ryder 30; Margaret [-?-] 30; Thomas 32, 104, 220, 233
Rankin, Catherine Walker 20; Dolly 20; George 19; Mary Bull 19; Mary Walker 20
Ratcliffe, Richard 38
Rathell, [-?-] 173; Ann West 173; David 172, 173, 174; Elizabeth 172, 173, 174; Elizabeth Russum 172, 173, 174; Isaiah 174; John 172, 173, 174; Joseph 172, 173, 174; Kirby 173; Lidia [-?-] 172; Mary 172, 173, 174; Mary [-?-] 174;

Index

Nancy 174; Pritchard 173; Rachel [-?-] 174; Rebecca 173; Richard 172, 173; Samuel 172, 173; Sarah [-?-] 174; Sarah Kerby 172; Thomas 172, 173, 174; William 173, 174
Rathrell. See Rathell.
Raughter, Elias 149
Raven, Avarilla 219, 220; Drusilla 219, 220; Elizabeth 218, 219, 220; Esther 220; Hester 218, 219; Isaac 218, 219, 220; Jane Long 141; Keziah 220; Letitia 219; Letitia Ward 218, 219; Letticia 220; Luke 81, 218, 219, 220; Maria 218, 219; Mary 218, 220; Millicent 220; Millla 220; Sarah 81; Thomas 141; William 220
Rawlings, Isaac 52; James 123; Jane 29; John 121, 230
Ray, Bridget 175; Mary [-?-] 175; Richard 175
Read, George 183; Katherine 176; Susannah 176
Reading, Maurice 181; Patience Rowles 181
Reaves, William 122
Reddell, John 56
Redding, Eliza M. Keirle 124
Redell, Eleanor Daughaday 56
Reed, [-?-] Atkinson 8; John 5; Samuel 8
Rees, Sarah 114
Reese, Daniel 14, 15; Elizabeth Bond 14, 15; Geo. 82
Reeves, Edward 25; Henrietta [-?-] Robinson Swanson Cannon 26; Margaret 122; William 103
Regan, John 84; Timothy 84
Reid, William 211
Rench, Margaret Watkins 228; Ralph 228
Renshaw, James [?] 112; Janes[?] 112
Rho(a)des, Catherine 17; Elizabeth 98; Henry 17; John 98; Mary 98; Mary Matthews 97, 98; Sarah Standiford 98; William 97, 98
Ricaud, Benjamin 176, 207; Elizabeth 176
Rice, James 228; Solomon 67
Richand. See Ricaud.
Richard. See Ricaud.
Richards, John 203; Joshua 201; Lewis 14, 28, 115, 124, 125, 190, 203; Lydia 203; Rebecca Scarborough 203

Richardson, Anthony 174; Daniel 72, 193; Elizabeth Welsh 72; Joseph 61; Mark 138; Mary 48, 66; Richard 199; Samuel 74; Tabitha 75; Thomas 182; Thomas Dickinson 174; William 31, 193
Richey, John 118; Mary 118
Ricketts. N. 5
Riddle, John 228
Ridgely, Charles 31, 73, 159; Henry 85; J. 30; Robert 84, 85
Rigbie, Cassandra 144; John 117; Nathan 75, 143, 144; Nathaniel 74; Sarah Giles 74, 75
Rigbie. See also Rigby.
Rigby, John 52; Nathan 78
Rigby. See also Rigbie.
Rigdon, [-?-] 184
Riley, John 202, 203; Martha Taylor 202, 203
Ringgold, James 3; Thomas 6
Risteau, George 95, 161; Isaac 29, 146; John 144, 160; Katherine Ogg Talbot 160; Talbot 59, 121; Thomas 237
Ritter, Anthony 95; Catherine 95; Catherine [-?-] 95; Henry 95
Roach, Ellizabeth Hambleton 78; William 78
Roads, John 133
Roberson, James 194
Roberts, Anne 105; Benjamin 11, 134; Comfort 10, 11; Eliza Corbin 41; Elizabeth 209; Elizabeth [-?-] 91; Grace 143; Henry 199; Jacob 218; John 11, 12, 91, 121, 134, 143, 183, 199; Mary [-?-] Ashley 6, 7; Richard 105; Robert 6, 7; Sarah [-?-] Barton 12; Thomas 41; William 19
Robertson, Eleanor Ward 217; Lettice Long 139; Samuel 212; Susannah 139
Robeson, Comfort Rowles 178; Oneall 178; Robert 97
Robey, James 154
Robinson, Alexander 165; Angelica Kauffman Peale 165; Comfort Rowles 178; Jacob 218, 219; Jonas 49; Lettice 138; Lettice Long 139; Mary [-?-] 178, 219; Mary Dashiell 112; Matthew 112; Priscilla 165; Susannah 138; Thomas 178; William 25, 90
Robotham George 75
Rockhold, John 196; Susannah 196

267

Index

Rode, Rich. 69
Roe, Anthony 3; Jane Parrott 3
Rogers, Abigail 175; Bridget 175; Daniel 175; Elizabeth 175; Elizabeth Denison 175; John 175, 176; Lucinda Thompson 176; Margaret 175, 176; Margaret Crane 175; Margaret Lee Clark 176; Martha 175, 176; Martha Whittingham 176; Mary 175; Mary [-?-] Contee Hemsley 175; Nathaniel 175; Nich 103; Nicholas 81, 214; Patience 175; Philip 237; Richard 175; Samuel 175; Sarah [-?-] 49; Susanna Whipple 175; William 175, 33, 49, 176, 191
Rohra, Catherine Whistler 113; John 113
Rohrbach, Adam 190
Roles. See Rowles
Rolles. See Rowles.
Rollo, Archibald 13; Temperance 13
Rolls. See Rowles.
Rooker, Henry 85
Rosenquist, Alexander 185; R. 186
Rossum, John Van 125
Roszenquest, Johanna Hull Smith 193
Rous(s)e, Thomas 59, 60
Roux, Paul 172
Rover, Elizabeth 151
Row, William 182
Rowland, James 116
Rowles, Airy 182; Ann 180, 181; Ann [-?-] 182; Ann Davice 178, 179; Ann Lynch 179; Anne 179, 181; Anne Gorswick 181; Arianna 182; Charles 177; Christiana [-?-] 182; Christopher 176, 177, 179; Comfort 178; Constant 135, 178; Constant Sampson 179, 181; David 178, 179, 180, 181; Davie 182; Elizabeth [-?-] 176, 178, 179, 180, 181; Elizabeth Dungan 181; Ely 180, 181; Jacob 177, 178, 179, 180, 181, 197; John 177, 178, 179, 180; Joseph 181; Levin 180; Martha 177; Martha [-?-] 180; Martha [-?-] Smith 195, 196; Martha Baker Snith 178, 179; Mary 178, 179, 181; Mary [-?-] 181; Mary Hill Crouch 177; Mary Scarf [-?-] 179; Matthew 181; Nance 180; Patience 181; Patience Stinchcomb Rowles 179; Rachel 178, 181; Reason 180; Rezin 180, 181; Richard 179, 181; Ruth 178, 179,
180, 181; Ruth 237; Sarah 178, 180, 181; Sarah Fisher 177, 178, 180; Sarah Joyce 180; Sophia [-?-] 181; Susanna 178, 180; Thomas 177, 178, 180, 181, 182; William 83, 177, 178, 179, 181, 182, 195, 196
Rozenquest, Alexander 192; Hanna Smith 192
Ruark, Patrick 58
Ruff, Daniel 70
Rumsey, Benj. 208
Ruse, Rachel 106
Rusk, Anne Carback 28; William 28
Russ, Richard 72
Russell, Alexander 78; Thomas 129
Russum, Elizabeth 172, 173
Rutledge, John 91; Thomas 16
Ruxton, Nicholas 119
Ryan, Dennis 186; Eleanor Simmons 186; Eleanor Simmons Morgan 186; Elinor 187
Ryder, Thomas 131
Ryland, Ann 23; Mary Burke 20, 21; Nicholas 21, 23
Ryley, Eliza 26
Saintee, Philip 3
Salmon, Thomas 34, 133
Salway, Thomas 60
Sampson, Abraham 16; Constant 179; Elizabeth [-?-] 135, 136, 179; Esther 78; Isaac 135, 136; John 9, 135; Richard 9, 135, 136, 179; Ruth 16
Samson. See Sampson.
Sanders, Henry 186, 187
Sanderson, Francis 142
Sands, Francis 61
Sappington, Mark Brown 208
Sater, Charles 161; George 55, 161; Helen 161; Henry 125; Mary [-?-] Stevenson 125; Rachel Hamilton 55
Saunders, Elizabeth 134, 187
Savory, William 140
Saylor, Henry 91
Scales, Sarah 39
Scarborough, Rebecca 203
Scarf(e), Hannah Taylor 202, 203; James 179; Mary [-?-] 179; William 202, 203
Schels. Peter 152
Schitz, Peter 151
Schranit. See Grangett.
Scott, Ann 130; Avarilla 130; Daniel 35, 73, 130, 205, 226; Hannah [-?-] 73;

Index

Hannah Butterworth 73; Jane 130, 226; Jane [-?-] 2; Jane Johnson 130; John 207; Sarah 130; Susanna [Drew?] 74; William 2

Scrivener, Elizabeth 167; Elizabeth Clark 167; John 167; Levi 167; Margaret 167; Mary A. 167; Mary Simmons 185; Philip 185; Polly 167; Rachel Purnall 167; Rezin 167; Sarah 167; William 167

Scudamore, Abigail Dixon 137; Penelope 138; Thomas 137, 139, 225

Scutt, Catherine [-?-] Carrington 31; John 31, 32

Seal, Hannah Cowan 46; James 46

Seigarsar, Felix 94

Selby, Edward 215; Enoch 87

Sellers, Anna 165; Coleman 165; Sophonisba Angusciola Peale 165

Sellman, John 179, 210; Leonard 20; Mary Walker Rankin 20

Serjeant, John 23

Sewell, Achsah 122; John 122; Mary Marriott 122

Seymour, John 175

Seyney, Morgan 108

Shadwell, Elizabeth 155; Elizabeth [-?-] 155; John 35, 136, 155; Michael 34, 136

Shadwell. See also Chadwell.

Shanks, Robert 170

Sharbutt, Thomas 187

Sharp, Peter 75; Susanna 13

Shaw, Assenal [-?-] Hamill 80; Catherine Chandler Hamill 79, 80, 81; Catherine Hamill 79; Christopher 34, 81; Christopher Durbin 80; Elizabeth Johnson 130; Jane 80; John 80, 130; Joseph 80; Susannah [-?-] 80; Thomas 181

Sheckeks, Sarah Simmons 188

Sheckells, Rebecca 188; Richard 188

Sheppard, John 191; Moses 123

Sheredine, Caroline 75; Cassandra [-?-] 74; Daniel 75; John 233; Nathan 74; Tabitha [-?-] 120, 191; Tabitha Long King 103, 139; Thomas 103, 104, 120, 139, 140, 191

Sherwood, Ann 174

Shields, David 151

Shipley, Adam 234; Benjamin 234; Catherine Ogg 161; George 160; Katherine Ogg 160; Lloyd 161; Mary Whipps 234; Rachel Whipps 234; Rebecca Ogg 160; Samuel 82; Uroth Whipps 234; William 160

Shockney, Charles 161; Sarah Ogg 161

Short, Ann 77; Naomi 77

Showers, John 95

Sick, Thomas 78

Sickelmore, Constant Love 183, 184; Elizabeth 183, 184; Hannah 183, 184; Katherine Harrington 183; Martha [-?-] 182; Prudence Hendon 182; Ruth Cammel 183; Ruth Sarah 183; Samuel 182, 183; Sarah 183; Sarah [-?-] 182, 183; Sutton 183, 184; Thomas Wriothesley 183

Sickelmoe. See also Sicklemore.

Sicklemore, Constant Love 21; Sarah 21; Sutton 21

Sicklemore. See also Sickelmore

Simes, Jane Ramsay Peale 166; Mary Jane 166; Samuel 166

Simmonds. See Simmons.

Simmons, Abigail 188; Abraham 184, 185, 186, 187 188; Ann 187; Basil 188; Benjamin 185, 186; Betridge 187; Chapman 187; Deborah 186; Deborah [-?-] 186; Debrugh 186; Diana 185; Eleanor 185, 186; Eleanor [-?-] 186; Elisabeth 166, 185, 186, 187; Elizabeth Knighton 185, 186, 187; Elizabeth Powell 106; George 11, 167, 184, 185, 186, 187; Isaac 184, 185, 186, 187, 188; James 186, 186, 187, 188; Jeremiah Chapman 187; Johanna 11; John 106, 186, 187; Knighton 186, 187; Margaret 186; Margaret [-?-] 186, 187;Martha 186; Martha [-?-] 185, 187, 188; Mary 184, 185, 188; Mary [-?-] 187; Mary Child 188; Mary Drury 188; Mary Lawrence 188; Priscilla Liles 188; Rachel 186; Rebecca Sheckells 188; Richard 186, 188, 210; Robert 22; Samuel 186, 187, 188; Sarah 184, 185, 186, 188; Sarah [-?-] 184. 185, 186, 187; Sarah Thornbury 188; Sophia 195; Thomas 188; Van 188; William 184, 186, 187, 210; William West 188

Simonds. See Simmons.

Simons. See Simmons.

Index

Simpson, Ann 189, 190; Ann [-?-] 188, 189, 190; Avarilla Simpson 190; Charlotta Elizabeth [-?-] 190; Eleanor 189; Eleanor [-?-] 189; Elizabeth 189, 190; Elizabeth [-?-] 189, 190; Elizabeth Buchanan 189, 190; Elizabeth Durbin William Andrew 190; Elizabeth Prebble 170; Gilbert 189; Hannah 189, 190; James 190; John 189, 190; Jonathan 189, 190; Joshua 189; Martha 189; Mary 189, 190; Mary Larrissee 189; Mary Smith 189, 190; Matthew 189; Nathaniel 190; Reuben 190; Richard 188, 189, 190, 191; Samuel 189, 190; Sarah 189, 191; Sarah Collins 189; Susanna 106, 188; Susanna Collins 106; Thomas 188, 189, 190, 191; Walter 191; William 170, 189, 190
Simson. See Simmons, and Simpson
Sinclair, William 157
Sindall, Mary 201; Philip 42
Sing, Frances Taylor 200, 201; Margaret 55, 199, 200, 201
Singclear, Michael 131
Sittlemyer, Elizabeth 142; Mary [-?-] 142; Sebastian 142
Sixsmith, William 201
Skelton, Phebe Ann 116
Skidmore, Edward 108, 206; Margrett 58
Skidmore. See also Scudamore.
Skillington, Thomas 75
Skinner, Adderton 64; Anne 65; Frederick 53, 54; John 37; Mary 17; Matthew 17
Slade, John 62; Jonas 178; Minerva 228; W. 227
Slater, Ellis 89; Margaret 168; Robert 141
Slaughter, John 64
Slemaker, Elizabeth Giles 74; James 74
Sligh, Ann [-?-] 192; Ann McLeod 192; Elizabeth 191; Elizabeth Sophia 192; Samuel 192; Sophia [-?-] 41; Sophia Wilkinson 191, 236; Thomas 29, 31, 41, 120, 191, 192, 219, 236; William 191, 192
Slubey, [-?-] 7; William 6
Slye. See Sligh.
Smallwood, [-?-] 165; Samuel 66
Smith, [-?-] Simpson 189; Aleth(i)a Dare 52; Alice [-?-] 195; Ann 131, 193, 194, 196, 201; Ann [-?-] 194; Ann Watkins 194; Anne [-?-] 195, 196; Anthony 192, 193; 194; Arthur Forbes 36; Bridget [-?-] Jones 100; Cassandra 73, 170, 195; Charles 49; Comfort 196; Cosman 83; Deborah [-?-] 19; Dinah 193; Dinah [-?-] Knighton 192, 193; Edward 100, 168; Eliza 193, 194, 195; Eliza [-?-] 193, 194, 195; Elizabeth 49, 193, 195; Elizabeth [-?-] 193, 194; Elizabeth Giles 74; Elizabeth Merryman Cox 49; Elizabeth Watkins 193 ; Emanuel 189; George 112; Hannah 192; James 28, 164, 194, 195, 196; Jane 159, 193; Jane Watkins 194; Jeremiah 67; Johanna Hull 192, 193; John 49, 149. 158, 178, 193, 194, 195, 196, 225; Joseph 19, 171; Margaret [-?-] 104; Martha [-?-] 195, 196; Martha Baker 178; Mary 189, 193, 194, 195; Mary [-?-] 168, 230; Mary Fowler 49; Nathan 184, 185, 232; Nathaniel 56, 129, 164; Philemon 194, 195,196; Philip 233, 234; Priscilla 229; Priscilla West 229; Rachel 49, 97; Richard 100, 131, 229; Sally 28; Samuel 49, 189, 193, 194, 195; Sarah Rowles 178; Susannah Rockhold Howard Crouch 96; Thomas 49, 67,182, 230; Walter 52, 54; William 22, 74, 97, 117, 128, 164, 178, 195, 196, 207
Smithson, Ann Scott 130; Thomas 130
Smoot, Barton 79; George 155; John 80; Josias 154; Samuel 154; William Groves 79, 80
Smyth, Richard 222
Snelson, William 70
Snider, Valentine 115
Snowden, Richard 85
Sollers, Ann Dare 53; Elizabeth Heighe 88; James 53; Mary Heighe Tongue 208; Robert 98; Sabrett 88, 208; Sabritt 208
Solomon, Samuel 24
Somervell, James 52, 53; John 52; Susanna Dare 52, 53
Somerville, John 52
Soumain, Samuel 64
Southard, Eliza 136
Spear, William 114
Spedde, Sophia 95
Spence, Archibald 167
Spencer, Charity Cobb 38. 143; Elizabeth Ward 220, 221; Jeremiah 45; William 151, 220, 221; Zachariah 37, 38, 143

Spenser, Charity Cobb 37
Spiers, Thomas 114
Spink(s), Sarah 116, 196
Sprigg, Richard 86
Spry, Johanna 137; Oliver 35, 129
Stackmous, Thomas 32
Stagers, Elizabeth 94
Staley, [-?-] 100; Mary Harrison Jones 100, 101
Stallings, Richard 88, 218
Standford. See Standforth.
Standforh, John 99, 232, 233; Phylothia 232; Susanna Whipps 232, 233; Susannah 233
Standiford, Esther [-?-] 62; James 98, 227; Martha 227; Martha Watkins 227; Sarah 98; Skelton 62
Stanford. See Standforth.
Stansbury, Abraham 220; Ann 141, 142; Catherine 202; Catherine [-?-] 202; George 49, 181; Isaac 141; James 141; Jane Hayes 139; John 141, 142; John F. 201; Josias 197; Luke 28, 135, 145, 202; Mary 219; Mary Raven 218, 220; Rebeecca 203; Richard 141; Richardson 140, 218, 219, 220; Ruth 202, 203; Thomas 10, 11, 139, 140, 202; Tobias 49
Stapleton, Edward 114
Starkey, Joshua 208
Stephens, Giles 133
Stephenson, Henry 202
Sterling, Thomas 87, 88
Sterrett, [-?-] 45
Stevens, Charles 177; Giles 133, 137; John 136, 169; Richard 149; William 155
Stevenson, Anne 201; Edward 50, 125, 126; George 102; Henry 126, 201; Jemima Merryman 126; Joshua 201; Mary King 125, 126; Nicholas 201; Rachel Plowman 127; Richard King 125, 126, 127, 128
Stewart, David 180; Robert 12; Robert S. T. 12; Sarah Rowles Snith 178; Susanna Rowles 178
Stiles, Nath. 136
Stinchcomb(e), Ann 29; Catherine [-?-] 147; Catherine McClain 148; John 30, 140, 147, 179, 180; Mary 179; Nathaniel 140, 179, 180; Patience 179; Patience Rowles 179; Sarah 179
Stirlng, Thomas 87
Stockdon, John 198
Stockett, Damaris Welsh 72
Stocksdale, Solomon 148; Thomas 148
Stoddard, James 72
Stokes, John 189
Stoler, John 92
Stone, Elizabeth [-?-] Sampson Bagford Hinton 9, 135, 136; Hugh 153; Mary 153; Samuel 212; Thomas 9, 135
Straughton, Ann Claypoole Peale 165, 166; William 165, 166
Street, William 60
Strowd, James 31
Sturtun, George 206
Sudden, John 12
Sudenant, Jery 98
Sullivan Jeremiah 98; Jenerate 98; John 26, 191
Summer, Michael 31
Summers, John 94; William 169
Summerson, John 40
Sumner, John 97; Mary [-?-] 97
Sutton, Joseph 15; Ruth Cantwell 27; Samuel 27; Thomas 184
Swan, Robert 192
Swann, E. H. 155
Swanson, Edward 25
Sweetin. See Sweeting.
Sweeting, Ann Bowen 198; Anna Barbara 115; Benjamin 197; Caroline Phillips 115; Catherine Wineman 114, 198; Edw. 181; Edward 189, 196, 197; Elizabeth 197; Elizabeth [-?-] 198; Mary 196, 197; Mary Pearle 196, 197; Mary Watts 197; Robert 179, 196, 197, 198; Ruth Trotten 197; Sarah Laine 197; Thomas 114, 115, 197, 198; William 197, 198
Swift, Jeremiah 82, 83
Swindell, Daniel 10, 11, 133, 134; Elizabeth [-?-] 10; Elizabeth [-?-] Cogell Dorman 133, 134
Symington, Deborah 45; James 45
Symonds. See Simmons
Symson. See Simpson
Synmons. See Simmons.
Syons, Joseph 42

Index

Tacker. See under Tucker.
Taillor, Thomas 71
Talbot, Edmund 49; John 51, 168; Katherine Ogg 160; Margaret 18; Richard 61; William 160
Talbott, Benjamin 81; Daniel 217; Edw. 81; Edward 176; Eliza Ward 217; John 21, 62, 81, 103, 176; Joseph 217; Mary Birckhead 217; Rachel 217
Talby, Samuel 48
Tally. See Tolley.
Tanihill, Andrew 65
Tanner, George 220
Tansey. See Tanzey.
Tanzey, Abraham 198, 199; Abram 199; Alexander 198, 199; Ann 198; Catharina 198, 199; Edward 199; Katherine 198; Leah 199; Martha 198; Mary 198; Mary [-?-] 198; Mary Parsons 198; Mary Pugh 199; Rebecca 198. 199; Rebecca [-?-] 199
Tanzy. See Tanzey.
Tapley, Christopher 25
Tarrence, Ann 170
Tasker, [-?-] (Esquire) 21
Tate(s), Elizabeth Coulter 44; James 44; Robert 80
Taylard, William 177, 186
Tayloe, Elizabeth Gwynn 230
Taylor, [-?-] Thompson 203; Ann 201, 202, 204; Ann Hook 96; Ann Stevenson 202; Anna 202; Anne Stevenson 201; Anne Tracey 199, 200; Anney 202; Barbara Hook 96; Catherine 203, 204; Catherine Stansbury 202, 202, 204; Christieanne 204; Clemency Thompson 203; Eleanor [-?-] 202; Elijah 201, 202, 203; Eliza Bell 204; Eliza S. 203; Elizabeth 21, 201, 203, 204; Elizabeth [-?-] 203; Elizabeth Emson Whitaker 143, 144; Elizabeth Thompson 202; Ellen V. Norris 204; Elmira G. 203; Everard 53; Frances 199, 200, 143, 144; Grace 144; Hannah 201; Hannah Eugenie 202, 203; Harriet W. 203; Henry 203; Isaac 7, 201, 202, 203, 204; Jacob 201, 202, 204; James 156; Jemima 200; John 21, 96, 182, 200; Joseph 54, 55, 57, 199, 200, 201, 202; Joseph Neal 200; Joshua 201, 202, 203; Juliann 201; Lorenzo 202; Lorenzo D. 203; Louisa Maria Dashiell 112; Lydia Richards 203; Margaret 147; Margaret Burke 21; Martha 201, 202, 203; Mary 200, 201; Mary [-?-] 200; Mary Ann 203; Mary Anne 202; Mary Gongo Trevitt 204; Milton N. 203; Nelson 202, 203, 204; Patience [-?-] 201; Patience Tipton 202, 203, 204; Rachel 144 200, 201, 201; Rebecca 202, 302; Rebecca Stansbury 203; Richard 54, 55, 199, 200, 201, 202, 203, 204; Richardanna 204; Ruth 201, 202; Ruth Stansbury 202, 203; Samuel 25, 200, 201, 202, 203, 204; Sarah 56, 200, 201, 201; Sarah [-?-] 53, 200, 203; Sarah Ann 201, 204; Sarah Gatch 202; Sarah Price 200, 202; Sarah Thompson 204; Susanna [-?-] 200; Thomas 32, 33, 50, 73, 74, 96. 143, 199, 200, 201, 202, 203; Thomas Dorsey 204; Thomas Wilkinson 202, 203; Thruston M. 112; Wilkerson 203; William 50, 131
Tayman, Benjamn 121
Teague, Susanna 46
Teal, Edward 32; Emanuel 148
Tealle, Jane [-?-] 141
Tealle, John 141
Teasdale, Christopher 38; Mary Carter 38
Tebedo, Faith 204; Jos. 204; Joseph 204. 205; Mary 204; Mary [-?-] 205; Peter 204, 205
Teegarden, Elizabeth 171; George 171; Rachel Prebble 171
Temple, Eleanor 205; Eleanor Laurenson 205; Elinor 205; Johanna(h) 205, 206; Michael 205;Phillis 206; Philissana 205; Susanna 205; Thomas 205
Templeton, Susanna 22
Tench, Thomas 185, 186
Tepedo. See Tebedo.
Teye. See Tye.
Tharp, William 2
Therrell, Katherine 129; Margaret [-?-] 129, 130; Richard 136, 137; Robert 129
Thomas, Alice 14; Alice Bond 15; George 79; James 14, 15; Jane [-?-] 211; John 66, 196, 211; Joseph 146; Samuell 60; William 3
Thompson, Ann Norrington 157; Cassandra Norrington 157; Catherine Levely 113, 114; Clemency 203; Daniel 168, 176;

272

Index

Elijah 16; Elizabeth 202; Frances Norrington 157; John 45; Mary [-?-] 176; Richard 66; Sarah 204; Thomas 185; William 15
Thornborough, Margaret 8; Roland 126, 127; Thomas 8
Thornbury, Francis 126; Sarah 188
Thornbury, See also Thornborough
Thurrell. See Therrell.
Thurrold. See Therrell.
Thurroll. See Therrell.
Thurston, Margaret 233; Thomas 143
Tibbens, Daniel 212
Tibbets. See Tebedo.
Tibbido. See Tebedo.
Tibbs, William 103
Tilden, John 6
Tilghman, James 40; Michael 169
Tillard, Martha Simmons 186; William 186, 187
Tillotson, John 3; Sarah [-?-] 3; William 3
Tilton, Keturah 124
Tilyard, John 57, 58; Mary [-?-] 58; Richard 58
Tinge. See under Tongue.
Tinges, John 142
Tipper, Edward 58
Tippeto. See Tebedo.
Tipton, Aquila 92; Gerard 55; John 92; Joshua 92; Mary [-?-] 202; Patience 202; Samuel 50, 202; Tabitha 92; Thomas 127
Todd, Elizabeth 103; James 103, 139; Penelope Scudamore 139; Sarah Wilkinson 236' Thomas 34, 126, 236
Tolley, Ann 208; Cordelia Hall 208; Edw. C. 208; Edward Carvill 208; Eliza 206; Elizabeth 207, 208; Elizabeth [-?-] 206, 207; Elizabeth Worthington 208; George 206, 207; James 36, 207, 208; John 206, 207; Martha 208; Martha Hall 208; Mary 206, 207. 208; Mary Freeborn 207, 208; Mary Garrettson 208; Mary Watkins 208; Sophia 208; Thomas 206, 207, 208; Thomas Garrettson 208; Walter 128, 206, 207, 208; William 206, 207
Tomlinson, Anna English 213
Tonge. See Tongue.
Tongue, Ann 210; Ann Cowman 210; Anne [-?-] 53, 209; Anne Harrison 210; Annie 210; Benjamin 210; Benjamin H. 210; Elizabeth 209, 210; Elizabeth Morgan 209; Elizabeth Roberts 209; Ellen 210; Harriet 210; Henry 210; James 53, 88, 99, 208, 210; John 210, 211; Mary 209, 210; Mary [-?-] 211; Mary Heighe 88, 208, 209; Sarah 210; Thomas 53, 88, 208, 209, 210, 211; Thomas R 210; William 211
Toogood, Josias 72; Mary Welsh 72
Toogood. See also Towgood.
Tool, Darby 20
Toon, Samuel 111
Topp, Edward 195
Towers, John 100
Towgood, Josias 193
Towgood. See also Toogood.
Townsend, Amy Norman McClain 147, 148; John 147
Towson, Abraham 31, 120, 121; Dorcas 121; Elizabeth Mahon 120, 121; Mary 121; William 121
Tracey, Anne 199; James 91; Joshua 50; Mary 91; Mary [-?-] 91; Samuel 34; Sarah 77; Teague 91
Tracey. See also Tracy, Trasey.
Tracy, Keziah Merryman 150; Mary [-?-] 185; Teague 185
Tracy. See also Tracey, Trasey.
Transum, [-?-] 168
Trasey, Samuel 133
Trasey. See also Tracey, Tracy.
Trevis, William 204
Trevitt, Mary Gongo 204; Robert 204
Trigg, Margaret 162
Troster, Jno. 87
Trott, James 204; Thomas 166
Trotten, Elizabeth Hayes Lenox 139; Luke 139, 140; Ruth 197; Susanna Long 140
Trotter, James 186
Trundle, John 192
Tschudi. See under Tschudy.
Tschudy. Barbara [-?-] 152 ; Elizabeth 151; Elizabeth Rover 151; Nicholas 151, 152; Winbert 151; Wingbert 151
Tucker, Ann 211, 212 213; Ann Palmer 213; Benjamin 212; Cassandra [-?-] 212; Charles 212; Clement Beck 213; David 220; Dorothy [-?-] Harrington 211, 212; Elizabeth 212, 213; Elizabeth [-?-] 213;

Index

Elizabeth Hitchcock 213; Hannah 213; Isaac 212; Jacob 211, 212, 213; James 213; John 211, 212, 213; Joshua 213; Joshua Fisher 213; Margaret 212, 213; Margaret [-?-] 118; Margaret Cobb 37, 38, 143, 212, 213; Mary 212, 213; Mary Ward 220; Nancy 213; Rebecca [-?-] 213; Richard 211, 213; Robert 212; Sarah [-?-] 213; Seaborn 37, 38, 118, 143, 211, 212, 213; Sole 213; Susanna(h) 213, 213; Susanna [-?-] 213; Susannah Kernut 213; Thomas 213; William 213, 218

Tuckin. See Tucker.

Tudor, John 81; Martha 125

Tully, Edward 55

Tunis, Phoebe 231

Turnbull, George 164

Turner, Ann 214; Ann [-?-] 214; Caleb 214; Chloe 214; Cloey 215; Durham 215; Elizabeth 214; Frances 214; Francis 214, 215; Jacob 214, 215; Joseph 214, 215; Joshua 214; Mary 215; Matthew 214, 215; Nancy Jane 15; Nathaniel 214; Polly 215; Rachel 214, 215; Robert 214; Sally 215; Sarah 214; Sarah [-?-] 214, 215; Sarah Maybury 214; William 143

Tydings, Pretiosa 150

Tye, Eleanor 91, 92; Elizabeth 91; George 91, 92; John 91, 92; Persosha Hitchcock 91; Porsoche [sic] Hitchcock 92; Presiota Hitchcock 91; Ruth [-?-] 92; Susana 91, 92

Tyer, Johanna [-?-] 3; Thomas 3

Usher, Thomas B. 151

Uty, George 137; Nathaniel 71

Vanroson, John 125

Vaughan, [-?-] 163; Benjamin 122; Christian 109; Christopher 122; Edward 109; Sarah 149; William 25

Vaughn, Abraham 50

Veale, Christopher 66, 99

Vernon, Christopher 211; Thomas 233; William 185

Vickory, Ann [-?-] 126, 127; John 126, 127; Richard 126; Richard Stevenson 126, 127, 128

Villett, Peter 153; Rebecca 153

Vincent, Mary 27

Vine, Godfrey 117; John 117; Sarah 117;

Sarah Litton Beddoe 117

Vines, William 82

Viney, Godfrey 1; William 1

Wade, Zachariah 167

Wagstaffe, John 215

Waites, [-?-] 136; Christiana 136, 224, 225; Jane [-?-] 136

Walder, Edward 136

Walker, Catherine 19; Catherine Ferguson 65; Delilah 171; Emily J, Keirle, 124; George 196; Isaac 65; James 178; Jean 36; John W, 124; Joseph 83; Mary 91; Nancy 95; Thomas 20

Wallace, Charles 19, 20; Mary Bull Rankin 19, 20

Waller, Elizabeth [-?-] 47; John 47; William 47

Wallis, Samuel 38; Thomas 1

Walston, John 67, 188

Walters. Thomas 224

Walton, John 94

Ward, [-?-] 184, 217; Allen 215, 216; Ann 215, 216, 220, 221; Avice 217; Avis 103, 217; Benjamin 218, 220, 221; Bridget 219; Bridget [-?-] 218, 219; Catherine [-?-] 220; Edward 215, 216, 217, 220, 236; Eleanor 218; Eliza 215; Elizabeth 217, 218, 219, 220, 221, 231; Elizabeth [-?-] 217, 218; Elizabeth Cox 218; Elizabeth Gover 216; Elizabeth Phillips 216; George 159; Hannah Lee 219, 220; Hannah Sickelmore 183, 184; James 220; John 140, 215, 216, 217, 218, 219, 220, 221; Joseph 193, 218, 219, 220, 221; Leititia 218, 219, 220; Mary 159, 217, 219, 220; Mary [-?-] 220; Mary Ann 220; Mary Gross 219; Mary Parkinson 219, 220; Nancy 219, 220; Phillizanna 216; Rachael 219, 220; Rachel Talbott 217; Rebecca 217; Rebecca Cox 216, 217; Richard 218, 219; Robert 212, 215, 216, 217, 218; Samuel\ 215, 216, 217, 218; Sarah 216, 218, 219, 220; Sarah [-?-] 218; Sarah Barber Moran 154; Sarah Burrough 219; Stephen 220; Susannah [-?-] 215; Sutton Sickelmore 183, 184; Talbot 220; William 215, 216, 217, 218, 219, 220

Warfield, Joshua 85; Richard 84

Warman, Stephen 216

Index

Warren, John 174; Mary [-?-] Rathell 173; William 173
Warron. See Warren.
Washington, [-?-] 86; Philip 196
Waskell, Isaac 134
Wastman, Jordan Nicholas 111, 112
Waters, Cephas 64, 665; Elizabeth Giles 7; Godfrey 18; Harriet 209; Harriet Tongue 210; Jacob F. 210; Joanna Giles 74; John 65, 71; Martha Bradford 18; Mary Edwards 64, 65; Mary Ijams 65; Philip 86
Waterton, John 35, 129, 130
Watkins, Allies Dicker 224; Ann 194, 228; Ann [-?-] 193 ; Ann Barkabee 227; Benjamin 227, 228; Christiana 225, 226; Christiana Waites 139, 224, 225; Daniel 227; Daniel Scott 226, 227, 228; Davis 221; Eleanor [-?-] 224; Elinor 24; Elizabeth 193, 217, 221, 222, 224, 226, 228; Elizabeth Hatten 228; Elizabeth James 228; Elizabeth Jones 228; Elizabeth Mead 227, 228; Elizabeth Pines 228; Ellen 228; Frances 221, 223, 224, 228; Frances [-?-] 224; Frances Hardesty 227, 228; Francis 10, 26, 35, 66, 130, 136, 139, 224, 225, 226, 227, 228; Isaiah 228; James 134, 224, 228; Jane 194, 226, 227; Jane Scott 130, 226; John 186, 193, 194, 216, 221, 224, 227, 228; John N. 210; Joseph 224; Margaret 193, 221, 223, 224 , 225, 226, 228; Margaret [-?-] 194, 221, 223, 224, 227, 228; Marie 224; Martha 221, 223, 224, 227, 228; Mary 208, 221, 223,224, 227; Mary [-?-] 224, 228; Mary Anne 227; Mary Wright 226, 227; Minerva Slade 228; Nathaniel 226, 227; Nicholas 229; Purify Greenfield 228; Ruth Guyton 228; Samuel 221, 222, 223, 224, 225, 226, 227, 228; Sara 224, 228, 229; Solomon 227; Sophia Biddison 228; Sosia Biddison 228; Susanna 228; Thomas 224, 227; Unity Green 228; William 221, 222, 223, 224, 227, 228; William Henry 228
Watson, Anthony 68; David 68; Jane Johnson Scott 130; John 130; Mary 68; Mary Chenoweth 130
Watters, Henry 18; John 72; Mary Bradford 18; Sarah 59
Wattes. John 205

Wattors. See Watters.
Watts, Edward 197; Frances Holland 197; John 197; Mary 197; Mary [-?-] 197; Mary Ann 95; Sarah [-?-] 197
Wayland. See Whayland.
Wayman, John 86
Wealand. See Whaylalnd.
Wealls, John 147
Weatherall. See under Wetherall.
Weaver, George 94
Webster, Elizabeth Giles 72; Hannah 74; Hannah [-?-] 157; Isaac 116, 144, 211, 214; John 100, 116, 157, 205; Mary 116; Webster, Michael 72; William 32
Wedill, Roger 211
Weems, Charles Howell 111; D. 186; John 53, 209
Weise, Augustus 116
Weise, Susannah Louisa [-?-] 116
Weitzel, Paul 9
Wekch, See Welch.
Welch, John 25, 30; Laban 96, 201, 202; Rachel Taylor 202; Robert 123; Sarah Mallonee 123
Welch. See also Welsh.
Wells, [-?-] 99, 137; Ann Carback 29; Benj. 180; Blanch 26; Charles 180; Frances 102; George 67, 90; Isaac 198; John 147; Joseph 29, 149; Richard 232; Sebell Jones 99; Sybil Jones 99; Thomas 63, 99
Welsh, Catherine Lewis 64; Catherine Stansbury 202; Damaris 72; Jemima 64; John 72, 185; Mary 72; Rachel Taylor 201; Robert 64; Sarah 72; Sarah Mallonee 122; William 126, 202
Wersler, Morice 191
Wessels, Elizabeth Tolley 207
Wessels, James 207
West, [-?-] (Rev. Dr.) 129; Ann 173, 229; Anna Pue 230; Arthur Pue 230; Eleanor "Ellen" Oden 230; Elizabeth 229; Elizabeth Maccubbin 229; Enoch 46; George 173; Hannah Williams 229, 230; Harriet Black 230; Jane 75; John 229; John Henry 229; Jone 75; Lotan 173; Maria Lloyd 230; Martha 229; Martha Hall 229; Mary 229; Mary Lloyd 230; Mary Magdalene 229; Priscilla 229; Rachel Sophia 230; Rebecca Ann 229;

Richard Williams 230; Robert 144, 229; Sarah [-?-] 144; Stephen 187, 229, 230; William 14
Weston, Willo. 19
Wetherall, Henry 98
Whalan. See Whayland.
Whaland. See Whayland.
Wharfe, Levy 25
Whayland, Ann 231; Catherine Lego 231; Catherine Matthews 97, 98, 230, 231; Elizabeth 231; Elizabeth Copeland 231; Elizabeth Ward 231; Henry 231; Isabel Wilson 213; James 231; Margaret 231; Martha 231; Martha [-?-] 231; Martha Dorney 232; Mary 231; Mary Caudrey 231; Mary Lego 231; Patrick 97, 98, 230, 231; Phoebe Tunis 231; Rebecca [-?-] 231; Sarah 231; Solomon 231; Stephen Mathews 231; Thomas 231; William 231
Whayleand. See Whaland.
Whaylum, Mary 138
Whealand. See Whayland.
Wheeler, Arabella 51; Benjamin 50; Mary 89; Rachel Taylor 200; Solomon 200
Whetcroft, Burton 20; William 20
Whipple, Susanna 175
Whipps, Abigail 232, 233; Anne 232; Benjamin 234, 235; Christopher 232; Cicelle 232; Eliza 233; Elizabeth 232; Elizabeth Medcaff 232, 233; Elizabeth Pierce 235; Ellen 232; Francis 232; Fraunces 232; George 234; Henrietta Pool 235; Jane 98, 232, 233; John 98, 160, 232, 233, 234; Katherine 234; Margaret Thurston 233, 234; Mary 234; Mary McComas 234, 235; Rachel 234; Robert 232; Roger 232; Ruth 234; Samuel 234, 235; Sara H. Lewis 235; Sarah 232, 233; Sarah Lucerne 160; Sarah Lucrese 234; Sarah Lucretia 235; Sarah Luctretia Ogg 234; Sarah Ogg 160; Susanna 233, 234; Susanna Rebecca Pierce 235; Susannah 232; Sybil Hodge 232; Thomas 232; Uroth 234; Ursula 234; Usley 234; Valite 235; William 232
Whips. See Whipps.
Whistler, Catherine 113; Esther 113; Ulrick 113

Whitacre. Abraham 17:Frances [-?-] 17; John 70; Peter 17
Whitaker, Abraham 205; Ann Hitchcock 71; Catherine [-?-] 144; Charity 144; Charles 206; Elizabeth Enson 143; Empson 144; James 144; John 70; Mark 143, 144; Mary [-?-] 206; Nancy Ann Hitchcock 70; Peter 206
White, James 38, 227; Jane Watkins 227; John 37, 38, 143, 211; Priscilla [-?-] 211; Priscilla Cobb 37, 38, 143; Priscilla Cobb Jones 143; Stephen 231; Thomas 47; Timothy 32
Whitecar. See Whitaker.
Whitehead, Francis 100, 196
Witham, Ruth Rowles 178
Whitseer. See Whitaker.
Whittingham, Martha 175
Whittop, Thomas 90
Whutacre. Whitaker.
Whyppe. See Whipps.
Wickes, Benj. 60; Elizabeth [-?-] 180; Jo. 109; John 6; Joseph 180;
Wiesenthal, Charles Frederick 129, 191
Wiesenythal. See wiesenthal.
Wilcoxen, John 65
Wild, Edward 206
Wilder, John 79, 80
Wiley, Ann 201; Margaret Sing 201; Margaret Sing Daughaday 55, 56; Richard 201; William 55, 201
Wilford, Eleanor 23
Wilkins, Frances Carback 29, 120; Francis 29, 120
Wilkinson, Ann 235; Ann Patrick 237; Anne 80, 236; Barbara Gorsuch Pickett 238; Betty Heighe 89; Caleb 237; Cassie 29; Eliza [-?-] 238; Elizabeth Clark(e) 236; Elizabeth Harryman 237; Fanny Peregoy; Hannah Eastwood 63; James 236; Jane 41; Jethro Lynch 181, 236, 237; John 138, 238; Joseph 89; Joshua 237; Moses 237; Philisanna 235, 236, 237; Phyllis 237; Rachel 237; 237; Rachel Lenox 236; Rebecca 238; Richard 237, 238; Robert 41, 235, 236, 237; Samuel 237; Sarah 236, 237; Sarah [-?-] 236; Sophia 191, 192, 235, 236; Tamar [-?-] 41, 80, 191; Tamar Love 235;

Index

Temperance Carback 29; Thomas 63, 237; William 29, 41, 80, 181, 191, 196, 197, 235, 236, 237
Williams, Charles 47; Hannah 229; Hezekiah 193; John 74; Judith Jones 47; Lodowick 235; Robert 96; Thomas 180
Williamson, William 138
Wilmot(t), John 91, 103, 177
Wil(l)son, Ann Skinner Ferguson 66; Ann Turner 214; Charles 162; Edward 89; Elizabeth 54, 111; Faith 184; George 314; Henry 54; Isabel 231; Jane 90, 102, 111, 162; John 26, 102, 153; Jonathan 153; Joseph 66, 89; Letitia Kenley 102; Rebecca Ferguson 66; Robert 225; William 66
Wilton, Ann 7
Wiltshire, John 36
Wimsett, Ann Ward 220, 221; James 220, 221
Winchester, William 42
Windley, Richard 34
Wineman, Anna Barbara Levely 113, 114, 115; Catharine 114, 115, 198; Henry 113, 114, 115
Wingfield, Elizabeth 23
Winter, Ralph 196
Witham, Ruth Rowles 178
Wolff, Johann 113; Michael 113; Salome [-?-] 113
Wood, Ann 154; Ann Watkins 228; Dorothy Jones Powell 99, 100; Elizabeth 46; Elizabeth [-?-] 46; Jane 154; John 79, 80, 99, 100; Joshua, 189; Margaret 154; Mary 154; Nancy 77; Peter 154; Robert 99, 185; Sarah 158; Susan 154; William 228
Wooden, George 125; Priscilla 100; Sarah 100; Sarah [-?-] 100; Solomon 100
Woodhead, George 65
Woodward, John 40
Woody, Sallie 26
Woolfe, Francis 212
Woolley, Rev. [-?-] 7
Worthington, Elizabeth 208; James 400; James Tolley 208; Martha 208; Mary Tolley 208; Samuel 208; Thomas 86; Thomas Tolley 208; Walter 208; William 132
Wotton, William 185
Wright, [-?-] 136; Bloyce 35; Elizabeth [-?-] 105; Elizabeth Barton 13; Elizabeth King 106; Francis 26; Jane 29; John 102; Leah Tanzey 199; Louisa Turpin 112; Mary 226; Solomon 163; Thomas 13, 105, 106, 178; William 130, 134, 199, 226
Wright. See also Waites.
Wriothesley, Henry 182, 183
Wroth, James 5; Kinvin 6; Martha 5; Mary 5
Yanston, Henry 9; Lawrence 9
Yeates, Jean 6; John Lloyd 166; Mary Jane Simes 166
Yeiser, Engelhard 113; Philip 113
Yellott, Coleman 228
Yeo, John 170
Yestwood. See Eastwood.
Yieldhall, Constant Rowles 178; Robert 178
Yoakley, Mary Morris 156
Yon, Henry 154
York, Edward 58; Elizabeth Debruler 58; George 58, 59; John 58; William 58, 59, 105, 106
Young, Clara 128; Clare 12; John Tully 55; Rebecca 12; Samuel 128; Sarah Morris 156; William 36, 76, 119, 183
Zeigler, Francis 94
Zuille, Matthew 5, 6

277

www.ingramcontent.com/pod-product-compliance
Lightning Source LLC
Chambersburg PA
CBHW071238230426
43668CB00011B/1486